Joseph Addison Alexander

The Gospel according to Matthew

Joseph Addison Alexander

The Gospel according to Matthew

ISBN/EAN: 9783337282295

Printed in Europe, USA, Canada, Australia, Japan

Cover: Foto ©Thomas Meinert / pixelio.de

More available books at **www.hansebooks.com**

THE

GOSPEL

ACCORDING TO

MATTHEW.

EXPLAINED BY

JOSEPH ADDISON ALEXANDER.

NEW YORK:
CHARLES SCRIBNER, 124 GRAND STREET.
1861.

PREFACE.

THIS volume presents the last work on which the pen of Dr. Alexander was engaged.

It is complete as a commentary to the close of Chapter XVI., and then, as though the author anticipated the approaching interruption of his earthly labours, it finds a quasi-completion in an analysis of the concluding chapters.

It may be of interest to the reader to know, that at the commencement of his analysis of Chapter XVII., the manuscript of Dr. Alexander contains this memorandum: "Resumed after five weeks' confinement and inaction, January 3d, 1860;" and that day by day pursuing the work, he records in his journal, "Wednesday, January 18th, Finished the Analysis of Matthew," and "20th, Read over my Analysis of Matthew XVII.–XXVIII.,"—just a week and a day before his death.

Of course not only is the volume deficient in the notes upon these concluding chapters, but also in the General Introduction, similar to that of his work on Mark, which he designed to have furnished.

It remains only to state, that as it was Dr. Alexander's desire to make the commentary on Matthew complete in itself, without reference to that on Mark, wherever parallel passages occur, he has in general simply transferred the notes in full from the latter volume, making only the necessary alterations to adapt them to the text of Matthew.

S. D. A.

NEW YORK, *December*, 1860.

THE

GOSPEL ACCORDING TO

MATTHEW.

CHAPTER I.

In pursuance of his purpose to demonstrate the Messiahship of Jesus by showing the exact correspondence of his life to the prophecies and types of the Old Testament, Matthew begins by tracing his descent, not only from David the first and greatest of the theocratic kings, but from Abraham the Father of the Faithful and the founder of the ancient church or chosen people. This important fact is established, not by mere assertion or historical narration, but by a technical and formal genealogy or pedigree, exhibiting our Lord's descent, not merely in the general but in detail, throughout the three great periods of the history of Israel (1–17). Having thus shown, as if by documentary evidence, from whom he was descended, the evangelist records the circumstances which preceded the Nativity itself, with particular reference to the difficulties springing from his mother's marriage and the mode of their solution (18–25).

1. The book of the generation of Jesus Christ, the son of David, the son of Abraham.

The two first words are to be read in close connection as forming one compound title, *generation-book*, *descent-book*, corresponding to the modern phrase, *genealogical table*, or to the one word *pedigree*, when used to denote, not the extraction or descent itself, but the written record or certification of it. The word translated *book* ($\beta i\beta\lambda o s$) has in Greek a much wider usage, being applied to any writing, and originally signifying one of the most ancient kinds of writing material, to wit, the inner bark of the *papyrus* plant, from which is derived our *paper*, although made of an entirely different substance. As here used it is nearly equivalent to *document* in modern English, or to *paper*, as denoting not the mere material but the writing, especially when it is official or authoritative, or important in relation to some special case or business, as for instance the "papers" in a suit at law. The other word (γενέσεως) in classical Greek means generation, in the proper sense of creation or procreation, but in Hellenistic usage birth (as in v. 18 below) or lineage, extraction, as in this verse. It is the genitive case of the name (*Genesis*) given in the Septuagint version to the first book of Moses, as containing the *Origines* of human history. There is no grammatical ellipsis to be here supplied, (*this is*) *the book* (Tyndale), so as to form a complete sentence. It is rather a title or inscription, either of the whole book; or, as some suppose, of the two first chapters, which contain the history of our Saviour's infancy; or of the first alone, which contains his genealogy and birth; or, as most interpreters are now agreed, of the genealogy alone (vs. 1–17). It may then be regarded as the original inscription of the pedigree, belonging to it in the register from which some suppose it to have been transcribed. This supposition, though unnecessary, is by no means inconsistent with the inspiration of the record, since the introduction or adoption even of a human composition by divine authority imparts to it the same infallibility which it would have if written by immediate divine suggestion. As a positive argument in favour of this supposition it may be alleged, that the entire structure of the genealogy is not what might have been expected in the opening of a history, but resembles rather a document prefixed to it, on which the writer then proceeds to comment, as a sort of text or theme, or from which he sets out as the starting-point of his whole narrative. This peculiar relation of the genealogy to the history in Matthew's Gospel is made still more striking by comparing it with Luke's, which is wrought into the texture of his narrative, so as to form an integral and inseparable part of it. (See Luke 3, 23–38.) *Jesus Christ* is here used not as a mere personal designation or proper name, although it had become so when this book was written, but with distinct reference to the meaning of both titles, and to the claim which they involve, that he to whom they are applied was the promised Saviour (see below, on v. 21) and Messiah, or Anointed Prophet Priest and King of Israel (see below, on v. 16). Even regarded as a title or inscription, this first sentence is equivalent to a formal declaration of our Lord's Messiahship, as the truth to be established in the following history, beginning with his lineal descent from Abraham and David, in default of which all other proofs would be unavailing. *Son* is here used in the wider sense of lineal descendant. (See below, on v. 20, and compare Luke 1, 5. 13, 16. 19, 9.) *Son of David* was among the most familiar designations of the Messiah in the dialect of the contemporary Jews. (See below, on 9, 27. 12, 23. 15, 22. 20, 30. 21, 9. 15. 22, 42, and compare Rom. 1, 3. Rev. 5, 5. 22, 16.) *Son of Abraham* may be construed with the nearest antecedent (*David*), but agrees more probably with the remoter (*Jesus Christ*), whose descent from both the Patriarchs (or founders of the royal race) is here asserted.

2. Abraham begat Isaac ; and Isaac begat Jacob ; and Jacob begat Judas and his brethren.

The form of expression here used and throughout the table (ἐγέννησε) is a literal translation of the one employed in Jewish genealogies, (יָלַד) the oldest specimens of which are those contained in Genesis (4, 18), particularly that in the fifth chapter; where we have substantially the same title or inscription as in this case, "the book of the generations of Adam" (Gen. 5, 1), and the same technical formula (*begat*), denoting not so much an act as a relation, and meaning simply that he was his father. A trace of the same genealogical usage may be found in Ps. 2, 7, where the words, "This day have I begotten thee," do not fix the date of the Messiah's sonship as beginning in time, but express a filial relation which existed from eternity. What is here affirmed is that Abraham was the father or progenitor of Isaac, Isaac of Jacob, Jacob of Judah, and so on, to the end of the whole pedigree. *Judas*, the Greek form of the Hebrew *Judah* (*Jehudah*), here distinguished from *his brethren* (or *brothers*), the other sons of Jacob, as the one from whose line the Messiah was to spring. (See below, on 2, 6, and compare Gen. 49, 10. Heb. 7, 14. Rev. 5, 5), though the rest were entitled to be named, at least collectively, as being Patriarchs or founders of the twelve tribes (compare Acts 7, 8. 9), each of which possessed a sort of royal dignity, and all of which together constituted the Theocracy or chosen people. (Compare Ps. 122. 4. Acts 26, 7.) As if he had said, 'Jacob was the father of the twelve, to whom the tribes of our theocracy trace their origin, and among these of Judah, who was the lineal progenitor of Christ himself, as shown in the detailed genealogy which follows.'

3. And Judas begat Phares and Zara of Thamar ; and Phares begat Esrom ; and Esrom begat Aram.

In the original narrative (Gen. 38, 29. 30), these names are written *Pharez, Zarah*, and *Tamar*. *Of* (out of, from, by) *Thamar*, the daughter-in-law of Judah (Gen. 38, 6). As this was an incestuous connection, and intentionally so on Tamar's part, it seems extraordinary that it should be prominent in the genealogy of Christ. But this only serves to prove the genuineness of the genealogy itself, as the same thing is apparent in the Jewish books, which undertake to account for it by representing the sins of Tamar, Rahab, and Bathsheba, as virtuous acts committed under the divine direction. But this solution is not only morally detestable, but far less probable on other grounds, than that which supposes these names to be introduced to humble Jewish pride and illustrate the divine sovereignty in choosing "base things of the world, and things which are despised . . . . that no flesh should glory in his presence" (1 Cor. 1, 29). *Esrom* and *Aram*, called in David's genealogy appended to the book of Ruth (4, 19), *Hezron* (compare 1 Chron. 2, 5) and *Ram*, which last may be only a contracted form of *Aram* (compare Job 32. 2. with Genesis 22. 21).

4. And Aram begat Aminadab; and Aminadab begat Naasson; and Naasson begat Salmon.

These names occur also in Ruth 4, 20, with a slight difference of orthography, (*Amminadab* and *Nahshon*.) The latter was a brother of the wife of Aaron (Ex. 6, 23) and the hereditary chief of Judah in the wilderness (Num. 2, 3. 10, 14.)

5. And Salmon begat Booz of Rachab; and Booz begat Obed of Ruth; and Obed begat Jesse.

In 1 Chr. 2, 11, *Salmon* is called *Salma* (*Salmah*), as another person is, in the same chapter (vs. 51–54). *Booz* is the *Boaz* of the Old Testament (Ruth 2, 1. 4, 21), and might have been conformed to it as *Jesse* (*Jessai*) is, in the translation. *Of Rachab, of Ruth*, the same form of expression as in v. 3 and there explained. There is no reason to doubt the identity of the former with the Rahab of the book of Joshua (2, 1. 6, 23. 25), which agrees well with the chronology, as Salmon, the son of Nahshon, was a man of mature age at the fall of Jericho. The difficulty which arises from the length of the interval, is not peculiar to this table, but common to it and the one in Ruth, which may also be abridged by the omission of some less important names (see below, on v. 17), as the verb (*begat*) does not necessarily denote immediate succession, but the genealogical relation of progenitor and descendant, like the nouns *son* and *daughter*. (See above, on v. 1, and compare the passages there cited.)

6. And Jesse begat David the king; and David the king begat Solomon of her (that had been the wife) of Urias.

David the king, by way of eminence, not only as the first but as the best and greatest of the theocratic sovereigns, who represented the Messiah's royalty and as it were kept his throne for him till he came (compare Ezek. 21, 27). The reign of Saul, although divinely authorized, was not theocratical but secular, designed to teach the people by experiment the natural effect of having a king like the other nations. (See 1 Sam. 8, 5. 20.) The reigns that followed, not excepting that of Solomon, are treated in the history as mere continuations of the reign of David, filling up the interval between him and the Great Deliverer, of whose Messianic royalty he was the constituted type and representative. This special relation between Christ and David is implied in the comparative frequency with which the latter is referred to in the later Scriptures, and his name sometimes applied to the Messiah himself (Ezek. 34, 23. 24. 37, 24. 25), while Solomon is never named in prophecy, and very seldom in the New Testament, and even then rather with disparagement than honour (see below, on 6, 29. 12, 42). These comparisons will throw light on the emphasis with which the evangelist (or genealogist) twice in this one sentence speaks of *David the king.* This repetition at the same time indicates that David was the close of one and the beginning of another cycle in the history of Israel. The theocracy which culminated in him begins to decline even under his successor. From Abraham to David all moves upwards, and from David to the Advent downwards. All idea of intrinsic merit, even in the man thus highly honoured, as a ground of the divine choice, is excluded by the mention of Bathsheba, suggesting the great complex crime of David's life, and the providential judgments which avenged it, but without disturbing his position as an instrument in God's hand and a type of the Messiah. This is the fourth female name introduced among our Lord's progenitors (see above, on vs. 3, 5), one of the four being of heathen origin, and the other three remembered chiefly for their sins. This remarkable fact may be connected with our Lord's vicarious subjection to reproach and his official share in the dishonour brought upon our race by sin. A more exact translation of the last words would be, *from* (or *by*) *the* (wife) *of Uriah.* (See the original history in 2 Sam. xi. xii.

7. And Solomon begat Roboam ; and Roboam begat Abia ; and Abia begat Asa.

Roboam and *Abia* are the *Rehoboam* and *Abijam* or *Abijah* of the Old Testament. (See 1 Kings 11, 43. 14, 31. 2 Chr. 12, 16. 13, 1.) They are named here only as connecting links in the chain of genealogical succession.

8. And Asa begat Josaphat ; and Josaphat begat Joram ; and Joram begat Ozias.

Josaphat and *Ozias*, called in the Hebrew *Jehoshaphat* and *Uzziah.* (See 1 Kings 22, 41. 2 Kings 15, 13.) Between Joram and Uzziah three kings are omitted, namely, Ahaziah (2 Kings 9, 29), Joash (2 Kings 12, 1), and Amaziah (2 Kings 14, 1). These omissions were no doubt intended to reduce the genealogy to the uniform limits mentioned in v. 17 below; and these particular kings may have been chosen as descendants of Jezebel, and as such representatives of the corruption wrought in Judah by alliance with Israel, and especially by intermarriage with the family of Ahab. This is far more probable than that the choice of names to be omitted was entirely arbitrary; but even this is less incredible than that the omission was an ignorant or inadvertent one, either on the part of the evangelist or on that of the original genealogist from whom this genealogy was borrowed (see above, on v. 1).

9. 10. And Ozias begat Joatham ; and Joatham begat Achaz ; and Achaz begat Ezekias ; and Ezekias begat Manasses; and Manasses begat Amon ; and Amon begat Josias.

In these two verses there are no omissions, but the royal genealogy is given without interruption. *Joatham, Achaz*, and *Ezekias*, are the *Jotham, Ahaz*, and *Hezekiah* of the Old Testament, where they follow each other in the same order. (See 2 Kings 15, 32. 16, 1. 18, 1, and compare 2 Chr. 27, 1. 28, 1. 29, 1.) *Manasses (Manasseh), Amon* (in one or two of the oldest copies, *Amos*), and *Josias (Josiah)*, are the next three kings in the original history. (See 1 Kings 21, 1. 19. 22, 1, and compare 2 Chr. 33, 1. 19. 34, 1.)

11. And Josias begat Jechonias and his brethren, about the time they were carried away to Babylon.

The omission of *Jehoiakim*, the son of Josiah and the father of *Jehoiachin* or *Jeconiah* (2 Kings 23, 34. 24, 6. 2 Chr. 36, 4. 8), has been variously explained. Some suppose *Jeconiah* to be the Greek form both of *Jehoiakim* and *Jehoiachin;* but this is at variance both with Hebrew and Septuagint usage. (Compare 2 Kings 24, 6. 12. 15. 25, 27. Ezek. 1, 2. with Esth. 2, 6. Jer. 24, 1. 27, 20. 28, 4, and both with Jer. 22, 24. 28. 37, 1, where the name is still further contracted to *Coniah*.) This objection applies no less to the supposition that *Jeconiah* means *Jehoiakim* in this verse and *Jehoiachin* in the next, which would moreover be at variance with the context, as the name of each progenitor, except the first, is twice inserted. Still less admissible is the assumption of an ignorant or inadvertent error in confounding the two names, which are less alike in Greek and Hebrew than in English, and could hardly be confounded in a formal genealogy. More probable than either is the supposition of an error in transcription from the same cause, as nothing is more common when two words are alike than the unintentional omission of one. And we find accordingly, in several uncial manuscripts and ancient versions, *Josiah begat Jehoiakim and Jehoiakim begat Jeconiah and his brethren*. This is rejected by the critics as a mere interpolation, because wanting in the oldest manuscripts now extant, which however are at least four hundred years later than the date of composition. It is also objected that Jeconiah had no brothers, or at least not more than one (1 Chron. 3, 16. 2 Chron. 36, 10.) This objection may be met by still another explanation, which supposes Jehoiakim to be omitted as the king by whose fault the monarchy was overthrown and the national independence lost (2 Kings 24, 4. 10), and the *brethren* of Jehoiachin (or Jeconiah) to denote the contemporary race who went with him into exile. (Compare the use of the word *brethren* in Ex. 2, 11. 4, 18. Num. 20, 3. Acts 3, 22. 7, 23.) The principal objection to this last assumption is the vague and unusual sense which it puts upon the verb *begat*. But any supposition seems more credible than that of a gross blunder, either on the part of the evangelist or on that of his genealogical authority, and of its passing unobserved until the time of Porphyry, who wrote against the Scriptures in the latter part of the third century. *About the time they were carried away* is a correct but needless paraphrase of three Greek words (ἐπὶ τῆς μετοικεσίας) literally meaning *on* (or *at*) *the migration*. The preposition (ἐπί) is explained by some as meaning *tow-*

ards or just before; but its usage elsewhere in construction with the same case rather requires the sense of *about* or *at*. (See Heb. 1, 1. 2 Pet. 3, 3, and compare Mark 2, 26. Luke 3, 2. 4, 27. Rom. 1, 10.) The genitive (*of Babylon*) can hardly denote motion to a place, but rather means belonging to it, as we say the Babylonian exile or captivity, in speaking of the national condition, or the Babylonian deportation, of the act or event which caused it.

12. And after they were brought to Babylon, Jechonias begat Salathiel; and Salathiel begat Zorobabel.

After the migration of Babylon, or Babylonian exile, i. e. after it happened or began, not after it was ended, as the Greek word does not signify the state or condition of the people there, but their removal thither, as in the preceding verse. It is therefore neither necessary nor admissible to give the preposition (μετά) here the sense of *in* or *during*, which is contrary to usage. The English version (*after they were brought to Babylon*) conveys the sense but not the form of the original. The divine declaration, that Jeconiah should be childless, means that he should have no immediate successor on the throne, as explained in the context of the prophecy itself (Jer. 22, 30.) *Salathiel*, the Greek form of the Hebrew *Shealtiel*, is repeatedly named in the Old Testament also as the father of *Zorobabel* (*Zerubbabel*, Ezra 3, 2. 8. Hagg. 1, 1), but in 1 Chr. 3, 19 as his uncle, which may either relate to a different person, like the two Zedekiahs in vs. 15. 16 of the same chapter, or to an adoption, or to a leviratic marriage of the kind prescribed in Deut. 25, 5. The Salathiel and Zorobabel of Luke 3, 27 can hardly be identical with those here mentioned.

13–15. And Zorobabel begat Abiud; and Abiud begat Eliakim; and Eliakim begat Azor; and Azor begat Sadoc; and Sadoc begat Achim; and Achim begat Eliud; and Eliud begat Eleazar; and Eleazar begat Matthan; and Matthan begat Jacob.

As these nine names belong to the interval between the Old and New Testament, we have no means of verifying or comparing them, but every reason to believe that they were found in the public archives of the tribe of Judah or the private genealogy of the family of Joseph. The number of generations corresponds sufficiently to that of years included in the interval referred to. If there is any disproportion, the excess is on the side last mentioned, and may be readily explained by the assumption that a few names are omitted, as in other parts of this same table. (See above, on v. 8, and below, on v. 17.)

16. And Jacob begat Joseph the husband of Mary, of whom was born Jesus, who is called Christ.

This conclusion of the genealogy shows whose it is, namely Joseph's; and at the same time why it is recorded, namely, because he was the husband of Mary; and also why her husband's pedigree has any historical interest or value, namely, because she was the mother of Messiah. As if it had been said, 'Since Jesus was the Son of Mary, and Mary the lawful wife of Joseph, and Joseph the lineal descendant of David, therefore Jesus was himself the heir of David, by legal right, as shown in the preceding table, no less than by natural descent, as appears from his mother's genealogy recorded elsewhere,' i. e. in Luke 3, 23–31. The *Heli*, there named as the father of Joseph, may have been so by adoption or by legal substitution (see above, on v. 12), but was more probably his father-in-law, i. e. the father of Mary herself, who is said to be so called in some Jewish books. *Jesus called the Christ*, or more exactly still, *the (one) called Christ*, is not, as some imagine, a suggestion of doubt (equivalent to saying, the reputed or alleged Messiah), nor on the other hand, a strong asseveration of the fact (so called because he was so, a use of the Greek verb now denied by the highest philological authorities); but a simple statement that he bore this title at the date of the history or genealogy, and was thereby distinguished from all those who shared with him the name of *Jesus* (or *Joshua*), which was one in common use among the Jews. *The Christ* has here its primary and full sense as an official title, and not its secondary and attenuated meaning as a personal or proper name (see above, on v. 1). *Was born*, the same verb that is used throughout the genealogical table in its active form (*begat*), but is applied, in Classical as well as Hellenistic usage, to both parents.

17. So all the generations from Abraham to David (are) fourteen generations; and from David until the carrying away into Babylon (are) fourteen generations; and from the carrying away into Babylon unto Christ (are) fourteen generations.

So, literally, *then* or *therefore*, a connective particle, referring back to the preceding genealogy, and summing up its statements, as an introduction to the history which follows. As if he had said: 'You see then from this table, that there are fourteen generations,' &c. This cannot mean that there were really, in point of fact, just fourteen generations in the several intervals here mentioned; for we know from the Old Testament, that four names are omitted in the second period, and have reason to believe that others may be wanting in the third. (See above, on vs. 8. 13.) It rather means the contrary, to wit, that although there were more generations in the actual succession, only fourteen are here given, for the sake of uniformity, in each of the three periods. So far from being a mistake or an intentional misrepresentation, neither of which can be imagined even in a skilful genealogist, much less in an inspired evangelist, it is really a caution to the reader against falling into the very mistake which some would charge upon the writer. As if he had said: 'Let it be observed that this is not a complete list of all the generations between Abraham and Christ, but that some names are omitted, so as to leave fourteen in each great division of the history of Israel.' *All the generations*, if extended to the whole verse, may then be understood to mean all that are here given; but if restricted to the first clause, which is a more probable construction, it may have its strict sense (absolutely all) and give a reason for selecting fourteen as the measure of the periods, namely, that there were really just fourteen generations in the first, and that the others were assimilated to it, either by the genealogist from whom the pedigree was borrowed, or by the evangelist himself. But how are the names to be distributed and reckoned, so as to leave fourteen in each division? The solution of this problem may be varied by counting David and Josiah once or twice, and by including or excluding Christ himself and his mother in the third division. But this only shows that the precise enumeration of the names is not the main thing, but their equal distribution, and that this must be determined by the real number in the first division, which remains the same in all these different arrangements. It is also evident that if the three fourteens can be made out in so many different ways, the writer cannot be mistaken in affirming their existence, although we may not be able to determine which mode of calculation he intended. But it still remains to be considered why he thus divided them at all. Some say that this was a customary formula appended to the ancient genealogies, designed to aid the memory, and here retained by the evangelist without change, as a part of the original document which he is quoting. Others suppose a mystical allusion to the name of David, the letters of which in Hebrew (דוד), when summed up according to their numerical value, make fourteen (4+6+4); or to the forty-two stations of the Israelites in the wilderness; or to the scriptural use of seven as a sacred number. Besides these mnemonical and mystical solutions, there is a chronological one, namely, that the periods are equal in years though not in generations, and two of the great cycles having been completed, he who was born at the close of the third must be the Christ. The only other supposition that need be stated is, that the writer's purpose was to draw attention to the three great periods in the history of Israel as the chosen people, one extending from Abraham as its great progenitor to David its first theocratical sovereign; another to the downfall of the monarchy and loss of the national independence; and a third from this disaster to the advent of Messiah. To this periodology attention would be drawn by the very effort to arrange the periods and the choice of methods in so doing. Thus understood, the verse may be paraphrased as follows: 'The foregoing table is divided into three parts, the first of which embraces fourteen generations, and the other two are here assimilated to it, by omitting a few names, in order to make prominent the three great eras in the history of Israel, marked and divided by the calling of Abraham, the reign of David, the Babylonian exile, and the birth of Christ, the end to which the previous succession pointed.'

18. Now the birth of Jesus Christ was on this wise: When as his mother Mary was espoused to Joseph, before they came together, she was found with child of the Holy Ghost.

Had the preceding pedigree been that of a mere man, it would have ended as it began with the usual genealogical formula, *Joseph begat Jesus.* But as this was not the fact, the true relation between them is distinctly stated in v. 16, namely, that Joseph was not the father of Jesus, though the husband of his mother. To this negative statement the evangelist now adds a positive statement of his real generation, connected yet contrasted with the previous genealogy by the connective (δέ), which has here its proper sense of *but*, or on the contrary. This connection of the sentences is weakened and obscured in the translation by the use of *now* instead of *but*, as well as by prefixing it to *Jesus Christ*, which in the Greek is rendered prominent by standing first. As if he had said: 'All these, from Isaac (v. 2) to Joseph (v. 16), followed one another in the natural sequence of ordinary generation; *Jesus Christ, on the contrary*, was born in a manner wholly different,' which the writer then goes on to describe (in vs. 18–25). Some of the modern critics omit *Jesus*, upon very doubtful manuscript authority, but with the supposed advantage of reserving the proper name or personal designation until after its prescription by the angel has been stated (in v. 21). But the name has been already mentioned twice (in vs. 1. 16), and cannot therefore be withheld as unknown to the reader. *Birth*, or rather *generation*, including also the *conception*. The Greek word in the common text is the noun (γέννησις) corresponding to the verb (ἐγέννησε), which is repeated nearly forty times in the preceding context (vs. 2–16). The oldest manuscripts and latest critics have a different though kindred form (γένεσις) of wider import, and which really includes the other, as the specific sense of birth or generation is involved in the generic one of origin, production. In either case there is a verbal reference to what precedes which cannot be preserved in a translation. If the latter reading (γένεσις) be preferred, the allusion is to v. 1, where the genitive case of the same name occurs. As if he had said: Such is the book of the Messiah's *generation*, or his whole descent; but his immediate *generation* was as follows: If the other (γέννησις) be retained, the allusion is to the repeated use of the cognate verb (ἐγέννησε) already mentioned. As if he had said: One of these *begat* another, in the natural and ordinary way; but the Messiah was *begotten* in a different manner. *On this wise*, or in modern English, *in this manner*, but in Greek a single word (οὕτως), meaning simply *thus* (or *so*), and here equivalent to our phrase, *as follows*. *For* (γάρ), omitted in the version, unless it is included in the phrase *when as*, is here equivalent in force to *namely*, or *that is to say*, but really refers to something not expressed. As if he had said: and the origin referred to was entirely unlike that of all the persons previously mentioned, *for*, &c. *When as*, another obsolete expression, analogous to *whereas*, which is still in use, but here a mere periphrasis for a participial construction, *his mother Mary having been espoused*, i. e. before the discovery here mentioned, as implied in the past participle (μνηστευθείσης.) The Greek verb strictly means to court or woo, but in the passive form to be engaged, betrothed (as in the Septuagint version of Deut. 22, 23. 25. 27. 28, compared with the active voice in Deut. 20, 7.) There are frequent allusions in the Old Testament to the marriage vow as a religious contract (Prov. 2, 17. Ezek. 16, 8. Mal. 2, 14), but the first mention of a written bond occurs in the Apocrypha (Tob. 2, 14.) According to the later Jewish books, the bride continued in her father's house for some time after her espousals. *Before* implies nothing as to what took place afterwards. Compare the use of the same phrase (πρὶν ἤ) in Mark 14, 30. Luke 2, 26. 22, 34. Acts 2, 20. 25, 16. *Came together*, cohabited as man and wife, either in the wider or the stricter sense, more probably the former, which includes the other, before he had even brought her home (see below, on v. 25.) *Was found*, not simply *was*, a Hebrew idiom alleged by some interpreters, but now rejected by the best authorities, nor does it mean *detected*, or discovered, against Mary's will; but simply *became known* to herself, and probably through her to others, or at least to Joseph, her betrothed husband. *With child*, literally *having in (the) womb*, an idiomatic phrase occurring also in v. 23, 24, 19. Luke 1, 31. 1 Th. 5, 3. Rev. 12, 2, and often in the Septuagint version (e. g. Gen. 16, 4. 5. 11. 38, 24. 25.) *Of*, *from*, or *by*, as the source and the efficient cause. (See below, on v. 20, and compare John 3, 6.) *Ghost*, the Saxon word for *Spirit*, still retained in German (*Geist*) and the cognate languages, but in modern English only used in this phrase, and in reference to the apparition of departed spirits, though it may be still traced in its rare but genuine derivative, *ghostly*, i. e. spiritual or religious. The whole phrase *Holy Spirit* does not signify an influence or power, but a person as in many other places, even where the article, as here, is omitted.* The indefinite form may have been adopted for the very reason that the phrase had become a personal or proper name.

19. Then Joseph her husband, being a just (man), and not willing to make her a public example, was minded to put her away privily.

Joseph, however (δέ), or on his part, as the other and apparently the injured party in this grave transaction. *Just* may be taken either in the strict sense of rendering to every one his due (*suum cuique*), or in the wider sense of *good* (as Horace uses *æquus*), including mercy

---

* See below, v. 20. 8, 11, and compare Mark 1, 8. Luke 1, 15. 35. 41. 67. 2, 25. 3, 16. 4, 1. 11, 13. John 1, 33. 7, 39. 20, 22. Acts 1, 2. 5. 2, 4. 4, 8. 31. 6, 3. 5. 7, 55. 8, 3. 9, 17. 10, 38. 11, 16. 24. 13, 52. 19, 2. 3. Rom. 5, 5. 9, 1. 14, 17. 15. 13. 16. 1 Cor. 2, 13. 12, 3. 2 Cor. 6, 6. 1 Th. 1, 6. 2 Tim. 1, 14. Tit. 3, 5. Heb. 2, 4. 6, 4. 1 Pet. 1, 12. 2 Pet. 1, 21. Jude 20.

and compassion no less than rigid conscientiousness and honesty. In the former case, the whole phrase, *just and not willing*, will mean, *just and (yet) not willing*, i. e. too just to retain her but too kind to expose her. In the other case the sense is, *just and (therefore) not willing*. The first construction is the simplest and requires no departure from the ordinary usage of the word *just*. *Willing* is not an adjective in Greek, but the participle of the verb to *will*. What is denied, therefore, is not a mere disposition, which he may have felt, but a volition or decided act of will, to which he could not bring himself. *To make an example of her*, by divulging her supposed offence, or making it the subject of judicial process. (Wiclif: *he was rightful and would not publish her.* Tyndale: *a perfect man.*) He was inclined, not he positively *wished*, still less *was determined*, both which expressions are too strong for the original verb (ἐβουλήθη.) *Put her away*, discharge, or free her. a term often applied elsewhere to divorce (see below, on 5, 31. 32. 19, 3. 7. 8. 9), but here used in the sense of a more private and informal separation. According to Philo and Maimonides, a betrothed woman possessed all the rights of a wife, and could only be repudiated with the same formalities. *Privily*, in modern English, *privately* or *secretly*, i. e. without judicial forms, by mere repudiation as prescribed in the Mosaic law (Deut. 24, 1), not without a written instrument, but without undue publicity, and possibly without specification of the cause. This shows that the last words of the verse preceding are the evangelist's own statement of the real cause, and not a part of what was found (εὑρέθη) or discovered at the time in question.

20. But while he thought on these things, behold, the angel of the Lord appeared unto him in a dream, saying, Joseph, thou son of David, fear not to take unto thee Mary thy wife; for that which is conceived in her is of the Holy Ghost.

While he thought, in Greek an absolute construction, *he revolving* (pondering, considering) *these things.* The original verb denotes an intellectual act, but with an implication of strong feeling (as in 9, 4. below.) *These things*, those related in the two preceding verses, with particular reference to the purpose mentioned in v. 19. *Angel* originally signifies a *messenger* (as in Luke 7, 24. 9, 52. James 2, 25), but is specially applied in scripture to the "ministering spirits" (Heb. 1, 14) sent forth to announce and execute the will of God. *Angel of Jehovah* is a title often given in the Old Testament to the second person of the Godhead; but this meaning would be here irrelevant. The angel sent may have been Gabriel, as in Luke 1, 19. 26; but it is not here asserted. *Appeared* is in the Greek a passive form originally meaning *was revealed* (or rendered visible), but constantly employed as a deponent verb.* *By dream* (κατ' ὄναρ) an ana-

* See below, 2, 7. 13. 19. 6, 5. 16, 13. 9, 33. 13, 26. 23, 27. 28. 24, 27. 30.

logous expression to *by day*, *by night*, and perhaps like them indicative of time, but commonly explained as a description of the mode of the divine communication. The Greek noun is used in the classics absolutely as an adverb, and by Homer is contrasted with another which denotes a waking vision (ὄναρ and ὕπαρ.) *Son of David*, not a pleonastic or superfluous expression, but one intended to remind him of his own descent and consequent relation to the Messiah, and perhaps thereby to make him the more willing to complete his marriage. The use of the nominative for the vocative is common not only in the Hellenistic but the Classical Greek writers. *Fear not*, either to do wrong or to incur injury. *To take* to thyself, into thy company, a frequent sense of the Greek verb (παραλαμβανειν), 2, 13–21. 4, 5. 8. 12, 45. 17, 1. 18, 16. 20, 17. 26, 37. 27, 27, and with special reference to marriage in Herodotus and Xenophon. *Mariam* (or *Miriam*), the original form of the Hebrew name, but only used by Matthew and Luke in the beginning of their Gospels.* *Thy wife*, not merely in anticipation, but *de facto* and *de jure*. (See above, on v. 19.) *Of the Holy Ghost*, as in v. 18 (compare acts 5, 39. Rom. 2, 29.)

21. And she shall bring forth a son, and thou shalt call his name JESUS: for he shall save his people from their sins.

It is a slight but significant difference between this and the similar assurance made to Zecharias (Luke 1, 13), that the pronoun (*to thee*) is omitted here, because our Lord was to be brought forth not to Joseph but to God. The second verb (*thou shalt call*) is neither an imperative future, as in the commandments, nor a mere prediction (*thou wilt call*), but something intermediate between them (*thou art to call*), implying both futurity and divine appointment. The naming of children is ascribed in Scripture to both parents (compare Gen. 29, 32–35. 35, 18, with Exodus 2, 22), and to Joseph here as the husband of Mary and the legal father of her offspring (see above, on v. 16). The name itself (*Jesus*) is the Greek form of the Hebrew *Joshua*, which may be variously analyzed, but always with the same essential meaning, that of *Saviour* or *Salvation*, and with reference to *Jehovah* as its author. (See Num. 13, 8. 16. 1 Chr. 7, 27. Neh. 8, 17.) This idea, suggested by its very etymology, is distinctly expressed in the remainder of the verse. The verb translated *save* means strictly to *preserve* or *keep safe*, but is secondarily applied to active rescue or deliverance from evil, whether natural or moral, being equally appropriate to bodily healing and to spiritual renovation. *His people* would be naturally understood by Joseph as referring to the chosen race, the family of Israel, not as a state or nation merely, but as a church or spiritual corporation, and as such including all who should believe in Christ as the appointed Saviour. *From their sins*, not merely from the punishment which they deserved and the effects which they produced, but from

* Luke 1, 27. 30. 34. 38. 39. 46. 56. 2. 5. 16. 19. 34.

the guilt and turpitude of sin itself. The word here used is properly a negative description of moral evil, as a failure or short-coming, from a verb which primarily means to aim wrong or to miss the mark. But as this deficiency or failure has respect precisely to what man owes and what God requires, it becomes in usage one of the strongest and most positive expressions for sin as a want of conformity to the law of God. This description of Christ's mission as a moral and religious, not a secular and civil one, affords a key to his whole history as well as a sufficient refutation of the silly notion, that the salvation here ascribed to him (and in Luke 1, 68. 71. 74) is emancipation from the yoke of Roman bondage, and the restoration of their former independence.

22. Now all this was done, that it might be fulfilled which was spoken of the Lord by the prophet, saying.

Here again, as in v. 18, the word translated *now* is the usual connective (δέ) corresponding to our *and* or *but*, and continuing the sentence without interruption from the verse preceding. This construction raises a presumption that the words which follow are those of the same speaker, namely, of the angel, a presumption which can only be destroyed by something in the words themselves forbidding it. But instead of this, they rather strengthen and conform it. The expression *all this*, or retaining the exact form of the Greek phrase, *this whole (matter)*, i. e. the betrothal and conception of Mary, is more natural if uttered by the angel at the time than if added by the evangelist long after. The verb too is in the perfect tense and properly means *has (now) come to pass* (or *happened*), and not, *did come to pass* (or *happen*) at some former time. This distinction between the perfect and the aorist is clearly marked, not only in the theory of the Greek verb and the practice of the classical Greek writers, but also in the usage of the New Testament where the perfect tense of this verb occurs more than sixty times, and with a few exceptions (such as Matt. 25, 6. Rom. 16, 7. Gal. 3, 17. 1 Thess. 2, 1. 1 Tim. 2, 14. Heb. 7, 16), some of which are doubtful, not only may but must be rendered by our perfect to express its full force, although rarely so translated (as in Acts 4, 16. Rom. 6, 5. 11, 25), being usually rendered by the simple past tense or the present passive.* The same thing is true of the participial, infinitive, and pluperfect forms,† and of some places where the oldest copies have a different reading (e. g. Matt. 19, 8. 24, 21. John 6, 25. 12, 30. 14, 22. Rom. 7, 13. Gal. 3, 24). That the two tenses are not simply convertible in either language, may be seen from Rev. 16, 17. 21, 6, where *it is done* means *it has come to pass*, and could not be exchanged for *it was done*, *it happened*, or *it came to pass*, without destroying, or at least obscuring the sense of the expres-

---

* See Mark 5, 33. 9, 21. 13, 19. 14, 4. Luke 14, 22. John 1, 15. 27. 30. 5, 14. Acts 4, 21. 22. Rom. 2, 25. 11, 5. 1 Cor. 9, 22. 13, 1. 5, 17. 12, 11. Gal. 4, 16. Heb. 3, 14. 5, 11. 12. 12, 8. Jas. 2, 10. 2 Pet. 2, 20.

† Mark 5, 14. Luke 2, 15. 8, 34–35. 56. 10, 36. 24, 12. John 6, 17. 12, 29. Acts 5, 7. 13, 12. Gal. 3, 17. 1 Tim. 5, 9. 2, 18. Heb. 7, 20–23. 11, 3. 1 John 2, 18.

sion. Such being the settled usage of the form here used, as signifying, not what *happened once* (ἐγένετο), but what *has happened now* (γέγονε), it may be added to the phrase before it (*all this*) as a further reason for regarding these as the words of the angel, and not of the historian. The conclusion thus reached is confirmed not only by the authority of Chrysostom and other Greek interpreters, to whom the nice distinction of the tenses must have been familiar, but also by the parallel cases in 21, 4. 26, 56 below, where the construction is precisely similar. *Fulfilled*, a verb originally meaning *filled full*, in the physical or proper sense (as in 13, 48. Luke 3, 5. John 12, 3. Acts 2, 2), and often applied figuratively to internal states or exercises,* and to completion or completeness, especially in reference to time,† but also to the full performance of a promise or an obligation,‡ and to the accomplishment or verification of a prophecy, as here and often elsewhere, but especially in Matthew's Gospel.§ *That it might be fulfilled* is the strict (and according to the highest modern philological authorities the only) sense of the original expression, as denoting purpose or deliberate intention. But besides this *telic* use (as the grammarians call it) of the Greek conjunction (ἵνα), some contend for an *ecbatic* use, denoting not design, but mere result or consequence, however unforeseen or accidental. As examples of this latter use are cited John 9, 2. Rom. 5, 20. 11, 11, and the case before us, with the many others like it, where the sense will then be, *so that it was fulfilled.* As the other sense, however, is at once the proper and the common one, the best interpreters consider it as doubly entitled to the preference in this case. It does not mean, however, that the prediction was the cause of the event, which some make an objection to the *telic* explanation, but that the event was necessary to the execution of the divine purpose as expressed in the prediction *which was spoken*, literally, *the (thing) spoken*, not merely written, but originally uttered viva voce. *Of the Lord by the prophet*, or as it might be rendered more explicitly and more agreeably to modern usage, *by the Lord* (as the prime agent or the ultimate author of the revelation) *through the prophet* (as the instrumental agent or the organ of communication). *The prophet* is Isaiah, as expressed in one old manuscript (the Codex Bezæ), in whose writings the quotation is still extant (see Isai. 7, 14), and of whose divine legation we have here inspired if not angelic attestation. This is the first appearance of a feature characterizing this whole gospel, namely the express quotation of Old Testament predictions which had been fulfilled in the life of Christ.

---

* See Luke 2, 40. John 3, 29. 15, 11. 16, 6. 24. 17, 13. Acts 2, 28. 5, 3. 13, 52. Rom. 1, 29. 15, 13. 14. 2 Cor. 7, 4. Eph. 3, 19. 5, 18. Phil. 1, 11. Col. 1, 9. 2 Tim. 1, 4. 1 John 1, 4. 2 John 12.
† See 23, 32. Mark 1, 15. Luke 7, 1. 9, 31. 21, 24. John 7, 8. Acts 7, 23. 30. 9, 23. 12, 25. 13, 25. 14, 26. 19, 21. 24, 27. Rev. 6, 11.
‡ See 3, 15. 5, 17. Luke 1, 20. Rom. 8, 4. 13, 8. 2 Cor. 10, 6. Gal. 5, 14. Col. 1, 25. 4, 17. Jas. 2, 23.
§ See below, 2, 15. 17. 23. 4, 14. 8, 17. 12, 17. 13, 35. 21, 4. 26, 54. 56. 27, 9. 35.

23. Behold, a virgin shall be with child, and shall bring forth a son, and they shall call his name Emmanuel; which being interpreted is, God with us.

The quotation is made almost precisely in the terms of the Septuagint version. One of the two variations (ἕξει for λήψεται) exists only in relation to the Vatican text of the Seventy, the Alexandrian agreeing with the text of Matthew. This difference is merely one of form, without the least effect upon the meaning. The other variation (καλέσουσι for καλέσεις) is of more significance, though really of little moment, as it merely substitutes the indefinite expression, *they shall call*, equivalent to *shall be called* (compare Luke 12, 20) for the definite address to the mother (*thou shalt call*), which is itself most probably a substitute for the third person (*she shall call*) of the Hebrew text.* The essential point is the act of naming, not the person who performed it. Another variation, both of the Septuagint and Gospel, from the precise form of the Hebrew text, is the substitution of the future (*shall conceive* or *be with child*) for the present, as implied though not expressed in the original construction, which is participial or adjective, not verbal. *Behold, the virgin pregnant* (or *with child*), as if actually present to the prophet's senses. But this too is a merely formal difference, the words confessedly relating to the future, whether proximate or distant. The Hebrew word translated *virgin* (παρθένος) is not the usual equivalent of those Greek and English terms, but one which properly denotes a girl, maiden, or young woman, and is so rendered by the other ancient Greek translators (νεᾶνις). Some suppose this difference in the old Greek versions to be connected with a different interpretation of the passage; but the two are really equivalent, as the Hebrew word (הָעַלְמָה) is always applied elsewhere to unmarried women,† and as the stronger terms, in Hebrew (בְּתוּלָה), Greek (παρθένος), Latin (*virgo*), are occasionally used of wives and mothers;‡ so that the idea of a virgin is as strongly expressed here as it could be. *A virgin* greatly weakens the original expression, which is definite in Greek (ἡ παρθένος) as well as Hebrew (הָעַלְמָה), and denotes *the* (particular) *virgin* in whom the prediction was especially verified. *Lo* (or *behold*), as usual, introduces something novel, unexpected, and surprising. The name in this case is descriptive, and was not to be actually borne in real life, as *Jesus* was. *They shall call*, i. e. they shall have cause or occasion, so to call him; he shall be entitled to the name *Immanuel*. *God with us* has both a lower and a higher sense, sometimes denoting a gracious or providential presence and protection,§ but in this case an essential and personal divine manifestation. *Interpreted*, translated out of Hebrew into

---
* (קָרָאת), as in Lev. 25, 21. Ps. 118, 23. Gen. 33, 11; but compare Gen. 16, 11, where the same form is undoubtedly the second person.
† See Gen. 24, 43. Ex. 2, 8. Ps. 68, 26. Prov. 30, 19. Song Sol. 1, 3. 6, 8.
‡ See Joel 1, 8. Homer Il. 2, 514. Virgil Ecl. 6, 47. Æn. 1, 493.
§ See Josh. 1, 5. Ps. 46, 7. 11. 89, 25. Jer. 1, 8. Isai. 43, 21.

Greek (Tyndale: by interpretation, *Cranmer: which, if a man interpret it, is as much as to say*), which some regard as a proof that Matthew was originally written in the latter language; but although this is probable for other reasons (see above, the general introduction p. 1), it does not follow necessarily from this clause which might have been inserted by the Greek translator. The application of this prophecy to Christ is not a mere accommodation, meaning that the words, originally used in one sense and in reference to one subject, might now be repeated in another sense and of another subject; for this does not satisfy the strong terms of the passage (*all this happened that it might be fulfilled*), nor would such a fanciful coincidence have been alleged with so much emphasis by Matthew, still less by the Angel. The only sense that can be reasonably put upon the words is, that the miraculous conception of Messiah was predicted by Isaiah in the words here quoted. This essential meaning is not affected by the question whether the prediction was a mediate or immediate, a twofold or exclusive one; that is to say, whether it was first fulfilled in the natural birth of a child soon after it was uttered, and the subsequent deliverance of Judah from invasion, but again fulfilled, and in a higher sense, in the nativity of Christ; or whether it related only to the latter, and presented it to Ahaz as a pledge that the chosen people could not be destroyed until Messiah came. Both these opinions are maintained by eminent interpreters, whose arguments, however, belong rather to the exposition of Isaiah than of Matthew. His authoritative exposition of the prophecy extends no further than the fact of its fulfilment in the miraculous conception of the Saviour.

24. Then Joseph, being raised from sleep, did as the angel of the Lord had bidden him, and took unto him his wife.

This verse records the execution of the order sent to Joseph through the Angel, in a form very common both in Homer and the Scriptures, i. e. by repeating the terms of the command from v. 20, in the same sense that was there explained. *His wife* (like *thy wife* in the verse referred to) may either simply designate the person (*her who was his wife*), or have the more emphatic sense of *as* (or *for*) *his wife*. The former construction is more natural, especially in this case, where Mary is not named, and is commonly adopted by the best interpreters. *Had bidden* is in Greek a verb originally meaning to arrange, array, and specially applied, as a military term, to the posting or stationing of troops, but also employed by the best Attic writers in the secondary sense of enjoining any thing on a person, or (without an accusative, as here) commanding him.

25. And knew her not till she had brought forth her first-born son: and he called his name JESUS.

This verse has been the subject of dispute for ages, not as to what it expresses, but as to what it implies. The question is not what the words directly mean, but what is the inference to be drawn from them. *Knew her not*, as his wife, cohabited with her only in the primary but wider sense of the expression, as denoting residence together. The remainder of the verse seems to limit this negation to the time which intervened between the divine communication made to Joseph and the birth of Christ. From this it is now inferred by some interpreters that after that event other children were born to Joseph and Mary, and that these are mentioned in the sequel as the brothers and sisters of our Lord.* This is supposed to be necessarily implied in Matthew's use both of the particle (*until*) and of the adjective (*first-born*).† But these implications, although plausible, are not necessary or certain. *Until*, and its equivalents in other languages (עד, ἕως, *donec*), affirm and deny nothing beyond the *terminus ad quem* which they are used to designate, but leave the rest to be discovered in some other way. The Greek interpreters assert this to be the usage of the word employed in this case (ἕως), and refer for proof to Gen. 8, 7 and Ps. 110, 1, to which others have added Isai. 42, 3, as quoted in Matt. 12, 20, where the meaning cannot be that after he has sent forth judgment unto victory he will begin to bruise the broken reed and quench the smoking flax. So too in 1 Tim. 4, 13, Paul cannot mean to say that after he comes Timothy must cease to read, exhort, and teach. Nor is the contrary affirmed in either case, but simply left to be determined by the context or the nature of the case. These examples are sufficient to establish the position, that the inference in question from the use of the word *till*, however natural, is not conclusive; or in other words, that this expression cannot prove the fact of subsequent cohabitation in the face of cogent reasons for disputing it. As to the word *first-born*, the mistake lies in making it a popular expression, to be interpreted by common usage, whereas it is a technical term of the Mosaic law, and as such familiar to the Jews of that day both in Greek and Hebrew, being constantly employed in the Septuagint version, to translate the Hebrew term applied to the firstling both of man and beast, but by way of eminence to the human child by which the womb was opened, or the woman first became a mother. Such children were devoted to God, partly in commemoration of the Hebrew first-born being spared when those of Egypt were destroyed.‡ Can it be supposed that the destroying angel on that memorable night passed by those Egyptian families in which there was a single child; or that the law for the redemption of the first-born was suspended till a second child was born? If not, the legal epithet *first-born* included not only the eldest but also only chil-

---

* See ch. 12, 46. 13, 55. John 7, 3. 1 Cor. 15, 7. Gal. 1, 19.
† Wiclif and Cranmer: *first-begotten.* Tyndale: *first son.* Geneva and Rheims: *first-born.*
‡ See Ex. 4, 22. 23. 11, 5. 12, 12. 29. 13, 2. 13. 15. 22, 29. 34, 20. Lev. 27, 26. Num. 3, 12. 13. 40-51. 8, 16-18. 18, 15-17. 33, 4. Deut. 15, 19, and compare Neh. 10, 36. Ps. 77, 56. 104, 36. 134, 8. 135, 10.

dren, and its constant use in this extended application in the law not only might but must have made it perfectly intelligible as applied to Jesus though he were the sole child of his mother. It is not true, therefore, as is frequently alleged by modern writers, that the use of either of these terms by Matthew necessarily implies the birth of other children. Equally groundless is the common allegation that no other inference would ever have been thought of, but for a superstitious reverence for the Virgin Mary, and an ascetic over-estimate of virginity as a holier state than that of marriage. Entirely apart from such corruptions and anterior to their appearance, there was a strong ground for believing the virginity of our Lord's mother to have been perpetual, afforded by the obvious consideration, that the same reasons which required it before his birth might possibly at least require it afterwards. This analogy is not at all dependent on the nature of those reasons, which to us may be inscrutable, but simply on the fact of their existence. If, *for any reason*, it would not have been becoming or expedient that the woman chosen to be the mother of our Lord should sustain the same relation to any other child before his birth, why was it any more becoming or expedient after he was born? This view of the matter may at least induce us to suspend our judgment on this delicate and interesting question, without any fear of popish or ascetic superstition, till the history itself shall furnish further data for a definite conclusion. (See below, on 10, 3. 12, 47. 13, 55. 28, 10.) In the mean time, all that this verse necessarily imports is that her virginity remained unimpaired, if not forever, yet at least *till she became a mother*, which is the essential fact expressed by the phrase, *brought forth her first-born son*, just as the corresponding term (*begat*) in the preceding genealogy denotes the analogous relation of paternity. (See above, on v. 2.) The omission of the word (πρωτότοκον) from which this whole discussion has arisen, in the oldest extant manuscript (the Codex Vaticanus) and in the old Egyptian versions, though regarded by the latest critics as a sufficient reason for expunging it, may be a mere attempt of the transcribers and translators to cut the knot which they despaired of loosing.

CHAPTER II.

In further prosecution of his purpose to demonstrate the Messiahship of Jesus, Matthew now relates his recognition by representatives of the Gentile world, closely connected, both in prophecy and history, with his birth in Bethlehem, and with his escape from the murderous designs of Herod, by being carried into Egypt, his return thence, and his subsequent residence in Nazareth, all which the Evangelist exhibits as the fulfilment of Old Testament predictions. The contents of this chapter have peculiar interest, not only on their own account, but also as affording the most striking illustration of the plan on which this Gospel is constructed, and of its distinctive character, as being not a mere history but a historical argument in favour of our Lord's Messiahship.

1. Now when Jesus was born in Bethlehem of Judea, in the days of Herod the king, behold, there came wise men from the east to Jerusalem.

The actual nativity of Christ is only recorded incidentally by Matthew, in the last verse of the preceding chapter, and again in this verse, as an event which had already taken place. A detailed account of the time, place, and other circumstances, is supplied by Luke (2, 1–20). The connective particle (δέ) makes this as a direct continuation of the narrative in ch. 1. 'He knew her not until she had brought forth her first-born son, and when he was brought forth,' &c. *Jesus having been produced,* i. e. conceived and born, both which ideas are included in the meaning of the Greek verb, and its corresponding noun (see above, on 1, 2. 18). *Bethlehem* (the house of bread), an ancient town belonging to the tribe of Judah, and as such distinguished from another of the same name in the tribe of Zebulon (Josh. 19, 15). It is still in existence, about six miles south or south-west of Jerusalem. Though not a town of large size or political importance, it was early famous as the residence of Jesse and the birth-place of David. (1 Sam. 16, 1. 17, 58. Luke 1, 11. John 7, 42.) *Herod,* commonly surnamed the Great, was the son of Antipater, an Idumean and the confidential counsellor of the last of the Maccabees or Hasmonean princes, who reigned in Judea from the time of Antiochus Epiphanes (B. C. 175) to the Roman conquest (B. C. 53). Herod, at a very early age, was governor of Galilee, but having taken refuge from his enemies at Rome, there enjoyed the favour of Mark Anthony and Octavian (afterwards Augustus) and by order of the Senate was crowned king of the Jews at the Capitol. With the aid of the Roman General Sosius, he obtained possession of his kingdom and reigned thirty-seven years, with great talent and success as a secular ruler, but with great severity and jealousy towards all competitors and rivals, not excepting his own children and the Hasmonean family with which he intermarried. Hence he is chargeable with acts of extreme cruelty, including the murder of his wife and three sons. His ruling passion was the love of architectural embellishment, which he indulged by rebuilding and beautifying many towns in Palestine and elsewhere, but especially by the renovation of the temple (see below, on 24, 1, and compare John 2, 20). *The days* is an indefinite expression applicable to his whole life or his long reign, but here applied to its conclusion. What is here recorded must, however, have occurred at least forty days before his death, as we know from Josephus that his last forty days were spent, not at Jerusalem, but at Jericho and the baths of Callirhoe. *Behold*, as usual, implies that their coming was unlooked for and surprising (see above, on 1, 23). *Came* is in Greek a verb without exact equivalent in English, strictly meaning *became near* (or *present*), but of course implying previous arrival. *Wise men* is Tyndale's vague translation of *Magi* or Magians, a word used by Herodotus to signify the learned tribe or caste among the ancient Medians or Persians, whose cultivation of astrology and other occult sciences gave rise to the derivative terms *magic, magical, magician*. A trace of this usage may be found in the phrase *Rab-mag* (chief magician) as the title of an officer or courtier at the camp of Babylon (Jer. 39, 3), perhaps the same place which was occupied by Daniel (2, 48). The word is here used without any implication of unlawful or disreputable practices. Wiclif translates it *astromyens* (astronomers), and the Rhemish version *sages*. That the providential representatives of heathendom were chosen from this class, may imply the existence of some old tradition, perhaps connected with the record or the memory of astronomical phenomena. (See below, upon the next verse.) The word translated *east* means originally *rise* or *rising*, and is elsewhere coupled with *the sun* (as in Rev. 7, 2. 16, 12), but here denotes that quarter of the heavens or the earth. The form is plural, as in 8, 11. 24, 27 below, where the term is also used in a vague but local sense. It cannot therefore be determined from the word itself whether these Magi came from Persia, Arabia, Babylonia, or some still remoter country. An old ecclesiastical tradition makes them three in number (from the three gifts mentioned in v. 11) and the representatives of as many countries. Caspar, Melchior, and Balthazar, are the names attached to them by this tradition, which also makes them kings of their respective countries. Hence "The Three Kings," is among the most familiar popular traditions of the old world, even on the signs of shops and taverns. *From the east* is construed by the best interpreters, not with the verb but with the noun, *wise men from the east*, i. e. originating or belonging there. *Jerusalem* (here *Hierosolyma*), anciently called *Salem* (Gen. 14, 18. Ps. 76, 2, and *Jebus* (Judg. 19, 10. 11), in an elevated situation nearly midway between the Mediterranean and the Dead Sea, conquered by David from the Jebusites (2 Sam. 5, 6–9), and thenceforth the political capital of Israel and seat of the theocracy. Having been destroyed at the Babylonian conquest (2 Kings 25, 8–10), it was rebuilt at the Restoration (Neh. 2, 5. 3, 1–32), and retained its metropolitan pre-eminence under Herod and the Romans. To this well-known centre the wise men from the east would of course resort in the first instance.

2. Saying, Where is he that is born King of the Jews? for we have seen his star in the east, and are come to worship him.

This verse assigns the reason of their visit, as given by themselves (*saying*). They assume the fact of his nativity as certain, and the time as known already (see below, on v. 7), and merely inquire for the place, as something not revealed or ascertainable from astronomical phenomena. *The (one) born*, already, as the past participle (τεχθείς from the verb used in 1, 25), denotes. The Geneva Bible follows the Peshito in construing the words thus, *that king of (the) Jews that is born*. But the common version (which is Tyndale's) agrees better with the form of the original. *King of the Jews*, the title applied to the Messiah in the New Testament by Gentiles (see below, 27, 29. 37, and compare John 18, 33). while the Jews themselves called him *King of Israel* (see below, 27, 42, and compare John 1, 50. 12, 13.) After the downfall of the kingdom of the ten tribes, and particularly after the return from exile, the whole nation being merged in Judah, the name *Jew* became a general one, especially with foreigners, and is applied in the New Testament, not only to the people of Judea in the strict sense, but to those of Galilee, in reference both to their religion and their national descent (as in Luke 7, 3. John 2, 6. Acts 10, 28, and elsewhere). As the throne of David had been vacant now for ages, the inquiry of the wise men had respect not to the actual sovereign, who was not an Israelite at all, but to the hereditary rightful sovereign who had just been born. This meaning of the question will account for the effect which it produced according to the next verse. *Have seen*, or more exactly, *saw*, i. e. on a particular occasion and some time ago. Even if they came no further than from Babylonia, they may have been as long upon the road as Ezra and his colony, to wit, four months (see Ezr. 7, 9); but this is quite uncertain and was not intended to be made known by this narrative. *His star*, i. e. one relating or belonging to him, either by a special revelation, or according to the principles of their astronomy, which partook no doubt of what we call astrology, i. e. prognostication of the future from the relative positions of the heavenly bodies. Their conclusions may however have been drawn from real astronomical phenomena, interpreted according to some old tradition, perhaps, that of Balaam (Num. 24, 17), or Daniel's prediction of the seventy weeks (Dan. 9, 24), both of which were probably preserved in the east, or at least in Babylonia. *Star* is in Greek a word applied to any luminary in the heavens, whether fixed star, planet, comet or meteor, all which have been supposed by different interpreters to be intended here. More than one eminent astronomer has understood it as referring to a remarkable conjunction of the planets Jupiter and Saturn in the sign of Pisces, which is said to have occurred three times in the year 747 after the building of Rome. The first of these conjunctions may have been observed in Babylonia and the last in Judea (see below, on v. 9). The star may then denote the conjunction itself, which is not inconsistent with the vague use of the Greek word, or the appearance of a new star, in the strict sense by which the conjunction may have been accompanied, as it was (according to Kepler) in the year 1604. By a singular coincidence Abarbanel, a famous Jewish writer of the fifteenth century, without alluding to the cases just referred to, speaks of a similar conjunction in the same sign of the Zodiac as having preceded the birth of Moses, and as having been repeated in his own day, (A. D. 1463), from which he infers that the Messiah was about to appear. The concurrence is in this case so remarkable, and the explanation recommended by such high scientific authority, that it would probably have been universally adopted, but for the foregone conclusion, in the minds of many, that the birth of Christ took place in a different year. But that assumption is so doubtful, and the views of the best writers so discordant, that it can scarcely be allowed to decide the question now before us, but may rather be decided by it. This astronomical solution is, at all events, both from its scientific character and from the high authority on which it rests, more satisfactory than the assumption of a transient meteor, a comet, or a purely miraculous appearance, which would here be less impressive than a natural phenomenon, coincident with such a juncture in the moral world, and showing both to be under the same infinitely powerful and wise control. This hypothesis moreover agrees best with the traditional devotion of the wise men of the East (i. e. of Babylonia and the adjacent regions watered by the Tigris and Euphrates) to astronomy, which would naturally lead them to observe such unusual appearances and perhaps to compare them with others of the same kind, preserved by the tradition of their science, and connected with previous critical conjunctures in the history of Israel, from which they might, erroneously or otherwise, infer that what they now saw was a premonition of the advent of that great deliverer, for whom, according to two Roman historians, the whole East had long been looking.* This is a testimony too explicit and unqualified to be explained away, as some modern sceptics have attempted, as a mere misapprehension or transcription of a passage in Josephus, where he disingenuously represents the Messianic prophecies of Scripture as pointing to Vespasian, who was proclaimed Emperor, on the death of Vitellius, by the army under his command in Palestine. What is most important, after all, however, is to distinguish even the most plausible conjectures from the simple statement of the wise men in the text, that they had seen what they regarded as *his star*, i. e. a heavenly phenomenon relating to him. *In the east* may be construed either with the subject or the object of the verb, *we* (while still) *in the east saw his star*, or, *we saw his star* (appearing) *in the east*, an ambiguity of syntax which leaves it doubtful in what part of the heavens they beheld it. Some interpreters evade the solution of this question by giving the Greek noun (ἀνατολή) its primary sense of *rise* or *rising* (see above, on v. 1), which it has in one place (Luke 1, 78), though translated *dayspring*. The principal objection to this explanation is the want of any reason for referring to the rise any more than to the culmination of the star. *Are come*, or more exactly, *came*, that is, just now, or lately, which is substantially the meaning of the common version. *Worship*, a Greek verb which orig-

---

* Percrebuerat Oriente toto vetus et constans opinio, esse in fatis ut eo tempore Judæa profecti rerum potirentur (*Sueton. Vespas. IV.*) Pluribus persuasio inerat, antiquis sacerdotum literis contineri, eo ipso tempore fore ut valesceret Oriens, profecti Judæa rerum potirentur (*Tucit. Annal V. 13*).

inally means to kiss the hand, the garments, or the ground before one, as an oriental method of expressing the profoundest reverence, and therefore specially applied to the act of doing homage to a Sovereign, which in ancient times, and in the east especially, was seldom free from some idolatrous ascription of divine honours even to a human being. There is therefore the less reason for explaining the word here of purely civil reverence or homage, to perform which could not well be the sole object of these Magi in their journey from the east, which would have been wholly out of place upon the part of Herod (see below, on v. 8). The meaning, therefore, must be that they came to do reverence and homage to a new-born child, as the Messiah, the long-expected *king of the Jews*, the benefits of whose reign were to extend to other nations also.

3. When Herod the king had heard (these things), he was troubled, and all Jerusalem with him.

The effect of this unexpected visit and inquiry was such as might have been expected. *And hearing* (*it*, or *this*, or *these things*), *Herod the king*, de facto, as distinguished from the king de jure, who had just been born. *Troubled*, disturbed, agitated, with jealous fear of a competitor, which is known to have been one of Herod's weaknesses, and one which seems to have continued with him till his death, as such infirmities often do, even when rendered most irrational by age or other circumstances. *All Jerusalem*, a natural and common figure for its whole population, which occurs again in 3, 5 below. *With him* may mean in sympathy with him, but more probably denotes mere coincidence of time and place. The causes of the agitation cannot have been perfectly identical. While Herod trembled for his throne, the people would naturally dread his violence, or the troubles incident to any revolution, or, as some suppose, the evils which were expected to precede the reign of the Messiah and were proverbially called his sorrows.

4. And when he had gathered all the chief priests and scribes of the people together, he demanded of them where Christ should be born.

That Herod understood their question as relating to the birth of the Messiah, now appears from the mode in which he answered it, not by a mere declaration of his own, but by appealing to the highest authority in all such matters. *Chief priests* the plural of the word elsewhere rendered *High Priest* (see below 26, 3. 51. 57. 58. 62. 63. 65), and denoting in the singular the hereditary head of the family of Aaron and of the sacerdotal tribe of Levi. Although this office could be held by only one person at a time according to the law of Moses, the Romans had usurped the power of appointing and displacing the High Priest at pleasure, so that there were often several who had enjoyed the dignity. These some suppose to be the *chief priests* mentioned in the Gospels. Others understand the term to designate the heads of the twenty-four courses into which the priesthood was divided by David (1 Chr. 24, 3–18), or the natural heads of the families descended from Aaron; or such priests as were members of the Sanhedrim, either by elective or hereditary right, equal perhaps in number to the Scribes and Elders, who had seats in the same body, i. e. twenty-four of each class, making seventy-two in all, a number borrowed from the seventy elders who assisted Moses in the wilderness (Numb. 11, 16. 24), and of whom this body may have claimed to be successors, though it probably originated in the exile. *The scribes* were the successors of Ezra, as conservators of the Old Testament canon, and as this office required a critical acquaintance with the text of scripture, the same persons would of course be its professional expounders. The name may have primarily signified their office as transcribers of the law, or it may be derived directly from the word meaning *Scriptures*, and denote a scripturist, or one employed about the sacred volume. *Scribes of the people* does not mean private unofficial scribes, but, on the contrary, national or public scribes, those who held the office, not for private advantage but for the general benefit and service. *All the chief priests and scribes* cannot, of course, be strictly understood, since they were scattered through the country, but must either mean all who were accessible, all then present in Jerusalem, or all who were members of the Sanhedrim. Most interpreters prefer the latter supposition, and regard this as a formal meeting of the Sanhedrim itself. The third class which composed it is not mentioned; but it is a common usage to describe the Sanhedrim by naming two of its component orders.* Or the scribes and priests may be particularly mentioned as the proper arbiters of such a question. *Christ*, the Christ, the Messiah, the anointed (see above, on 1, 1). *Should be born*, or more exactly, *is born* as an abstract proposition, without reference to time, so as to leave it undetermined whether the event had actually taken place or was still future. (For a similar use of the indefinite present, see 1 Cor. 15, 35. John 7, 42.)

5. And they said unto him, In Bethlehem of Judea: for thus it is written by the prophet.

This is the reply of the chief priests and the scribes to Herod's question, returned no doubt by the whole body through their official representatives, and not promiscuously by the individual members. The answer seems to have been given without any hesitation, as a matter perfectly well understood and settled by divine authority. *By* or *through* (as in 1, 22) *the prophet*, too well known to Herod and the other Jewish hearers to require specification. (See Micah 5, 1. 2, where the passage is still extant.) *For* assigns the reason of their prompt decided answer, and imparts to it a meaning or an emphasis

---

* Compare 16, 21. 26, 3. 59, with 20, 19. 27, 1.

equivalent to that expressed by our phrase "of course." *Thus* may either mean *as follows*, or more probably, *as just said*, referring to the immediately foregoing designation of the place of the Messiah's birth. As if they had said: where should he be born except at Bethlehem, the place expressly fixed by God himself speaking through his inspired prophet. *It is written,* more exactly, *has been written,* the perfect tense suggesting the additional idea of its having been not only uttered long ago, but ever since on record and awaiting its fulfilment.

6. And thou Bethlehem, (in) the land of Juda, art not the least among the princes of Juda: for out of thee shall come a Governor, that shall rule my people Israel.

The retention of the particle at the beginning shows that this was meant to be a formal quotation, not a mere allusion or a paraphrase. *Thou,* or *as for thee,* in reference to what immediately precedes, not here, but in the original connection (Mic. 5, 1). Instead of *Ephrath* (or *Ephrata*), an old name of Bethlehem (Gen. 48, 7), which distinguished it from Bethlehem in Zebulon (Josh. 19, 15), the evangelist or the scribes themselves distinguished it still more expressly by the phrase *land (of) Judah.* Some suppose *land* to be here used for *town* or *city,* as it sometimes is in the Septuagint version. Others take it in a wider although still restricted sense, as including both the town and the surrounding district. (See below, on v. 16.) But the simplest explanation is that which makes it an elliptical expression meaning (*in*) *the land of Judah,* just as we add the name of the state to that of the town (e. g. *Princeton, New Jersey*). *Not the least,* or more emphatically, *not at all* (or *not by any means*) *the least.* This peculiar form of speech suggests a sort of contrast or antithesis, as if it had been said, 'thou art not the least after all,' or, 'as thou wast of old described,' implying that both accounts were just, and that while it was the least in one sense, it was not the least, or (by a natural litotes or meiosis) was the greatest in another. This furnishes a key to the apparent disagreement between Micah and Matthew, and removes the necessity of charging the supposed inaccuracy on the Sanhedrim, whose words the evangelist reports without correction. Besides the extreme improbability of such an error or perversion, on the part of such a body, on so public and important an occasion, its retention would be utterly at variance with the plan of this evangelist, whose gospel is constructed on the very principle of choosing such events as proved or exemplified the fulfilment of prophecy, a design which could not have been promoted by the record of a false citation. The variation was no doubt intentional and meant to be a sort of gloss or comment on the obscure language of the prophet *little to be among* (i. e. too little to be named or reckoned among) *the thousands of Judah,* i. e. the divisions of the tribe (as in Judges 6, 15. 1 Sam. 10, 19). It is, to say the least, a singular coincidence, that Bethlehem is not named among the cities of Judah in the Hebrew text of Josh. 15, 59, although inserted with ten others by the Greek translators, who to make the text and context uniform, subjoin the summary "eleven cities with their villages." This is now regarded, by the highest critical authorities, as one of many instances in which these old translators sought to rectify the errors and supply the omissions of the Hebrew text, as they considered them. To say nothing of the other ten, the absence of Bethlehem from the official list is in striking agreement with its external insignificance as testified by all tradition, and explicitly asserted by the prophet in the passage quoted. The greatness here set off against it is entirely moral, and arises from the fact that Messiah was to be a native of this otherwise obscure and unimportant place. It is not to be overlooked, however, that this contrast had already been partially presented in the type, though it could only be completed in the antitype. David, the first and greatest of the theocratic sovereigns, and the most honoured representative of the Messiah as a king before he actually came, was born and spent his early life at Bethlehem. That the two things were connected, not only in the divine purpose, but in the popular belief and expectation, may be gathered from John 7, 42, compared with Luke 2, 4. 11, and with the original history in the sixteenth chapter of First Samuel. *Princes*, leaders, governors (10, 18. 27, 2. 11. 14. 15. 23. 27. 28, 14), are put for the original term *thousands* (Sept. χιλίασιν), by a sort of personification in which the heads of families represent the families themselves and the places of their residence. There is no need therefore of explaining the Greek word (ἡγέμοσιν) as an adjective agreeing with a noun understood and meaning *chief* (*towns* or *cities*), which is moreover not sustained by usage. Still less admissible is a change in the Hebrew text, or rather in its pointing, so as to read *chiefs* (אַלֻּפֵי) instead of *thousands* (אַלְפֵי). This is not only needless and gratuitous, but inconsistent with the usage of the former word (אַלֻּפִים), which does not mean a chief in general, but a duke of Edom, the distinctive term happily employed in the English version of Gen. 36. 15–43. 1 Chr. 1, 51–54, the only place where the word occurs, except a few times in the later prophets (Jer. 13, 21. Zech. 9, 7. 12, 5. 6.), when the primitive usage may have been corrupted, or perhaps alluded to by way of contrast (e. g. in Zech. 9, 7, 'like an Edomitish chief in Judah'). *For* introduces or assigns the reason why the same place could be least and not least among the thousands of Judah. *Out of thee shall come* may have the strict sense of local derivation and progression, or the figurative one of birth and genealogical extraction, which is a common one in Hebrew. (See Gen. 17, 6. 46, 26. Isai. 39, 7, and compare Heb. 7, 5.) That the relation thus described is not immediate but remote, i. e. not birth at Bethlehem but mere descent from ancestors who lived there, is a figment invented by the later Jews to justify their application of the passage to Zerubbabel, who was no doubt born in Babylonia. (See Ezra 2, 1. 2.) The obvious meaning of the word is that Bethlehem itself, considered as a place, was to be magnified by giving birth to an illustrious personage, who is then described in the remainder of the sentence. *A governor*, chief, leader, not the word translated *princes* in the first clause, but of kindred origin, the essential idea being in both cases that of leading, taking the lead, acting as a leader. As the other is a noun (ἡγεμών) answering to *leader*, so this is properly a participle (ἡγούμενος) and denotes *a leading* (*man* or *person*), although variously rendered elsewhere.* One of the oldest versions (the Peshito) uses *king* for both words. The general description is then specified by indicating where and among whom he was to be a leader. *Rule* is in the margin of the English Bible *feed*, neither of which conveys the full force of the Greek verb (ποιμανεῖ), derived from a noun (ποιμήν) meaning *shepherd*, and itself denoting the whole office of a shepherd, which includes not only feeding but protection and control. Both in the literal and figurative usage of the term, the first of these ideas sometimes predominates (as in John 21, 16. Jude 12. Rev. 7, 17), sometimes the other (as in Rev. 2, 27. 12, 5. 19, 15), sometimes both are meant to be included (as in Luke 17, 17. Acts 20, 28. 1 Cor. 9, 7. 1 Pet. 5, 2). The figurative representation of civil rulers, and especially of kings, as shepherds, is natural and common in the classics, as appears from the favourite Homeric phrase, "shepherds of the people," from Xenophon's explicit affirmation of the likeness, and from the saying of Tiberius preserved by Suetonius, and worthy of a better origin, that the part of a good shepherd is to feed his flock, not to devour it. The same application of the term occurs in Scripture, even where the English reader may suppose a reference to spiritual functions only, as the pastors and shepherds, so often spoken of by Jeremiah and other prophets,† are not religious ministers, at least not exclusively, but also civil rulers. This last clause, *who shall rule* (or *feed*) *my people Israel*, is not formally contained in the original, though really involved in the first words of Micah 5, 4 (*he shall stand and feed in the strength of the Lord, in the majesty of the name of the Lord his God*). These words imply that the ruler, who was to come forth from Bethlehem, was not to be a secular chief merely, but to wield a sacred and divine authority, which, with the words *in Israel* (Mic. 5, 2), correspond in substance to the last clause of the verse before us, notwithstanding the omission of the words *to* (or *for*) *me*, i. e. for my service and by my authority, which are sufficiently implied in the expression *who shall rule my people Israel*, i. e. the old theocracy or Jewish Church. As the question put by Herod to the Sanhedrim had reference only to the *place* of the Messiah's birth, they quote only what relates to this point and the identification of his person, omitting what is said of his eternal generation (in the last clause of Micah 5, 2) and the allusion to his mother (in the next verse), although both these are most interesting and important features of the passage as a Messianic prophecy, and both would naturally be suggested to a Jewish hearer by the formal quotation even of a part.

7. Then Herod, when he had privily called the wise

* E. g. *chief* (Luke 22, 26. Acts 14, 12. 15, 22), *governor* (Acts 7, 10), *them that have the rule* (Heb. 13, 7. 17. 24.)
† Jer. 2, 8. 3, 15. 10, 21. 12, 10. 22, 22. 23, 1. 4. 25, 34. 50, 6. Mic. 5, 5. Nah. 3, 18. Ezek. 34, 2. 8. 10. Zech. 10, 3. 11, 3. 5. 8.

men, inquired of them diligently what time the star appeared.

The prompt and authoritative answer of the Sanhedrim to Herod's question (in v. 4) would naturally lead him to inquire whether this prediction had been really fulfilled, or whether there was any recent birth at Bethlehem, on the ground of which the fact of such fulfilment could be plausibly asserted. In order to determine this important point, he seeks to know on what grounds these astronomers believed the event, so long expected both by Jews and Gentiles (see above, on v. 2), to have taken place. They had already given as a reason for their coming the appearance of a star, which they connected, in their science or their superstition, with the birth of a great personage among the Jews, to whom though Gentiles, they had come to render civil homage, if not religious worship. *Then*, i. e. after the response recorded in v. 6, and no doubt immediately, the Greek word (τότε), which is one of Matthew's favorite expressions, sometimes denoting even simultaneous actions or occurrences (see below, on v. 16). *Privily*, privately, or rather secretly, a word sometimes applied to any thing insensible or imperceptible, but commonly denoting, in the best Greek usage, fraudulent or treacherous concealment. *Calling* or *having called*, does not necessarily denote a peremptory summons, but in this connection rather a courteous invitation to a private conference, the secrecy relating to all but the Magians themselves, who might consider themselves honoured by this private audience. The motive for concealment may have been a wish to avoid further popular excitement before he had discovered all the facts; or it may no less naturally be referred to that instinctive fondness for concealment, which belongs to men of jealous and suspicious temper, or of treacherous intentions, even where there is no rational occasion or necessity for secret measures. We have then a striking instance of verisimilitude, which could not have occurred to a fictitious writer, for the very reason that the act was the result, not of reasoning or calculation, but of a spontaneous impulse. *Inquired diligently*, not the phrase so rendered in v. 16, but a single Greek word (ἠκρίβωσε), meaning to render accurate, or do exactly, and applied in usage to arrangement, information, inquiry, and many other acts of which exactness, accuracy, or precision may be predicated. The idea of diligence, or industry, derived by all the English versions from the Vulgate (*diligenter didicit*), is entirely foreign from the meaning of the Greek word and its cognate forms both here and elsewhere.* *Of them*, from them, as the only source of information upon this point. The literal translation of the last clause is, *the time of the appearing star*. As the word translated *time* is one applied to periods rather than to fixed points (compare Acts 1, 7), the question may have been not when the star was seen first, but how long it had been seen since, which implies that it had remained visible (but

---

* See below, on v. 16, and compare Luke 1, 3. Acts 18, 25. 26. 22, 3. 23, 15. 20. 24, 22. 26, 5. Eph. 5, 15. 1 Thess. 5, 2.

see below, on v. 9). *Appeared*, or retaining the original form, *appearing*, is a Greek participle now adopted as an English noun, *phenomenon*, appearance, or rather something that appears. The idea of rarity or strangeness forms no part of the essential meaning. Herod's motive for making this inquiry was not to consult his own astrologers, as some suppose, in reference to the birth of which he had just heard, but rather to arrange the murderous design by which he hoped to render it innocuous.

8. And he sent them to Bethlehem, and said, Go, and search diligently for the young child ; and when ye have found (him), bring me word again, that I may come and worship him also.

The construction is the participial one so common in this context, and so constantly resolved by our translators into the past tense, *sending them to Bethlehem, he said*.* So too in the next clause, *going*, or *having gone*, or *journeyed*, as the Greek verb commonly denotes not mere motion but departure to a distance. The participle is not pleonastic, nor conditional (*if ye should go*), but a substantive part of the command or exhortation, pointing out a necessary means to the proposed end of exact investigation. This is of no importance here, but may throw light upon another instance of the same construction (see below, on 28, 19). *Diligently*, thoroughly, exactly, an adverb corresponding to the verb in the preceding verse. *Search*, a verb which originally means to *verify* or ascertain as true (ἐτάζω from ἐτεός), here used in a compounded form (ἐξετάσατε) suggesting the additional idea of searching *out*, extracting or eliciting the truth in difficult and doubtful cases. The same verb is applied to persons in the sense of close or strict examination (see below, on 10, 11, and compare John 21, 12), and is used in the Septuagint version of Deut. 19, 18 with the same adverb as in this case (ἀκριβῶς). *Search for*, though essentially correct, is not the precise sense of the Greek phrase, which means rather to *examine* (or *inquire of*) others with respect to the child (περὶ τοῦ παιδίου), i. e. not only to discover his person, or find where he was, but also to learn all about him. *Young child* is in Greek a single word (παιδίον), explained by some to mean a suckling, as distinguished from a new-born babe (βρέφος), and a boy or lad (παῖς); but that such terms are to some extent convertible, is clear from Luke 18, 15–17, where two of them are actually interchanged. *When* is not as in the preceding clauses, introduced by the translators, but a literal translation of the Greek (ἐπὰν δέ), which sometimes indicates a slight antithesis (see Luke 11, 22. 34), but here suggests only a contingency, like our *whenever*, i. e. whether sooner or later. *Found*, as the result of the search just commanded, and perhaps implying doubt as to the issue.

---

* See above, 1, 18. 20. 2, 1. 3. 7, in all which places *when*, or *while*, represents a participle in the original.

Bring (me) word again, in Greek a single but compounded verb, meaning sometimes simply to *announce* (as in 8, 33. 12, 18. 14, 12. 28, 8. 10. 11), but sometimes more specifically, to *report* or carry back news (as in 11, 4. Luke 14, 21. Acts 5, 22. 12, 26), which additional idea may however be suggested by the context, as in this case, where the word *again* is not in the original, but Herod must of course be understood as bidding them to come back or return, in order to communicate the fruit of their inquiries. *I* and *also,* separated in the version, stand together in the Greek, or rather form a single word (κἀγώ) and might be translated *I too,* i. e. as well as you and others. Whether *worship* be here taken in its civil or religious sense (see above, on v. 2), it cannot be supposed that Herod really intended either to adore the child or do him homage, but his words must be either hypocritical, intended to conceal his murderous intentions, or ironical, expressive of his scorn and spite towards his infant rival. Here again, we are not to assume too much of a rational and settled purpose, but must make allowance for unreasoning suggestions of strong passion or inveterate affection. (See above, on v. 7.) *Come and worship* is another resolution of the Greek participial construction, which appears to have been foreign from the English idiom in the days of King James, or at least of Tyndale, from whom all these unnecessary changes have been borrowed. Even the most fastidious ear and taste would probably take no offence now at the literal translation, *so that I too coming may adore him.*

9. When they had heard the king, they departed; and lo, the star, which they saw in the east, went before them, till it came and stood over where the young child was.

But they, on their part (οἱ δέ), *having heard the king,* waiting of course till he had ended his instructions, as recorded in the verse preceding. *Departed,* set out on their journey, or resumed it, from Jerusalem to Bethlehem. *Lo, behold,* introduces something new and unexpected, like our own phrase, "strange to say," &c. *The star,* luminary, heavenly phenomenon, whatever it may have been (see above, on v. 2). *Saw* may be either the imperfect tense implying a repeated or continued vision, or the aorist, denoting that they saw it at a certain time, or on one particular occasion. *Went before them,* a Greek verb which originally means to *lead forth* or *bring forward* (as in Acts 12, 6. 16, 30. 25, 26), but in common usage, to lead the way, precede, or go before, whether the object be implied (as in 21, 9. Mark 6, 45. 1 Tim. 5, 24. Heb. 7, 18), or expressed (as in 14, 22. 21, 31. Mark 10, 32, and here). It does not necessarily denote in this place, that a luminous appearance moved in front of them until they reached the house. It may mean merely that the star was visible before them as they went towards Bethlehem. So too the statement, that it *stood over where,* or *above* (*the place in*) *which, the child was,* is a natural expression of the fact that as they journeyed towards it, the star was visible in that part of the heavens. This explanation is entirely consistent with the use of the word *came* (or *coming*), which at most can only denote change of place or relative position, since they last observed it. It is not said, nor intended, that the star pointed out the house, which is not even mentioned, and which was no doubt ascertained, as in all such cases, by inquiry. Josephus in like manner speaks of a star as *standing over* the city of Jerusalem before its downfall. The miraculous, in either case, is represented as belonging to the star itself, and not to its position over the place indicated. The oldest manuscripts and latest editors have a passive form (ἐστάθη) which strictly means, *was placed* (or *stationed*), but is equivalent in usage to the common reading (ἔστη) *stood.*

10. When they saw the star, they rejoiced with exceeding great joy.

And (or *but*, omitted in the version) *seeing* (or *having seen*, resolved, as usual, into *when they saw*) *the star*, implying, it should seem, that they had not beheld it during their long journey. Or the reference may be to its new position as described in the preceding verse. *Seeing the star* (in this apparent station), they *rejoiced a great joy—very* (or *exceedingly*). This collocation of the words gives great force to the intensive adverb which stands last in Greek. The combination of the cognate verb and noun (*rejoiced a joy*) is not a peculiar Hebrew idiom, as sometimes represented, but is found occasionally in the classical and modern writers. It is slightly different in form from the construction with the dative (see John 3, 29. 1 Thess. 3, 9), though translated in the same way. (Compare 1 Kings 1, 40, and the marginal translation of Jonah 4, 6.) The common version coincides with the Rhemish. Wiclif has, *full great joy;* Tyndale, *marvellously glad;* Cranmer, *exceeding glad;* and the Geneva Bible, *exceeding great gladness.* This extreme joy was most natural, not only in relation to the object of their search, but to the truth of their calculations and conclusions, in which they would naturally feel an intellectual and scientific pride.

11. And when they were come into the house, they saw the young child with Mary his mother, and fell down, and worshipped him: and when they had opened their treasures, they presented unto him gifts; gold, and frankincense, and myrrh.

Coming (or *having come*) *into the house*, where the holy family was then residing. This does not necessarily imply their permanent abode at Bethlehem, as the house might be merely one in which they had temporary lodgings (see below, on v. 23). *Saw*, or according to some ancient copies, *found*, with apparent reference to the words of Herod in v. 8. *The (young) child with Mary his mother*, not the Madonna and her child, as in the Romish Mariolatry, and the artistical tradition founded on it. The same incidental mention and subordinate position of the Virgin may be noted in vs. 13. 14. 20. 21. *Falling (down) worshipped him*, the same verb that is used to express civil homage in the Septuagint version of Gen. 42, 6. 43, 25, and both combined in that of 2 Sam. 1, 2, unless we assume that all such homage in the ancient east included a religious or idolatrous devotion, like that paid to the emperors of Rome and China. At all events, the homage here described implied that they who paid it recognized the child as something more than "king of the Jews." *Opening* (or *having*) *opened their treasures*, which may either mean their costly wares or their vessels which contained them, as the Greek word, from which ours is derived, is applied not only to the contents (as in 6, 19–21. 13, 44. 19, 21. 2 Cor. 4, 7), but also to the receptacle, whether fixed or portable. (See 12, 25. 13, 52, and compare the wooden treasure (ξησαυρον ξύλινον) of Josephus. It is an old but fanciful opinion, that these three gifts were presented to the infant Jesus in as many different characters, gold as a king, incense as a God, and myrrh as a sufferer. Another notion of the same kind, is that the three gifts were presented by as many magi, who were therefore three in number, representing three countries of which these were the products, while a further combination with the prophecy in Ps. 72, 10. Isai. 60, 6, led to the conclusion that the three were kings of their respective countries. Hence arose the legend of the Three Kings, one of the most fixed and familiar in the popular traditions of the old world, though without foundation in the narrative before us, which is silent both as to the rank and number of the magi, and describes the gifts as a collective or promiscuous offering from all together. The gifts themselves were valuable products of the east, but not confined to single countries, and are here combined, like those in Gen. 43, 11, as a suitable present to a recognised superior, before whom, according to an ancient oriental usage, mentioned by Seneca and other classics, the inferior must not appear empty-handed. (Compare 1 Sam. 9, 7. 8.) *Incense*, in its widest sense, is any sacrificial burning, but is specially applied to aromatic fumigation, as an act of worship. The Greek word here denotes one of the substances so used, an odoriferous transparent gum distilling from a tree in Arabia. In the classics this word (λίβανος) means the tree and a derivative form (λιβανωτός) the gum; but in the Greek of the New Testament, the latter means a censer (Rev. 8, 3), and the former is applied to the gum itself (Rev. 18, 13). *Myrrh* in Greek *Smyrna*, which appears elsewhere as the name of a city in Asia Minor (Rev. 1, 11. 2, 8). As an appellative it also signifies an aromatic gum, exuding from a thornbush in Arabia, extremely bitter, and employed by the ancients both as a spice and a perfume. (See Mark 15, 23. John 19, 39, and compare the Septuagint version of Ps. 45, 9. Song Sol. 3, 6. 5, 5.)

12. And being warned of God in a dream that they should not return to Herod, they departed into their own country another way.

Here the Greek participial construction is retained. Showing that it was avoided in the previous context only as a matter of taste, and not because it would have been a violation of the English idiom (see above, on v. 8). *Being warned of God*, in Greek a single word, originally meaning to deal or transact business, more particularly that of a pecuniary nature (χρηματίζω from χρήματα); then to negotiate, or confer on state affairs; and then, to give an answer after such negotiation, in which sense it is used by Demosthenes and Xenophon. By a further elevation and extension of the meaning, it is applied to the responses of the oracles, and in the Scriptures to Divine communications, especially those made to individuals. The sense of warning is required by the context here as it is in Heb. 8, 5. 11, 7. 12, 25, but probably without the implication of a previous prayer or consultation as in Acts 10, 25, and in the Vulgate here (*responso accepto*). For a still further deviation from the primary sense, see Acts 11, 26 and Rom. 7, 3. *By dream* (κατ' ὄναρ), as in 1, 20.* *Not to turn back*, or retrace their steps, an absolute or reflexive use of the verb also found in Plato, and in Heb. 11, 15. Acts 18, 21, where it is construed with the same proposition. *They departed*, not the verb so rendered in v. 9 (and *go* in v. 8), but one suggesting the additional idea of withdrawal or retreat, being the verbal root or theme of *anchorite*. Besides the verse given here (and in 4, 12. 14, 13. 15, 21. 27, 5. John 6, 15), it is variously rendered, *give place* (i. e. make room, 9, 24), *turned aside* (v. 22 below), *withdrew himself* (12, 15), *went aside* (Acts 23, 19. 26, 31). It here implies not the mere act of departure or removal, but escape from danger as the motive. *By* (or *through*, omitted in the version) *another way*, different from that by which they came; perhaps a more direct one since they visited Jerusalem, not because it lay in the way, but because it was the capital, at which they would of course expect to find the new-born king, or at least to obtain news of him. Into their own *place* (χώραν, a kindred form to the preceding verb), land, territory, region, country, 4, 16. 8, 28. Luke 21, 21. John 4, 35), not that subject or belonging to them, as its sovereigns (see above, on v. 11), but simply that of their nativity or residence. Whether this was Persia, Babylonia, or Arabia is not revealed and cannot be determined by conjecture. (See above, on v. 1.)

13. And when they were departed, behold, the angel of the Lord appeareth to Joseph in a dream, saying, Arise, and take the young child and his mother, and flee

---

* According to Wiclif, the whole phrase means to *take an answer in sleep*.

into Egypt, and be thou there until I bring thee word: for Herod will seek the young child to destroy him.

Another participial construction, but resolved as usual into the past tense with *when*. *They having retreated* (or *withdrawn*), the same verb that was used in the preceding verse and there explained. The next clause is repeated from 1, 20, but with the substitution of the narrative or graphic present (*appeareth*) for the past tense (*appeared*). This mode of revelation or divine communication seems to be the lowest mentioned in the sacred history, being confined in that before us to the Magi, Joseph, and the wife of Pilate (see below, on 27, 19, and compare 20, 13. 31, 24). In the Old Testament, it seems at times to characterize the revelations of false prophets as distinguished from the true (as in Deut. 13, 1. Jer. 23, 25. 27, 9. 29, 8. Zech. 10, 2), once those of lower prophets as compared with Moses (Numb. 12, 6). We find it also in the case of Solomon (1 Kings 3, 5) and Daniel (7, 1), who, although inspired men, were not official prophets. The verb translated *arise* originally means to raise or lift up (as in 12, 11), then to rouse from sleep (as in 8, 25), and by a natural figure from the sleep of death (10, 8. 11, 5). The strict sense of the passive form here used is, *being roused*, awakened, i. e. not when you awake as usual in the morning, but at once, immediately, without delay. *Take* (to thyself, or with thee, in thy company), the verb translated *take unto thee* in 1, 20, and *took unto him* in 1, 24. *The (young) child and his mother*, nearly though not precisely the same phrase with that in v. 11. *Flee*, a stronger term than that in the first clause of the preceding verse, and one expressing still more fully the necessity of haste and the existence of danger. *Egypt*, the nearest point of which was probably not more than sixty miles from Bethlehem. That country, although subject to the Romans, was beyond the reach of Herod, and was extensively inhabited by Jews, whose fathers had been settled there by one of the first Ptolemies or Greek kings of Egypt. It was here that the religion and philosophy of Greeks and Jews were first brought into contact, the Old Testament translated into Greek, and the Platonising Judaism of Philo and his school invented. So numerous were these Egyptian Jews, that a temple was erected for them under the priesthood of Onias (B.C. 150), which detracted in some measure from the exclusive claims of the legitimate sanctuary at Jerusalem. Near the site of this Egyptian temple, at a place called Metacca, an old tradition fixed the place of our Lord's temporary residence. Besides the reasons just suggested for selecting Egypt as the place of his retreat, there was another of more moment, which is afterwards expressly mentioned (see below, on v. 15). *Be thou* (continue or remain) *there till I tell thee* (otherwise or further), or *till I say to thee* (what thou shalt do). This is the literal translation of the words corresponding to Tyndale's paraphrase, *until I bring thee word*. *Will seek*, or is about to seek, the first verb (μέλλει) having no equivalent in English, and denoting mere futurity, but with more distinctness than the future tense. *Seek* has here its proper sense of *search* or *look for*, with a view to the discovery of his home or hiding-place. *To destroy*, or (for the purpose) *of destroying*, an idiom sometimes represented as a Hebraism, but found also in the best Greek writers. *Him*, literally, *it*, the word translated *young child* being of the neuter gender.

14. When he arose, he took the young child and his mother by night, and departed into Egypt.

This verse simply states the execution of the order in the one before it, which was even more prompt than the English version seems to represent it. *When he arose* might seem to mean that he waited till his ordinary time of rising; whereas the literal translation is, *being aroused*, or *having risen*, i. e. instantly, without delay. This idea is moreover suggested by the phrase *at night*, or *in (the) night*, which would be unmeaning if he waited till the morning. *Departed* is the verb already twice used in relation to the retreat of the wise men, and denoting something less than flight, but something more than mere departure. (See above, on vs. 12. 13.)

15. And was there until the death of Herod: that it might be fulfilled which was spoken of the Lord by the prophet, saying, Out of Egypt have I called my Son.

This verse describes Joseph as passively no less than actively obedient to the words of the angel. He not only went into Egypt, but remained there (*was there*), a correlative expression to the one in v. 31 (*be there*). *Till the death*, literally *end*, i. e. end of life, a term occurring only here in the New Testament, but used in the Septuagint version (Gen. 27, 2) and the best Greek writers as an euphemism for death. That of Herod took place in the spring of 750 U. C., the year being fixed by an eclipse of the moon about the same time, which, according to the highest astronomical authorities, could not have occurred in any other year within a reasonable compass. The physical cause of Herod's death, according to Josephus, was a loathsome and most painful malady. *That it might be fulfilled*, the same formula essentially with that in 1, 22, but without the emphatic preface, *all this happened*. The words here quoted are still extant in Hos. 11, 1, and more exactly rendered here than in the Septuagint version, which, instead of *my son*, reads *his children*. But the first person was correctly given in the other old Greek versions of Aquila, Symmachus, and Theodotion. Between the extreme of making this a case of mere accommodation, and that of making the original passage an exclusive prophecy of Christ, the most satisfactory interpretation is the one which supposes an intended typical relation between the history of Israel and that of the Messiah, as the Body and the Head. This significant analogy, which may be readily traced in the later sufferings and temptations of both parties is also visible in the commencement of their several careers. As the national existence of Israel began with the exodus from Egypt, so the early life of the great antitype sets out from the same point of departure. The same thing would be true essentially if Bengel's exposition were the true one. *From the land of Egypt* (i. e. ever since he dwelt there) *I have called* (*him*) *my son.* Compare Exodus 4, 22. 23. Hos. 12, 9. 13, 4.)

16. Then Herod, when he saw that he was mocked of the wise men, was exceeding wroth, and sent forth, and slew all the children that were in Bethlehem, and in all the coasts thereof, from two years old and under, according to the time which he had diligently inquired of the wise men.

Having related the escape to Egypt and the residence there, Matthew now returns to Herod and describes the effect produced upon him by the failure of the Magi to return as he had ordered or requested (see above, on v. 8). It agrees remarkably with Herod's character, as known to us from other sources, that he is here described as acting not from politic nor even from malignant motives merely, but also from a sense of injured dignity and wounded pride. His cruelties indeed, atrocious as they were, appear to have been prompted not so much by natural blood-thirstiness as by a jealous and suspicious temper, especially in reference to rivalry or competition. In this respect a parallel might easily be drawn between his downward course from bad to worse and that of Saul in his jealous enmity of David, but with this advantage on the part of Saul, that he was jealous in behalf of his own children, whereas Herod, with a sort of insane selfishness, committed his worst cruelties upon his own sons, which gave rise to the famous witticism of Augustus, that he would rather be Herod's hog (in allusion to the Jewish abstinence from swine's flesh) than his son, a still more pointed sarcasm if, as some suppose, it was pronounced in Greek and with a play upon the likeness of the words denoting *hog* ($\tilde{v}_{\varsigma}$) and *son* ($v\iota\acute{o}s$). By a singular anachronism, Macrobius, a Roman writer of the fourth century, confounds this saying and the act by which it was occasioned with the prominent massacre recorded in the verse before us, as if Herod's own son was among the children slain at this time, whereas he was put to death after he had reached maturity. Matthew's narrative is also in acordance with the general teaching of experience, that few important actions, whether good or bad, are prompted by a single unmixed motive. This accounts for the diversity with which historians explain the same facts, and for the mystery overhanging the whole subject of historical causes and effects, where the result depends on human agency. *Seeing*, perceiving, that is, inferring from the non-appearance of the Magi, on their homeward route from Bethlehem (see above, on v. 12). *Mocked* is in Greek a compound verb derived from a noun meaning *child*, and itself denoting childish sport or play, but also used by the classical writers in the secondary sense of fooling, duping, and by the

Hellenists in that of scoffing or derisive insult, being thus applied to the cruel derision of our Lord before his crucifixion.* The idea here is not that of mere deception, i. e. breach of promise or disappointment of his expectation (Wiclif, *deceived*), but that of contemptuous slight or insult, as expressed in the common version, *mocked of* (i. e. *by*) *the wise men*. Even the Rhemish version (*deluded*) really includes the notion of derision, although lost in modern English usage. *Exceeding wroth*, in modern English, *very angry*, or more exactly, *very (much) enraged*, as the last word is in Greek a passive verb, derived from a noun meaning passion, and particularly that of anger.† The remainder of the verse describes the acts to which this fury prompted him. *Sending forth*, commissioning, the verb from which *apostle* is derived. It is here used absolutely or intransitively, as in 14, 35. 27, 19 below. There is no need, therefore, of supposing a grammatical ellipsis and supplying *messengers* or *men of war* (as Cranmer does). *Slew*, a Greek verb strictly meaning to *take up* or *take away* (as in Heb. 10, 9), but commonly employed, like our *despatch* or *make away with*, as a sort of euphemism for the act of killing. Except in this place and the one just cited, it is used exclusively by Luke, occurring in his two books twenty times, and always in the secondary sense of slaying or destroying. The Rhemish version renders it too strongly, *murdered*, which, though true in fact, is not necessarily included in the import of the word itself. *Children*, i. e. male children (Geneva), men-children (Rheims), the sense being limited to one sex by the masculine adjective and article (πάντας τοὺς) and by the usage of the Greek noun (παῖδας), which is the nearest equivalent to our word *boy*, and like it sometimes used both for *son and servant*. (See below, on 8, 6. 12, 18. 14, 2. 17, 18.) *Coasts*, confined in modern English to the maritime borders of a country, but of old denoting boundaries in general, and in Scripture sometimes the territory bounded or enclosed between them.‡ It may here mean either the immediate outskirts (suburbs) or the district dependent upon Bethlehem as its chief town. In either case, the tract intended must have been a small one (see above, on v. 6). *From two years old*, in Greek an adjective (διετοῦς) meaning biennial (or of two years), and agreeing with some noun understood, such as *time* (from the age of two years), or *child* (from the boy of two years), or used abstractly, as in the Vulgate version (*a bimatu*).§ *And under*, a comparative form of the adverb (κάτω), *down* (see below,

---

* See below, on 20, 19. 27, 29. 31, 41, also Mark 15, 20. Luke 23, 11, and compare the use of the derivative nouns *mockery* and *mocker* in Heb. 11, 36, 2 Pet. 3, 3. Jude 18.

† See Luke 4, 28. Acts 19, 28 (compare 12, 20). Rom. 2, 8. 2 Cor. 12, 20. Gal. 5, 20. Eph. 4, 31. Col. 3, 8. Heb. 11, 27, and the Book of Revelation *passim*. *Exceeding* in old English is an adverb, and is so used to translate the same Greek word (λίαν) in 4, 8. 8, 28, below, while in 27, 14, it is rendered *greatly*.

‡ See below, on 8, 34. 15, 21, and compare Ex. 10, 14. 19. Deut. 2, 4. 16, 4· 19, 3.

§ It occurs only here in the New Testament, but cognate forms and similar constructions may be found in the Septuagint version (e. g. 1 Chr. 27, 23. 2 Chr. 31, 16. Ezra 3, 8), as well as the Apocrypha (2 Mac. 10, 3), and even in Herodotus.

on 4, 6. 26, 51), and here denoting *lower down* not in reference to space but time, i. e. *under* or *below* the age just mentioned. Wiclif has *within*, i. e. within the limits just defined. *Diligently inquired*, in Greek a single word, the same that was employed above in v. 7 and there explained (Vulg. *exquisierat*). This does not imply that Jesus was just two years old at this time, but rather that he was not, as appears from the word *under*. In the former case, it would be hard to account for the long delay of the wise men either in beginning or in finishing their journey. The true sense is that two years was the maximum or highest age consistent with the statements of the Magi, while the real age was no doubt far below it. That the tyrant should allow himself margin in this devilish infanticide, and choose rather to destroy too many than too few, is in perfect keeping with his sanguinary habits, when influenced by jealousy or hatred. The silence of Josephus with respect to this slaughter of the innocents, as it is beautifully called in the traditions of the early church, has been made a ground of cavil by some modern sceptics. But the difficulty, if it be one, is not only purely negative as founded on the silence of a single writer, but susceptible of easy explanation from the obvious consideration, that the male children under two years, in so small a town as Bethlehem (see above, on v. 6), or even in the tract of which it was the centre, must have been very few, and that the interest imparted to the massacre by its connection with the infant Saviour would be wholly wanting to a Jewish writer, who could view it only as a small drop in the bloody stream of Herod's cruelties. On the other hand, the truth of the occurrence here related is confirmed by its analogy to one which Josephus does record among the last acts of this jealous tyrant, namely, his command that a number of the chief men should be put to death as soon as he expired, in order that there might be mourning, or at least no rejoicing, at his own departure.* The motive of the massacre, as we have seen was partly politic and partly passionate. While this appeared to be the only way in which a feared and hated rival could be reached, it seemed at the same time to gratify the tyrant's proud and bestial resentment. This agreement between Matthew and Josephus, as to Herod's character, even in relating wholly different events, is the more remarkable because he appears here only for a moment as it were before his final disappearance from the field of action, thus affording a strong though incidental proof of authenticity.

17. Then was fulfilled that which was spoken by Jeremy the prophet, saying,

This too was the fulfilment of a prophecy still extant in the Hebrew Scriptures (Jer. 31, 15). The formula of reference is not so-

---

* The truth of this too has been called in question, but with as little reason as the other, and the sceptical critics are constrained to own that both events are perfectly in keeping with the life and character of Herod, and at least serve to illustrate the Italian proverb, *se non vero ben trovato*.

strong as that in 1, 22, nor even as that in v. 13 above. The expression here is not, *that it might be fulfilled*, but simply that *it was fulfilled*. Hence some infer that this is a case of mere accommodation or a new application of words originally uttered in relation to a subject altogether different. But the difference of form is not such as to warrant this distinction, since a mere accommodation is not more at variance with the statement of design or purpose (*that it might be fulfilled*) than it is with the positive assertion of the fact (*then it was fulfilled*). The question whether the fulfilment was a real or fictitious one must be determined, not by the prefatory formula, but by the meaning of the prophecy itself and by its correspondence with the facts which are said to have fulfilled it.

18. In Rama was there a voice heard, lamentation, and weeping, and great mourning, Rachael weeping (for) her children, and would not be comforted, because they are not.

The original passage, by a fine poetical personification, represents the mother of Joseph and Benjamin (Gen. 30, 24. 35, 18) as mourning over the captivity of Israel at Ramah, where Nebuzaradan, the captain of the Babylonian guard, appears to have assembled the exiles, as a sort of rendezvous, before they actually left the country (Jer. 40, 1). The name *Ramah* properly means *high*, and is so understood here by Wiclif (*on high*) and Tyndale (*on the hills*). It is commonly agreed, however, that it here denotes a particular place, namely, Ramah in Benjamin near Judah, so called from its elevated site, five or six miles north of Jerusalem, between Gibeah and Bethel (Judges 19, 13). It is now called *Erram* and is not to be confounded with another Ramah, the birth-place and residence of the prophet Samuel (1 Sam. 1, 19. 2, 11. 7, 17). Rachel, though not the mother of Judah, was buried near Bethlehem (Gen. 35, 16. 19), where her grave is still shown, and is therefore not inappropriately introduced in this place as renewing her old lamentation over this new calamity occurring near her resting-place. She may even be conceived of as rising from her tomb, disturbed in her long rest by this new and strange catastrophe. It is not however merely this poetical conception that is here embodied, but a real affinity between the cases. The point of resemblance may be that in either case the temporary suffering was the precursor of a joyful future. As the Babylonish exile was soon followed by the Restoration (see Jer. 31, 16–40) so the massacre at Bethlehem was followed by the ministry of Christ and his salvation. The quotation varies somewhat from the Septuagint version. *Rachel* may be construed with a verb before or after (*was heard* or *refused*) but more naturally as an independent nominative. *Lamentation, weeping*, and *mourning*, may be either explained as synonyms, or as denoting articulate, inarticulate, and silent sorrow. The first of the three is omitted in several manuscripts and versions. *Would not*, was not willing, did not choose, refused. *Are not*, or as it is more fully expressed both in Greek and English, *are no more*, i. e. no longer living. The force of this description would be greatly heightened by the recollection of the circumstances which attended Rachel's own death (Gen. 35, 16–20).

19. But when Herod was dead, behold, an angel of the Lord appeareth in a dream to Joseph in Egypt,

But (or *and*) *Herod having ended* (his life). This elliptical use of the verb, the only one which occurs in the New Testament (see below, 9, 18. 15, 4. 22, 25), is also found in the best Greek writers from Herodotus to Xenophon (compare the cognate noun in v. 15 above). As this event, according to Josephus, took place about the Passover, and was preceded by an eclipse of the moon, astronomers are able, by these data, to define the year, viz., 750 after the building of Rome, and four years earlier than the vulgar idea of the birth of Christ, which was introduced by Dionysius Exiguus more than five hundred years after the nativity itself. This error, which is now universally admitted, although its exact extent is still disputed, has had no effect, as Bossuet well observes, upon the mutual relation or the chronological succession of events, or the correctness of men's views respecting them. (See above, on v. 2.) *Lo*, behold, or strange to say (as in vs. 1. 9. 13). *In Egypt*, where he had been ordered to remain till this time (see above, on v. 13), where the same form of expression is employed, except a slight change in the order of the words.

20. Saying, Arise, and take the young child and his mother, and go into the land of Israel : for they are dead which sought the young child's life.

The first clause agrees exactly with the second of v. 13, till we come to the word *flee*, which is exchanged for *go*, or rather *journey*, set out (see above, on v. 9), because what is here described was not a flight but a return home. *Land (of) Israel*, without the article, precisely similar in this respect, though not in case or syntax, to *land (of) Judah* in v. 6 above. The phrase here signifies the whole country, two of the provinces or parts of which are there distinguished in the next verse. The general name is derived from the inhabitants, like the older designation *land of Canaan*, which however is commonly restricted to the country west of Jordan,* and is supposed by some to be a physical description of it as *lowlands*, and in contrast with the *highlands* of Libanus and Syria. *Palestine* is properly the Greek form of *Philistia*, denoting strictly the south-western portion,† but extended by the Romans, and in modern usage, to the entire land

---

* See Gen. 12, 5. 6. 37, 1. 50, 13. Ps. 105, 11. 12. Ezek. 16, 3, and compare Num. 33, 51. Josh. 22, 9. 11.

† See Ex. 15, 14. Isai. 14, 19. 21, and compare the Septuagint version of Ps. 60. 8. 87, 4. 108, 9.

of Israel. *Are dead*, or more exactly, *have died*, i. e. since you came away, the perfect to be strictly understood as usual (see above, on 1, 22). The plural form, *those seeking* (i. e. those who once or lately sought), has been variously explained as referring to Herod and his counsellors as agents, or to Herod and his son Antipater, who resembled him in cruelty, and had still more reason to be jealous of a rival, though eventually put to death five days before his father. Others regard it as a majestatic plural, often used by kings in speaking of themselves, but wholly inappropriate as applied to Herod by an angel. A more palpable hypothesis is that of a generic plural, sometimes used in reference to a single object.* Somewhat different from this is the indefinite plural, supposed to be exemplified in Luke 12. 20. 16, 9, and in Ex. 14, 19, which appears to be alluded to, if not directly quoted, in the verse before us, and may therefore have determined its peculiar form. Upon any of these suppositions, the essential fact is still the death of Herod himself. *Young child*, in Greek a single word, but a diminutive in form, the same that is employed above in vs. 8. 11. 13. 14. *Life*, a word which properly denotes the vital principle or living substance, and is therefore sometimes used to distinguish the *soul* from the *body* (as in 10, 28, and perhaps in Luke 12, 20), but is here and elsewhere properly translated *life*.†

21. And he arose, and took the young child and his mother, and came into the land of Israel.

This is the simple execution of the order in the verse preceding, and exactly similar in form to v. 14 above, excepting that *by night* is here omitted, there being no necessity for hasty flight in this case, and that *retired into Egypt* is exchanged for *came into (the) land (of) Israel*, the same phrase that occurred just before (in v. 20) and was there explained. The indefinite form in both cases might be represented in English by the idiomatic combination, *Israel-land*.

22. But when he heard that Archelaus did reign in Judea in the room of his father Herod, he was afraid to go thither: notwithstanding, being warned of God in a dream, he turned aside into the parts of Galilee;

But hearing, on the way, or after his arrival in the land of Israel. *Archelaus*, the eldest son of Herod the Great, by his Samaritan wife Matthace, to whom he bequeathed his crown and royal title, but Augustus only partially confirmed the will, confining his dominions to Judea, Idumea, and Samaria, and requiring him to bear the title *ethnarch* till he should prove himself worthy to be called a king.

---

* The examples usually cited being Matt. 26, 8 (compared with John 12, 24) and 27, 44 (compared with Luke 23, 39), together with the less striking cases found by some in 9, 8. 12, 4. 21, 27. 24, 26. Acts 7, 42. 13, 40. 16, 16.
† See below, on 6, 25. 20, 28, and compare Acts 20, 10. Rom. 11, 3.

After reigning eight or nine years he was summoned to Rome to answer charges of oppression and cruelty, and afterwards banished to Vienne in Gaul. *Did reign*, literally, *reigns*, is reigning, the form of expression which would have been used by Joseph himself, or by those who told him of the fact. There is no need of taking the verb *reign* in a diluted sense, as it may here have reference to the time immediately succeeding Herod's death, before his will was broken and his successor's title changed, at which time, as we learn from Josephus, Archelaus was congratulated as already reigning (ἤδη βασιλεύοντα). *In* (or rather *over*) *Judea*, the received text (ἐπί) being retained by the latest critics, and having the same sense as in Rev. 5, 10, where the construction is the same, and in Luke 1, 33. 19, 24. 27. *In the room* (Tyndale's version) is in Greek a preposition (ἀντί) often rendered *for*, but really denoting either substitution or retaliation.* *Was afraid*, a passive verb, was frightened, or alarmed, which is the original import also of the English word (*affrayed*), the noun derived from which and still in use (*affray*), though popularly used of any fight, denotes in law, according to Blackstone, only one which alarms the vicinage. The passive form could not be retained here in the version, because our idiom does not allow it to be construed with an infinitive. The explanation of the words as meaning that he did go, but with fear, is wholly at variance with usage, and directly reverses the true sense of the expression. *To go*, or more exactly, to *go away*, implying that his natural course would have been to go elsewhere, which agrees exactly with Luke's account of Mary's previous residence at Nazareth. (See Luke 1, 26. 2, 4.) *Thither*, literally *there*, an interchange of prepositions equally familiar to the Greek and English idiom, though commonly expunged in our translation.† *Notwithstanding* (Tyndale's version) is in Greek the usual connective (δέ), and is here little stronger than our *and*. *Warned of God in a dream*, the same words that were used above in v. 12, and there explained. *Warned* must here be understood as meaning admonished or instructed with authority. *Turned aside* (Tyndale's version) is the verb rendered *departed* in vs. 12. 14, but in all three places meaning retired, retreated, with an implication of escape from danger. *Parts of Galilee*, not portions of that province, but that part of the country so called.‡ *Galilee*, a Hebrew word which originally means a ring (as in Esth. 1, 6. Song Sol. 5, 14) or circle, and like the latter term is applied to geographical divisions, being sometimes rendered (in the plural) *coasts* (Joel 3, 4) and *borders* (Josh. 13, 2), but commonly applied as a proper name (*Galilee*) to the northernmost province of the land of Israel, as divided by the Syrians and Romans, lying between Phenicia and Samaria, the Jordan and the Mediterranean.§ The remoteness of this dis-

---

* See below, 5, 38. 20, 28, and compare Luke 11, 11. Rom. 12, 17. 1 Th. 5, 15. Heb. 12, 2. 16. 1 Pet. 3, 9.

† See the original of Jno. 18, 3. Lu. 24, 28. Jas. 3, 4. Deut. 1, 37. 4, 42.

‡ Compare the local use of the same plural noun in Acts 2, 10. 20, 2, and also in 15, 21. 16, 13 below, and Acts 19, 1, where it is translated *coasts*, in the sense before explained. (See above, on v. 16.)

§ See Josh. 20, 7. 21, 32. 1 Kings 9, 11. 2 Kings 15, 29.

trict from Jerusalem and its proximity to the heathen, perhaps with some mixture of the population, as expressed in the name *Galilee of the nations* or *the Gentiles* (Isai. 9, 1. Matt. 4, 15), seem to have lowered it in Jewish estimation (John 7, 41. 52), although the Galileans professed the same religion and frequented the same sacred places (John 4, 45. 7, 2. 11, 56).

23. And he came and dwelt in a city called Nazareth: that it might be fulfilled which was spoken by the prophets, He shall be called a Nazarene.

Having stated why he took up his abode in Galilee and not in Judea, Matthew now explains the choice of a particular locality within the first-named province. *Coming*, or *having come*, is not a pleonasm or superfluous expression, but a distinct statement of his arrival in the province, followed by his settlement in Nazareth. As if he had said, for these reasons he came to Galilee and not Judea, and having come he dwelt, or rather settled, took up his abode. The Greek verb does not of itself denote either permanent or temporary residence, but rather the act of settling or beginning to reside, as in 4, 13. 12, 45. Luke 11, 26. Acts 2, 5. 7, 2. 4, whether the subsequent abode be temporary (as in Heb. 11, 9) or permanent (as in Acts 9, 32. 17, 26, and often in the Book of Revelation.) *In*, literally *into*, a familiar idiom where previous motion is implied though not expressed.* *A city*, in the wide sense, or *a town*, in its proper English acceptation, as including villages and cities, both which terms are applied in the New Testament to Bethlehem. (Compare Luke 2, 4. 11 with John 7, 42.) The indefinite expression (*a town* or *city*) implies that it was not a place universally well known like Jerusalem or even Bethlehem. There is no doubt, however, as to its identity, since it has been visited by travellers and pilgrims almost without interruption from the time of Christ until the present day. It is situated on the northern edge of the great central plain of Jezreel or Esdraelon, into which it opens through a narrow pass in the wall of hills by which it is surrounded. The name *Nazareth* seems to be an Aramaic form (נצרת) of a Hebrew word (נצר) meaning a shoot or twig, and applied by Isaiah (11, 1) to the Messiah as a shoot from the prostrate trunk or stem of Jesse, i. e. to his birth from the royal family of Judah in its humble and reduced estate. This coincidence of name, as well as the obscurity of Nazareth itself and the general contempt for Galilee at large, established an association between our Lord's humiliation and his residence at this place, so that various predictions of his low condition were fulfilled in his being called a Nazarene. This is, on the whole, more satisfactory than any other explanation of this difficult and doubtful passage. That which supposes an allusion to the Nazaritic vow of the

---

* Compare Mark 1, 39. 2, 1. 13, 9. 16. Luke 11, 7. 21. 37. John 9, 7. Acts 7, 4. 8, 39. 40. 13, 21. 21, 12. 13. 23, 11.

Old Testament (see Numbers 6, 1–21); or to Samson in particular as one of that class (Judg. 13, 5), and a type of Christ, is at variance with our Lord's mode of life, which was not that of a Nazarite (see below, on 11, 19), and with the usual orthography of that word in the Septuagint version. Still less admissible is the reference, assumed by some, to another Hebrew word which means a crown, or the supposition of some early writers that the passage quoted has been lost from the Hebrew text by negligence or expunged by fraud, both which contingencies are utterly forbidden by the care with which that text has been preserved and guarded both before and since the time of Christ. On the other hand, if we admit a reference to various predictions of our Lord's humiliation with particular allusion to his birth from the humbled house of David, as foretold by Isaiah (11, 1), this accounts both for the plural and indefinite form (*the prophets*), and for the stress laid upon the local name, which is identical with that applied to the Messiah in the particular prediction just referred to. This was not the fortuitous result, but the providential purpose of Christ's residence at Nazareth. The meaning is not that Joseph so designed it, but that God so willed it. The formula of reference is the same with that employed in v. 15, there explained. *He shall be called*, not merely in the sense of being entitled to be so called (see above, on 1, 23), but in that of actually hearing the name here imposed in real life, as we know the Saviour to have done, though the fulfilment of this prophecy is rendered less clear to the English reader by the constant substitution of the paraphrase *Jesus of Nazareth*, which occurs only twice in the original (John 1, 46. Acts 10, 28) for the exact phrase elsewhere used, *Jesus the Nazarene*. Even in the mouth of the Apostles and of Christ himself, this phrase has reference to its original derisive import, *Jesus of Nazareth*, i. e. whom you have treated with contempt by that name.* This explanation of the purpose for which Joseph was led to take up his abode at Nazareth, is perfectly consistent with the fact of his previous residence at that place as alleged by Luke (1, 27. 2, 4. 39. 51). That it was not before mentioned arises from the peculiar plan of this first gospel, the grand design of which is to demonstrate the Messiahship of Jesus, and which introduces only such historical events as have a bearing on this purpose, which the early residence of Joseph and Mary at Nazareth had not.

* See John 1, 45. 46. 18, 5. 7. 19, 19. Acts 2, 22. 3, 6. 4, 10. 6, 14. 10, 38. 22, 8. 26, 9.

CHAPTER III.

Having recorded the genealogy and birth of Christ, with the events which led to his residence at Nazareth, the evangelist now proceeds to describe his public ministry, beginning, however, with that of John the Baptist, which preceded it and introduced it. Omitting, as already known, or unimportant for his special purpose, the early history of John himself, Matthew introduces him abruptly at the beginning of his public work, with an exact specification of its scene (1) and subject (2), its relation to prophecy (3) and to the habits of the ancient prophets (4), its effect upon the people (5. 6), and a specimen of John's fidelity and earnestness in dealing with all classes (7), exhorting them to reformation (8), warning them against false confidence (9) and impending judgments (10) and defining his position as a baptizer with respect to his superior who was to follow (11), and whose coming must be either saving or destructive to the souls of those who heard him (12). To this description of John's ministry in general is added a particular account of his principal official act, which also forms a natural transition to the ministry of Christ himself (13–17). This was his own baptism, as to which we are informed of the localities (13), of John's refusal (14), of our Lord's reply and John's compliance (15), and of the divine recognition of our Lord as the Messiah, addressed both to the eye (16) and to the ear (17) of the spectators. This view of the narrative contained in the third chapter will suffice to show that it is in its proper place, between the account of his nativity and infancy that goes before, and that of his temptation and the opening of his ministry that follows.

1. In those days came John the Baptist, preaching in the wilderness of Judea.

In those days, an indefinite expression, used not only in the Scriptures (as in Ex. 2, 11. Isai. 38, 1), but by the best Greek and Latin writers (as Herodotus, Virgil, and Livy), in reference either to a period of a few days (as in Acts 1, 15), or of many years, as in the case before us, where there is a blank of nearly thirty years (see Luke 3, 2. 23), filled elsewhere only by a single incident (Luke 2, 42-52), and that removed from what is here recorded by an interval of eighteen years. This protracted period of private discipline and preparation in the life both of Christ and his forerunner, is in striking contrast with our own impatience even under the most hurried superficial processes of education. The reference of *those days* to the Saviour's residence in Nazareth, although not necessarily included in the meaning of that vague phrase, is true in fact, and with the continuative particle ($\delta \epsilon$) serves to connect what is here said with the immediately preceding context (2, 23). It is also in accordance with the usage of the phrase itself, which, even when most indefinite, always has respect to something previously mentioned. *In those days*, i. e. while he was still resident at Nazareth. The corrupted or apocryphal Gospel of the Hebrews, as we learn from Epiphanius, had here the full but false specification, "in the days of Herod the king," from which some groundlessly suppose the clause before us to have been abridged, without regard to its inaccuracy. That the phrase (*in those days*) cannot mean at the precise time mentioned in 2, 23, is plain from what follows and from a comparison of Luke's more exact chronological specifications (3, 1. 2. 23), which may be used to illustrate the narrative before us, but are not to be incorporated with it, because not included in the plan and purpose of Matthew's Gospel. *Came* is in Greek the graphic present, *comes*, arrives, or, retaining the precise sense of the compound verb, *becomes near*, at hand, or present. The same form is common in the Septuagint version, and another of the same verb is applied in the Apocrypha (1 Macc. 4, 46) to the future or prospective appearance of a Prophet in Israel, after the long suspension of the office. In like manner it is used of Christ's appearance (Heb. 9, 11), and here of John the Baptist, not as a private person, but a preacher and baptizer. *John*, a Hebrew name, the etymology of which suggests the idea of divine grace or favour. The circumstances of its imposition, with the other incidents of John's conception and nativity, omitted here by Matthew, because not essential to his argument in proof of the Messiahship of Jesus, are detailed with great particularity by Luke (1, 5–25. 57–66), as necessary parts of a methodical biography or history. *The Baptist* (or *Baptizer*), a definite description, presupposing some acquaintance with his name, as that of a historical person on the part of the original readers. Some of the older writers understood him to be so called simply as the person who baptized our Saviour, *John the Baptizer* (*of Jesus*). But this, although the most important and most honourable act of his official life, is only one out of the many that entitled him to bear the name in question, which describes him, not by that one act, but by the rite which distinguished his ministry from all before it, and is, therefore, sometimes used to designate it as a whole.* *Preaching*, a verb so rendered more than fifty times in our version, but four times *publish* (Mark 5, 20. 7, 36. 11, 10. Luke 8, 39), and twice *proclaim* (Luke 12, 3. Rev. 5, 2). It properly denotes the act of a public crier, or a herald, announcing or proclaiming something by authority. This primary and strict sense of the term must not be superseded by the technical and modern usage of the word *preaching*, as applied to formal and official religious teaching. In this sense, it is probable that neither John nor the Apostles preached, while Christ was with them (see below, on 10, 7.) It is at least not the main act here ascribed to John, which is rather that of announcing, giving notice, that the long-expected advent of the Messiah was at last approaching or arrived, as expressed more fully in the next verse. *Wilderness*, like the corresponding word in Hebrew, does not

---

* See below on 21, 25, and compare Acts 1, 22. 10, 37. 18, 25. 19, 3. 4.

necessarily or always signify a sandy desert, nor even an unbroken forest, but merely the uncultivated land as distinguished from that under tillage, but consisting often of rich pastures, and inhabited, though not so densely as the other portions. Hence we read of men residing, and of towns or cities, in the wilderness. (See Josh. 15, 61. 62. Judg. 1, 16. 1 Sam. 25, 1. 2). The first two passages just cited, and the title of Ps. 63, mention the *wilderness of Judah*, or, as it is here called, *Judea* (see above, on 2, 1. 6). This cannot mean the country, as distinguished from the towns or cities, of that province, which is altogether contrary to usage. Nor does it mean that John was traversing the less frequented portions of the country. The ministry here spoken of was stationary, and the wilderness must therefore be a definite locality. It does not mean, however, the great desert stretching from Tekoa to the Persian Gulf, which could not have been called *the desert of Judea* simply because it begins or ends there, but denotes specifically that part of Judea itself which is adjacent to the Dead Sea and the Jordan, without any very definite limits, as none such probably existed. Josephus, in describing the course of the Jordan from the lake of Genessaret to the Dead Sea, speaks of it as traversing much desert territory ($\pi o \lambda \lambda \dot{\eta} \nu\ \dot{\alpha} \nu \alpha \mu \epsilon \tau \rho o \acute{\nu} \mu \epsilon \nu o s\ \dot{\epsilon} \rho \eta \mu \acute{\iota} \alpha \nu$). This relates to the upper or external valley of the Jordan, while the inner or immediate bed has always been luxuriantly fertile. It was not merely optional or accidental, but a material part of John's commission, that he should make his appearance as a herald and forerunner far from the ordinary haunts of men, and instead of seeking them should be sought by them. In this respect he symbolized or represented the segregation of the Jewish church from other nations under the restrictive institutions of the old economy.

2. And saying, Repent ye ; for the kingdom of heaven is at hand.

This verse gives the subject or substance of John's *preaching*, in his own words, not as uttered upon any one occasion, much less as repeated without change on all occasions, but as a summary and sample of his constant proclamation or announcement. *And saying* is a direct continuation of the sentence from the verse preceding, *preaching and saying*, i. e. proclaiming by (or in the act of) saying (what immediately follows). This, though sometimes represented as a Hebrew idiom, is a simple and natural expression equally at home in any language. *Repent*, a Greek verb properly denoting afterthought, reflection, and then change of mind, including both the judgment and the feelings, upon moral subjects, with particular reference to one's own character and conduct, with an implication of improvement or reform in both. Evangelical repentance is not mere amendment nor mere sorrow for sin, but comprehends them both. The latter is expressed by a distinct Greek verb, which is used to denote even the remorse of Judas (see below, on 27, 3). The repentance to which John the Baptist called the Jews was a total reformation of both heart and life, as an immediate preparation for the advent of Messiah. The same necessity is urged not only in the prophecies (especially in Mal. 4, 5. 6), but also in the later Jewish books, and particularly in the saying, that when Israel repents a single day, the Messiah will immediately appear. *The kingdom of heaven* is a favourite expression in this gospel, parallel and equivalent to *kingdom of God* in the others.* It appears to be derived from the prophecies of Daniel, where it is applied to the kingdom which God himself was to erect upon the ruins of the four great empires, the successive rise and fall of which are so explicitly foretold in that book. This final and everlasting reign is that of the Messiah, both in its inception and its consummation, one of which is sometimes prominent, sometimes the other. *Heaven* (or *heavens*), in this phrase, is not put for God himself (as some explain the same word elsewhere), nor for a state of perfect blessedness hereafter (as it sometimes does mean), but for that heavenly condition of society or of the church, which was to commence at Christ's first advent and to be completed at the second. *Is at hand*, literally, *has approached* (or *come near*) i. e. lately and in consequence of recent changes, namely, the conception, birth, and adolescence of Messiah. The idea is not that his reign was once near but is so no longer, nor that it is now near and has always been so, but the intermediate notion that it has lately become nearer than it ever was before.

3. For this is he that was spoken of by the prophet Esaias, saying, The voice of one crying in the wilderness, Prepare ye the way of the Lord, make his paths straight.

Some regard these as the words of John himself, who is certainly represented elsewhere (John 1, 23) as applying the same prediction to his own ministry. There is no objection to this construction from the use of the demonstrative pronoun (*this*), which would then be precisely the same as in John 6, 50. 58. But most interpreters suppose the citation to be made by the evangelist, as in the parallel accounts (Mark 1, 3. Luke 3, 4). *For* assigns the reason of his uttering the words in the preceding verse, to wit, because he was the herald foreordained to do so. *This*, the person just described as so proclaiming. It is not necessarily implied that the prediction was fulfilled in John alone, but merely that he was the last in the succession of forerunners, and in some respects the greatest (see below, on 11, 11). The use made of the prophecy is not an "elegant accommodation," but an authoritative exposition of its true sense and a legitimate application to its real subject. The present tense (*is*) does not show these to be the words of John, or necessarily refer to the preceding verb (*has come near* or *approached*). It may just as well have reference to the present (*comes*, appears) in v. 1, or to the general fact of John's position in

---

* See below, on 5, 3. 19. 20. 10, 7. 11, 11. 12, and compare Mark 1, 14. 15. 4, 11. 9, 1, &c.

the scheme of prophecy and history. *The (one) spoken of* or *mentioned by*, (as in 2, 17), or, according to the Syriac version and the latest critics, *through* (as in 1, 22. 2, 5. 15), i. e. by his instrumental agency, or through him as a medium or an organ of communication. *The prophet Isaiah*, not a certain prophet so called, but the well-known and illustrious prophet of that name. The passage quoted is still extant in the Hebrew text (Isai. 40, 3) and in the Septuagint version, from which it is here taken with little variation. *Saying* might seem in English to agree with *this;* but there is no such ambiguity in the original, where the form of the word shows that it agrees with *the prophet Isaiah*, all these words being in the genitive singular masculine. *The voice*, or, more exactly, *a voice*, may be construed with a verb understood, *(there is) a voice*, or *a voice (is heard)*; but it is rather an abrupt exclamation or ejaculation, as if he had said, 'Hark, a voice,' perhaps with the additional idea of a long-continued previous silence. John is supposed by some, perhaps too fancifully, to be called a *voice*, i. e. a transient, momentary utterance, as contrasted with the *Word*, or permanent revealer of the Father who came after him (John 1, 1. 8). It may also be an undue refinement, though a pleasing one, to suppose that he is here represented as a voice, because his life was vocal no less than his lips, the whole man being as it were a sermon. *Of (one) crying* is the Rhemish translation of a word (βοῶντος) variously rendered in the older English versions, *of him that crieth* (Geneva Bible), *of a crier* (Wiclif, Tyndale, Cranmer). In Greek it is the participle of a verb which means to cry aloud, and is especially applied to the roaring or bellowing of certain animals, and therefore used, as some suppose, to signify the vehemence and harshness of John's ministrations. The original construction in Isaiah seems to be *a voice crying;* but the genitive construction, here adopted from the Septuagint, conveys substantially the same idea. *In the desert* is connected by the Hebrew accents with what follows (in *the wilderness, Prepare*, &c.), and the same construction is here possible, though not so natural as that which couples it with *voice* and *crying*.* But they both amount to the same thing, what is formally expressed in one case, being really implied or incidentally suggested in the other. If the command was uttered in the desert, it was in order to its being there obeyed or carried into execution (Bengel: *ubi vox ibi auditores*), as if it had been said, 'Here prepare,' &c. *The wilderness* primarily meant in the original prediction is a metaphorical or moral one, to wit, the spiritual desolation of the church or chosen people, through which God is represented as returning to them, a common figure in the Scriptures for the restoration of his favour or his gracious presence, after any interruption caused by sin. The twofold allusion, assumed by most interpreters, to the restoration from the Babylonish exile, and to the ancient oriental usage of opening and clearing roads before armies on the march or sovereigns upon journeys, is by no means certain or necessary. The latter is no peculiar local usage, but one which may be practised anywhere

---

* For a similar departure from the Masoretic accents, compare Heb. 3, 7.

in case of need.* The former rests upon a dubious assumption as to the connection between the thirty-ninth and fortieth chapters of Isaiah, and is countenanced by no explicit reference to Babylon, or to the captivity there, in the text or context. The terms of the prophecy may be applied to any reconciliation between Jehovah and his people, but are especially appropriate to that which was expected to accompany the advent of Messiah and the change of dispensations. When the "fulness of the time" for those events was come (Gal. 4, 4), the moral condition of the Jews might well be represented as a wilderness or desert, through which the way of their returning God must be prepared anew. But while this was the primary and full sense of the prophecy, which could only be morally accomplished, the literal fulfilment of its terms by John's actual appearance in a wilderness, seemed both to identify him as its subject and to prepare the minds of men for its fulfilment in a higher and more spiritual sense. Examples of the same twofold accomplishment, intended to secure the same end, are by no means unknown to the history of Christ himself, and more particularly of his passion.† At the same time John's appearance, not in the temple or the synagogue or even in the streets of the Holy City, but in an accessible though somewhat distant solitude, enhanced his fitness as a living symbol of the law, in its contrast with the Gospel, as explained above (on v. 1). *Prepare*, in the original prediction, means a particular mode of preparation, namely, the removal of obstructions, corresponding to the English *clear*, in reference both to roads and houses.‡ The obstructions here meant, being of a moral kind, could only be removed by reformation or repentance (see above, on v. 1), or as one of the Greek commentators beautifully phrases it, by gathering from the surface of the desert the thorns of passion and the stones of sin. *The Lord*, not the Lord Jesus Christ, at least exclusively, but as in the original prophecy, *Jehovah*, the peculiar name of God considered as the national and covenanted God of Israel (see Ex. 6, 3), a name represented in the Greek of the Septuagint and of the New Testament by the phrase (ὁ κύριος) *the Lord*, denoting sovereignty. The second person of the Godhead is, however, not excluded, since it is in Christ, not only *by* him as an instrument, but *in* him as a person, that God reconciles the world unto himself (2 Cor. 5, 19), or, exchanging apostolic for prophetic forms, returns to his forsaken people. *Straight* may be opposed either to obliquity of course (as in Acts 9, 11), or to unevenness of surface, which last is the meaning in Isaiah, as appears from the next verse (40, 4), omitted here but introduced by Luke (3, 5), and exhibiting the ways as rectified or made straight (Wiclif, *right*) by the levelling of mountains and the filling up of valleys, a description also

---

* It is described by Diodorus in the case of Semiramis, by Suetonius in that of Caligula, and by Strabo, Justin, Plutarch, and Josephus, in more general terms.
† See below, on 21, 4. 16. 27, 9. 34. 35.
‡ Compare the use of the same Hebrew verb in Gen. 24, 31. Lev. 14, 36. Isai. 57, 14. 62, 10. Mal. 3, 1.

found in classical poetry.* *Paths*, in Greek a noun (τρίβους) derived from the verb (τρίβω) *to rub*, and therefore strictly meaning ways worn by the feet. In the Greek of the Scriptures it occurs, besides this place and the parallels, only in Gen. 49, 17. 1 Sam. 6, 12. But the corresponding Hebrew word denotes a highway or an artificial causeway, thrown up above the level of the land through which it passes.

4. And the same John had his raiment of camel's hair, and a leathern girdle about his loins ; and his meat was locusts and wild honey.

The same John seems equivalent in English to *the said* (or *the aforesaid*) *John;* but the literal translation is, *and John himself,* perhaps employed as a transition from the prophecy to the fulfilment. As if he had said, 'the John thus described in prophecy, when he actually came himself (or in fact), *had his dress,*' &c. This last phrase denotes more than that he had *a dress* of the kind described, suggesting the additional idea that his dress was a peculiar or distinctive one. *Raiment* is in Greek a noun peculiar to the Hellenistic dialect, but derived from a verb used in the classics. *Of camel's hair,* literally, *from hairs of a camel,* the preposition (ἀπό) indicating the source and the material. The reference is not to camel's skin with the hair, which would be too heavy, and has never been in use for clothing, although Clement of Rome, in his epistle, adds it to the *sheepskins and goatskins* of Heb. 11, 37. Nor is the stuff meant *camlet*, i. e. the fine cloth made in the east of camel's hair, much less the woollen imitation of it made in Europe, but a coarse sackcloth made of the long shaggy hair of the camel, which it sheds every year. Such cloth has always been extensively used in the east, both for tents and clothing, especially among the poor, and as a sign of mourning, being generally black in co'our (Rev. 6, 12). It seems to have been used as a proverbial designation of the cheapest and coarsest kind of dress. Thus Josephus says that Herod used to threaten the ladies of his court, when they offended him, that he would force them to wear hair-cloth. The garb of John the Baptist, here described, was not worn merely from frugality, or in contempt of fashionable finery, like that of Cato as described by Lucan,† but in imitation of the ancient prophets, who are commonly supposed to have been distinguished by a *rough* (or *hairy*) *garment* (Zech. 14, 3), or rather of Elijah in particular, who is described in the Old Testament (2 Kings 1, 8) as *an hairy man* (Sept. ἀνὴρ δασύς), or more exactly, *a possessor* (i. e. wearer) *of hair* (meaning *hair-cloth*, as above). The epithet *hairy* is not only as appropriate to his dress as to his person, but its reference to the former

---

* ...... At vos, qua venit, subsidite montes,
    Et faciles curris vallibus este viæ !—OVID.

† Hirtam membra super Romani more Quiritio Induxisse togam.—PHARSAL. 2, 386-7.

agrees better with the mention of the leathern girdle which immediately follows it in that case, as it does in this. As the words of Zechariah above cited are the only intimation that the prophets were distinguished by an official dress, and as Ahaziah, upon hearing the description above quoted (2 Kings 1, 8), appears to have recognized it, not as the prophetical costume, but as the dress of a particular prophet, it is on the whole most likely that Elijah wore it, not merely *ex officio* as a prophet, but for some special reason growing out of his own prophetic ministry as a Reprover and Reformer in the apostate kingdom of the ten tribes (1 Kings 18, 21. 19, 14). It may then have been a kind of mourning for the sin and the impending ruin of his people, which is much more likely than the supposition that it indicated an ascetic life, of which we find no trace in the prophetic history. Now John the Baptist's ministry not only bore a strong resemblance to that of Elijah, but is expressly represented by the Angel who announced his birth as a continuation or renewal of it (Luke 1, 17), and had been so represented in the last prophetic utterance of the Old Testament (Mal. 4, 5. 6), as expounded and applied by Christ himself (see below, on 11, 14. 17, 10–13). The dress of John may therefore be regarded, like his preaching in a literal desert (see above, on v. 3), as an outward coincidence intended to identify him as the subject of an ancient prophecy and the successor of an ancient prophet, while the prophecy itself had a wider scope and a more complete fulfilment, not in his external habits merely, but in the whole purpose of his ministry to reconcile the fathers and the children, i. e. to bring back the chosen people to the spirit and the practice of the old theocracy, so far as this was absolutely necessary as a moral preparation for Messiah's advent. (See above, on v. 1.) This view of John's relation to Elijah is by no means inconsistent with the supposition, that his coarse dress and food had also a practical use as an example to the penitent, as well as a symbolical significance as representing the austerity and rigour of the law in its demands upon those who were subjected to it.* The girdle, worn to bind the flowing oriental dress together, being necessary to all active movement, is a natural and common figure both for energy and preparation.† But in this case, as in that of Elijah (2 Kings 1, 8), the emphasis is not so much on *girdle* as on *leathern*. The important fact is not that John the Baptist wore a girdle, which was no doubt true of all his neighbours and acquaintances, both male and female, but that this universal article of dress, instead of being costly in material or decoration, was composed, not even of what we call leather, but most probably of undressed hide, an idea not so readily suggested by the authorized as by the older versions (*of a skin*). Such a girdle was in keeping with his shirt of haircloth, and his whole dress with the coarse and frugal fare described in the remainder of the verse. *His meat*, not flesh or animal food,

---

* A rabbinical tradition represents Elijah as arrayed in sheepskins, and to this, as the usual prophetical costume, some suppose an allusion in our Lord's denunciation of *wolves in sheep's clothing* (see below, on 7, 15).
† See 2 Sam. 22, 40. Ps. 65, 6. 93, 1. Prov. 31, 17. Isai. 45, 5. John 21, 18.

which is the meaning of the word in modern English, but *his food* in general, by which term it is rendered twice (Acts 14, 17. James 2, 15), but always elsewhere *meat*. The change of usage as to the word is remarkably exemplified in the phrase *meat-offering*, which is employed by our translators to describe precisely that kind of oblation into which *meat* (in its modern sense) could never enter.* *Locusts*, an insect of the grasshopper family, exceedingly destructive in the east, but allowed to be eaten by the law of Moses (Lev. 11, 22), and actually so used among many nations, both in earlier and later times. From some mistaken notion as to such food, and in strange oblivion of the legal grant just cited, some of the older writers tried, by arbitrary change of reading or by forced interpretation of the common text, to change these *locusts* into crabs or fishes, wild pears, nuts, cakes, or the boughs and leaves of trees. One of the strangest grounds of this gratuitous perversion was that John had not time or means to cook the locusts in the desert, which, however, is a very simple process, and continually practised by the Bedouins and other dwellers in the desert. Others, with more plausibility, but still without sufficient reason or necessity, explain *wild honey* to mean a sweet gum which distils from certain trees or shrubs, and is supposed to be so called in a few doubtful passages of ancient writers. The necessity of all such explanations is precluded by the clear and frequent mention, both in Scripture and the classics, of honey, in the strict sense, as produced by wild or unhived bees, and therefore found in trees and rocks, and situations still more unexpected.† It may have been in reference to these wild spontaneous products, rather than those secured by human care and labour, that the Holy Land was said to flow with milk and honey.‡ The fare of John the Baptist here described was not the ordinary diet of the country, as distinguished from the luxury of towns and cities, but one of more than usual simplicity and abstinence, and although not miraculously furnished, yet resembling Elijah's (1 Kings 17, 6. 18, 6) in its difference from that in ordinary use. In consequence of this abstemious mode of life, our Lord himself describes John as *neither eating nor drinking*, in comparison with his own less rigid practice (see below, on 11, 18). That it was not, even upon John's part, mere ascetic rigour, but commemorative and symbolical imitation, is apparent from the fact that he does not appear to have enforced this mode of life on others. Even the frequent fasts of his disciples seem to have been borrowed from the Pharisees and not from John (see below, on 9, 14).

5. Then went out to him Jerusalem, and all Judea, and all the region round about Jordan.

* See Lev. 2, 1. 5, 13. 6, 14. 14, 10. Num. 7, 13. 15, 6. 1 Chr. 21, 23.
† See Deut. 32, 13. Judg. 14, 5. 1 Sam. 14, 25. Ps. 81, 6.
‡ Ex. 3, 8. 17. 13, 5. 33, 3. Josephus also speaks of the region about Jericho as fed with honey (χώρα μελιτότροφος), which would hardly be said of that produced by domesticated bees.

Then, at the same time that is mentioned in the foregoing context, i. e. while John was thus living and thus preaching. Or the sense may be, after he had made his first appearance, as described in v. 1. *Went out* (or *forth*) from their homes into the wilderness. *Jerusalem* is put for its population by a natural and common figure also used by Cicero.* *All Judea*, i. e. all the rest of it, besides the capital and holy city. (Compare the frequent combination, *Judah and Jerusalem*, Isai. 1, 1. 2, 1. 3, 1). *The country round about Jordan* may be either a particular specification of the general terms just used (all Judea and especially that part about the Jordan), or an extension of the previous description (all Judea and those parts of the other provinces which are adjacent to the Jordan), so as to include a part of Galilee, Samaria, Perea, and Gaulonitis, all which had their points or lines of contact with the river. The phrase however is most probably indefinite and popular, denoting an indefinite but well-known region, not a technical expression of political or physical geography. Some would restrict it to a particular district called in the Old Testament the Plain of Jordan (Gen. 13, 10. 11. 1 Kings 7, 46. 2 Chr. 4, 17), or to the whole bed of that river, either from its source or from its leaving lake Gennesaret to its entrance into the Dead Sea, a tract now called by the inhabitants *El Ghor* (*the Valley*). The *all* in these two clauses is explained by some as a hyperbole for *most* or *many*, such as they suppose to be exemplified in 4, 18. 24. 10, 22. Mark 1, 37. Luke 7, 29. John 12, 32. Acts 4, 21, and elsewhere. But in all such cases there is more danger of attenuation than exaggeration, and in that before us we have reason to believe that the strong expressions of the text were literally true, or at least that a very large proportion of the whole population were drawn forth into the wilderness, by what they had heard of John the Baptist's early history and his peculiar mode of life, as well as by his earnest appeals to the conscience, which in every age have had a strange fascination, even for those whom they condemn or force to sit in judgment on themselves. From all this it is probable that John for some time, the precise length of which cannot now be determined, was an object of general curiosity, and even universally acknowledged as a messenger from God. (See below, on 11, 7–15. 21, 23–27.)

6. And were baptized of him in Jordan, confessing their sins.

The sentence is continued, without interruption or a change of subject, from the verse preceding, *they went out and were baptized*. The imperfect tense of both verbs shows that this concourse was not merely once for all, on some particular occasion, but repeated and continued for a length of time not here determined nor recorded elsewhere. The act or rite here mentioned is the one from which John derived his title *Baptist* or *Baptizer* (see above, on v. 1). Baptism is neither washing nor immersion simply, but symbolical or ceremonial washing, such as

---

* Mihi ipsa Roma obviam procedere visa est.—ORATIO IN PISONEM.

the Mosaic law prescribed, as a sign of moral renovation, and connected with the sacrificial rites of expiation, to denote the intimate connection between atonement and sanctification. It was from these familiar and significant ablutions that John's baptism was derived, and not from the practice of baptizing proselytes, the antiquity of which, as a distinct rite, is disputed, since it is not mentioned by Philo or Josephus, and first appears in the Gemara or later portion of the Babylonish Talmud. If really as ancient as the time of Christ, it was no doubt one of the traditional additions to the law made by the Pharisees, like the tithing of garden-herbs and the baptism of beds and cups. (See below, on 23, 23, and compare Mark 7, 4.) The extravagant importance afterwards attached to this rite in the case of proselytes, so as even to make it more essential than circumcision itself, and necessary to the validity and value of that ordinance, confirms the view just taken of its origin. The stress laid by the same traditional authorities on total immersion as essential to this baptism savours also of the oral law, and may perhaps have some connection with a similar confusion of the essence and the mode in Christian baptisms. In the written law of Moses, on the other hand, as in the primitive or apostolic practice of the Christian church, the essence of symbolical or ceremonial washing was the application of the purifying element. Some modern writers have carried this perversion so far as to deny the reference to cleansing altogether, and to make the dipping or immersion every thing, as symbolizing burying, death, depravity, or condemnation. There is far more truth, though not unmixed with fancy, in another modern notion, that John first excommunicated the whole people as unclean before God, and then on their profession of repentance purified them by his baptism. We may at least be certain that this rite was recognized by those who underwent it as a new form or modification of the purifying rites with which they were familiar, as appointed symbols of repentance and regeneration. As to the mode, the very doubt which overhangs it shows it to be unessential, and the doubt itself does not admit of an etymological solution. Even admitting that the word *baptize* originally means to dip or plunge, and that the first converts were in fact immersed—both which are doubtful and disputed points—it no more follows that this mode of washing was essential to the rite, than that every *elder* must be an old man, or that the Lord's *supper* can be lawfully administered only in the evening. The river Jordan is the only considerable stream of Palestine, rising near the base of Mount Hermon, flowing southward in a double bed or valley with a deep and rapid current, through the lakes of Merom and Tiberias, into the Dead Sea. Recent surveys and measurements have shown that the valley of the Jordan, with its lakes, is much below the level of the Mediterranean. This famous river formed the eastern limit of the province of Judea, and was probably the nearest water to the desert tract where John had made his first appearance. It was on account of this contiguity, and for the accommodation of the crowds attending him (John 3, 23), that John baptized there, and not for the convenience of immersion. They submitted to John's baptism, not as an unmeaning form, but at the same time *confessing their sins*, the Greek verb being an intensive compound, which denotes the act of free and full confession or acknowledgment. This, which is prescribed as a condition, although not a meritorious ground of pardon (Prov. 28, 13. 1 John 1, 9), and was therefore required even under the Mosaic law (Lev. 5, 5. 16, 21. 26, 40. Num. 5, 7), is at the same time one of the best tokens of repentance. The confession in the case before us, was neither public nor auricular, but personal and private. Whether it was general or particular, and uniform or various in different cases, are questions which we have no means of certainly determining. As John's whole ministry was only introductory to that of Christ, and his baptism not immediately effectual, but only *for* (or with a view to) *the remission of sins*, as Mark (1, 4) and Luke (3, 3) express it, it is possible, though not to be insisted on as certain, that the confession here referred to was a general acknowledgment of personal and national defection from the principles and practice of the old economy, to which the people must be brought back, as an indispensable condition or prerequisite of the Messiah's advent. See above, on v. 4. and compare Mal. 4, 5. 6 (in the Hebrew text 3, 23. 24), where this change is ascribed to the instrumental agency of Elijah, i. e. John himself (see below, on 17, 10–13).

7. But when he saw many of the Pharisees and Sadducees come to his baptism, he said unto them, O generation of vipers, who hath warned you to flee from the wrath to come?

We learn from this verse, that the concourse to John's ministry and baptism was not confined to either of the great religious sects, or rather schools, into which the Jewish church was then divided; and that John reproved and warned them both with impartial faithfulness, without respect of persons or of parties. The *Pharisees* and *Sadducees* differed, not only as to certain doctrines and the observance of the oral law, but also in their national and patriotic feelings, and their disposition to assimilation with the Gentiles. The name *Pharisee*, though otherwise explained by some, most probably means *Separatist*, not in the modern sense of *schismatic*, nor in allusion to mere personal austerity and strictness, as distinguishing a few ascetics from the masses of the people, but rather as defining the position which they occupied in reference to other nations, by insisting upon every thing peculiar and distinctive, and affecting even to exaggerate the difference between the Gentiles and themselves. This, which was at first, i. e. after the return from exile, when these divisions are first traceable in history, and even later, under the first Maccabees or Hasmonean princes, the true national and theocratic spirit, by degrees became corrupt, losing sight of the great end for which the old economy existed, and worshipping the law, not only that of Moses, but its traditional accretions called the Oral Law, as a system to be valued for its own sake, and designed to be perpetual. The opposition to this school or party arose chiefly from the *Sadducees*, a name of doubtful origin, derived by the early Christian writers from the Hebrew word for *righteous* (צָדִיק), but by the Jewish books from a proper name of kindred origin (צָדוֹק) *Zadok*, said to be that of the original founder. At first, they seem to have objected merely to the narrow nationality of their opponents, and to have aimed at smoothing down, as far as possible without abandoning their own religion, the points of difference between Jews and Gentiles, so as to reconcile the faith of Moses with the Greek philosophy and civilization, and renouncing or suppressing whatever appeared most offensive or absurd to the cultivated heathen. But this dangerous process of assimilation could not be carried far without rejecting matters more essential; and we find accordingly, that the Sadducees, before the time of our Lord's public ministry, had abjured, not only the Oral Law or Pharisaical tradition, but the doctrine of the resurrection and of separate or disembodied spirits, no doubt on the pretext of their not being expressly taught in the Old Testament.* This liberal or latitudinarian party was composed, according to Josephus, of persons in the more refined and educated classes, while the Pharisees included the great body of the people. For between these schools or parties the whole nation was divided, unless we except a third, called by Josephus the *Essenes*, and described as an ascetic class, inhabiting the desert near the Dead Sea, and leading a life not unlike that of the later Christian monks. The absence of all reference to this class in the Gospels is explained by some, upon the ground that they were merged in the vast multitude of those who followed John the Baptist and our Lord himself. But as they are not mentioned here and elsewhere, where the other schools and parties are referred to, it is probable that what Josephus tells us of the Essenes is only true of a temporary association, growing out of transitory local causes, and without a permanent distinctive character, like that of the two great bodies named by Matthew in the verse before us. If the Essenes, however, had a permanent and organized existence, they were no doubt entitled to the appellation of a *sect*, in the ordinary sense of that expression, as implying a distinct organization and a separate worship. But for that very reason it is not at all appropriate, though commonly applied, to the Pharisees and Sadducees, who, notwithstanding their diversities of doctrine and of practice, were professors of the same faith, and, so far as now appears, joined in the same worship. Their mutual relation may be therefore more exactly represented by the word *schools* or *parties*, the one suggesting difference of doctrine, and the other that of discipline or practice. The mutual relation of these parties in the Jewish church and state (which were inseparably blended) was analogous to that of Whigs and Tories, or of High and Low Church, for the last two hundred years, in England; each obtaining the ascendancy in turn, or at the same time sharing it between them. Such vicissitudes and rivalries may be distinctly traced in the history of the Has-

---

* See below, on 22, 23, and compare Acts 23, 8. 1 Cor. 15, 12.

monean dynasty before the Roman conquest, as for instance in the fact, that Alexander Jannæus charged his widow on his death-bed, as the guardian of her sons and regent during their minority, to transfer her political connections from the Sadducees, with whom he had himself been acting, to the Pharisees, as being not only the more numerous and powerful, but also the more national and patriotic party. From all these facts it will be seen that the Pharisees and Sadducees are here named, not as select classes, large or small, distinct from the body of the people, but as the two great schools or parties, into which that body was itself divided, so that *many* refers rather to the aggregate number, which is there described by its component parts. As if he had said, 'seeing a great multitude, consisting both of Pharisees and Sadducees.' From this it also follows, that when Luke (3, 7) represents John as uttering the same words *to the crowds* or *multitudes* (τοῖς ὄχλοις), there is no mistake in either statement, nor the least inconsistency between them, nor the slightest need of forced constructions, as, for instance, that he spoke to the Pharisees and Sadducees before the people, or *at* the former although *to* the latter, but a twofold yet harmonious statement of the simple fact, that the *crowds* who came out were both *Pharisees and Sadducees*. *To his baptism,* i. e. both to witness and receive it, not merely to the place of its administration. The sense of opposition or hostility (*against his baptism*) is at variance both with usage and the context. To both these parties, so unlike and even opposite in character and spirit, and little accustomed to be thus confounded, John addressed himself in terms of undistinguishing severity. *Generation* is in Greek a plural, and is so translated by Wiclif and in the Geneva Bible, both of which have *generaciouns*. The plural may have reference either to variety of species or to multitude of individuals. The word itself denotes any product, whether animal (as here) or vegetable (as in 26, 29, below, and in Luke 12, 18). It is commonly translated *fruit*, which has the same double use in English. (Besides the passages just cited, see Mark 14, 25. Luke 3, 7. 22, 18. 2 Cor. 9, 10.) *Generation* occurs only here and in the parallels (12, 34. 23, 33. Luke 3, 7). The Rhemish version has a more poetical expression, but equivalent in import, *vipers' brood*, i. e. offspring or progeny of vipers. As a mere expression of abhorrence or contempt, this language would be unaccountable, if not unworthy of the man who used it. If the notion thus conveyed were that of craft or cunning, the form would still be a surprising one. The only satisfactory solution is afforded by assuming an allusion to the protevangelium or first promise of a Saviour after the Fall (see Gen. 3, 15), in which the *seed of the woman*, i. e. Christ and his people, are contrasted with the *seed of the serpent*, or the devil and his followers, both men and demons, throughout all ages, as composing two antagonistic powers, which were to be long at war, with various fluctuations and vicissitudes of fortune, including temporary partial advantages on one side, but an ultimate and total triumph on the other. This prediction gives complexion to all later history, which is really the record of its gradual fulfilment. This war of ages was now approaching to its crisis or catastrophe. The heads of the two parties were about to be brought into personal collision.* In the mean time the forerunner of the conqueror denounces the great body of the people who came forth to hear him, and especially the leaders of the two great parties into which they were divided, as belonging to the hostile army. The mere change of expression, from *seed of the serpent* to *brood of vipers*, is entirely insufficient to outweigh the historical and other arguments in favour of this explanation, which converts a harsh and almost passionate vituperation into a solemn and impressive recollection of a prophecy coeval with the fall of man and interwoven with the whole course of his subsequent experience. *Who hath warned you*, or retaining the strict sense of the aorist, *who did warn you*, or *who warned you*, i. e. just now, or before you came out hither? The Greek verb, elsewhere rendered *forewarn* (Luke 12, 5), *shew* (Luke 6, 47. Acts 9, 16. 20, 35), originally means to show secretly or partially, both which ideas are suggested by the particle (ὑπό) with which it is compounded, and may therefore be expressed by our phrase, to give a glimpse of any thing. Here (as in some of the passages just cited) it denotes a slight intimation or suggestion, as distinguished from a full disclosure. 'Who has given you a hint of the impending danger?' The infinitive which follows may be variously construed, as denoting either the necessity of flight, or possibility of rescue. 'Who has shown you that you must flee?' 'Who has shown you that you can escape?' In either case, the words express surprise; on the former supposition, at their having been alarmed; on the latter, at their venturing to hope. The first is probably the natural impression made on most unbiassed readers, though the other is preferred by some interpreters, and one even understands the words to mean, that if they had been warned, they would no doubt have fled. The *wrath*, i. e. the manifestation of God's anger against sin and his determination to punish it.† *To come*, in Greek an active participle, *coming*, or about to be, the verb denoting mere futurity and having no equivalent in English (see above, on 2, 13). *The coming wrath* is an expression elsewhere used by Paul (1 Thess. 1, 10), and in the same sense, namely that of future and impending judgments, without specification of their form or nature.

8. Bring forth therefore fruits meet for repentance:

Bring forth, literally, *make*, i. e. produce or bear (Rhem. *yield*). The same use of the verb occurs in Gen. 1, 11, and 7, 17. 18. 21, 43 below. *Fruits*, or, according to the critics, *fruit*, in the singular number, but without a change of meaning. *Meet*, the word so rendered Acts 26, 20. 1 Cor. 16, 4. 2 Th. 1, 3, and *due* (*reward*) in Luke 23, 41, but usually *worthy*, which would have been better here. *Fruits worthy of repentance*, i. e. such effects as it may justly be expected to

---

* See below, on 4, 1, and compare John 12, 31. 14, 30. 16, 11.
† Lev. 10, 6. Num. 1, 53. Deut. 9, 7. Josh. 9, 20. 2 Kings 23, 26. 1 Chr. 27, 24. 2 Chr. 19, 2. Ezra 5, 12. Neh. 13, 18. Job 21, 20. Isai. 54, 8. Jer. 21, 5. Hab. 3, 2. Zech. 7, 2. Rom. 2, 5. Eph. 2, 3. 1 Th. 5, 9. Rev. 6, 16.

produce. The margin of the English Bible has *answerable to amendment of life.* The Peshito, or old Syriac, has *conversion.* *Therefore,* because you have been warned, or because you have come forth to be baptized, professing your repentance, which includes at least the purpose of reformation, act accordingly. As this is not a continuation of the figure in v. 7 (*generation of vipers*), but an introduction to the one in v. 9 (*trees*), *fruit* is to be taken in a vegetable not an animal sense, though appropriate to both (see above, on v. 7), and therefore furnishing a natural transition from the one to the other.

9. And think not to say within yourselves, We have Abraham to (our) father; for I say unto you, that God is able of these stones to raise up children unto Abraham.

Think not to say is explained by some as a mere pleonasm, meaning nothing more than *say not*, as the same verb used in Mark 10, 42, is omitted in the parallel passage (20, 25 below). Others run into the opposite extreme of making it mean *wish* (Vulg. *ne velitis*), *begin* (Luther), *presume* (Geneva), *delight* (Rhemish), none of which ideas is suggested by the Greek verb. It simply means, *do not even think of saying*, as expressed by Tyndale's paraphrastic version (*see that ye once think not to say*), and a little differently in Cranmer's (*be not of such mind that ye would say*). The act prohibited is not simply that of speaking, but of thinking or intending so to speak. *In yourselves*, or as it is expressed in Hebrew, *in your hearts* (see Ps. 4, 6. 10, 6. 14, 1), i. e. secretly and mentally, not vocally or audibly, implying that they might be disposed to think, what they would not care to utter upon this occasion. (*As a*) *father*, founder, or progenitor, *we have Abraham*, a proud boast afterwards expressly uttered by the Jews in opposition to our Lord himself (See John 8, 33. 37. 39). What was then denied by him, and by John the Baptist in the case before us, was not the fact of their descent from Abraham, which was notoriously true, but their reliance upon that fact, as securing the divine favour, irrespective of their character and conduct. This arrogant and impious reliance, which was secretly or openly cherished by the Jews of that day, found expression afterwards in maxims, some of which are still preserved in the rabbinical tradition, for example that of the Bereshith Rabbah, that Abraham sits at the gate of hell, and suffers no one of his circumcised descendants to go down there. *For* assigns a reason why they should not entertain this national hereditary trust, viz., because it presupposed that God was bound to that one race as his chosen people, and could not, if he would, reject them. In opposition to this wicked and absurd illusion he assures them, in a tone almost ironical, that if they perished, God was able to supply their place, and that from the most unpromising and unexpected quarters. *Of* (out of, from among) *these stones*, not a figure for the Gentiles as worshippers of stocks and stones; nor in allusion to the monumental stones of Gilgal; but a simple designation of the loose stones lying on the surface of the ground, to which the Baptist may have pointed as he spoke. There is no need of supposing an allusion to the stony soil of the Arabian desert, from which one part of it derives its name (*Arabia Petræa*), as *wilderness* does not necessarily denote a barren waste (see above, on v. 1). The expression would be natural in any situation where loose stones happened to be lying around. They are mentioned at all as the least obvious and likely source of such supply, and therefore necessarily implying an immediate divine agency in its production. The same idea might have been expressed in general terms, but with far less emphasis, by saying, 'If all the natural descendants of the Patriarch were swept away, God could supply their place at once from any quarter even the least promising.'* There is a possible though not a necessary reference to Isai. 51, 1. It matters little as to John's essential meaning, whether *children to* (or *for*) *Abraham* be understood of natural or spiritual offspring. If the former, the assertion is, that God could easily renew the Jewish race, in case of its perdition; if the other, that he could as easily substitute a better. On either supposition, the vocation of the Gentiles, although not expressly represented by the stones, is tacitly implied as possible. *Raise up*, or retaining the original import of the Greek verb (see above, on 2, 13. 14. 20, 21) *arouse*, awaken from inanimate existence into life.† *I say unto you*, with emphasis on both pronouns, as in 5, 28 below, and often elsewhere. 'Whatever you may say to me or to yourselves about your proud prerogatives as natural descendants of the faithful Abraham, the Friend of God, *I tell you* in return that God has no need of your services, but with the same ease that he made you or Abraham or Adam, can convert the very stones beneath your feet into worthier sons of Abraham than you are.'

10. And now also the axe is laid unto the root of the trees: therefore every tree which bringeth not forth good fruit is hewn down, and thrown into the fire.

And now also, not at some period remotely or indefinitely future, but *already*, even while I speak, the judgment is impending.‡ *The axe*, which in Homer always means a battle-axe, but in the later classics, as with us, an instrument for felling trees, is here a figure for divine judgments, possibly suggested by the reference to *fruit* in the preceding verse. *Is laid*, literally *lies*, is lying, as the original verb is a deponent one. The passive form, employed in the translation, seems to mean that some one is now laying (or applying) it to the tree, i. e. actually felling it; whereas the neuter form of the original may possi-

---

* For a similar strong figure, very differently applied by Christ himself, see Luke 19, 40.

† Compare the application of the verb *raise up* to human generation in Gen. 38, 8. and in 22, 24 below.

‡ *But also*, or *but even* (δὲ καί) is a favorite combination of Luke's (3, 9. 12. 14. 8, 36. 16, 1. 18, 1. 9. 16. 23, 38.

bly have been intended to convey the idea of its lying there as yet inactive, in immediate proximity (at, close to, πρός) and ready to be used at any moment. This is indeed all that the words necessarily denote, although more may be implied or suggested by the context. Upon this point depends another question as to the precise sense of *the root*, which may either mean the bottom of the tree, *at* which the axe *is lying* in readiness for future use, or the radical and vital portion of the tree, to which it is already actively applied, with a view to its complete excision, or as that idea is expressed in prophecy, with reference to this very period and these very judgments, so as to leave neither root nor branch (Mal. 4, 1. Hebrew text, 3, 19). The essential meaning, upon either supposition, is that of imminent complete destruction. The combination of the singular and plural (*root* and *trees*) may have no separate significance, or may specifically signify the common root of all the trees, with reference perhaps to the national dependence or descent from Abraham, as cherished by his individual descendants. *The trees* of this verse, corresponding to the *fruits* of that before it, must of course denote those from whom fruit was expected and required, namely, those to whom John the Baptist was now speaking, the crowds who came forth to his baptism and consisted both of Pharisees and Sadducees. *Therefore*, because the axe is laid there for the very purpose. *Bringing forth*, literally, *making*, i. e. yielding or producing, as in v. 8. *Good fruit*, there described as *fruit meet for* (answerable to, or worthy of) *repentance*, but here by its intrinsic quality as *good*, both in the sense of right or acceptable to God, and that of salutary, useful, to the doer and to others. *Is cut down*, not is commonly or generally cut down, as a matter of course, which is forbidden by the preceding *therefore*, but now, in this case, upon this occasion, at this time, or as it might be expressed in the English of the present day, *is being cut down*, as something actually passing, according to one sense of the verb *lies*, as explained above; but if the other be preferred, the present may be used to represent a certain and proximate futurity (*is cut down*, i. e. sure and just about to be so). *Hewn down*, so translated in the parallel passage (Luke 3, 9) and in 7, 19 below, but twice *cut down* (Luke 13, 7. 9), and thrice *cut off* (18, 8. Rom. 11, 22. 2 Cor. 11, 12), and once *hindered* (1 Pet. 3, 7), means strictly *cut out*, and is so translated in a single instance (Rom. 11, 24). It is here used to denote, not the mere felling, but the complete excision of the tree, i. e. its being cut up by the root. (See below, on 13, 29. 15, 13, and compare Luke 17, 6. Jude 12, in all which places the idea of eradication is expressed, but without that of cutting). *Is cast* (or *thrown*), not in general, but now, the present having the same sense as in the verb immediately preceding, rendered more emphatic, in the Greek, by its position at the end of the whole sentence (*into fire is cast*). *Into fire*, (not *the fire*), an indefinite description of the element made use of to consume the tree, and representing, as a figure, the wrath of God, already mentioned (in v. 7), or its ruinous effect, upon the unforgiven sinner (compare Heb. 12, 29).

11. I indeed baptize you with water unto repentance: but he that cometh after me is mightier than I, whose shoes I am not worthy to bear: he shall baptize you with the Holy Ghost, and (with) fire.

But though John uttered these severe denunciations, it was not in his own name, or by his own authority. He was only a forerunner, not a principal. The very rite which he administered was only emblematical of something to be actually done by his superior, between whom and himself there was a greater disparity than that between a master and his meanest slave. A contrast or antithesis is indicated by the very structure of the sentence, which is balanced, in the usual Greek manner, by the corresponding particles, *indeed* (μέν) and *but* (δέ), equivalent, when thus combined, to our expressions, 'on the one hand and the other.' The first introduces a description of himself and his own ministry, the second that of his superior or principal. *Indeed*, or it is true, a sort of concession or acknowledgment that they were right in thinking him a messenger from God, commissioned to baptize with water, literally, *in water*, as the element or fluid, which no more implies immersion than our common phrases to rinse or wash in water. But though both were to baptize, it was in a manner and with an effect immeasurably different, a difference corresponding to the infinite disparity between them as to rank and nature. The sum of what is here said is, that John's whole ministry was relative, prospective, and preparatory; that he was not a principal but a dependent; further removed from his superior in rank than the humblest domestic from his master; and that the same disparity existed between the ministry and acts of the two parties. John did indeed baptize them for (or with a view to) repentance; but even this he only did as a forerunner. *The (one) behind me coming* seems to presuppose their knowledge of the fact, that he was to be followed by another, though they might not be aware of the precise relation which the two sustained to one another. *Mightier*, more powerful, implying not only a diversity of rank but also of efficiency and actual performance. The first of these ideas is then stated still more strongly and distinctly. The difference was not merely that of first and second, but of master and servant; nay, it was still more marked and distant. For the meanest slave might bring or carry his master's sandals; but this humblest of all services, as rendered to John's master, was too great an honour even for the man whom all Judea and Jerusalem had come forth to honour. *Worthy*, or as the Greek word strictly means, *sufficient*, i. e. good enough. *Shoes*, literally, *underbindings*, i. e. sandals, soles of wood or leather, fastened by a strap, particularly mentioned in another form of this repeated declaration, which has been preserved by Mark (1, 7). *To bear*, or carry, with particular reference, as some suppose, to a journey or the bath. To an oriental audience words could hardly have expressed the idea of disparity in a stronger or a more revolting manner. That John should have made such a profession of his own inferiority, not once but often, in the presence of the people, and at the height of his own popularity, implies a disposition, on the part of others, to rest in him as the expected Saviour; his own clear view of the subordinate relation which he bore to Christ; and his sincere and humble resolution to maintain it, even in the face of popular applause and admiration, and amidst the most enticing opportunities of self-aggrandizement. What was thus true of the persons was no less true of the acts which they performed and the effects which they produced. If John was less, compared with Christ, than the lowest slave compared with his own master, what he did, even by divine authority and as our Lord's legitimate forerunner, must be proportionately less than what his principal would do, as to intrinsic worth and power. *He shall baptize you in holy spirit*, or (the) *Holy Spirit;* for although the article is not expressed in either of the Gospels, the constant use of this phrase to denote a divine person has almost rendered it a proper name, and as such not requiring to be made definite by any prefix, like a common noun. The antithesis is then not only between water and spirit but between dead matter and a divine person, an infinite disparity. Now this extreme incalculable difference seems to be predicated of baptism as administered by John and Christ. But Jesus baptized only by the hands of his disciples (John 4, 2), and this was no less water-baptism than that administered by John. The contrast, therefore, cannot be between John's baptism as performed with water, and that of Christ (or his disciples) as performed without it. Nor can it be intended to contrast Christ's baptism, as attended by a spiritual influence, with John's as unattended by it; for the latter is proved to be essentially identical with Christian baptism by its source, its effects, and its reception by our Lord himself. There are still two ways in which the comparison may be explained, and each of which has had its advocates. The first supposes the antithesis to be, not between the baptism of John and that of Christ, which were essentially the same, but simply between the administering persons. 'I baptize you in water, not without meaning and effect, but an effect dependent on a higher power; he will baptize you in the same way and with the same effect, but in the exercise of an inherent power, that of his own spirit.' This construction, though it yields a good sense and conveys a certain truth, is not so natural and obvious as another, which supposes no allusion to the outward rite of Christian baptism at all, but a comparison between that rite, as John performed it, and the gift of spiritual influences, figuratively called a baptism, as the same term is applied to suffering (see below, on 20, 22. 23). The meaning then is, 'I indeed bathe your bodies in water, not without divine authority or spiritual effect; but he whose way I am preparing is so far superior, both in power and office, that he will bathe your souls in the effusion of the Holy Spirit.' And as this divine influence is always described in the Old Testament either as unction or effusion, and the figurative baptism must correspond in form to the literal, we have here an incidental proof that the primitive baptism was not exclusively or necessarily immersion.

With fire, not the fire of divine wrath, as in v. 10, but the powerful and purifying influences of the Spirit so described elsewhere. (See Isai. 4, 4. 64, 2. Jer. 5, 14. Mal. 3, 2. Acts 2, 3.)

12. **Whose fan (is) in his hand, and he will thoroughly purge his floor, and gather his wheat into the garner ; but he will burn up the chaff with unquenchable fire.**

To the figure of a fruitless tree cut down and burnt (in v. 10), John now adds that of chaff destroyed in the same way, but with distinct reference to the saved as well as lost, the former being represented by the corn or wheat, the latter by the chaff, straw, or stubble, separated from it. *Fan*, or winnowing instrument, whatever may have been its form, whether that of a shovel or a fork, with which the grain was thrown up to be cleansed by the wind. (*Is*) *in his hand*, i. e. in readiness for use, or just about to be employed. Or without supplying any verb, we may explain the phrase as a descriptive one, analogous to *sword in hand*, and others like it. The axe could only represent one part of the judicial process, the excision of the wicked, while the fan suggests both, as its very use was to separate the wheat and chaff, in order to the preservation of the one and the destruction of the other. *And* (being thus armed or equipped) *he will* (certainly, or is just about to) *cleanse thoroughly*, in Greek a single word meaning to *cleanse through and through*, or from one end to the other. *Floor*, not in the usual or wide sense, but in the specific one of *threshing-floor*, as the corresponding Hebrew word is sometimes rendered (see for example Gen. 50, 10. 11, where both forms are used to represent precisely the same word in the original). The oriental threshing-floor is not a floor at all, in our customary sense of the expression, but a hard flat piece of ground, on which the grain is either threshed with sledges or the feet of cattle, or exposed to the wind, to which last method there is here allusion.* *To cleanse the floor* is either to cleanse the grain upon it by removing all impurities, or to cleanse the floor itself by the removal of the grain thus purified, in which case these words are descriptive of the end of the whole process. *Gather*, collect, or bring together, first from its dispersion, at the harvest, and then from its mixture with the chaff and other refuse, at the winnowing or threshing. *His wheat*, or his own wheat, that belonging to him, which implies its value, while the chaff belongs to no one, because worthless. *Garner*, granary, in Greek *depository*, or the place where any thing is laid up for safe-keeping. From this word, through the Latin, comes *apothecary*, and the word itself (*Apotheke*) is used in German to denote a druggist's shop or store. Its specific application to a barn or granary is in accordance with the classical usage, though Herodotus applies it to the thing deposited, a twofold usage similar to that of *store* in English. It might here be not inaccurately rendered *store-house*. The remaining clause presents

---

* See Deut. 25, 4. 2 Sam. 24, 22. 1 Chr. 21, 23. Isai. 23, 27. 28. 41, 15.

the contrast under the same figurative form. *But* (while he thus secures his wheat in the appropriate place) *the chaff* (or whatever is not nutritive and therefore valuable) *he will burn up*, literally, *burn down*, both denoting entire consumption, but the latter being applicable in our idiom, which differs from the Greek in this point, only to houses, or to something which the fire reduces and disorganizes as well as destroys. *With fire unquenchable*, or more exactly *unquenched*, i. e. never quenched or put out, which amounts to the same thing, as the fact that it is not quenched implies that its extinction is impossible. The Greek word is a favourite with Homer, but most frequently applied in a figurative sense to what is endless or unceasing, such as fame or laughter, and by Æschylus even to the ceaseless flow of ocean. The word itself has now been anglicized (*asbestus*) to denote natural or artificial substances considered incombustible, whereas it really describes them as perpetually burning. (Compare Mark 9. 43. 45, where the same Greek word is paraphrased, *that never shall be quenched*.) With a freedom in the use of figures which is characteristic of the Scriptures, the same persons who in v. 10 are consumed as trees are here consumed as chaff, while the careful preservation of the wheat represents the destination of the saved.* In most other instances, the prominent idea is that of chaff scattered by the wind, to which is here superadded that of burning, both which agencies, as some suppose, were often visibly connected at the threshing-floor, the wind to separate the chaff and fire to destroy it.

13. Then cometh Jesus from Galilee to Jordan unto John, to be baptized of him.

The transition from John's ministry to that of Christ is furnished by the baptism of our Lord himself, as the most important act of the former, and an immediate preparation for the latter. At the same time, it afforded the most striking confirmation of what John himself had taught as to his own inferiority (see above, on v. 11), by an express divine recognition of our Lord as the Messiah. But this was not the only nor perhaps the chief end of our Lord's subjection to this ceremonial form. Though without sins of his own to be repented of, confessed, or pardoned, he identified himself by this act with his people whom he came to save from sin (see above, on 1, 21), and gave them an assurance of that great deliverance; † avowed his own subjection to the law as the expression of his Father's will (see below, on v. 15); and put honour upon John as a divinely inspired prophet and his own forerunner. An ingenious living writer supposes an allusion to the cleansing rites required by the ceremonial law not only in the

---

* For similar images applied to the same or kindred subjects compare Job 21, 18. 39, 12. Ps. 1, 4. 35, 5, Isai. 5, 24. 17, 13. 29, 5. 41, 15. Jer. 23, 23. Dan. 2, 35. Hos. 13, 3. Zeph. 2, 2. Mal. 4, 1 (in Hebrew 3, 19).

† Sic enim baptizatus est, ut circumcisus est, ut purificatus in templo cum matre, ut flagellatus, ut crucifixus; nobis hæc omnia passus est, non sibi.—ERASMUS.

case of personal impurity, but in that of even accidental contact with the unclean.* *Then*, or in those days (Mark 1, 9), i. e. while John was thus preaching and baptizing, without any intimation of the length of his ministry, which cannot, however, have been very long. The conclusion reached by highly probable, though not entirely conclusive combinations, is, that from John's public appearance to his death was a period of about three years, at least one half of which was spent in prison. (See below, on 14, 1–12.) *Cometh*, the same word that is used above (in v. 17) to describe John's own appearance as a preacher and baptizer   In this place, as in that, it strictly signifies arrival, but perhaps with the accessory idea of a sudden unexpected coming forward into public view, for he was not baptized in secret or alone, but in the presence, if not in the company of others. (Compare Luke 3, 21.)   *From Galilee*, that is to say, from Nazareth in Galilee (Mark 1, 9), where Joseph and Mary lived before the birth of Christ (Luke 1, 26. 27), and where they again took up their abode on their return from Egypt. (See above, on 2, 22. 23, and compare Luke 2, 39. 51.) *To the Jordan* (as the place, and) *to John* (as the person), a distinction marked in Greek by the use of different prepositions (ἐπί and πρός), but which can only be expressed in English by approximation (*to John at* the Jordan). For a brief description of this river, and the reason of John's being there, see above, on v. 5. *To be baptized*, in Greek a genitive construction (for the sake or purpose *of being baptized*), from which we learn not only that he was baptized (Mark 1, 9), but that this was no fortuitous occurrence or mere after-thought, but the express design with which he left home and appeared among John's hearers. *Of him*, or in modern English, *by him*, as the visible and real agent in baptizing, though the act was performed under a superior authority, and, therefore, only *through* him as an instrumental agent, just as prophecies are sometimes said to have been uttered by and sometimes through the prophets. (See above, on 1, 22. 2, 5. 15. 17 23.)

14. But John forbad him, saying, I have need to be baptized of thee, and comest thou to me ?

Although we have no less than three accounts of our Lord's baptism, it is only from the one before us that we learn the fact of John's at first declining to perform it. *Forbad*, in Greek the verb to *hinder* or *prevent*, compounded with a preposition (διά) meaning *through*, which may either give the verb the local sense of stopping, not permitting him to pass (of which there is a clear example in the apocryphal book of Judith 12, 7), or the intensive sense of thoroughly or utterly forbidding him, as in the similar compound of the verb *to cleanse*, in v. 12. But in either case, the main idea is not so much that

---

* See Lev. 15, 5. 22, 6. 5, 2. 6, 27. 7, 21. 11, 8. 31. 15, 19. Num. 19, 11. 22, 1. 31, 19. Deut. 14, 8, and compare Hagg. 2, 13. 14.

of verbal prohibition, which is commonly suggested by the verb *forbid*, as that of physical obstruction, hindrance, or arrest, the act of holding back or stopping with the hand or by some movement of the body. The imperfect tense implies that this was more than a momentary act, being still persisted in till Jesus spake the words recorded in the next verse. *John was stopping him* (and) *saying, I have need*, etc.. (when) *Jesus answering said* (see below on v. 15). *I have need*, a synonymous but stronger phrase than *I need*, being more suggestive of continued and habitual necessity. (Compare its use in 6, 8. 9, 12. 14, 16. 21, 3. 26, 65.) *Of thee*, i. e. *by thee*, as in v. 13. *Comest thou*, a question, or *thou comest*, an exclamation, both expressive of surprise, as in John 13, 6. *To me*, i. e. to be baptized by me, as fully expressed in the preceding verse. This surprise of John implies his previous acquaintance with the person, or at least the character, of Jesus, and perhaps a personal belief that he was the Messiah, which is perfectly consistent with his saying elsewhere, that he knew him not, i. e. was not assured of his Messiahship, until he had received the promised sign from heaven (John 1, 33). The spirit of John's language is, 'If either of us is to receive baptism from the other, I should be baptized by thee as thy inferior (see above, on v. 11, and compare Heb. 7, 7), and as being really a sinner needing pardon and repentance, whereas thou art thyself the Lamb of God which, taketh away the sin of the world (John 1, 29. 36). This shows how far John was from regarding his own baptism as a magical charm, or as intrinsically efficacious, and how clearly he perceived and represented it to be significant of something altogether different and dependent on a higher power. For it is only upon this ground that he could have seen any incongruity in his administering it even to his own superior, who might have submitted to the rite, or performed it as an *opus operatum*, no less than others, but who seemed to be entirely beyond the reach and the necessity of that which the baptismal washing signified, to wit, the need of pardon and of moral renovation. (See above, on v. 6.)

15. And Jesus answering said unto him, Suffer (it to be so) now: for thus it becometh us to fulfil all righteousness. Then he suffered him.

The participial construction, commonly resolved by our translators into a past tense (see above, on 2, 8), is here retained with great advantage as it is in 2, 12 above. The two first words of our Lord's answer (ἄφες ἄρτι) are perceptive or imperative; the rest assigns the ground or reason. *Suffer* is in Greek a verb originally meaning to *let go* or (more actively) to *send away*, in which sense Matthew uses it below (13, 36); then to *let alone* or leave undisturbed (as in 15, 14. 27, 49); then to *leave*, in the proper local sense, to go away from (as in 4, 11. 20. 22, and often elsewhere); then to *leave with*, or give up to (as in 5, 40); then to *leave out* or omit (as in 23, 23); then to *leave unpunished*, pardon, or forgive (as in 6, 12. 9, 2. 12, 31. 18, 21); and lastly to *permit*, allow, or suffer (as in 19, 14. 23, 13). Among these various shades of meaning there is only one entirely inadmissible in this case, namely that of simply leaving or forsaking, since we cannot understand our Lord as telling John to leave him, when he had just come to be baptized by him. But he might say, in accordance with the context and the circumstances, *let me go*, i. e. into the water, from which John was keeping him; or *let me alone*, meddle not with my proceedings; or *yield to me*, give up to my expressed wish; or *omit*, dispense with, these gratuitous objections; or even *pardon me*, excuse me, as a formula of condescending courtesy; or finally *permit me*, suffer me to do what I am doing, which is the sense preferred by most interpreters and well expressed in our translation (*suffer it to be so*), though the true grammatical construction may require the ellipsis to be otherwise supplied (*suffer me to do so*). As John's surprise and hesitation necessarily imply that there was something strange in the request or application, so this one word of our Lord implies that there was really some cause of wonder, and that what he now proposed was an exceptional extraordinary act, and as such to be borne with and submitted to. The next word suggests the kindred but additional idea, that it was a temporary act, or rather one to be performed once for all (*hac una vice*). It is not the common adverb of time (νῦν) exactly answering to *now* (at present, or at this time), but another (ἄρτι) corresponding rather to *just now* and *presently*, sometimes referring to a time already and yet scarcely past (as in 9, 18 below and 1 Th. 3, 6); sometimes to a proximate immediate future (as in 26, 53 below and John 13, 37); sometimes to the present moment, as a passing one, in contrast either with the past (as in John 9, 19. 25) or with the future (as in John 13, 7. 19). This last is here to be preferred, not only as by far the most common and familiar sense, but also as best suiting the connection, and especially the word immediately preceding (ἄφες), as it has been just explained. The two together then mean that the act proposed, although unusual and mysterious, was to be allowed and acquiesced in for some temporary reason. But as this might have seemed to represent it as a necessary but a real violation of the order constituted by divine authority, our Lord precludes this misconception by affirming the contrary, or giving as a reason for his present conduct its conformity to right and to the will of God. *For thus* (i. e. by acting in this very way) *it becometh*, literally, *is becoming*, seemly, congruous, i. e. precisely suited to our character and relations, which implies without expressing the idea of duty or moral obligation. Instead of saying, in so many words, *we ought* (or *we are bound*) *to do it*, he suggests the same truth less directly and with the additional idea of a fitness or suitableness springing from their personal and mutual relations, what they were in themselves, to one another, and to God. (Compare the application of the same term, *becoming*, in Heb. 2, 10. 7, 26.) *To fulfil*, the verb applied to prophecy in 1, 22. 2, 15. 17. 23 above, but here used in the sense before explained (on 1, 22) of making good, completing, satisfying, or discharging moral obligations. In the same sense it is said below (5, 17) of the entire law, which Christ came not to abrogate but to obey, and here, with a difference rather formal than substantial, of *all righteousness*, or *all right*, meaning all that is right, and as such incumbent, because pleasing in the sight of God, if not explicitly required by him. There may also be a reference to the doctrinal meaning of the same word as employed by Paul (Rom. 3, 21. 22) to signify God's mode of justifying sinners, or his method of salvation, into which Christ's baptism did unquestionably enter, as a link in the long chain of connected means by which the end was to be brought about. But even in the vague sense proposed above of all that is right and therefore binding upon us, the clause assigns a satisfactory reason for requiring John's consent, to wit, that if withheld it would leave something undone, which it was becoming should be done and done by them. *For us* (ἡμῖν) might possibly be taken in a wide sense as denoting men in general, but much more probably denotes specifically those immediately concerned in this case, i. e. John and Jesus. *It becometh* (or is suitable for) *us* (i. e. for me and thee as my forerunner) to accomplish all that is required by God, and therefore right, as well as necessary to the execution of his method of salvation by freely justifying all believers. *Then*, on hearing this conclusive and authoritative answer, (*John*) *permits* (or *suffers*) *him*, another instance of the graphic present (see above, on vs. 1. 13, and compare 2, 19). The meaning of the verb here is of course determined by its meaning in the first clause, and according to the several alternatives there stated, might be rendered, lets him go, lets him alone, yields to him, excuses him, or suffers him, which last is probably the true sense in both cases, *suffers him (to be baptized)*. This expresses more than *he baptized him*, since it represents the baptism as in some sense the act of the baptized and not of the baptizer, who was really more passive than the subject of the rite, by whose authority, and in direct obedience to whose positive command, it was administered. That John obeyed in silence, though a probable suggestion, is not a necessary inference from that of the historian, who might naturally hurry over all that John said further, as without importance for his purpose, to describe the baptism itself, or rather the divine recognition and attestation of our Lord as the Messiah, by which it was accompanied and followed. The pronoun here expressed (*suffers him*) determines the construction of the same verb as elliptically used above.

16. And Jesus, when he was baptized, went up straightway out of the water : and lo, the heavens were opened unto him, and he saw the Spirit of God descending like a dove, and lighting upon him.

The baptism itself was followed by a visible and audible divine recognition of our Lord as the Messiah. *Having been baptized*, not *when he was baptized*, which is not only a gratuitous departure from the form of the original, but leaves the order of events in doubt, as *when* might be equivalent to *while*, whereas the past tense of the Greek verb (βαπτισθείς) determines it. *Jesus ascended* (went or came up) *straightway* (forthwith or immediately) *from*, i. e. *away from*, as in vs. 7. 13. and in 2, 1. 4, 25. 5, 29. not *out of*, which would be otherwise expressed, as it is in v. 9, and in 2, 6. 15. 7, 5. 8, 28. much less *from under*, which is not the meaning of the particle in any case, nor here suggested by the context. *Ascended from the water* evidently means went up from the bed of the river, in which he had just been standing, whether baptized by immersion, or affusion, as the most convenient method, even in the latter case, especially for those who wore the flowing oriental dress, and either sandals (see above, on v. 11) or no covering of the foot at all. But even if John did submerge, in this and other cases, this was no more essential to the rite than nudity, as still practised by the bathers in the Jordan, and at least as much implied in this case as immersion. The two things naturally go together, and immersion without stripping seems to rob the rite in part of its supposed significancy. *And behold* (or *lo*), as usual, implies a sudden unexpected sight (see above, on 1, 20. 23. 2, 1. 9. 13). *The heavens*, a plural form explained by some as an allusion to the fact or popular belief of several successive heavens, one of which seems to be spoken of by Paul (in 2 Cor. 12, 2); but much more probably a Hellenistic imitation of the corresponding Hebrew word which has no singular, and simply equivalent to sky or heaven. *Were opened*, an entirely different word from that employed by Mark (1, 10), and meaning *torn* or *rent*, though rendered by the same word as the one before us in the text of the translation. This cannot possibly denote a flash of lightning, or the shining of the stars, or a sudden clearing of the sky, or any thing whatever but an apparent separation or division of the visible expanse, as if to afford passage to the form and voice which are mentioned in the next clause. (Compare the similar expressions of Isai. 64, 1. Ezek. 1, 1. John 1, 52. Acts 7, 56.) In all these cases the essential idea suggested by the version is that of renewed communication and extraordinary gifts from heaven to earth. *To him* is commonly explained as meaning to his view or to his senses, and by some referred to John, who elsewhere speaks of having seen this very sight, and for whose satisfaction and direction it would there seem to have been imparted (see John 1, 33). But although it was an attestation not to John alone but to the people (see Luke 3, 21), the only natural construction here is that which refers the words to Christ himself, the nearest antecedent, especially if the pronoun (αὐτῷ) be regarded as the dative, not of object merely, but of use or profit (*opened for him*, i. e. for his service and advantage). The same is true of the next verb (*and he saw*), which is referred to John by some, who understand the previous clause of Jesus; but all analogy and mode are in favour of an uniform construction, i. e. of assuming the same subject in both clauses, *the heavens were opened to him, and he saw* (i. e. to Jesus, and Jesus saw). This is perfectly consistent with John's seeing the same objects, as asserted by himself (John 1, 33), but not with the idea that this whole scene was a visionary one, restricted to the mind or the imagination either of the Baptist or of Christ himself. The harmonious variation of the two accounts in this respect may possibly have been intended to prevent this error, and to show the objective reality of the scene described in both these places. *The Spirit of God* cannot be an attribute or influence, which could not be embodied or subjected to the senses, but denotes a divine person still more certainly and clearly than in v. 11 above. *Descending*, the correlative expression to *ascended* in the first clause, being compounds of the same verb with the prepositions *up* and *down*. *Like* is in Greek a compound particle made up of the words *as* and *if*, and equivalent in meaning to the phrase, *as if it had been*, which does not necessarily imply that it was not so, though it cannot be employed to prove the presence of a real dove, much less of one which accidentally flew by or over, and was viewed by John the Baptist as an emblem of the Holy Ghost! Equally groundless is the notion that the point of the resemblance or comparison is not the shape or figure but the motion of the dove, as being either swift or gentle, or in any other way peculiar. The uncertainty and vagueness of the image thus presented, renders this interpretation as unnatural and foreign from the context here, as it is inconsistent with the more explicit terms employed by Luke (3, 22). The natural expression, and indeed the strict construction of the words, is that there were was an appearance of a dove, most probably a form momentarily assumed, in order to make visible the union of the Spirit with the Son on this august occasion. The selection of this form has been referred by some to the natural qualities belonging to the dove, such as gentleness and purity; by others to its hovering and brooding motion, used in Gen. 1, 2, according to an ancient Jewish exposition, to describe the generative or productive agency of the Divine Spirit in the first creation. Instead of this, or in addition to it, some suppose a reference to the dove of Noah (Gen. 8, 8–11) and to the sacrificial use of this bird, as prescribed or permitted by the ritual in certain cases (Gen. 15, 9. Lev. 14, 22. 21, 6. Luke 2, 24). Whether all or any of these reasons entered into the divine plan of our Lord's inauguration as the Christ, can only be conjectured, and is wholly unimportant in comparison with what must be regarded as the certain and essential fact recorded, namely, that the incarnate Son did see the Spirit in a bodily form (Luke 3, 22), not only descending from the open heavens, but coming to and on himself, as the central figure in this glorious scene, and as the person with whom the Divine Spirit, though essentially one with him, now entered into new relations, with a view to that mediatorial work in which they were to be respectively the Saviour and the Sanctifier of mankind.

17. And lo, a voice from heaven, saying, This is my beloved Son, in whom I am well pleased.

The visible presence and communication of the Spirit was attended by an audible testimony from the Father. *Lo* (or *behold*) again introduces something strange and unexpected. There is no need of supplying *came* from the parallel accounts (Mark 1, 11. Luke 3, 22), as *lo* is often followed by a nominative absolute (i. e. without a verb), forming not a complete sentence but an exclamation.* *A voice*, not visionary or imaginary, nor heard only by our Lord himself, nor that mysterious echo which the Jews call *Bath-kol*, but a literal and real sound, corresponding to the bodily appearance (Luke 3, 21) by which it was preceded (see above, on v. 16). That the voice was audible to others, may be learned from the analogous occurrence at the Transfiguration, where the added words (*Hear ye him*) were addressed directly to the three disciples (see below, on 17, 5). *From*, or more exactly, *out of*, (see above, on v. 16, where the usage of the prepositions ἐκ and ἀπό) is explained. *Heaven*, literally *the heavens*, as in the preceding verse, though here (and in Mark 1, 11) needlessly assimilated in the English version to the singular form used by Luke (3, 22). *This is*, as if still addressing others, whereas Mark and Luke have *thou art*, as addressed to Christ himself. This variation in reporting words expressly used on a particular occasion, although made a ground of cavil here and elsewhere,† is susceptible of easy explanation on the principle which all men recognize, if not in theory in practice, that one witness may report the substance and another the exact form without any inconsistency or violation of the truth. *This*, i. e. this man now before you, upon whom the Spirit has descended in your presence. *My Son*, the words applied to the Messiah in the promise made to David (2. Sam. 7, 14), and in his own prophetic psalm founded on it (Ps. 2, 7). Hence the *Son of God* became one of his standing designations (see below, on 4, 3. 6. 8, 29. 14, 33. 26, 63. 27, 40. 54), corresponding to his other title, *Son of Man* (Dan. 7, 13. Matt. 8, 20. 9, 6. 10, 23. 11. 19 &c.), each implying more than it expresses, *the Son of God* (who is the Son of Man), *the Son of Man* (who is the son of God). The filial relation thus ascribed to the Messiah, far from excluding, presupposes his eternal sonship. *My beloved Son*, is more emphatically worded in the Greek, *my Son, the Beloved*, as a sort of proper name or distinctive title. (Compare the similar but not identical expression in Eph. 1, 6.) As this epithet could not be applied, in the same sense, to any other being, it is really coincident, though not synonymous, with *own son* (Rom. 8, 32), *only son* (Gen. 22, 2. 12, where the Septuagint uses the same Greek word), *only begotten*, as applied to human relations by Luke (7, 12. 8, 42. 9, 38), and to divine by John (1, 14. 18. 3, 16. 18. 1 John 4, 9), and Paul (Heb. 11, 17). The combination of these epithets by Mark (12, 6) and Homer (μοῦνος ἐὼν ἀγαπητός), far from proving them synonymous, explicitly distinguishes between them. This divine love is not to be deemed as the ground or cause, but the effect or co-eternal adjunct of the sonship here ascribed to Christ. The remaining words are also borrowed from a Messianic prophecy, still extant in Isaiah (42, 1), and expressly quoted and applied by Matthew elsewhere (see below, on 12, 18). *In whom*, or as Luke (3, 22) and the latest text of Mark (1, 11) read *in thee* (see above, on the preceding clause). *I am*

---

* See below, on 7, 4. and compare Luke 5, 12. 19, 20. Acts 8, 27. Rev. 4, 1. 6, 2. 7, 9.
† See below, on 9, 11. 15, 27. 16, 6. 20, 33. 21, 9. 26, 28. 39. 27, 37. 28, 5.

well pleased is in Greek a single word, the aorist of a verb used sometimes to express volition, and then construed with a following infinitive, but sometimes perfect satisfaction or complacency, the object of which is then denoted by a noun or pronoun following.* According to the theory and usage of the Greek verb, both in the classics and in Scripture (see above, on 1, 22), the aorist (εὐδόκησα) is to be confounded neither with the present, *I am (now) well pleased*, nor with the perfect, *I have (ever) been well pleased*, but has respect to a specific point of time, *I was (once) well pleased*. Although the deviations from this strict rule are sufficient to authorize a liberal construction when required by exegetical necessity, the latter is precluded in the case before us by the obvious allusion to the Son's assumption of the Mediatorial office, which is here presented as the ground or reason of the Father's infinite complacency or approbation, as distinguished from what may be called, for want of any better term, the natural affection or intense love, which enters into our conception of the mutual relation of paternity and sonship. There is therefore no tautology in these two clauses, but the first describes our Lord as the beloved Son of God from all eternity; the second as the object of his infinite complacency and approbation as the Son of Man, the Mediator, the Messiah. In this voluntarily assumed or adopted character, the Son of God was recognized and set forth at his baptism. Though himself the only Son of God by nature or inherent right, he is here offered to us as a pledge of our adoption, so that through his mediation we may all become the Sons of God, "to the praise of the glory of his grace, wherein he hath made us accepted in the Beloved" (Eph. 1, 6, compare Col. 1, 15. 20. 1 John 3, 1). This sublime and solemn recognition of our Lord in his official character, involves a striking exhibition of the threefold personality in the divine essence, the Father audibly addressing and the Spirit visibly descending on the incarnate Son, as he assumes his Messianic Office.

CHAPTER IV.

Continuing his narrative of the events immediately preceding our Lord's public ministry and serving as preliminaries to it, Matthew now records his conflict with the Tempter in the wilderness, and triumph over him (1–11). He then begins the history of our Lord's prophetic ministry in Galilee, which opens where the ministry of John the Baptist closes, and is shown to have been long before predicted by Isaiah (12–17). At Capernaum, the chosen centre of his operations, he se-

---

* Compare Luke 12, 32. Rom. 15, 26. 2 Cor. 5, 8. Gal. 1, 15. Col. 1, 19. 1 Thess. 2, 8. with 1 Cor. 10, 5. 2 Cor. 12, 10. 2 Thess. 2, 12. Heb. 10, 6. 8, 38. 2 Pet. 1, 17.

lects four fishermen to be his personal attendants, and eventually his Apostles (18–22). This is followed by a summary account of his itinerant labours, as a teacher and a healer, with the consequent concourse from all quarters, both of Palestine and the adjacent countries (23–25).

1. Then was Jesus led up of the Spirit into the wilderness, to be tempted of the devil.

Then, a favourite connective in this gospel, where it occurs thrice as often as in all the others put together, a minute but strong proof that inspiration did not supersede the peculiar modes of thought and speech by which the sacred writers were distinguished. As it may mean either *afterwards* or *at the same time*, and in the former case may denote either longer or shorter intervals, it can here prove nothing by itself as to the chronological relation of the incidents which it connects in Matthew's narrative, namely our Lord's Baptism and Temptation. It does, however, raise a presumption that they were immediately successive, and this presumption is confirmed by the more explicit language of the parallel accounts (Mark 1, 12. Luke 4, 1). *Jesus*, who had just been recognized as the Son of God by a voice from heaven and the visible descent of the Holy Ghost (see above, on 3, 17). *Was led up*, as if passively, and in obedience to an impulse distinct from his own will, though not opposed to it. *Of* (i. e. *by*) *the Spirit*, as the source or author of the impulse just referred to. *The Spirit* does not mean his own mind or the evil spirit, but the Holy Ghost, as a divine person, often simply so described, which had just descended visibly (3, 17) and rested on him (John 1, 32), and of which he was now full (Luke 4, 1), i. e. occupied, endowed, and governed by it, not merely as a man, but as the God-Man or Mediator, in which character or office he sustained a peculiar relation to the third person of the godhead, as the author of all spiritual good in the hearts and lives of men, and in his own as their surety and their representative. *Into the wilderness*, not in the wide sense of the term before explained (on 3, 1), namely that of an uninhabited or even an uncultivated tract, however fertile or luxuriant; but in the strict sense of a *desert*, yielding no supplies, and far from the abodes of men, frequented only by wild animals (Mark 1, 13). Whether the wilderness here meant was the interior and wilder portion of the one where John appeared (3, 1), so that our Lord, though in the wilderness already, might be said to have gone (i. e. to have gone further) into it; or a distinct and wilder solitude, extending from the Jordan in the neighbourhood of Jericho to Bethel (Josh. 16, 1); or the wilderness of Sinai, where the Israelites wandered, and where Moses and Elijah fasted (Ex. 34, 28. 1 Kings 19, 8), are questions not determined by the text or context, and of little exegetical importance, as the only essential fact, because the only one recorded, is that these transactions took place in a desert, far from all human aid and sympathy. *Led up*, i. e. as some understand it, towards Jerusalem, in reference to its physical and moral elevation, but much more probably, from the depressed bed or valley of the Jordan into the mountainous solitudes of Bethel or the Dead Sea, where tradition designates the spot by the name of *Quarantaria*, in allusion to the forty days' fast recorded in the next verse. *To be tempted*, not as a mere incidental consequence (*so that he was tempted*), but as the deliberate design or purpose (*that he might be tempted*). not of his own mind, which at least is not directly meant, but of the Father who had sent him, and the Spirit who now led him. *To be tempted* means originally nothing more than to be tried, proved, or (in modern English) tested, i. e. shown to possess or want certain qualities, to be determined by comparison with some prescribed and well-known rule or standard. In a material sense the term is thus applied to the precious metals, in a moral sense to human character, as proved or tried by God himself, or as solicited to sin by men or devils, in which sense God can no more tempt than he can be tempted (James 1, 13). The great tempter of mankind is the prince of demons (9, 34. 12, 24), or the chief of fallen angels (25, 41), by whom our first parents were betrayed into transgression (2 Cor. 11, 3), and who is therefore called *Satan* or the *Adversary* (Mark 1, 13), and the *Devil*, slanderer or false accuser (Luke 4, 2). It was by this enemy of God and Man that Jesus now went up into the desert to be tempted, as a necessary part of his own human discipline and humiliation (see above, on 3, 15); as a lesson to his people of what they must look for, and an assurance of their own escape and triumph; but besides all this, as a premonition of the great decisive crisis in the war between the "seed of the woman" and the "seed of the serpent" (see above, on 3, 7), the heads and representatives of both which parties were now to be brought personally into contact. Our Lord's susceptibility of temptation was no more inconsistent with his sinlessness than that of Adam, and is insisted on in Scripture as essential to his office, and especially as necessary to a real sympathy between him and his tempted people (Heb. 2, 18). This scriptural idea has been variously amplified, embellished, and extended, by ingenious and in some cases fanciful comparisons between the three temptations here recorded and the threefold bait presented to Eve (Gen. 3, 6), the threefold description of worldly lusts by the Apostle (1 John 2, 16), the successive temptations of Israel in the wilderness, those peculiarly belonging to the three great periods of human life, and to the corresponding stages in the progress of the race or of particular nations; to which has recently been added an analogy between these temptations and the three great offices of Christ on one hand, and the three great Jewish sects or parties on the other. As such comparisons admit of an indefinite multiplication, and depend upon the taste and fancy of the individual interpreter or reader; they are not to be forced upon the text as a part of its essential meaning, whatever use may be made of them as striking and illustrative analogies.

2. And when he had fasted forty days and forty nights, he was afterwards an hungered.

And having fasted, not in the attenuated sense of eating little, or of abstaining from all ordinary food (see above, on 3, 4); but in the strict and proper sense of eating nothing (Luke 4, 2). *Forty days and forty nights,* i. e. forty whole days of entire privation, not merely half days of such abstinence with intervening periods of indulgence, such as the later Jews, according to their own traditions, practised in their stated fasts. This protracted fast of Christ, being clearly miraculous or superhuman, affords no example to his people, and can be imitated by them only in the way of thankful and reverent commemoration. A yearly fast of forty days, whatever it may have to recommend it, can never be made binding on the conscience by this extraordinary incident occurring once for all in the biography of Jesus. *Was an hungered,* an unusual phrase even in Old English, corresponding to a single word in Greek, and that an active verb, meaning nothing more nor less than *hungered,* or in modern phrase, *was hungry. Afterward,* a relative expression which can only be referred to the preceding clause, and must mean therefore when the forty days were ended. This implies that while they lasted he was free from hunger; and this again that his fast was not a painful act of self-denial, but an abnormal preternatural condition, having no analogy in our experience, and therefore not a proper object of our imitation. As here recorded it has reference, not so much to bodily mortification, or even spiritual discipline, as to intimate and exclusive intercourse with God, like that of Moses and Elijah, when called to the solemn task of legislation and of reformation (see above, on v. 1). To these great historical examples there is evident allusion in the mention of the forty days, an external circumstance alike in all three cases. As the abstinence from food for such a length of time evinced an interruption or suspension of the ordinary laws of life, so the hunger which followed showed the suspension to be at an end, and the humanity of Christ to be no less real than that of the Great Lawgiver and Reformer of the old economy.

3. And when the tempter came to him, he said, If thou be the Son of God, command that these stones be made bread.

As it is not said that this was the beginning of our Lord's temptation, there is no inconsistency with the account of Mark (1, 13) and Luke (4, 2), that he was tempted forty days. Both may be reconciled by simply assuming that the three temptations here recorded were the last of a long series, and perhaps the only ones in which the tempter became visible. The sense of Matthew's narrative will then be, that after having otherwise assailed him, in a way perhaps which could not have been comprehensible to us, the tempter now approached him visibly, and took advantage of the natural hunger which succeeded his extraordinary abstinence. *The tempter,* literally, *the (one) tempting,* i. e. the one who was to tempt our Lord on this occasion, but not without allusion to his character and practice, as *the (one) tempting* (others also) or *the tempter* (of mankind in general). The idea that the tempter mentioned here, is a mere personification of our Lord's own thoughts and dispositions, is as impious as it is absurd. That the tempter, though a real person, was a human one, the High Priest, or a member of the Sanhedrim, or one of the emissaries sent to John the Baptist (John 1, 19) now on his way back to Jerusalem, are notions which, if ever seriously entertained, have long since been exploded. The impression made by the terms of the narrative itself for ages upon every unsophisticated reader is undoubtedly the true one, namely, that *the tempter* who appears in this transaction, was a personal but not a human being, or in other words an evil spirit, and the one emphatically called *the Devil* (see above, on v. 1). *When the tempter came to him* is not, as it might seem in English, a mere note of time, but a substantive part of the transaction, *coming to* (approaching) *him, the tempter said.* The voice which spake was not that of an unseen speaker, or uttered from above or from below, but by a person coming up to him, perhaps as a stranger, or a casual passer by. This supposes him, however, to have exhibited an ordinary human form, whereas some think that he was transformed into an angel of light (2 Cor. 11, 14), and others that he wore a shape peculiar to himself, or at least to fallen angels. There is nothing in the text or context to decide this question, which is rather one of curiosity than of exegetical importance. *If a son thou art of God* would be the strict translation; but as the usage of the article in this phrase varies, even where the sense remains unchanged,* the indefinite form is not to be insisted on. The division of the chapters tempts the reader to regard this scene as wholly unconnected with the one before it in the narrative, although they were immediately successive (see above, on v. 1), and the first words of the tempter, here recorded, seem to contain an allusion to the solemn recognition of our Lord as the Son of God by a voice from heaven (see above, on 3, 17), of which Satan may have been himself a witness. This clause may be either understood as expressing a doubt (if thou art really the Son of God), or as admitting that the fact was so (since thou art the Son of God), which last is no less in agreement with Greek usage. On the former supposition, the remainder of the verse prescribes a test by which the truth of his pretensions might be tried; on the other, it simply makes a proposition or request, which could not be complied with, if he were not really the Son of God.—*Command that*, literally, *Say* (or speak, in order) *that*, for the purpose of seeing this effect. (As to the usage of the Greek conjunction, see above, on 1, 22). *These stones*, perhaps the same to which John the Baptist pointed (see above, on 3, 9), or at least of the same kind, i. e. loose stones scattered on the surface of the desert.—*Be made*, or more exactly, *may become*, begin to be, i. e. be changed into (see above, on 1, 22).—*Bread*, literally, *breads*, i. e. loaves or cakes, a usage similar to that of the French (*pains*). This plural form renders it less probable that *bread* as some suppose, and as it does in 15, 2 below and else-

---

* Compare the original of 8, 29. 14, 33. 16, 16. 26, 63. 27, 40. 43.

where stand for food in general, the different varieties of which would hardly be denoted by the plural (*breads*). The strict interpretation is confirmed, moreover, by the proverbial antithesis or contrast between stone and bread (or stones and loaves) both in Scripture (see below, on 7, 9), and in the classics. The suggestion of the tempter then was not that he should supply himself with dainties or varieties of food to gratify his appetite, but simply with the staff of life, to satisfy his hunger.* If so, the first temptation was not to the sin of gluttony, as some have strangely fancied, which could not have been committed by eating bread when hungry, and after a fast of forty days, and to which our Lord's reply in the next verse would be wholly irrelevant. Nor was the temptation to a vain and ostentatious exhibition of miraculous endowments, which would have been thrown away in such a spot, and to which the answer would be no less inappropriate. The only sin, which satisfies the terms of the whole context, is that of distrusting God and refusing to rely upon his providence, by undertaking to supply one's own wants and sustain one's own life, in the exercise of an extraordinary power.—As to the motive or design of this temptation, some regard it as a mere desire to induce our Lord to sin, and in a way suggested by his actual condition, which was one of hunger. Others suppose it to have been a more specific wish to ascertain the truth of his pretensions, by inducing him to act in a manner inconsistent with them.—Another point which may be variously understood, because entirely conjectural, is the knowledge which the tempter had of Christ's divinity, or the sense which he attached to his acknowledged Sonship. Though the title *Son of God* was applicable to him in the highest sense, as denoting community of nature or participation in the essence of the Father (see above, on 3, 17), it admitted also of a lower application to his human nature, to mankind in general, to angels both as creatures and as objects of divine affection; and the tempter may have been in ignorance or doubt as to which of these relations was denoted by the phrase when uttered by the voice from heaven, or, as some suppose, applied by Jesus to himself in previous conversations during the forty days preceding this direct and overt demonstration of hostility. In favour of such ignorance or doubt is the extreme improbability that Satan would have dared, or thought it possible, to tempt a divine person; whereas *a Son of God*, in some of the inferior senses which have just been mentioned, might be capable of falling into sin as the apostate fiend himself had done (John 8, 44. Jude 6). This seems to be a more satisfactory solution of his conduct upon this occasion, than to resolve it into the fatuity which naturally clings to all depravity, and which therefore might betray even the most crafty and sagacious of all finite spirits into the absurdity of tempting God to sin, as he had no less foolishly attempted to resist him, or to be his rival. All this, however, is mere matter of conjecture or imagination, as the narrative itself affords no hint of any thing but what was actually said and done, and the whole subject of Satanic agency is too

---

* Lev. 26, 26. Ps. 105, 16. Isai. 3, 1. Ez. 4, 16. 5, 16. 14, 13.

mysterious and too imperfectly revealed, to be successfully subjected to a process of reasoning or of speculation.

4. But he answered and said, It is written, Man shall not live by bread alone, but by every word that proceedeth out of the mouth of God.

The contrast is not between material and spiritual food, which would be wholly inappropriate to this temptation, but between ordinary food, represented by bread, and any other food which God may prescribe or promise. This is clear from the connection here and in the passage quoted (Deut. 8, 3), where the reference is plainly to the manna, not as immaterial food, which it was not, but as a succedaneum for the usual kind of nourishment, by which the Israelites were taught to rely upon Providence not only for the customary means of subsistence, but for extraordinary supplies in rare emergencies. The application intended by our Saviour to his own case evidently is, that in providing for himself by miracle, he would be guilty of the same sin which the ancient Jews so frequently committed, that of questioning God's willingness and power to supply them. *But* (on the other hand, and in reply to this suggestion) *he* (Jesus) *answering said, Not on bread only* (or *alone*), i. e. in reliance or dependence on it as the only practicable means of sustenance, *shall man live,* i. e. is he, by divine appointment and the law of his condition, to subsist, *but on* (or according to the latest critics, *in,* i. e. in the use of) *every word proceeding through the mouth of God,* or uttered by him. *Word* neither means *thing* (a usage now denied by eminent philologists) nor *truth,* which, as we have already seen, would be irrelevant in this connection, but, must be taken in its strict and proper sense of *something spoken,* as appears further from the added words, *by* (or *through*) *the mouth of God. Proceeding,* coming (or going) out, i. e. uttered or pronounced, whether in the way of precept or decree or promise. (Compare Num. 30, 12. Deut. 23, 23. Judg. 11, 36). *It has been written,* long ago, and still remains on record (see above, on 2, 5). By thus appealing to the Scriptures, Christ not only gives his attestation to the Pentateuch and to the Book of Deuteronomy, as part of a divine revelation, but instructs us, by example, in the proper method of repelling such temptations, namely by opposing truth to error, and the word of God to the suggestions of the Evil One. (See below, on vs. 7. 10).

5. Then the devil taketh him up into the holy city, and setteth him on a pinnacle of the temple,

Then, sometimes loosely or indefinitely used, but here, no doubt, meaning in the next place, and indicating the exact order of events, which is reversed by Luke (4, 5. 9), in order to accommodate his own plan or purpose. *Then* may also mean immediately, as in v. 1 above, though some suppose an interval between the two temptations, as if he had said, *afterwards*, or at another time, or on a different occasion. It has even been imagined that this second onset took place when our Saviour was returning from the desert to Jerusalem. But this, though possible, is not the natural impression made upon most readers, who regard the temptations as immediately successive. *Takes him along* (or with him), in his company, a verb of frequent use in the New Testament, and always, when applied to persons, in the same sense, without any necessary implication of coercion, or even of authority, though one or both may sometimes be suggested by the context.* Here, however, there is nothing to imply compulsion, and the verb means merely that they went together, but at Satan's instance, which is no more inconsistent with our Lord's divine or human dignity, than his submitting to be scourged and crucified by Satan's agents. In either case it was a part of his voluntary humiliation as a Saviour and a substitute, the height or depth of which consisted not in his permitting Satan to conduct him from place to place, but in submitting to be tempted by him.—*The Devil*, slanderer, or false accuser (see above, on 4, 1). *Up*, though not in the original, is found in all the English versions except Wiclif's. *Into the holy city*, i. e. Jerusalem, so called because it was the seat of the theocracy and sanctuary, or as our Lord himself expressed it afterwards, "the city of the Great King" (see below, on 5, 35). There is nothing here to intimate a visionary or ideal journey, but the natural impression made is that of a corporeal external entrance from without, perhaps directly from the wilderness or desert. *Sets him*, literally, *stands him*, i. e. makes him stand, but here again without implying force or authority, the essential notion being that of causing him to stand, but whether by request or otherwise, is not expressed (see below, on 18, 2. 25, 33). *A pinnacle*, in Greek *the wing*, supposed by some to be the roof of the temple itself, so called from its gradual inclination upon either side, like the folded wings of a bird, perhaps an eagle, which word is itself applied thus in Greek writings. But according to Josephus, the summit of the sacred edifice was armed with spikes to prevent birds from alighting on it. A more obvious and natural interpretation gives to *wing* its ordinary sense in architecture, namely, that of a lateral projection from the main edifice or body of a building. In this sense it may be applied either to the vestibule or porch of the temple properly so called (ὁ ναός†) which was higher than the temple itself, or to one of the vast porticoes or colonnades surrounding the whole area of the temple, two of which overlooked deep valleys, namely, Solomon's porch,‡ upon the east side, looking down into the valley of Jehoshaphat or Kedron, and the Royal Porch, upon the south side, looking down into the valley of Hinnom. This last is represented by Josephus as a dizzy height, which would agree well with the context and the circumstances in

---

* See above, on 1, 20. 24. 2, 13. 20. and below, on 12, 45. 17, 1. 18, 16. 20, 17. 24, 40. 41. 26, 37. 27, 27.
† See 23, 16. 17. 21. 35. 26, 61. 27, 5. 40. 51.
‡ See John 10, 23. Acts 3, 11. 5, 12.

the case before us. *The temple*, one of the words so translated, and denoting the whole sacred enclosure, not the sanctuary only, but the courts by which it was surrounded.*

6. And saith unto him, If thou be the Son of God, cast thyself down, for it is written, He shall give his angels charge concerning thee : and in their hands they shall bear thee up, lest at any time thou dash thy foot against a stone.

Here again some suppose the sin to which our Lord was tempted to have been a vain display of his miraculous power, not as in the other case without spectators, but before the multitude who thronged the courts of the temple, and by whom he might be recognized as the Messiah. But as no such purpose is referred to in the narrative, or in our Lord's reply to the temptation, a more probable interpretation is the common one, which makes this the converse of the former case, and as that was a temptation to distrust, explains this as a temptation to presumption, or a rash reliance upon God's protecting care in situations where he has not promised it, and where the danger is a voluntary or a self-produced one. *Cast thyself down*, from the summit of the temple to the pavement of the court below, or from the lofty porch into the deep valley which it overlooked. This he is solicited to do without necessity, or fear of the result, confiding in the promise of divine protection and angelic care. As the ground of this rash confidence, the tempter, borrowing the weapon which had just disarmed him, cites a passage from the ninety-first Psalm (vs. 11. 12), an inspired composition, the whole drift of which is to illustrate the security of those who put their trust in God, even with reference to temporal calamities. It relates to the Messiah, not exclusively, but by way of eminence. The argument suggested is *a fortiori*, namely, that if all God's people are thus cared for, much more will his Son be. The quotation is recorded in the words of the Septuagint version, which is here a correct transcript of the Hebrew. The plural (*angels*) shows that there is no allusion to a guardian angel attending each individual believer, but merely to the angels collectively, as " ministering spirits," the instrumental agents of God's providential care over his people (Heb. 1, 14). The promise here given does not extend to dangers rashly incurred or presumptuously sought, and was therefore no justification of the act to which our Lord was tempted by the Devil. That the mere omission of the words, *in all thy ways*, was a part of that temptation, or designed to wrest the passage from its true sense, though a very ancient and still prevalent opinion, seems to be a gratuitous refinement, as our Lord himself makes no such charge ; as the first words of the sentence would of course suggest the rest ; and as *ways*, in the original, does not mean ways of duty, but of Providence. Neither the tempter's argument nor Christs' reply to it

* See below, on 12, 5. 6. 21, 12. 14. 15. 23. 24, 4. 26, 55.

would be at all affected by the introduction of the words suppressed. Bearing or carrying on the hands seems intended to denote a tender care like that of nurses, an allusion frequently found elsewhere.* *Lest at any time* is all expressed in Greek by one word (μήποτε), which may also be explained as denoting mere contingency, *lest haply* or *by chance*.† *Dash*, knock, or strike, in walking, i. e. stumble. *Against*, is twice expressed here by the same particle (πρός), once before the verb and once before the noun. *The stone*, i. e. the one which happens to be lying in the way. A smooth path and unobstructed walk is a natural and common figure for prosperity and safety. "Then (if thou keep wisdom and discretion) thou shalt walk in thy way safely, and thy foot shall not stumble" (Prov. 3, 23).

7. Jesus said unto him, It is written again, Thou shalt not tempt the Lord thy God.

Our Lord here uses the same method of resistance as before, repelling the temptation by a dictum of the Scriptures, drawn from another passage of the same book (Deut. 6, 16). *Again*, does not mean, on the contrary (or other hand), in reference to the tempter's allegation from the Psalms, but *once more*, in another place, with reference to his first quotation, or to both together.‡ *Tempt*, not the simple verb so rendered elsewhere,§ but an emphatic compound meaning to *try out*, to draw out by trial, to try thoroughly.|| As applied to God, it means to put him to the proof, to demand further evidence of what is clear already,¶ as in this case by requiring him to show his watchful care by an extraordinary intervention in a case of danger wilfully and needlessly incurred. The precept has a double edge or application, to the Saviour, as a reason why he would not tempt God, and to the Devil, as a reason why he should not tempt Christ. As if he had said: I will neither tempt God by presuming on his providence, nor suffer you to tempt me by presumptuous solicitation.

8. Again, the devil taketh him up into an exceeding high mountain, and sheweth him all the kingdoms of the world, and the glory of them.

Again, as in the verse preceding, although here used to distinguish not the quotations but the temptations from each other. The same question here arises as in v. 5, with respect to the interval between the two assaults; but here too the impression made on all un-

---

* See Num. 11, 12. Deut. 1, 31. Isai. 49, 23. Acts 13, 18. 1 Th. 2, 7.
† See below, on 5, 25. 7, 6. 13, 15. 20. 15, 32. 25, 9. 27, 64.
‡ See below, on 5, 33. 13, 44. 45. 47. 18, 19. 19, 24. 21, 36, and compare Heb. 1, 5. 6. 2, 13. 4, 5. 7. 10, 30.
§ See above, on v. 1, below, on 16, 1. 19, 3. 22, 18. 35.
|| Compare its use in Luke 10, 25. 1 Cor. 10, 9.
¶ See Ex. 17, 2. Isai. 7, 12. Mal. 3, 15. Acts 5, 9. 15, 10. 1 Cor. 10, 9.

biassed readers is no doubt that of immediate succession. *Taketh*, i. e. along or in his company, precisely as in v. 5. This part of the transaction is supposed to have occurred in vision, even by some who understand what goes before as literally true. But such a difference is highly arbitrary and unnatural; nor is there any more necessity for such a supposition here than in the other cases. The *very high mountain* is not named, and can only be conjectured. The scene of this temptation is supposed by some to have been Nebo (Deut. 34, 1), and by others Tabor (see below, on 17, 1); but as *very high* is a comparative or relative expression, it may just as well have been the Mount of Olives (see below, on 21, 1. 24, 3. 26, 30), immediately adjacent to the Holy City, or some point in the highlands, between Jericho and Bethel, or in those adjacent to the Dead Sea (see above, on v. 1, and on 3, 1). *Sheweth*, causes him to see, not upon a map or picture, which might just as well have been presented elsewhere; nor by an optical illusion, which the tempter had no right or power to practise on the Saviour's senses; but either by a voluntary and miraculous extension of his vision on his own part, or by a combination of sensible perception with rhetorical description (*show* being elsewhere used to express both visual and oral exhibition, as in 8, 4. compared with 16, 21), an actual exhibition of what lay within the boundary of vision, and an enumeration of the kingdoms which in different directions lay beyond it, with a glowing representation of their wealth and power (*and the glory of them*). Upon either of these latter suppositions, *all the kingdoms of the world* may be strictly understood, instead of being violently explained away, as meaning the different provinces of Palestine, or even of the Roman Empire.

9. And saith unto him, All these things will I give thee, if thou wilt fall down and worship me.

Having thus exhibited the bait, the tempter actually offers it. *These* (*things*), *all* (*of them*), which I have now shown or described to thee, to wit, the kingdoms of the world with their glory, i. e. all that renders them attractive to the love of power, pleasure, wealth, and honour. *To thee will I give*, implying that he had a right to do so, not inherent but derivative (Luke 4, 6). This is not to be regarded as a sheer invention, but a statement at least partially correct, and shown to be so by the frequent reference to Satan as the prince or god of this world (John 12, 31. 14, 30. 16, 11. 2 Cor. 4, 4). How far this delegated power extends, in what way it is exercised, and by what checks it is restrained, are questions which we have not data to determine, but which cannot nullify the fact itself so clearly revealed elsewhere. The charge of simple falsehood, therefore, is as groundless here as that of misquotation in v. 6, the force of the temptation lying deeper in both cases. The condition annexed to this seductive offer is supposed by some to be religious adoration, i. e. idolatry or rather devil-worship;* by others a mere civil homage or acknowledgment of

---

* See Lev. 17, 7. Deut. 32, 17. 2 Chr. 11, 15. Ps. 106, 37. 1 Cor. 10, 20. Rev. 9, 20.

sovereignty (see above, on 2, 2. 8. 11). But in this case the two acts are necessarily coincident if not identical, as no one does or can pay allegiance to the Devil as his sovereign, without making him his god, and worshipping him as such. The falling down was merely the external recognition of his right to this two-fold homage. The sin to which our Lord is here solicited is not a simple but a complex one, including secular ambition and idolatry, not only that covetousness which is idolatry (Col. 3, 5), but also apostasy from God as the true sovereign and the only object of religious adoration, and the substitution of his most malignant enemy in both these characters. To this same complicated sin, the ancient Israel was tempted, and with a very different result (Lev. 17, 7. Deut. 32, 17).

10. Then saith Jesus unto him, Get thee hence, Satan: for it is written, Thou shalt worship the Lord thy God, and him only shalt thou serve.

Then, as in vs. 1, 5, corresponding to *again* in vs. 7, 8, both meaning *once more*, and marking repetition and succession. *Get thee hence*, in Greek a single word (ὑπαγε=*apage!*) *begone*, *avaunt*, *out of my sight!* a strong expression of abhorrence, not only for the person of the tempter, but particularly for the impious audacity of his last temptation. Some of the old manuscripts and late editions add *behind me*, which is probably, however, an interpolation from 16, 23 below. *Satan*, adversary, enemy of God and Man, in which light he had now unmasked himself, and is therefore here addressed by name, as well as driven from the Saviour's presence. This climax both in the temptation and in the repulse, may serve to show that Matthew's order is that of the occurrences themselves, whatever may have been Luke's reason for inverting it (see above, on v. 5). But not content with naming the tempter and bidding him begone, our Lord once more opposes scripture to his vile solicitations, drawing still upon the same part of the Pentateuch, as if to put peculiar honour in advance upon a book which was to be especially assailed by modern infidelity. The passage is found in Deut. 6, 13, and is here given in the words of the Septuagint version. *Alone* is not expressed in the original passage, but is necessarily suggested by the context, and is therefore introduced not only in the lxx. version, but by Josephus and by Aben Ezra, one of the most famous of the rabbins (see also 1 Sam. 7, 3). *Serve*, a verb used in classic Greek to signify mercenary labour, work for hire, but in Hellenistic usage transferred to religious service. The distinction which the Church of Rome would make between this and the lower service which she pays to images, is utterly precluded by the text before us, which prohibits not *latreia* merely, but even *proscynesis*, to be paid to any other object than to God alone. This scripture also has a double edge or application, as if he had said: 'Instead of being asked to worship thee, I am entitled to be worshipped by thee.'

11. **Then the devil leaveth him, and behold, angels came and ministered unto him.**

Then, after the conclusion of this last assault and its repulse. *Leaveth him*, or letteth him (alone), the Greek verb used above in 3, 15, and there explained. The idea here expressed is not that of mere locomotion or departure, but of cessation from disturbance and annoyance, not forever but until a a future time (Luke 4, 13). The departure of the Devil coincides with the appearance or return of holy angels, who would seem to have withdrawn during this mysterious conflict, that the honour of the triumph might be Christ's alone. *Came*, literally, *came up*, or *came to* (*him*), which naturally, although not necessarily, suggests the idea of a visible appearance. *Ministered*, or as the Greek specifically signifies, waited on him, served him, with particular reference to food.* This angelic ministration is in contrast both with the Satanic onset and with the abstinence and hunger which preceded it. From the privations of the desert and the solicitations of the devil, the transition was immediate to the society and help of angels.

12. **Now when Jesus had heard that John was cast into prison, he departed into Galilee.**

Having thus recorded the preliminaries of the Saviour's ministry, Matthew now proceeds to the ministry itself, which he seems, like Mark and Luke, to describe as beginning in Galilee, the northern province of the land of Israel, divided from Judea by the district of Samaria (see above, on 2, 22). But we learn from John (1, 19-52. 2, 13-25. 3, 1-36. 4, 1-42), that he was publicly recognized by his forerunner, and began his own work, in Judea. This has been malevolently represented as a contradiction; but in neither of the first three gospels is it expressly said that this was absolutely his first appearance as a public teacher, but only that he now appeared as such in Galilee. Matthew, moreover, as well as Mark (1, 14), explicitly confines his narrative to what happened after John's imprisonment, leaving room at least for the assumption that something previous is omitted because not included in the writer's plan. Luke too speaks of Jesus as returning to Galilee *in the power of the Spirit* (Luke 4, 14), i. e. of the same Spirit who had prompted and directed his official functions elsewhere. The only question is why the first three gospels should have omitted what took place in Judea, and begun with his appearance in Galilee. A sufficient answer seems to be, that his appearance in Judea was intended merely to connect his ministry with that of John, by letting the two co-exist or overlap each other, like the two dispensations which they represented. As the forms of the Mosaic law were still continued in existence, long after they were virtually superseded by the advent of Messiah and the organization of his kingdom, as if to show that the

---

* See below, on 8, 15. 25, 44. 27, 55. and compare Luke 10, 40. 12, 37. 17, 8. 22, 27. John 12, 2. Acts 6, 2. Heb. 6, 10.

two systems, although incompatible and exclusive of each other as permanent institutions, were identical in origin, authority, and purpose, the one being not the rival or the opposite, but simply the completion of the other; so our Lord, whose presence was to supersede the ministry of John, appeared for a time in conjunction with him, and received his first disciples from him (John 1, 37), as a proof that John had only begun the work which Christ was to accomplish. When this joint ministry, if it may be so called, was terminated by the imprisonment of John, our Lord retired or retreated into Galilee, where he had been brought up, and where he was to be rejected by his neighbours and acquaintances, as well as to perform the greater part of his prophetic functions. The imprisonment of John is barely mentioned here, as suggesting the time and the occasion of our Lord's withdrawing from Judea, the events which led to the imprisonment itself, being reserved by Matthew for another place (see below, on 14, 3–5). *Hearing* or *having heard*, seems to imply that he was at some distance from the place of John's arrest or seizure. *Cast into prison* is more correctly rendered in the margin, *delivered up*, i. e. by Herod to the jailer (compare Luke 12, 58. Acts 8, 3. 22, 4), or by Providence to Herod himself (compare Acts 2, 23). *Departed*, the verb used in 2, 12. 13. 14. 22. above, and corresponding more exactly to *withdrew*, retreated. It does not necessarily denote escape from danger, as in the places just referred to, where that idea is suggested by the context. It is here precluded by the statement that our Saviour went directly into Herod's jurisdiction, and that his danger in Judea could not be increased by John's imprisonment. The meaning rather is that he withdrew from Judea, where his ministry had already roused the jealous party spirit of the Pharisees (John 4, 1), into Galilee, where John's removal left an open field for Christ's own ministry and missionary labours. It is unnecessary therefore to take *Galilee* in the specific sense of Upper Galilee, or as denoting any other portion of the province as distinguished from the rest; which would be perfectly gratuitous and contrary to usage, as well as inconsistent with the context, which requires *Galilee* to be contrasted, not with itself or any part of itself, but with the other provinces of Palestine.

13. And leaving Nazareth, he came and dwelt in Capernaum, which is upon the sea-coast, in the borders of Zabulon and Nephthalim.

Leaving Nazareth, which had been his home since his return in infancy from Egypt (see above, on 2, 21–23), and which might have been expected to become the seat and centre of his operations. Without explaining why this expectation was not realized, as Luke does most minutely (4, 16–31), Matthew hurries on to speak of his settlement at Capernaum, in which a signal prophecy was verified. *Coming* (or *having come*) is not a pleonastic or superfluous expression, but a distinct statement of the fact, that he not only went to Capernaum, as he often did at other times, but took up his abode there. *Dwell*, or rather *settled*, the Greek verb denoting an incipient residence (as in 4, 13. 12, 45. Luke 11, 26. Acts 7, 2. 4), whether eventually permanent (as in Acts 9, 32. 17, 26), or temporary (as in Heb. 11, 9). What is here recorded is our Lord's adoption of Capernaum instead of Nazareth, as the centre of his ministry, from which he went forth on his missions or official journeys (see below, on v. 23). *Capernaum the maritime*, in Greek an adjective denoting what is on or by the sea, as correctly paraphrased but not translated in the English Bible. It is so called, not to distinguish it from any other place of the same name, for no such place is known to have existed, as in the case of Bethlehem (see above, on 2, 1. 6), but because its situation was important to identify it as the subject of the prophecy recited in the following verses. *Capernaum* itself is no longer in existence, and its very site is now a subject of dispute; but Dr. Robinson has clearly shown that it was always understood to be marked by a village now called Khan Minyeh, till the 17th century, when travellers began to seek it at a place called Tell Houm an hour further to the north-east, but with nothing to support its claims except a very faint resemblance to the ancient name. This was variously written, Capharnaum, Cepharnome, Caparnaum, Capernaum, &c. The place is not named in the Old Testament, which probably, though not necessarily, implies a later origin. Josephus mentions the town once by the name of Cepharnome, but applies the form Capernaum (or Capharnaum) only to a fountain. The most probable site of the city was near the northern edge of the small but fertile district called Gennesaret* on the eastern shore of the lake which forms the eastern boundary of Galilee, and through which the Jordan passes (see above, on 3, 6, and below, on v. 18). *Borders*, or boundaries, in Scripture sometimes means the region bounded, or the area within the borders;† but the same town could not be within two tribes, except by being on their confines or borders in the strict sense. *Zabulon* and *Nephthalim* are slight modifications of *Zebulon* and *Naphtali*, the names of two of Jacob's sons (Gen. 30, 8. 20), and of the tribes descended from them (Num. 1, 8. 9). The precise bounds of the territory occupied by these tribes cannot now be ascertained; but what is known from the books of the Old Testament agrees exactly with the language of the verse before us. There can be no doubt that they were contiguous and settled in the northern part of the country (Josh. 19, 10–16. 32–39), and the later Jewish books represents the Sea of Galilee as belonging or adjacent to the tribe of Naphtali. The design of this minute topographical description of Capernaum, as situated on the sea and also on the confines of these two tribes, is disclosed in the next verse.

14. That it might be fulfilled which was spoken by Esaias the prophet, saying,

* See below, on 14, 34. and compare Mark 6, 53. Luke 5, 1.
† See above, on 2, 16. and below, on 8, 34. 15, 22. 39. 19, 1.

The formula here used is the same with that in 1, 22. but without the prefatory phrase, *all this came to pass* (or happened), and with a distinct mention of the prophet's name. The passage quoted is still extant in Isaiah (8, 23. 9, 1), from whose text it is here translated into Greek, and not borrowed from the Septuagint version, which is exceedingly corrupt, and in some points wholly unintelligible. This is the fifth prophecy alleged by Matthew to have been fulfilled in the life of Christ (see above, on 1, 22. 2, 15. 17.23), besides the one implicitly applied to him in 2, 6. It is no doubt with a view to this fulfilment that our Lord's removal to Capernaum is so distinctly stated, although other circumstances, in themselves of more importance, are omitted (see above, on v. 12, and on 2, 22). The words quoted from Isaiah are the close of a prophetic passage, in which the old theocracy is threatened with divine judgments, to be afterwards succeeded by extraordinary favour, to be specially experienced by that part of the country which had suffered most in the preceding trials. The evangelist cites only what was necessary to his purpose. beginning with the last words of a sentence, which he introduces to identify the subject and describe the scene, in order to connect it with the local habitation of the Saviour.

15. **The land of Zabulon, and the land of Nephthalim, (by) the way of the sea, beyond Jordan, Galilee of the Gentiles.**

Land (of) Zebulon and land (of) Naphtali may be taken, either as nominatives or vocatives. In the former case, there is an absolute construction of the noun without a verb, equivalent in sense but not in form to our phrase (*as to) the land of Zabulon*, &c. On the other supposition, the form is that of an apostrophe addressed to those two regions. (*Oh*) *land of Zebulon*, &c. The question is entirely grammatical, without effect upon the meaning of the sentence, as this clause is only introduced to show of what region the prophet was speaking. *Way of the sea*, is not in apposition with these phrases. *way* being in the accusative case (ὁδόν), and according to the usual construction, governed by a preposition understood (κατά), as expressed in the English version (*by way*, i. e. near, adjacent to). Some understand it to mean that Capernaum was *on the way to the sea*, i. e. the Mediterranean; but the previous description of it as *upon the sea* (in v. 13), requires *sea* to be here taken in the same sense as denoting the sea of Galilee. *Beyond* is in Hebrew a noun originally meaning *passage* or *crossing*, then the side or bank of a stream, whether the nearer or the further side. In the Old Testament it usually means the country east of Jordan, but in some cases no less certainly the west side.* As here used, it is understood by some to mean the country east of Jordan (called in Greek *Peræa*), and to describe a different tract from those mentioned in the previous clauses. But more probably it

---

* Compare Num. 32,19. 32. 34,15. Josh. 1,14. 15. with Deut. 11,30. Josh. 7,7. 12,1.

means the country lying along Jordan, on the west side, and is in apposition to what goes before, i. e. descriptive of the same tract or region, namely, the land of Zebulon and Naphtali, which was partly adjacent to the Sea of Galilee and partly to the river Jordan. *Galilee of the Gentiles*, a name given to the northern part of Galilee, on account of its proximity to the Syrians and Phenicians, or perhaps an actual mixture of the population.

16. The people which sat in darkness, saw great light ; and to them which sat in the region and shadow of death, light is sprung up.

The people, not a plural meaning persons, but a singular denoting a community or nation, here that portion of the Jews who were settled in Galilee. *The (people) sitting*, not merely being, but continuing, dwelling, yet with due regard to the metaphor or image, drawn from a sedentary posture, as implying permanent inaction. *Darkness*, a familiar figure in the dialect of Scripture, not only for intellectual evils, such as ignorance and error, but for the moral depravity and the misery resulting from them. *Saw* or (*have seen*), a prophetical description of the change, which although future when Isaiah wrote, was absolutely certain, and when Matthew wrote actually past. *Light*, a metaphor answering to *darkness*, and of course denoting its opposite or converse, intellectual and moral. The ideas necessarily included are those of truth, knowledge, moral purity, and happiness.* *Great light*, i. e. bearing due proportion to the darkness which it scattered; a light sufficient to dispel the thickest darkness, intellectual and moral, such as that described in the foregoing sentence. The strong terms of this first clause become stronger still in that which follows. *To those* (or to the persons) *sitting* (i. e. inactively and helplessly remaining) *in the* (very) *region* (place or country) and *shadow of death*, a much more emphatic form of speech than *darkness*, though intended to express the same essential meaning. *Region and shadow of death* may either be explained as independent figures, meaning *region of death* and *shadow of death*, or as an instance of the figure called hendiadys, equivalent to *region of the shadow of death*, i. e. the place or region where his shadow falls. According to the other construction, the two ideas are suggested of death's region (where he dwells or reigns) and his shadow (the darkness which he produces). In either case the main idea is that of the profoundest shade, such as belongs to death, as its effect or its precursor. Even to such *light arose* (or *sprung up*) in the prophet's view as future, and in the evangelist's as past. The Greek verb is the one corresponding to the noun translated *east* in 2, 1. 2. 9. and *rising* elsewhere (Rev. 7, 2. 16, 12). It is specially appropriated to the rise of heavenly bodies,† although sometimes otherwise ap-

---

* See Job. 30, 26. Ps. 112, 4. Ecc. 2, 13. Isai. 5, 20. 42, 16. 45, 7. 50, 10. John 1, 5. Acts 26, 18. Rom. 13, 12. 1 Pet. 2, 9. 1 John 1, 5. 2, 8.
† See below, on 5, 45. 13, 6, and compare Mark 16, 2. Jas. 1, 11. 2 Pet. 1, 19.

plied (Luke 12, 54. Heb. 7, 14). The verse in its original connection has respect to the degraded and oppressed state of the Galileans, arising from their situation on the frontier, their exposure to attacks from without, and their actual mixture with the Gentiles. The same description is transferred by Matthew to the spiritual darkness which they shared in common with the other Jews, and the peculiar ignorance with which the other Jews reproached them (John 7, 41. 49. 52). That the Galileans were in fact more barbarous, corrupt, and ignorant, though often said, is neither susceptible of proof nor intrinsically probable, as their intercourse with strangers tended rather to improve them, and the ancient writers represent them as a turbulent and martial race, but not as peculiarly or grossly wicked. Yet even their alleged inferiority in mind and morals made it more remarkable that it was among them, in this remote and relatively dark part of the country, that the great Prophet or Revealer manifested forth his glory (John 2, 11). Nay, it was in the very midst of this benighted or calumniated region, that he fixed the seat of his prophetic ministry, not indeed at Nazareth, but at Capernaum.

17. From that time Jesus began to preach, and to say, Repent; for the kingdom of heaven is at hand.

From that time, i. e. the time mentioned in v. 12, the time of John's arrest, and the consequent cessation of his ministry. The words are not intended to define the date with chronological precision, but to draw the line by which the public work or the official life of Christ was bounded in relation to the previous or preparatory ministry of John the Baptist. The essential fact is not one of chronology but history, to wit, that one opened when the other closed, which is perfectly consistent with the visible and temporary co-existence, previously mentioned as evincing their identity of origin, authority and purpose (see above, on v. 12). And accordingly we find that in the apostolical history the public life of Christ, is measured or computed from "the baptism (i. e. from the ministry) of John."* But besides this chronological succession between John and Jesus, there was also an extraordinary sameness in the subject or the substance of their preaching, as described in 3, 2. and the verse before us. Both are in fact described as uttering the same call to repentance and presenting the same motive, namely, the approach of the Messiah's kingdom. (For the meaning of all these expressions, see above, on 3, 2). But that this was only the beginning, not the whole, of our Lord's preaching, is expressly intimated here by saying, *he began to preach*. In other words, what constituted John's whole message was but the beginning of his own. He took it up where his forerunner laid it down, resumed the thread where it had seemed to be abruptly broken by the violence of Herod, but only, if we may so say, to spin it out indefinitely further. So far then is the preaching or official proclamation of the two divine

* See below, on 21, 25, and compare Acts 1, 22. 10, 37. 13, 25. 19, 3. 4.

messengers from being here described as co-extensive, that the very opposite is really suggested by the statement that our Lord *began* where John had ended. This view of the passage sweeps away all pretext for regarding the *began* as pleonastic or superfluous, as well as the opposite extreme of making it mean more than it does or legitimately can, to wit, that he began afresh, began a second time, began in Galilee, &c. We have seen already that his earlier appearance in Judea, although full of striking incidents and proofs of his divine legation, was preliminary to his ministry or preaching, properly so called, which now began, when he resumed and carried on the interrupted work of John, and became as it were for a time his own forerunner, or acted as the herald of himself as king. By this arrangement, though at first sight paradoxical or accidental, the precise relation of John's ministry to that of Christ was more distinctly set forth than it could have been if he had ended his preparatory work before his principal appeared at all, leaving a doubtful interval between them, or if, on the other hand, our Lord had fully entered on his own work during John's captivity, thus holding up the two together in a kind of rivalry or competition.

18. And Jesus, walking by the sea of Galilee, saw two brethren, Simon called Peter, and Andrew his brother, casting a net into the sea; for they were fishers.

Although it formed no part of our Lord's personal mission upon earth to re-organize the church, a change which was to rest upon his own atoning death as its foundation, and must therefore be posterior to it, he prepared the way for this great revolution by selecting and training those who should accomplish it. This process was a gradual one, beginning with the first introduction or acquaintance, followed up by an express call to personal attendance, and resulting in the ultimate formation of the persons thus selected into an organic body of Apostles. Passing by the first steps of this gradual vocation, which were afterwards supplied in part by John (1, 35-52), the other three evangelists proceed at once to the second, the actual vocation of the first Apostles to be followers or personal attendants of the Saviour. Hence they are naturally spoken of as if before unknown to him, though not expressly so described, and therefore in agreement with the previous occurrences preserved in John's supplementary account, but not included in the plan and purpose of the other gospels. *Walking about*, not listlessly or idly, but no doubt in the performance of his work as a proclaimer or announcer of the kingdom. *By* (or *along*) *the Sea of Galilee*, the lake through which the Jordan flows, along the east side of the province so called (see above, on 3, 5. 4, 13). This use of the word *sea*, though lost in modern English, is retained in German (*See*) with specific reference to inland lakes. It is here, however, the exact translation of the Greek word (θάλασσαν), which in classical usage is applied both to lakes and oceans. The one here meant is also called *Gennesaret* (Luke 5, 1), in Hebrew *Cinnereth* (Deut. 3, 17), or *Cinneroth* (1 Kings 15, 20), from a city and a district on the western shore. (See above, on v. 13, and compare Josh. 19, 35. Num. 34, 11). A third name is the sea (or lake) of *Tiberias*, from a city built by Herod on the south-west shore, and named in honour of the Emperor Tiberius. (See John 6, 1. 21, 1). The lake is about twelve miles long and half as many wide, in a deep basin surrounded by hills. It is still famous, as of old, for its clear pure water, abundant fish, and frequent storms. From among the fishermen on this lake Christ selected his first followers, four of whom are here named, being two pairs of brothers. *Simon*, a later form of *Simeon* (Gen. 29, 33), which, however, is sometimes retained in reference to the same and other persons (Luke 2, 25. 3, 30. Acts 13, 1. 15, 14. 2 Pet. 1, 1. Rev. 7, 7). *The (one) called Peter*, i. e. not only the person so called, but the Simon so called, to distinguish him from others of the same name, which was very common. This second name or surname had its origin, however, not in accident or popular usage, but in the words of Christ himself when Simon was first brought into his presence by his brother Andrew (John 1, 43). The name *Cephas* then imposed is the Aramaic synonyme of the Greek *Petros*, both denoting a rock or stone. This is sometimes explained as having reference to Peter's constancy and firmness; but these are attributes in which he was remarkably deficient, not only in his immature or pupillary state (see below, on 26, 40. 75), but even after the effusion of the Spirit, as appears from a remarkable incident preserved in one of Paul's epistles (Gal. 2, 11). His true characteristics were ardor and boldness, often degenerating into rashness and a blind self-confidence (see below, on 14, 28. 16, 22. 26, 33–35); but these are not suggested by the figure of a stone or rock. It is, therefore, a more probable opinion, that he was so called as the first stone in the Apostolic basis or foundation which our Lord was then about to lay, and on which, in due subordination to himself, the church was to be built up in its new Christian form. (See below, on 16, 18, and compare Eph. 2, 20). As the Apostles were to be the founders of the church, so Peter was to be their foreman, a position for which he was naturally fitted by the very qualities already mentioned, which are not however indicated by the name itself. That this priority was not a primary or permanent superiority in rank and office, but a purely ministerial and temporary leadership, intended for the benefit of others, and contributing to humble rather than exalt himself, will be clearly seen when we come to the organization of the Apostolic body (see below, on 10, 1. 2). *Andrew* is itself a Greek name (*Andreas*), the Hebrew etymology assumed by some being forced and far-fetched. It may serve to illustrate the familiar use of the Greek language even in the east from the time of the Macedonian conquests, and the Jewish practice of adopting Gentile appellations, either exclusively or in conjunction with their native names. (See Acts 1, 23. 9, 40. 12, 12. 13, 1. 9). Which was the elder brother, we have no means of determining, as Simon may be first named in prospective reference to his priority as an Apostle, or his greater eminence in after life; whereas Andrew was the means of introducing him to Jesus, to whom he had himself been introduced by John the Baptist (compare John 1, 49). *Casting a net*, a Greek noun derived from the preceding verb, and meaning something cast around (the body) as a garment, or (in the water) as a net of large size, which sense of the word occurs in Hesiod and Herodotus. That he *saw* them thus employed is perfectly consistent with the fuller narrative of Luke (5, 1–10), describing the symbolical miracle by which the call of these Apostles was attended, while that before us, and the parallel account in Mark (1, 16), speak only of the call itself. So far from discrediting each other, these harmonious variations serve to show that the evangelists, though perfectly consistent, because under one divine direction, were so far independent of each other as to have their several designs and plans, determining the choice of their materials, or the insertion and omission of particular events and topics. *For they were fishermen*, not only upon this occasion, but as their stated occupation and the means of their subsistence. This is not to be exaggerated as a proof of abject poverty and social degradation, because fishermen, in some countries or in some states of society, hold such a position, or because an old Greek proverb makes a fisher's life the type of hardship and of destitution. In the part of Galilee adjacent to the lake, this was probably a common and a profitable business, as it is now on the banks of Newfoundland and coasts of New England. The first Apostles seem to have been chosen out of this class, not as the lowest and the most illiterate, in order to enhance the proof of a divine authority attending the religion which they propagated; nor as the hardiest and most accustomed to exposure, fitting them for what they were to suffer in their master's service; but as representing the body of the people in that part of Palestine, and no doubt possessing at least an average amount of natural intelligence and such religious training as was common to the whole population, even of Galilee, who, although treated with contempt by the people of Judea, frequented the same feasts (John 4, 45), and attended the same spiritual worship in their synagogues (see below, on v. 23), and received the same instruction from their scribes in every town of Galilee (Luke 5, 17). The inference which some of the old writers draw from their being thus employed when called, to wit, that we have most reason to expect the call of God when busily engaged in our lawful occupations, though unexceptionable in itself, is historically neither so important nor so clear as the fact that these men, after having been in company with Christ and recognized as his disciples, had returned to or continued in their former business, no doubt under his direction, and perhaps expecting such a call as the one here recorded. This would render more intelligible, or at least more natural, their prompt obedience to the summons, and confirm what has been said already of the gradual progressive plan by which our Lord collected the materials of his apostolic structure.

19. And he saith unto them, Follow me, and I will make you fishers of men.

MATTHEW 4, 19. 20.

This verse contains the call itself, for which they had no doubt been waiting, and by which the whole course of their life was now to be determined. *Come after me*, or more exactly, *hither! behind me*, not only in the literal and local sense, but in the moral and figurative sense of close adherence and subordination. This is far more natural and satisfactory than to suppose an allusion to the practice of teachers literally walking about with their pupils behind them. Even if there were no such practice in the east, as there was among the restless and mercurial Greeks, the language here used would explain itself, as suited to the outward circumstances in which it was uttered, and at the same time as expressive of the intimate relation which these men were to sustain to their new master. With a beautiful allusion to their former occupation, at which he had found them busy, he describes their new employment as essentially the same, but dignified and sublimated in its ends, and in the means by which they were to be secured. They were still to be fishermen, but not of fishes; they were henceforth to employ their art on higher and more valuable prey. This metaphor like others must not be unduly pressed; but the main points of resemblance cannot be mistaken, such as the value of the object, the necessity of skill as well as strength, of vigilance as well as labour, with an implication if not an explicit promise of abundance and success in their new fishery. All this was dependent not upon themselves, but on the power and authority of him who called them. *I will make you* (*to become*, Mark 1, 17) *fishers of men*. As the business of their lives had hitherto been only to provide for the subsistence of the body, by securing the bodies of inferior animals for food; so now they were to seek the souls of men, not to destroy but save them, in the way of Christ's appointment and for the promotion of his glory. Though it cannot be supposed that he selected fishermen to be his first Apostles merely for the purpose of drawing this comparison, he may have called them from the actual labours of the fishery, in order to employ it as an emblem of their future work, as well as with a view to its miraculous illustration, as preserved by Luke (5, 1–10).

20. And they straightway left (their) nets, and followed him.

The effect of this abrupt call, as it seems to be if we look only at this narrative and that of Mark, without Luke's more particular account of what preceded it, is here described as instantaneous, not only because they were expecting and prepared for such a summons, but because they were divinely moved to answer and obey it. This unhesitating response to the divine call is represented elsewhere as an equitable test of true devotion to the Master's service (Luke 9, 57–62). *Leaving*, letting them lie, or letting them alone, the Greek verb used above in 3, 15, and there explained. *The nets* (not the word so rendered in v. 18, but the generic term of which that is a specification),

i. e. the nets which they were casting into the sea, either to wash them (compare Luke 5, 1), or for a draught of fishes (compare Luke 5, 4. 5). It is implied, though not expressed (as in the version) that the nets belonged to them. The immediate act described is that of leaving their nets then and there; but this implies their leaving them forever, both as property and sources of subsistence. (See below, on 19, 27.) *Followed*, not the phrase so rendered in v. 19, but the usual Greek synonyme of *follow*, and expressing the same sense as in the other case, but in a less pointed and emphatic manner.

21. And going on from thence, he saw other two brethren, James (the son) of Zebedee, and John his brother, in a ship with ᴵZebedee their father, mending their nets : and he called them.

Another pair of brothers was to be called to the same service at the same time and place. *Advancing*, going forward in the same direction, from the spot where Simon and Andrew had been called, and now perhaps attended by them, although this is not a necessary supposition, as the boats were near together (Mark 1, 19), and the fishery a joint one (Luke 5, 10). *Them too* (he saw, as he had seen the others) *in the boat* (as Wiclif renders it, the less exact term *ship* having been introduced by Tyndale.) The Greek word (πλοῖον from πλέω) properly means any thing that sails, corresponding more exactly to the English *craft* or *vessel*. Those here meant were probably mere fishing smacks, propelled both by sails and oars, and drawn up on the shore when not engaged in active service. *James the (son) of Zebedee*, a name occurring also in the Jewish books (*Jacob Bar Zabdi* or *Zabdai*), and supposed by some, but without much probability, to designate the same person. The first name has always been a common one among the Jews, as that of their national progenitor, and the other seems to be identical with names which occur in the Old Testament (Zabdi, Josh. 7, 1 ; Zebadiah, 1 Chr. 8, 15). That the relation here denoted by the genitive is that of father and son, is not only probable from usage, but rendered certain by the distinct mention of the father in the next clause, as present in the boat, and no doubt managing the fishery. *John his brother*, commonly regarded as the other disciple of John the Baptist, who with Andrew followed Jesus when acknowledged by their master as the Lamb of God, (John 1, 35, 37.) *Mending*, repairing, what is worn or broken, is the usual meaning of this Greek word in the classics, though according to its etymology and Hellenistic usage, it may have the wider sense of making perfect or complete, putting in order, making ready for use, or in familiar English, fixing.*
In one way or the other, both these pairs of brothers were preparing for their daily work or actually busied at it, when the master *called them*, using probably the same formula in both the cases, though recorded only in the first (v. 19).

* See below, on 21, 16, and compare Luke 6, 40. Rom. 9, 22. 1 Cor. 1, 10. Gal. 6, 1. 1 Th. 3, 10. Heb. 10, 5. 11, 3. 13, 21. 1 Pet. 5, 10.

22. And they immediately left the ship, and their father, and followed him.

Here again the effect was an immediate one, and rendered still more striking by the fact that they left not only the nets and the boat but their father who was in it. *And they* (or *they too*), i. e. the sons of Zebedee no less than those of Jonas (see above, on v. 20). Even from what is here said it might naturally be inferred that Zebedee was present, not as a passenger or mere spectator, but as the chief-fisherman, and this is confirmed by the mention of hired men in the parallel account of Mark (1, 20). There is therefore no ground in the text or context for the notion that they left their father by himself, or destitute or helpless from extreme old age, all which are fanciful embellishments, without even probability to recommend them. On the contrary, the natural presumption is that Zebedee, instead of being utterly dependent on his sons for his subsistence. furnished them employment as he did to others, and that when they left him, it was not to starve, but to continue his old business with the aid of others. Even in the imaginary case just mentioned, the express command of Christ would have suspended every other claim and obligation; but no such case appears to have existed, and we have neither right nor reason to invent it. That the family of Zebedee was not one of the lowest rank, may also be inferred from John 18, 15, as commonly interpreted. That the miracle which Luke records (5, 1-7) occurred at this time, is apparent from his mentioning the call and their response to it (5, 10. 11), which cannot be supposed to have occurred on more than one occasion.

23. And Jesus went about all Galilee, teaching in their synagogues, and preaching the gospel of the kingdom, and healing all manner of sickness, and all manner of disease among the people.

This is not a statement of what took place upon any one occasion, or a direct continuation of the narrative immediately preceding, but a general description of our Saviour's ministry in Galilee, after he had fairly entered on it (as related in vs. 12-17), and had selected certain persons to attend him (as recorded in vs. 18-21). Being thus provided with the necessary aids, he began the systematic work which was continued till he bade farewell to Galilee, and set out upon his last journey to Jerusalem (see below, on 19, 1). This ministry is here described as itinerant or ambulatory, not confined to one spot or a few, but covering the whole of Galilee, no doubt in the widest sense of the expression (see above, on 2, 22. 4, 12-15). *Went about*, a verb originally meaning *led about*, of which sense there is only one example in the Greek of the New Testament (1 Cor. 9, 5). In every other case it has the neuter sense of going about, which some regard as an ellipsis for the phrase *led (himself) about*, but which more probably implies that he led others, that he did not go about alone but as a leader, with a suite or retinue, composed in this case of the four disciples whose vocation is recorded in the previous context (vs. 18–21), and perhaps of others. This is a summary description of our Lord's prophetic ministry, with its two great functions, which are there distinctly and particularly mentioned. *Teaching*, imparting knowledge, i. e. as the context here demands, religious knowledge, or the knowledge necessary to salvation, not in the completed form subsequently given to it in the apostolic preaching and epistles, but in such a measure as to make those who received it wise unto salvation. (See below, on 5, 1.) *In their synagogues*, i. e. those of Galilee, the country being put for its inhabitants (see above, on 3, 5). *Synagogues*, a Greek word which originally means *collection*, and is properly applied to things, but in the Hellenistic dialect to persons also, like our English *meeting*. It is frequently applied in the Septuagint version to the whole *congregation* of Israel, as an aggregate and corporate body. During the Babylonish captivity, it seems to have been transferred to the divisions of this body, in their separation and dispersion, and more especially to their assemblies for religious worship. After the second great dispersion of the Jews, occasioned by the Roman conquest and destruction of Jerusalem, the synagogues assumed the form of organized societies, with a peculiar constitution and discipline, from which that of the Christian Church is commonly supposed to have been copied. It is doubtful, however, whether synagogues, in this later sense, existed in the time of Christ and the Apostles, when the word, though sometimes, like the English *church, school, court*, etc. transferred to the place of meeting, properly denoted the meeting itself, not as an organic body, but as an assembly of the people for a special purpose. In Jerusalem, where multitudes of foreigners were gathered, to attend the feasts or as permanent settlers, it was natural that those of the same race and language should convene together, both for worship and for social intercourse; and this accounts for the extraordinary number of synagogues, alleged by the Jewish tradition to have existed in Jerusalem before its downfall (480), an incredible number if we understand by synagogues distinct organizations of a public and a formal nature, but possible enough if nothing more be meant than gatherings of the people, in larger or smaller circles, for religious purposes. Of this truly national and sacred usage, that of meeting on the sabbath for religious worship, our Lord immediately availed himself, as furnishing the most direct and easy access to the body of the people. The service of the synagogue appears to have been eminently simple, consisting in prayer and the reading of the Scriptures, with occasional or stated exhortation. That our Lord was permitted to perform this duty without any seeming opposition or objection, may be owing to a customary license of instruction, or to his universal recognition as a gifted teacher and a worker of miracles (compare Luke 4, 46. Acts 13, 15). *Preaching* (announcing or proclaiming) *the gospel* (glad news or glad tidings) *of the kingdom* (the Messiah's reign, the new economy or Christian dispensation). This was one great function of his ministry; the other is described in the remainder of the verse. *Healing*, a Greek word which originally means *serving* or attending (as a servant does a master); then *tending*, nursing (with particular reference to sickness); and then *healing*, curing, which last word (derived from *curo*) primarily means to take care, but like the Greek one here used is specially applied to the treatment and removal of disease. *Sickness*, the Greek corresponding to *disease* in English, while the one so rendered means originally *softness*, and then languor, weakness, or infirmity. Some suppose a distinction to be here intended between chronic and acute disease; others between positive disease and mere debility or sickness; but most probably the two terms are combined as synonymous, or nearly so, in order to exhaust the whole idea of sickness or disease. *All manner*, i. e. every kind, is not a version but a paraphrase, intended to preclude the extravagant idea that our Saviour really healed all the sickness then existing. This is better than the old device of making *all* mean *many*, which it never does directly, though it often denotes all within a certain limit, then suggested by the context. So in this case, *all disease and all infirmity* may mean all that was brought within his reach or presented to his notice by the sufferers themselves or by others representing them; the rather as there is not the remotest intimation that the Saviour ever finally rejected such an application. (See below, on 9, 35, where the very same words are translated, *every sickness and every disease*.)

24. And his fame went throughout all Syria : and they brought unto him all sick people that were taken with divers diseases and torments, and those which were possessed with devils, and those which were lunatic, and those that had the palsy ; and he healed them.

Having thus related the beginning of Christ's ministry, and described in general terms its two great functions, the didactic and the thaumaturgic, Matthew tells us the effect of his appearance in these official characters, i. e., as a Teacher and a Healer. This effect was an extensive fame or reputation (literally, *hearing*), not confined to Galilee, nor even to the land of Israel, but penetrating into the surrounding region on the north and east, here denoted by the vague but comprehensive name of *Syria*, as applied to the great Roman province, of which Palestine was then a part or a dependency. Its precise limits are not only doubtful but of little exegetical importance, as the fact recorded is the wide extension of our Lord's fame, not to a specific distance but in a particular direction. The effect and proof of this celebrity was a vast concourse needing his Divine help, either for themselves or others. Here again the pronoun (*they brought*) has respect not to the formal antecedent (*Syria*), but to that for which it stands, the whole surrounding population. (See above, on v. 23.) *Sick people*, literally, *those having badly*, i. e., having themselves (or being) ill. These miraculous cures were not confined to any one form of disease, but included all varieties. *Divers*, a Greek word, originally signifying parti-colored, piebald, but used by the best writers in the wider sense of various, different in kind. This phrase may be grammatically construed either with what goes before (having themselves ill with various diseases), or with what follows (with various diseases seized); but the latter construction is preferred by the best philological authorities. *Torments*, a word which originally means a touchstone for the trial of the precious metals; then any mode of inquisition or discovery, especially by torture; and then discarding the original idea, and retaining only that of torment or extreme pain. It is here applied to painful bodily diseases, as it is to the pains of hell in the only other place where it occurs in the New Testament (Luke 16, 23–28). *Taken*, seized, or, as the stronger term in Greek suggests, held fast, confined, oppressed.* To show still further the variety of cases thus presented to our Saviour as the Great Physician, the evangelist enumerates three classes, as among the most severe and yet the most familiar. Those which were possessed *with devils*, six words answering to one in Greek, which may be rendered *demonized*, i. e., subjected to the power of demons. This specific malady is mentioned on account of its extraordinary prevalence at that time, its peculiarly distressing character, its strange complication of moral and physical disorder, and, above all, its mysterious connection with the unseen world and with another race of spirits. These are called *unclean* or impure in a moral sense, essentially equivalent to *wicked*, but suggesting more directly the idea of corruption, as existing in themselves and practised upon others. These are the *angels* or ministering spirits of the devil, who fell with him, have since been added to him, as believers are added to the Lord and are co-operating with him as the tempters and accusers of mankind. To these fallen and seducing spirits our race has ever been accessible and more or less subjected; but when Christ was upon earth, they were permitted to assume a more perceptible, if not a more complete ascendency, extending to the body and the mind, and thus presenting the worst forms of insanity and bodily disease combined. That these demoniacal possessions are not mere poetical descriptions of disease or madness, but the real acts of spiritual agents, is apparent from the personality ascribed to them, as well as from their being so explicitly distinguished from all other maladies, as in the case before us; while the fact that they did really produce disease abundantly accounts for their being sometimes so described and constantly connected with corporeal illness. The extraordinary prevalence of these disorders in the time of Christ, while we scarcely hear of them in any other period of history, may be partly owing to the fact, that what is always going on in secret was then brought to light by his authoritative interposition; and partly to the fact, that the stupendous strife between the

---

* Compare Luke 8, 37. 45. 12, 50. 19, 43. 26, 63. Acts 7, 57. 18, 5. 2 Cor. 5, 14. Phil. 1, 23.

"seed of the woman" and the "seed of the serpent" (Gen. 3, 15), which gives complexion to all human history, then reached its crisis, and these demoniacal possessions were at once the work of Satan, as a means of doing evil, and of God, as a means of doing good, by glorifying him whom he had sanctified and sent into the world. (See John 10, 36. 17, 1. 5.) Every expulsion of a demon by our Lord himself, or in his name by his Apostles, was a triumph over his great enemy, not only in the unseen world but upon earth, in the sight of men as well as angels (Luke 10, 17. 18. John 12, 31. 16, 11). This immediate relation of these strange phenomena to Christ's person and official work, accounts for their absence both before and since, as well as for the impotent resistance of the evil ones themselves, and their extorted testimony to the character and rank of their destroyer. (See below, on 8. 29–32. Mark 5, 7. 9, 26. Luke 4, 33–35. 41. 8, 28. 29.) It explains likewise the distinct mention of this class of miracles, both here and elsewhere (e. g. 8, 16. 28, 33. Mark 1, 34. 6, 13. 16, 17. 18. Luke 8, 2. 36), as being in themselves the most surprising of all cures, and at the same time the most palpable of all attestations to the Messiahship and Deity of Jesus. *Those which were lunatic*, another single word in Greek, which might be rendered *moonstruck*, i. e. morbidly affected by the changes of the moon, applied in English (*lunatic* from *luna*) to insanity, but in Greek to epilepsy. (See below, on 17, 15, the only other instance of the term in the New Testament.) The word may here be used in its secondary sense, without regard to its original import, just as we use *lunatic* for *madman*, without even thinking of its derivation; or it may denote a real physical connection, which, although inscrutable to us, is not more incredible in itself than the effects of the moon upon the tides, or of certain atmospheric changes upon some constitutions. At all events, there is no ground for the charge of connivance at a popular or superstitious error, any more than in the case of demoniacal possessions. *Those that had the palsy*, literally, *paralytics*, a word which seems not to have obtained currency in English when the Bible was translated, as we never meet with it or its cognate noun, *paralysis*, but always with its earlier corruption, *palsy*. Another difference of usage in the Greek itself is that the corresponding verb (*to paralyze*) is used exclusively by Luke (5, 18. 24. Acts 8, 7. 9, 33.) and Paul (Heb. 12, 12), while the adjective is equally peculiar to the other Gospels,* The Greek words, according to the medical authorities, denote all morbid relaxation of the nerves, including what the modern nosology distinguishes as paralysis and apoplexy. *And he healed them*, without any limitation as to number or implied discrimination, which omission, although in itself merely negative, must be interpreted by what was positively said before, viz., that *he healed every sickness and disease*, not merely some of every kind, but every case presented to him. (See above, on v. 23.)

---

* See below, on 8, 6. 9, 2. 6. Compare Mark 2, 3. 4. 5. 9. 10.

25. And there followed him great multitudes of people from Galilee, and (from) Decapolis, and (from) Jerusalem, and (from) Judea, and (from) beyond Jordan.

This is not a mere tautology or varied repetition of the statement just made, but the record of another fact of great importance, serving to connect the previous description of Christ's ministry with the great discourse contained in the ensuing chapters. This important fact is, that besides the multitudes who came to obtain healing for themselves and others, there was soon formed a permanent or constant body of disciples in the wide sense, who not only came to him while in their neighbourhood, but *followed him* from place to place, of course with many fluctuations and mutations as to individuals, so as to keep him constantly surrounded by a multitude. This is one of the most singular yet certain facts of our Lord's ministry, to wit, that even in his most profound retirements the multitude was never very far off.* *Great multitudes*, literally, *many crowds*, i. e. promiscuous assemblies, as distinguished from organic bodies or selected companies, whether great or small. *From* is not to be connected with the verb (*followed*), but denotes the quarters whence the multitudes or crowds came, who did follow or attend him in his journeys throughout Galilee. Besides the three great divisions of the land of Israel, at that time, Galilee, Judea, and Perea (beyond Jordan), which have been already mentioned,† Matthew specifies *Decapolis*, a Greek word meaning *Ten Towns* and analogous in form to *Tripolis*, *Tetrapolis*, and *Pentapolis*, all of which occur in Greek geography, as names of tracts in different countries, so called from their having three, four, or five important towns respectively.‡ Pliny and Ptolemy enumerate the ten towns here meant, coinciding as to eight (Scythopolis, Hippos, Gadara, Dion, Pella, Gerasa, Philadelphia, Canatha), but differing as to the remaining two. This difference does not necessarily imply mistake upon the part of either, as the ten towns may not have been always reckoned in the same way, or Decapolis may have been a vague and popular rather than a technical and certain designation. All the cities named by Ptolemy and Pliny, except one (Scythopolis), lay east of Jordan, and south of the sea of Galilee. They seem to have been all Greek cities, i. e. chiefly occupied by Gentiles, some belonging to Perea, some to Coelesyria, and here collectively referred to, not for the sake of geographical precision, but to show that this great confluence of hearers and disciples was made up both of Jews and Gentiles. How soon the concourse reached its height is not recorded either here or elsewhere; but the words of Matthew, taken in their whole connection, seem intended to suggest that it was at this interesting juncture, when the

---

* See below, on 5, 1. 8, 1. 18. 11, 7. 12, 15. 13, 2. 14, 14. 15, 10. 30. 17, 14. 19, 2. 20, 29.
† See above, on 2, 1. 22. 3, 13. 4, 12. 15.
‡ The first name was also used in reference to a single town, composed of three parts, and is still the name of cities both in Africa and Asia.

tide of popularity was at its height, and the representation of the regions and the races most complete, that he delivered for the first time the remarkable discourse recorded in the next three chapters.

CHAPTERS V.—VII.

The next three chapters are occupied with a continuous discourse, traditionally known, from the place of its delivery, as the Sermon on the Mount. Different opinions have been entertained in reference to its connection with the previous context, and with Matthew's entire narrative. The obvious presumption is, that he is here recording what our Saviour said on one particular occasion. Besides the negative proof afforded by the want of any intimation to the contrary, this assumption is confirmed by the simple historical form of the narration, and the accompanying circumstances mentioned in the two first verses.

In opposition to this simplest and most natural presumption, some prefer to regard the Sermon on the Mount as a summary and sample of our Lord's instructions during the whole course of his public ministry. This hypothesis agrees well with our previous conclusion, drawn from other premises, that the immediately preceding context is a general description of that ministry, and not of its commencement merely; so that we might naturally expect what is there said of his miracles and journeys, to be followed by a similar account of his preaching. It also agrees well with what is now very commonly admitted to be Matthew's practice of combining matters of the same kind, whether consecutive in time or not. It is supposed to be further recommended by the light which it appears to throw upon the fact, that many of the dicta comprehended in this long discourse are also met with elsewhere in the Gospels, and often in what seems to be their original historical connection. This phenomenon, however, is susceptible of other explanation, at least in reference to some expressions which are aphoristical in form, and which our Lord appears to have employed in various applications and connections.

This same hypothesis is further recommended by the aid which it is thought to afford in the solution of another difficult inquiry as to the mutual relation of the Sermon on the Mount contained in Luke and Matthew. The old and obvious assumption, that these passages are two reports of one and the same sermon, is adhered to by the modern sceptical school of critics and interpreters, not only on the old ground, that they both begin and end alike, and have the same general drift and tone, and are followed by an account of the same miracle, but also on account of its affording an occasion and a pretext for disparaging the verbal inspiration of the two evangelists, by showing how they disagree in their report of the very same transaction. But even granting what is thus assumed, there is really no contradiction, nor even any variation, whether of the form or substance, which may not be reconciled by simply assuming what is natural and matter of experience in all such cases, namely, that one witness may preserve the substance and the other reproduce the very form, or both record the former only without any deviation from the truth of history or from the credit of the several historians. But although the difficulties which attend this supposition are by no means insurmountable, in case of exegetical necessity excluding every other, it cannot be denied that they are quite sufficient to command our preference of any doctrine unencumbered with them. Such is the theory that both Luke and Matthew's Sermon on the Mount are general descriptions of Christ's public teaching, gathered from his various discourses, and including many things recorded elsewhere in their true historical connection. This hypothesis admits of being modified without essential change by supposing only one to have this general comprehensive character, and the other to be really a record of a particular discourse delivered upon one occasion. The latter description may be then applied to Luke, while Matthew is supposed to have added many kindred sayings uttered upon different and various occasions. Still another view of the relation between these discourses is, that though originally one, they have been fully given only by Matthew for his Jewish readers, while much that was appropriate to them is omitted or curtailed by Luke as less appropriate to Gentiles. But as this diversity of purpose cannot be distinctly traced in all the variations, some still prefer the ingenious hypothesis suggested by Augustine, that the two discourses are entirely distinct though delivered on the same occasion; that preserved by Matthew on the mountain-top to a select circle of disciples, that by Luke upon the plain below to the whole multitude. This not only makes it easier to account for the omissions, as of matters not well suited to the ear of a promiscuous assembly but also enables us to reconcile the seeming disagreement of the two accounts as to the place where the discourse was uttered, without resorting to the less obvious though not impossible assumption, that he went up and down repeatedly, or that the place described by Luke was not a plain, as distinguished from a mountain, but a *level place* upon the mountain itself. It cannot be denied, however, that Augustine's supposition of two versions of the same discourse, delivered in immediate succession and almost upon the same spot, and to some of the same hearers, although not impossible or inadmissible in case of urgent exegetical necessity, is far from being obvious or natural, and therefore not to be insisted on, if any simpler and more probable solution of the facts can be suggested.

Such a solution seems to me to be afforded by a due consideration of the fact, that Christ's discourses were delivered not to one fixed audience or congregation, but to shifting multitudes, who all however were in need of substantially the same instruction, which would naturally lead him, not to utter new discourses upon every new occasion, like a settled pastor or a fashionable preacher, afraid or ashamed to repeat himself, nor yet to reiterate with slavish uniformity a fixed liturgical type or formula; but intermediate between these two extremes, to dispense the same substantial truth with that familiar mixture of diversity and sameness, to which even uninspired teachers are accustomed, who have frequent occasion to inculcate one unwritten lesson upon different assemblies and at various times and places. If the truth embodied in the Sermon on the Mount was needed by one multitude, it must have been by others, and it cannot be supposed, without detracting from the Master's wisdom and benevolence, that he dispensed it once for all, instead of frequently repeating it, at less or greater length, and with many unessential variations of expression. Two such variations on the same theme are preserved to us by Luke and Matthew; by the former as delivered in connection with the final designation of the twelve apostles, as a sort of inaugural discourse or ordination sermon; by the latter, as the very beginning of our Lord's public teaching, although its *position* in the Gospel may be rather historical than chronological.

On any of these suppositions, this discourse presents a sample of his preaching, and discloses to us what was its design and character, whether actually spoken upon some one occasion, or collected from his preaching upon many. Viewed in this light, it is important to observe that the Sermon on the Mount is not a system of theology or exhibition of the Christian doctrine in its full development, which was to rest upon his death and resurrection as its basis, and could only be matured by his apostles after his departure, but under his express authority and the direction of his Spirit, so that it is equally absurd and impious to draw invidious distinctions between what was taught by Christ himself and his apostles, as unequal in authority, whereas the only difference is that between an order uttered *viva voce*, and the same transmitted by a letter or message. The error here corrected is a common one with sceptics and half infidels, who are neither willing to renounce all faith in Christ as an authoritative teacher, nor to receive all the teachings of his revelation. Another error, which prevails more among Christians, is that of regarding this discourse as a system, not of religious doctrine, but of ethics or morality, and endeavouring to find in it specific formal rules of duty for the various emergencies of common life, an end which can only be attained by forced and paradoxical constructions. It is true that the discourse is full of the most invaluable moral and religious truth, but in a shape more rhetorical than systematic; clothed in paradox and figure rather than in rule and definition, and conveyed incidentally rather than directly, as the primary immediate end in view, which was neither to expound the doctrines of religion, nor to lay down rules of conduct, nor to teach the true way of salvation, but to show the nature of Messiah's kingdom, which was near at hand, and by which the completed revelation of all saving truth was to be made known and perpetuated. Thus viewed, the Sermon on the Mount is here precisely in its proper place, if not chronologically yet methodically, as a fuller exposition of the theme which had already been propounded, as treated of our Lord's preaching and of John's before him, "Repent, for the kingdom of heaven is at hand." As to the nature of this kingdom there were various errors current, and to these the form of the discourse has reference throughout, but more especially to the almost universal error of supposing that the moral requisitions of the law were to be set aside, and the standard of duty as established by it lowered in Messiah's kingdom. In opposition to this fatal Antinomian delusion, it is here taught that the standard was rather to be raised than lowered, by a spiritual exposition of the law's demands, and a full recognition of its whole extent and constant obligation, so that no one must press into the Messiah's kingdom in the hope of sinning more securely. This brings the Sermon on the Mount into connection with the giving of the law at Sinai, which some writers push to an extreme as comprehending even the minutest outward circumstances. Other delusive expectations, no less really though less conspicuously combated and rectified in this discourse, are those of the bigoted Jew who thought the Gentiles could not possibly be saved; of the revolutionary zealot who expected all distinctions and relations to be utterly subverted in the change of dispensations; of the censorious moralist whose piety consisted in detecting and condemning the defects of others; and of the formalist who trusted in a ritual ceremonial righteousness. These and some other current notions with respect to the Messiah's kingdom, are corrected not always by formal refutation, but in part by pointed aphorism, vehement apostrophe, and striking figurative illustration. The plan or form of the discourse is determined not by technical or abstract method, but by natural association; so that the opposite charges of utter incoherence on the one hand, and of a plan so artificial on the other, as to show that the discourse was never actually spoken in its present form, but afterwards composed by the historian, neutralize and nullify each other. The multiplicity of ways in which the passage has been analyzed, with various degrees of plausibility, confirms the fact already stated, that it is neither desultory nor precise in its arrangement, but at once coherent and inartificial. Another consequence and proof of this is, that many of the schemes which have been thus proposed are perfectly compatible with one another, and may be combined as an assistance to the memory. The conventional division of the text throws the sermon into three great parts. The first, coincident with chapter V., shows for whom the kingdom is designed, defines their relation to the world, and that of the Messiah to the law, showing that the moral standard of his kingdom would be higher than that recognized by the Scribes and Pharisees. The second, answering to chapter VI., pursues the same course with respect to great religious duties, which must be performed to God, and not to man; then extends this principle to every thing in life, and shows that this is the true remedy for anxious cares. The third part, chapter VII., after reproving the censorious contempt of Pharisaical hypocrites for others, prescribes prayer as the true expression of the faith before required, and encourages it by a cheering promise; then sums up all that has been said as to the law; exhorts to self-denial as essential to salvation;

warns against false guides and false profession, and the fatal error of not acting upon these instructions. The details of this analysis can only be presented step by step as we proceed in the interpretation.

CHAPTER V.

THIS first division of the Sermon on the Mount, after giving the historical occasion of its utterance (1. 2), describes the characters or classes which had reason to rejoice in the approach of the Messiah's kingdom (3–10), the poor in spirit (3), mourners (4), the meek (5), the hungry and thirsty (6), the merciful (7), the pure in heart (8), the pacific (9), the persecuted in a good cause (10); all of whom are here pronounced blessed or happy in the prospect of the coming change. The last of these beatitudes is then applied directly to the hearers (11–12), which affords occasion to define their relation to the world, under the figures of salt (13) and light (14. 15); and to exhort them to good works (16). This, in its turn, suggests the moral claims and requisitions of the kingdom, and its relation to the law, which is declared to be unchangeable—no less binding in the new than in the old economy (17–19). Nay, the moral standard in Messiah's kingdom should be vastly higher than that of Pharisaical Judaism (20). This is then stated in detail with reference to several prevailing sins, which, far from being treated more indulgently, would meet with a severe censure (21–48). These are murder (21–26); adultery (27–30); unauthorized divorce (31. 32); unlawful swearing (33–37); revenge (38–42); and hatred (43–47); the whole enumeration being wound up by presenting the divine perfection as the standard of morality and the model to be copied in the kingdom of Messiah (48).

1. And seeing the multitudes, he went up into a mountain : and when he was set, his disciples came unto him :

This verse is to be read in the closest connection with the one before it. *There followed him great multitudes* . . . *and seeing the multitudes,* i. e. the same which had just been mentioned, any other reference being wholly arbitrary and unnatural. This construction, however, decides nothing as to the chronology, since the last verses of the preceding chapter are not descriptive merely of the first crowds which attended him, but of the concourse which attended his whole ministry. Those who regard Luke and Matthew as reporting the same sermon, adapt the chronology of one to the other, and insert here various incidents recorded elsewhere. But even upon that hypothesis, we cannot improve Matthew's narrative by introducing what he was directed or permitted to leave out. It was a part of his plan to put together what we find together in the text, and all additions *aliunde* belong not so much to the interpretation as to a chronological synopsis. *He went up,* ascended, not habitually, but, as the form of the Greek verb denotes, on one particular occasion. *A mountain,* literally, *the mountain,** which may either mean the one above the place where the people were assembled, or the highlands as distinguished from the lowlands of Palestine, in which generic sense the Hebrew word for mountain frequently occurs.† If a particular mountain is intended, it cannot be identified, and for that very reason is of no importance. The tradition of the church of Rome has designated as the Mount of the Beatitudes, a hill of singular configuration, now called the Horns of Hattin; but as the Greek church has no similar tradition, and the Roman cannot be traced further than the thirteenth century, it is probably a mere conjecture of some medieval traveller. It is not even certain, as interpreters infer from 8, 5, that it was near Capernaum, since the intervals of time are not determined by the text or context. *Having sat down,* either for repose, or as the customary posture of a teacher. *His disciples,* not in the restricted sense of his apostles (as in 10, 1. 11, 1, and elsewhere), who may have been appointed (compare Luke 6, 12. 13), but have not yet been referred to in this narrative (see below, on 10, 2); but in the wider sense of hearers, pupils, those who listened to him as a teacher come from God (John 3, 2). Some suppose him to have gone up to avoid the multitude, but to have been followed by them, as their presence is implied in the statement at the end of the discourse. (See below, on 7, 28.) Others understand him simply to have gone up higher on the hill-side so as to address the multitude below more easily. If *disciples* be here taken in its widest sense, no distinction may be needed between them and the multitude, who were all, for the time being, his disciples, i. e. learners in his school or listeners to his instructions. *Came to him,* as he sat upon the mountain, not implying that they had been absent and now joined him, but that they came nearer or followed him when he changed his place. This might be said either of a smaller number, or of the whole multitude.

2. And he opened his mouth, and taught them, saying,

Opening (or *having opened*) *his mouth,* is not a pleonasm, i. e. an unmeaning phrase; nor simply a periphrasis for *spake* (or *began to speak*); nor in antithesis to silent teaching by his looks or deeds (Chrysostom); nor an intimation that he meant to speak long (Augustine); but, as every reader feels, although he may not be able to

---

* See below, on 14, 23. 15, 29. Mark 6, 46. Luke 6, 12. 9, 28. John 6, 3, and compare Ex. 2, 15. Num. 11, 27. Deut. 18, 16. Matt. 13, 2.

† See Gen. 12, 8. 14, 10. 19, 17. Num. 13, 29. Deut. 1, 2. Josh. 9, 1. 14, 12. 15, 48.

express it, a formula denoting the commencement of a solemn and authoritative utterance on an important subject. This is not only in agreement with Scripture and Hebrew usage,* but with that of the classics, the same expression being found both in Æschylus and Aristophanes, and with the circumstances of the case before us, in which the nature of Messiah's kingdom was about to be set forth by the Messiah himself. *Taught*, in the imperfect tense (*was teaching*), may appear to favour the assumption of a general description of his ministry, rather than of a particular discourse; but it may also denote continued speech as distinguished from a momentary utterance.

3. Blessed (are) the poor in spirit: for theirs is the kingdom of heaven.

The exposition of the nature of his kingdom opens with a designation of the characters and classes, who had reason to rejoice in its erection. Not the rich and worldly, not the prosperous and selfish, not the formal and self-righteous, would be rendered happy by the great approaching change, but the opposite of all these, who are now described in a series of *beatitudes* or *macarisms*,† so called from the word with which they severally open (vs. 3–11). That there are seven of these beatitudes, has been sometimes reckoned a significant circumstance, connected with the frequent use of seven as a sacred or symbolical number. The beatitudes are so far uniform in structure, that each begins with a description of the class or character, pronounced by the Saviour to be blessed, and concludes with a statement of the ground or reason of the benediction. *Blessed*, a word originally applicable to the divine blessedness, and that of men admitted, as it were, to share it, but often used in the New Testament to represent the welfare or felicity of men in this life, yet always probably with reference to its dependence on the divine favour, as expressed in English by the participle blessed, rather than the adjective *happy*. The first beatitude (v. 3) seems intended to correct the false impression, that the blessings of Messiah's kingdom were reserved for the rich and higher classes of society; whereas it was intended more particularly for the *poor*, but not in the more obvious and ordinary sense of the expression, which is therefore qualified by the addition of the phrase *in spirit*. Of the various constructions which have been proposed, e. g. 'blessed to the Spirit,' i. e. in God's estimation—'blessed in spirit,' though distressed in body—the only one that is entirely natural, is that which has been commonly adopted in all ages, and which construes *in spirit*, not with *blessed*, but with *poor*, of which it is the necessary limitation, as the blessing here pronounced is not on poverty as such, or as a mere outward state, but on poverty of spirit, or, in modern phraseology, spiritual poverty. This does not mean intellectual weakness or destitution, but

---

* See Judg. 11, 35. 36. Job. 3, 1. 33, 2. Acts 8, 35. 10, 34. 2 Cor. 6, 11. Eph. 6, 19.

† Μακαρισμός, Rom. 4, 6. 9. Gal. 4, 15.

a conscious deficiency of moral goodness and of spiritual advantages. The antithesis to outward wealth and worldly prosperity, lies not in the unlawfulness of that condition, or the merit of its opposite, but partly in the well-known fact of general experience, that spiritual poverty more generally coincides with that of an external kind, than with its opposite, and partly in the scriptural usage of the term *poor*, and some of kindred import to denote the people of the Lord collectively as sufferers, and inevitably destitute of much that is essential to the worldling's happiness. The poor, in this sense, and in that of feeling their own want of spiritual food, and consequent dependence on divine grace, are pronounced in this verse blessed ; happy, because those for whom that grace is in reserve, and on whom it is now to be conferred by giving them the kingdom, for which Israel had so long been waiting, as their own rightful indefeasible possession. *Theirs*, belonging to them, as their own—so far from being forcibly shut out of it, they are the very men for whom it is intended and prepared. (See below, on 25, 34). *The kingdom of heaven*, literally, *of the heavens*, an allusion, not to the later Jewish notion of a definite series or succession of heavens (compare 2 Cor. 12, 2. Eph. 4, 10), but to the plural form of the Hebrew word (שָׁמַיִם) which has no singular ; a like case being that of water, (מַיִם), which has led to the frequent use of *waters* in the Greek of the New Testament, where the sense is simply that of *water*. By *heavens*, therefore, we are here to understand nothing more than *heaven*, and by this the local residence of God, or that part of the universe where he sensibly manifests his presence to his creatures. And as the residence of earthly sovereigns is continually used to represent themselves or their authority, as in the phrases, the Sublime Porte, the court of St. James's, and a multitude of others equally familiar, so heaven, as the abode of God, is sometimes put for God himself (see Dan. 4, 26. Luke 15, 18. 21), and the *kingdom of heaven*, is precisely what Matthew elsewhere, and the other evangelists everywhere, call the kingdom of God (see above, on 3, 2. 4, 17, and compare Mark 1, 14. 15. Luke 4, 43. John 3, 3. 5. Acts 1, 3), with particular reference to its approaching restoration or erection by the hands of Christ himself, and on the principles set forth in this discourse, beginning with the pointed declaration here made, that its rights and benefits were not to be monopolized, or even shared, as a matter of course, or of prerogative by the rich, but appropriated to the poor, i. e. the poor in spirit, whether rich or poor in outward circumstances and condition.

4. Blessed (are) they that mourn : for they shall be comforted.

Another contradiction to the cherished expectations of the worldly Jews. The Messiah's kingdom, far from being regulated by existing differences of condition, would, in many instances, reverse and nullify them. What was said before of poverty, is now said of sorrow, its habitual concomitant. *Blessed*, in the same sense as above, i. e. blessed of God, or rendered happy by his favour. The verb, which is not expressed in Greek in either case, is not to be supplied in the future, but the present form, as in the English version. The declaration is not that they shall be happy, but that they are already so, in certain prospect of the coming consolation. Here again the limitation of the terms expressed in the preceding verse must be considered as implied or understood. Those *mourning*, the (ones) mourning, in a spiritual manner, both for sin and for the evils which flow from it. *They*, in the last clause, is emphatic, because not necessary to the sense in Greek as it is in English. It is therefore equivalent to *even they*, the very persons who seem now least entitled to be called or reckoned happy.

5. Blessed (are) the meek : for they shall inherit the earth.

Another popular mistake to be corrected in relation to Messiah's kingdom, was the notion that its honours and advantages were in reserve for those who could contend for them and claim them, the ambitious, arrogant, courageous class, who commonly monopolize the benefits of earthly kingdoms. In antithesis to this erroneous expectation, Christ pronounces his third blessing on a character the opposite of all this. *Blessed*, happy in the prospect of Messiah's reign, and as its chosen and most favoured subjects (*are*) *the meek*, or mild and gentle (Wiclif, *mild men*), as opposed by an apostle (1 Peter 3, 4) to a vain ostentation and connected with a quiet spirit, as of great price in the sight of God, which seems to imply that it is not so in the sight of men, who rather pity and despise than value or admire this temper. More especially is this the case, where courts and kingdoms are in question, so that prophecy makes this a characteristic point of difference between Messiah's kingdom and all others (see below, on 21, 5. and compare Zech. 9, 9.), that its sovereign was to come to it, not as a warrior and a conqueror, but as a meek and gentle man of peace. No wonder, therefore, that a kindred spirit is here represented as a preparation for the benefits and honours of that kingdom, here expressed, in accordance with the usage of the old dispensation, by inheriting the land, i. e. the land of Canaan, as the sum and local habitation of all blessings, secular and spiritual, promised to the old believers. It is unnecessary, therefore, to adopt the wider meaning (*earth*), in reference either to the universal spread of the Messiah's kingdom, or to the renovated earth as the literal and future heritage of all true Christians.

6. Blessed (are) they which do hunger and thirst after righteousness : for they shall be filled.

The fourth class, paradoxically represented as the destined heirs and subjects of Messiah's kingdom, are the hungry and thirsty, as contrasted with the rich and well supplied. As this is really a mere specification of the poverty already mentioned, by presenting in relief and in a strong light, one of its familiar incidents, we learn that these are not be regarded as precise definitions of distinct conditions which exclude each other, but as varied aspects of the same great object. The relation of the clauses is precisely similar to that in v. 3, and expresses what is only implied in the intervening verses. The first words, taken by themselves, might seem descriptive of an outward condition, that of extreme destitution even of the ordinary sources of subsistence, and a promise of relief from this, as one main purpose of the coming kingdom. But lest this should be received in too confined and low a sense, it is immediately explained by adding *righteousness*, i. e., conformity to God's will as a title to his favour, and making this the object, both grammatical and moral, of the hunger and thirst upon which our Lord had just pronounced his blessing. This remarkable construction, as well here as in v. 3, besides its rhetorical beauty, answers the important purpose of extending the beatitude to those who literally suffer, while at the same time it suggests the necessity of higher aims and of more spiritual tastes and appetites. As if he had said: 'Do not imagine that my kingdom is meant only for those now in the possession and enjoyment of abundance, to the utter exclusion of those suffering for want; it is designed for these especially, but only on condition that their hunger and their thirst extend to spiritual objects also, to conformity with God's will and experience of his favour. Those who have this hunger, whether rich or poor, shall assuredly be filled (Cranmer, *satisfied*—Rheims, *have their fill*). The last verb ($\chi o \rho \tau a \sigma \theta \eta \sigma o \nu \tau a \iota$) is applied to the older classics only to the feeding of animals, but in later Greek to that of human subjects also, and in every case with the accessory idea of full feeding or satiety. The sense here is not a different one from that which the verb has elsewhere (see below, 14, 20. 15, 33–37), though applied by a lively figure, to the satisfaction of a moral or spiritual appetite.

7. Blessed (are) the merciful: for they shall obtain mercy.

This is not a general declaration of the principle so clearly stated elsewhere, that a forgiving disposition is an indispensable condition of our own forgiveness (see below, 6, 14. 15), which would here be out of place; but a continued designation of the characters or classes, for whose benefit the kingdom was to be erected, although commonly excluded from all such advantages. The most successful and distinguished in the kingdoms of this world are too often the revengeful and implacable, the clement and forgiving being, as it were, disqualified for such distinction by this very disposition. But in my kingdom it shall not be so. Happy already, in the prospect of its prompt erection, are the merciful, the very class so shamefully neglected in all other kingdoms, but in mine to be treated according to their nature. As they have been merciful to others, so will I be merciful to them. As they have spared others, so will I spare them, and give them a distinguished place among my subjects.

8. Blessed (are) the pure in heart: for they shall see God.

There is more obscurity in this verse than in those immediately preceding, both as to the meaning of the clauses and their mutual relation, or the reason given for the benediction. *Pure in heart* (Rheims, *clean of heart*) is a phrase precisely similar to *poor in spirit* (v. 3), and determines its true construction, as the dative here (τῇ καρδίᾳ) must qualify the adjective before it, by denoting where the purity required resides, or wherein it consists. But although the words admit of only one grammatical construction, there is some diversity of judgment as to the precise sense of the whole phrase, *pure in heart*, which may be taken either specifically, as denoting freedom from particular impurities, or more generically, as denoting freedom from the polluting influence of sin. On the former, which is the more usual supposition, the particular impurity denied is commonly assumed to be what the Scriptures call *uncleanness*, comprehending all violations of the seventh commandment, in heart, speech, or behaviour. Some, however, who admit the specific import of the phrase, apply it to hypocrisy, deceit, and falsehood, and by *pure in heart* understand sincere and guileless; while a third interpretation gives it the generic sense of sinless, holy. The first, which is the usual explanation of the phrase, assumes as the necessary meaning of the word *pure* what is rather a modern limitation of its import, and is also less in keeping with the context, as we have no reason to believe, that any of Christ's hearers thought that the lascivious or incontinent would have any advantage over the modest and the chaste in his kingdom. The same objection lies in some degree against the third interpretation, as too vague and comprehensive, and as no one could imagine that impurity in this wide sense would profit them as subjects of the kingdom. The remaining sense of freedom from deceitfulness and falsehood avoids both objections, being sufficiently specific or descriptive of a particular moral quality, and that one which is too much slighted and too often outraged in the kingdoms of this world.—It may be that the cunning and the hypocritical are commonly successful, and that the honest and sincere are losers by that very quality; but I say, happy are the pure in this respect, for they shall see God. Some who understand *pure in heart* as meaning free from carnal lusts, suppose an intimate connection between that exemption and the capacity to see God, or a peculiar tendency of such sins to obscure the view of His divine perfection. But however correct this may be in point of fact, it is irrelevant in this connection, where analogy requires that this clause should assign a reason for the class in question being counted happy; and as the corresponding clauses in the five preceding verses all express in various forms the fact that those referred to shall experience the divine favour in the reign of the Messiah, the most natural interpretation of the clause before us is, that the sincere and undisguised shall stand in the divine presence as his honoured servants and the objects of his special favour. There is then no allusion to the beatific vision, or to chastity as specially preparing the soul for it, but a simple intimation that sincerity and simplicity of purpose, which often shuts men out from the service and the presence of an earthly sovereign, will in this case have the contrary effect of enabling and entitling those who practise it to *see God.*

9. Blessed (are) the peacemakers : for they shall be called the children of God.

Another current fallacy in reference to the kingdom of Messiah, was the notion that like other kingdoms it must rest on war and conquest, with the necessary consequence that those who *make war* are its most distinguished subjects, and entitled to its highest honours. Our Saviour teaches, on the contrary, that this pre-eminence belongs to the opposite character of those who *make peace,* not merely in the secondary sense of practising or cherishing it, but in the primary and proper sense of reconciling those who are at strife. Xenophon and Plutarch use the same word of ambassadors commissioned to negotiate a peace. This, while it includes the other sense of peaceable, pacific, strengthens the expression by suggesting a positive act, strongly demonstrative of such a disposition. Nothing can so clearly prove one to be peaceful in his own temper and practice as an effort to make peace or maintain it between others. The English version therefore is correct, and to be taken in its proper sense.—There is no need of assuming any definite relation between this specific character and the reward promised to it in the last clause; as if the peaceable were in any peculiar sense the sons of God. According to the context, this is only another varied statement of the fact, that those who have this character, instead of being slighted as in earthly kingdoms, shall be highly favoured. As the pure in heart shall see God, i. e. be admitted to his royal presence, so the peacemakers shall be reckoned as his sons and heirs. *Shall be called* is not a Hebrew idiom for *shall be,* but suggests the additional idea, in the present case, of oral recognition, and perhaps of formal registration. They who practise and make peace, however little honoured in the kingdoms of this world, shall be named, and accosted, and proclaimed in the kingdom of Messiah, not only as the servants but the sons of God!

10. Blessed (are) they which are persecuted for righteousness' sake : for theirs is the kingdom of heaven.

The last class mentioned, who might seem to be excluded from the honours of a kingdom, but whom Christ exalts to high distinction in His own, are *the persecuted,* those vindictively pursued by enemies superior in power. The figure, borrowed from the chase and war, denotes not simply violence, however cruel, but persistent enmity and power to indulge it. Men are not said to be persecuted by inferiors, nor with strict propriety by equals, but by those above them, as by a hostile government or ruler. This concluding macarism or beatitude may seem at first sight out of keeping with the rest, as it describes not a character but a condition arising from the act of others. But a sufficient bond of union or assimilating circumstance, is the supposed unfitness of the class described to share the honours of a mighty kingdom. As the poor, the sorrowful, the meek, the hungry, the sincere, the peaceful, are the least likely to attain distinction in an earthly state, the same may be still more emphatically said of those who are under its displeasure, nay, subjected to its persecution. Another answer to the same objection, which is merely one of form and not of substance, is that the condition mentioned in the first clause is converted into a description of character by the qualifying words that follow. The blessing is not pronounced on all who suffer persecution for whatever cause, but on those who are pursued for righteousness' sake, i. e. because of their own rectitude, or conformity to the divine will, as in v. 6 above. There can be no reference here to justification or to justice in the abstract, but to what is *right* in character and conduct, as opposed to what is *wrong*. So far are such from being shut out of the Messiah's kingdom, as the Jewish rulers might imagine in relation to their own rebellious subjects that the kingdom really belonged to them, was theirs, the same expression that had been applied already to the poor in spirit (v. 3). Thus, by a beautiful reiteration of his own expressions, he comes back to the point from which he started, in declaring for whose sake His kingdom was to be erected, or of whom it was to be composed.—Not the rich, the gay, the fierce, the full, the cunning, the warlike, or the favourites of earthly rulers, were as such, to be distinguished in His kingdom; but the poor, the sorrowful, the meek, the hungry, the sincere, the peaceful, and the persecuted, who endured all this for His sake, and who longed for spiritual no less than for secular relief.

11. Blessed are ye, when (men) shall revile you, and persecute (you), and shall say all manner of evil against you falsely, for my sake.

Thus far the macarisms have a general or abstract form, without special reference or application to the hearers. But our Lord now takes occasion, by the sudden introduction of the second person plural, to remind them that these vague propositions, as they may have seemed to them, had a specific and a proximate bearing on their own condition. This he does by repeating and applying to themselves the last benediction in the series, but by implication making the same use of all the others. Having said in general, that even the persecuted, if for doing right and not for doing wrong (compare 1 Peter 2, 20. 3, 17), are to be counted happy on account of their prospective honours in his kingdom, he turns as it were, suddenly to his disciples, in the wider sense of such as listened to his teachings with respect, and tells them that this is true of them as well as others. *Blessed are ye*, happy are you, when this is your experience. This is at once an intimation that the previous instructions are not merely theoretical but practical, and a benignant warning to his followers of what they must expect if they continued in his service. 'I speak of persecution as of something real, something known to the experience of men, and hereafter to be not unknown to yours, but entitling you to share in the blessing which I have just uttered.' *When*, &c., is in Greek a more contingent expression than in English, the verb being not in the future, but the aorist and the whole phrase approaching very near to the English, 'if they should at any time revile,' &c., but suggesting more distinctly the idea that they certainly will do so. The full sense may be thus expressed in paraphrase: 'if they ever should revile you, as they will,' &c. The form of expression is still more indefinite in Greek, where *men* is not expressed, nor even *they*, the person and number being indicated by the verbs themselves. *They* is, however, more exact than *men*, which makes the statement too generic, as relating to mankind at large; whereas the pronoun already suggests the real subject of the verbs, to wit, the unbelieving Jews, and more especially their rulers. *Revile*, reproach, abuse you, to your face, as distinguished from the backbitings afterwards referred to. *Persecute*, may either be generic, and include the other form of evil treatment mentioned in this verse; or, which agrees better with its intermediate position, a specific term, denoting acts of persecution, not expressed by either of the others, or active as distinguished from oral persecution. *All manner of evil*, literally, *every wicked word*, which last ($ῥῆμα$) is omitted by the latest critics, and by most interpreters explained as an example of the Hebrew idiom, which uses *word* as an equivalent for *thing*. But such cases, which have been unduly multiplied even in Hebrew, are extremely rare in the New Testament, and not to be assumed without necessity, which certainly has no existence here, as the strict sense is entirely appropriate, and far more expressive than the secondary and diluted one. The epithet *wicked* then applies, not to the conduct charged by the calumniator, but to the malignant calumny itself. *Falsely*, literally, *lying*, is omitted by the latest critics, but on insufficient grounds, and is necessarily implied, if not expressed. *For my sake*, because (or on account) of me, i. e. as being my disciples, or believers in my claim to the Messiahship, and therefore avowed subjects of my kingdom. Such is the treatment which he warns them to expect, as his professed followers, and such the consolation which he gives them. They must have tribulation in his service; but for that very reason he pronounces them blessed.

12. Rejoice, and be exceeding glad : for great (is) your reward in heaven : for so persecuted they the prophets which were before you.

So far was this premonition of their sufferings in his cause from requiring or justifying grief, that they were positively bound to glory and rejoice in the assurance, as he here encourages and orders them to do. *Be exceeding glad* (the adverb wanting in the older versions) is a paraphrastic version of a single word ($ἀγαλλιᾶσθε$), a Hellenistic verb, supposed by some to be made out of a Hebrew one, and often used in the

Septuagint version to represent one of the synonymous expressions for extreme joy or triumph. Combined with the ordinary Greek word for rejoicing (χαίρετε), it denotes the highest and most active exultation, as opposed to the depression and alarm, which such a prospect might naturally be expected to produce. The reason of this paradoxical command is given in the next clause. *Reward* here means compensation or indemnity for what they were to suffer, without any implication of legal merit or even moral worthiness. *In heaven*, not in a state of future blessedness, which makes the consolation too remote, but in the court or presence of God (see above, on v. 3), and in his present favour. Rejoice even in your sufferings, because there is abundant compensation in reserve for you, secured by the divine decree, and ready for you in the divine presence. The last clause may be dependent in construction, either on the first or second. On the latter supposition, it assigns a reason why their compensation would be great; on the former, an additional reason for rejoicing, namely, that they only shared the fate of the best men before them. The subject of the verb here is the same as in the first clause, to wit, the unbelieving Jews, as represented by their wicked rulers. *Those* (literally *the*) *before you* is an explanatory phrase subjoined to specify *the prophets*, though the reference is of course, and necessarily, to those who went before them, unless we assume an implied allusion to the prophets, or inspired men, who were yet to suffer. From the mention of the prophets, some infer that these words are addressed to the apostles, or to such as were to hold that office, and who might be represented as successors to the prophets. But it seems more natural to understand the prophets as the representatives of all good Jews, or of the spiritual Israel, and the priority ascribed to them as simply chronological, and not that of official succession. The sense will then be, that the followers of Christ had no cause to despond, or even to be cast down, in the prospect of inevitable suffering for his sake, since the same distresses had befallen the most pious of their predecessors, as they well knew from the history of the ancient prophets in the books of the Old Testament. Another purpose answered by this verse, besides that of direct encouragement, is that of intimating to the hearers, the connection of the new kingdom now to be established with the old theocracy or Jewish church, whose most authoritative representatives the prophets, are here mentioned as belonging to the same class and experiencing the same opposition as awaited all the followers of Christ.

13. Ye are the salt of the earth: but if the salt have lost his savour, wherewith shall it be salted? it is thenceforth good for nothing, but to be cast out, and to be trodden under foot of men.

Having now applied directly to his hearers and disciples the preceding promises and benedictions, and particularly that which had respect to persecution, our Lord takes occasion to define still more precisely the relation of his followers, as a separate body, to mankind at large. Their distinct existence, as a peculiar people, if not as an organized society, had been implied already in the warning against persecution, presupposing two antagonistic parties, and at once suggesting the inquiry, how are they related to each other? The solution of this question, far from being designed merely to indulge an idle curiosity, is strictly and immediately promotive of our Lord's main purpose in this whole discourse, which was, as we have seen, to set forth the true nature of his kingdom, and the principles on which it was to be administered. To this end it was obviously necessary that his hearers should be taught, of whom the kingdom was to be composed, and what effect it was to have upon the world around it. This is here propounded in two beautiful comparisons, or rather metaphors, derived from every-day experience, and admirably suited to illustrate the important truth to be communicated and enforced (vs. 13–16.) The first of these similitudes is given in the verse before us. *Ye*, not the apostles, of whose organization we have yet had no account, much less the Christian ministry, except so far as what is true of the whole body is emphatically true of its chief members. The immediate objects of address are still *the multitudes*, or rather *the disciples*, of the first verse, i. e. such, among his many hearers, as acknowledged his authority to teach, and received his doctrine as divinely sanctioned. The scope of the discourse is greatly narrowed, and its force impaired by making it a mere official charge, while every advantage that can be regarded as attending that mode of interpretation, is abundantly secured, without the loss of others equally important, by a simple application of the principle already stated, that the same thing which is absolutely true of all, may be specially or relatively true of some. *Ye* (or *you*) then, who now hear me, or at least so many of you as believe my teachings and profess to be my followers. This is the first trace of a distinguishing profession in the narrative, although the separation may have taken place before and only been formally recognized on this occasion. *Are*, not are to be or shall be, but already are, and that not merely in my purpose and your own destination, but in actual and present influence, implying that the sifting process had begun, and that the line was drawn between the world and the church, though not yet so expressly called. (See below, on 16, 18. 18, 17.) *Salt* is among the most familiar and necessary substances employed in common life, and therefore admirably suited to illustrate truth, for the instruction of a great mixed multitude, like that which Christ addressed on this occasion. The domestic use of salt is twofold; first, to season that which is insipid; and then, to preserve that which is corruptible. In both respects there is an obvious analogy between the physical effects of salt and the moral influence exerted by the church or the collective body of Christ's followers. They give, or ought to give, a spiritual relish or sapidity to what would otherwise be stale, flat, and unprofitable, in the knowledge, occupations, and enjoyments of mankind; and by so doing, they preserve society, or what the Scriptures call the world, from that disintegration and corruption, to which all that is human naturally tends, except so far as this destructive tendency is counteracted by the antiseptic remedies which grace employs, and among which is the influence exerted by the followers of Christ considered as *the salt of the earth*. This last expression does not imply, that salt is here referred to as a manure or fructifying substance in the processes of husbandry. The phrase *cast out*, which afterwards occurs, points rather to domestic uses, the idea naturally suggested to the mind of every reader; and the word *earth*, as in many other cases, may be put for its inhabitants, and correspond exactly to the *world* of the next verse. All this is readily suggested by the metaphor itself, as given in the first clause. But in order to prevent their looking merely at the honour and distinction necessarily implied in the position thus assigned them, he proceeds to set forth, still more fully and expressly, the responsibility and danger which accompany this eminence, employing for this purpose the same figure which he had already used, and carrying out into detail the metaphor of salt. The first clause, by itself, supposes that the salt performs its office and accomplishes its purpose; but the next suggests the possibility of failure and its necessary consequence. *But*, introducing quite a different hypothesis from that of the preceding clause, *if*, implying not a certain but a possible contingency, *the salt*, employed for either of the purposes before described, *have lost his savour*, or in modern phrase, *its taste* (Cranmer, *saltness*.) This is a paraphrastic version of a single Greek word (μωρανϑῇ), a passive verb derived from an adjective (μωρός) which commonly means *foolish* (as in v. 22 below), but is also applied to inanimate objects, in the sense of *tasteless* or *insipid*, by the same natural analogy which leads us to employ the noun *taste*, to describe both mental and bodily impressions. It matters not which of these uses is regarded as the primary, and which as the derivative. The verb, according to its etymology and form, means to deprive of sense in one case, and of taste or savour in the other; and the passive tense, here used in reference to salt, can only mean, *be made insipid, rendered tasteless*, or, to coin a single word for the occasion, *be unsalted*. There is no need of appealing to the fact, alleged by travellers, that large masses of such saltless salt have been actually met with in the east. The force of the comparison does not depend upon the literal occurrence of such changes, but is rather enhanced by their supposed impossibility. Even supposing that salt cannot lose its savour, and that its doing so is merely mentioned as a monstrous and imaginary case, it only serves the better to illustrate the contingency, here meant to be suggested, of a body or society created to preserve and season all around it, and itself becoming destitute of what it was intended and commanded to impart to others. The question which follows has been variously interpreted. Tyndale's version (*what can be salted therewith?*), and Cranmer's (*what shall be seasoned therewith?*), not only weaken, but entirely change the sense, and are wholly ungrammatical, without an arbitrary change of text (τί for ἐν τίνι.) The Geneva Bible renders it, *wherewith shall one salt?* (or, as it might have been translated more exactly, *wherewith shall be salted?*) i. e. if the salt have lost its saltness, what can be substituted for it in the seasoning of food or in its preservation? This is a possible construction and a good sense, but less striking and emphatic than the one extracted from the words by the oldest and most usual interpretation, which makes salt itself the subject of the verb, and understands the question to be, what shall season it, when it has lost its savour? *Wherewith*, literally *in what*, i. e. in (the use of) what (means)? *Shall it be* is not so strong as *can it be*, but more expressive, as the impossibility is really suggested by the certain futurity. What never will be virtually never can be. The inevitable answer, Nothing, is more forcible when left to be supplied, than if it were expressed. But in the last clause it is amplified and carried out in positive expressions, which apply directly to the salt, but more remotely to the person or the body which it represents. *Thenceforth*, literally, *yet*, still, longer, i. e. after it has lost its saltness. *Good for nothing*, the phrase used in all the English versions, but the oldest (Wiclif, *to nothing it is worth over*) is an idiomatic or proverbial expression, not exactly corresponding to the form of the original, which strictly means not *good* but *strong*, suggesting the idea not of worth or value merely, but of strength or efficacy. *It avails* (ἰσχύει) *for nothing more*. This negation is made still more striking by a sort of ironical exception in the last clause. *But* (not δέ or ἀλλά, but εἰ μή), except, if not, *to be cast out*, &c. It is only good enough and strong enough to be thrown away, and instead of being used, *to be trampled on*, or trodden under foot. *Of* (i. e. *by*) *men*, does not seem to be emphatic, unless the definite expression, *the men*, be supposed to mean the very men who might have used it or did actually use it till it lost its savour. The allusion, which some find here, to the formal degradation of unworthy ministers, supposes a restricted application of the passage, which has been already shown to be untenable, and is only true as a particular example of the general truth taught, that when the church, or any of its members, fail to exercise the salutary influence for which they were created, they become not only absolutely worthless, but just objects of contempt to those who ought to have revered them, and been benefited by them.

14. Ye are the light of the world. A city that is set on a hill cannot be hid.

To the metaphor of *salt* is now added that of *light*, a still more essential element of comfort in domestic life. The form of the declaration is the same as in v. 13, with the single change of *earth* to *world*. The Greek word (κόσμος), which primarily signifies order or symmetrical arrangement, is applied to the structure and harmonious system of the universe (as in 13, 35. 24, 21 below); then to that part of it which man inhabits (as in 4, 8 above); and by a natural metonymy to men themselves, as in the case before us. There is no prominence here given (as in John 17, 9. 14, and often elsewhere) to the fact that this world is a wicked world, though really implied or presupposed. The main idea is that of mankind or of human society, of which our

Lord declares his followers to be *the light*. In this, as in the other case, the reference is not to recondite or latent but to obvious and familiar points of correspondence. The thought necessarily suggested to the mass of hearers would be that of communicating knowledge, rectifying error, and dispelling the gloom which is inseparable from a state of spiritual ignorance, implying alienation from the only source of truth and goodness. This office was to be performed, this influence exerted, by the followers of Christ, as individuals and as a body. But again, as in the former case, the simple lesson, taught by the similitude itself, is amplified and guarded against all abuse, by carrying the illustration out into detail. What is thus added is essentially the same in either case, to wit, that the agency which fails of its effect is worthless. Salt, in order to be valuable, must have saltness. Light, in order to be valuable, must be seen. The illuminating influence of Christ's disciples is a nullity without actual diffusion upon their part, and actual perception on the part of others. To claim the character without acting in accordance with it, were as foolish as to build a town upon a hill and then expect it to be unseen. Its position is designed to make it more conspicuously visible, and any thing at variance with this design is not only inconsistent but self-contradictory and suicidal. It is in vain, therefore, for the church or any part of it, in theory or practice, to repudiate the very end for which it was established. If it is not a visible and bright church, it is not a church at all. *Set on an hill* is better rendered in the Rhemish version, *situated on a mountain*. The first word strictly means *lying*, and the last word is applied to the highest as well as to the lowest elevations, which is not the modern usage of the English *hill*. The opinion of some writers, that our Saviour had particular allusion to the lofty situation of the city Saphet, then perhaps in full view, is refuted by the fact that it was not yet built. It is moreover perfectly gratuitous, and most improbable, that all or any of our Saviour's illustrations of divine truth were suggested, as it were, at random, by fortuitous and unexpected sights or sounds. It is enough that they were drawn from real and familiar life, without ascribing to them an impromptu character, which might perhaps do credit to the genius of an uninspired teacher, but which only detracts from the honour of omniscience.

15. Neither do men light a candle, and put it under a bushel, but on a candlestick: and it giveth light unto all that are in the house.

The preceding illustration drawn from a city on a mountain, by its very beauty and sublimity, departs from the domestic character of what had just been said in reference to salt. From this momentary deviation the discourse is now brought back by the addition of a second illustration, to the same effect with that just given, but derived from rdinary household habits. The essential meaning still is that an object, which exists in order to be seen, must be seen, or it fails of its effect, and might as well not be at all. The illustration here is from the obvious absurdity of lighting a candle and then hiding it from view. *Neither* connects it with the last clause of v. 14, as another negative proposition of the same kind but distinct in form. As if he had said, 'equally unheard of is it in domestic life to light,' &c. *Men* is here put indefinitely, as in v. 11, for the simple pronoun *they*, which is continually so used in colloquial English, as a succedaneum for the French *on* and the German *man* (on dit, man sagt, they say), which last is identical in origin with *men*, as here used in the English Bibles. *Light*, the Greek verb usually rendered *burn*, but sometimes causative in meaning (make burn, kindle). *Candle*, a word denoting any movable artificial light, whether candle, lamp, or lantern, any of which terms may represent it, though the first is entitled to the preference from long familiarity. The corresponding Greek word in the next clause is related to this, as *candlestick* to *candle*, *lamp-stand* to *lamp*, although nothing is gained by the substitution of the latter. *Put* (or *place*), not on any one occasion but habitually, it is not the custom of men so to do. *The bushel*, or in Greek *the modius*, with the definite article to designate the measure found in every house as one of its utensils. The precise capacity of that here mentioned is of no importance. That it really came nearer to our *peck* than our *bushel*, can have no effect upon the meaning of the passage, which would be the same if the word used had been *basket, box,* or *bed* (as it is in Mark 4, 21). The point of comparison is not the size but the concealing power of the subject, so that the dimensions of the modius are of as little exegetical importance as those of the bed. *A candlestick*, or more exactly, the candlestick, i. e. the one found of course in every house, not only in the East but elsewhere. *And* (then, in that case, when put into its proper place), *it giveth light*, a single word in Greek, the theme or root of the noun *lamp*, which may be here translated *shines*, as the same verb is in v. 22, and 17, 2 below, and several times elsewhere. Stripped of its figurative dress, the meaning of the verse is, that as Christ's disciples are to be a source or channel of divine and saving knowledge to the world, they must not endeavour to defeat the very end of their existence by concealing or withholding what they have received, not only for themselves but for the benefit of others.

16. Let your light so shine before men, that they may see your good works, and glorify your Father which is in heaven.

The original order of the words, disturbed by Tyndale, has been partially preserved in the Rhemish version (*so let your light shine*), and still more perfectly by Wiclif, although scarcely in accordance with our idiom (*so shine your light*). *So* is not to be construed merely with what follows (so as, so that), but with what precedes, *thus*, likewise. As men do with lamps or candles in their houses, so must you do with the light of truth in this dark world,

Your light, in the tropical or moral sense, represented in the context by the literal material light of lamps or candles. 'So let the saving knowledge you possess be spread abroad to others also.' *Before*, i. e. before their faces, not behind their backs, or wholly out of sight, as if a lighted candle should be covered with a peck or bushel measure. *The men*, i. e. other men, or more specifically, those within your reach, or under your immediate influence. The last clause urges a new motive for so doing in addition to that drawn from the very nature and design both of material and moral light. That it was light, was enough to show that men must see it or they could not profit by it. But a higher reason for the same thing is presented. By a beautiful transition we are led, through a laudable regard to our own credit, up to the ultimate and most coercive principle of action. *That they may see your good* (fair, beautiful, fine) *works* (or actions). This undoubtedly implies that we are not to do good, as a general rule, by stealth, but with a view to being seen by others; and that in this sense a regard to character or reputation is not only lawful, but incumbent upon all disciples. Lest, however, they should rest in this as the supreme end to be aimed at, he defines this end in the closing words by adding, *and may glorify your Father* (*the one*) *in heaven*, literally, *in the heavens* (see above, on v. 3), as distinguished from all earthly fathers or superiors whatever. The term *Father* tenderly suggests the new and intimate relation which was to exist through Christ himself, between his followers, and that God who without his intervention is not only inaccessible to man but "a consuming fire." (Heb. 12, 29. See below, on 6, 9.) *Glorify*, a Greek verb derived from a noun which originally means *opinion*, whence the verb in classical Greek usage means to think or to be of opinion. But as the noun acquired the more specific sense of the opinion entertained by one man of another, and especially a favourable, flattering opinion, admiration, reputation, fame, or glory; so the verb, in Hellenistic usage, means to promote or propagate this glory. When applied to God, as it usually is in the New Testament (compare 6, 2 with 9, 8. 15, 31), it means to give him glory, in the only intelligible sense of that expression, not to make him glorious in himself, which is impossible, but in the sight of creatures, by acknowledging and praising him as glorious. Thus the Saviour winds up this division of his great discourse, by leading his disciples through the homeliest and most familiar every-day analogies of common life, to the sublime and final end of all action and of all existence

17. Think not that I am come to destroy the law, or the prophets: I am not come to destroy, but to fulfil.

In opposition to the notion entertained by some, that this is an abrupt transition, and that no connection can be traced with the foregoing context, either because Christ spoke incoherently, or because the words were never uttered in this order; there is no need of insisting on a formal logical progression in the thought, as some have done, and thereby been betrayed into a forced and disingenuous construction of the passage. The association of ideas, if there is one, must be on the surface, not concealed beneath it, and it seems to be afforded by the phrase *good works* in the preceding sentence. Down to that clause, the allusion seemed to be to knowledge rather than to practice, and by letting their light shine the disciples might have understood exclusively the diligent diffusion of the truth in their possession. This is undoubtedly the primary import of the figure, but our Saviour, with consummate wisdom, guards against the natural proclivity to rest in speculative wisdom or divorce it from its natural effect upon the life and conduct, by introducing, as a necessary part of the illumination which they were to practise, the exhibition of a luminous example, *so that men may see your good works and* (by them be led to) *glorify your Father in heaven.* This reference to *good works,* as a necessary means of glorifying God, in the new as well as in the old economy, would naturally raise a question as to their mutual relation, and particularly as to the continued force of the Mosaic law under the reign of the Messiah. Now to this point, we have reason to believe, related one of the most prevalent and dangerous delusions of the day, to do away with which was a main design of the discourse before us. This was the idea, natural in all such cases, and often actually reproduced in revolutionary times, both civil and religious, that the new régime would bring with it, not merely the correction of abuses, but a change of moral principles, a relaxation of the claims of justice, and a greater license of indulgence in things hitherto forbidden. This spirit of libertinism, which was afterwards revived in the period of the Reformation, and again in that of the French Revolution, is the natural spontaneous growth of man's aversion to restraint, promoted by a no less natural confounding of restraints imposed by human tyranny with those imposed by divine authority.* As human nature is the same in every age and country, it is not surprising that this Antinomian delusion should have mingled with the Jewish hopes of the Messiah's advent, or that Christ should have devoted to its refutation an extensive space in this great exposition of the nature of his kingdom, beginning with the verse before us. *Think not* implies a disposition so to think, and may therefore be considered an implicit confirmation of the previous statement as to the existence of the error here referred to. *That I came,* when I appeared among you as "a teacher come from God." (John 3, 2.) A direct allusion to his Messianic office is less probable so early in his ministry, although that sense would necessarily be put upon his words by his disciples at a later period, as in other cases where we are expressly told that what he said was not fully understood till rendered clear to them by subsequent events.†

* An instance of the same thing may be seen among ourselves, in the almost frantic opposition of some foreign residents to the protection of the Sabbath, as an imposition perfectly analogous to those from which they have escaped in Europe.

† See for instance John 2, 22, "When therefore he was risen from the dead, his disciples remembered that he had said this unto them, and they believed the Scripture and the word which Jesus had said."

Came to destroy, a combination of the finite and infinitive familiar to our idiom, in which the second verb defines the end or object of the first. In this connection, the whole phrase relates to the design of the Messiah's advent, and by parity of reasoning, to the principles or nature of his kingdom. *Destroy,* so rendered also elsewhere in this gospel (see below, on 26, 61. 27, 40), is in Greek peculiarly expressive, as originally signifying dissolution or disintegration, the destruction of a whole by the complete separation of its parts, as when a house is taken down by being taken to pieces, the very act denoted by the verb in the passage just cited. In the same sense, but with a figurative application, Paul employs it to describe the dissolution of the body (2 Cor. 5, 1), and of a system of belief and practice (Gal. 2, 18), which last is precisely its use here. *To destroy the law* is not to break it, in the way of personal transgression, which would be otherwise expressed, as it is elsewhere (Rom. 3, 23. 25. 27), but to abrogate (or as Wiclif says, *undo*) it, as a whole and as a system. *The law* would of course be understood to mean the law of Moses, under which they lived, and from the restraints of which the class here addressed were longing to be free. That it does not mean the ceremonial law, as such, or as distinguished from the moral law, is evident, not only from the want of any such distinction, which is therefore wholly arbitrary and gratuitous, but also from the words expressly added, *or the prophets,* which may either mean the prophets in the strict sense, as expounders of the law, or more indefinitely, all the inspired writers of the Old Testament, by whom, and not exclusively by Moses, the law, as the expression of the will of God, had been revealed to Israel. The disjunctive (*or*) is not, as some explain it, here equivalent to *and*, but has its proper force, expressing an alternative negative, 'neither in the narrower nor in the wider sense, the law as originally given by Moses, or as afterwards expounded in the later Scriptures.' Not content with warning them against this error, he solemnly propounds the corresponding truth, both in a negative and positive form. *I am not come,* the same verb that occurs in the first clause (ἦλθον), and which strictly signifies *I came,* i. e. when I appeared officially among you, and began my public ministry; or possibly there may be a remoter reference to his incarnation and nativity, of which he elsewhere speaks as his coming forth from the Father (John 16, 28). In either case the phrase describes the object of his Messianic work and mission, which was *not to destroy* (in the sense before explained) *but to fulfil.* The object of the verbs is suppressed, not only because it is so easily supplied from the preceding clause, but because the proposition here is a more general one. He did not come to abrogate the law or the prophets; for the end and design of his whole work was not destructive but completory. *Fulfil,* from its restricted use in English, is less ambiguous than the Greek verb, which usually means to *fill* or *fill up* (see above on 1, 22. 2, 15. 17. 23. 3, 15. 4, 14), either in a literal or figurative sense. Its precise sense here must be determined by the obvious antithesis or contrast to *destroy.* As that does not mean simply to transgress or violate, so this cannot simply mean to *keep* or *obey.*

And as that means to abrogate or undo the whole system, this must mean the opposite, not only to continue its existence, but in some sense to perfect or complete it. This fulfilling of the law, however, may be either subjective or objective, the supplying of omissions and defects in the law itself; or the supplying of omissions and defects in its observance or its execution. The first of these ideas is at variance with the nature of the law, as a divine revelation and economy, as well as with the uniform teaching of both Testaments.* Even as an expression of God's will for a temporary purpose, it cannot be called imperfect or defective; for it is of that expression that the Scriptures predicate perfection. To complete the law, then, cannot mean to make it better, but to cause it to be better kept and carried out, which is the very thing required by the connection, as our Lord is combating the false idea, that the law would be relaxed or disregarded in the kingdom of the Messiah.

18. For verily, I say unto you, Till heaven and earth pass, one jot or one tittle shall in no wise pass from the law, till all be fulfilled.

Not only was the mission of our Lord completory and not destructive in its end or purpose, but the law itself, as the expression of God's will which is immutable, must be essentially perpetual and constant. This proposition is co-ordinate to that in the last clause of v. 17, and not dependent on it; so that the *for* assigns another reason why they should not think he came to abrogate the law, to wit, because it was not, in the sense which they attached to the word *destroy*, susceptible of abrogation. This is not simply stated in didactic form, but solemnly propounded as a most important principle, with all the authority belonging to the speaker as a teacher come from God. *Amen*, here translated *verily* (or *truly*), is a Hebrew adjective, originally meaning *sure* or *certain*, but employed as an ejaculatory particle of assent or concurrence, at the close or in the intervals of prayers, benedictions, curses, vows, or other forms of a religious kind, when uttered by one or more persons in the name of others. (Num. 5, 22. Deut. 27, 15. 1 Kings 1, 36. 1 Chr. 16, 36. Ps. 106, 48. Jer. 28, 6. Matt. 6, 13. 1 Cor. 14, 16. Rev. 5, 14. 22. 20.) But besides these cases, and some others where the word is retained without translation, there are many more in which it is translated *verily*, and stands not at the end but the beginning of a sentence. This is one of the most marked characteristics of our Saviour's manner which have been preserved to us, especially by John, who always writes it twice, a form not found in any of the other gospels. In the case before us, as in others, it invites attention to the following words as uttered on divine authority, and therefore truth itself. The same idea is often expressed

---

* Compare Ps. 19, 7 (the law of the Lord is perfect, converting the soul) with Rom. 7, 12 (the law is holy and the commandment holy and just and good).

in the Old Testament by a divine oath. *I say unto you* is an expressive formula, too often overlooked as pleonastic, but containing two emphatic pronouns. I, the Son of God, and yet the Son of man, declare to you, my hearers and disciples. The declaration thus impressively announced is, that the law shall never cease to be authoritative and obligatory. This idea is expressed by a comparison, familiar to the style of the Old Testament, with the frame of nature or the constitution of the universe, a standing emblem of immutability. The meaning cannot be that as the heavens and the earth shall one day be destroyed, so the law shall then be nullified, but not till then. Such an assurance, even if it could be naturally thus expressed, would be irrelevant in this connection, the whole drift of which requires an absolute assertion of immutability. The changes which the universe is yet to undergo are either left entirely out of view, or reckoned as mere changes of its form without annihilation of its substance, and therefore not unfitting it to be the emblem of unchanging perpetuity. *Pass*, or more exactly, go by, pass away, become invisible, and by implication cease to be. *Jot or tittle*, in the oldest editions of King James's Bible written *iote and title*, are expressions borrowed from the art of writing, and peculiarly appropriate in speaking of a written law, not even the minutest point of which should fail of its effect or be abolished without answering its purpose. As we in such a case might say, not a word, syllable, or letter, so the ancients said not an iota, the smallest Greek letter, corresponding to the Hebrew yod, from which it also takes its name. The other word (κεραία), translated *tittle*, properly denotes a little horn, but is applied to the minute points and projections by which similar letters are distinguished. *In no wise*, or by no means, not at all, is an intensive or emphatic formula, here used to represent the double negative in Greek (οὐ μή), which instead of cancelling enhances the negation. *Pass* (pass away) *from the law*, i. e. cease to be a part of it, or be obliterated from it. This is a natural hyperbole, which every reader understands at once as meaning that the law shall abide in its integrity without the least deduction from its actual contents and substance as a well-known systematic whole. That this is the true meaning of the strong expressions, is apparent from what follows. *until all be fulfilled* (or done, come to pass, or happen). Not literally every point and stroke of the writing, which are separately insusceptible of such fulfilment, but the whole law as a system, without any derogation or deduction from its absolute completeness. We have here another proof that to destroy and to fulfil in the preceding verse do not mean to obey and to transgress particular precepts, but to perpetuate or abrogate the law considered as a whole. Divested of its peculiar form, and intended to arouse attention and enforce the truth, our Saviour's declaration is that the law, from which they hoped to be delivered, should remain in its integrity and undiminished force, until its purpose was accomplished. This last phrase seems to solve the question how these strong expressions could be predicated of the ceremonial law, which was to be and was abolished by Messiah's advent. That peculiar system was a sensible and temporary form of the divine law, not the law itself, so that its abrogation when its purpose had been answered was a part of the fulfilment here predicted, not a deviation from it or a contradiction of it. It must be also observed, in explanation of this point, that Christ is evidently rectifying errors in regard to something deeper and of more intrinsic moment than the ceremonial law. He is refuting the erroneous and most dangerous impression, that the change of dispensations was a change not only of external institutions but of moral principles, in opposition to which error he declares that these can never change.

19. Whosoever therefore shall break one of these least commandments, and shall teach men so, he shall be called the least in the kingdom of heaven: but whosoever shall do, and teach (them), the same shall be called great in the kingdom of heaven.

This is a practical and personal improvement of the principles just laid down, which might otherwise have been considered merely speculative, or at least without immediate bearing on the characters and lives of individuals. Our Saviour thus far has been speaking of the law as a whole or as a system, and of his own relation to it as an abrogater or fulfiller. But the immutability of God's law could not be a matter of indifference to those who heard him, and he now applies it in the most explicit manner. *Therefore*, since the law can never lose its binding force. *Whosoever* (or in modern phrase, *whoever*), without any personal distinction or exception. *Shall break* is in Greek a more contingent phrase (ὃς ἐὰν λύσῃ), whoever may (at any time), &c. *Break*, the simple verb, of which a compound occurs twice in v. 17, where it is rendered by *destroy*. The essential idea is still that of loosening and dissolving, but without the preposition (*down*), suggesting the idea of a structure taken down or pulled to pieces. We are not therefore to identify the two verbs, and make that here used mean likewise to annul or abrogate the system. This is also forbidden by the express mention of a single precept as the thing dissolved, and not of the whole law or congeries of precepts, as in v. 17. The only dissolution that can be affirmed of one such precept is its violation by the individual, so that the term *break*, used in all the English versions, is correct, although the same word would be incorrect in rendering the compound verb before employed. We are not to overlook the exact use of *precepts* or *commandments*, as distinguished from the whole law. *Least*, not in compass or external form, which sense has been applied by some to the Decalogue or Ten Commandments, as the summary or basis of the whole law, an idea just the opposite of that conveyed to every unsophisticated reader, who can only understand by least commandments those of least importance either really or in the estimation of mankind. But however little in itself or in proportion to the whole law, if it really form part of it, the obligation to obey it is complete, and its wilful violation is a virtual violation of the whole, according to the apostolic dictum, that he who offends in one point is guilty of all (Jas. 2, 10). *And teach men so*, by precept or example leading others into the same false depreciation of the law, or even of what seem to be its least important precepts, as no longer binding in the kingdom of Messiah. That this last is the idea necessarily implied though not expressed, is clear from the form of the penalty denounced, which is not that he shall perish or be cast forth into outer darkness, but that he *shall be called* (i. e. recognized, described as being, see above, on v. 9) *least in the kingdom of heaven*, i. e. under the new dispensation or the reign of the Messiah (see above, on v. 3). The reference is therefore not to soul-destroying error or to absolute rejection of the truth, but to theoretical and practical offences which might be committed by those waiting for the kingdom, or admitted to it. Such an offender shall be justly designated *least*, not *the least*, in comparison with every other, but one of the least, belonging to the lowest class of those who are in any sense the subjects of Messiah's reign. This form of expression would be wholly unaccountable and unintelligible if we did not know from the preceding context, that our Lord is combating erroneous views upon the part of some who were impatiently expecting the Messiah and a simultaneous relaxation or entire abrogation of the law, as the rule of human duty. Such are here admonished that by the slighting even the minutest precept of the law, they would certainly degrade themselves to the lowest rank in that kingdom where they hoped to be pre-eminent. Their admission to it is assumed or presupposed, the alternative of salvation or perdition being not at all in question. If it had been, our Lord would not have represented them as least in the kingdom, but as utterly shut out of it. The last clause is the converse of the one before it, adding emphasis and clearness to the solemn affirmation. *Great*, i. e. one of a superior rank, corresponding to the indefinite superlative before used.

20. For I say unto you, That except your righteousness shall exceed (the righteousness) of the Scribes and Pharisees, ye shall in no case enter into the kingdom of heaven.

The discourse now takes a wide step in advance, and enters on a new and spacious field, but by a natural and obvious transition from the previous context. Thus far the Saviour had been speaking of the law and of its precepts, as they were in themselves, without any reference to the form under which his hearers were familiar with them, and on which their views of the divine law must be founded. This peculiar form had been imparted to the law by the traditional accretions and the superstitious practice of the Pharisees, the great prevailing sect or party (see above, on 3, 7), and the official or professional instructions of the Scribes, the leaders of that party and the spiritual guides of the people (see above, on 2, 4). They were ostensibly the strictest moralists, and much of the intolerable burden under which the people groaned, arose from their unauthorized additions to the law which their followers confounded with the law itself. These naturally looked upon the Scribes and Pharisees as too good, "righteous overmuch" (Ecc. 7, 16), and hoped for a new state of things, in which this irksome and excessive righteousness would be dispensed with. But our Lord here warns them that instead of having less they must have more of this conformity to right and to the will of God, than any of their spiritual guides, and that as a condition not only of pre-eminence but even of admission to the kingdom. Here is the point of contact or connection with the previous context. He had told them who should be called *least* and *great* in the Messiah's kingdom. He now tells them who should be admitted to it or excluded from it. That the violator even of the least divine command should take a low place in the kingdom, was sufficiently alarming to these Antinomian expectants of Messiah's advent. But immeasurably more so was the declaration that instead of being freed from the intolerable task of trying to be righteous, they must be more righteous than the very Scribes and Pharisees themselves, or forfeit all participation in the blessings of the coming change. As if a Popish devotee should now be told that instead of looking to the supererogatory merits of his holiest superiors to eke out his own defects, he must surpass them all in holiness himself. The form of expression is intentionally paradoxical, requiring explanation of the terms before it could be fully or correctly understood. The *prima facie* meaning seemed to be, that they must imitate the Scribes and Pharisees, and go beyond them in the same direction, or they could not be admitted to the kingdom. The meaning, as afterwards explained, was that the Pharisees and Scribes, instead of having too much, had too little, nay, had nothing, of the quality required, so that instead of trying to be like them, they must seek in this respect to be as different as possible. *For* connects this sentence with the declarations in the three preceding verses. *I say unto you*, although without the *verily* of v. 18, gives solemnity and form to the expression. *Righteousness* is not to be taken in any technical or abstruse sense, but as simply meaning rectitude, conformity to some acknowledged standard, which with all Jews was the real or supposed will of God. There is no question here as to the method of salvation, or the Christian doctrine of justification, but simply as to a participation in the reign of the Messiah. *Shall exceed*, the same expression as v. 19, which might be rendered more exact by omitting the auxiliary verb. Tyndale's version (*exceed*), retained by all the Protestant translators, is inferior in strength not only to the Greek but to the Vulgate and its copyists in English (Wiclif, *be more plenteous than*. Rheims, *abound more than*). Their righteousness must be abundant absolutely, and also in comparison with the Scribes and Pharisees. *In no case*, the same Greek form (οὐ μή) that occurs in v. 18, and is there translated *in no wise*.

21. Ye have heard that it was said by them of old time, Thou shalt not kill; and whosoever shall kill shall be in danger of the judgment.

Having said in general, that the customary or prevailing righteousness, exemplified and sanctioned by the Scribes and Pharisees, was insufficient to secure admission into the kingdom of Messiah, our Lord proceeds to show this in detail, by contrasting the Pharisaic doctrine as to several most familiar sins, with his own requisitions in regard to the same matters, the result of the comparison in each case being, that the standard of morality in his church or kingdom would be vastly higher than among the strictest Jewish moralists of that day, so that no man need resort to him in the hope of greater license or indulgence as to moral duties. This important head of the discourse extending to the close of the fifth chapter, is subdivided by the different sins, which are successively brought into view, as differently treated by the Pharisaic and the Christian ethics. These are murder (vs. 21–26), adultery (vs. 27–30), unauthorized divorce (vs. 31. 32), unlawful oaths (vs. 33–37), revenge (38–42), hatred (vs. 43–48). Common to all these subdivisions is the general idea running through them, that the sins enumerated would be still more strictly censured and forbidden in the new than in the old theocracy. There is also a general similarity of form, without punctilious and unnecessary sameness, the method being to present first the Jewish theory and practice as to each particular, and then the Christian in emphatic contrast. Some of the formulas, employed alike in every case, will of course need only to be once explained, to wit, when they first occur, leaving merely what is new or peculiar to be subsequently noticed. *Ye have heard*, not the perfect but the aorist ($\dot{\eta}\kappa o \acute{\upsilon} \sigma \alpha \tau \epsilon$), which, according to the theory and strict rule of Greek syntax, means *ye heard* (or *did hear*) at a given time, but is often employed, even in the classics, and still more in Hellenistic usage, to denote an act repeated or continued to the present time, especially in verbs which have no perfect tense in common use. The idea here suggested evidently is, that they had often or habitually heard it, and not merely once for all, on some particular occasion. The reference, which might be to mere minor or colloquial information, is determined by the context to the hearing of official or professional instruction. They had often heard it from the Scribes and Pharisees, already mentioned as their standards and exemplars of true righteousness or goodness; what follows, therefore, is the customary representation, whether true or false, of these acknowledged leaders. *It was said* (or *spoken*), in the way of a command, as appears from the words quoted. That it was so said, is not here affirmed directly either by our Lord or the evangelist, but given as an affirmation of the Scribes and Pharisees, familiar to the hearers upon this occasion. *Them of old time*, an unnecessary circumlocution representing two Greek words which simply mean *the ancients*, here referring to the fathers of the nation, and especially to that generation which received the law through Moses. The original expression never denotes personal age (Acts 21, 16 being only an apparent exception), much less official dignity or eldership, but always a relation to some former period or previous state of things; as *the ancient prophets*, i. e. those of the Old Testament (Luke 9, 8. 19); *the old world*, namely, that before the flood (2 Pet. 2, 5); *the old (things)*, the state of man before conversion (2 Cor. 5, 17); *the old* (or ancient) *serpent*, i. e. the same that figures in primeval history (Rev. 12, 9. 20, 2); to which may be added the adverbial phrase, *from ancient days*, or *generations* (Acts 15, 7. 21). This determinate usage is sufficient by itself to condemn the construction put upon the clause before us in the text of our translation (*by them of old time*), and to recommend that of the older English versions (*to them*), now omitted or found only in the margin. For by what *ancients* could this be said to have been uttered? The Scribes would never have attributed the precept to the whole body of the people, or applied the term *ancients* either to Moses or to God himself; while its application to contemporary *elders* is not only contrary to usage, but involves the incongruity of making these elders cite themselves. 'Ye have heard (from the elders) that it has been said by the elders.' But apart from these considerations, this construction is precluded by the fact, that in every other case where the same passive form is followed by the dative, that case denotes not the speaker but the hearer. Rom. 9, 12, it was said *unto her* (ἐρρήθη αὐτῇ)—ib. v. 26—it was said *unto them* (ἐρρήθη αὐτοῖς)—Gal. 3, 16—*to* Abraham were spoken the promises—Rev. 6, 11. it was said *unto them*—Rev. 9, 4—it was commanded them, literally, said *unto them*. According to this usage, which is uniform and constant, the words now before us can only mean, *it was said to the ancients*, i. e. to the generation which received the law (Acts 7, 53). This was probably a formula in common use among the Scribes and rabbies when they made a quotation from the law of Moses. *Thou shalt not kill*, the sixth commandment, here recorded in the words of the Septuagint version (Ex. 20, 13). *And* or *but* (δέ) introduces something added to the simple precept in the way of comment or interpretation, either by the Scribes and Pharisees themselves, or a part of the original legislation as reported by them. In the former case the phrase, *it was said unto the ancients*, extends only to the precept as it stands in the decalogue. 'It was said of old, thou shalt not kill, and we say in accordance with it, he that kills, etc.' On the other supposition, both these clauses are described as part of the original command, preserved in the Oral law or "tradition of the elders" (see below, on 15, 2). The latter is in perfect keeping with the doctrine and the practice of the Pharisees, but not the necessary meaning of the language, nor perhaps the most obvious in this connection. As to the words themselves, thus added to the sixth commandment, whether by tradition of the elders or by later Pharisaic comment, they are either an unmeaning paraphrase, in which case they would hardly have been quoted, or an exposition of the sense in which the precept was to be applied. The only way in which the latter supposition can be justified is by laying stress upon the verb in its precise sense, which is that of murder or malicious homicide, as in the Hebrew of the sixth commandment. The whole may then be paraphrased as follows. 'You have (often) heard (it said by the Scribes and leading Pharisees), that our fathers were commanded not to murder, and that consequently only he who murders (in the strict sense of the term) is liable to be condemned and punished under this commandment.' This agrees not only with the obvious import of the terms and with the previous connection, but presents exactly such a limitation of the precept as our Lord appears to combat in the next verse. *Shall kill* is too categorical a form, like those in vs. 19. 20, and might be translated more exactly *may kill*, or still better by the simple present (*kills*) which is often used contingently in modern English, and is so used by our own translators in the next verse (*whosoever is angry*), although not to represent the same original construction. *Shall be*, on the other hand, exactly represents the next verb, which is future (ἔσται). *In danger of*, obnoxious, liable, exposed to, the original expression primarily signifying *held in*, and then *bound by*, with particular reference in usage to judicial or forensic obligation. There is no need of giving to *the judgment* here its highest sense of final and eternal condemnation, or its lowest of a local secular tribunal. Far more obvious and suited to the context is the usual and wide sense of judicial process, without specification of the time, place, or form, in which it is conducted. ' Whoever murders (and no other) shall be liable to trial and conviction in due course of law.'

22. **But I say unto you, That whosoever is angry with his brother without a cause shall be in danger of the judgment : and whosoever shall say to his brother, Raca, shall be in danger of the council : but whosoever shall say, Thou fool, shall be in danger of hell-fire.**

Having stated the traditional or Pharisaic gloss upon the sixth commandment, which restricted it to actual malicious homicide, our Lord now gives his own far wider and more stringent exposition of the same law, reaching beyond the overt act to the malignant dispositions out of which it springs. *But I say unto you*, in opposition not to the Mosaic precept, but to this unauthorized confinement of its prohibitions to the ultimate result of murderous affections. *Whosoever is angry*, or retaining the peculiar form of the original, *every (one) angered* (or *enraged*). The qualifying adverb (εἰκῇ) usually means in the New Testament *in vain*, i. e. without effect, to no purpose (Rom. 13, 4. 1 Cor. 15, 2. Gal. 3, 4. 4, 11); but in one other place at least (Col. 2, 18), it has the sense in which Polybius and Xenophon employ it, to wit, idly, inconsiderately, causelessly, unreasonably. The Vulgate and its followers omit it here entirely, in which they are sustained by the latest critics, who suppose it to have been introduced by certain copyists, in order to avoid an absolute condemnation of all anger, which is inconsistent both with apostolic precept (Eph. 4, 26) and with Christ's example (Mark 3, 5). It would seem to follow, therefore, that the limitation is implied if not expressed, which makes the textual variation exegetically unimportant. The truth, however, is that the question here is not between a groundless and a reasonable anger, but between all anger, as an inward affection of the mind, and its outward manifestation in unlawful acts of violence. As if he had said, men are to be judged, not only by their murderous acts, but by their murderous feelings. This is directly stated in the first clause, and then indirectly in the others, where instead of anger itself, we have natural and usual expressions of it in abusive and contemptuous language. This essential import of the terms is not affected by the specific sense attached to each, although the obvious and common explanations are no doubt the best. *Racha* (which Wiclif renders *fy*) is probably an Aramaic word (רֵיק or רֵיקָא), meaning vain, empty, which occurs in the later Jewish books as an expression of contempt. *Fool* is used for the same purpose in all languages, evincing pride of intellect to be an universal passion. There is no need, therefore, of attaching to the term the peculiar sense ascribed to corresponding Hebrew words, in which wickedness and folly seem to be identified. The whole question as to the specific import of these terms is without exegetical importance, as the meaning meant to be conveyed is simply, that the sixth commandment, as interpreted by Christ, forbids, not only the extreme act of murder, but the anger which impels to it, and the words by which that anger is betrayed, whatever be their primary or proper meaning. The disposition to insist upon that meaning is connected with an ancient and an almost universal notion of a climax in this sentence, which has led to many forced constructions, and obscured if not perverted its whole meaning. According to this usual assumption, we have here three gradations of unauthorized and sinful anger, with as many measures or degrees of punishment assigned to them respectively. The first degree of sin is simple anger (or according to the common text, unreasonable, groundless anger) not expressed at all; the second the expression of such anger by the use of the word *raca;* and the third, by the use of the word *fool.* The first or lowest form of punishment, attached to these offences, is *the judgment,* which is commonly explained to mean the local or inferior tribunal which existed in all Jewish towns, composed of three or seven judges. The next is *the council,* or synedrion, the Greek term commonly applied to the supreme court or national tribunal of the Jews (see below, on 10, 17. 26. 59). The third is the *fire of hell,* or more exactly, the *gehenna of fire,* a later Jewish name for the place of future torment, being really a Greek word made up of two Hebrew ones, originally meaning the *Valley of Hinnom.* As a local designation, it described the valley on the south side of Jerusalem, famous of old as a favourite place of idolatrous worship, and especially of the horrid service paid to Moloch by causing children to pass through the fire (Lev. 18, 21. 20, 2. 2 Kings 23, 10. 2 Chr. 33, 6. Jer. 19, 2. 32, 35). Hence in times of reformation, and especially under Josiah, the last good king of Judah, this valley was defiled, probably by being made a place of deposit for the refuse and offal of the city (2 Kings 23, 10). It is often added that to consume this refuse fires were kept perpetually burning; but there is no sufficient evidence of this fact, and the latest writers suppose the sacrificial fires of Moloch to have given rise to the peculiar usage of the *Gehenna*, to denote the place of future torment, or what in modern English is called *hell*. This view of the passage, though entitled to respect from its antiquity and general reception, is unquestionably open to some serious objections. In the first place, it assumes a gradation in the sin condemned, which is not readily suggested by the terms employed. Interpreters have found it so impossible to show the greater guilt of calling a man *fool* than *raca*, or of saying either than of cherishing a silent but malignant anger, that they have been forced to put the most unnatural constructions on these words, without effect, because the difficulty still remains essentially the same, whatever be their meaning. In the next place, there is an offensive incongruity in coupling two degrees of Jewish criminal proceedings with eternal torments as the third degree of the same scale. However palliated or disguised, the transition here is felt to be a *salto mortale*. It is really an indirect acknowledgment of this, that some propose to make the *judgment* and the *council*, although properly denoting human courts, mere figures for inferior degrees of what is afterwards called *hell-fire*. How gratuitous and arbitrary this is, may be gathered from the fact, that others just reverse the process, and make *hell-fire* a strong, Oriental figure for the worst or highest form of punishment in this world. Feeling the difficulties which attend the supposition of a climax, yet unwilling to renounce it, some have recently proposed to substitute an anti-climax by reversing the gradation both of sin and punishment, or, what may be regarded as the furthest possible extreme in this direction, to assume a climax in the one case and an anti-climax in the other. Such diversities of judgment and extravagant inventions on the part of wise and learned men imply an error in the principle or basis of the exposition, which can only be rectified in this case by discarding the idea of a climax altogether, and explaining the three clauses as substantially equivalent though formally dissimilar expressions of the same idea, namely, that the law of God forbids not only murder but malignant anger and its oral manifestations. 'So far is this commandment from relating only to the act of murder, that it makes internal anger an offence deserving punishment. Yes, even such a word as raca, if expressive of an inward spite, may be a crime, obnoxious to the highest censures; and the use of the word fool may spring from such a state of mind, that he who utters it may be condemned to endless torments.' Retaining this as the essential meaning, there is some room for latitude of judgment as to the particular expressions. It is even admissible, though not so natural, to understand the judgment and the council as denoting human censures, while the fire of hell denotes the wrath of God, provided these unequal sanctions be connected, not with different degrees of sin, but with the same, as making men obnoxious both to present and to future, both to human and divine retributions. *Into hell-fire*, i. e. liable to be thrown into it. The lesson taught then as to murder is, that the law against it would be far more rigidly interpreted and executed under the Messiah's reign than under the Mosaic law, as expounded and enforced by the contemporary Scribes and Pharisees.

23. Therefore, if thou bring thy gift to the altar, and there rememberest that thy brother hath aught against thee ;

The next four verses (23–26) contain a practical improvement of the view just taken of the sixth commandment, or the law of murder, rendered still more pointed and direct by the use of the second person singular, as if addressing some one individual among those present. If the law extended in its prohibitions to internal feelings and apparently unmeaning words, the mutual alienations of men ceased to be a matter of indifference, and demanded speedy reconciliation. This is first expressed (23. 24) by making such an act obligatory even in comparison with external duties of religion, as well as a prerequisite to their acceptance. *Therefore*, since the law of God takes cognizance of angry and revengeful feelings no less than of murderous acts. The word translated *bring* may either have its usual and general sense, or be technically used to denote the act of presentation (corresponding to the Hebrew הִקְרִיב). In the latter case the sense is stronger, as the worshipper is then supposed to be not merely drawing near but actually at the altar and engaged in the first act of oblation. *And there rememberest*, after thy arrival at the altar, which implies that it had not occurred to him before. *Thy brother*, not thy neighbour merely, but some still more near and intimate connection. *Hath aught* (any thing) *against thee*, i. e. any ground of litigation or complaint. It is not necessarily implied, though possibly intended, that the fault is on the side of the person here addressed. One may have something against another, i. e. something to say or to demand, though really his claim is groundless. Nay, the case is stronger upon that supposition, as the worshipper is then advised to come to an agreement even with a captious and unjust opponent, rather than incur the risk of hating him and murdering him in his heart.

24. Leave there thy gift before the altar, and go thy way ; first be reconciled to thy brother, and then come and offer thy gift.

Rather than incur this fearful risk of murderous affections, it is better to postpone or interrupt even a religious service which may be performed hereafter, while the opportunity of reconciliation may be lost forever. *There*, before the very altar and in the divine presence. It is evident that this is not suggested as a case at all likely to occur in real life, or even as a formal rule to be observed if it should occur, but rather as a strong assurance that it would be right and proper thus to act, if there were no other means of accomplishing the end required. The same mode of statement, still more strongly marked, occurs below in vs. 29, 30. *Go thy way*, an old English phrase, equivalent to *go away*, though it may seem to convey more to a modern ear. *First* and *then*, indicate the order of the acts prescribed. *Be reconciled*, not merely passively consent to be so, but use active means to bring about a reconciliation. *Come and offer*, literally, *coming* (having come for the purpose) *offer*, thus resuming and completing the act interrupted in the verse preceding.

25. Agree with thine adversary quickly, whiles thou art in the way with him ; lest at any time the adversary deliver thee to the judge, and the judge deliver thee to the officer, and thou be cast into prison.

By a natural transition and association, the imaginary case of an offended brother is exchanged for one of litigation, the vexatious incidents of which are then urged as a motive for preferring certain compromise to doubtful triumph in the courts of law. Both suppositions are intended to enforce the duty of avoiding alienations and enmities, as really at variance with the law of God, and, therefore, attended by the rise, or rather certainty, of his displeasure. Reduced to the form of a comparison, in which both sides of the analogy are fully stated, it may thus be paraphrased: 'As in the case of a contested law-suit, it may sometimes be expedient to make peace by sacrificing even your just rights, because these would be dearly purchased by the risk of failure, condemnation and imprisonment, perhaps forever; how much more ought such an issue to be sought when there is nothing to be gained and every thing to lose by cherishing the enmity of others.' There is no need then of making this a parable, in which the adversary (i. e. adverse party in a law-suit) represents either God or the offended brother of the previous context, and specific meanings are assigned to the judge and officer. It seems more natural to take it as an argument a fortiori, founded on a very common incident of real life, and not admitting of an emblematical interpretation. *Agree*, literally, be well minded or disposed, i. e. to reconciliation. *Quickly*, soon, without delay, before it is too late. *Whiles*, an old form of the common *while* or *whilst*, here used to render a phrase strictly meaning *until when* (or *what time*), followed by the present indicative (ϵi) because referring to an actual condition, not a future or contingent one. *In the way with him*, i. e. to the place of trial. Seize even that last opportunity of compromise and reconciliation. *Lest at any time*, the strict translation of a particle ($\mu \acute{\eta} \pi o \tau \epsilon$), which often denotes mere contingency without distinct reference to time (see below, on 7, 6. 13, 15. 29. 15. 32. 25, 9. 27, 64.) *Deliver to the judge*, by prosecution or complaint, or by insisting on the judges giving sentence. *Deliver to the officer*, by passing sentence and ordering the ministerial attendant of the court to execute it. *Deliver*, in both cases, means to put it in the power of the judge or his executive officer to do their duty, or perform their functions in the case. There is of course no allusion to tyrannical or fraudulent betrayal of the prisoner by one of the parties named into the power of the other. *Be cast*, literally, *shalt be cast*, a deviation from the form of the original directly opposite to that in vs. 19. 20. 22, but equally gratuitous and needless. *Thou shalt be cast*, i. e. in that case, if that happen.

26. Verily, I say unto thee, Thou shalt by no means come out thence, till thou hast paid the uttermost farthing.

This verse might seem to be the mere completion of the ideal case described in the preceding verse, suggesting no unusual conclusion of such matters. But the solemn formula at the beginning, like that in v. 18, and still stronger than the one in v. 20, seems to show that while the words relate directly to the case supposed, they are intended to apply to the more awful case elucidated by it, and to remind the hearer that perpetual imprisonment for debt on earth is but a shadow of perpetual imprisonment in hell for sin, of which he is in danger, not only when he commits murder, but whenever he indulges feelings of hostility in which the germ of that great crime is latent, and from which it may eventually be developed; or continues wilfully a state of alienation which, however negative or harmless it may seem, is murderous in principle already, and may one day become murderous in actual effect. *Till thou hast*, though it implies the possibility of payment, at the same time suggests the debtor's hopeless incapacity to make it. The coin mentioned is of still less value than a British farthing, or our own cent, and therefore was adopted to convey what is here the essential idea, that of an infinitesimal residuum.

27. Ye have heard that it was said by them of old time, Thou shalt not commit adultery.

The next sin to which our Lord applies his discriminating process is adultery, pursuing the same course as in the case of murder, i. e. first contrasting his interpretation of the seventh commandment with the common one (27. 28), and then deducing from this contrast an impressive moral lesson (29. 30.) The first sentence (v. 27), although not elliptical in form or syntax, is abridged in substance, and to be interpreted according to the parallel in v. 21. In itself considered it is simply a quotation of the seventh commandment, nearly in the words of the Septuagint version (Ex. 20. 14). But it cannot be with this commandment that he here contrasts his own more rigid rule (v. 28); for this would be at variance with his own relation to the law, as just before defined (v. 17), and with the whole structure of this passage, which is obviously directed, not against the law itself, but against the customary Pharisaic view of it, although this object is more fully stated in some parts of it (e. g. in v. 21 above and v. 43 below, where the corrupt gloss is expressly cited), than in this place and in vs. 31. 33. 38, where only the commandment is expressed, but the erroneous view of it sufficiently disclosed by what is said in refutation of it. In the case before us, the form of expression may be thus assimilated to the one in v. 31 : 'Ye have heard that it was said to the ancients, Thou shalt not commit adultery, and therefore only he who does commit adultery, in the strict sense of the term, is a transgressor of the law.' This completion of the sense not only brings the passage into harmony with those before and after it, but furnishes the requisite antithesis to v. 28, which otherwise contains no comparison at all between our Lord's interpretation of the law and any other, which, as we have seen, is here the very drift of the discourse.

28. But I say unto you, That whosoever looketh on a woman to lust after her, hath committed adultery with her already in his heart.

But I say unto you, precisely the same formula employed in v. 21, and therefore to be understood in opposition, not to the commandment which had been expressly quoted, but to the usual interpretation of it, which is tacitly implied, as perfectly familiar to the hearers. *Whosoever looketh*, literally, *every (one) looking*, not simply *seeing*, which is otherwise expressed in Greek as well as English, but voluntarily and actively directing the sight towards an object. This idea of deliberate, spontaneous action is expressed still more distinctly by the words that follow, *to lust after* (or more simply, *to desire*, or as Wiclif renders it, *to covet*) *her*, in which the form is not that of a bare infinitive, but the stronger one of an infinitive preceded by an article and preposition ($\pi\rho\grave{o}s\ \tau\grave{o}\ \epsilon\pi\iota\vartheta\upsilon\mu\tilde{\eta}\sigma\alpha\iota$) and denoting purpose in the clearest manner, not merely *so as to*, but *with a view to*, the indulgence of illicit and corrupt desire.* *A woman* is more definitely rendered by Tyndale (*a wife*), and interpreted by Cranmer (*another man's wife*), which agrees well with the fact, that in Greek, as in French, the ordinary word for *wife* is simply *woman* ($\gamma\upsilon\nu\acute{\eta}$, *femme*), which is more than eighty times so rendered in our version. (See below, 22, 24–28, where both words are correctly used in the translation of the same brief passage.) It is also recommended by the fact, that adultery is properly a violation of the marriage vow. But as the Greek word is in itself indefinite, and as our Saviour evidently puts a wide construction on the law, dealing rather with its spirit than its letter, it is not only morally more safe, but philologically more exact, to give the term the widest sense which it will bear, and which is really its proper meaning, the specific sense of *wife* when ap-

---

* The reading of some uncial manuscripts and critical editions ($\alpha\grave{\upsilon}\tau\tilde{\eta}s$ for $\alpha\grave{\upsilon}\tau\acute{\eta}\nu$) has no effect upon the sense but only on the form of the construction.

propriate being always suggested by the context. On the other hand, the verb (μοιχεύσεις, ἐμοίχευσεν) has in usage a specific meaning (*to commit adultery*) and must not be adjusted to the wide sense of the noun (*a woman*), so as to denote fornication, or illicit intercourse in general. The extension of the doctrine here laid down to other cases besides breaches of the marriage vow is not to be secured by tampering with the words, but by parity of reasoning, and by observing the extensive application of the principle involved. In form, the declaration relates only to adultery; in principle and spirit, to all *lechery* (as Wiclif here translates it), i. e. all illicit intercourse between sexes. *Already*, before any overt act takes place. *In his heart*, as the seat of the affections, or more generally, yet in strict accordance with the usage of the Greek word, *in his mind*, as distinguished from his body (see below, on 13, 15). The doctrine here taught in relation to adultery is identical with that laid down in v. 22 respecting murder, namely, that the prohibition of the law extends, not only to the overt act, but to the inward disposition, provided this be truly murderous in one case and adulterous in the other. Thus explained, it is only a deduction from the principle, which all acknowledge, that external acts derive their moral character entirely from the motive which impels to them. If this be so, it is impossible that the guilt of any action should begin with its actual performance, and the sin may justly be described as already committed, in the sight of God, as soon as the purpose is distinctly formed, or even the unlawful wish deliberately cherished. In reference, therefore, to the two great cardinal offences, Christ here vindicates his kingdom from the foul aspersion of establishing a lower standard than the one erected by the Pharisees and Scribes in their theoretical and practical interpretation of the law.

29. And if thy right eye offend thee, pluck it out, and cast (it) from thee: for it is profitable for thee that one of thy members should perish, and not (that) thy whole body should be cast into hell.

Here again, as in v. 23, the plural pronoun is abruptly changed into the singular, as if the object of address were no longer the whole multitude, or even the disciples who formed part of it (v. 2), but some one individual hearer. The design of this change, which the English reader is too apt to overlook from his habitual confusion of the numbers in colloquial usage, is in either case to give a pointed, personal directness to the practical advices which now follow, and to render it impossible for any one who hears or reads the words to treat them as mere barren generalities. As if he had said, 'Such is my interpretation of these two commandments, which I state to all of you collectively; and now I will tell each one of you how he ought to act in consequence.' In this respect our Lord affords a model to his ministers, who ought neither to neglect the general exhibition of sound doctrine, nor to pretermit its practical and personal enforcement. The advice itself is similar, in form and substance, to an exhortation which has been preserved by Mark (9, 43–48), as uttered on a subsequent occasion, and by Matthew himself (18, 8. 9), perhaps upon a third, a striking instance of our Lord's didactic method of repeating the same lessons, more or less modified, to different assemblies. Of the three forms in which this exhortation is recorded, that before us is the briefest, and most probably the oldest, thus exhibiting the theme, of which the others are majestic variations. Common to all, because essential to his purpose, is the solemn warning against being tempted and betrayed into sin by any thing belonging to themselves, however highly valued and however fondly cherished. This idea he expresses in a manner which may be described as characteristic of his teaching, i. e. by assuming an extreme case and supposing that a man's own members, even those which he particularly prizes, and to lose which would be little less than death itself, are incurable, incorrigible causes or occasions of transgression against God. The case is not presented as a real one, or one which there is reason to anticipate in actual experience; but if it should occur, if the only alternative presented to a man were deliberate habitual transgression or the loss of his most valuable members, what would be his choice? If he prefer his bodily integrity and purchase it at such a price, he has reason to believe himself a reprobate. But if in the extreme case here supposed, he would be ready to choose mutilation rather than a life of sin, that choice includes all minor cases, as the whole includes the part, and as the greater comprehends the less.

In the verse before us, the antithesis presented is between the loss of one eye, with salvation or admission into heaven, and the use of two eyes, with perdition or the everlasting pains of hell. That this is the original connection or occurrence of this striking passage, may be gathered from the otherwise unimportant circumstance, that the eye, which stands last in the other cases (Matt. 18, 19, Mark 9, 47), here stands first, in obvious and beautiful connection with the previous condemnation even of an unchaste look as virtual adultery. We thus learn, as it were, the very *genesis* or origin of this divine injunction, as developed in the natural succession of our Saviour's thoughts and words in his organic or inaugural discourse, and afterwards repeated in an amplified and finished but essentially unaltered form on different occasions. *The right eye* seems to be particularly mentioned as commonly reckoned the most valuable, either from a natural difference or one produced, in all the double members of the body, by more constant use. *Offend*, not in the ordinary modern sense of displeasing or alienating in affection, but in the Latin and old English sense of stumbling or being made to stumble. The nearest root or theme to which it can be traced in classic Greek, denotes a trap or snare, but in the Hellenistic dialect a stumbling-block or any hindrance in the path, over which one may fall. In like manner the derivative verb means to make one fall or stumble, a natural figure both for sin and error, and often representing both as commonly connected in experience. 'If thy very eye, and that thy right eye, incurably betrays thee into sin.' The present tense ($\sigma\kappa\alpha\nu\delta\alpha\lambda\iota\zeta\epsilon\iota$) brings the supposition home with great force to the hearer's actual experience. Not 'if it should so do hereafter,' but 'if it is so doing now.' *Cast it from thee*, with abhorrence and contempt, not only as a small price to be paid for your deliverance from sin, but as intrinsically hateful on account of its supposed abandonment to sin itself. *It is profitable* (or *expedient*, as the Rhemish Bible renders it), i. e. comparatively, as appears from the remaining clause, but is not expressed in the verb itself, though so translated in the older English versions (*better it is*, Tyndale, Cranmer, Geneva). *Perish*, or be lost, suggesting the idea of perdition or eternal misery, though strictly inapplicable to an amputated or exscinded member. *And not*, i. e. not expedient, profitable, good for thee, conducive to thy happiness. *Cast*, the same word that was previously applied to the eye, and thus suggesting the immense disparity of loss and gain, the disproportion between voluntary rejection of a single member and coercive or compulsory rejection of one's self forever. *Hell*, an English word originally meaning the unseen world, or the world of spirits, or the state of the dead, and thus corresponding to the Greek word *hades* (see below, on 11, 23. 16, 18), but in later usage limited to the place of future torment, and employed to represent the Greek *gehenna*, which has been explained already. (See above, on v. 22.)

30. And if thy right hand offend thee, cut it off, and cast (it) from thee: for it is profitable for thee that one of thy members should perish, and not (that) thy whole body should be cast into hell.

The same supposition is then made as to the *right hand*, with an exhortation to *cut it off* (or more exactly *out*, which is a stronger expression) in the case assumed, to wit, if it cannot be retained without a certainty of sinning against God. The remainder of the verse is an exact repetition of the twenty-ninth, except that the conjunctive particle (και) with which it opens indicates the close connection and resemblance of the two, whereas that at the beginning of the verse preceding (δέ) rather introduces an addition somewhat different in form, or marks the transition from our Saviour's doctrine to its application. It is not necessary to repeat that this is no formal rule of duty, or provision for a case to be expected in real life, but the strongest possible expression of the principle which ought to govern even the extremest case conceivable, much more the usual emergencies of every-day experience. That principle is simply the unsparing and indignant sacrifice of any thing, however dear and to appearance indispensable, which necessarily incites to sin. The special reference in this connection is, of course, to all indulgences, however lawful in themselves, which experience has shown to be promotive of unhallowed passion.

31. It hath been said, Whosoever shall put away his wife, let him give her a writing of divorcement.

Closely connected with the sin of adultery, and often leading to it, as explained below, was the practice of the Jews as to Divorce, which is the next topic in the series of comparisons between the Pharisaic and the Christian ethics. Here again the abridged form of citation is employed, the words actually quoted being those of the law itself, and the false interpretation being only given indirectly in the refutation. The idea entertained by some, that in these cases there is nothing omitted or to be supplied, but the antithesis is simply between Christ and Moses, is not only inconsistent with our Lord's position as defined by himself in this discourse (v. 17), but utterly destructive of the symmetry which so remarkably distinguishes this portion of the Sermon on the Mount. It is indeed incredible, without the clearest demonstration, that while other things are so exactly balanced, this should have been left at random; or that while our Lord begins and ends by combating the Pharisaic exposition of the law, and placing his own interpretation in the strongest contrast with it, he should in the intervening parts attack the law itself and introduce a rival legislation. This hypothesis is immeasurably more improbable than the supposition that the introductory formulas are in some places more laconic than in others, and in that case to be supplemented from the parallels. Where so simple an assumption removes all the difficulties of the case and makes harmonious what would otherwise be hopeless discord, every principle of sound interpretation, and indeed of common sense, requires that it should be made. But although we are authorized by these considerations to supply the tacit reference to the prevalent corruption of this precept, it does not follow that the corruption was itself the same as in the other cases. This is a point to be determined by the circumstances and connection of the case before us, with due regard to the precise meaning of the first clause. *It was said* (to the ancients in the law) *that* (the Greek particle of citation not expressed in English) *whosoever shall,* the same use of the future as in the translation of vs. 19, 20, 22, which might be more exactly rendered, *whoever puts away.* This phrase, however, is much stronger than the Greek verb (ἀπολύσῃ), which is variously rendered elsewhere, send away (Matt. 14, 15), loose (18, 27), release (27, 15), let depart (Luke 2, 29), forgive (Luke 6, 37), let go (Luke 14, 4), dismiss (15, 30), and set at liberty (Heb. 13, 23). It is another compound of the verb used in vs. 17, 19, with the same essential sense of loosening or undoing, to which the preposition (ἀπό) gives the accessory notion of releasing (as an object bound by untying), letting go, without the implication of violent expulsion, which can hardly be separated from the phrase *put away.* But whatever be the import of the term in general usage, it is certainly employed here to describe repudiation or divorce. The precept quoted is still found in Deut. 24, 1, the form here given being that of the Septuagint version. *Writing of divorcement* answers here to a single Greek word (ἀποστάσιον), which in Attic law denoted the apostasy or criminal defection of a freedman from his patron, but is used in the Septuagint with *writ* or writing (βιβλίον ἀποστασίου),* to translate

---

* This full form is retained by Mark (10, 4), and by Matthew himself in another place relating to this subject. (See below, on 19, 7.)

a Hebrew phrase (סֵפֶר כְּרִיתֻת), which strictly means a writ of excision, the certificate or document required in the law (Deut. 24, 1) to be given to the wife by her repudiating husband. According to the Jewish traditions, it was, even in the time of Christ, a controverted question between the schools of Hillel and Shammai, whether the obscure phrase (עֶרְוַת דָּבָר), rendered *some uncleanness*, but literally meaning *nakedness of word* (or *thing*), was to be taken in a moral sense as meaning lewdness, or in the vague sense of something disagreeable. The latter doctrine (that of Hillel) is said to have been afterwards carried by the famous Rabbi Akiba so far as to allow a man to put away his wife on finding one who pleased him better. That the bill or writing was not a charge of infidelity, but rather a certificate of innocence in that respect, is clear, because it was to be delivered to the wife herself, and because the law required an adultress to be punished (Num. 5, 31), not to be thus quietly dismissed. The *writing of divorcement*, therefore, was itself no hardship, but a benefit, protecting the divorced wife from unfounded imputations, and declaring her repudiation to be founded upon something less than violation of her marriage vow. This was the requisition of the law; but what was the corruption or the false interpretation of it, tacitly implied and afterwards refuted? This, we learn from a fuller declaration of our Saviour on a different occasion, which has been preserved by Mark (10, 2-12), consisted in regarding the Mosaic precept as a license to repudiate at will; whereas it was a merciful provision in behalf of the repudiated woman, designed to mitigate the hardship of divorces, even when unlawful. It was not a general permission to repudiate, but a stringent requisition that whoever did so should secure his wife from injury by certifying that she was not chargeable with unchaste conduct, but divorced upon some minor pretext.

32. But I say unto you, That whosoever shall put away his wife, saving for the cause of fornication, causeth her to commit adultery: and whosoever shall marry her that is divorced, committeth adultery.

In opposition to this prevalent perversion of a merciful provision in the law, our Saviour teaches that so far from making divorce easier, he intended to forbid it altogether as the law did, with the single exception of those cases where the contract had already been annulled by the conduct of one party, i. e. by desertion (1 Cor. 7, 15) or adultery. The latter is here designated, not by a specific term (μοιχεία) corresponding to the verb in the last clause and to the kindred one in v. 27 above,* but by a more generic term (πορνεία), which however is not incorrect, as it does not properly mean fornication in the strict

---

* This term is used elsewhere, both by Matthew (15, 19) and other New Testament writers. (Mark 7, 21. John 8, 3. Gal. 5, 19.)

sense, as distinguished from adultery, but lechery or whoredom, as including both. *Saving because of*, literally *outside of the word* (cause or reason) *of unchastity*. The exceptive particle (παρεκτος) belongs to the later Greek or Hellenistic dialect, and is only used in this figurative way. *Causeth*, literally *makes*, a use of the verb common to both idioms. *To commit adultery*, i. e. to violate her marriage vow against her will, by forced separation or compulsory desertion. Or the words may have prospective reference to the case mentioned in the last clause, that of a re-marriage on the part of the repudiated wife, who thereby violates the vow by her own act, but by the procurement, if not under the coercion, of her husband. The Church of Rome regards this as an absolute prohibition of re-marriage, even in the case here mentioned, that of fornication in the wide sense, which in the case of married persons is adultery. The Protestant and Oriental Churches hold re-marriage to be lawful in all cases where divorce is, and explain this verse accordingly. (See below, on 19, 9.)

33. Again, ye have heard that it hath been said by them of old time, Thou shalt not forswear thyself, but shalt perform unto the Lord thine oaths.

The next item in this catalogue of sins is that of swearing or unlawful oaths, in reference to which there seem to have been two prevailing errors in the theory and practice of the Jews. The first was the opinion or belief, that no swearing was unlawful except false swearing; the other, that no swearing was unlawful except swearing by the name of God. In opposition to these errors Christ here teaches that the sin, where there is any, consists not in swearing falsely, which is a distinct offence punished both by God and man, nor in any particular form of oath, but in swearing at all without necessity or warrant. The introductory formula is here the same as in v. 21, with a single word prefixed (*again*), making the transition to another prohibition of the law. This is not found in the decalogue, nor *totidem verbis* elsewhere in the Pentateuch, but is a pregnant summary which the people may have often heard from their instructors as the teaching of the law upon the subject. The first or prohibitory clause (*thou shalt not perjure* or *forswear thyself*, i. e. swear falsely) is an abridgment of the precept in Lev. 19, 12: "Ye shall not swear by my name falsely, neither shalt thou profane the name of thy God. I (am) the Lord;" or, as the second member of the sentence might be rendered, "and (thereby) profane the name of thy God, (even) me, Jehovah." The second or preceptive clause (*thou shalt perform*, literally *pay* or *give back*, *to the Lord thine oaths*, not merely what has been directly promised to himself, but all engagements sanctioned by an oath in his name) is a paraphrase or condensation of the command in Numb. 30, 2 (Heb. 3): "If a man vow a vow unto the Lord, or swear an oath to bind his soul with a bond (literally, to bind a bond upon his soul), he shall not break (literally, profane, the same word that occurs in the citation from Leviticus) his word; according to all that proceedeth out of his mouth (see above, on 4, 4) shall he do." The same command is found in Deut. 23, 23, in a more general form, "That which is gone out of thy lips thou shalt keep and do," which the last clause then applies to a specific case already mentioned in the context. Of these commands, both negative and positive, the verse before us is a correct summary. To assume that our Lord is combating the law itself, we have already seen to be absurd, and it is doubly so in this case, as his own injunction in the following verses does not contradict this precept in the least, and must therefore be directed against some erroneous explanation of it, not expressly stated but implied in his correction of it. This erroneous view of the law in question seems to have arisen from the fact, that in Leviticus (19, 12) the sin forbidden is the profanation of the name Jehovah by false swearing. Hence it was inferred that where either of these elements was wanting, or in other words where the swearing was neither false nor expressly by the name of God, there was no sin at all committed.

34. But I say unto you, Swear not at all : neither by heaven ; for it is God's throne.

In opposition to this too restricted view of the divine prohibition, he declares, as its true import and the sense in which he should himself enforce it, that they should not swear *at all* (ὅλως), wholly, altogether, an adverb which qualifies the negative and makes it absolute, as in the somewhat different phrase here used in English. The only question has respect not to its meaning but to the extent of its application. By a possible construction, *not at all* (μὴ ὅλως) may have reference to the form of the oath, as being in the name of God or not—'I forbid not only oaths in the divine name, but others which are really disguised forms of the same thing,' and of which he then proceeds to give examples. By another possible construction, *not at all* refers not to the form but to the act of swearing. This, which is the usual construction, really includes the other, since a prohibition of all forms of swearing is a prohibition of swearing itself. The particular oaths which follow are no doubt familiar samples of those then in common use, and must be understood as representing the whole class of frivolous and uncommanded modes of swearing. *By heaven*, literally, *in the heaven*, a Hebrew idiom, the preposition (בְּ) usually answering to ἐν being also used in other combinations, and among the rest in swearing. (Gen. 22, 16. בִּי נִשְׁבַּעְתִּי, *by myself have I sworn*.) In other parts of the New Testament we find the classical construction of the same verb with the preposition κατά (Heb. 6, 13) and with the accusative (Jas. 5, 12). *The throne of God*, a beautiful description of heaven, also found in the Old Testament (Isai. 66, 1). It is not here given as a reason why heaven is too holy to be sworn by, but to show that swearing by it is in fact to swear by God himself. An oath, as a religious act, consisting in the solemn invocation of an omniscient witness to attest the truth of what is uttered, cannot, from its very nature, terminate on any creature, much less on a lifeless and material object. Swearing by heaven, therefore, either has no meaning, or derives it from the fact that heaven is the residence, the court, the throne of God. (See above, on v. 3.) This is designed to show that an unlawful oath, judicial or colloquial, is not divested of its criminality by any euphemistical evasion or disguise of the divine name, which is really involved, not merely in the form but in the substance and the very definition of the oath itself. Hence the simple phrase, *I swear*, or its equivalents, is as real and direct an appeal to God, as if his names and titles were expressly uttered.

35. Nor by the earth; for it is his footstool: neither by Jerusalem; for it is the city of the great King.

The same thing is here said of the earth, described as God's footstool (or retaining the pleonastic form of the original, *the footstool of his feet*) in the sublime passage of Isaiah (66, 1) previously quoted or referred to. The design is not poetical embellishment, but the suggestion through a familiar part of Scripture, that as the throne and its accompanying footstool derive all their dignity from him who sits above them, so the heavens and the earth, which bear a similar relation to the Most High, are entirely dependent upon that relation for the least significancy in religious acts, and more especially in that of swearing. In other words, he who swears by the earth either swears by God or does not swear at all. In the last clause the same thing is said of Jerusalem, but with a slight change of expression not retained in the translation, namely, the substitution of another preposition (εἰς) which properly means *into* after verbs of motion, but has frequently the weaker sense of *to* or *towards*, expressive of direction without actual entrance. This is probably the meaning here, involving an allusion to the ancient although uncommanded practice of praying towards the holy city. (See 1 Kings 8, 38. 42. 44. Dan. 6, 10.) As if he had said, 'neither swear (turning) towards Jerusalem,' which is the more natural as uttered by our Lord in Galilee. *Because it is the city of the great king*, the capital or royal residence of Jehovah, as the immediate head of the theocracy, and owes to that relation all its sanctity and even its significancy as an object to be sworn by; so that he who swears by it either swears by God or does not swear at all.

36. Neither shalt thou swear by thy head, because thou canst not make one hair white or black.

The third and last familiar form of oath prohibited is by a man's own head; but here the reason given is not only more obscure, but at first sight altogether different from that suggested in the other cases. Instead of showing the relation of the object to the majesty of God, he points out its relation to the littleness of man, and his utter incapacity to exercise the least controlling power over it. However true this may be, it does not at once commend itself to every mind as a sufficient reason for the prohibition. The difficulty may be somewhat lessened by explaining *white or black* as a proverbial expression, meaning any kind whatever, and giving to the verb its strongest sense, that of creation. 'Thou canst not make (or bring into existence even) one hair (whether) white or black.' It is then a denial of man's power, not to change the colour of his hair, which is continually done by artificial means, but to produce one of any colour, which, however trivial the effect may be, is a creative act. The object of the clause may then be to suggest, in an indirect and possibly proverbial form, the correlate or converse of this proposition, namely, that the head of man is not a creation of his own but of God, and exclusively at God's disposal; so that if it can be sworn by, it is only as a needless and an uncommanded oath by God himself, the more to be avoided because destitute of even that slight pretext which might seem to justify the oaths just mentioned by his throne, his footstool, and his royal city, all which may be used to represent him in a way that seems entirely inappropriate to the human head.

37. But let your communication be, Yea, yea; Nay, nay: for whatsoever (is) more than these cometh of evil.

But to what conclusion does all this point? That the forms of swearing here forbidden were irreverent and needless substitutes for solemn oaths by God himself, and, therefore, ought to give place to the latter? This is certainly included, and if this were all, it would determine *not at all* in v. 34 to mean in none of these accustomed forms, but only in the name of God. The passage then would be a simple prohibition of all indirect and covert modes of swearing, as if these could lessen or destroy the guilt of either perjury or blasphemy. But that this is not the true sense, or at most the full sense of the prohibition, becomes absolutely certain from the verse before us, which is to be taken in connection with the first clause of v. 34, the intervening clauses being mere specifications of familiar modes of swearing comprehended in the prohibition. 'But I say unto you, swear not at all (not even by the use of customary petty oaths), but let your word (talk, form of speech) be yea, yea, nay, nay' (or in modern English, yes and no), the duplication of the terms denoting frequency or constancy. 'Be always saying yes or no, and nothing more.' If the preceding context were a simple prohibition of the customary oaths there mentioned, with an implied permission or encouragement to use the solemn form of oath by God himself, the verse before us would be utterly irrelevant if not directly contradictory to such a purpose. The conclusion must have been in that case, 'let your oaths be in the name of God alone,' whereas it is in fact, 'let your speech be without oaths,' with a positive suggestion of the simple affirmations and negations which should take their place. *Whatsoever (whatever,* or simply *what) is more than these* (or more exactly, *the abounding,* the excess, of these), i. e. whatever goes beyond these simple affirmations and negations. *Cometh of,* literally, *is from* or *out of*, which is obviously meant to indicate the source or origin of such expressions. *Evil* is definite in Greek, *the evil*, or *the wicked*, and agreeably to usage may be either abstract, *out of wickedness*, from moral evil (as in Rom. 12, 9. 1 Thes. 5, 22. 2 Thes. 3, 3. Jas. 4, 16), or personal and concrete, *from the evil (one)*, so called by way of eminence, because he was the tempter of mankind and the source of human sin and misery (as in 1 John 2, 13. 14. 3, 12. 5, 18). See below, on 6, 13, where the same ambiguity exists. In either case, the habit of exceeding the most simple forms of affirmation is prohibited, not merely by an arbitrary rule or absolute authority, but as intrinsically evil in its source and moral quality. Unless we deny to the discourse all coherence and consistency, in which case it would not be worth interpreting, we must admit that vs. 34 and 37, taken together, do contain a prohibition of all swearing. But in what sense and with what extent of application? As to this point there has always been a great variety of judgments, which however may be readily reduced to these four classes. 1. The Quakers and some others understand the passage as an universal prohibition of all oaths, or appeals to God in attestation of the truth, as well judicial as colloquial. 2. Some suppose the prohibition to be absolute, but applicable not to the existing state of things but to a future condition of society, when the Messiah's reign shall reach its consummation. 3. The great mass of Christians in all ages have understood the prohibition as extending only to the use of oaths in conversation, or to their irreverent and needless use in courts of justice and in other public offices. 4. A fourth view of the passage understands it as prohibiting all voluntary swearing, both judicial and colloquial, the latter being never right, the former only when imposed by adequate authority, and in prevention of a greater evil. The first of these opinions is refuted *a priori* by the fact that an oath is a religious act and therefore cannot be intrinsically evil, or at all unless universally prohibited; that such a prohibition is at variance with the oaths so constantly ascribed to God himself in Scripture,* and with the practice of our Lord himself† and that of his apostles. The second explanation is refuted by its fanciful and arbitrary character, the same assumption being equally admissible in reference to every prohibition of the decalogue, and by the danger thence arising of an universal relaxation of the principles of morals, founded on the pretext that society is still imperfect; and by the arbitrary treatment of a simple categorical prohibition, as being practically no prohibition at all. The objection to the third and common view is, that it leaves too great a license to judicial swearing, and apparently connives at the most hideous abuses in official practice. All these objections are avoided by the fourth interpretation, which sufficiently provides for all official and judicial oaths when really expedient, but condemns perversion and excess in these, as well as all oaths used in conversation, and is further recommended by the

---

* See for example Gen. 22, 16. Ps. 95, 11. Heb. 6, 13. 7, 21.
† See below, on 26, 63. and compare Rom. 1, 9. 2 Cor. 1, 23. Phil. 1, 8. 1 Thes. 2, 5. 10.

obvious analogy of the sixth commandment, which prohibits homicide in terms as strong and universal, though almost unanimously understood not only to excuse the act of killing under certain circumstances, but to require it as a duty under certain others.

38. Ye have heard that it hath been said, An eye for an eye, and a tooth for a tooth.

A fifth sin, as to which they were to look for less indulgence in Messiah's reign than under the corrupt administration of the law by scribes and pharisees, was the indulgence of a vengeful and vindictive spirit. The legal pretext under which this vice was practised was the *lex talionis*, or rule of retribution found in Ex. 21, 24. Lev. 24, 20. Deut. 19, 21. *Ye have heard* (from the expounders of the law) *that it was said, eye for eye, tooth for tooth.* The indefinite article need not be expressed, and weakens the whole sentence. Here again, there is assumed a false interpretation of the dictum, which is really a part of the Mosaic law, and an erroneous practice founded on it. What this prevailing error was has been disputed, some supposing that it was the transfer of a rule designed to govern the proceedings of the magistrate to private life, the substitution of personal revenge for public punishment. Another supposition is that it consisted in regarding as a rule at all, to be acted upon even in judicial process, what was only a proverbial expression of the general principle of righteous retribution underlying all law, and repeatedly exhibited in that of Moses rather *in terrorem* than as something to be carried out in practice. This opinion is defended on the ground of the severity and cruelty supposed to be involved in such a principle of punishment; by the difficulty of applying it in practice; by the absence of any one recorded instance of its execution; and by the reason of it given in Deuteronomy (19, 20), "those which remain shall hear and fear, and shall henceforth commit no more any such evil among you." But the terror here referred to is that arising from the execution, not from the mere threatening, of retaliation. The rule, moreover, stands recorded in the midst of laws which were evidently meant to be literally understood and acted on. See Ex. 21, 22-26. Lev. 24, 17-21, in the latter of which places it is moreover clothed in as direct and positive a form as any proper law could be—"breach for breach, eye for eye, tooth for tooth; as he hath caused (literally, given) a blemish in the man, so shall it be done to (literally, given in) him." If these considerations are not sufficient to outweigh those previously stated, and to prove conclusively that the *lex talionis* was a law in the proper sense and habitually carried into execution; it may at least serve to deter us from too hastily asserting the contrary, and lead us to adopt an explanation of the passage now before us, not involving either supposition as to the precise design of this terrific law or the fact of its literal execution. This seems to be the case with the first interpretation mentioned which, without deciding the disputed question either way, assumes merely that the *lex talionis*, whatever its legitimate design and use, had been adopted as a rule of private justice, authorizing every injured person to redress his own wrongs, an abuse not peculiar to the east but singularly rife there, as appears from the practice of the Bedouins at this day. It is essentially the same wild justice that is known among ourselves as lynch-law, whether administered by one or many, and too often justified, not merely by the clamor of excited mobs, but by the verdict of enlightened juries. It is needless to observe that what is eminently right and wholesome in the hands of a divine or a divinely aided judge, may be the height of tyranny in any other.

39. **But I say unto you, That ye resist not evil: but whosoever shall smite thee on thy right cheek, turn to him the other also.**

But I say unto you, in opposition not to the lex talionis as a maxim of the law, but to this abuse of it as justifying personal revenge. *That ye resist not* is in Greek simply *not to resist*. *Evil*, the same ambiguous expression that occurs above in v. 37, and admitting here too of the same constructions, namely, *evil* (in the abstract), or *the wicked* (man), by whom you have been injured. *But*, on the contrary, so far from thus retaliating. This is then more positively and specifically stated by supposing a familiar case which might occur in any man's experience, and therefore furnishes a surer test of the dispositions here required. The only question of interpretation is one running through the next three verses, which are filled with other cases of the same kind, calling for the application of the same rule and the display of the same spirit. This question is, whether the duty here enjoined is that of absolute and passive non-resistance in all cases of oppression or injurious treatment. The affirmative can be defended only on the general principle or law of language, that its obvious and proper sense must always be entitled to the preference, and can only be deprived of it by positive considerations, showing that some other sense was really intended. The question, therefore, is whether there are any such considerations in the case before us, and how far they go in weakening the general presumption and antecedent probability in favour of the literal and strict sense. 1. The first consideration of this nature that presents itself is one derived from general experience, the fact, that the commandment, strictly understood, has never been habitually carried into execution, even by the most devoted exemplary Christians. The apparent exceptions to this statement have been either too confined or shortlived to affect its general truth, or have extended only to the negative command of non-resistance, without including the more positive injunction to encourage and solicit further injury. Now a precept which has never been reduced to practice must be impracticable or impossible, and cannot therefore have been uttered in the sense thus put upon it. 2. To this argument *a posteriori* may be added another *a priori*, drawn from the unreasonableness and injustice of the law, as thus explained, as violating general principles of right, deliberately sacrificing that of the injured and oppressed, facilitating and encouraging injustice, and subverting all the principles on which society has been constructed. 3. A third consideration adverse to the strict interpretation, is that Christ himself did not act upon his own rule thus explained, but when smitten by a servant of the High Priest, instead of courting further outrage, arrested it by strong expostulation (John 18, 22. 23); and that Paul, when treated in like manner, still more earnestly resented it (Acts 23, 2. 3). 4. It should also be considered, that the use of strong and paradoxical expressions, to arouse attention and provide for extreme cases, is not only an occasional phenomenon but a standing characteristic of our Saviour's *didache* or mode of teaching, not without examples in this very chapter, which creates a presumption opposite to that arising from the general law of language now in question. 5. Lastly, the peculiar structure of this part of the Sermon on the Mount, makes it almost if not absolutely certain, that in this, as in the similar injunctions which precede, we are not to look for absolute or abstract rules, extending to all cases, but to some peculiar case, suggested in the context. What that case is, we may learn from the preceding verse, where the text or theme of this particular passage is the *lex talionis*, with its popular perversion as a legal pretext for revenge. If there be any kind of logical coherence or consistency between the two successive verses, the second no less than the first, must have respect to this specific sin, and the abstinence commanded must be, not from simple self-defence or self-protection, but from such as would be necessarily vindictive or revengeful in its character. The limitation really implied though not expressed, is probably the same as in vs. 29. 30. where the language is still stronger and more paradoxical, and, therefore, more available in explanation of that now before us. As no sane man has ever understood those verses as a formal rule of ordinary duty calling for the literal excision of the eye or hand as soon as either has become the cause or instrument of sin; so no sane man has any right or reason to insist upon a similar interpretation of the words before us. Nor would any such disparity of treatment ever have existed, if the duty supposed to be enjoined had been equally startling and revolting in both cases. But the man who is fanatical enough to let himself be robbed and beaten, in supposed obedience to our Lord's command, though few have ever gone so far as to turn the other cheek, or press the spoiler to take more, may not be quite fanatical enough to amputate his own right hand, though no less explicitly required by the very same authority and almost in the very same form. But even if it be admitted, as a negative conclusion, that the precept now before us is not to be strictly understood as a general and formal rule of duty, it may still be asked how we must understand it and obey it? The solution of this question is afforded by the same analogy already cited, that of vs. 29. 30. If, as we have seen already, what is there said has respect to an extreme case, not to be expected, much less sought for, in our every-day experience, namely, that of an incurable incompatibility between obedience to the will of God and the retention of our dearest members, and in that case requires us to exscind them without mercy; so the words before us may be understood to mean that rather than become our own avengers, or indulge a spirit of vindictive retribution, we must suffer any form or measure both of wrong and insult; whether that recorded in the last clause of the present verse, or those enumerated in the three that follow, which are mere additional specifications or examples of the rule propounded here. Should it be objected that this explanation arbitrarily restricts a precept general in form, by introducing a specific application, not required or indicated in the text, the answer is, that this specific application is the very subject of the passage as propounded in v. 38, and that the notion of an absolute and general command could only have arisen from the insulation of the precept and habitual neglect of its connection.

40. And if any man will sue thee at the law, and take away thy coat, let him have (thy) cloak also.

Rather than indulge the revengeful spirit here condemned, be ready to endure not only personal indignity but legal wrong. *If any man will sue thee at the law* is a needless paraphrase, made more enfeebling by the constant use of *will* in modern English as a mere auxiliary, whereas it is here an independent verb, and the participial construction definite and unconditional. *To the (one,* or *the man) wishing to sue thee,* or *to go to law with thee.* The Greek verb primarily means to separate, discern, distinguish, then to decide or exercise discriminating judgment; then to try judicially, to judge, to sentence. The middle voice, which here occurs, is used by Homer in the sense of fighting or contending, either by a transfer from the forum to the field of battle, or, as the lexicographers prefer, by immediate deduction from the first sense of separating, differing, &c. *Willing* or *wishing,* i. e. desiring, and by necessary implication here, insisting on the litigation, the subject or occasion of which is then brought home to every bosom as involving the most necessary articles of dress or clothing, which consisted in the east of two chief garments, the χιτών and the ἱμάτιον, here translated *coat* and *cloak,* but more exactly corresponding to our *shirt* and *coat.* The form and shape are unimportant, as the two are only put together to express the general idea of necessary clothing. *And* (wishing, as the object of his suit) *to take thy inner garment* (shirt or tunic). *Let him have* is Tyndale's version, less exact and expressive than the Rhemish, *let (it) go to him.* The Greek verb is the one employed above in v. 24, as well as in 3, 15. 4, 11. 20. 22, and there explained. *Thy* is not repeated in Greek, but the first (σου) may be regarded as extending to both nouns (*the coat and cloak of thee*). The case here stated would have more effect upon a Jewish audience, because the upper garment was expressly exempted in the law of Moses from the claims of creditors in ordinary cases, partly for the reason that the poor at least used it also as a covering at night (Ex. 22, 26. 27). The idea really suggested therefore, would be that of giving up even what the law reserved for the use of the unfortunate debtor. Even this must be abandoned, though it might be legally retained, if its retention or defence would be a gratification of the natural resentment at such conduct, on the ground of the *lex talionis*, as the Pharisees and Scribes explained it. This injunction of our Lord undoubtedly condemns much defensive litigation, which appears to be prompted by a simple sense of justice, but is really vindictive in its origin and spirit.

41. And whosoever shall compel thee to go a mile, go with him twain.

A third specification of the general command to suffer wrong rather than assert right in a spiteful or revengeful spirit. This allusion is derived from an ancient Oriental custom, of which there may have been some recent instance known to our Lord's hearers. The usage was that of pressing man and beast into the public service for the purpose of conveying news with greater speed. This, which seems to be the germ or origin of modern posting, in the wide sense of the term as used in Europe, is ascribed by Greek historians both to Cyrus and Xerxes, under whom there seems to be a trace of its existence still preserved in Esther 8, 10. 14. The public couriers, or bearers of despatches, who possessed this power of impressment, when required to furnish the relays of horses and of horsemen, were called by a name of Persian origin (ἄγγαροι), from which was derived in later Greek the verb here used (ἀγγαρεύω) in the sense of forcing one to go upon a journey. *Shall compel,* not *will,* as in v. 40, because here there is but one verb in the future tense. The arbitrary will expressed in that case by the *will* is here included in the meaning of the verb itself. *Mile,* the Roman mile of a thousand paces (which is Wiclif's version here), and according to the latest authorities, about 140 yards shorter than the English. The important point in this case is the proportion between *one* and *two.* Rather than refuse, in an angry and vindictive spirit, to go one mile by constraint, go two and make the hardship double. *Twain,* an old form for *two,* retained in all the English versions here, and in a few other places. (See below, on 19, 5. 6. 27, 21. 51.)

42. Give to him that asketh thee, and from him that would borrow of thee turn not thou away.

To these occasional and rarer instances of hardship or annoyance, he now adds one of less violence, but more intolerable if continued or repeated often. The precept must be understood with the same qualification as the others. Rather than refuse from a vindictive motive, or to gratify a spirit of retaliation, *give to the (one) asking thee.* This may denote free gifts as distinguished from the loan referred to in the last clause, as the latter may be merely an expansion of the other. *The one wishing,* willing, perhaps with the same implication of persistency and overbearing urgency as in v. 40. Here again, the change of usage should be noted, *would* being not a mere auxiliary, but an independent verb. *Borrow*, a Greek verb meaning to *lend*, but in the middle voice, to have lent to one, to receive on loan. According to the lexicons, it *always* means in classic Greek to lend on interest, the absolute sense (which here occurs) belonging only to the Greek of the New Testament. But a trace of its earlier existence may be found in the fact that Demosthenes adds *on interest* (ἐπὶ τόκοις), which would be superfluous and therefore out of place in so concise a writer, if the verb itself included that idea. *Turn not away*, in Greek a passive, strictly meaning, *be not turned away*, but according to the best grammarians used in the middle sense of *turn not thyself away*. The passive in such cases is peculiarly expressive, having nearly the same force as if it had been said, 'do not let thyself be turned away.' (Compare σώζητε, Acts 2, 40.)

43. Ye have heard that it hath been said, Thou shalt love thy neighbour, and hate thine enemy.

The last particular here specified, in which the moral standard of Messiah's kingdom was to be far higher than the one then recognized among the Jews, was that of friendship or benevolence to others. In this case the distinction is clearer than in any of the others, between the requisition of the law and its perversion by the Scribes and Pharisees. *Ye have heard* (from these your spiritual leaders) *that it was said* (through Moses, to your fathers), *thou shalt love thy neighbour*, an abridged form of the precept still recorded in Lev. 19, 18, from which our Lord afterwards derived the second part of his reply to the question, which was the great commandment of the law (see below, in 22, 39). As it was not his intention to remind them of this clause exclusively, and as it would at once suggest the rest to any well instructed Jewish hearer (see above, on 4, 6), it will aid us in interpreting the passage now before us to complete our Lord's quotation and transcribe the whole verse in Leviticus, "Thou shalt not avenge nor bear any grudge against the children of thy people, but thou shalt love thy neighbour as thyself; I (am) the Lord." The prohibition of revengeful grudges in the first clause makes the connection still more close and obvious between this part of Christ's discourse and that before it. It may even lay bare the association of ideas which occasioned the transition in his thoughts and words to the concluding topic in this long enumeration. Here, too, as in the case immediately preceding (see above, on v. 38), the simple recital of the law in its original connection, shows at once the source of the perversion which our Lord condemns. In its letter and its primary design, this precept was intended to promote benevolent affections among the chosen people, or from one Jew to another, as appears from the specific phrase, *the sons* (or *children*) *of thy people*. This specification had been always open to abuse, but more particularly after the rise of Pharisaism, even in its earlier and purer form, which was that of an exclusive nationality and dread of all assimilation with the heathen (see above, on 3, 7). Before and at the time of Christ this spirit had become one of fanatical antipathy, not only to the faith and worship, but to the persons of all Gentiles, founded on a plausible though false deduction from the precept of the law just quoted. As its requisition of benevolent affections is expressly limited to fellow Jews ("the children of thy people"), it was easy for the Pharisees, and even for the Scribes of their persuasion, in the exposition of this law, to argue from its silence as to others their express exclusion, nay to make a duty and a virtue of regarding them with positive hostility, as enemies of God and of his people. This perversion, which could scarcely be avoided in the case supposed, or rather known to have existed, is precisely the one indicated in the last clause of the verse before us (*and thou shalt hate thine enemy*). It is not necessary to assume, nor even probable, that such a proposition, in its revolting harshness, ever formed a part of their religious teaching. It is sufficient to regard it as our Lord's own summary expression of the substance and spirit of that teaching, or the practical conclusion to which their less revolting glosses and distinctions tended: 'You have heard that as the law commands you only to love the children of your people, you are of course at liberty, if not in some sense bound, to cherish opposite affections towards all others.' Such a spirit of national repugnance could not fail in its turn to generate analogous antipathies between one class and another even of the chosen people, and eventually also between man and man; so that the Pharisaic doctrine finally assumed the character, in which it is here set forth, "thou shalt love thy neighbour and hate thine enemy." The word translated *neighbour* properly means *near*, but is as old as Homer in its application to persons, and especially to those with whom we have more intimate relation than with others, whether the precise connection be a local, a domestic, or a national one. This relative and wide use of the term affords occasion for our Saviour's beautiful reply to the question, Who is my neighbour? as recorded in another gospel, with immediate reference to this precept of the law (Luke 10, 27. 29. 36), and will also throw some light upon his teaching in the present instance.

44. **But I say unto you, Love your enemies, bless them that curse you, do good to them that hate you, and pray for them which despitefully use you, and persecute you.**

But I say unto you, in opposition to this false and wicked corollary added by the Pharisees to the Mosaic law of love. *Love your enemies*, not only national but personal, private as well as public. By this wide interpretation of the law all pretext for invidious exceptions and distinctions is precluded. But is not this an extension of the law itself, as well as a correction of the false gloss put upon it? Can the precept in Leviticus be truly said to mean all this, without a violation of its very terms, which so particularly name *the children of thy people*, as the *neighbours* to be loved and cherished? This is an important question, as relating to the last ground on which it can be plausibly maintained, that our Lord, in this discourse, is not merely showing the true sense but supplying the deficiencies of the law itself (see above, on v. 17). It may be answered by reverting to the ground and purpose of the separation between Israel and the other nations, which was not perpetual but temporary, and intended not to aggrandize the chosen people, but to make them instruments of good to the whole race. This is clear from the patriarchal promises; from the means used to keep up the remembrance of their œcumenical relations in the minds of the more favoured race; from the representative character assigned to them, as being not so much the church of God as a peculiar people representing it; and from the continual reproof and refutation of their narrow prepossessions, not merely in the New Testament, but in the Prophets, and the law itself. The virtues which they were required to practise, then, among themselves, were exhibitions on a small scale of the duties which they owed to all alike, and not the right side of a picture, the reverse of which was turned to others. The true correlative of the love required between Jew and Jew, was not contempt or hatred of the Gentiles, but a still more comprehensive love to them too, bearing the same proportion to the first that national or social charities sustain to the more intimate affections of the family. The pious Jew was not required to love the Gentiles as he loved the Jews, but still to love them, not to hate them; and the least degree of love is the negation of all hatred. The bare correction of this error would have been a vast advance upon the Pharisaical theory and practice of benevolence. But Christ goes vastly further still, and shows that the Mosaic (i. e. the divine) law of love extends not only to multitudes whom they considered as excluded by their birth or nationality without regard to personal demerit, but to those whose personal demerit was the greatest possible, not only against God but towards themselves. After saying generally, *love your enemies*, which might be negatively understood as meaning those who are not your friends by any social, national, or private tie, he specifies this vague term by adding as synonymous expressions, *those cursing you . . . . those hating you . . . . those insulting you . . . . those persecuting you.* This cuts off all misapprehension and evasion as to the extent, not only of our Lord's own requisition, but of the Mosaic law, as he expounds it. The same end is secured in reference to the positive and active nature of the love required, by coupling with each hostile act (already quoted) a corresponding act of friendship or benevolence. Bless those cursing you, do good to those hating you, and pray for those *despitefully using you*, or more exactly, *insulting* or *abusing you*. The Greek word always has specific reference to speech or words, and originally means to threaten, from which the transition is an easy one to contumelious talk as the expression of a spiteful scorn in general. Besides the parallel passage in Luke (6, 28), it occurs only once again in the New Testament (1 Pet. 3, 16), where it is too specifically rendered, *falsely* *accuse.* It seems to be here joined with *persecute*, in order to express the two ideas of hostile speech and hostile action.*

45. That ye may be the children of your Father which is in heaven : for he maketh his sun to rise on the evil and on the good, and sendeth rain on the just and on the unjust.

The true law of benevolence having been laid down in all its length and breadth, and in contrast with the narrow Pharisaic rule and practice, is now shown to be reasonable from analogy. The appeal is a twofold example, that of God and man. The demonstrative power of the first rests not merely on the general principle of God's perfection and authority as the standard and exemplar of all excellence, but also on the filial relation borne to him by all believers, and here obviously assumed by Christ as necessarily belonging to his true disciples. As if he had said, 'In coming to me, you come to the Father, not mine merely but your own; for if you believe in me. you are his children, and the child must imitate the father in all imitable qualities and acts. But he does not confine his rain and sunshine to the good or righteous, i. e. those who are conformed to his will, but gives them also to the wicked and unrighteous.' The implied conclusion is that we are not to regulate our love by the merit of the object but extend it to all. From this it follows that the love here meant is not the love of complacency, involving moral approbation, but the love of benevolence, involving only a desire of the object's welfare. *Maketh to rise*, an unavoidable periphrasis of one Greek verb (ἀνατέλλει), which is used both in a transitive and intransitive sense (see above, on 4, 16, and below, on 13, 6), the former of which is applied in the classics to the growth of plants, the rise of water, and the shedding forth of light. *Sendeth rain* (Tyndale, *his rain*), on the other hand, might be more simply and exactly rendered *rains* (or *raineth*). *Evil and good, just and unjust*, are not be carefully distinguished, but regarded as synonymous descriptions of the one great universal contrast which exists in human character.

46. For if ye love them which love you, what reward have ye? do not even the publicans the same?

The other analogy is drawn from human conduct, and that not of the best but rather of the worst men in the hearers' estimation, publicans and Gentiles. Even these could feel and act with kindness towards their friends and nearest relatives; and therefore Christian charity must reach further and rise higher, namely, to the love of enemies, before enjoined. The logical connective (*for*) refers back, not to the

---

* The textual variations in this verse have no effect upon the sense, but only on the fulness of expression.

immediately preceding verse, but to the one before it. We have here the reason, not for God's impartial gifts to all his creatures, but for man's imitation of it as required in v. 44. *Them which love you* is in Greek a participial construction like that in v. 44, *those loving you.* · *Reward*, not merely compensation as in v. 12, but implying merit and a condign retribution. What claim to extraordinary approbation and to the advantages attending it? *Have ye*, more exact than Tyndale's and the Rhemish version, *shall ye have*, which supposes the reward to be wholly future; whereas the reference is to present right and security in the sight of God. *Publicans*, whose very name was a proverbial expression for the want of character and standing in society. This excommunication of a whole class or profession arose from the singular political condition of the Jews at this time. The Romans, to whom they had been virtually subject since the occupation of Jerusalem by Pompey, and particularly since the coronation of Herod as king of the Jews by order of the senate, with their usual wise policy, suffered them in most things to govern themselves. The two points in which their domination was most sensibly felt were the military occupation of the country and the oppressive system of taxation. This branch of the imperial revenue was farmed out to certain Roman knights, and by them to several gradations of subordinate collectors, each of whom was required to pay a stated sum to his superior, but with the privilege of raising as much more as he could for his own benefit. This financial system, which still exists in some oriental countries, must from its very nature be oppressive, by offering a premium for extortion and rapacity. To this was added in the case before us the additional reproach of being instruments and tools, not merely of a foreign despotism, but of a gentile or heathen power. The odium thus attached to the office of a publican, or Roman tax-gatherer, prevented any Jews from holding it except those of the most equivocal and reckless character, who, being thus excluded, by their very occupation, from respectable society, were naturally thrown into that of wicked and disreputable men. Thus a business, not unlawful in itself, and only made oppressive by the cupidity of those engaged in it, came by degrees to be regarded by devout Jews as intrinsically evil, and gave rise to that familiar but without reference to these facts unintelligible combination, "publicans and sinners." To do no more than such men did implied a very debased moral standard, or at least a very narrow view of what our Lord required in his disciples. The two interrogations in this verse are much more pointed than a simple denial that they had no reward, and a simple affirmation that the Publicans did likewise.

47 And if ye salute your brethren only, what do ye more (than others) ? do not even the publicans so ?

This is a rhetorical reiteration of the last verse with a slight change of expression. Instead of *love*, we have *salute* (or *greet*), as one of its habitual expressions. Our version here correctly substitutes a literal translation of the Greek verb for the gloss of Tyndale (*if ye be friendly*) and of Cranmer (*if ye make much of your brethren*). *Brethren*, not merely *brothers* in the strict sense, but near relatives. (See above, on 1, 25, and below, on 12, 46. 13, 55.) *What more*, literally, *what abundant* (or *excessive*), i. e. what beyond the ordinary practice, even of the worst men. The original expression (περισσόν) is the same as that in v. 37. Tyndale and his followers, who there translate it *more than*, have here the paraphrase or gloss, *what singular thing do ye?* Instead of *Publicans* (τελῶναι), the Codex Vaticanus and some others, followed by the latest critics, here read *gentiles* or *heathen* (ἐθνικοί), which not only varies the expression without varying the sense, but anticipates the striking combination in 18, 17 below, where an excommunicated brother is required to be treated as *a heathen and a publican*. As *so* is here equivalent to *the same* in the preceding verse, the sense is not affected by their transposition in some ancient copies and the latest critical editions. The argument contained in these two verses is, that the benevolence required in the law, as expounded and enforced in the Messiah's kingdom, must be something more than that habitually practised, from the force of selfish motives or mere natural affection, by the very classes whom the Jews regarded as the most abandoned and most desperately wicked.

48. Be ye therefore perfect, even as your Father which is in heaven is perfect.

In conclusion of his argument, if such it may be called, in favour of a large benevolence, vastly transcending. both in quantity and quality, the natural, conventional, or selfish kindness practised by the worst of men, our Lord reverts to the divine example, previously set forth in v. 45, and to the filial relation of his followers to God, as making that example an authoritative standard. It is not, however, a mere repetition of the language before used, but a generic statement of the principle there partially applied to one specific case of human conduct and divine administration. All that was there said was that, as God does not confine his providential gifts to those who in any sense deserve them, so his people need not be afraid of sinning if they love their enemies, repaying their most hostile enmity with acts of kindness. The great truth there implied is here propounded in its whole extent and simple grandeur. They were not to copy the imperfect models furnished even by the best of men, much less those furnished by the worst, but the perfect model set before them by their heavenly Father, i. e. by God, not as an absolute sovereign or inexorable judge, but in that parental character which he sustains to all the true disciples of his Son. The imperative form used in all the English versions (*be ye*), though it gives a good sense and may be defended by the passive meaning of the Hebrew future in the ten commandments, and throughout the law of Moses (see above in vs. 21. 27. 33. 43), must nevertheless yield to the exact form of the Greek verb which is future (ἔσεσθε), and may here be taken in its strict sense as denoting not so much what should or must as simply that which is to be. The ideas of certainty, necessity, and moral obligation, may be all implied, but they are not expressed; nor would they here be so appropriate to the context as the purpose of the whole discourse, which is not, as some imagine, to enact laws or prescribe rigid rules of conduct, but to set forth the true nature of the coming kingdom, and especially to rectify the false impressions which prevailed respecting it, even among many who were soon to enter it and rise to high distinction in it. Having shown, in execution of this purpose, that instead of lowering the standard of morality erected by the Pharisees and Scribes in their interpretation of the law, he should enforce it in a far more comprehensive, spiritual, stringent sense, and having urged them to the practice of an almost superhuman charity, transcending that of sinful man, and resembling that of God himself; he now explains this paradoxical and startling requisition, by assuring them that what he had prescribed was no empirical expedient to secure a special end in some extraordinary case, but the organic law or constitution of his kingdom, the fundamental principle of Christian ethics, making God the model and his will the rule, and suffering even the imperfect to aim only at perfection. *Therefore*, because all human models are essentially imperfect, and unfit to be copied even by those who in this respect resemble them. *Ye are to be* (in my kingdom and my service), i. e. must be in your aims and efforts now, and shall be really through grace hereafter, not essentially deficient in your principles and motives, as the best of men are when abandoned to themselves, but *perfect*, or complete, wanting nothing that is absolutely necessary to your ultimate perfection, because acting on the same principles, and aiming at the same ends, *as your Father in heaven*, or according to the latest text, *your heavenly Father*.

CHAPTER VI.

HAVING set forth the difference between the standard of morality acknowledged by the Scribes and Pharisees and that to be erected in the kingdom of Messiah, and exemplified this difference in the treatment of several prevailing sins, our Lord proceeds, in this division of the Sermon on the Mount, to do the same thing with respect to several religious duties, namely, charity or almsgiving (1–4), secret prayer (5–15), and private fasting (16–18). Assuming the necessity of all these duties, he exposes the hypocrisy and ostentation which characterized the Pharisaical performance of them, and exhorts his followers to avoid this error by performing them exclusively to God and not to man, and in the single hope of a divine reward, without the least view to mere secular advantage. This advice is then extended to the whole course of life, which can be truly happy only when the object of supreme affection is an undivided and a heavenly one (19–21). This is illustrated by an analogy derived from the economy of human sight (22–23), and by another from domestic service, with a formal application to the case in hand (24). Far from losing by this undivided consecration, they would gain immunity from wasting care by trusting in God's constant care of them, which is established by two arguments of opposite descriptions, from the greater to the less, and from the less to the greater. He who gave us life and bodies will not fail to supply food and raiment (25), and he who provides for the inferior creation, animal and vegetable, will not fail to do the same for man (26–30). Undue solicitude is not only useless (27) but irreligious, heathenish, dishonouring to God (31–32); whereas by seeking first to do his will and to promote his glory, these inferior favours may be best secured (33). And as these considerations ought to banish from the minds of Christ's disciples all excessive care about the present, they ought still more to prevent it in relation to the future, which instead of lessening can only multiply the evil by accumulation (34).

1. Take heed that ye do not your alms before men, to be seen of them : otherwise ye have no reward of your Father which is in heaven.

There is no want of coherence or abrupt transition here, but an obvious extension of the previous teachings about certain sins to certain religious duties, highly valued by the Jews, as they are now by the Mahometans, with whom they constitute almost the whole external part of their religion. The connecting thought may be thus supplied : 'such is the difference between the treatment of these sins by me and by the Scribes and Pharisees; but you must also learn to differ from them in the performance of religious duties.' *Take heed*, a Greek verb strictly meaning to *apply*, i. e. to hold one thing to another, and with a corresponding noun, to apply the mind, to attend; then elliptically even when the noun is not expressed, to take heed, to be cautious. As the reference is commonly to danger, physical or moral, it is usually rendered in this Gospel by the English verb *beware* (7, 15. 10, 17. 16, 6. 11. 12), and elsewhere by take heed (Luke 17, 3), give heed (Acts 8, 6), give attendance (1 Tim. 4, 13), have regard (Acts 18, 11), in all which versions the original idea of applying the mind to any object is distinctly traceable; nor is it wholly lost in 1 Tim. 3, 8, where it is rendered, *given to* (much wine), but really means, *giving*, i. e. giving one's attention, or one's self, to that indulgence. Its use at the beginning of this verse suggests at once the importance of the caution and the difficulty of observing it. It cannot be denied that the reference to alms is here somewhat abrupt, and that there is something like tautology in the recurrence of the same word at the opening of the next verse. Although these are mere rhetorical minutiæ, not affecting the essential meaning, it is worthy of remark that they are both removed by what the latest critics give us as the true text, instead of *alms* (ἐλεημοσύνην) reading *righteousness* (δικαιοσύνην), on the authority of the Vatican and Beza manuscripts, the oldest Latin versions, and some Fathers. This external testimony is remarkably confirmed by the internal evidence, i. e. by the improvement in the sense, or at least in the symmetrical structure of the passage, which then opens with a general precept as to all religious duties (v. 1), and afterwards proceeds to alms-giving, as the first specification (v. 2). There is no need therefore, of making the two terms synomymous, as in the later Hebrew usage. It is altogether better to give *righteousness* its full generic sense of right doing, or conformity to the will of God, with special reference in this connection to religious duties. (See above, on 3, 15. 5, 6. 10. 20.) *Your righteousness*, that which you habitually practise and acknowledge as incumbent on you. *That ye do not*, more exactly, *not to do*, the infinitive depending in construction on the verb (*take heed*) at the beginning of the sentence. 'Be careful not to practise your religious duties in the sight (before the face) of men,' i. e. of other men, but not without a sensible antithesis with God, as mentioned in the other clause. The consistency of this charge with the positive command in 5, 16, is saved by the difference of end or motive. There it was to glorify God; here it is, not merely to be *seen* by men, but to be gazed at as a show or spectacle, the Greek verb (ϑεαϑῆναι) being that from which come *theatre, theatrical*, &c. (See below, on 11, 7. 22, 11. 23, 5.) The idea of deliberate intention, as distinguished from a mere fortuitous result, is expressed precisely as in 5, 27, by a preposition and an article prefixed to the infinitive (πρὸς τὸ ϑεαϑῆναι). The general precept then, even as to external duties, is that although men may see them, and in certain cases ought to see them (see above, on 5, 16), they are never to be done directly, much less solely or supremely, for that purpose. This prohibition equally extends to the religious duties subsequently mentioned, and by parity of reason to all others. The ground or motive is assigned in the last clause of the verse before us. *Otherwise* (the older English versions have *or else*), literally, *but if not*, with a particle annexed (εἰ δὲ μήγε) which can scarcely be expressed in English, but is used in Greek to qualify or limit what is said, and often corresponds very nearly to our phrase, *at least*. 'Take heed . . . or at least if you do not,' &c., which is nearly equivalent to saying, 'take heed if you regard your own true interest, as well as duty.' *Reward*, not meritorious or condign recompense, as in 5, 46, but simply compensation or retributive advantage, as in 5, 12. 'If you do not guard against this formal ostentation in religious duties, you have nothing to expect from them in the way of a divine blessing.' *With your Father*, i. e. laid up, in reserve for you, in his presence or his purpose. The idea is the same with that expressed in 5, 12 by the phrase *in heaven*. *The* (one, i. e. *the Father*) *in the heavens*, as distinguished from all human parents, whether natural or spiritual (see above, on 5, 16).

2. Therefore when thou doest (thine) alms, do not sound a trumpet before thee, as the hypocrites do, in the

synagogues, and in the streets, that they may have glory of men. Verily, I say unto you, They have their reward.

The negative precept as to alms is then repeated in a more specific form. Or according to the other text already mentioned, the generic rule relating to all duties is now specially applied to one. *Therefore*, because all such duties must be done to God and not to man. *When thou doest*, implying that it would be done and must be done of course, provided it were well done. *Alms* is itself a contraction, technically called a corruption, of the Greek word here used (ἐλεημοσύνη), and of which we have a more direct derivative in the somewhat uncouth adjective, *eleemosynary*.* The Greek noun, according to its etymology, means first *mercifulness*, then its exercise, especially in the relief of want. An analogous usage is that of *charity* in English, as denoting both a disposition or affection of the mind and its material effect or product. The pronoun (*thine alms*) is supplied by the translator from v. 4 below. The translation of the next words (*cause not a trumpet to be sounded*), is still more paraphrastic than the version in the text. Better, because more exact, than either would be, *trumpet not before thee*, if the English verb (*to trumpet*) could be used without an expressed object. There is no need of resorting to the doubtful and improbable assumption of a literal trumpeting, in ancient times or Oriental countries, either by the beggars or their benefactors; much less to the farfetched and unnatural allusion to the trumpet-shaped money-boxes in the temple-treasury, and to the ringing of the coin as it fell into them! The phrase requires no elucidation beyond that which it receives from the figurative use in various idioms of the trumpet, as a loud and brawling instrument, to represent an ostentatious boastful exhibition of ourselves or others. *Before thee* is a trait derived no doubt from actual military usage, or the general practice of trumpeters preceding those whom they announced or heralded: 'Do not give alms, as a general goes to battle, or a king before his people, with a trumpeter to lead the way and arouse attention.' In the last clause this negative command is made still more specific by presenting, as the thing to be avoided, the habitual practice of a certain class, apparently referred to as well known to all the hearers. *The hypocrites*, a Greek noun, the verbal root of which means properly to answer or respond, e. g. as an oracle, or in dramatic dialogue, from which last usage the derivative acquires the specific sense of *actor*, one who acts a part, to which the later Hellenistic usage † added the moral application to dissemblers, false pretenders, which is the only meaning of the word in modern languages. It is here applied by implication, as it elsewhere is expressly (see below, on 23, 13–29) to the whole class of Pharisees and Scribes, with whose false morality and spurious religion, our Lord,

---

* The *s* in *alms* is therefore radical, and not necessarily the plural termination; so that the phrase *an alms*, employed by our translators (Acts 3, 3), is perfectly grammatical. See Trench on Revision, p. 43.

† See the Septuagint version of Job 34, 30. 36, 13, where it is used to represent the Hebrew חָנֵף.

throughout this passage (from 5, 20 to 6, 18), is contrasting the morality and piety which were to be required and promoted in the kingdom of Messiah. *Do*, i. e. habitually, as a constant and notorious practice. He is evidently not communicating new and unknown facts, but fearlessly appealing to his hearers as the witnesses of what he says, q. d. 'as you well know that the Pharisees and Scribes do.' *In the synagogues*, or meetings for religious worship (see above, on 4, 23), which have always been the chosen scenes for the display of formal ostentatious piety. *And in the streets*, a Greek word which in the early classics has a meaning altogether different (that of violent or rushing motion), but in later and especially in Hellenistic usage, has obviously acquired the meaning here attached to it by all translators. From a supposed antithesis to *broad ways* (πλατεῖαι) in one passage (Luke 14, 21), it is there translated *lanes*, and commonly explained to mean narrow and confined streets. But the contrast even there is doubtful, as the terms may be substantially synonymous, and does not occur either here or in Acts 12, 10; while in Acts 9, 11, the only other instance of its use in the New Testament, the implication is the other way. Nor is it probable that these ambitious formalists, who sought the honour that proceeds from men and not from God (John 5, 44), would seek it in the lanes and alleys of the Holy City, as distinguished from its wider streets and open places. As connected here with *synagogues*, the word more readily suggests the thought of crowded thoroughfares, if not as its specific import, yet as comprehended in its wider sense of streets in general. This ostentatious charity was not fortuitous or unsought, but deliberately purposed. *Have glory* is in Greek a passive form of the verb translated *glorify* in 5, 16, *that they may be glorified by men*, i. e. admired, applauded, flattered, not in private but in public. With significant allusion to his own words in the close of the preceding verse (*ye have no reward*, &c.), he affirms the contrary of these theatrical religionists, and with a solemn formula suggestive of some deep and hidden meaning. *Verily* (*amen*, as in 5, 18. 26) *I say unto you*, and with authority, as claiming your attention and belief of something paradoxical yet true, and of the highest moment. *They have*, not the simple verb commonly so rendered (as in v. 1), but a form compounded with the preposition (ἀπό) *from*, away from, and therefore frequently denoting distance (15, 8. Luke 7, 6. 15, 20. 24, 13), but in other cases giving an intensive force to the essential meaning of the verb, by suggesting the accessory idea of completeness, fulness (see Luke 6, 24. Phil. 4, 18. Philem. 15). According to this second usage, it may here mean that *they have already*, or already full, without the prospect of increase hereafter. *Their reward*, i. e. all that they can claim or hope for, namely, the applause of men. As this is all that they have sought in their devotions, it is all they are to have, in the way of benefit or personal advantage. In this verse, as in 5, 23. 29. 36. 39, there is a sudden change from the plural to the singular, as if to give the exhortation more point by addressing it to one and not to many.

3. But when thou doest alms, let not thy left hand know what thy right hand doeth.

This verse presents, in contrast with the Pharisaic mode of giving alms, the Christian manner of performing the same duty. The personal contrast is more prominent in Greek, because the pronoun stands at the beginning of the sentence. *When thou doest*, or retaining the original construction, which is that of the genitive absolute, *thou doing alms*, or practising the grace of charity. The last clause seems to be proverbial and expressive of the utmost secrecy, so close that one part of the body may be said not to know the movements of another. This is still more striking when affirmed of parts so much alike and near together as the double members. The force and beauty of this clause are greatly weakened by supposing a continued allusion to the trumpet, held in one hand while the other gives the alms, or even to the more familiar act of taking money with the right hand from the purse held in the left, or vice versa, or to that of pouring small change from the one into the other. The very strength of these expressions might have taught interpreters that they are not a formal rule of duty, but a hyperbolical negation of all morbid appetite for vain publicity and popular applause in the performance of religious duties. 'Far from trumpeting your charities, or doing them in order to be seen of men, let the very members of your body keep the secret from each other.' The idea that the right hand means the man himself, and the left hand those who are his nearest and most intimate associates, is not only gratuitous, but unsupported either by Scriptural or classical usage. Such a mode of treating proverbs, with their strong and often paradoxical expressions, would be quite destructive of their point and power, as well as offensive to a truly refined taste.

4. That thine alms may be in secret: and thy Father which seeth in secret, himself shall reward thee openly.

To those who had been brought up under a formal, ostentatious system, like that of the Scribes and Pharisees, it might have seemed that the foregoing precept nullified the main design of charitable giving, namely, that of exhibiting a charitable spirit. But our Lord here teaches that this loss of notoriety is not an incidental evil, but an object to be aimed at. *So that*, expressing not merely the result, but the purpose of the action. *Thy alms*, as distinguished from the alms of the hypocrites denounced in v. 2. *In secret*, literally, *in the hidden (place)*, again suggesting not an accidental but an intentional concealment. The remainder of the verse assigns the motive or inducement for this sacrifice of notoriety and human praise. The principle involved is, that as all religious duty is performed to God, and is dependent on his blessing for its good effects, it matters comparatively little whether man is cognizant of it or not. It is enough if God beholds it and will bless it. *Thy father, the (one) seeing in secret*, no less certainly and clearly than in public, being independent of man's efforts either to disclose or hide. This is set forth in the Old Testament as a necessary incident of God's omniscience (Ps. 139, 12). *Himself* (omitted in the older versions), without reference to human knowledge or opinion, *will reward*, or rather *will repay thee* (so the Rhemish Bible), will make good whatever loss may seem to be sustained by thus relinquishing the praise of man. *Openly*, in public, corresponding to *in secret* in the other clause. This seems to circumscribe the promise too much, and may therefore have been added to the text by ancient copyists, as it is not found in the Vatican and Beza codices, and is omitted by the latest critics.

5. And when thou prayest, thou shalt not be as the hypocrites (are) : for they love to pray standing in the synagogues, and in the corners of the streets, that they may be seen of men. Verily, I say unto you, They have their reward.

The same rule is now applied to prayer, which from its very nature is addressed to God not man, so that whoever acts as if the latter were the case, thereby proves himself a hypocrite, a mere performer, one who acts the part of a true worshipper of God, but in his heart is courting the applause of man. Such an example, only too familiar to his hearers, Christ exhorts his followers to shun. *When thou prayest*, assuming that they would pray and must pray, not merely in obedience to a positive command, nor even as a necessary means of spiritual growth, but as a vital function of the new life, which can no more be dispensed with than the body can live without breath or without blood. *Thou shalt not be*, or the future may be taken as in 5, 48, *thou art not to be*, this is not what I look for and require in the subjects of my kingdom, for the reason given in the next clause. *Because* (ὅτι) *they love*, implying not an error of judgment but a perverse will and a corrupt state of affection. They delighted in theatrical and ostentatious worship, which to them was the essence of devotion, so that secret prayer was none at all and therefore probably neglected altogether, as it often is where ritual religion reigns. *The synagogues* are not named as improper places of devotion, for which end they were established, but simply as the places where these hypocrites exhibited their formal worship. *The corners of the streets* were in themselves unsuited to devotion, as the noisiest and most crowded parts of every city, so that the very choice of such a place for prayer betrayed a want of the right spirit and a disposition to worship man rather than God. The word here rendered *streets* is not the one employed in verse 2, but the one referred to in the note there as denoting strictly *broad* (*ways*), wide streets. These are evidently mentioned as the most frequented, which confirms our previous conclusion that the other word does not mean lanes or alleys, which the hypocrites would scarcely have selected for their alms, while they prayed at the corners of the widest thoroughfares. *Standing* is no part of the hypocritical display, which would rather have affected genuflexion in the public highway, but is simply mentioned as the customary posture of the Jews in prayer, ascribed by our Lord elsewhere, not only to the boasting Pharisee, but also to the broken-hearted Publican (Luke 18, 11–13). *That*, not merely so that, but in order that, to the intent that, *they may be seen of* (more exactly *may appear to*) men. The use of this verb may be intended to suggest that they *appear* to pray when in truth they are only acting. *Verily I say*, the same solemn formula as at the close of the preceding topic, in the last clause of v. 2, and with the same return to the plural pronoun (ὑμῖν), though the singular is used before and after.

6. But thou, when thou prayest, enter into thy closet, and when thou hast shut thy door, pray to thy Father which is in secret; and thy Father, which seeth in secret, shall reward thee openly.

Here, as in reference to alms, the description of the practice of the hypocrites introduces a prescription of the method to be used by Christ's disciple. *But thou*, in opposition to the ostentatious prayers which he had just described. *Closet*, an English word denoting properly a room within a room, and here used to translate a Greek one meaning *store-room*, the essential idea being that of an innermost and most retired apartment. *Thy closet*, that belonging to thyself and subject to thy own control. *Having shut the door*, not only closed but fastened it, which is the proper meaning of the Greek verb. No one perhaps has ever deemed that the external acts here mentioned are essential to acceptable devotion, or that the Lord's Prayer cannot lawfully be used in any place but a closet, or even there with open doors. All feel that these are merely strong expressions for the strictest privacy, although consistency requires the same strict interpretation here that some would put upon the strong terms of other precepts in the Sermon on the Mount, e. g. 5, 34. 39. The promise in the last clause is precisely similar to that in v. 4, with the same doubt overhanging the last words as a possible interpolation. These expressions limit the whole passage to personal or private prayer and make it wholly inapplicable to common prayer or public worship, which is a distinct and independent duty, resting on express divine command. It may however be a question, whether we are not here forbidden to confound the two kinds of devotion by performing private prayer in public places so as to attract attention and be "seen of men."

7. But when ye pray, use not vain repetitions, as the heathen (do): for they think that they shall be heard for their much speaking.

Having taught precisely the same lesson with respect to alms and prayer, to wit, that they must be performed to God and not to man, and, therefore, unless otherwise required, in private not in public; our Lord goes further with respect to prayer, and adds a warning against heathenish as well as pharisaical abuses. In this additional instruction, he resumes the plural form, which had been dropped at the close of the first verse, excepting only the repeated formula, *Amen* (or *verily*) *I say unto you* (vs. 2. 5). This remarkable interchange of number without visible necessity, would seem to point to one of two conclusions; either that the difference of number in the second person is itself unmeaning, and that the later Greeks had begun to use the singular and plural indiscriminately, as we now do; or that what follows has respect to common not to private prayer. The latter view is favoured by the circumstance, which always has to some appeared surprising, that the plural form is used throughout the Lord's Prayer (vs. 9–13), while in the subsequent directions as to fasting (vs. 16–18), both are used successively. *But when ye pray* might also be translated, *praying moreover*, (δέ), i. e. in addition to the previous warning against ostentation and formality. *Use not vain repetitions* is a paraphrase and gloss but not a version, giving probably the sense but not the form of the original, consisting of a single word, a verb unknown to classic Greek and variously derived, the older writers tracing it to Battus, a Cyrenian king and stammerer, mentioned by Herodotus; the moderns making it what the grammarians call an onomatopoetic word, i. e. formed in imitation of the natural sound, like *babble*, which is here used by Tyndale and his followers. This is expressly represented as a heathen practice, of which two remarkable examples are preserved in Scripture; that of the priests of Baal, in Elijah's time, who "called on the name of Baal from morning even until noon, saying, Oh Baal, hear us!" (1 Kings 18, 26); and that of the worshippers of Artemis or Dian at Ephesus, in Paul's time, who "all with one voice, about the space of two hours, cried out, Great is Diana of the Ephesians" (Acts 19, 34). *The heathens*, or *gentiles*, not the noun which is commonly so rendered (ἔθνη) and which properly means *nations* (see above, on 4, 15), but an adjective derived from it and strictly meaning *national*, but absolutely used in the same sense as the primitive noun, or possibly with more explicit reference to individuals. (See above, on 5, 47, where the latest critics substitute it for the common reading, *publicans*). The last clause gives the origin or motive of this heathen practice. *For they think* (are of opinion) *that in* (i. e. in the use or in consideration of) *their much speaking* (or loquacity), in Greek a single but compound word (πολυλογιά, polylogy). *They will be heard*, or listened to, a compound verb, applied especially to audience in prayer and implying a favourable answer. (See Luke 1, 13. Acts 10, 31. Heb. 5, 7, but compare 1 Cor. 14, 21.) This notion is but one form of the wide-spread heathen error, which has also found its way into the Christian world, that religion, and especially that prayer or worship is rather a magical charm than a rational or reasonable service (Rom. 12, 1), and that as the *opus operatum* has intrinsic efficacy, its effect will bear proportion to the quantity, and hence the value of mere repetition. It has often been remarked that in corrupted Christian churches one of

8. Be not ye therefore like unto them: for your Father knoweth what things ye have need of before ye ask him.

Therefore, because the practice is thus heathenish, and rests upon an ethnic superstition. *Be not like them* is in Greek still stronger from the passive form and meaning of the verb, *be not likened* (or *assimilated*) to them, i. e. by your own act, or by voluntarily following their example.* The last clause gives a still deeper reason for the vain repetitions of the heathen, which is at the same time a more cogent reason why the Christian cannot practise them, to wit, because they rest upon a grovelling and contracted view of the divine perfections, an idea that the wants of men can only be made known to God by constant iteration. The disciple must not, therefore, do as they do, for he has not even their excuse of ignorance. *Your father,* not an empty form of speech, but intended (as in 5. 16. 45. 48. 6, 1. 4. 6) to remind them of the filial relation which, as Christ's disciples, they sustained to God, and which is here peculiarly appropriate in speaking of their wants and his ability and willingness to help them. This relation was familiar to the saints of the Old Testament. "Like as a father pitieth his children, so the Lord pitieth them that fear him" (Ps. 103, 13). *Before ye ask him,* or before your asking him, so that if prayer were intended to inform him of our wants, it would be altogether useless and absurd; how much more the notion, that he needs not only to be told, but to be often told, of man's necessities. The true use and effect of prayer, though fully explained elsewhere, it was no part of our Lord's design to set forth here, but only to deny that it had any such design as that which lay at the foundation of the heathenish battology.

9. After this manner therefore pray ye: Our Father which art in heaven, Hallowed be thy name.

Not contented with the negative injunction which precedes, our Lord provides his hearers with a positive preservative against the vain repetitions of the heathen, by giving them a specimen of brief, simple, comprehensive prayer, adapted in its form to their actual position on the threshold of the new dispensation, and therefore containing no direct allusion to himself or his peculiar work, yet so constructed as to furnish for perpetual use a framework into which all lawful prayers might readily be fitted, or a model upon which they might be newly fashioned. But the primary design of the Lord's Prayer, as it is tra-

---

* For another application of the same verb in our Lord's parabolical diction, see below, on 7, 24. 11, 16. 13, 24. 18, 23. 22, 2. 25, 1.

ditionally called, was to show the disciples, by example no less than by precept, how the ethnic battology might be avoided. *Therefore, because you will not be permitted to use vain repetitions. After this manner* is Tyndale's paraphrastic version of the single Greek word meaning *thus* or *so*, and here referring, not, as it sometimes does, to what precedes (e. g. 5, 16. 19), but wholly to what follows. *Pray ye,* with stress upon the pronoun, which is not required in Greek to indicate the person, and must therefore be regarded as emphatic. *Ye*, my followers and disciples, as distinguished from the ignorant and superstitious heathen. That this is not a requisition of punctilious adherence to the form, much less of its exclusive use, is clear from the existence of two equally authoritative forms (see Luke 11, 2–4), a circumstance which has occasioned much embarrassment to scrupulous liturgists. *Our Father, the (one) in the heavens*, a description repeatedly employed by Christ before in this discourse, and now put into the mouths of his disciples, as an explicit recognition of their filial relation to God, not only as their maker and their providential benefactor, but as the Father of our Lord himself, through whom they are adopted into a more intimate and spiritual sonship, which is here by implication represented as their only warrant for approaching him. *Hallowed*, sanctified, made holy, i. e. treated as such, recognized as sacred, reverenced and thereby glorified, a corresponding use of which verb may be seen above in 5, 16. *Name* is not to be diluted or explained away, as meaning every thing by which God is made known to his creatures, but to be primarily taken in its proper sense of title, appellation, with particular allusion to the name *Jehovah*, by which he was distinguished from all false gods and described not only as a self-existent and eternal being (which that name denotes), but also as the God who was in covenant with Israel, the God of revelation and the God of grace, or in New Testament language, the God and Father of our Lord Jesus Christ (2 Cor. 11, 31). Thus understood, the name of God can be hallowed only by his reverent and believing recognition as the Saviour, no less than the maker, judge, and ruler of the world. It is one of the most prominent and striking features of this model-prayer, that it begins with God's own glory, as the great end to be sought, with the necessary means of its promotion, and then, as something secondary or subordinate, asks those things which relate to the petitioner himself. This is not to be regarded as an accidental circumstance, but as a practical lesson with respect to the comparative importance of divine and human interests, and to their relative position in our prayers, as the expression of our wishes and our governing affections.

10. Thy kingdom come. Thy will be done in earth, as (it is) in heaven.

Thy kingdom, that of the Messiah, which was now about to be erected. This expression shows that the Lord's Prayer was originally designed and suited for the actual condition of affairs, before the church was formally reorganized and the written revelation of divine truth closed; so that whatever light may be reflected upon its language from events of later date, we must not lose sight of its historical occasion and its primary sense, as understood by those to whom it was first given. *Come*, into existence, into view, as something introduced *ab extra*, as descending from above. This petition virtually comprehends all the ulterior effects of the Messiah's advent, and may be legitimately used by us with special reference to these, provided that in formally interpreting the prayer in its historical connection, we distinguish what has thus been added to it from its simple meaning as originally uttered. There is less difficulty as to this point in the third petition, which is couched in universal terms, no more restricted then than now, and having no specific reference, even in expression, to a temporary state of things. *Thy will*, a Hellenistic noun derived from a classical Greek verb of frequent use and in conformity to classical analogy and usage as to termination. In this connection it of course means neither the faculty nor exercise of will, but its objective product, that which is willed, as embodied in the law, or made known through a revelation. *Be done*, a passive form, referring more directly to the agency of man than the original (γενηϑήτω), which is also passive but derived not from the active verb *to do*, but from a neuter verb (γίνομαι) originally meaning *to become*, or to begin to be, and so to happen, come to pass, in which sense it is very common but is variously rendered (see above, on 1, 22. 4, 3. 5, 18. 45). The passive form adds to the idea of occurring, happening, that of its being brought about by the agency of other beings, although not so strongly or distinctly as our English passive (*done*), which however is substantially correct. The recognition of God's name and the erection of God's kingdom, although not identical, are certainly coincident with the fulfilment of his will. *In earth as* (*it is*) *in heaven* is the sense but not the form of the original, in which the order is reversed, the model being placed first and the copy afterwards, *as in heaven, also upon earth*. As the reference is evidently not to mere physical results, but also if not chiefly to the moral accomplishment of the divine will, *heaven* and *earth* may be explained as meaning the abode of angels and of men respectively, *as by angels, so by men*. The *as* may be understood as expressing similarity in kind and in completeness. 'Let thy will be done as cheerfully and fully in this lower world as in the upper.'

11. Give us this day our daily bread.

Here begins the second part of the Lord's Prayer, relating to the wants of the petitioners, which, though subordinated to the glory and the sovereignty of God, are not in conflict with them, but included in them, and are now allowed to occupy the brief space which remains of this divine epitome. The first prayer, under this head, is for bodily subsistence, represented, as it often is, by food, and this again by bread, the staff of life, and the main staple of subsistence among all but the most degraded nations. The epithet prefixed to it is one of the most doubtful and disputed words in Scripture. Of the various meanings which have been attached to it, interpreters are mainly divided between two, both which are very ancient, and both founded on the etymology. The first supposes the original expression (ἐπιούσιον), to be made up of a preposition (ἐπί) and a noun (οὐσία) denoting essence or substance, and the whole phrase to mean that which is required for support. The objection to this explanation, which affords a very good sense, and agrees well with the context, lies not in the form of the compound, which is justified by usage, but in the sense ascribed to the compounded noun (οὐσία), which properly means essence or substance, not subsistence. The other explanation derives the word from a participle (ἐπιοῦσα) coming, coming on, an elliptical expression for the coming or ensuing day (ἡμέρα ἐπιοῦσα). The objection to this is the apparent incongruity of asking for to-morrow's bread to-day. The Vulgate cuts the knot by copying the form of the original (*panem supersubstantialem*), and the Rhemish Bible follows it as usual (*give us to-day our supersubstantial bread*). Apart from this unmeaning imitation, there is little choice between the two interpretations, each of which affords a good sense and appropriate in this connection, nay, a sense which would have been suggested by the context if the doubtful word had been omitted. The bread for which we pray is of course that which supports us, and of which we stand in daily need. The prayer for spiritual nourishment may either be considered as included in the wide term *bread*, or as suggested by an obvious association and analogy, which furnishes a natural transition to the prayer of the next verse.

12. And forgive us our debts, as we forgive our debtors.

This petition has respect to the greatest and most urgent of all wants, the forgiveness of sin. *And remit to us*, the same verb that occurs above in 4, 40, in the sense of *let go*, here applied by a natural figure to the remission of the claims of justice upon an offender. *Our debts*, another natural expression for moral delinquency or breach of obligation, though the Greek word, in the only other place where it occurs (Rom. 4, 4), is no less naturally used to signify the obligation itself. The last clause is not conditional but comparative, explaining the remission asked as just the same with that habitually practised in the case of human debtors. This supposes the word *debtors* to have here its strict commercial sense, and the reference to mutual forgiveness of offences generally to be first made in v. 14. But as that purports to be an explanation of something previously said, which can only be the cause before us, most interpreters take *debtors* in a sense analogous to that of *debts*, to wit, offenders or transgressors. This may seem to make mutual forgiveness a condition of divine forgiveness; but it necessarily means no more than that those who ask for pardon must be ready to bestow it.

13. And lead us not into temptation, but deliver us from evil. For thine is the kingdom, and the power, and the glory, for ever. Amen.

The sixth petition is for preservation and deliverance from future sin and its effects. *Temptation* means originally *trial*, but in usage more specifically moral trial or a test of character, especially by giving men the opportunity of choice between sin and obedience. A still stronger sense, predominant in modern usage, is that of direct solicitation to evil. In this sense, God is said to tempt no man (James 1, 13), while in the others, it is expressly predicated of him (Gen. 22, 1). The word here cannot mean mere trials, in the sense of troubles and afflictions, not even considered as tests of faith, but must include the opportunity of sinning and the peril of it, as an evil to be deprecated and if possible escaped. *Lead us*, not merely as the sense of letting us be led by others, but in that of providentially involving us in circumstances which afford us opportunities and motives to transgress, without coercing us to do so. *But*, not a separate petition, but an antithetical division of the same, and as such necessary to complete it, the two parts interpreting each other. If temptation here means only trial in the lower sense of trouble and affliction, then the *evil* of the last clause must be natural evil or distress. But as temptation has respect to sin as well as suffering, evil must at least include that of a moral nature, whether we take it as an abstract or a concrete term, *evil* in general, or *the evil (one)*, considered as the author of sin and as the tempter of mankind, which last idea agrees well with the prayer against temptation in the other clause. *Deliver*, rescue, save by drawing to thyself, a beautiful and most appropriate idea, which the Greek verb expresses in the usage of the classics. *For* assigns the ground of the whole prayer, or of its being addressed to God. 'We ask all this of thee because.' &c. *Thine*, belonging to thee, as thy right, and as thy actual possession. *The kingdom*, the right to reign and actual dominion; hence the prayer, 'thy kingdom come.' *The power*, the ability to answer these petitions and to grant these gifts, implying absolute omnipotence. *Glory*, the acknowledgment or recognition of inherent excellence, the thing prayed for in the first petition, which is here justified by this ascription of it to the Father as his right and his prerogative. *Forever*, literally, *to the ages*, in Greek a word which properly denotes *duration*, sometimes definite, as an age, a lifetime, or a dispensation, but when limited by nothing in the context, indefinite and even infinite duration. *Amen*, the Hebrew word which occurs so often at the beginning of a sentence and is then translated *verily* (see above, on 5, 18. 26. 6, 2. 5), but here used as a particle of assent or concurrence, often found at the close of prayers and other forms of a religious kind when uttered by one or more persons in the name of others.* This doxology is wanting in some an-

---

* Num. 5, 22. Deut. 27, 15. 1 Kings 1, 36. 1 Chron. 16, 36. Ps. 106, 48. Jer. 28, 6. Matt. 6, 13. 1 Cor. 14, 16. Rev. 5, 14. 22, 20.

cient codices (especially the Vatican and Beza), and omitted in quotation by some ancient writers, which has led the modern critics to regard it as an addition from some old church liturgy. Its great antiquity, however, and its constant use for ages, make it safer to retain it till some light is thrown upon the four centuries, or more, which intervene between the date of this gospel and the oldest extant manuscript.

14. For, if ye forgive men their trespasses, your heavenly Father will also forgive you ·

15. But, if ye forgive not men their trespasses, neither will your Father forgive your trespasses.

The next two verses, as already stated, purport to give a reason for something in the previous context, which can only be the last clause of v. 12. As if he had said, ' In asking for forgiveness, you must stand prepared to exercise it also, for unless you are, you cannot be forgiven, not because the one is the condition of the other, but because the two must go together, and the absence of the one proves the absence of the other.' The verb four times repeated here is the same with that in v. 12; but instead of the word *debts*, another figure is employed, that of a fall or false step, rendered in the English versions, *trespass*, and intended to express the same idea, that of sin, which may be considered either as a debt due to the divine justice, or as a lapse from the straight course of moral rectitude. The fulness and precision with which the alternative is here presented may appear superfluous, but adds to the solemnity of the assurance, and would no doubt strengthen the impression on the minds of the original hearers. In this, as in the whole preceding context, God is still presented in his fatherly relation to all true believers; as if to intimate that even that relation, tender as it is, would give no indulgence to an unforgiving spirit.

16. Moreover, when ye fast, be not as the hypocrites, of a sad countenance : for they disfigure their faces, that they may appear unto men to fast. Verily, I say unto you, They have their reward.

The contrast between formalism and genuine religion is now carried out in reference to a third great duty, that of fasting, the continued exercise of which, like that of charity and prayer, is here assumed, without distinguishing between the true and false mode of performing it, a subject treated by our Saviour elsewhere. (See below, on 9, 14. 15.) The plural form, resumed in the preceding verses, is continued through the one before us, after which it again gives place to the singular precisely as in vs. 2 and 6 above. Here too, as there, the practice of the hypocrites is first described, with an injunction to avoid it. *Be not*, or more exactly, *become not*, the Greek word being not the simple verb of existence (as in v. 5), but the one explained above in v. 10, and employed here to suggest the idea of a change from their ordinary look and manner. *Of a sad countenance* (Geneva Bible, *look not sour*), in Greek a single word, denoting angry, sullen, or morose, not merely in feeling but in aspect, as the derivation of the term implies. This allusion to the habits of the Pharisees, though probably intelligible of itself to most of our Lord's hearers, is explained by the addition of a positive description. *For*, I say like the hypocrites, because, &c. *Disfigure*, literally, cause to disappear or vanish, either by changing the appearance, as in this case, or by destroying, as in vs. 19. 20. *Appear to men to fast* is neither the construction nor the sense of the original, or is at least ambiguous, as it may mean that they would seem to fast when they do not, whereas the meaning of the Greek is that they may appear to (or as the same verb is translated in v. 5 above, *be seen of*, i. e. by) *men (to be) fasting*. The fault here charged is not that of a false pretence, but that of ostentation. They did fast, and they took care that it should be known by their austere and mortified appearance. The last clause is the same as in vs. 2. 5, the emphatic repetition giving to this part of the discourse a rhythmical or measured structure, suited not only to impress the hearers at the time, but also to engrave it on the memory.

17. But thou, when thou fastest, anoint thy head, and wash thy face ;

18. That thou appear not unto men, to fast, but unto thy Father, which is in secret : and thy Father, which seeth in secret, shall reward thee openly.

We have here the usual antithesis or contrast (as in vs. 2. 6) between Pharisaical and Christian practice, with the usual transition to the singular number. *But*, in opposition to this hateful ostentation, *thou*, my individual disciple, not only as opposed to the hypocritical formalist just described, but as distinguished from the aggregate body of believers. *When thou fastest*, literally, *fasting*, at the time or in the act of fasting. There are two ways of interpreting the last clause, both of which are perfectly grammatical. The first and probably the common one is founded on the fact that fragrant unguents were a favourite luxury at ancient feasts, and that anointing is a frequent figure in the Scriptures for rejoicing. (See for example Ps. 45, 7. Isai. 61, 3, where the "oil of gladness" and the "oil of joy" are identical in Hebrew.) In accordance with this usage the command before us is to shun the sanctimonious ostentation of the Pharisees by going to the opposite extreme ; instead of looking sad or sour, appearing to be more than usually gay and cheerful. The obvious objection to this is, that it prescribes a course of conduct inconsistent with that state of mind, of which religious fasting is the index and the counterpart, as stated by our Lord himself upon a subsequent occasion. (See below, on 9, 14. 15.) To require external mirth and gaiety of men who are suffering the pangs of spiritual grief, would be a mockery unworthy of our blessed Master, and without a parallel in his teachings elsewhere. But besides this incongruity between the inward state supposed and the outward acts enjoined, the requisition, thus explained, is one of positive deception, which is still more inconceivable. To let men see that they were fasting was hypocrisy in those who did it; how much more to seem to be rejoicing when they were in fact distressed. These objections do not lie against the other explanation, which supposes washing and anointing to be here not extraordinary festive usages, but ordinary acts of cleanliness and neatness, and the requisition to be simply to appear as usual, instead of that neglect or positive disfigurement, which told to all around that the religionist was in a state of spiritual discipline or conflict. Even in this case there would be concealment; but concealment is not falsehood; nor are we bound by any principle of morals or religion to disclose our secret exercises to the view of others. All this, however, presupposes that the fasting here intended, like the prayer in v. 6, is a personal and private duty, without any reference to public services of that kind to which we may be called in company with others. This presumption, founded on the context and the language of v. 17, becomes a certainty in that which follows, where the same reason for consenting to be unseen by the eye of man is given with respect to fasting, that was previously given with respect to alms and prayer in vs. 4. 6.

19. Lay not up for yourselves treasures upon earth, where moth and rust doth corrupt, and where thieves break through and steal:

20. But lay up for yourselves treasures in heaven, where neither moth nor rust doth corrupt, and where thieves do not break through nor steal.

There is no more incoherence or abruptness here than in 5, 17 above, though both transitions have been so described. In either case, the nexus and association of ideas, if not obvious and patent to the superficial reader, may be readily detected, and, when once pointed out, seems natural and easy. The great principle propounded in the foregoing context, as the law which ought to govern our religious duties, is, that they are not performed to man, but to God, and that he alone can recompense, or make them fruitful. But this, though originally introduced to show how certain duties ought to be performed, admits of a much wider application. It is, in fact, a fundamental principle of all religion, and the secret of all happiness and comfort, even in the present life. To show this, is the drift of the discourse in the remainder of this chapter, the principle being first laid down in vs. 19–21, and then elucidated and applied in vs. 22–34. The connection, then, is this, that as almsgiving, prayer, and fasting, must, in order to have any value, or accomplish any good, be performed as duties which we owe to God, and in reliance on his blessing, so the same is true of every thing in life, and of the whole course of life itself, the entire security and happiness of which depend upon our doing all for God, and in dependence upon him exclusively. This is strikingly and beautifully set forth in the verse before us, under the figure of amassing wealth, i. e. providing for our future welfare. (See the same idea carried out in one of our Lord's parables, preserved by Luke, 12, 16–21.) *Lay not up treasures*, is in Greek more pointed and expressive, because the verb and noun are kindred forms, *store not away stores*, or, retaining the derivative equivalent in English, *treasure not up treasures*, as the verb is actually rendered elsewhere (Rom. 2, 5), and by Wiclif here. *Upon earth*, not merely of an earthly nature, but dependent on this present life, and terminating with it. (Compare Paul's analogous expression, *worldly lusts*, Tit. 2, 12.) Divested of its figurative dress, the precept is, not to let our future happiness depend upon any thing belonging merely to the earth, or to the present life. The reason given in the next clause may be stated in the same way to be this, that such provision for the future shares in the precarious uncertainty and brief duration of the sphere from which it is derived, and to which it is restricted by its very nature. The figurative dress with which this reason is invested, has respect to the main figure in the other clause. Treasures of money and of clothing, almost equally valued in the ancient East, whose flowing garments, not exposed to the vicissitudes of fashion, were even transmitted by inheritance, are liable to be destroyed by rust and moths, respectively, or secretly abstracted by the thief and robber. The word translated *rust*, according to its etymology, means *eating*, and is used metonymically, both in Classical and Hellenistic writers, to denote what is eaten. (John 4, 32. 6, 27. 55.) Here it may mean *corrosion*, and particularly that of metals, though the old Greek translator, Aquila, applies it to the moth, in Isa. 50, 9. (Compare with this clause James 5, 2. 3.) *Corrupt*, the word translated *disfigure* in v. 16, and originally meaning to remove from sight, or cause to disappear, as in Jas. 4, 14, but continually used in the best writers, by a kind of euphemism, for destruction. Thus, Thucydides applies it to the razing of a house, and the erasure of a writing; Herodotus and Xenophon to the secret execution of state prisoners; with which may be compared the English phrases, to despatch, to make away with, and the Greek, to lead away, as used in Acts, 12, 19. Tyndale's word (*corrupt*), retained by all the later English versions, is not only contrary to usage, but suggests to the modern reader the incongruous idea of putrefaction. Here again the oldest English version is the best (Wiclif: distrieth—destroyeth). *Break through*, literally, *dig through* (Wiclif: *delven out*), with probable allusion to the mud walls and the unburnt brick often used in eastern houses. *Thieves*, in old English, like the corresponding Greek word, has a wider meaning than the one which we attach to it, including all who lawlessly deprive men of their property, by force or fraud, including what we commonly call robbery. (See below on 21, 13. 26, 55. 27, 38, where the same word is employed to represent a very different Greek one.) The meaning of the clause is, that the usual forms of human wealth are liable to loss, both from natural and human depredation.—V. 20 is the converse of v. 19, written with a solemn repetition of its terms, like that already noticed in v. 15, and intended to produce the same effect. The point of variation, upon which the contrast turns, is the phrase, *in heaven*, corresponding to *on earth*, and meaning just the opposite, to wit, beyond the sphere of this world and of this life, in the presence of God, and in his gracious purpose. (See above, on 5, 11.) Provision thus made for the future, is beyond the reach of change or loss, the necessary incidents of earthly good and secular advantages.

21. For where your treasure is, there will your heart be also.

This verse gives a still deeper insight into the great principle or law of human conduct laid down in the two foregoing verses. It was not, as might have been imagined without this addition, merely as a safeguard against loss, that Christ advised his followers to make provision for the future, not in this world, but a better. It was also as a necessary means of fixing their supreme affections on the proper objects, and of thus determining their character and destiny. The principle here stated is the obvious but momentous one, that what men value they will love, and that the two things cannot be divided in experience. Theoretically, this may seem to be an identical proposition, or, at least, a truism; but experience demonstrates its necessity, and man's native disposition practically to deny it, as evinced by their professions to love God supremely, while the objects which they value most belong to this world. To this universal, soul-destroying error, Christ opposes a familiar truth, which all admit in theory and all deny in practice, namely, that the two things thus divorced must go together; that the man who loves God will inevitably seek his happiness in him, both for the present and the future, while the man that seeks it in this life, thereby proves himself a lover of the world, and not of God, which two affections are declared by an apostle to be wholly incompatible.* The reference, of course, is not to friendly or benignant dispositions, but to governing affections, as in Luke 14, 26, one of the strongest of our Saviour's divine paradoxes, and intelligible only in the light of the great principle here laid down, that the treasure and the heart will always go together; that the quarter to which men now

---

* See James 4, 4, where all the English versions weaken the expression by the use of the terms *friend* and *friendship*, instead of *love* and *lover*, which are here required by the nature of the subject, though the others are always employed elsewhere.

look for happiness is that in which they place their best affections. *Where* and *there*, are terms properly belonging to the figure of a local treasure, but admitting of an easy application, in all languages, to spiritual subjects and relations. The distinction in the tenses, here, is not unmeaning, but indicates a necessary logical connection. 'Where your treasure now is — where you now look for the sources of your future happiness — there will your heart, or your supreme affections, as a necessary consequence, be found to be.' Thus completed, the whole doctrine of these verses (19–21) is, that not in reference merely to religious duties, such as alms, and prayer, and fasting, but to all religion, and to all life, the only security for future good, is to be found in God—in absolute reliance on him, and in absolute devotion to him.

22. The light of the body is the eye : if therefore thine eye be single, thy whole body shall be full of light.

Here again it has been not unusual to imagine an abrupt transition, or a total breach of continuity, arising either from the incoherence of our Lord's discourse, or from the fragmentary manner in which Matthew has reported it. The whole assumption is gratuitous and groundless. Without seeking any subtle artificial means, which would be as much displaced and out of character as desultory unconnected talk, it is easy to demonstrate an association of ideas between this and the foregoing context, amply sufficient to repel the charge of total incoherence, without any violence to the thought or language. This desirable result may be attained by simply viewing the remainder of this chapter (22–34) as an extended illustration and enforcement of the truth taught in the three preceding verses (19–21). The illustration, properly so called, is twofold, being partly drawn from the animal economy of man (22–23), and partly from his domestic habits and relations (24). The part of the human constitution thus made use of is the sight, and that not in a technical or scientific, but a popular and superficial way, as usual in Scripture, which refers to natural phenomena and facts, not as philosophers explain them, but as other people see them. The particular fact here used to illustrate spiritual truth, is the familiar one, that sight is simple, that the eye, in order to perform its office, must concentrate its visual power on the object, and that whatever tends to mar this unity by making it see double or confusing its perceptions, tends to vitiate its action and defeat the very end of its existence. The reason for selecting this particular comparison is intimated in the first clause of the verse before us, namely, the importance of the eyesight in the animal economy. *The light*, or luminary, source of light, the same word that is used above in 5, 15, and there translated *candle*, as it is here in the Rhemish Bible, and by Wiclif *lantern*. The meaning obviously is that this part of the body is the only one by which man can enjoy the light, by which he must be guided in his movements and made acquainted with external objects. *Therefore*, since this is the office and importance of the eye in the human constitution. *Thine eye*, suddenly returning to the singular pronoun, as in v. 17, and no doubt for the same purpose of impressive individualization. *Single*, in the strict and proper sense as opposite to double or to manifold, the only meaning justified by usage or the context. The sense of *sound* or *healthy*, given by some writers, is a mere conjectural deduction from the supposed meaning of the corresponding epithet, which, as we have seen before (on 5, 11. 37. 39. 45. 6, 13), may denote either physical or moral evil, and must therefore, it is hastily concluded, when applied to a bodily organ, mean diseased, disordered, and the parallel of course can only mean the opposite condition. But the true deduction is the inverse one, from the specific to the vague term. As the former (ἁπλοῦς) certainly means simple, single, the indefinite term evil means of course defective or diseased in this particular respect, i. e. double, mixed, confused. Or rather this is not the specific meaning of the adjective itself, but only the restriction of its meaning as required in this connection. The indefinite sense put upon the term by some not only violates all usage and the laws of lexicography, but utterly obscures the connection, and affords a pretext for the charge of incoherence. If there is no allusion to simplicity or singleness of sight, but only to its sound or healthy state, the illustration loses all its point, and must be treated as a mere digression or interpolation. On the other hand, if *single* have its proper sense, and *evil* be interpreted according to it, the comparison is perfectly adapted to its purpose, namely, that of showing, by a physical analogy, the vast importance, nay, the absolute necessity, of such a single and exclusive trust and love to God as had been just before enjoined upon our Lord's disciples. *Full of light* is Tyndale's paraphrase of our word simply meaning *light* or *luminous*, and better though not perfectly expressed by Wiclif (*lightful*) and the Rhemish version (*lightsome*). The essential meaning is that if the eye be single it will answer its purpose or perform its office with respect to the whole body, which is not represented as all eye (1 Cor. 12, 17), but merely as deriving through the eye from the light whatever benefit that element or substance was intended to impart. The future (*shall* or *will be*), as in v. 21, denotes a necessary consequence.

23. But if thine eye be evil, thy whole body shall be full of darkness. If therefore the light that is in thee be darkness, how great (is) that darkness!

This is the alternative or converse supposition of an evil eye, not in the moral application of that phrase occurring elsewhere (see below, on 20, 15, and compare Mark 7, 22. 2 Pet. 2, 14), but in the physical sense of a bad eye, i. e. one diseased, and here still further specified by *single* in v. 22, so as to mean destitute of that simplicity or singleness essential to the healthy function of the organ and its undisturbed effect upon the animal economy. *Full of darkness* is still more objectionable here than *full of light* in the preceding verse, because it seems necessarily expressive of a total obscuration or stark blindness, which is not the natural effect of the duplicity, complexity, or confusion here supposed. The difficulty lies exclusively in Tyndale's paraphrase, retained by all the Protestant translators. The original expression is a single word (σκοτεινόν) corresponding exactly to the English *dark*, and so translated in these very versions of Luke 11, 36, although in v. 34 of the same chapter, it is rendered as it is here, *full of darkness!* These capricious variations ought to make us vigilant in constantly comparing even the most perfect versions with the one inspired original. *Thy whole body shall be dark* is here the true translation, i. e. not entirely destitute of light or vision, but obscured, confused, and dimmed in its perceptions, by the want of singleness or oneness in the visual organ. As in v. 23, this is said of the whole body, only as losing the advantage which it would have otherwise enjoyed. When the whole frame suffers from the darkness of the eye, it may, almost without a figure, be itself described as dark. *Therefore*, since the safety and the comfort of the whole frame thus depend upon the singleness and clearness of the vision. *The light (the one) in thee*, not the light in general, but that part of the animal economy by which its blessings are secured to the whole body. *Darkness*, the correlative of *light*, and used in the same way, not to denote absolute privation, but any obscuration, caused by the diseased state of the organ. That it is not to be absolutely understood, appears from the very exclamation or interrogation in the last clause, which would then contain an anticlimax, the darkness being first described as total and then apostrophized as very great; whereas, if the body is first spoken of as dark, and then the darkness as a great one, there is a natural and striking climax. There is something in the very collocation of the Greek verbs here peculiarly impressive:—*the darkness, how great!* i. e. how great is it! The interrogative construction, *how great (is it)?* is essentially the same, the exclamation, in such cases, being only an impassioned question. But the main force and beauty of the last clause arise from its relating not so much to the physical case supposed as to the spiritual case which it was brought in to illustrate. Without any formal application of the figure, which would only have impaired the illustration, the divine instructor far more forcibly suggests it by an exclamation, applicable both to the imaginary and the real case, but infinitely more impressive in relation to the latter. This rhetorical device, if it may be so called without detracting from its godlike authority and wisdom, may be rendered clear, though necessarily enfeebled, by a paraphrase of this kind. 'Such is the effect of double or confused sight on the body, not unlike that of a double or divided heart upon the soul. How great must be the darkness even in the one case, but how infinitely greater and more fatal in the other! Let your heart and treasure therefore be together; not on earth, where both must one day perish, but in heaven, in God, beyond the reach of such a danger; not divided between both, which is indeed impossible, for though you may imagine that you love God while you seek your happiness in this world, you will one day know, and by your own experience, whether saved or lost, that where your treasure is, there will your heart be also.'

24. No man can serve two masters: for either he will hate the one, and love the other; or else he will hold to the one, and despise the other. Ye cannot serve God and mammon.

Another illustrative argument in favour of an undivided trust in God and devotion to him, is derived from a familiar fact in social or domestic life, to wit that the efficiency and value of a servant are dependent on a like concentration of his powers and affections in the service of one master. The apparent inconsistency between this statement and familiar cases of a different description, where a man does seem efficiently to serve more than one employer, may be easily removed by two considerations. The first is, that the service here described is that of a slave, the Greek verb meaning, both in classical and Hellenistic usage, to be a slave or to act the part of one. What might be true, then, of a freeman labouring for hire, now in this man's service, now in that man's, or in both at once, would be untrue and impossible of one whose time and labour are the property of another. The only way in which such a bondman could serve two masters is by virtue of a partnership between them. But this is precluded by a second consideration, namely, that the two masters here are evidently two whose rights and interests and orders are in conflict, as appears from the alternative prediction in the second clause. The first case there supposed is stronger than the second, love and hatred indicating more disparity than simply cleaving to the one and looking down upon the other. The former verb is used in the classics to denote a special devotion to some one god, and more correctly rendered in our Bible than by Tyndale and his followers, who use the weaker and more inexact form, *lean to*, or by the Romish versions, which follow the Vulgate in translating it *sustain*. The meaning seems to be that even where there is not love and hatred, in the strict sense, to the different masters, there will be a preference of one and a correspondent slighting of the other, when their orders or their wishes are in conflict. The application here is more express than in the previous illustration. Instead of using terms directly applicable to the case of real human service and leaving the hearers to apply it to the higher case illustrated by it, he winds up by expressly and most pointedly declaring, *Ye cannot serve (both) God and Mammon*. This last, written in some manuscripts with one m (μαμωνᾶ), is an Aramaic word applied to *wealth* or riches, but according to the most probable etymology, originally meaning *trust* or confidence, and thus describing wealth, not simply in itself as a material condition, but in its moral aspect as a ground of hope, which brings the passage into beautiful agreement with our Lord's explanation of his own paradoxical assertion that a rich man cannot enter the kingdom of heaven (Mark 10, 24). Mammon being here referred to as a master, is of course personified or treated as a person; but that such a god was actually worshipped by the Syrians, like the Plutus of the Greek mythology, has never been established, though familiarized to all minds by the poetry of Milton, which has given personality, not only to this Aramaic word, but to the Hebrew *Belial*, meaning good-for-nothing, worthless.

"Thus Belial, with words clothed in reason's garb,
Counselled ignoble ease and peaceful sloth,
Not peace; and after him thus Mammon spake."
PARADISE LOST, Book ii., vs. 226-228.

25. Therefore I say unto you, Take no thought for your life, what ye shall eat, or what ye shall drink; nor yet for your body, what ye shall put on. Is not the life more than meat, and the body than raiment?
A natural and almost unavoidable misapprehension of the foregoing exhortation to live only for God and heaven was the notion, that it necessarily involved the loss of every thing belonging to this life; whereas it was in fact a deliverance from all care, and the strongest possible assurance that even their earthly wants would be provided for. *Therefore*, literally, *for this*, i. e. for this cause, for this very reason. So far was entire devotion to God from leaving those who practised it in want or in danger of it, that it was the strongest reason for dismissing all anxiety about the subject, because he who serves God will be cared for by him. *I say unto you*, as my disciples, with the authority belonging to me as your master. *Take no thought for*, an old English phrase, employed by Bacon and Shakspeare in the sense of being anxious or excessively solicitous. The idea of excess is here essential, so that ordinary thought or care is not excluded. *Life*, in Greek a word which signifies the soul considered as the vital principle, and therefore rendered both by *life* and *soul* in different connections. Compare 2, 20 above with 10, 28 below, where being in antithesis to *body*, it is rendered *soul*. The same combination occurs here, and therefore *soul* would seem to be the proper version. The only objection is that as food belongs no less than clothing to the body, the antithesis would be a false one. This objection might perhaps be met by the scriptural use of *soul* and *heart* for the inner as distinguished from the outer man; but on the whole it may be better to remove the difficulty, if there be one, by assuming no antithesis, but simply a distinct mention of the life and body, because dress is not essential to the life, as food is, although needed for the decency and comfort of the body. *Shall eat* and *shall drink*, English futures used to represent the aorist subjunctive, which is properly suggestive of doubt and contingency. Perhaps the best translation as to sense, although not perfectly exact in form, would be, *what ye are to eat and drink*. The last clause is an argument from greater to less. He who gives us life may be expected to sustain it; he who made the body may be trusted to protect it and provide for it. Instead of being stated as a formal proposition, this reasoning is made at once more pointed and more popular by being compressed into a question. The same interrogative form is employed by Paul in an argument of precisely the same kind, though relating to the most "unspeakable" of all gifts. (Rom. 8, 32.)

26. Behold the fowls of the air: for they sow not, neither do they reap, nor gather into barns; yet your heavenly Father feedeth them. Are ye not much better than they?

This is an argument from less to greater. He who cares for the inferior creation cannot fail to provide for his intelligent creatures, and especially for those who serve and trust him. This argument, extending through v. 30, has a beautiful symmetry almost poetical in form, arising from a twofold parallelism of the sentences, the first illustration being drawn from the animal kingdom and relating to the care for food, the second from the vegetable world and relating to the care for raiment (28–30). *Behold*, look at, an expression strengthened by a double preposition, one before the verb and one before the noun, implying close attention, searching observation. *Fowls*, now restricted to edible, domesticated birds, was used in old English to denote birds in general, and is here employed to represent a Greek word strictly meaning *winged* or *flying* (*things*). The *air*, literally, *the sky* (or *heaven*) here put, as often in the classics, for the space above the earth, the visible expanse, the atmosphere, through which the birds fly. *Sow not*, &c., they do not even use the means which man is bound to use and does use, but are wholly dependent on their instincts and the bounties of their Maker. Sowing, reaping, and ingathering, are the three stages of agricultural employment and provision for the food of man, all which are here denied in reference to the birds, which is equivalent to saying that they use no means at all for the production of their own food. *Your heavenly father* is not a mere periphrasis for God, but suggestive of an almost infinite disparity between the cases. Instead of saying, *their heavenly father feedeth them*, which, in a lower sense, would be correct, he says, *your heavenly father*, intimating that the God who thus provides for the inferior animals, is bound by a peculiar fatherly relation to provide for man, and still more for those men who, as his Son's disciples, are his children in the most intimate and strictest sense. The conclusion from these premises is indicated in the last clause, and again in the form of an interrogation. *Are ye not much better*, Tyndale's version of an idiomatic Greek phrase not susceptible of close translation, the verb meaning properly to *differ*, with an adverb meaning *more*, and thus determining the difference to be in favour of the subject, which is then represented as excelling, being worth more, than the object of comparison (Wicl., *more worthy*—Rheims, *more of price*). The reasoning involved in this comparison and question is that he who thus takes care of what is less valuable, will of course take care of what is more so. *Barns*, in Greek, a wider term denoting any kind of storehouse or deposit (see above, on 3, 12).

27. Which of you by taking thought can add one cubit unto his stature?

Before proceeding to his second analogical argument, our Lord corroborates the first by adding a suggestion as to the entire inefficiency and uselessness of anxious care in reference to human life, which cannot thereby be extended or prolonged. The form is still that of a question, here implying strong negation. *By taking thought*, in the original, a simple participle, *caring*, being anxious. *Can*, a distinct and independent verb in Greek, *is able*. *To add*, or put to, as the original expression etymologically signifies, *Stature*, a secondary meaning of the Greek noun, which primarily relates to time and corresponds to *age* in English, but is also used to denote corporeal growth, as an effect and sign of advancing age. There is a twofold objection to the version *stature ;* first, that Christ is here speaking of the life and of food as necessary to sustain it, and passes in the next verse to the body and its raiment; a consideration of the more importance from the regular and balanced structure of the passage, as already noticed. In the next place, the addition of a cubit to one's stature is a very great one ; whereas the one here mentioned is described in a parallel passage (Luke 12, 26) as "that which is least." The only objection to the version *age*, is that *cubit* is not a measure of time but of space, being derived, like most measures of length, from the average dimensions of the human body (compare foot, pace, ell, handbreadth, span, &c.) *Cubit* originally means the *fore-arm*, from the elbow to the wrist; then, as a standard of measure, from the elbow to the tips of the fingers, usually reckoned as a length of eighteen inches, or a foot and a half, more or less. But how could such a measure, the precise extent of which varied in practice and is wholly unimportant, be applied to time, or to the length of human life? Only with tacit reference to the figure of a race or journey, often used in Scripture and familiar in all languages: 'Who by anxious care can add even a foot or two to his appointed course on earth?' We then have the advantage of giving to the Greek noun (ἡλικία) its primary meaning, and one perfectly consistent with the parallel in Luke ; for though a cubit is a very large addition to one's stature, it is a very small one to the length of a journey, and still less to the duration of a lifetime.

28. And why take ye thought for raiment? Consider the lilies of the field how they grow ; they toil not, neither do they spin.

Here begins the second illustration or comparison, which has respect to clothing and is drawn from the vegetable kingdom. The form of direct prohibition, used in v. 25, is here exchanged for that of interrogation, so predominant in this whole context, and implying a negation no less pointed than the other. *Take thought*, the same verb as in v. 25, and meaning anxious care, undue solicitude. *Consider*, an intensive compound of the verb to *learn*, originally meaning to learn thoroughly, and then, as a necessary means, to study closely, to observe attentively, a secondary sense as old as Herodotus. The use of the word here suggests that what is thus proposed is not a mere indulgence of the taste or curiosity, but a moral lesson to be learned by studying the works and providence of God, a method of instruction practised long before by Solomon (see Prov. 6, 6–8. 30, 24–31), to which there may be here an intentional allusion as his name is introduced just afterwards. *Study the lilies of the field*, wild flowers, without human care or cultivation. All speculation, as to the precise kind of lily here intended, is gratuitous and exegetically unimportant. There is no need of assuming an allusion to a gorgeous purple lily, found in some parts of the east, on account of the comparison which follows, and which is no less relevant and true of the most ordinary species. The point of comparison is not the colour, but the luxuriant growth and native beauty. *How they grow*, a use of the active verb found only in the later Greek, the older writers giving it the transitive or causative sense of making grow or causing to increase, which is also found in 1 Cor. 3, 6. 7, while always elsewhere, as in this case, it is used as an intransitive or neuter.* The Greek verbs are in the singular number, but agree, according to a well-known idiom of the language, with a plural subject of the neuter gender. But the latest critics give the verbs a plural form, as found in the Codex Vaticanus and some others, and as quoted by Chrysostom and Athanasius. The difference is merely one of form, requiring no change in the English version. *Toil* and *spin* may either be generic and specific terms, denoting work in general and one familiar form of it; or toil may have the more restricted sense of work relating to the preparation of clothing, in addition to the primary operation of spinning, such as weaving, sewing, and the like. These terms then correspond with beautiful exactness to the processes of husbandry employed for the same purpose in the other illustration or comparison (v. 26).

29. And yet I say unto you, That even Solomon in all his glory was not arrayed like one of these.

And yet is not too strong a version of the particle (δέ) here used to introduce a comparison or contrast. *But*, although they use no means to furnish their own clothing. *I say unto you*, implying not so much the importance of the thing said as its seeming improbability, requiring an authoritative asseveration to command belief. *Even Solomon*, with possible allusion, as already hinted, to his similar method of enforcing moral truth, but with a much more certain one to the proverbial splendour of his reign, still traditionally cherished in the East as the type of a magnificent Asiatic monarch. *All his glory*, great and unexampled as it was. *Glory* has here no reference to moral excellence, but only to external splendour, which is a frequent sense of the Greek word in the Septuagint version and of the corresponding Hebrew noun (כָּבוֹד), even when applied to God, describing not his absolute perfection, but his sensible manifestation to his creatures, as in the *Shechinah*,

---

* The converse of this change may be observed in the English *grow*, which was originally neuter, but in later usage often has the active sense of cultivating, raising, or producing, when applied to vegetable products.

or cloud of the divine presence in the tabernacle and temple, and still earlier in the patriarchal and primeval theophanies. Here it means the royal state of Solomon, especially his regal costume or official dress. *Not even Solomon was arrayed*, literally, *thrown about* or cast around, i. e. with clothing. *Like*, as, i. e. so splendidly and beautifully. *One of these*, not these collectively, or in the aggregate, but any one of them deserves to be compared with Solomon in all his glory.

30. **Wherefore, if God so clothe the grass of the field, which to-day is, and to-morrow is cast into the oven, (shall he) not much more (clothe) you, O ye of little faith?**

The premises or data having been recited, the argument from less to greater is now stated, but again in the form of an interrogation. *Wherefore*, the logical connective between this and the preceding verses, is the word above translated *and yet* (in v. 29) and elsewhere *but* or *and*, as in vs. 16. 20, or omitted altogether, as in v. 27. *If* does not express a doubt or a contingency, but simply sets forth what is actually true as premises from which to argue, and is nearly equivalent to *since* or *whereas*, in English. *Grass*, a Greek word originally meaning an enclosure, then applied especially to pastures, and by another natural transition, to the grass itself. The term is here used in the wide sense of herbage, so as to include the smaller plants, as distinguished both from trees and from the larger shrubs or bushes. The point of comparison is fragility and brief duration, as expressed directly in the next clause. *To-day* and *to-morrow*, put for one day and the next, or by a natural figure of speech, for any two points of time not distant from each other. *Is*, literally, *being*, i. e. existing, living, and by necessary implication, flourishing, luxuriating, as before described. *Cast into the oven*, the precise shape or size of which has no effect upon the meaning, as the point of the comparison is nothing peculiar to the ovens of the East, but that which is common to all ovens from their very nature and design, to wit, that they are heated, and that this requires fuel. More peculiar to the East may be the use of withered grass and flowers for this purpose, as alleged by archæologists and travellers. The argument seems here to be drawn from the different duration of the human and the vegetable subject; but this is only mentioned to enhance the vast disparity between them, which extends to many other more important points of difference. *Clothe*, a distinct verb from the one in v. 30, but analogous in composition and in use. *Shall he not clothe*, supplied by the translators, weakens the expression, though it gives the sense correctly. *Oh ye of little faith*, in Greek a single word, a compound adjective, without exact equivalent in English. It has here specific reference to faith or confidence in God's protecting and providing care.

31. **Therefore take no thought, saying, What shall**

we eat ? or, what shall we drink ? or, wherewithal shall we be clothed ?

The practical application of the argument from God's care of inferior creatures. *Therefore*, since that care ensures a still more tender care for you. *Take no thought*, as in vs. 25. 27. 28, be not anxious, or excessively solicitous. The interrogative form is again used, but in this case as a natural expression of an uneasy doubt as to bodily provision and support. The future, as in v. 25, is not the form of the original, which more exactly means, *what may* (or *can*) *we eat?* but may be rendered as before, what are we to eat, or drink, or wear?

32. For after all these things do the Gentiles seek: for your heavenly Father knoweth that ye have need of all these things.

This verse assigns a further reason for not cherishing an anxious spirit, namely, that at bottom it is heathenish. *The Gentiles*, literally, *nations*, i. e. all besides the Jews. *Seek after*, a compound form of the verb rendered *seek* in the next verse, and probably intended to suggest the accessory idea of eagerness, solicitude, and importunity. Some throw this first clause into a parenthesis and connect the last directly with the prohibition in v. 31. But as such constructions are now regarded by the best philological authorities as very rare, it seems better to explain the first clause as a new and additional reason, and to connect the last with something not expressed though necessarily implied. 'I say be not thus anxious, for the heathen are so, and that for a reason which ought not to exist in your case, namely, a doubt of God's omniscience. You can have no such motive; for,' &c. *Your heavenly father*, as such and because he is such, with the genuine affection of a father towards his children. *Have need of* is in Greek a single word (*ye*) *need*. *All these* (*things*), literally, *these all*, a concession that the things of this life must be had and therefore may be sought, but not with an overweening estimate of their importance or a sceptical solicitude to gain them.

33. But seek ye first the kingdom of God, and his righteousness; and all these things shall be added unto you.

Having now prohibited, at great length and in various forms, the indulgence of a sceptical solicitude about even necessary things belonging to the present life, he shows them how it is to be avoided; not by mere negation, or attempting simply to abstain from such anxiety and unbelief, but by positively doing something else which will immediately correct the evil. This remedy for unbelieving doubts and cares consists in constantly subordinating all such personal considerations to the higher interests of the divine service, not as excluding all provision for this life but as including and securing it. *Ye* is not separately expressed in Greek, and therefore not emphatic as in vs. 9. 26, because there is here no comparison between different classes of agents, but only between different modes of action. *The kingdom of God*, as then about to be erected, and the cause which they were bound, as Christ's disciples, to promote. *His righteousness*, that which he esteems right or has made right by requiring it, conformity to God's will as the only rule of right. The more specific sense of *justification* is obtained by parity of reasoning or reflection from the apostolic teaching; but the simple meaning of the words as understood, and intended to be understood, by the original hearers, is that by seeking to do God's will and promote his cause, they would most effectually further their own interests, not only spiritual and eternal, but secular and temporal. *All these (things)*, an expression twice used in the verse preceding, and applied to the necessary things of this life, with particular reference to food and clothing, as the subject of the previous context. *Added* (the same verb as in v. 27) i. e. given over and above the spiritual good directly flowing from devotion to God's service. The whole prescription, therefore, is, instead of anxiously and passionately hunting, like the heathen, for the good things or even the necessaries of this life, as if God were not aware of their necessities or able to supply them, to aim first, in time and preference, at those things which concern his service, and believe that by so doing, what appears to be neglected will be certainly secured.

34. Take therefore no thought for the morrow: for the morrow shall take thought for the things of itself. Sufficient unto the day (is) the evil thereof.

The most important question here, is in regard to the precise connection between this verse and the previous context. The more obvious, and probably more common view of this connection, is, that we have here a summary recapitulation of the whole discourse about the cares of life, with an additional reason for avoiding sceptical solicitude. This may seem to be favoured by the logical connective (*therefore*), and the similarity of form between this and the exhortation in v. 31. Against it may be urged the qualifying phrase, *for the morrow*, to, or towards, or with a view to, the ensuing day, which does not occur before, and which seems designed to introduce another class of cares, to wit, those for the future as distinguished from those for the present. It may be plausibly replied, that all care has relation to the future, though it may not be a distant one, and that the cares previously described by their objects (raiment, food, &c.), are here described in reference to time—for the morrow as a proximate futurity. But even granting this, which is by no means certain, there is a still more serious objection to the supposition that this verse relates precisely to the same cares that had been already more than once forbidden.

This objection is, that the reason here assigned is altogether different from any that had been before expressed or implied, and one peculiarly appropriate to future, or more distant cares, as distinguished from proximate, or present cares. That reason is, that by letting our anxieties thus run ahead, we only accumulate the evil, and impose on each successive day, not only its own burden, but the burden of the days that follow. This seems to favour, though it does not conclusively establish the opinion that our Saviour, having wound up his warning against unbelieving cares in general, adds, as a sort of corollary, a specific warning against cares about the morrow, or the future, as distinguished from the present. *Therefore* (too), or on the same grounds, and by parity of reasoning, *be not anxious for the morrow*, or in the prospect of remoter wants or dangers. The next clause cannot mean, as it has sometimes been explained, that the morrow (or the future) will provide for itself, and need not, therefore, be provided for beforehand. The verb does not mean to provide, but to be anxious, and unduly anxious, being identical with that in the preceding clause, and in vs. 25. 27. 28. 31. The only meaning that the words will bear, is, that the morrow will be just as anxious as to-day, so that by anticipating its anxieties, the present has a double load to bear. *The* (*things*) *of itself* is an exact translation of what might be more idiomatically rendered, *its own* (things or affairs) as opposed to those of the preceding days.* *Sufficient* is not to be grammatically construed with *evil*, as the two words are, in Greek, of different genders; but the former, which is neuter, must be taken by itself, as meaning *a sufficient thing*, or in a single word, *enough*. *Unto* does not answer to a preposition, but is simply the sign of the dative case, and as such, might have been translated *for*. *The day*, in this connection, evidently means each or every day, as it arrives. *Evil*, like the cognate adjective, and the synonyme employed above, in vs. 13. 23, may denote either natural or moral evil, either suffering or sin, and more particularly malice. The former seems to suit the context here, and to afford a good sense, namely, that the suffering of each day is as much as it can bear, without gratuitously adding what belongs to others. In favour of the other explanation is the constant usage of the word in the New Testament, there being ten other cases of the moral sense, and not one of the natural.† It also adds point to the sentence by carrying out the personification of the day to the end. 'Sufficient for the day is its own malignity or mischief, without seeking to incur that of others.'‡ It cannot be denied, however, that the other is a simpler and more natural construction, and the argument against it from New Testament usage, may perhaps be outweighed by

---

* The latest critical editions follow the Vatican and several other uncial copies, in omitting the article and simply reading, *for itself*.
† See Acts 8, 22. Rom. 1, 29. 1 Cor. 5, 8. 14, 20. Eph. 4, 31. Col. 3, 8. Tit. 3, 3. James 1, 21. 1 Pet. 2, 1, 16.
‡ Wicl. It sufficeth to the day his own malice. Tynd. The day present hath ever enough of his own trouble. Geneva B. The day present hath ever enough to do with its own grief. Cranm. Sufficient unto the day is the travail thereof.

the twofold application of the cognate adjective,* and by the occasional occurrence of the noun itself, to denote suffering in the classics, the Septuagint, and the Apocrypha.† *The evil thereof*, means nothing more than *its evil*, this possessive pronoun never being used in our translation; but the former version gives a more sonorous close, retaining, at the same time, the order of the words in Greek.

CHAPTER VII.

The first part of this chapter seems to be addressed to the censorious Pharisees, who were disposed to treat with a contemptuous rigour, the disciples of our Saviour, but are warned that he would judge themselves with equal severity, and that the correction of their own faults should precede, if not prevent, the condemnation of others (1–5). He then warns his followers not to expose themselves or the gospel to the spiteful or ignorant contempt of such men, without evident necessity (6). From this digression he returns to the subject of provision for the future (5, 34), and teaches them to banish unbelieving cares by a childlike trust in God, expressed in prayer, with a cheering assurance of success, derived from God's paternal kindness, as compared with that of men (7–11). He then, in winding up his whole discourse, reverts to the fulfilment of the law and prophets (5, 17), showing how they are to do their part (12); exhorts them to pursue the course of right and safety, however self-denying (13. 14); warns them against their faithless spiritual leaders, proved to be so by their influence on others (15–19); against false profession in their own case (20–23); and against the fatal error of hearing without practising what he had taught them (24–27). To the sermon on the Mount, which closes here, is added an account of its effect upon the people (28. 29).

1. Judge not, that ye be not judged.

2. For with what judgment ye judge, ye shall be judged: and with what measure ye mete, it shall be measured to you again.

It is commonly agreed that the connection of this chapter with the foregoing context, and of its parts among themselves, is less clear than

---

* Compare Rom. 13, 3. and 14, 20. 1 Cor. 13, 5. and 15, 33. Rev. 2, 2. and 16, 2.
† Thucyd. 3, 58. Ecc. 7, 14. 1 Macc. 10, 46.

in the previous divisions of the Sermon on the Mount. Hence some abandon the idea of connection altogether, and regard what follows as an incoherent, or at least a desultory series of advices, either added by our Lord, as a conclusion to the more continuous discourse which he had been delivering, or thrown together by the historian, as a further sample of his mode of teaching, not at any one time, but on different occasions. But besides the general presumption against such compilations, and in favour of a regular connected train of thought, there is a special presumption of the same kind here, arising from the ease with which the thread of the discourse can be detected and maintained unbroken in the two preceding chapters. It is highly improbable from all analogy, as well as from the general laws of thought and language, that a composition, so methodical to this point, should at once and altogether be deprived of its coherence. It becomes us, therefore, who have found an obvious plan and purpose in the previous part, to take for granted that it still exists and governs the remainder of the sermon, though it may not be so easily discerned, and ought not to be violently made out by gratuitous assumptions or unnatural constructions of the language. It is also proper in such doubtful cases to allow a certain latitude of judgment and liberty of choice between the different hypotheses which may be urged with any show of plausibility. Among these, one supposes that our Lord here turns to another class of those who were impatiently expecting the Messiah's kingdom, but with false conceptions of its nature, and corrects their errors as he had before corrected those of other classes (see above, on 5, 3). The class here addressed would then be that of the censorious moralists, whose whole religion lay in finding fault with others, and who may have anticipated ample scope for the indulgence of this morbid appetite amidst the changes which the church was now to undergo. As this is a character which shows itself in every time and place, and one that was particularly apt to be engendered by the pharisaical abuse of the Mosaic system, there is nothing in the fact assumed by this interpretation that is antecedently or intrinsically improbable. Nor is there much weight in the sole objection, that if such had been our Lord's design, he would have carried it out earlier in the discourse, and in immediate connection with the other misconceptions there corrected. This would be to demand, not mere coherence in the thoughts, but a rhetorical preciseness and formality of method altogether out of keeping with the free and natural, though rational arrangement of his thoughts and language, which would not be in the least disturbed by such a separation of the topics, especially if suited to promote the general design of his discourse, or if susceptible of explanation from the known or even the conjectured circumstances of the case. Such explanation is afforded by the supposition, which is nothing more, and not to be relied on as a certain fact, that on this as on many similar occasions, there were foes as well as friends among his hearers, representing the great Pharisaical interest and ready to express their disagreement and contempt by looks if not by language. That this is no imaginary state of things, we learn from Luke's explicit statement on a subsequent occasion, that as he spake unto the people, "the Scribes and Pharisees began to urge him vehemently, and to provoke him to speak of many things" (Luke 11, 53), and again, "the Pharisees also, who were covetous, heard all these things, and they derided him" (Luke 16, 14). This parallel is the more exact, because among the things then spoken and derided was the very doctrine about serving God and Mammon which is laid down here in the preceding chapter (6, 24). If they derided it at one time, why not at another? And if at this time, what can be more natural than the assumption, that our Lord, perceiving their contempt, both of his doctrine and disciples, addresses them directly in the first part of this chapter, though in terms admitting of a wider application. That the primary object of address was rather a censorious enemy than even a mistaken friend, is rendered still more probable, though not entirely certain, by the harsh term applied to him in v. 5, which we shall examine more particularly when we reach it. The first verse, however, as in 5, 21. 27. 32. 33. 38. 43. 6, 1. 7. is in the plural form, making it a general rule or admonition; while the personal application in the singular number follows in the next verse. The reappearance of this somewhat singular interchange of numbers, which has been already noted as a characteristic of the Sermon on the Mount, affords a further proof, if any were required, that the passage now before us forms part of a systematic whole, and of the same which we have been considering, and not of a fragmentary, miscellaneous compilation added to it. The first clause contains a prohibition or dissuasion and a motive for it, which is then more fully stated in the second verse. There can of course be no allusion either to official judgment and judicial functions, or to the mere formation of opinion, both which lie beyond the reason here suggested for not judging, and neither of which could be forbidden absolutely. The reference must, therefore, be to something intermediate between these, something neither unavoidable, like personal opinion, nor obligatory, like official judgments, but dependent on the will and dispositions of the person judging. This applies exactly to voluntary and censorious judgments upon others, not required by personal or public duty. *That ye be not judged*, assigns the reason why they should not sit in judgment upon others. If you would not be judged, do not judge 'yourselves.' The only question of importance is, what judgment is referred to in the second clause, that of man, or that of God? If the former, this is a prudential maxim, warning us that we may look for treatment at the hands of others similar to that which they received from us. However true this may be, and important as a rule of worldly wisdom, and however it may seem to correspond to the positive command in v. 12, it is not the kind of motive commonly presented in the Sermon on the Mount, or elsewhere in our Lord's discourses. This appears to recommend another answer to the question, namely, that the judgment against which we are here warned is that of God himself; not merely as it is to be pronounced hereafter, but as it is conceived and executed now. The meaning then is, 'be not forward to condemn the character and acts of others; for a still severer standard will be faithfully applied to your own by a judge who cannot err.' We are not here taught that by shunning such censorious judgments of others, we can wholly avoid that of God in our own case, but simply that the latter will be rendered more severe by an uncharitable rigour towards our neighbours. (See above, on 6, 14. 15.) This is more fully set forth in the second verse, where we learn that the same high standard, which all men recognize in judging of their neighbours, will be faithfully applied to their own conduct in the divine judgment. This presupposes a familiar fact in the experience of men, to wit, that however lenient they may be in judging their own acts and motives, they are always exacting in their estimate of others. Even he who denies all moral distinctions in the abstract or in reference to his own responsibility, will eagerly resent and punish any wrong or insult offered to himself. *Judgment* and *measure* are literal and metaphorical expressions for the same thing, to wit, the mode of estimating character and conduct.

3. And why beholdest thou the mote that is in thy brother's eye, but considerest not the beam that is in thine own eye?

Here, as frequently before, the exchange of the plural for the singular announces a more close and pointed application of the general rule to individual cases. The change is still more striking in the present instance if, as was hinted to be not improbable, this part of the discourse was immediately suggested by the presence and the looks, if not the words and actions, of censorious Pharisees, to one of whom, a real or ideal person, the discourse is now suddenly addressed. *And,* or *but,* if this be so, if thou art to be tried by the same rule and measured by the same standard, why art thou so censorious and exacting as to others, when thy own defects are not only equal but far greater? This idea is expressed, perhaps with some allusion to the figures of 6, 22. 23, under the image of an eye disordered by the presence of a foreign body, such as a dry particle of wood, in one case a minute chip or mere splinter, compared with which the other may be hyperbolically called a beam. The word *mote,* used in all the English versions, is well suited to express the difference of size, but not the close correspondence as to substance or material, suggested by the usage of the Greek word, which although it properly means something dry, is specially applied by Herodotus and Aristophanes to dry sticks and twigs, such as birds use in the making their nests. *Beholdest* is in all the other English versions *seest;* but the true sense is that of looking at, of observing, taking notice of as a voluntary and officious act. The original construction is like that in 5, 16, *the mote, the (one) in the eye of thy brother,* not merely of thy fellow-man, but of one sustaining a more intimate relation to thee, social or domestic. (See above on 5, 22. 23. 24. 47.) The interrogation implies that there was no need of observing it at all, which shows again that the judgment here condemned is not official but officious. *But,* on the other hand, in reference to thy own case. *Considerest*, an emphatic compound verb in Greek, analogous to that in 6, 28, although derived from an entirely different root and meaning primarily to understand thoroughly, and then, as a necessary means, to observe attentively. The antithesis between the verbs is not to be neglected. The censor had no occasion even to look at or to see the slight obstruction in his brother's eye, but every reason to observe and scrutinize the great one in his own. The hyperbole in *beam* is not to be explained away or softened down by any modification in the meaning of the Greek word, which is the same in Attic and Homeric usage. The case supposed is not a real but an ideal one, and the impossibility of this trait serves to strengthen the impression of a vast disparity. The language is proverbial, as in 19, 24. 23, 24, the hyperbole, instead of belonging to the artificial language of rhetoric, being really most frequent in the dialect of common life.

4. Or how wilt thou say to thy brother, Let me pull out the mote out of thine eye; and, behold, a beam (is) in thine own eye?

This verse presents another aspect of the case, introduced by the disjunctive (*or*). *How wilt thou say?* a more correct translation than the *sayest thou* of all the other English versions which mistake the future (ἐρεῖς) for a present form. The import of the question is, how canst thou have the face to say? How canst thou be so inconsistent and self-ignorant or self-indulgent as to say? The prohibition is not one derived from real life, but a translation into words of the supercilious and censorious spirit cherished by too many moralists. *Let me pull* (Tynd. *suffer me to pluck*; Cranmer, *suffer me, I will pluck*), is in Greek an imperative prefixed to a subjunctive, strictly meaning, *suffer (that) I pull (cast) out*. The first verb has the same sense as in 3, 15, where it twice occurs. (For its other meaning, see above, on 4, 11. 20. 22. 5, 24. 40. 6, 12. 14. 15.) *Pull out*, literally, *cast out* or expel, as in v. 22 below and often elsewhere. The essential idea is that of forcible removal. *And behold*, an expression of surprise, introducing something strange and unexpected. (See above, on 1, 20. 23. 2, 1. 9. 13. 19. 3, 16. 17. 4, 11.) As if he had said, 'who could have believed that this man, so officious in discovering a small speck in his neighbour's eye, has a greater but an unobserved obstruction in his own?'

5. Thou hypocrite, first cast out the beam out of thine own eye; and then shalt thou see clearly to cast out the mote out of thy brother's eye.

Having pointed out by means of the foregoing questions the absurdity of such officious meddling, he proceeds in this verse to prescribe a better course, with an additional reason for it, i. e. over and above the one involved in the inconsistency and folly of the contrary proceeding. (*Thou*) *hypocrite*, explained above on 6. 2. 5. 16, a word found in the three first Gospels, once in Mark, four times in Luke, and fifteen times in Matthew. In all these places, with the possible exception of Luke 12, 56, it is applied to the unbelieving Jews, the enemies of Christ, and is not likely therefore to be here used of his followers and friends. This strengthens the assumption that the passage now before us has immediate reference to Pharisees then present, and perhaps cherishing the very spirit here translated into words and held up to contempt. At the same time, the language is so chosen as to make the lesson one of wider application, and even more remotely to charge with hypocrisy, not only the original offender, but all who are guilty of the same self-righteous and censorious inconsistency. *Hypocrite* has here its proper sense of one who acts a part, or personates a character not really his own, to wit, that of a rigid moralist and just judge, who impartially condemns sin where he finds it; while in fact he indulges in himself a greater evil of the same kind that he mercilessly spies out and rebukes in others. The prevalence of this hypocritical morality among the Jews, and the obstruction which it offered to the progress of the Gospel, may be learned from the Epistle to the Romans, where the second chapter, specially addressed to Jews (see v. 17), is an expansion of the very thought suggested in the verse before us. Instead of formally exposing the hypocrisy and inconsistency of such a practice, our Lord attains the same end more impressively by telling the censorious hypocrite in what way the reproach might be avoided, and his judgments at the same time rendered more correct. *First*, before condemning others, sit in judgment on thyself. This idea is conveyed by a continued use of the same figures introduced in the preceding verse. *And then*, when thou hast thus begun at home and brought thy own sins to as strict a standard as the one applied to others. *See clearly*, literally, *see through*, i. e. through all obstructions and concealments. This is mentioned as a further incidental benefit to be derived from an impartial self-examination and self-judgment, but not as the main reason why it should be undertaken. It is not merely, nor even chiefly on account of the obscuring influence of sin upon the moral judgment, that we are required to condemn it in ourselves before attempting to discover it in others; but because it concerns us more, and is essential to our own salvation. At the same time it is none the less true that the process of self-scrutiny and self-arraignment does prepare the mind for similar functions in the case of others, when we are legitimately called to them. But no amount of such improvement in capacity to judge aright, will justify an uncalled and censorious interference with the character of others, which is the error here immediately in question.

6. Give not that which is holy unto the dogs, neither cast ye your pearls before swine, lest they trample them under their feet, and turn again and rend you.

If the view just taken of our Lord's immediate purpose in the five preceding verses be correct, the natural connection with the sixth verse seems to be, that he here turns from the 'hypocrite,' addressed in vs. 3–5, to his own disciples, and exhorts them not to expose themselves, and that wherewith they were intrusted, to the ignorant or wicked scorn of unbelievers, without obvious necessity or urgent duty. With a boldness and severity, which only his omniscience and supreme authority could justify, and which is, therefore, no example for his followers, except to so far as they repeat or expound his own words, he describes the impure and ferocious enemies of truth and of his kingdom by the hateful epithets of *dog* and *swine*, the two species of domesticated animals for which the Orientals had the greatest abhorrence. The Oriental dog is more gregarious and savage than the western, less attached to man, and, being chiefly fed on garbage, more disgusting in its habits and appearance. Hence the dog is chiefly spoken of in Scripture as an object or expression of contempt. To swine, besides their natural and universal habits, there attached a religious odium as an unclean animal, excluded not only from the altar but the table. The two may either be promiscuously blended as a joint type of all that is abhorrent in human character; or so far separated that the dog shall represent the class of violent and savage foes, the swine those peculiarly impure and degraded. In favour of the former explanation is the fact, that both these species were regarded by the Hebrews as unclean, and that both are almost equally disgusting in the east, and then, that the very structure of the sentence makes it difficult to separate them altogether. *The dogs* and *swine* differ as to definiteness only in the version; the article standing before both in Greek. *That which is holy*, Tyndale's periphrastic version of *the holy*, or *the holy (thing)*, here meaning no doubt any thing made sacred by appropriation to God's service, such as sacrificial food, which is here suggested by the context (see above, on 4, 6. 5, 25), as well as by the use of the word *give*, while in the other clause, where pearls not food are mentioned, the expression is to *cast before*. There is no need of supposing an allusion to the similarity between pearls and any kind of food for swine, and an intention to deceive them. The antithesis is clearly between things the most highly valued among men, and animals incapable of using or enjoying them. The last clause gives the reason of this prohibition, i. e. a reason in addition to the one arising from the contrariety of nature. *Lest* is in Greek a compound particle, and strictly means, *lest ever* (or *at any time*); but later usage gradually weakened the reference to time and left that of contingency the prominent idea. *Under their feet*, literally, *in their feet*, an idiomatic phrase, which may mean in the use of them (see above, on 3, 11. 5, 13), which is substantially equivalent to *with them*, or by means of them. Or *in* may be intended to suggest more strongly the incongruous confusion of the costly pearls amidst the food and feet of the filthy swine. *Turning* away from what they cannot taste or value, or perhaps *turning on you*, as the object of attack. *Rend*, a Greek verb, which strictly means to break, but is applied by Æschylus to the tearing of a veil or robe, and by Pindar to the wounding of the human body. Some suppose this last clause to refer specifically to the dogs, a construction which has even been expressed in some of the old English versions (Tyndale and Cranmer, *and the other turn again*). But most interpreters either restrict it to the swine, as often savage and always voracious, or suppose both species to be meant, the distinction having been lost sight of. The essential ideas are those of blind contempt for what is really most sacred and most precious, and ferocious enmity towards those from whom it is received or offered. The lesson taught is, that even saving truth must be withheld from those who would certainly reject it with contempt and savage hatred. As cases of this sort are rare, and not to be assumed without necessity, the passage furnishes no pretext for an indolent or cowardly suppression of the truth in order to avoid a personal danger. The primary reason is the trampling of the pearls under feet; the risk of laceration is but secondary. Where there is no danger of the gospel being treated with a blasphemous contempt, the mere exposure of its preachers or professors to the violence of such despisers does not seem to warrant a withholding of the message.

7. Ask, and it shall be given you ; seek, and ye shall find ; knock, and it shall be opened unto you :

This is one of the abrupt transitions here assumed by those who relinquish or repudiate the attempt to trace an unbroken train of thought or thread of the discourse. Admitting, as before, the comparative obscurity of the connection, and attempting only a conjectural solution of the problem, we may at least assist the memory, if not the understanding, by continuing the previous assumption or suggestion, as to the possible occasion and immediate object of address in the preceding verses. If, as we have there supposed without affirming it, that passage has respect to the censorious contempt of Pharisees then present, which became apparent at this stage of the discourse, there is nothing to forbid, though nothing to require, the further supposition, that as soon as this interruption, so to speak, had been disposed of, he resumes the thread which had been dropped or broken at the close of the sixth chapter, and completes what he had there left unfinished, in relation to the heathenish and Christian method of providing for the future. The absolute and peremptory prohibition of extreme solicitude and anxious care might seem to the disciples, as it has appeared to some interpreters, to cut off all endeavours to secure the divine bounty and protection, upon which they were required so implicitly to trust. But as Augustin said, in answer to this exegetical misgiving, that trust and prayer are not at variance but coincident, the one being only the expression of the other ; so our Lord himself, according to the view now taken hypothetically, may be understood as guarding in this verse against the same misconception. Having pointedly forbidden unbelieving anxieties in general (6, 31), and more particularly their accumulation by far-reaching apprehensions and forebodings (6, 34), he may now, at least without unnatural perversion of his plan or language, be supposed to add that as the remedy for such forbidden cares is faith in God's paternal love, so the source as well as the expression of that faith is found in prayer. 'Instead of carking cares about the future, as if all depended upon chance or fate, ask him who can alone provide for you, and it shall be given you.' This is of course to be restricted and explained by the consideration that all true prayer, being prompted by divine grace, is in strict accordance with the divine will. The same thing is then expressed in other forms, one literal, the other metaphorical. *Seek*, not as the heathen seek (6, 32), but as he had already taught his followers to seek (6, 33), giving his cause the preference, but even in promoting it securing their own interests, for time as well as for eternity. The last clause reiterates this thought a third time under the image of a door, behind which or within which lie the mercies that we need, and at which we are, therefore, called to knock, as the ancient and customary mode of gaining entrance.

8. For every one that asketh, receiveth; and he that seeketh, findeth: and to him that knocketh, it shall be opened.

Lest the strong but general assurance of the preceding verse should be neglected as a customary or unmeaning form of speech, it is repeated here in terms still stronger and more universal, not as a promise to be verified in future, but as a fact of actual experience. The change from the future to the present, therefore, is significant, and not to be neglected in the exposition. 'I say, not only that you shall receive hereafter what you ask, but that, in point of fact, whoever does ask, does receive accordingly.' That is to say, believing prayer is never vain or unsuccessful, and the knowledge of this truth is among the most efficient antidotes to sceptical misgivings and excessive care. The force of this remarkable assurance is enhanced in this connection by its formal correspondence to the threefold promise in the verse preceding, which is very slightly, if at all impaired by the reappearance of the future in the last clause (*shall be opened*), which may be intended to remind us that the general fact here stated is a pledge that it shall continue to be so, and, therefore, to all intents and purposes, a promise.* The future of the common text, like that in v. 8, may be either construed with a noun understood (door, gate), or impersonally, as in our version.

9. Or what man is there of you, whom if his son ask bread, will he give him a stone?

10. Or if he ask a fish, will he give him a serpent?

---

* Even this appearance of irregularity is done away if we adopt the reading of the Codex Vaticanus (ἀνοίγεται), as received into the text by Lachmann.

Lest even the preceding declaration should not satisfy them that it is so, he now shows them that it must be so; a necessity arising from the fatherly benevolence of God, and proved by the effect of analogous affections in the case of sinful, fallen man. The argument, like that in 6, 26-30, is from less to greater. *Or,* if this is not sufficient to convince you, view the matter in another light. The favourite form of interrogation is again resumed, implying strong negation. *Who is there?* is equivalent to 'there is no one.' *Of you,* from among you, one of those now present. *What man,* i. e. what mere man, with the ordinary instincts of humanity about him. The original order of the words is, *Who is there among you, a man* (or though a mere man)? The grammatical authorities suppose two questions, or two forms of question, to be here confounded. But however intricate the syntax, there is perfect clearness in the sense. *Bread,* probably the round cake now used in the east, and bearing some resemblance to a smooth, flat stone. The same resemblance may be traced between some kinds of serpent and some kinds of fish. The form of the interrogation in both cases, is that employed in Greek when a negative answer is expected, and therefore nearly equivalent to saying, he will not, will he?

11. **If ye then, being evil, know how to give good gifts unto your children, how much more shall your Father which is in heaven give good things to them that ask him?**

This is the formal argument or inference from the facts indirectly stated in the two preceding verses. This connection is indicated by the *therefore. Ye, being evil,* i. e. ye mere men, and fallen, sinful men. *Know (how)* is not simply equivalent to *can,* as rendered in the older English versions, but suggests the distinct idea that they understood the matter from their own experience. *Good gifts,* in reference to this life, and in opposition to the evil gifts just mentioned. *How much more,* the difference is not defined, being indeed infinite. *Your Father, the (one) in heaven,* an essential description here, because the argument itself is one from the parental love of men to that of God. *Shall give,* or certainly will give, must give, from his very nature, and the relation which he bears to all believers, as his spiritual offspring. *Good (things),* a mere abbreviation of the phrase *good gifts,* in the preceding clause. The absolute use of the adjective without the substantive, is much more frequent in the Greek than in the English idiom. *To them that ask him,* literally, *to those asking him,* a phrase which seems not only to suggest the indispensable condition of God's favours, but to bring back this part of the discourse to the point from which it started (in v. 7), the necessity of prayer as a preventive of unbelieving and excessive care.

12. **Therefore all things whatsoever ye would that**

men should do to you, do ye even so to them: for this is the law and the prophets.

The connection is more difficult to trace at this point than at any other in the whole discourse; and yet the supposition of an abrupt transition seems precluded by the logical connective (*therefore*). As we have neither right nor reason to assume that this is used without a purpose, and as sound philology condemns all tampering with its meaning, we are under the necessity of looking for some natural if not very obvious association with the previous context. The prima facie meaning of the language is, that because God is more disposed to give what is good than earthly parents to their children, therefore, Christ's disciples ought to do to others what they would that others should do to them. It must be admitted that although the premises and the conclusion are both clear, the logical connection is obscure. One of the latest commentators has attempted to establish a connection by departing from the old and universal understanding of the verse before us, which refers *even so* to the preceding clause, and makes it mean, as they do, or as you wish that they should do, to you. The writer here referred to, on the contrary, refers it to the verse preceding, and supposes it to mean, as God does, i. e. freely and abundantly. 'Therefore, because God thus gives, do ye in like manner give to others whatsoever ye desire that they should do to you.' This ingenious construction has the great advantage of establishing a logical connection and removing all appearance of abruptness. The objections to it are, that it puts a meaning on the sentence which it probably has never yet suggested to an ordinary reader; and that it makes the first clause of the verse before us quite superfluous, if not irrelevant. If the meaning of the whole verse is, that men should do to others as God does to them, it is only obscured and interrupted by a reference to what others do or ought to do to them, which introduces an entirely different standard of comparison. 'Whatever you desire men to do to you, do ye to them, as God does,' is a very confused sentence both in thought and language. And yet there seems to be no other method of connecting this verse logically with the one before it. It is better, therefore, to renounce the thought of so immediate a nexus, and to seek for a remoter one. If this is done, by far the simplest and most natural hypothesis is that which makes this a deduction from the whole preceding context, the beginning of a general conclusion to the whole discourse. This is not only agreeable to usage in all long discourses, but particularly recommended here by the recurrence in the last clause to the language of 5, 17, the text or theme on which he has been preaching. Having there disclaimed all purpose to invalidate the law or the prophets, and shown that on the contrary he came to honour and fulfill them, he now begins to wind up his whole argument by saying what the law and prophets are, i. e. how they may be best fulfilled in practice. Not by rigorous obedience to the letter, while the spirit is denied or slighted; not by doing as little for others and exacting as much from them as we can; but by doing to them as we desire that they should do to us; in other words, by loving our neighbour as ourself, which Christ has elsewhere represented as the second great commandment of the law (see below, on 22, 39), and Paul as the sum and substance of the second table (Rom. 13, 9). This explanation, while it yields the best sense and in perfect harmony with other Scriptures, requires no forced constructions or gratuitous assumptions, but a simple pause between the verses, and the commencement, in the one before us, of our Saviour's peroration or conclusion of his whole discourse. As if he had said: 'This, then, is the sum of what I have been saying. I have shown you that I came not to destroy the law or lower its demands, but to enforce them in their true and full sense. I have taught you that your alms and prayer and fasting, and the whole course of your lives, must have a reference to God and his exclusive service, that your anxious cares must be devolved on him, that you have only to ask, as children ask a father, with still greater certainty of being heard, and now I tell you, in review of all this, that the only way to keep the law and prophets is by doing to others as you wish that they should do to you.' This sentence has too commonly been insulated as an independent maxim, and even as peculiar to the Christian system; whereas the sentiment occurs in heathen writers of an earlier date,* and derives its value here from its connection with our Lord's interpretation of the law and his directions how to keep it.

13. Enter ye in at the strait gate: for wide (is) the gate, and broad (is) the way, that leadeth to destruction, and many there be which go in thereat:

What precedes was to many a 'hard saying' (compare John 6, 60); or rather Christ's whole doctrine, as to the spiritual import and perpetual obligation of the law, was unwelcome and discouraging, even to the mass of those who were disposed to follow him. A merely human teacher, even of the truth, might have been tempted to extenuate the difficulty by concealment or by softening the harshness of the requisition. But our Lord, with merciful severity, discloses the whole truth, and far from representing this painful self-denial as an accidental or a temporary thing, or as dispensable in certain cases, holds it up, in the conclusion of this great discourse, as something absolutely necessary to discipleship in his school and to citizenship in his kingdom. What was afterwards announced by Paul and Barnabas to their Gentile converts as a formal proposition. that 'we must through much tribulation enter into the kingdom of God' (Acts 14, 22), is here declared by Christ himself to his Jewish disciples, in the form of an earnest exhortation

---

* The closest parallel is the dictum of Isocrates: ἃ πάσχοντες ὑφ᾽ ἑτέρων ὀργίζεσθε ταῦτα τοῖς ἄλλοις μὴ ποιεῖτε. The one ascribed to Aristotle by Diogenes Laertius is more restricted in its scope, having reference to the treatment of friends. The advice of Seneca (*ab altero expectes alteri quod feceris*) belongs to a later period.

and a positive command. 'Instead of drawing back because the entrance is so narrow and the way so hard, strive the rather upon that account to enter in.' *Enter*, go or come in, i. e. into my kingdom, as the new theocracy, begun on earth to be completed in heaven. *At* (literally, *through*) *the strait* (or *narrow*, not to be confounded with *straight*, which is the opposite of *crooked*) *gate*, used in Greek as in English for the entrance to a town or large enclosure, as distinguished from the *door* (θύρα) of a house or room. (See above, on 6, 6, and below, on 16, 18. 25, 10. 27, 60.) The image here presented, therefore, is not that of a palace to be entered at once, but of a city, or perhaps a country, passes into which the Greeks called gates, with a path or road beyond it. Homer indeed uses *way* for the *way into*, entrance, which would make the two things here identical. But it seems more natural and makes the imagery richer and more varied, to distinguish the gate, or original entrance, from the way, or path to be afterwards pursued, before arriving at the final destination. Some reverse this order, which is that of the text itself both in this verse and the next, and understand the way to be that leading to the gate, which then denote respectively the way or journey of the present life, conducting to the gate of death or of heaven. But the usual construction is more natural, which makes the gate the entrance to the way of life. *The narrow gate*, a definite expression which implies that there is also a wide one. This is then explicitly affirmed. *Wide* (*is*) *the gate*, or there is a wide gate, so that you must choose between them. *Broad*, in Greek a compound, meaning ample as to space or room (Vulg. *spatiosa*), and showing that the way is something more extensive than the gate, to which this epithet could scarcely be applied. This spacious way, with its easy entrance, would be naturally more attractive; but the reason for not taking it is given in the rest of the description, *the* (*one*) *leading to destruction*. The figure of two ways, to represent the life and destination of mankind, is introduced, with great force and beauty, at the close of the first Psalm. *Leading*, in Greek more expressive, *leading off* or *away*, suggesting the idea of great distance, and of scenes altogether different from the present. That the sense is not that of misleading, or leading out of the right path, appears from its application in the next verse to the way of life. *Destruction*, loss, perdition, an indefinite expression, applicable both to temporal and eternal ruin, and intentionally used here so as to suggest both, as included in the issue of this wide and crowded pathway.* A more exact translation of the last clause is, *and many* (*are*) *those entering* (or *going in*) *through it*. It is not to be avoided, therefore, either because difficult of access or unfrequented, but because, as just before said, leading to destruction. These last words are not to be connected with the gate alone, because they speak of going in; for though the gate was the entrance to the way, the way itself was the entrance to destruction.

---

* The Peshito here employs a word substantially the same with the Hebrew *Abaddon*, which John introduces and translates in Rev. 9, 11. Luther has the strong but too exclusive term, *damnation*.

14. Because strait (is) the gate, and narrow (is) the way, which leadeth unto life, and few there be that find it.

Some of the oldest manuscripts and versions here read τί, instead of ὅτι, which is then supposed to be an exclamation (*how strait the gate!* So the Vulgate and Peshito). But as this usage of the Greek word is denied by the philologists, another explanation makes the sentence interrogative, *why (is) the gate narrow*, &c.? an expression either of surprise or sorrow. But the latest critical editions have restored the common text (*because*), which makes this verse co-ordinate with the second clause of v. 13, 'because there is a broad way, and because there is a narrow way,' a twofold reason for the exhortation to press into the latter. *Narrow* in Greek is not a simple synonyme of *strait*, but more expressive, being a passive participle strictly meaning squeezed, compressed, contracted, and suggesting the idea of a difficult as well as inconvenient entrance. To a Greek reader it would also seem significant, that this verb is the root of the noun translated *tribulation*. (See below, on 13, 21, and again compare Acts 14, 22.) *The* (other) *way* (to wit) *the* (one) *leading off* (or *away*, i. e. from this world) *into life*, literally, *the life*, i. e. life by way of eminence, eternal life, the opposite of *destruction*. This exact correspondence in the terms of the description makes it more remarkable and certainly significant, that in the last clause there is a departure from this uniformity. Instead of saying, in exact antithesis to v. 13, *few (are) those entering* (or *going in*) *through it*, the expression here is, *few (are) those finding it*. As we have no right to consider this an accidental or unmeaning variation, so, on the other hand it greatly strengthens both the thought and the expression, by suggesting the additional idea, that not only few gain entrance to this narrow path and way, but few so much as find it. While the broad way of destruction is conspicuous and easy of access, the narrow way of life, besides being difficult of entrance when discovered, is not even discovered by the greater number. This agrees exactly with the moral or spiritual truth intended to be set forth by these figures. The course of life which ends in ruin, being simply the indulgence of man's natural desires, needs neither search to find it nor exertion to pursue it, but is perfectly familiar and accessible to all alike. The course of life which leads to blessedness hereafter, being contradictory to human wisdom and to human inclinations, calls for a twofold painful effort, of the understanding to determine what it is, and of the will to choose it when it is discovered.

15. Beware of false prophets, which come to you in sheep's clothing, but inwardly they are ravening wolves.

The danger of mistake as well as difficulty, hinted in the last words of the verse preceding, would suggest, by obvious association, the necessity of guidance, with its natural correlative, the risk of being misled to destruction. This fearful peril would be greatest where the guides possessed authority, and enjoyed the confidence of those whom they conducted. This was really the case with the religious leaders of the Jews, the Scribes and Pharisees, to whom there seems to be immediate reference, although, instead of being named, they are described in terms derived from the Old Testament, where false religious teachers, claiming a divine authority, are called *false prophets.* As prediction of the future is not even the original and primary functions of a prophet, but authoritative teaching in the name of God, the phrase is perfectly appropriate to those here characterized by it. At the same time it admits of a wider application to false teachers of a later date, confirmed by the constant use of *prophet* in relation to the Christian church.* *Beware*, the verb employed above in 6, 1, and there explained. *Of*, away from, so as to avoid connection or communication with them. *Which come*, not such of them as come, as if this were only true of some false prophets, but *who as such* (or because they are such) *come*, &c. This is the true force of the pronoun here used (οἵτινες), which is carefully distinguished in Greek usage from the ordinary relative (οἵ). The highly figurative terms which follow are derived from the habits of pastoral life, with which many of the hearers were familiar from experience or observation. As the wolf is the natural enemy of sheep, it is elsewhere used as a figure for the cruel enemies of Christ's flock (see below, on 10, 16. and compare John 10, 12. Acts 20, 29). But the stronger and more complete figure of a wolf disguised as a sheep, conveys the idea of deceit and treachery combined with cruelty and savage fierceness. *In sheep's clothing*, or garments of sheep, does not mean in literal sheep-skins, in allusion to the dress of the old prophets; first, because this custom is assumed without proof; then, because this explanation would either destroy the correspondence of the clauses, or require us to understand the whole description literally, which would be absurd. The true sense is, that these false prophets come to (or approach) the people, claiming to be like themselves in point of harmlessness, simplicity, and intimate connection with the church or chosen people, often represented as the flock of God; † while in reality, *within*, inside (Vulg. *intrinsecus*), as distinguished from the outside appearance or profession, they are *wolves*, destructive enemies, and *ravening* (i. e. eagerly seizing and devouring) *wolves*. *Within*, or more exactly, *from within*, which may either be taken as equivalent to *inside*, an interpretation justified by classic usage, or explained more strictly as suggesting the idea of movement or action from within (*ab intra*). 'In appearance they are sheep, but by the actions which proceed from within, or by their inward character, as wrought out in their conduct, they are seen to be rapacious wolves.' This severe accusation was repeated and sustained at length near the close of our Lord's ministry. (See below, on 23, 13–29.)

* See below, on 23, 34. and compare Acts 11, 27. 19, 6. 21, 9. 1 Cor. 12, 28. 14, 29. Eph. 4, 11. Rev. 11, 10. 22, 9.
† See Isai. 40, 11. 63, 11. Jer. 13, 17. Ezek. 34, 6. Mic. 7, 14. Zech. 9, 16. 10, 3. 11, 17.

16. Ye shall know them by their fruits: Do men gather grapes of thorns, or figs of thistles?

That the terms of the preceding verse were highly metaphorical, must have been self-evident to every hearer; but if any doubt remained, it would be removed by the total change of figure in the verse before us, where the savage beasts are suddenly converted into worthless plants, the ravening wolves into thorns and thistles. *Fruits*, taken by itself, might be applied to offspring (as in Acts 2, 30); but the vegetable meaning of the figure is determined by the other clause, where thorns and thistles, grapes and figs, are particularly mentioned. The severe denunciation of their spiritual guides as unworthy of their confidence required some criterion of character, some test by which to justify their disobedience. This is here afforded in a figurative form. *Know*, not the simple Greek verb, but a compound, meaning sometimes to recognize, to know again (as in 14, 35 below, Mark 6, 33. Luke 7, 37. Acts 3, 10. 4, 13. 12, 14. 28, 1), sometimes to discover or detect (as in Mark 2, 8. 5, 30. Luke 1, 22. Acts 19, 34), which seems to be the meaning here. *By*, literally, *from*, in reference to the premises, from which the conclusion is to be deduced. The form of interrogation, in the last clause, like the one in vs. 9. 10, presupposes or anticipates a negative answer, they do not gather, do they? It is, therefore, equivalent to a strong denial, rendered more emphatic by appealing to the hearer's own experience in proof of it. *Men* is applied, as in 5, 15, not with any distinctive meaning as opposed to women or to other beings, but as simply representing the indefinite subject of the verb (*they gather*), which is used in various languages to signify the act of reaping or plucking fruit, with or without reference to that of storing it away. (See below, on 13, 28. 48. and compare the cognate verb in 3, 12. 6, 26. 13, 30.) *Thorns* and *thistles* are in Greek generic and specific terms, the former representing the whole class of armed or prickly plants, the latter a particular variety so called from being *three-pronged*. The distinction is of no importance here, where the two are put together as familiar instances of fruitless and forbidding plants, while grapes and figs are named as the best known and most highly valued fruits of Palestine. The fact thus interrogatively and figuratively stated, is that men know better than to look for valuable fruit on plants which cannot from their nature yield it.

17. Even so every good tree bringeth forth good fruit; but a corrupt tree bringeth forth evil fruit.

Even so, or so, too, in like manner, introduces an extension of the previous statement, as to different species, so as to embrace individuals of one and the same species. A plant, in order to bear fruit, must not only belong to a fruit-bearing species, but itself be fruitful. *Good* is here used to translate two Greek adjectives, which differ somewhat in their primary import, but in general usage are almost synonymous. The former means originally good in its kind, adapted to its purpose;

the other, beautiful, or pleasing to the sight; but both are constantly employed where we say 'good,' both in a physical and moral sense. In this case, we may either treat them as synonymous, or understand the first as meaning good for bearing, and the other fine, attractive to the senses. *Bringeth forth*, literally, *makes*, produces, in which sense and application the Greek verb is used by Aristotle and Theophrastus. The present tense denotes a general or universal truth, as if he had said, 'always bears good fruits.' The plural form of the noun is needlessly relinquished in the version, here and in the next verse, though retained in vs. 16. 20. That no particular significance attaches to the plural form, appears from the occurrence of the singular in v. 19, as well as from the use of the plural in speaking of a single tree. In the last clause, which is simply the converse of the first, there is also a difference in the epithets, but here retained in the translation. *Corrupt*, literally, rotten or decayed, which can hardly be intended in its strict sense, as a rotten or decayed tree bears no fruit at all, but rather in the somewhat wider sense of spoiled or vitiated, bad in quality, the simple opposite of *good* in the preceding clause. *Evil*, the adjective applied to sinful men in v. 11 above, and in 6, 23 to a disordered eye, has here too, from the nature of the case, the sense of physical defect or worthlessness. The general fact here asserted is that plants, as well as animals, produce their like, so that the quality of the tree may be determined by the fruit, and *vice versa*.

18. A good tree cannot bring forth evil fruit, neither (can) a corrupt tree bring forth good fruit.

The fact asserted in the previous verse not only is so, but it must be so. The bad tree not only does not but cannot produce good fruit, or the good tree bad fruit. This may seem at variance with the fact that even good trees are liable to fail, or to bear fruit of an inferior value. But the reference is not to failures or exceptional cases, but to the legitimate and normal operation of the cause. The natural and proper product of a good or bad tree cannot differ from its source in quality. This is strictly true, and all that is intended. The four epithets occurring in v. 17 are here repeated, not at random, but with great precision, in accordance with their previous application, although not in the same order, which implies that they were meant to be distinctly understood, according to the proper sense of each.

19. Every tree that bringeth not forth good fruit is hewn down, and cast into the fire.

The appeal to observation and experience is here carried a step further, so as to include not only the habitual estimate of trees according to their fruits, but the practical issue of that estimate, the treatment of the tree according to its fruits. Here again the present form of the verb denotes what is usual among men in such cases. *Every tree not making* (or *producing good*) *fruit*, i. e. never doing so, since men do not destroy trees for a single failure. *Hewn down*, literally *out*, implying absolute excision and removal from its place. The same verb is translated in the same way in 3, 10, but in 5, 30 where it is applied to members of the body, *cut off*. The last words indicate the use, to which the tree thus felled was commonly applied, to wit, as fuel. This specification of a custom so familiar makes the sentence more impressive, without excluding other purposes for which a barren fruit-tree might be cut down. 'How many a tree, which failed to answer its original purpose, have we seen hewn down and converted into fuel?' The specific reference to this use is intended to suggest the destiny of such false teachers.

20. Wherefore, by their fruits ye shall know them.

Wherefore, not to be confounded with the similar word *therefore*, or at least not here used to represent the same Greek particle, but one, which, although an illative or logical connective, seems to point out a remoter antecedent, or to indicate an inference, but not from what immediately precedes. So here, the reference to human practice having been extended further than the point of comparison originally mentioned, namely, that men usually estimate trees by their fruit, our Lord now reverts to that point, for the purpose of applying the comparison to the case in hand. *So then* (as I was saying but a little while ago) *by their fruits*, i. e. by the fruits of these false prophets *ye shall know* (recognise, discover, or detect) *them*. It has sometimes been disputed whether *fruits* here means false doctrine or erroneous practice founded on it. It is clear, from the whole drift of the comparison that *fruits*, in the application, means the moral effect produced by the false teachers here denounced, both on the doctrinal belief and on the lives of their disciples: 'That they are false prophets and rapacious wolves, you may easily convince yourselves, by looking at the influence exerted by them on your own character and that of others.' The allusion commonly assumed to the personal character and conduct of the Scribes and Pharisees themselves, can only be admitted, if at all, as included in the general description of their influence, but not as the criterion itself, by which they must be judged; for this would make their character the test or touchstone of itself, and be equivalent to saying, 'you may know that they are wicked by their being wicked,' which is reasoning in a circle; whereas no such objection can be made to the prescription, 'you may know that they are wicked by their making you and others so.'

21. Not every one that saith unto me, Lord, Lord, shall enter into the kingdom of heaven; but he that doeth the will of my Father which is in heaven.

The foregoing premonition might have seemed to be directed only against open enemies. But here our Lord proceeds to warn his hearers, that even some of his professed disciples would be finally re-

jected. This was the more important because many of the very class
which he had been describing had assumed the name and language of
his followers, either under shallow and short-lived impressions, or with
the purpose of deliberate deception. Even in the college of Apostles
this class had its representative, well known and tolerated by the Master, as a means of greater good than could then be effected by an earlier
exposure and expulsion. (See John 6, 64. 70.) So here he plainly intimates the presence of hypocrites and false professors in the ranks of
his nominal disciples. (See below, on 13, 24.) This was a most important and appropriate winding up of his organic or inaugural discourse, now drawing to a solemn and impressive close. *Not every one*,
in classic Greek, might seem to be equivalent to *no one*, thus excluding
all who profess to acknowledge Christ as Lord from admission to his
kingdom. But this absurd sense is avoided by a due regard to the
Hebrew idiom which, like our own, uses the phrase *not every one* to
intimate that some but not all who made such a profession would be
saved. *Saying unto me*, so addressing or accosting me. *Lord*, i. e.
master, sovereign, the repetition making the acknowledgment more
earnest and emphatic, or perhaps denoting frequent and habitual action,
'not all who are continually calling me their Lord and Master.' It is not
improbable that this practice had already become common among those
disciples whom our Lord knew to be hypocrites or false professors.
That it was not of itself to be a ground of condemnation, but is here
denounced only as insufficient without action answering to the profession, is expressly taught in the remainder of the verse. *But the (one)
doing*, practising, *the will of* (what is willed and required by) *my
father, the (one) in heaven*, literally *heavens* (see above, on 5, 8). The
same limitation or specification of the vague term *father*, so as to exclude all human paternity, had been used before to describe the spiritual sonship of believers (see above, on 5, 16. 45. 48. 6, 1. 9. 7, 11), and
is now applied, in a still more strict and proper sense, to that of Christ
himself, implying oneness of nature and coincidence of will, so that his
kingdom was the kingdom of the Father, and obedience to its law obedience to the Son himself. *The (one) doing*, not in contrast to *the
(one) saying*, for the two things are entirely compatible, but the one
both saying and doing, or 'of those who call me Lord, the one who at
the same time does my Father's will.'

22. Many will say to me in that day, Lord, Lord,
have we not prophesied in thy name? and in thy name
have cast out devils? and in thy name done many wonderful works?

The exclusion just predicted would bring with it the severest disappointment to many now professing to be Christ's disciples. There is
no need of supposing that the very dialogue here given will be ever
verbally repeated in the case of any one, much less of every one, belonging to the class in question. It is equally admissible, and more in

keeping with our Lord's accustomed mode of speaking on such subjects, to regard this as a lively embodiment in words of what will certainly take place in fact. (See below, on 25, 31–48.) Their surprise and disappointment will be such as might be naturally clothed in these words. *In that day*, an indefinite expression, purposely employed to make a vague but powerful impression on the hearers, while to us it conveys a more specific sense, determined and made clear by later revelations. Those immediately addressed might not, as we do, instantly associate the words with the idea of a final judgment or a great day of account, though this is really their import as interpreted to us, whereas to them they might suggest little more than if it had been said, 'the day is coming when many will be ready to exclaim.' The tone is that of serious and alarmed expostulation, rendered bold by the imminent danger of exclusion. The reiteration (*Lord, Lord*) is not only a renewal, as it were, of the original profession, but a natural evidence of present earnestness and importunity. *Have we not*, or retaining the original construction, which implies an interval, greater or less, between the acts described and this appeal to them, *did we not*, when thou wast upon earth, and we among thy followers. *In thy name*, may be strictly understood as meaning called and known by thy name, thy professed disciples; or agreeably to constant usage as denoting an appeal to Christ, an invocation of his name, as the authority by which they acted (see below, on 10, 41. 18, 5. 20. 21, 9. 23. 39. 24, 5); or both these senses, which are perfectly compatible, may be combined; as bearing thy name and invoking it, i. e. as nominal disciples and official messengers. *Prophesy*, not necessarily predict, though that might be included (as in Acts 11, 28. 21, 10), but authoritatively teach in the Church and under a commission from our Lord himself, authenticated by the gift of miracles. Of these the most remarkable is stated by itself, and then a general expression follows. See above, on 4, 24, where the participle (*demonized*) is a derivative of the word here rendered *devils*, although not correctly, as the Scriptures recognize but one *Devil*, so called as the slanderer and false accuser of mankind (see above, on 4, 1), while the other fallen angels are collectively described as *demons*. This word, in its primary form ($\delta\alpha\iota\mu\omega\nu$), means a *deity* (in Latin, *numen*), or rather any superhuman being, whether god, or gods, or demigods, &c., in which sense Socrates applied it to the genius, or good angel, by whom he believed himself to be attended. From this noun comes a corresponding adjective ($\delta\alpha\iota\mu\acute{o}\nu\iota os$), divine or superhuman, the neuter form of which, and not a diminutive as some have thought, is used absolutely, here and elsewhere, to denote the fallen spirits who were suffered to possess, or occupy and influence, the bodies and the souls of men, and whose expulsion was the strongest proof of Christ's superiority and triumph, as the seed of the woman, over the seed of the serpent (Gen. 3, 15), or the devil and his angels. (See below, on 25, 41.) That this power was not an incommunicable one, but actually imparted by our Lord to his disciples, is expressly stated in 10, 8 below. *Wonderful works*, an inexact and needless paraphrase of one word, literally meaning *powers* (or as Wiclif, following the Vulgate, here translates it, *virtues*), but applied in usage to miraculous performances, as fruits and proofs of superhuman power, and therefore well translated in the other English versions, *miracles*. This is a generic or collective term, added to the specific one before it, so as to make dispossession prominent among the other wonders wrought, or claimed to have been wrought, by them. There is no need of supposing this to be itself a false profession, since we have reason to believe that miracles, as well as prophecy, were sometimes placed at the disposal of ungodly men.

23. And then will I profess unto them, I never knew you: depart from me, ye that work iniquity.

As before suggested, this may be regarded either as the actual reply in some one case, or every case, to such expostulations; or, with more probability, as a translation into words of what will be impressed upon the minds of such unhappy hypocrites, in answer to their own unfounded claims. *And*, continues the description without interruption, so that *and then* is nearly equivalent to *forthwith* or immediately, though *then*, taken by itself, is the correlative of *that day* in v. 22, and to the same extent indefinite to those who originally heard it. *Confess*, a verb originally meaning to *speak together*, or the same thing with another, i. e. to assent, agree, to what is spoken. In this connection, it may either have the vaguer sense, in which it is occasionally used, of solemnly declaring, or be taken as a sort of solemn irony, 'I will assent to what you say, but only by denying it.' Or the verb may mean to *profess*, and there may be a strong antithesis between his profession and their own. As they had professed him, so he would profess them, but only by declaring that he never knew them. (See below, on 10, 33.) *Never*, not even when I seemed to recognize your claims by suffering your presence. *Knew*, i. e. knew you to be mine, which is equivalent to saying, that he always knew them to be none of his. *Depart*, a Greek verb which denotes far more than locomotion, namely, separation and desertion, in which sense it is the root of the noun *anchorite*, meaning one who retires, or retreats, or is secluded from the world. (See above, on 2, 12. 4, 12, and below, on 27, 5.) It here means, separate yourselves from my disciples, take your true place as my enemies. The ground of this severe denunciation is then added, as a designation or description of the persons so denounced. *Ye that work*, literally, *the (ones) working*, or *those working*, not simply doing once for all, or even habitually practising, but *working at it* as your daily business, or *working it out* as the product of your labour. (See below, on 21, 28. 25, 16.) *Iniquity*, or more exactly, *lawlessness*, the opposite of righteousness, conformity to law or to the will of God. (See above, on 3, 15. 5, 6. 10. 20. 6, 33. and below, on 21, 32.)

24. Therefore, whosoever heareth these sayings of mine, and doeth them, I will liken him unto a wise man, which built his house upon a rock:

There was still a danger to which many were exposed who could not be accused of hypocrisy or false profession in the strict sense of the terms. Even after hearing all that Christ had said in correction of prevailing misconceptions and of practical abuses, some might after all content themselves with having heard it, and make no attempt to act upon it. Such he warns, in the ensuing verses (24–27), that mere knowledge of the truth and human duty without corresponding practice, only aggravates the doom of those who have it. This idea is beautifully carried out in parabolic form, by supposing two familiar cases, perhaps well known to the hearers. There is certainly no reason for regarding them as fictions. *Therefore* draws a conclusion not from what immediately precedes, but from the whole discourse; *therefore*, since all these things are so. *Does them*, acts upon them, acts them out, in his habitual conduct. *I will liken*, i. e. I will now compare, by way of illustration. *Wise*, a Greek word strictly meaning sane, not insane, but applied also to other less extreme intellectual distinctions, as in this case to discretion, practical prudence. *Who*, the compound relative explained above (on v. 15), and which would readily suggest to a Greek reader the idea, *who (as such)*, i. e. as being wise, because he was wise. *Built*, in Greek the aorist, referring to a definite past, and not the present, setting forth a general truth. This makes it the more probable that we have here a reference to real incidents, perhaps fresh in the memory of some who heard him. *A rock*, literally, *the rock*, not a rocky fragment, but a mass or bed of rock, as we sometimes speak of excavation in the living rock.

25. And the rain descended, and the floods came, and the winds blew, and beat upon that house; and it fell not: for it was founded upon a rock.

This verse describes the value of so solid a foundation, even in the midst of peril. *Rain*, in Greek a word denoting a shower or a storm of rain. *Floods*, the common word in Greek for rivers, here put for inundations, freshets, which is a frequent sense of the English plural. *Came*, as something extraordinary, not continually present. *Beat upon*, a good sense and good English, but not the exact original expression, which exhibits two cognate verbs, a simple and a compound. They *fell* upon it, but it *fell* not. *Was founded upon a rock*, or more exactly, *had been founded upon the rock*, which may here mean in addition the rock previously mentioned.

26. And every one that heareth these sayings of mine, and doeth them not, shall be likened unto a foolish man, which built his house upon the sand:

This is simply the converse of the case first stated, or its counterpart in real life. The same form of expression is retained, except in those parts where the contrast or antithesis must be brought out.

Here, as in v. 4, he does not simply say *my words*, but *these my words*, i. e. those uttered upon this occasion, which confirms our previous conclusion as to the unity of the discourse and its delivery at one time (see above, on 5, 1). Instead of *I will liken* we have here the passive, *shall be likened*, which may either be considered a synonymous expression, or express the additional idea that the likeness shall not be confined to this description, but extend to the reality, or be verified in actual experience. *Foolish*, a negative rather than a positive description, the Greek word, when applied to material objects, meaning tasteless or insipid (see above, on 5, 13), when to intellectual, senseless or irrational (see above, on 5, 22). The reference is here to want of common prudence or discretion in providing for one's own security. *The sand*, exactly corresponding to *the rock* in v. 24, each denoting not a definite or separate portion, but the substance or material itself. The contrast, as to this point, is made far more striking by the sameness of the other terms employed in the description.

27. And the rain descended, and the floods came, and the winds blew, and beat upon that house ; and it fell : and great was the fall of it.

The test applied to the foundation is again described precisely as before, or with a single variation, and even that does not appear in English. *Beat upon* is here a more exact translation than in v. 25, the Greek verb being different, and literally meaning, *struck against*, the double sense of falling being not expressed at all in this case. The antithesis is perfect, both in form and substance, *and it fell not . . . . . and it fell;* but in the added words there is a marked and striking difference. Instead of telling why it fell (as in the other case), to wit, because it had been founded on the sand, our Lord looks away from the cause to the effect, and intimates the total ruin of the baseless edifice, by simply adding, *and its fall was great.* The force of this fine apologue is greatly marred by giving a specific sense to each of its details, the rock, the sand, the wind, the rain, the floods, &c. Such minute interpretations may indeed be endlessly extended and diversified, to suit the taste or meet the wants of readers and expounders; but they must not be forced upon the text as any part of its essential meaning and design, which is to set forth, by familiar but impressive analogies from real life, the simple but momentous truth, that mere religious knowledge, without corresponding practice, is a baseless fabric doomed to swift destruction.

28. And it came to pass, when Jesus had ended these sayings, the people were astonished at his doctrine :

29. For he taught them as (one) having authority, and not as the scribes.

That the Sermon on the Mount, which closes with the verse preceding this, is not a mere collection of our Saviour's sayings upon different occasions, put together to illustrate his peculiar mode of teaching, but a single continuous discourse delivered at a certain time and place, is clear not only from the way in which the writer introduces it (see above, on 5, 1), and from its structure and contents, but also from the statement here made as to its conclusion and effect. *And* resumes the narrative suspended (5, 2) for the purpose of recording this discourse at length. *It came to pass* (or *happened*) is not a mere unmeaning superfluity, but tantamount to our familiar phrases, 'the result was this,' or 'thus it turned out.' *Had ended* is in Greek an aorist, *when he ended*, finished, or completed, an emphatic compound properly denoting an entire accomplishment or consummation. Here again the language presupposes a continuous coherent whole, something that had a beginning and must have an end, expressions which could scarcely be applied to a desultory series of disjointed dicta. The effect described is that produced upon *the people*, or as it should have been translated, *the multitudes*, the vast promiscuous assemblage mentioned in 4, 25 and 5, 1. and not upon any select class among them. A highly important feature in the history of Christ's ministry is the impression or effect of his teaching on the multitudes who heard it. This is here described in reference to one particular occasion, but in terms admitting of a general application, and substantially repeated elsewhere. (See below, 13, 54. 22, 33, and compare Mark 6, 2. 11, 18. Acts 13, 12.) The grand effect was that of wonder or astonishment, *they were struck*, literally *struck out*, driven from their normal or customary state of mind by something new and strange. The object or occasion of this wonder was *his doctrine*, not his *learning*, as Tyndale renders it in Mark 1, 22. unless he uses that term in its old sense (now regarded as a vulgarism) of *teaching*, which is Wiclif's version; nor the truth taught, which is now the common use of *doctrine:* but as the Greek word usually means in the gospels, either the act or mode of teaching. That this is the meaning here, we learn from the reason given for their wonder. This is stated in the last clause negatively, *for he was* (then as habitually) *teaching them not as the Scribes*. His instructions are here brought into direct comparison with those of a certain well-known class, who must of course be teachers. This is a sufficient refutation of the error that the Scribes were either clerks to the magistrates, or mere transcribers of the Scriptures. As the successors of Ezra, the first Scribe of whom we read in this sense (Ezra 7, 6), they were the conservators and guardians of the sacred text and canon, which implies a critical acquaintance with them, such as qualified the Scribes above all others to be expounders of the Scripture likewise. Although rather a profession than an office, they exerted a commanding influence on public opinion, and are repeatedly referred to as authoritative teachers of religion. (See below, on 23, 2-4, and compare Mark 12, 35. Luke 11, 52.) The point of difference is indicated in the positive statement that *he taught* (or *was teaching*) *them as* (one) *having authority*. This cannot refer to a dogmatical authoritative manner, as to which the Scribes most probably surpassed all others. Nor does it mean *powerfully*, as explained by Luther. The only sense consistent with the usage of the terms and with the context is, that he taught them, not as a mere expounder, but with the original authority belonging to the author of the law expounded. This is not a description of mere outward manner, but of that self-evidencing light and self-asserting force, which must accompany all direct divine communications to the minds of creatures. Even those who were most accustomed and most submissive to the teachings of the Scribes, must have felt, as soon as Jesus spoke, that he was speaking with authority, declaring his own will, and expounding his own law, not that of another. The distinction, therefore, is not merely between traditional and textual instruction, but between two forms or methods of the latter. Some of the old manuscripts here read, *their Scribes* (adopted by the latest critics), to which others add, *and the Pharisees.*

CHAPTER VIII.

HERE begins a series of miracles extending through the next chapter, those recorded in the present being five in number, with a general account of many more. Of the five recounted in detail, only one is accompanied by any statement of our Lord's words, beyond what is necessarily included in the description of the miracle itself. This remarkable succession of miraculous performances, uninterrupted by discourse or teaching, is sufficient of itself to create a presumption that the incidents here given are not arranged in reference to the time of their occurrence, but to some other purpose in the mind of the historian. This presumption is strengthened by the fact, that several of these miracles are given in the other gospels in a different chronological connection. All appearance of discrepancy is removed by the absence in such cases of any chronological specification on the part of Matthew. The true ground or principle of his arrangement is the illustration of our Lord's miraculous ministry by chosen specimens, succeeding the great sample of his teaching in the Sermon on the Mount, and preceding the mission of the twelve apostles with the same didactic and miraculous functions. The precise relation of the several occurrences here given to the parallel accounts, and of the general course of the history, as well as the probable grounds for their selection, will be stated in expounding each successively. The order of the topics in this chapter is as follows. After stating the continued concourse which attended our Lord's ministry (1), the history records the healing of a leper (2–4); that of a paralytic at Capernaum, the servant of a Roman officer (5–13); that of a case of fever in the family of Peter (14. 15); and of many others on the same day, not related in detail, but described in general terms, and in connection with an ancient prophecy respecting the Messiah's mission (16, 17). This is followed by a dialogue, intended to exemplify the false impressions of that mission, entertained by some who called themselves disciples (18–22), and at the same time to introduce two signal miracles which actually followed it, one evincing sovereign power over nature and the elements (23–27), the other over demons and demoniacal possessions of the most malignant character (28–34).

1. When he was come down from the mountain, great multitudes followed him.

Having described the Sermon on the Mount as occasioned by and uttered to a vast promiscuous assemblage (5, 1), and recorded the effect which it produced upon them (7, 28), the historian now informs us that this concourse did not cease with the discourse, nor even with our Lord's descent from the mountain or the highlands (see above, on 5, 1) where it was delivered, but continued after his return to the lake-shore and the city of Capernaum. The statement of the fact here seems designed to qualify the whole series of miracles recorded in this chapter, which we are, therefore, to conceive of as performed in the presence, or at least in the vicinity of multitudes. The connection with the foregoing chapter is made still more clear by the original construction of the first words, *and to him descending from the mountain*, the dative case required by the verb in Greek being afterwards repeated (*followed him*), which makes the first almost equivalent to a genitive absolute, *he descending* (or *having descended*), the sense of which, though not the form, is correctly given in the English versions (*when he was come down*) *great multitudes*, the Rhemish version, more exact than the older one, *much people* (Geneva Bible, *great press of people*), but admitting of still further improvement by the literal translation, *many crowds*, i. e. promiscuous assemblages, the plural perhaps indicating not more individuals, but groups and gatherings from various quarters.

2. And, behold, there came a leper and worshipped him, saying, Lord, if thou wilt, thou canst make me clean.

This first miracle appears to be selected on account of the peculiar nature of the evil which occasioned it. *A leper*, one afflicted with the *leprosy*, a painful and loathsome cutaneous disorder, which, although a natural disease, appears to have prevailed in a preternatural degree among the ancient Hebrews, so that heathen writers represent it as a national affection, and the cause of their expulsion from Egypt. The identity of this disease with any now known has been much disputed; but the latest testimonies favour the belief that it continues to prevail, and in an aggravated form, defying all attempts to cure it, even by the most improved and scientific modern methods. But even if the same disease, we have every reason to believe that it prevailed of old far more extensively, and in a more terrific shape than it ever does at present. The design of this extraordinary prevalence, if real, was to furnish a symbol of the loathsomeness of sin, considered as a spiritual malady, and by the rites connected with its treatment, to suggest the only means of moral renovation. The rules of procedure in such cases form a prominent part of the Mosaic law (Lev. xiii. xiv.), and were still in full force at the time of Christ's appearance. Besides the formal periodical inspection of the patient by the priest, and the purifying ceremonies incident even to a state of convalescence, the leper was excluded from society, required to dwell apart, and to announce his presence and condition by his dress, his gestures, and his words. That this law was applied without respect of persons, is apparent from the case of King Uzziah, who was smitten with the leprosy to punish his invasion of the priestly office, and though one of the most able and successful of the kings of Judah, spent the remainder of his life in a several (or separate) house, the government being administered by his son, as Prince Regent (2 Kings 15, 5. 2 Chr. 26, 16–21). The lepers, therefore, were a well-defined and well-known class of sufferers, distinguished from all others by the circumstances which have just been stated, and holding a sort of middle place between demoniacal possessions and mere ordinary ailments. There was no doubt much curiosity in reference to the course which our Saviour would pursue with respect to these unfortunates, who were not considered as entitled even to approach him. This may be the reason that Matthew relates the healing of a leper as his first particular example of the Saviour's miracles. *Worshipped*, a Greek word properly descriptive of an outward or corporeal action; in the first instance that of kissing, more especially the hand, or kissing the hand to one, as an act of homage; then applied by Herodotus to homage as performed in oriental courts by kissing the ground or by entire prostration; and then to homage or obeisance in general, whether civil or religious, which is also the old usage of the English *worship*, as preserved in the Marriage Service, and in 'worshipful,' 'your worship,' as official titles. There is no reason to suppose that this leper meant to do more than express the profoundest reverence and most earnest importunity. The precise acts of homage, as we learn from the other gospels, were those of kneeling (Mark 1, 40) and falling on the face (Luke 5, 12). This implies near approach, if not immediate contact, in direct violation of the Jewish usage. The beautiful expression in the last clause is expressive of the strongest faith in Christ's miraculous power, and only a reasonable doubt of his willingness to exercise it upon such an object. To us it seems a matter of course that he should cleanse the lepers as well as heal the sick; but it was in fact a very doubtful question till determined in the case before us. *Wilt* and *canst* are not mere auxiliaries but distinct and independent verbs, *if thou art willing thou art able*. To *cleanse* (or *purify*) *me*, i. e. to free me from the leprosy, considered not as a mere disease, but as a symbolical and actual defilement.

3. And Jesus put forth (his) hand, and touched him, saying, I will; be thou clean. And immediately his leprosy was cleansed.

Under the influence of human sympathy, as well as of divine condescension, he complies with the request of the poor leper, both by deed and word. The deed, that of stretching out the hand and touching him, had no magical intrinsic power, being frequently dispensed with; but it visibly connected the author with the subject of the miracle, and at the same time symbolized or typified the healing virtue which it did not of itself impart. The words which accompanied this gesture correspond to those of the leper himself, but with a point and brevity which make them still more beautiful and striking. If thou wilt, ... I will. Thou canst cleanse me, ... Be cleansed. The version, *be thou clean*, though perfectly correct in sense, mars the antithesis between the active and the passive voice of one and the same verb (καθαρίσαι, καθαρίσθητι). The effect, as usual, was instantaneous, and is here described by the concise expression, that *his leprosy was cleansed*, which is equivalent to Mark's more explicit statement, that "the leprosy departed from him," and he was cleansed or purified, as he had asked and Christ had promised, both in a physical and moral sense. By being freed from the literal corporeal foulness of this loathsome malady, the leper became *ipso facto* free from the social and religious disabilities which the ceremonial law attached to it, and needed only to be recognized as thus free by the competent authority.

4. And Jesus saith unto him, See thou tell no man; but go thy way, shew thyself to the priest, and offer the gift that Moses commanded, for a testimony unto them.

It is characteristic of the miracles of Christ, that they were neither preceded nor followed by unnecessary words or acts; but as soon as the desired change was wrought, the subject was dismissed, to make way for another. So here, the leper is no sooner cleansed than he is sent away, with an earnest exhortation and important direction. *See*, i. e. see to it, be careful, be upon thy guard. *Man*, supplied in such cases by the English version limits the sense too much, unless explained as an indefinite pronoun, like the same form in German. The charge here given was not one of absolute and permanent concealment, which was not only needless but impossible, from the sudden and complete change in the man's appearance and the subsequent effect upon his social relations. The prohibition was a relative and temporary one, and had respect to the more positive command which follows. Until that direction was complied with, he was to say nothing. This connection is suggested by the order of the sentence, "see thou tell no one . . . . but go," &c., i. e. remain silent till thou hast gone. This was no doubt intended to secure his prompt performance of a duty which he might otherwise have postponed or omitted altogether. This was the duty of subjecting himself to the inspection of a priest, and obtaining his official recognition of the cure which had been wrought upon him. That recognition would of course be followed by the offerings prescribed in the Mosaic law for such occasions. (Lev. 41, 1–32.) By this requisition Christ not only provided for the full authentication of the miracle, but as it were, defined his own relation to the ceremonial law, as a divine institution, and as being still in force. This was important, both as a preventive of malicious charges, and as a key to the design of his whole ministry or mission, which belonged, at least in form, to the old and not the new economy, and was only preparatory to the outward change of dispensations. (See above, on 5, 17.) This is the meaning put by some upon the last words *for a testimony* (Tyndale *testimonial*) *to them*, i. e. as a proof that I reverence the law and comply with its requirements. More probably, however, it refers to the fact of the man's being cleansed, which could be fully ascertained by nothing but official scrutiny and attestation.

5. And when Jesus was entered into Capernaum, there came unto him a centurion, beseeching him,

Of the natural diseases which prevailed among the Jews when Christ was upon earth, one of the most common seems to have been palsy or paralysis (the former word being a corruption or modification of the latter), either in the strict sense of the modern nosology, or in a wider one including what is now called apoplexy. The Greek terms, *paralysis* and *paralytic*, denote according to their etymology, a relaxation of the nerves on one side. This class of our Lord's miraculous healings furnishes the next case in the series now before us. It is also remarkable as having been performed at the request and on the servant of a Roman officer, as well as for the praise bestowed by Christ himself upon his strong and discriminating faith. It is likewise an example of miraculous restoration without personal contact or immediate presence. These circumstances are sufficient to account for its selection as an item in this catalogue, without regard to its chronology, which Luke expressly fixes as immediately subsequent to his version of the Sermon on the Mount, and, therefore, as we have already seen, somewhat later than the similar discourse preserved by Matthew. (See the introduction to chs. 5–7.) There is no inconsistency, however, as Matthew gives no such chronological specification as the one in Luke (7, 1), but simply says, *when he went into Capernaum*, literally, *to him entering*, as in v. 1, and with the same pleonastic repetition of the pronoun (αὐτῷ). Now as Capernaum was the centre of his operations, to which he frequently returned from his itinerant missions (see above, on 4, 10), the expression here used is an indefinite one, and necessarily means nothing more than, *as he was (once) entering Capernaum*. Besides this chronological specification, Luke adds some circumstances not preserved by Matthew, and, therefore, not essential to his purpose. It is no part of the interpreter's office to insert what the writer has thought fit or been directed to leave out, as if his narrative were incomplete without it, though we may employ it to illustrate and explain what is recorded, and especially to reconcile apparent contradictions. It will be sufficient, therefore, to observe that Matthew's brief account of the centurion's application to our Lord, as if it had been made in person, is by no means at variance with Luke's supplementary account of the intermediate agency by which it was presented. All that was necessary to the purpose of the former was the main fact that a Roman officer did so apply, and as he simply paves over the channel of communication, but says nothing to exclude it, there is no ground for the charge of contradiction or a variant tradition. The form of expression used by Matthew that he came to (or approached) him, said to him, &c., is completely justified not only by the legal maxim sometimes quoted (*qui facit per alium facit per se*), but by all analogy and usage, where the speaker or writer wishes to direct attention simply to the act, and not to its attendant circumstances. How readily and naturally might one writing of the recent war in Europe, speak of communications as directly passing between Louis Napoleon and Francis Joseph, when in fact they were conveyed by diplomatists or aides-de-camp, and how absurd would be the charge of contradiction, if a later and more regular historian should introduce these intermediate agencies omitted, and perhaps not thought of, by the former writer. This will suffice to meet the charge of inconsistency between the parallels. The minute examination of Luke's supplementary details belongs to the exposition of that gospel. *A centurion*, or commander of a hundred men, used perhaps with some degree of latitude for the leaders of divisions in a Roman legion. The one here referred to was most probably in Herod's service, and stationed at Capernaum. It is possible, however, that the Roman Emperor, the real sovereign of the country, had his military representatives even in the districts nominally governed by the tetrarchs. *Beseeching him*, a Greek verb originally meaning to *call on* (for aid), or in, to one's assistance, but secondarily *to call to*, in the way of exhortation and encouragement, which justifies its being sometimes rendered *comfort* (as in 2, 18. 3, 4 above), while here it has its strict and proper sense.

6. And saying, Lord, my servant lieth at home sick of the palsy, grievously tormented.

This is the centurion's description of his servant's case, as sent to Christ through the elders of the Jews (Luke 7, 3). It is not easy to determine in particular cases, how strong a meaning was attached to the word *Lord* (κύριε) by those who used it. As on one hand it is the Greek equivalent or rather substitute for the name *Jehovah*, both in the Septuagint and New Testament; so on the other it was a common title of respect or expression of civility, like *Domine* in Latin and *Sir* in English. Intermediate between these is a sense nearly corresponding to *my Lord*, and implying an acknowledgment of more than ordinary dignity and rank, even where there is no intentional ascription of divine honours. This is perhaps the true sense here and in many other cases, where our fixed associations with the title lead us naturally to assume a higher meaning than the speaker really intended to convey. *Servant,* literally, *boy,* an idiom found also in the Hebrew (נַעַר), French (*garçon*), and certain English phrases (e. g. *post-boy*), as well as in the use of *boy* itself for slave in our southern States. This usage in the Scriptures throws some light upon the application of the term to Christ himself, as both the servant and the son of God. (See below, on 12, 18.) *Lieth,* lies, is lying, in Greek a perfect passive meaning *has been thrown* (*down*), or in modern phrase, *prostrated,* whether figuratively by disease, or literally on a sick bed. *At home,* the phrase used in all the English versions except Wiclif, which retains the Greek form, *in the house,* i. e. my house. *Sick of the palsy,* in Greek, *paralytic,* a word which does not seem to have been used in English when the Bible was translated. It occurs only in the two first gospels (see above, on 4, 24), Luke employing a participle of the cognate verb (παραλελομενος), just as we say *paralyzed* as well as *paralytic*. *Grievously,* or, as the Greek word originally means, fearfully, terribly. *Tormented,* tortured, in extreme pain, a verb formed from the noun translated *torments* in 4, 24. and there explained.

7. And Jesus saith unto him, I will come and heal him.

Saith, in modern English *says,* the historical or graphic present, calling up the scene as actually passing. *To him,* i. e. to his messenger (Luke 7, 6). *I will come and heal him,* literally, *I coming* (or *having come*) *will heal him,* i. e. I am ready or about to do so, unless hindered, as he knew that he would be; so that the future does not express actual intention, but mere willingness. The verb translated *heal* is that employed above in 4, 23. 24. and there explained.

8. The centurion answered and said, Lord, I am not worthy that thou shouldest come under my roof: but speak the word only, and my servant shall be healed.

And answering, the centurion said, i. e, by his messenger, as Christ approached (Luke 6, 6). *Worthy,* literally, *enough,* of sufficient value, good enough. *Come under my roof,* or honour my dwelling with thy presence. *Speak the word,* i. e. the word of command necessary for the purpose; or rather, as the article is not expressed in Greek, *speak a word,* i. e. a single word, as all-sufficient, which is substantially the meaning of the dative (λόγῳ) now adopted by the latest critics, (*in*) *a word,* or in the use of one word only

9. For I am a man under authority, having soldiers under me: and I say to this (man), Go, and he goeth; and to another, Come, and he cometh; and to my servant, Do this, and he doeth (it).

This verse assigns his reason for believing that a word from Christ would be sufficient without personal proximity or contact. *For I am* is the imperfect version of the Geneva Bible; Tyndale and Cranmer have it more exactly *for I also myself am.* "I know the effect of an authoritative order, from one who has a right to give it, by my own experience as a soldier, being accustomed both to command and to obey." These two ideas are expressed by the words *under authority*, (i. e. the authority of others, and in my turn) *having soldiers under me.* *I say*, i. e. habitually, I am wont to say, in the exercise of my authority as a commander. *To this man*, literally, *this (one)*, an expression simply used in opposition to *another.* *Go* and *come* are idiomatic or proverbial terms for action in general. *Servant* in the last clause may either mean a soldier in attendance on an officer (see Acts, 10, 7), or a domestic, as distinguished from the soldiers before mentioned. The latter is more probable, because the Greek word (δοῖλος) properly denotes a slave, and because the reference is here to doing, i. e. serving, and not, as in the other clause, to going and coming, i. e. marching. The whole is a lively and laconic picture of brief command and prompt obedience.

10. When Jesus heard (it), he marvelled, and said to them that followed, Verily I say unto you, I have not found so great faith, no, not in Israel.

The original order is, *and hearing, Jesus wondered.* To reconcile omniscience with surprise is no part of our privilege or duty. All such seeming contradictions are parts of the great mystery of godliness, God manifest in the flesh (1 Tim. 3, 16), the union of humanity and deity in one theanthropic person. However incomprehensible to our finite faculties may be the co-existence in one person of the divine logos and a human soul, the possession of the latter, if conceded, carries with it all the attributes and acts of which a perfect human soul is capable. While to Christ's divinity or eternal spirit there could be nothing new or strange, to his humanity surprise and wonder were familiar. It may also be explained as meaning simply that he saw what would have produced a wonder in a mere man. But the strict sense is more natural, and no more incompatible with deity than the astonishment imputed to Jehovah in still stronger terms by Isaiah (50, 16. 63, 5). The main fact here is that the case was wonderful, and for the reason given in the next clause, with the prefatory formula of strong asseveration, *Verily* (Amen) *I say unto you*, and addressed *to those following*, not merely his attendants and the messengers from the centurion (Luke 7, 6), but probably the multitude, which seems to have been never far off upon such occasions. (See above, on v. 1.) The order of the Greek is, *not even in Israel* (the chosen people and the church of God, in which such faith might well have been expected) *so great* (or *so much*) *faith have I found* (or met with). The best interpretation of these words appears to be tho simplest and most obvious, to wit, that this was the first instance of a strong faith in Christ's power to heal even at a distance, and that this instance occurred not among the Jews but the Gentiles. That the centurion was a proselyte, i. e. a professed convert to the true religion, is neither affirmed nor necessarily implied. The contrast with Israel rather implies the contrary, and the representation of the Jewish elders (Luke 6, 5), only proves that like Cornelius (Acts 10, 1) he was one of the devout and serious class of Gentiles, who treated the religion of the Jews with respect and perhaps attended their worship.

11. **And I say unto you, That many shall come from the east and west, and shall sit down with Abraham, and Isaac, and Jacob, in the kingdom of heaven:**
Nor was this a solitary, accidental case, but only a specimen of what was to occur thereafter on a grand scale. The repetition of the formula, *I say unto you*, is very significant. 'Not only do I solemnly declare this Gentile to be more enlightened, as to my authority and power, than any Jew whom I have met with; but I also solemnly declare that this superiority of faith will one day be exhibited by multitudes.' *Shall come*, are to come hereafter, from a distance or *ab extra*, implying that at present, or by nature, they have no right to the privilege here promised or predicted. *From east, and west,* literally, *from risings and settings*, also used in the classics to denote these quarters of the earth and heavens, and here put for all directions, or rather for the opposite extremes, between which all are comprehended. *Sit down,* literally, lie down or recline, a luxurious posture introduced among the later Greeks and Romans from the east. Among the ancient Greeks as well as Hebrews sitting was the universal posture, as it still continued to be in the case of women and children, while the men, by whom alone convivial entertainments were attended, leaned on their elbows, stretched on beds or couches. This was also the fashion of the Jews, when our Saviour was among them, and the use of the words *sat, sat down, sat at meat*, in all such cases, is a mere accommodation to our modern usage, the very same verbs being rendered *lay* or *lying* when the reference is to sickness (as in Mark 30, 2. 4. 5, 40. Luke 4, 25. John 5, 3. Acts 9, 33. 28, 8), and in one instance *leaning*, where the true sense is the common one of lying or reclining (John 13, 23). The image here presented is commonly supposed to be that of a sumptuous banquet or luscious feast, representing the enjoyments of Messiah's kingdom. But although that mode of description occurs elsewhere (e. g. Isai. 25, 6), the essential idea here would seem to be simply that of near domestic intercourse, admission to the family and all its intimate relations, as denoted by participation in its usual repasts, or as we say, sitting at the same table, without explicit reference to dainty food or to extraordinary festivities. *Abraham, Isaac, and Jacob*, the three original patriarchs, still represented as presiding over the great family descended from them. As this family for ages was the

chosen people or visible church, the admission here predicted is not merely to national or civil rights, but chiefly to religious and spiritual advantages. This is therefore a distinct premonition of the great revolutionary change to be wrought in the condition of the Gentiles by the advent of Messiah.

12. But the children of the kingdom shall be cast out into outer darkness : there shall be weeping and gnashing of teeth.

But even the admission of the Gentiles to a free participation in the rights and honours of the chosen people, however repugnant to the narrow selfish prepossessions of the carnal Jews, would have been comparatively little without what is here distinctly foretold, namely, that the change would be an exchange or an interchange of places. Not only were the Gentiles to be brought in from without, but the Jews to be cast out from within. *The children of the kingdom*, those who seem entitled to its honours by hereditary right, as the descendants of the Patriarchs already mentioned, but disqualified or disinherited by not partaking of their faith. (See Rom. 4, 11. 16.) *Will be cast out*, or expelled, with primary reference to the figures of the preceding verse. While strangers from the most remote and opposite directions are to take their places, as it were, at the patriarchal table, and to be received into the patriarchal household, its natural, hereditary members will be forcibly excluded from it. *Into outer darkness*, or retaining more exactly the original construction, *into the dark, the outer*, i. e. outside of the house. The antithesis is not so much with the brilliant lights of an extraordinary feast as with the ordinary necessary light of any comfortable home, the loss of which suggests that of all other comforts, to which our Lord adds the prediction of more positive suffering, denoted by *weeping and gnashing* (grinding, grating) *of teeth*, as natural expressions of despairing grief for what has thus been lost or forfeited. The primary conception, not to be lost sight of in our other applications of the language, is that of children violently torn from the table and ejected from the house of their father, and heard giving vent to their grief and rage in the outside darkness. This beautiful but fearful picture is greatly marred by taking *outer* in the modern sense of *utter* or *utmost*, i. e. uttermost, extreme. *Utter*, as used in the older English, is synonymous with *outer*. This prediction of our Saviour makes the case of the centurion a type of national and social changes of the highest moment, and accounts for the prominence assigned to it in the history of his miracles. The absolute expressions of this verse are neither to be understood as simply meaning many, nor as excluding individual exceptions, but as denoting the excision of the chosen race, as such, and as a whole, " because of unbelief." (See Rom. 11, 1. 20, 32.)

13. And Jesus said unto the centurion, Go thy way ;

and as thou hast believed, (so) be it done unto thee.
And his servant was healed in the selfsame hour.

Having made this didactic and prophetic use of the centurion's faith as typifying the conversion of the Gentiles, our Lord does not forget to give it present and immediate effect in the case before him. *Go thy way*, an old English phrase used by all the Protestant translators to express a single Greek word (ὕπαγε) meaning simply *go* (as Wiclif and the Rhemish Bible render it), depart, begone. (See above, on v. 4, and on 4, 10. 5, 24. 41, in all which cases the original expression is identical.) *As thou hast believed,* or *didst believe,* in making this request. As in the fourth petition of the Lord's Prayer (see above, on 6, 12), the words are not conditional but comparative. The sense is not, because thou hast believed, as a meritorious ground or title to acceptance, but in accordance and proportion to thy faith, I grant thee what thou hast desired and believed me able to bestow. It is worthy of remark that in this as well as later instances, the faith to which our Lord accorded gifts of healing, was not that of the subject or the patient, but of one who represented him and interceded for him. This affords, if not a formal argument, a beautiful analogy, in favour of baptizing children on the faith of their parental sponsors, or of others standing *in loco parentis.* The immediate effect is stated in the last clause. *Hour* is a modification or corruption of the Greek word here used and originally meaning any definite period of time, whether long or short, especially if measured by some natural standard. Thus it is applied to the seasons of the year and the divisions of the day, especially the twelve parts of the natural day from sunrise to sunset, or from dawn to dusk. (See John 11, 9.) Here, however, and in other like cases, it would rather seem to mean a *moment,* or more indefinitely, *time,* without regard to its precise duration, 'at that very time (or instant'). At any rate, it does not mean that the cure took place within what we now call an hour, or a space of sixty minutes, but that it was instantaneous. (Compare Luke 7, 10.)

14. And when Jesus was come into Peter's house, he saw his wife's mother laid, and sick of a fever.

The next miracle is one of a more private and domestic character, performed in the bosom of a family with which our Lord had now contracted intimate relations, that of Simon Peter, whom we thus learn incidentally to have been married and a householder at Capernaum, in conjunction with his brother Andrew (Mark 1, 29). This is not inconsistent with the mention of Bethsaida elsewhere (John 1, 45), as "the city of Andrew and Peter." They are not here said to have been natives of Capernaum, nor even to have long resided there. As the very name *Bethsaida* means a fishery or place for fishing, and was common to more villages than one upon the lake (Mark 6, 45), it is probable that Peter and his brother lived there while engaged in that employment, and removed to Capernaum when Jesus chose it as the centre of his operations. It is even possible that Simon opened a house there for the convenience of his Lord and Master in the intervals of his itinerant labours. *When Jesus was come*, literally, *Jesus coming*, which means nothing more than *as he once came*, without determining the time, which is fixed in the parallel accounts (Mark 1, 29. Luke 4, 38) as immediately after the expulsion of a demon in the synagogue and probably soon after the vocation of the first apostles. (See above, on 4, 18–22.) Its position here is not chronological but topical, i. e. determined by the writers' purpose to give specimens of Christ's early miracles, exemplifying different kinds and classes of such wonders. *Wife's mother* is in Greek a single word corresponding to our compound, *mother-in-law*. *Laid*, in Greek a stronger word, *cast*, thrown down, prostrate, or confined to bed, the participle of the perfect passive used above in v. 6. *Sick of a fever*, Tyndale's version of another participle, from a verb without exact equivalent in English (Vulg. *febricitantem*), though akin to our adjective *feverish*, q. d. *fevering*, or having fever (Wiclif: shaken with fevers. Rhemish Bible: in a fit of a fever). This is one of the most usual and universal forms of disease, and is several times mentioned in the New Testament as the subject of miraculous healing (Besides the parallels, see John 4, 52. Acts 28, 8.)

15. And he touched her hand, and the fever left her: and she arose, and ministered unto them.

As in the case of the centurion's servant the cure was wrought by a word spoken at a distance, showing our Lord's independence of all outward means in the exercise of his extraordinary power; so here, and in most other cases (compare Luke 4, 40), he was pleased to indicate by touch and gesture the connection of the cure, as the effect produced, with himself as the producer, a connection which might otherwise have been disputed or uncertain. *Left her*, a much stronger word in Greek, the same that is employed above in 4, 11. 20. 22. 5, 24. 40. and might here be rendered, *let her go*, released her. *Arose*, in Greek a passive form ($\dot{\eta}\gamma\acute{\epsilon}\rho\vartheta\eta$) strictly meaning, *was aroused*, as if from sleep or stupor. (See above, on 2, 13.) *Ministered unto them*, or waited on them, served them, with specific reference to food. (See above, on 4, 11.) For *them*, some manuscripts and editors read *him*, thus confining her attendance to the person of our Lord himself. Here again we may observe that the effect was instantaneous and complete at once, without convalescence or progressive restoration, thus distinguishing the miracle from all natural or artificial cures; and also that as soon as it was wrought, the subject was restored to her original position, and resumed her ordinary household duties. (See below, on 9, 25.) This is a striking illustration of the apostolical paradox, "the foolishness of God is wiser than men." (1 Cor. 1, 25.)

16. When the even was come, they brought unto him

many that were possessed with devils: and he cast out the spirits with (his) word, and healed all that were sick;

One of the commonest and grossest errors in relation to the miracles of Christ is, that they were few in number, or that they are all recorded in detail. To guard against this very error, after recording two particular miracles of healing, Matthew adds a general statement of his other miraculous performances about the same time, from which we may obtain a vague but just idea of their aggregate amount. In the evening of the same day upon which he cured the fever in the house of Simon, all the sick of the city were collected there. (Mark 1, 33.) The mention of the evening and of sunset does not imply any scruple on our Lord's part as to healing on the Sabbath, which he had already done in this case, and both did and justified in other cases. (See below, on 12, 9–13.) It might more probably imply such scruples in the minds of the people, who would then be represented as deferring their request for healing till the close of the Sabbath, at the setting of the sun. Even this, however, is unnecessary, as the fact in question is sufficiently explained by two more obvious considerations: first, that the cool of the day would be better for the sick themselves, and secondly, that some time would be requisite to spread the news and bring the sick together. *Possessed with devils*, literally *demonized*, or under the control of demons, producing by their personal presence either bodily disease or mental alienation, or the two together. *All those having* (themselves) *ill*, or being in an evil condition. (Rhemish version, *ill at ease*.) This may either denote bodily disease, as distinguished from mental and spiritual maladies, or, still more probably, disease in general, of which the most distressing form is separately specified. The demoniacal possessions were undoubtedly diseases, but of a preternatural description, as occasioned by the presence and personal agency of evil spirits.

17. That it might be fulfilled which was spoken by Esaias the prophet, saying, Himself took our infirmities, and bare (our) sicknesses.

The great distinctive feature of this narrative now reappears, the demonstration of the Messiahship of Jesus, by showing the fulfilment of the ancient prophecies in his experience. Reckoning 4, 14. as the fifth direct argument of this kind, that before us is the sixth, and is the more remarkable, because entirely wanting in the parallels (Mark 1, 34. Luke 4, 40), which give the same account of the healing at Capernaum, with still greater fulness, whereas Matthew seems to abridge that statement, as if to make room for his favourite prophetical quotation. The continual recurrence of this difference shows clearly the individuality and independence of the writer, and the existence of a definite, consistent purpose in the narrative before us, and confirms the otherwise most probable conclusion, that it was designed, in the first instance, not for Gentile but for Jewish readers. The passage quoted is still extant in Isai. 53, 4. forming part of the clearest and most direct prediction of Messiah's sufferings as a sacrifice for sin. The translation was made by the evangelist himself, being much more exact than the Septuagint Version. The only departure even from the form of the original is in the substitution of the specific term *diseases*, in the last clause, for the more generic *pains* or *sorrows*. This is justified, however, not only by the wider use of the Greek word (νόσος) in the early writers (such as Hesiod), but alsó by the obvious correspondence of the Hebrew word to one in the preceding verse which properly means *sickness*, although evidently put for pain and suffering in general. *Took*, received, a vague term rendered more specific by the context, which suggests the idea of taking upon him or assuming as a load. This is clearly expressed by the other verb which in Greek usage comprehends the acts of lifting, carrying, and removing, in all which it exactly represents the Hebrew. The terms are evidently drawn from the Mosaic law of sacrifice, a necessary part of which is the substitution of the victim for the actual offender, so that the former *bears* the sins of the latter, and the latter, in default of such an expiation, is said to bear his own sins.* The application of these words by Matthew to the cure of bodily diseases cannot involve a denial of the doctrine of vicarious atonement, which is clearly taught in 20, 28. Nor is it a formal exposition of the passage quoted in its full sense, but, as Calvin well explains it, a hint that the prediction had begun to be fulfilled, because already its effects were visible, the Scriptures always representing sorrow as the fruit of sin. The miracles of Christ were not intended merely to relieve human suffering; for then why should they have been limited to three short years and one small country? They were also designed to authenticate his mission, and to furnish his credentials as a teacher come from God (John 3, 2); to rouse attention and prepare the minds of men for the reception of the truth (John 6, 2); and to serve as types and pledges of spiritual changes, often actually connected with them in experience (see below, on 9, 5). Another thought suggested by this passage is, that all the philanthropic means employed by individuals or by society at large for the relief of human suffering, and especially of that produced by bodily disease, are but continuations of the work begun by Christ himself. The medical profession, more especially, when governed by right principles and actuated by becoming motives, bears the same relation to our Lord, as the Physician of the body, that the ministry ought always to sustain to him, as the Physician of the Soul. And neither this profession, nor the charities of life in general, can ever hold their proper place or have their proper influence, till brought into a due subordination and dependence upon Him who 'Himself took our infirmities and bare our sicknesses.'

---

* See Lev. 5, 1. 17. 17, 16. 24, 15. Num. 9, 13. 14, 33. Ex. 23, 38. Lev. 10, 1. 7 16, 22. and compare Lam. 5, 7. Ezek. 18, 19.

18. Now when Jesus saw great multitudes about him, he gave commandment to depart unto the other side.

Matthew seems here to interrupt his list of miracles, for the purpose of recording a brief conversation which has no direct relation to them, and is not even chronologically connected with what goes before, but of a later date, as appears from Mark's explicit statement (4, 35), that the miracle which followed the dialogue here given was performed in the evening of the same day upon which our Lord delivered several parables recorded by Matthew in his thirteenth chapter. The difficulty is not one of discrepancy as to time; for Matthew gives us no date, merely saying, *when Jesus saw the multitudes about him*, i. e. once on seeing them, he said, &c. The only difficulty is a seeming deviation from the plan which we have been assuming, and a consequent exposure to the charge of incoherence. If he is giving us a series of miracles, as samples of Christ's wonder-working ministry, and purposely abstaining from unnecessary mention of his teachings or discourses, how shall we account for the abrupt anticipation of a dialogue, in which the miracles are not referred to, and which seems to have occurred long after the occurrences just mentioned? Why is it introduced at all in this catalogue of miracles, and why just here? It might be reckoned a sufficient answer to the former of these questions, that the evangelical tradition, as attested both by Luke and Matthew, represents this conversation as immediately preceding the miraculous stilling of the storm, and that Matthew, wishing to record the latter, did so with the well-known preface, although not strictly necessary for his purpose. We may, however, take another step and give a reason for his introducing this occurrence with its inseparable adjunct just at this point of his argument. Having, in strict accordance with his customary method, cited a passage of Isaiah, representing the Messiah as a sufferer, and sharing in the sufferings of others, he shows us how far this view of his mission was from being entertained even by some who sought or offered to be his disciples. This is effectually done by recording the two incidents or dialogues preceding the next miracle; and thus, without resort to any forced constructions or fortuitous assumptions, a twofold nexus is established, first, between the foregoing miracles and that which follows; secondly, between the dialogue which precedes the latter and the previous quotation from the writings of Isaiah. In other words, the stilling of the storm is introduced for its own sake as a signal and peculiar miracle; the dialogue preceding it is introduced because inseparable from it in tradition and the memory of men; and both are introduced just here, because suggested by the words quoted from Isaiah and applied to our Lord's miracles of healing. *Seeing many crowds about him*, as he did very often, so that this expression does not necessarily refer to the time of the preceding incident, but may be understood as meaning, seeing once, or at a certain time, &c. *Gave commandment* is in Greek a single word, *commanded*, i. e. his disciples or immediate followers, now in habitual attendance on him, of whom four are known to us from 4, 18–22. *Depart*, go away, i. e. from Galilee on the west side of the lake and river. *The other side*, an expression almost always used by the classics in reference to water, and constantly applied in the Gospels to the east side of the river Jordan or the lake of Gennesaret, which division of the country thence derived its Greek and Roman name, *Perea*. (See above, on 4, 15. 25. where the same word is translated *beyond*.)

19. And a certain Scribe came, and said unto him, Master, I will follow thee whithersoever thou goest.

This passage of the lake is particularly mentioned, not as any thing extraordinary in itself, but on account of the miracle to which it gave occasion; and also of the conversation which preceded it, from which it was inseparable in the first tradition of the gospel, and which at the same time has a natural connection with the previous quotation from Isaiah (in v. 7). That quotation represents the Messiah as a sufferer, assuming our distresses as the fruit and penalty of sin. But this was far from being the usual or prevalent impression, even among those who offered or professed to be the followers of Christ. This is here exemplified by a single instance, in which a Scribe, an educated and professional expounder of the law (see above, on 2, 4. 5, 20. 7, 29.) offers to follow him wherever he may go, expecting, as we learn from our Lord's reply, to share in the advantages and honours of the kingdom about to be erected. This implies at least a partial conviction that our Lord was the Messiah. That such belief was not a common one among the class to which this man belonged, appears to be suggested by the numeral *one*, which can hardly be a mere equivalent to our indefinite article (*a Scribe*) or pronoun (a *certain Scribe*). For even granting such an usage in the later Greek, why should it occur in this and a few other cases, some of which are doubtful, as they might as well have been translated *one*.* So in this case, *one Scribe*, or a single Scribe, suggests that among the many who about this time became the followers of Christ, there was one belonging to this large and influential body, which as a whole, was among the strongest counteracting influences which he had to fight against. *Master*, in the old and proper sense of *teacher* (*magister*), which involves a recognition of our Lord by this official teacher as his own superior. *Follow*, not in the bare sense of locomotion, but of personal attendance and adherence as a disciple. (See above, on 4, 20. 22.) *Whithersoever*, to whatever place, into whatever situation, even the most dangerous, but no doubt on the tacit condition that he should participate in the Messiah's triumphs and the glory of his kingdom. (See below, on 20, 22.) *Goest*, or more exactly, *mayest go*, the idea of contingency being suggested both by the form of the verb, which is subjunctive, and by the indefinite particle before it. (See above, on 5, 11.) It is not, therefore, simply an offer to go with him on the voyage or journey

---

* See above, on 5, 41. and below, on, 27, 14. 15. and compare Mark 4, 8. 20. 14, 51. Acts 4, 32. 1 Cor. 6, 5. Jas. 4, 13. Rev. 15, 21. 19, 17. 22, 2.

now before him, which would not have been so formally and solemnly proposed, but to adhere to him in every change of place and circumstances, until his kingdom should be finally established.

20. And Jesus saith unto him, The foxes have holes, and the birds of the air (have) nests; but the Son of man hath not where to lay (his) head.

It is only from this answer to the Scribe's proposal, that we learn its real character and spirit. Taken by itself, it might have seemed to be a perfectly disinterested offer; but in that case the reply would hardly have been natural or relevant. The reply itself is not, as it is often understood, a description or complaint of abject poverty or total destitution, which is inconsistent with the certain fact, that our Lord had many friends, that some of these possessed the means of comfortable living, and that some devoted themselves wholly to the care of his person and supply of his necessities.* Nor is such privation ever named among the griefs or sufferings with which he was acquainted or familiar as the "man of sorrows" (Isai. 53, 3). The words before us are nothing more than a proverbial description of an unsettled, homeless life, in contrast with the life which this "one Scribe" may have hoped to lead as his disciple. *Foxes* and *birds* are mentioned as familiar representatives of the lower animals generally, just as birds and lilies, in the Sermon on the Mount, are put for animals and plants. (See above, on 6, 26. 28.) The essential meaning of the clause is that even the most unimportant animals have more of a settled home than Christ himself. The language is of course hyperbolical but natural and beautifully graphic. *Holes*, caves or dens (so Wiclif here). a word used in the classics to describe the lairs and haunts of wild beasts, and especially of bears. *Birds of the air*, literally, *of heaven*, as in 6, 26. where the Greek words are the same. and where they are explained. *Nests* is too specific a translation of a Greek word meaning *shelters*, places of repose and safety, whether nests in the strict sense, or the branches of thick trees, or any other similar resort. *Son of man* cannot simply mean *a man*, or a mere man, for this would be untrue in fact, since the want in question does not pertain to men as such; nor could any reasons be assigned for this circuitous expression of so simple an idea. The sense of *man by way of eminence*, the model man, the type and representative of human nature in its unfallen or restored condition, is by no means obvious or according to the analogy of Scripture, and at most an incidental secondary notion. The true sense is determined by Dan. 7, 13. where the phrase is confessedly applied to the Messiah, as a partaker of our nature, a description which itself implies a higher nature, or in other words, that he is called the Son of man because he is the Son of God. This official application of the term accounts for the remarkable and interesting fact, that it is never used of any other person in the gospels, nor of Christ by any

* See below, on 27, 57, and compare Luke 8, 3. 10, 28. John 11, 1.

but himself. Even Acts 7, 56 is scarcely an exception, since the words of Stephen are a dying reminiscence of the words of Jesus, and equivalent to saying, 'I behold him who was wont to call himself the Son of man.' This exclusive use of the expression by our Lord may be accounted for by the consideration that it is not in itself a title of honour, but of the opposite, and could not therefore be employed without irreverence by any but himself, while he was upon earth, or in a state of voluntary humiliation. *Hath* (or *has*) *not*, in the proper sense, possesses not or owns not, or at least, has not at his own disposal or control as a mere man or a member of society. The words are often understood as if he had said, *knows not*, or as if he had meant, has not within reach, has not access to; which, as we have seen, would be at variance with the known facts of the case. We have no reason to believe that our Lord ever suffered for the want of a night's lodging, except when he voluntarily abstained from sleep for devotional or charitable purposes. Even when the bigoted Samaritans refused to entertain him, we are told that he "went to another village" (Luke 9, 56). *To lay*, in Greek another case of the subjunctive syntax, strictly meaning, *where he may* (or *can*) *lay* (literally, *lean, incline*), *his head* (for rest and sleep). The view which we have taken of these singular expressions has not only the advantage of making them consistent with the facts of our Lord's history, but also that of making them appropriate in answer to the Scribe's proposal, prompted, as our Lord at once perceived it to be, by a selfish and secular ambition. However simple and demure its letter, its spirit was, 'I am prepared to follow thee through conflict to a post of honour in thy kingdom when established.' The spirit of the answer is, 'My kingdom is not of this world, in which I am a transient pilgrim and without a home.'

21. And another of his disciples said unto him, Lord, suffer me first to go and bury my father.

There is nothing in the form of the expressions here used, or in Matthew's usage, to forbid the supposition that this second dialogue or conversation took place at another time, and that the two are put together on account of their resemblance, and their serving to illustrate the same general fact. But this last, as we shall see, is not exactly the case, and as both are joined by Luke as well as Matthew, and by both placed just before the stilling of the storm, it is much more probable that they occurred as here recorded, at the same time when our Saviour was about to cross the lake. That two such offers should have been made on one occasion, is altogether natural, especially at such a time of concourse and excitement. Indeed the one may have prompted the other, but with a qualification or condition, which might seem to make it less extravagant. While the first offers to go anywhere without restriction, the second does the same, but with a limitation as to time. We learn, however, from the parallel account (Luke 9, 59), that there was still another and more striking difference between the case, namely, that in one our Lord repelled a voluntary offer, while in the other the

MATTHEW 8, 21. 22.   235

disciple made conditions in obeying a command from Christ to follow him. This circumstance is not preserved by Matthew, showing that he merely joins the two occurrences as having taken place at the same time and being generally similar, although the second does not, like the first, illustrate the prevailing false impressions of Messiah's kingdom. *Another of the disciples*, not in the restricted but the wider sense of those who attended his instructions and acknowledged his authority, all which is implied in the use of the word *Master* by the Scribe in v. 19, and that of the word *Lord* by the disciple in the case before us. *Suffer*, not the verb so rendered in 3, 15. and *let* in the next verse here, but one originally meaning to turn over upon, then to turn over to, commit, entrust, and lastly to permit, which is its usual sense in the Greek of the New Testament. *First* does not qualify this verb ('permit me first, and I will obey afterwards'), but the verb that follows ('first to go away and then to follow thee'). *Bury*, in the wide sense, both of the Greek and English verb, including not the mere act of interment, but all funeral honours, the entire ceremonial practised in disposing of dead bodies, which among the Greeks, but not among the Jews, included burning. Some have understood this of a duty still indefinitely future, 'let me go away until my father dies and I have buried him.' But this, besides that it is not the obvious sense conveyed by the expression, would be both absurd and disrespectful in reply to an immediate summons. 'I will follow thee at once, if I may first go and wait until my father dies.' The only natural construction is the common one assuming that his father was already dead and his remains awaiting burial.

22. But Jesus said unto him, Follow me ; and let the dead bury their dead.

Paradoxical and difficult as this reply has always been considered with respect to its particular expressions, its essential meaning is entirely clear, to wit, that even the most tender obligations and most sacred duties, represented here by that of a son to honour his father with a decent burial, must yield to the paramount demand of the Messiah's service, and especially to his immediate positive command. This we are to hold fast, as the certain import of the passage, in considering its dubious details. The only serious exegetical question to be solved is, whether *dead* is to be taken in two different senses, or twice in the same sense. Both opinions are ancient; but the former has by far the greater weight of authority, being indeed almost universally adopted. There is scarcely less unanimity in reference to the first sense here attached to *dead*. The notion that it means grave-diggers, or the buriers of the dead, is only entitled to be mentioned as an exegetical monstrosity. With this exception nearly all who give the word two senses are agreed that it first means spiritually and then naturally dead: 'Let those who are dead in spirit (or in sins) bury their friends who are dead (in body).' The meaning supposed to be conveyed by this command or exhortation is, that there are men enough in a natural impenitent condition to take care of such things, without drawing away those who have a special call to the Messiah's service. There are two objections to this common understanding of the passage, neither of which can be regarded as conclusive, although both are entitled to deliberate attention. The first is, that it seems unreasonable and at variance with the spirit of true religion, to devolve the duty here in question upon those who are in a state of spiritual death and exempt all others from it. This objection may be met by explaining the words as a hyperbolical expression of the thought, that if either class may be excused from such a duty, it is those who owe conflicting obligations to the Saviour. The other objection is one founded on the general law of language and canon of interpretation, that the same word must be taken in the same sense when repeated in the same connection and especially in close succession, without some urgent necessity for varying it. The existence of this necessity in this case is the real point at issue. In other words, the question is, whether by taking the word twice in the same sense (that of naturally, literally dead), we obtain an intelligible meaning, or as good an one as that afforded by the usual but more artificial construction. The only meaning yielded by the former process is, that the dead should be left to bury themselves or one another, rather than withhold a disciple from immediate obedience to his Lord's commands. That the thing required is impossible, only shows that the form of the command is paradoxical, or that the case proposed is an extreme one as in 5, 29. 30 above and in 19, 24 below. It is then equivalent to saying, but in the strongest and most striking manner possible, that if the dead cannot otherwise be buried than by drawing Christ's disciples from obeying his express commands, they had better not be buried at all. It is probable that these two explanations will continue, as in time past, to commend themselves to different judgments as entitled to the preference. It is the more important, therefore, that the great principle evolved by both, and independent of the question in dispute, should be held fast on either side. *Let*, the verb translated *suffer* in 3, 15. *leave* in 5, 24. *let have* in 5, 40. *forgive* in 6, 12. and as here in 7, 4. All these meanings are reducible to one radical idea, that of letting go, and all combine to make the word in this case specially significant, by necessarily suggesting, over and above that of remission, the idea of leaving or abandoning, which might indeed have been included in the version by employing the word *leave* instead of *let*.

23. And when he was entered into a ship, his disciples followed him.

The evangelist continues his enumeration or exemplificati of Christ's miracles by adding one demonstrative of his cont over material-nature or the elements, to which the foregoing d logues were introductory, not only in tradition, but in point fact. In other words, they really preceded it, or took place just as was setting sail, or rather on his way to the vessel for that purpo

(Luke 9, 57). The original construction is like that in vs. 1 and 5, *to him entering,* literally, *stepping in,* a kindred compound to the one in v. 1, and specially applied in classical usage to the act of going aboard a vessel, so that it might here be rendered, *embarking.* *Ship,* in the wider sense of *vessel,* here applied to a fishing-boat, as explained above, on 4, 21. The Greek noun has the article, not *a boat,* but *the boat,* meaning either one which stately transported passengers, like what we call a ferry-boat, or one habitually used by our Lord and his disciples, perhaps that of Andrew and Peter (4, 18. Luke 5, 3), or another specially provided for the purpose (Mark 3, 9). *His disciples* might be understood to mean the two, with whom he had been just conversing (vs. 19–22) who are so described, expressly or by implication, in the first clause of v. 21, and who are then represented as adhering to him, notwithstanding the discouragement which they had met with. And these two disciples followed him, as one had offered and the other been commanded. But the usual or rather universal understanding of the words, and, therefore, the more obvious, as well as that suggested by the parallels (Mark 4, 36. Luke 8, 22), refers them to those who were already his habitual attendants, such as Simon and Andrew, James and John (4, 18–22), and perhaps Philip and Nathaniel (John 1, 43–45), or the whole body of the twelve, if we suppose that Matthew here relates the incident by anticipation, and that its chronology is more exactly given by the other two evangelists. (See above, on v. 18.) *Followed* must then be taken, not in the higher sense of adherence or discipleship, but in the lower one of joint locomotion or companionship, nearly corresponding to *attended* or *accompanied.* Here, for the first time since the call of the two pairs of brothers (4, 18–22), we have a threefold narrative of one occurrence, and shall make use of the parallel accounts, not to improve or even to complete the one before us, for it stands in need of neither process, but, as far as may be necessary, to illustrate and explain it. (See above, on v. 5.)

24. And behold, there arose a great tempest in the sea, insomuch that the ship was covered with the waves: but he was asleep.

Behold (or *lo!*) as usual prepares the way for something new and unexpected.* *Arose,* was, began to be, or happened.† *Tempest,* Tyndale's version of a word which usually means an *earthquake* and is always so translated elsewhere,‡ but which, according to its etymology, means any great commotion, whether in the water, air, or earth. It is not the same with the *storm of wind* mentioned in both parallels (Mark 4, 37. Luke 8, 23), but rather its effect upon the waters of the lake, which were vehemently moved and shaken. (Wiclif: *a great*

---

* See above, on 1, 20. 23. 2, 1. 9. 13. 19. 3, 16. 17. 4, 11. 7, 4. 8, 2.
† See above, on vs. 13. 16. and on 1, 22. 4, 3. 5, 18. 45. 6, 10. 16. 7, 23.
‡ See below, on 24, 7. 27, 54. 28, 2.

stirring.) *Insomuch that,* a now obsolete equivalent to *so that,* used below (v. 28) to represent the same Greek particle (ὥστε), which serves to connect two verbs, when the second expresses the effect or consequence of the first. The last verb is usually in the infinitive, a form which may be retained in English when the verb is active (so as to cover), but when it is passive, as in this case (so as the vessel to be covered), must be modified as in the common version. This might seem to mean the occasional washing of the waves over a deck, or what is technically called in English sea-phrase, 'shipping seas;' but there was probably no deck to these boats, and we learn from the parallels that the one in this case was already filled, and therefore in great danger (Mark 4, 37. Luke 8, 23). *But he,* with emphasis, in contrast with the rest who were awake and full of terror. *Was asleep,* literally, *slept,* was sleeping, not merely in appearance, but in reality. His human nature was refreshed by sleep, like that of other men, while his divinity (as Calvin says) was watching. As this sleep, although natural, was subject to his will, we may assume that he indulged it for the very purpose of enhancing the impression to be made by the ensuing miracle.

25. And his disciples came to (him), and awoke him, saying, Lord, save us: we perish.

Left to themselves in this extremity, they naturally look to Jesus for protection. For *his disciples* some editions read (without the pronoun) *the disciples;* others omit *disciples* altogether; while the very latest also omits *coming to (him),* on the authority of the Codex Vaticanus and several of the oldest versions. The text will then be simply, *they awoke him,* raised him up, aroused him. (See above, on v. 15. 2, 13. 3, 9.) *Lord,* the same indefinite expression, used so often in the Gospels and explained above (on v. 5), but here determined by the parallels to mean their own Lord, or Master, i. e. teacher (Mark 4, 38) and overseer or prefect (Luke 8, 24). *Save us* here means rescue us, deliver us from this impending danger; which differs only in its application or the nature of the peril from the higher sense of salvation. These two words (σῶσον ἡμᾶς) are also omitted in the Vatican and Paris codices and in the latest critical editions. *We perish,* not in general, at some time, but at present, *we are perishing,* at this time, even while we speak. This word (ἀπολλύμεθα) is common to all three accounts, which is the more remarkable because the others vary, though without effect on the essential meaning. The verb itself is that used actively in 2, 13 *(to destroy),* and as here in 5, 29, 30. It is equivalent to saying, we are lost, or we are going to destruction. The connection with the preceding verb is not the conditional or alternative one expressed in the refrain of Heber's beautiful hymn, *Save or we perish.* This is really implied but not expressed in the original, the last verb there denoting not a mere contingency or even a certain futurity, but a present reality, to wit, that they were perishing already, as a reason for invoking him to save them.

26. And he said unto them, Why are ye fearful, O ye of little faith? Then he arose, and rebuked the winds and the sea ; and there was a great calm.

The word here rendered *fearful*, has in Greek a strong and bad sense, that of *cowardly* or craven, so that in the dialect of Homer it is sometimes secondarily employed to mean wretched on the one hand or worthless on the other. There is a near approach to this in the only other instance of its use in the New Testament besides the one before us and its parallel in Mark 4, 40. namely, Rev. 21, 8. where it stands first in a catalogue of characters, whose portion is the lake of fire and the second death. But even there it has not so much the classical as the scriptural meaning, as suggested by the next word, *unbelieving*, which is not to be diluted into faithless or unfaithful, but taken in its usual and proper sense, as meaning destitute of faith, and thus explaining *fearful* which precedes it to mean fearful from that very destitution. This agrees exactly with the case before us, where the question implies censure and disapprobation, not because there was no danger, or because they had no right to be alarmed, but because their danger, although real (as expressly stated in Luke 8, 53), and their alarm, although natural and not irrational, ought to have been neutralized and nullified by his presence, and by confidence in his ability and willingness to save them. This trust may have been weakened or suspended by the fact that he was then asleep; but this could only prove the weakness of their faith in limiting his power to a wakeful state. *Oh ye* (supplied by all the English versions since Tyndale) *of little faith*, a single compound word in Greek, the same with that in 6, 30. and here as there implying the possession of some faith, however feeble, which must be allowed to define and qualify the seeming intimation of the contrary in Mark 4, 40. or fishermen would not have been alarmed and talked of danger: little faith is faith after all; but ought to become great faith.* *Then*, after thus rebuking their excessive unbelieving fear, which shows that the next word, although strictly meaning *roused*, does not relate here to his waking but to his rising, as in v. 15 above, and is therefore correctly given in the English version as to sense, although the form in Greek is participial (*arising, having risen*), belonging to the verb in the preceding verse. *Rebuked*, not merely in act, as the corresponding Hebrew verb does sometimes mean, but in word, as if addressed to rational agents, from which some infer that the storm was raised by Satan and his demons, who were then the real objects of the objurgation. This may seem to be favoured, and was perhaps suggested, by the sameness of our Lord's words as recorded by Mark (4, 39) and those addressed to a demoniac in the same gospel (1, 25). *There was*, began to be, or came to pass, *a great calm*, i. e. a perfect stillness of the sea, so lately agitated by the wind.

---

* Wiclif's version of this clause, although antique in form, is strikingly expressive: *What ben ye* (i. e. why are you) *of little faith aghast?*

(Wiclif: *a great peaceableness.*) γαλήνη from γελάω. cf. leni plangore cachinni (Catullus), and κυμάτων ἀνηριθμον γελασμα (Aeschylus).

27. But the men marvelled, saying, What manner of man is this, that even the winds and the sea obey him!

Here again, *the men* might be supposed to mean the two new followers or disciples of vs. 19-22 (see above, on v. 23), so described to distinguish them from those of longer standing—'and the (two) men wondered.' This is certainly at first sight more natural than to apply the phrase to all our Lord's disciples, even if we understand *the men* to mean *the (mere) men*, as distinguished from himself. A third explanation, now perhaps the current one, at least among the Germans, understands by *the men* the crew or sailors of the vessel, as distinguished from the passengers. The objection to this is not that there were no such men there, which is a dubious assumption, but that in both the parallels (Mark 4, 41. Luke 8, 25), the same words seem to be expressly or by necessary implication put into the mouths of the same persons who had roused our Lord and been upbraided by him for their unbelieving fear. On the whole, therefore, it seems best to understand *the men* as a collective or indefinite expression for the whole ship's company, or all those present, without attempting to determine whether it consisted solely of our Lord's disciples, or whether among these are to be reckoned the two mentioned in the previous context. *What manner* (i. e. *kind*) *of man* is found substantially in Wiclif and exactly in Cranmer; whereas Tyndale has *what man?* and the Rhemish Bible *what an one?* The Greek word strictly means what countryman, belonging to what place or region, but as early as Demosthenes had got the wider sense attached to it in this place, though the other is not inadmissible, as they may possibly have meant to ask precisely whence or from what land he was. In either sense, the words are not unnatural or misplaced even in the mouths of the disciples, who are not then to be understood as expressing any ignorance or doubt as to the person of their master, but unfeigned astonishment at this new proof of his control, not only over demons and diseases, but also over winds and waves, which they had seen like human slaves, obey him at a word. How appropriate to fishermen! *That* seems here equivalent to *so that,* which is not however an authorized usage of the Greek word (ὅτι), meaning properly *because*, and here perhaps assigning a reason for the question which precedes—'(We ask this) because the winds and sea obey him?' *Even*, or as Tyndale renders it, *both winds and sea;* but as the wonder was not that the wind as well as the sea obeyed him, for if one did the other might be expected to do likewise, but that the winds and sea, as well as demons and diseases, thus obeyed him. the best translation of the particle is *too* or *also* ('the winds and sea too obey him'), which is equally accordant with Greek usage, and only differs from the common version (*even*) in being more specific. *Even the winds and sea* (as well as other things not specified.) *The winds and sea too* (in addition to things previously mentioned). *Obey*, an expressive compound Greek verb originally meaning *to hear under*, i. e. to listen with submissiveness. The English verb is only deficient in suggesting the radical idea of the Greek one, that of hearing, which in Hebrew also often runs into the notion of obeying. This last clause may suggest the evangelist's reason for adducing this particular example of Christ's miracles, to wit, that he might thus complete his series of examples, not promiscuously taken but selected out of many, for the purpose of presenting in a new light his dominion over every form of evil, as well natural as moral.

28. And when he was come to the other side, into the country of the Gergesenes, there met him two possessed with devils, coming out of the tombs, exceeding fierce, so that no man might pass by that way.

All three evangelists agree in placing next to this miraculous stilling of the storm, as having actually and directly followed it in time, an extraordinary case of dispossession, claiming on several accounts to be selected and distinguished from the many cures of this sort which our Lord appears to have performed. (See above, on v. 16, and on 4, 24.) Of the three accounts, Mark's is much the most detailed, and Matthew's the most concise, which shows that some of the particulars recorded by the others were not necessary for his purpose; and we are not at liberty to destroy the distinctive character of the narrative by embodying in its text what the writer chose or was directed to leave out, although we may employ it to illustrate and explain what is inserted. The grand peculiarity of this transaction, common to all three accounts, is that it consisted in the dispossession of a multitude of demons, and their entrance into lower animals, with Christ's permission, or at his command. The scene of this remarkable occurrence was on the east side of the lake called by Mark (5, 1) and Luke (8, 26) the land or district of the *Gadarenes*, so named from *Gadara*, a strong and wealthy city of Perea, not mentioned in Scripture but described by Josephus as a Greek town, i. e. probably inhabited by Gentiles. It was attached to Herod's jurisdiction by Augustus, but annexed to Syria both before and afterwards. The highest modern geographical authorities identify it with extensive ruins at a place called Umkeis, on a mountainous range east of Jordan, near the southern end of the lake and overlooking it. The district appears to have had other names, derived from towns or tribes, one of which has been preserved by Matthew, though the reading here is doubtful. The common text is *Gergesenes* (Γεργεσηνῶν), probably identical with (Γεργεσαιῶν), the Septuagint form of the Hebrew *Girgashite* (גִּרְגָּשִׁי), one of the Canaanitish tribes destroyed by Israel at the conquest of the Promised Land (Gen. 15, 21. Deut. 7, 1. Josh. 24, 11). According to Josephus, only the name survived, and, therefore, might be used here to describe the tract or region, as that possessed by the Girgashites of old, without assuming the existence of a town called *Gergesa*, which seems to rest upon the unconfirmed authority of Origen, and may have been imagined or invented by him, to support his emendation of the text, consisting in the substitution of the present reading (*Gergesenes*) for what he represents himself as actual and ancient readings (*Gadarenes* and *Gerasenes*). The first of these, which he describes as found in only a few copies, is now the reading of the Vatican and Paris codices, of the Peshito or old Syriac version, and of the latest critical editions, which in Mark and Luke have *Gerasenes*. This last appears to have been the text of Matthew also, as exhibited by most old copies in the time of Origen, and still found in the Vulgate and Salcidic versions, and in citations of the verse by Athanasius and Hilary. It has reference to *Gerasa*, a town of the Decapolis (see above, on 4, 25), near the eastern frontier of Perea, and the edge of the desert, described by Josephus, as rich and populous, in which he is corroborated by existing ruins at a place which bears the slightly altered name of *Jerash*. The objection to this reading, that the town in question was too distant from the lake-shore where the miracle is said to have been wrought, can only be disposed of by assuming that a large tract, locally adjacent or politically subject to the city, bore the same name, which may seem to be confirmed by Jerome's statement, that in his day the name of *Gerasa* was given to the ancient Gilead. This whole question, although critically curious, is exegetically unimportant, since there can be no doubt as to the main fact, that what is here recorded took place on the east side of the lake and opposite to Galilee (Luke 8, 26). *Possessed with devils*, literally, *demonized*, the same expressive participle used above in v. 16, and previously in 4, 24. The statement here that there were *two*, is not a contradiction but a simple addition to the narratives of Mark and Luke who mention only one, but without excluding the idea of plurality, as Matthew does when he says *one Scribe* (v. 19), or *one fig-tree* (21, 19). Had either of the parallels, in either of these cases, introduced two Scribes or two trees, there would have been at least some colour for the charge of inconsistency. But in the case before us, Mark and Luke employ no numeral but simply use the singular. No one pretends that this is a direct contradiction; but some urge the gross improbability that if there had been two, the others would have mentioned only one. A serious error, into which those sceptics who *honestly* insist upon this circumstance have fallen, is, that they require the construction put upon the passage to be perfectly natural and easy; whereas it is sufficient, in a case confessedly so dubious, and presenting but a choice of difficulties, to show the possibility of reconciling the accounts by any admissible construction of the language. The antecedent improbability of such a difference in such a case is more than outweighed by the improbability, that such a contradiction could have been misunderstood or overlooked by the early readers and assailants of the Gospels. That it was not fastened on before the days of Julian or Porphyry, shows clearly that the narratives were not originally looked upon as inconsistent, whether we are able or unable to ascribe specific reasons for the difference in question. That such reasons are not wholly wanting may be shown by two considerations, the first explaining how Mark and Luke could mention only one, the other why Matthew should have mentioned both. The first, is that one was really sufficient for the common purpose of all three historians, especially if one demoniac, as we may readily assume, although of course we cannot prove, was more ferocious and alarming than the other.* But if one was sufficient, why should Matthew mention both? First, because though one might be sufficient, two could do no harm, and the historian is not restricted to the statement of what is absolutely necessary to his purpose. Secondly, because, though Matthew's narrative, in this and many other instances, is less detailed than either of the others, it is one of his distinctive habits, not as some have strangely said to see things double, but to record them when they actually were so. (See below, on 9, 27. 21, 2.) This, though malevolently represented as a habitual departure from exact truth, is nothing more than a particular example of the general fact, that one observer naturally notes particulars, and classes of particulars, which others overlook, or less attentively consider, even when they see and know them. Other examples of the same thing are Mark's frequent mention of Christ's looks and gestures, Luke's of his personal devotions, John's of certain favourite expressions, such as the reduplicated *Amen* (Verily, Verily), precisely parallel to which is Matthew's accurate specification of the number two, even when unnecessary to his purpose and when omitted, although not excluded, by the other Gospels. This conformity to general experience and the laws of human nature may be even used to convert this seeming discrepancy into an unstudied but convincing proof of strict veracity in all the witnesses, each testifying in accordance with his own peculiar mode of observation, and not that of others. *To him coming*, i. e. as he landed (Luke 8, 27), not merely after he had done so, which would admit of an indefinite interval, whereas the landing and the meeting were simultaneous or immediately successive. *Met him*, or came to meet him, possibly with some unfriendly purpose. *Out of the tombs*, a Greek word originally meaning memorials, then monuments, then tombs or sepulchres. As these were usually in the shape of houses, or of chambers hewn in the rock (see below on 27, 60), they would easily afford a haunt and refuge in such cases as the one here mentioned. Thus far the case resembled multitudes of others which our Lord had previously dealt with, excepting in the circumstance suggested by the words, *out of*

---

* "Here the maxim of Le Clerc holds true: *Qui plura narrat, pauciora complectitur; qui pauciora memorat, plura non negat.* Something peculiar in the circumstances or character of one of the persons, rendered him more prominent, and led the two former Evangelists to speak of him particularly. But their language does not *exclude* another.—A familiar example will illustrate the principle. In the year 1824, Lafayette visited the United States, and was everywhere welcomed with honours and pageants. Historians will describe these as a noble incident in his life. Other writers will relate the same visit as made, and the same honours as enjoyed, by *two* persons, viz. Lafayette and his son. Will there be any contradiction between these two classes of writers? Will not both record the truth?"—*Robinson's Harmony of the Gospels, note on § 57.*

the tombs. But here we begin to see a fearful singularity in this case, as compared with all the other demoniacal possessions mentioned in the Gospel history, and accounting in some measure for its being singled out and separately stated. Elsewhere such cases are exhibited as aggravated forms of disease, preternaturally caused, but under the control and care of others. Here, on the contrary, the sufferers were outcasts from society, not only dwelling in the tombs, but wholly uncontrollable (as fully stated in the parallels), *exceeding* (or exceedingly, extremely) *fierce,* a Greek word strictly meaning *hard,* i. e. difficult, but specially applied in classic Greek to things which are hard to bear, and to persons who are hard to deal with, ill-disposed, malignant, cruel or ferocious. A graphic stroke is added to the picture, as minutely painted in the other gospels, by the circumstance here added, that these mad men were the terror of the country, *so that no one was strong (enough) to pass by* (i. e. journey, travel) *through that road (or way).* The original construction of the first verb and particle is like that in v. 24; the verb itself is that employed in 5, 13, and there explained.

29. And behold, they cried out, saying, What have we to do with thee, Jesus, thou Son of God ? art thou come hither to torment us before the time ?

Behold is here almost equivalent to 'strange to say,' or 'who could have believed it?' namely, that these fierce demoniacs, who had long made the very roads impassable, instead of flying at the bold intruder, orally addressed him and acknowledged his superiority. But at the same time, they implicitly deny his right to interfere with them at present, by the question, *what to us and to thee?* i. e. what is there common to us or connecting us? Thy domain or sphere is wholly different from ours. What hast thou to do with that mysterious world of spirits, to which we belong, and which, though suffered to exert a physical and moral influence on man, are of a species altogether different, and therefore not amenable to thee? The plural pronoun (*us*) may be referred either to the evil spirits, as a body or a race, distinct from that of man; or still more probably, because more simply, to the multitude of demons who possessed them (Mark 5, 9. Luke 8, 30), or perhaps to the plurality, not only of the demons but of the demoniacs, as described by Matthew. As to the title, *Son of God,* and the sense in which the demons here apply it, see above, on 4, 3. *Didst thou come here* (or *hither*) is the proper form of the Greek aorist. *Before the time* should have stood next, as it does in the original and Wiclif's version. The article is not expressed in Greek, which therefore means *before-time,* i. e. prematurely or too soon, without direct reference to any set time in particular. *To torment us,* the active voice of the verb applied in v. 6 to excruciating pain of body. (For its derivation, see above, on 4, 24.) It has here the wider sense of agonizing punishment, as applicable even to spirits without bodies. This interrogation is a vehicle of earnest and even insolent expostulation, and when taken in connection with the one before it, involves an indirect denial of our Saviour's right to interfere with them, which seems to show that even when they called him *Son of God*, they had no knowledge of his true divinity.

30. And there was a good way off from them a herd of many swine, feeding.

A good way off, in Greek a single word, *afar*, but really an adjective agreeing with *way* understood, and therefore nearer to the English form than it might seem at first sight. There is no contradiction between this account and Mark's (5, 11), because *there* and *nigh* (literally, *at*, adjacent to) are relative expressions, and the same distance which is called *far* in a room would be considered nothing in a landscape or a journey. If the herd was beyond reach, it was *far off;* if in sight, it was near; if either, it was *there.* All these expressions might be naturally used by the same witness in succession, much more by two distant and independent witnesses. Nor would such a variation, when susceptible of such an explanation, be considered contradictory in any Anglo-Saxon court of justice, although so esteemed in many a German lecture-room. According to our rules of evidence, it might even serve to strengthen both accounts, as really though not ostensibly harmonious. *Many swine,* i. e. about two thousand (Mark 5, 13). *Feeding,* or *being fed,* as the form may be either middle or passive, and we know from v. 33 that there were persons tending them. As swine's flesh was forbidden and the swine an unclean beast according to the law of Moses (Lev. 11, 7. 8. Deut. 14, 8); as the law in general, and especially its ceremonial distinctions, were punctually observed at this time; as the use of swine's flesh is eschewed by all Jews at the present day, and there is no trace of any other practice in the interval: it is highly improbable that these swine were the property of Jews, unless their consciences allowed them to provide forbidden food for Gentiles, and it is simpler to assume that the Gentiles provided it for themselves, which agrees well with the statement of Josephus, that Gadara, the chief town of this district, was a Greek city (see above, on v. 28). The question would be one of little moment if it had not been connected by some writers with their vindication of our Saviour's conduct upon this occasion (see below, on v. 34).

31. So the devils besought him, saying, If thou cast us out, suffer us to go away into the herd of swine.

So, the usual connective (δὲ) rendered *and* in v. 30. *Devils,* i. e. *demons,* as explained above (on 4, 24). How they communicated with our Lord is not revealed, but can create no more difficulty than the similar communication between him and Satan as the tempter (see above, on 4, 3). As they were not yet driven out when this request was made, they may still have made use of the men's vocal organs, though they spoke no longer in their name but in their own. Matthew records the very words, and not the substance only, of this strange request. Mark also makes it a direct address (5, 12), while Luke gives it indirectly (8, 32), like the classical historians in reporting very short discourses. Mark's expression, *send us*, seems a peremptory demand, but involves a recognition of his power to dispose of them, which Matthew and Luke express by using the verb *permit*, and Matthew by recording the conditional expression, *if thou cast us out*. *To go away (from the men) into the swine*, and take possession of their bodies just as they had entered into the demoniacs (Luke 8, 30). Those who laugh at this request as mere absurdity, and therefore never uttered, only show their incapacity to estimate the craft and cunning which suggested it. Having begged to be left undisturbed and been refused, they now apparently relinquish their pretensions to the human victims, and content themselves with leave to take possession of inferior natures. But this mock humility is only a disguise for their malignant wish to bring reproach and danger on their conqueror and judge. If it be asked, in what sense, and to what extent, could evil spirits take possession of a herd of swine, the answer is, precisely so and so far as the nature of the swine permitted. As that nature was not rational or moral, no intellectual or spiritual influence could be exerted; but the body with its organs and sensations, the animal soul with its desires and appetites, could just as easily be wrought upon by demons as the corresponding parts of the human constitution. The difficulty lies in admitting demoniacal influence at all, and not in extending it to lower animals, so far as they have any thing in common with the higher.

32. And he said unto them, Go. And when they were come out, they went into the herd of swine: and behold, the whole herd of swine ran violently down a steep place into the sea, and perished in the waters.

It is not improbable that they expected this request, like the first, to be refused, as they could scarcely hope to conceal from Christ the motive, whether mockery or malice, which had prompted it. But in the exercise of that divine discretion which so often brought good out of evil, making the wrath of men (and devils) to praise him, and restraining the remainder which would not have that effect (Ps. 76, 10), he immediately permitted them, and no doubt actively coerced them into doing what they had themselves proposed. *Go*, a happy improvement on the older Protestant versions, which as usual have, *go your ways!* (See above, on vs. 4. 13.) *And going out* (from the demoniacs, or *having gone out*), *they went away, entered into the herd of swine*. The reality of this transition was evinced by a violent and sudden movement of the swine in the most dangerous direction, from which instinct, uncontrolled, would have preserved them. *The whole herd rushed down the precipice* (or overhanging bank, as the Greek word means according to its etymology) *into the sea* (or *lake*), between which and the hills (or highlands) they were feeding. Of all neological absurdities the silliest is the notion that this verse is a poetical description of madmen running through a herd of swine and driving them into the water! To destroy one thus would have been hard enough; but the evangelist describes a simultaneous movement of about two thousand, the number being introduced just here by Mark (5, 13), to shut out all perversion or unfounded explanation of the fact recorded. *Perished*, literally, *died*, of course by drowning or strangulation, as expressly mentioned in the parallels. It is a circumstance of some importance that they all without exception perished, an additional proof of supernatural agency in their destruction.

33. And they that kept them, fled, and went their ways into the city, and told every thing; and what was befallen to the possessed of the devils.

And those feeding them fled, astonished and affrighted at the sudden loss of their whole charge, *and reported*, carried back word to the place from which they came, i. e. *into the town* (or *city*) where the owners of the swine resided (compare Luke 15, 15). There is something very significant in the original form of the last clause, *all* (*things*) *and the* (*things* or *affair*) *of the possessed* (or *demonized*). They told the whole story, and began no doubt with the destruction of the swine, but did not fail to add the extraordinary change which they had witnessed in the famous madmen or demoniacs.

34. And, behold, the whole city came out to meet Jesus: and when they saw him, they besought (him) that he would depart out of their coasts.

And (καί) *behold*, introducing the last wonder to be told in this connection. *The whole city*, a natural hyperbole for its inhabitants, the same employed above in 3, 5. *To meet Jesus*, on his way to the city, and prevent his entrance. *Depart* (pass, from one place to another) *out of their coasts*, in the old English sense of borders, bounds, or confines, often put for all that is contained within them. (See above, on 2, 16.) This is so unlike the usual effect of our Lord's miracles and teachings that it seems to call for explanation, which may be derived from two considerations. The first is, that the miracle, although a signal miracle of mercy to the demoniacs themselves, was one of injury and loss to the owners of the swine; so that the whole mass of the population (Luke 8, 37) was not only filled with awe, but apprehensive of some more extensive damage. The other is that Gadara was a Gentile city (see above on v. 28), and the great mass of the Gadarenes throughout the district either wholly heathen or extensively mixed with them. Now, although the influence exercised by Christ was not necessarily confined to Jews, yet as his mission was to them (see below, on 15, 24), and they alone could fully understand his claims as the Messiah, it is not surprising that a Gentile population should have been less favourably impressed by this one miracle, the benefits of which extended only to two individuals, or at most to the circle of their friends, whereas the incidental evils, either actual or apprehended, were more general. We learn from the parallel accounts in Mark and Luke, that the miracle in question, while it led directly to our Lord's exclusion from this province, incidentally supplied his place by a zealous and devoted substitute, who would also have it in his power to counteract, if necessary, any false impressions with respect to the destruction of the swine. Our Saviour's agency in this destruction is not to be vindicated on the ground that Jews had no right to keep swine and were therefore justly punished by the loss of them. Even admitting that these men were Jews, their violation of the law would hardly have been punished so circuitously and without the slightest intimation of their crime. The act was one of sovereign authority, attested by the miracle itself, and so far as we can learn, not disputed even by the persons injured, however much they might lament their loss and wish to avoid its repetition. There is no more need of any special vindication here than in the case of far more serious inflictions of the same kind by disease or accident. The personal presence of the Saviour could not detract from his divine right to dispose of his own creatures for his own ends, even if these ends were utterly unknown to us, much less when they are partially perceptible. For, however sciolists and sceptics may deride this occurrence as absurd and unworthy of the Saviour, it answered an important purpose, that of showing his dominion over every class of objects, and of proving the reality of personal possessions, by exhibiting a case, in which the demons, abandoning the human subjects whom they had so long tormented, and leaving them entirely free from all unnatural excitement, instantaneously betrayed their presence and their power in a multitude of lower animals, impelling them, against their own instinctive dispositions, to a sudden simultaneous movement ending in their own destruction. Admitting the external facts to be as Matthew here describes them, they are wholly unaccountable except upon the supposition of a real dispossession such as he affirms, and the extraordinary novelty of which, without discrediting his narrative, explains his having given a conspicuous place in it to this signal proof of superhuman power.

CHAPTER IX.

The exemplification of Christ's miracles, begun in the preceding chapter, is continued through the one before us, but with more admixture of other matter associated with these in the writer's memory. After stating his return from the voyage mentioned in the previous context

(1), the evangelist relates the healing of another paralytic at Capernaum, with the conversation which grew out of it (2–8); his own vocation as a follower of Christ, and a conversation which occurred in his own house, with respect to our Lord's treatment of the publicans and sinners (9–13); another conversation with John's disciples in relation to fasting (14–17); the resuscitation of a ruler's daughter, and the healing of a diseased woman on the way (18–26); the healing of two blind men (27–31), and of a dumb demoniac (32–34); after which we have another general description of our Lord's itinerant labours and his miracles in general, with a strong expression of his pity for the people and desire to relieve them (35–38). This narrative, taken by itself, would naturally seem to be chronologically arranged, and in parts is expressly said to be so; but by comparison with the other Gospels, we find that in several instances this order is departed from. It might be sufficient, here as in the previous chapter, to account for this by simply referring it to Matthew's purpose, which required things of the same kind to be brought together, whether immediately successive or not. We have it happily, however, in our power to go further and explain, in part at least, why the existing order was adopted. This we shall attempt below in the detailed interpretation.

1. And he entered into a ship, and passed over, and came into his own city.

The division of the chapters here is very unfortunate, not only separating what belongs together, but creating an appearance of chronological inaccuracy which is instantly removed by putting this verse in its proper place at the close of the preceding narrative, completing the account of our Lord's visit to the east side of the lake and his return to Galilee. *And stepping into*, or embarking on, the same verb that is used above in 8, 23, and there explained. *A ship*, as in that case, should be *the ship* (or *boat*), here referring to the one in which he came, and which was no doubt waiting for him. *Passed over*, crossed, a Greek verb commonly applied to the passage of seas or rivers, an idea here expressed in the Vulgate version (*transfretavit*). *His own city*, not that of his birth (Bethlehem). nor that of his early long-continued residence (Nazareth), but that which he had chosen as the centre of his operations (Capernaum), and the circumstances of his settlement in which have been already mentioned. (See above, on 4, 13.) Here the narrative beginning at 8, 18, closes, and the next verse opens one entirely different.

2. And, behold, they brought to him a man sick of the palsy, lying on a bed: and Jesus seeing their faith said unto the sick of the palsy; Son, be of good cheer; thy sins be forgiven thee.

As already hinted in the introduction to the chapter, we are able
11*

to assign a more specific reason than in many other cases for the introduction of this miracle just here. The next in chronological order, as appears from a comparison of the three accounts, was the twofold or complicated miracle described below in vs. 18–26. But with that transaction Matthew had peculiar personal associations, from the fact, that when the ruler sought our Lord to heal his daughter (see below, on v. 18), he found him eating in the house of Matthew himself (see below, on v. 10), and engaged in a most interesting conversation, which was no doubt deeply graven on the memory of his entertainer. What could be more natural, therefore, than that the latter, before giving us the miracle, should record the conversation that preceded it, and that before doing this, he should record the fact of his own vocation, though it may have taken place much sooner. But this vocation, as we learn from all three gospels (see below, on v. 9), was immediately preceded by the healing of the paralytic, which accounts for his beginning with that miracle, though in itself sufficiently remarkable to find some place in any list or exemplification of our Lord's miraculous performances. This connection of the topics in the narrative before us is of some importance, as a proof that the evangelist, even when he seems to interrupt the chronological arrangement, does not do it at random, but for reasons which imply a definite purpose and a systematic method, and which, being sometimes, as in this case, ascertainable, may reasonably be assumed, even where we cannot trace it so distinctly. The separation of the first verse from its proper context (see above, on v. 1) necessarily produces the impression on the reader who is naturally influenced by these divisions, though entirely conventional and often wrong, that the verse in question gives the date of the occurrences that follow, or, in other words, that the healing of the paralytic took place on our Lord's return from the excursion, during which he stilled the storm and dispossessed the demoniacs of Gadara, as described in vs. 18–34 of the preceding chapter. But the first of these miracles is placed much earlier both by Mark (2, 1) and Luke (5, 17), namely, after the healing of the leper, which Matthew himself expressly represents as immediately following the descent from the mountain after the delivery of the Sermon on the Mount (see above, on 8, 1). But if 9, 1 belongs to the preceding context, there is no mark of time whatever in respect to the ensuing miracle, the first words of the verse before us simply meaning, that *they* (*once*) *brought to him a paralytic*. (See above, on 8, 5, where there is a similar transition.) This may seem to be forbidden by the words *and lo*, apparently connecting what follows in the closest manner with what goes before. But this impression is occasioned partly by the false division of the chapters, almost forcing these two verses into intimate connection, and partly by a disregard of Matthew's settled usage, which exhibits many instances of similar appearance, where we know that the two things were not immediately successive, and where all suspicion of mistake or variant tradition is precluded by the fact that there is no chronological specification, but a mere presumption founded upon juxtaposition. Throwing the first verse back into the former chapter where it properly belongs, and regarding that before us as the opening of a new context, *and* is simply a historical connective resuming and continuing the narrative, according to the Hebrew idiom which employs it even at the beginning of a book, although the English version usually softens *and* to *now* or *then*.* *Behold*, merely indicating something new and unexpected, is as much in place at the beginning as in any other portion of the narrative, and here amounts to saying, 'another proof of his extraordinary power was afforded on a different occasion when they brought,' &c. It would seem, from an expression used by Luke (5, 17), that other miracles of healing were performed at this time, but that one is recorded in detail, on account of the remarkable circumstances which attended it, and of the no less remarkable discourse to which it gave occasion. Of the three accounts, as in the case of the demoniacs at Gadara (see above, on 8, 28), the most concise is Matthew's, one of many proofs that the ancient and still current notion as to Mark's abridging Matthew is entirely groundless. As in other cases of the same sort, we must carefully avoid confounding the three narratives and destroying the distinctive character of either, while endeavouring to make them interpret and elucidate each other. *They brought to him*, an indefinite expression, meaning certain persons, whom it was unnecessary further to describe, but whom we know from other sources to have been men (Luke 5, 18) and four in number (Mark 2, 3). The next six words represent a single Greek one, which might now be rendered no less briefly in English by the use of the word *paralytic* (see above, on 8, 6). *Lying*, literally, *thrown*, or prostrate (as in 8, 6. 14). *A bed*, or couch, any thing on which one lies for rest. According to oriental usage, it was probably no solid framework like our bedsteads, but a simple pallet, rug, or blanket. *Seeing*, not merely in the exercise of his divine omniscience, but perceiving by external signs, fully described in both the other gospels (Mark 2, 4. Luke 5, 18). *Their faith*, not merely that of the sufferer, though this may be included, which distinguishes this case from that of the centurion (see above, on 8, 13). The *faith* directly meant in both cases is belief in Christ's ability and willingness to work the cure (see below, on v. 28). The commendation of their faith is not addressed to all, but to the sufferer alone, and in a form at once affecting and surprising. *Be of good cheer*, i. e. cheer up, take courage (Rhemish Bible, *have a good heart*). The same use of the same Greek word (θάρσει) occurs repeatedly in Homer, and sometimes in connection with the same endearing epithet. *Son*, or rather *child*, the Greek word being neuter, and in usage common to both sexes, even when the reference is to one, as here, and in 21. 28. Luke 2, 48. 15, 31. The same affectionate address is used by Christ to his disciples in the plural number (10, 24.

---

* Leviticus and Numbers are the only books in which the initial particle is rendered *and;* Genesis, Deuteronomy, First Chronicles, and Nehemiah the only historical books, properly so called, which do not open with it in Hebrew. It is taken for granted, here and in the text above, that the *vav* in all these cases is the copulative (*and*), and not an augment, like the ε and η in Greek, as some ingenious modern has suggested.

John 13, 33), and a synonymous form elsewhere (John 21, 5). It is here intended to express, not only kindness and compassion, but a new spiritual kindred or relation, which had just been formed between the speaker and the man whom he addressed. *Be forgiven*, like the Greek verb, is ambiguous, and may be either a command or an affirmation. It is now held by the highest philological authorities that the original word (ἀφέωνται) is an Attic, or more probably a Doric form of the perfect passive signifying something that is done already. *Thy sins have* (already) *been remitted*, the verb corresponding to the noun (*remission*) in 26, 28 below. There is no need of supposing, as some do, that this man's palsy was in some peculiar or unusual sense the fruit of sinful indulgence; much less that our Lord conformed his language to the common Jewish notion, that all suffering was directly caused by some specific sin, a notion which he pointedly condemns in John 9, 3. Luke 13, 2-5. Bodily and spiritual healing was more frequently coincident than we are apt to think, the one being really a pledge and symbol of the other. Saving faith and healing faith, to use an analogous expression, were alike the gift of God, and often, if not commonly, bestowed together, as in this case, where the singularity is not the coincidence of healing and forgiveness, but the prominence given to the latter by the Saviour, who instead of saying, 'be thou whole' (compare 8, 3.) or 'thy disease is healed,' surprised all who heard him by the declaration that his sins were pardoned. This paradoxical expression was no doubt designed to turn attention from the lower to the higher cure or miracle, and also to assert his own prerogative of pardon, in the very face of those whom he knew to be his enemies.

3. And, behold, certain of the Scribes said within themselves, This (man) blasphemeth.

We here see for whom this unexpected declaration was intended, not for his friends and disciples, but for others whom he knew to be present as spies and censors of his conduct. *Some of the Scribes*, i. e. of the large class or profession mentioned in 2, 4. 5, 20. 7, 29. 8, 19. These expounders of the law, and spiritual leaders of the people, had already been invidiously compared with Jesus by the crowds who heard him, and were therefore predisposed to regard him as a rival. Those who assembled now on his return to Capernaum were not merely residents of that place, but collected, as Luke strongly phrases it (5, 17), from every village of Galilee and Judea, as well as from Jerusalem. However hyperbolical these terms may be, the essential fact is still that these unfriendly Scribes came from various quarters, thereby showing the importance which began to be attached to Christ's proceedings, especially by those who were at once the jurists and the theologians, the lawyers and the clergy, of the Jewish nation. *Within themselves* might also mean *among themselves*, and here denote discussion, or an interchange of views (as in 16, 7. 21, 25, below); but this idea is excluded by the words in Mark (2, 6), *in their hearts*, so that what is here described is not reciprocal communication, but the secret working of their several minds, unconscious of the eye that was upon them. *This* is commonly supposed to be contemptuous, being often in classic Greek equivalent to *this fellow*, and occasionally so translated in our Bible. (See below, on 12, 24. 26, 61. 71.) *To blaspheme*, in classic Greek, is commonly applied to evil speaking among men, such as slander or vituperation, but sometimes to irreverent or impious language to or of the gods, which last (in application to the true God) is its exclusive sense in Hellenistic usage. The ground of this charge, here implied, is expressed in both the parallels (Mark 2, 7. Luke 5, 21) namely, that the power to forgive belongs to God alone. The principle involved in this interrogation is a sound one, and appears to have been a sort of axiom with these learned Jewish Scribes, who were also right in understanding Christ as acting by his own authority, and thereby claiming divine honours for himself. A mere declaratory absolution they could utter too, and no doubt often did so, but the very manner of our Lord must have evinced that in forgiving, as in teaching, he spoke with authority, and not as the Scribes. (See above, on 7, 29.)

4. And Jesus knowing their thoughts said, Wherefore think ye evil in your hearts?

These cavils and repinings, though not audible, were visible to him who had occasioned them, and now detected them by his omniscience without waiting till they were betrayed by word or action. *Knowing*, an idea borrowed from the parallels (Mark 2, 8. Luke 5, 22), where as the word here used means *seeing*, and is so translated in v. 2, as well as in all the older versions of the one before us. *Why*, literally, *for what*, i. e. for what cause or reason. *Think*, is stronger in Greek, meaning *ponder* or *revolve*, and according to the parallels to *reason*, reckon, calculate, a term implying coolness and deliberate forethought, not a sudden violent excitement. *Evil* is in Greek a plural adjective, *evil* (*things*), the same that is repeatedly employed above to denote both physical and moral evil. (Compare 6, 23. 7, 17, with 5, 37. 6, 13. 7, 11.) Here it can only have the latter sense. *In your hearts*, not merely in your minds, but in your inner parts, or secretly. The question has the force of a severe rebuke, 'what right have you to entertain such thoughts?'

5. For whether is easier, to say, (Thy) sins be forgiven thee; or to say, Arise, and walk?

This is one of the most striking instances on record of our Lord's consummate wisdom in the use of what appears to be a strange and paradoxical method of reasoning or instruction. As instead of pronouncing the man healed he unexpectedly pronounced him pardoned, so, instead of meeting their objections by a formal affirmation of his own prerogative, he does so by a subtle but convincing argument, disclosing at the same time why he had so spoken. They denied his power to forgive sins, and could not be convinced of it by any sensible demonstration. But they might equally dispute his power to heal, unless attested by a visible effect. If then his commanding the paralytic to arise and walk should be followed by his doing so, what pretext could they have for doubting his assertion that the same man's sins were pardoned? *For* assigns the reason of his calling their thoughts evil. *Which* (in old English *whether*) *is easier?* You may think it easy enough to pronounce his sins forgiven, whether they be so or not; but it is equally easy to pronounce him healed, or to demand of him the actions of a sound man, and if this should prove effectual, you must acknowledge that the other is so too, although the pardon of sin cannot be made palpable to sense like the cure of a paralysis.

6. But that ye may know that the Son of Man hath power on earth to forgive sins, (then saith he to the sick of the palsy,) Arise, take up thy bed, and go unto thine house.

'That you may know by what authority I tell this man that his sins have been forgiven, I will show you what authority I have over his disease, that the possession of the one may demonstrate the existence of the other, for both belong to me as the Messiah.' Having stated his argument, he now applies it, by exhibiting the very proof of his authority to pardon sin which he had shown to be conclusive. To forgive sin and to heal disease are superhuman powers, to claim which is equally easy, and to exercise them equally difficult. If I pronounce this man forgiven, you may deny it, but you cannot bring my declaration to the test of observation, since forgiveness is a change not cognizable by the senses. But if I assert the other power, you can instantly detect the falsehood of my claim, by showing that the paralysis continues. If, on the contrary, it disappears at my command, the proof thus furnished of the truth of one claim may convince you that the other is no less well founded. Thus far he had addressed the Scribes; then turning to the palsied man, *Arising* (probably *lying down and raised up*), *take up thy couch and go away into thy house.*

7. And he arose, and departed to his house.

Familiar as we are with this astounding scene, it is not easy to imagine the solicitous suspense with which both the enemies and friends of Jesus must have awaited the result. Had the paralytic failed to obey the summons, the pretensions of the new religious teacher were refuted by the test of his own choosing.

8. But when the multitudes saw (it), they marvelled, and glorified God, which had given such power unto men.

The effect upon the crowds was that *they wondered*, or according to another reading, found in the Vatican and Beza codices, as well as in the Vulgate and Peshito versions, *were afraid*, i. e. filled with a religious awe at such an exhibition of divine power over the worst forms of disease. *Glorified God*, or made him glorious by praising him (see above, on 5, 16. 6, 2). *Which had given*, literally, *the* (*one*) *giving* (or *having given*), *such*, not merely as to quality or kind, but *so great*, so much, which is the usage of the word in Greek. *Power*, including the ideas of physical capacity and moral right. (See above, on 7, 29. 8, 9.) This must here be understood as applying, not only to the miracle of healing, but to the forgiveness which it proved to have been also granted. *Unto men*, collectively or as a race, of which they looked on Jesus as the representative. (See above, on 8, 20.) This expression seems to show that they had no conception of his divine nature. There is another explanation of the plural (*men*) as referring to our Lord and his disciples, the whole company of which he was the leader.

9. And as Jesus passed forth from thence, he saw a man named Matthew, sitting at the receipt of custom : and he saith unto him, Follow me. And he arose, and followed him.

As the first four of his personal attendants were fishermen, so the fifth, whose vocation is recorded, was selected from among the publicans, and called from the actual discharge of his official functions. The three evangelists, by whom this interesting incident has been preserved, agree in making it directly follow the miraculous cure of the paralytic. *Passing by* or *along*, from Capernaum, where the preceding miracle was wrought (Mark 2, 1) to the lake-shore (ib. v. 13), he saw a person acting as a publican. (See above, on 5, 46.) *Receipt of custom*, or, as most interpreters explain the term, the place of such receipt, not necessarily a house, perhaps a temporary office or a mere shed, such as Wiclif calls a tolboth (*toll-booth*), a name transferred in Scotland to the common gaol. At this place, perhaps upon the water-side, he saw a person sitting and engaged in his official duties, whom he called to follow him, a call which he instantly obeyed, abandoning his former business (Luke 5, 28). It is not affirmed, or even necessarily implied, that this was his first knowledge of the Saviour. The analogy of the calls before described (4, 18–22) makes it not improbable that this man, like his predecessors, had already heard him, and perhaps received an intimation that his services would be required. It can scarcely be fortuitous in all these cases that the persons called, though previously acquainted with the Saviour, had returned to or continued in their former occupation, and were finally summoned to attend their Master while engaged in the performance of its duties. The person here called, Luke names *Levi*, Mark more fully, *Levi, son of Alpheus*. In none of the four lists of the apostles is the name of *Levi* found, but in one of them (10, 3), a publican is mentioned by the name of *Matthew*, the very name which an old and uniform tradition has connected with that gospel as its author. The combination of these statements, which some German writers in their ignorance of practical and public jurisprudence, represent as contradictory, no judge or jury in America or England would hesitate or scruple to regard as proving that the Matthew of one gospel and the Levi of the other two are one and the same person. This same diversity exists in relation to the hypothesis or theory, by which the difference of name may be accounted for. While one class treats it as a mere harmonical device without intrinsic probability, the other thinks it altogether natural and in accordance with analogy, that this man, like so many persons in the sacred history, Paul, Peter, Mark, &c., had a double name, one of which superseded the other after his conversion. In this case it was natural that Matthew himself should use the name by which he had so long been known as an apostle, yet without concealing his original employment, and that Mark and Luke should use the name by which he had been known before, when they relate his conversion, but in enumerating the apostles should exchange it for his apostolic title. This hypothesis is certainly more probable than that of a mistake on either side, or that of a confusion between two conversions, those of Levi and Matthew, both of whom were publicans, and one of whom was an apostle, but confounded by tradition with the other!

10. And it came to pass, as Jesus sat at meat in the house, behold, many publicans and sinners came and sat down with him and his disciples.

Having gone back to record his own vocation, Matthew now reverts to what may have occurred long after, on our Lord's return from the eastern shore, where he had exorcised the demoniacs. The chronological order is here easily determined by the parallels (Mark 5, 21. Luke 8, 40), both which represent what follows as immediately subsequent to the return just mentioned, whereas Matthew gives no such specification and must therefore be elucidated by the others. It is only an apparent disagreement with them, that he puts the feast and conversation in immediate juxtaposition with his own vocation. He does not say they were immediately successive, and his order is readily accounted for by simply assuming, what is altogether natural, that Matthew, when about to mention what occurred in his own house, pauses a moment to explain how Jesus came to be there. This is still more natural when we consider that the feast in question was attended by a multitude of publicans, to which class Matthew had himself belonged. It is as if he had said, writing in his own person, 'I remember well when Jesus went with Jairus, for he left my own house where he had been answering the cavils of the Pharisees against his keeping company with publicans, many of whom were at my table, as I had myself been one of them, and was actually serving as such, when the Master called me, as he came out of Capernaum after healing the paralytic.' *The house* might be either that of Jesus or of Matthew; but the ambiguity is solved by Luke (5, 29) who tells us that the publican apostle made a great reception (δοχήν) for him in his house, a circumstance modestly omitted in his own account of these transactions. We have then a double reason for the fact that many publicans and sinners sat (reclined) at meat with Christ and his disciples; first, the one expressed by Mark, that this unhappy class was very numerous, and very generally followed Christ, to hear his doctrine and experience his kindness; and then, the one implied by Luke, that he who gave this entertainment was himself a publican, and therefore likely to invite or to admit his own associates in office and in disrepute. *Sat at meat*, literally, *lay down* or *reclined*, then the customary attitude at meals, as explained above (on 8, 11).

11. And when the Pharisees saw (it), they said unto his disciples, Why eateth your master with publicans and sinners?

The unavoidable publicity of almost all our Saviour's movements, and the agitated state of public feeling with respect to him, would necessarily prevent a private and select assemblage even in a private house. It is only by neglecting this peculiar state of things that any difficulty can be felt as to the presence of censorious enemies at Matthew's table or within his hospitable doors, if not as guests, as spectators or as spies. These unwelcome visitors were Pharisees or members of the great ceremonial party (see above, on 3, 7. 5, 20). Nothing could be more at variance with their hollow ceremonial sanctity than Christ's association with these excommunicated sinners and apostates, and especially his free participation in their food, on which the Jews of that age especially insisted as a means and mark of separation from the Gentiles (Acts 10, 28), and from those among themselves whom they regarded as mere heathen (see below, on 18, 17). Unprepared as yet to make an open opposition to the Saviour, and perhaps awed by his presence, they present their complaint in the indirect form of an interrogation addressed not to him but his disciples. The supposed extravagance of Christ's pretensions was aggravated, in the eyes of his accusers, by a seeming inconsistency of his behaviour with respect to friendships and associations. While he claimed an authority above that of any prophet, he consorted with the most notorious violators of the law, who were excluded by all strict Jews from their social and ecclesiastical communion.

12. But when Jesus heard (that), he said unto them,

They that be whole need not a physician, but they that are sick.

The original construction is, *but Jesus hearing*. Though addressed to the disciples, the objection is replied to by our Lord himself, and as usual in an unexpected form, presenting the true question at issue, and suggesting the true principle or method of solution. Their reproach implied a false view of his whole work and mission, which was that of a physician; the disease was sin; the more sinful any man or class of men were, the more were they in need of his attentions. The very idea of a healer or physician presupposes sickness; they that are whole (or well, in good health) need no such assistance. *Be* and *are* must here be taken as exact equivalents, the former being in old English, an indicative as well as a subjunctive form, and no such distinction being made in the translation of the parallels, where *are* is twice repeated (Mark 2, 17. Luke 5, 31). In all three places the original construction is the participial one, so constantly avoided in our English versions, and in this case really forbidden by our idiom, *those being strong, those having (themselves) ill*. For the usage of this last phrase, see above, on 4, 24 and 8, 16.

13. But go ye and learn what (that) meaneth, I will have mercy, and not sacrifice: for I am not come to call the righteous, but sinners to repentance.

It is highly characteristic of this Gospel that although it has thus far differed from the other two in this passage only by omitting some things which they give, it here makes an addition to their text, and one precisely like that in 8, 17, consisting of a quotation from the prophet Hosea (6, 6), which is introduced as something with which they were familiar in the letter, although culpably ignorant of its spirit and true meaning. *Go*, literally, *going*, or still more exactly, *having gone* (away for the purpose). This is not a pleonastic phrase, but adds to the severity of the reproach by sending them away, as if to school, or to their books, to learn what they should have known already, and what some of them were bound ex officio to make known to others. *What that meaneth*, literally, *what (it) is*, or connecting it directly with what follows, *what is, I will have mercy*. The sense is given in the English version, but without the peculiar form which is foreign from our idiom. The quotation is made in the words of the Septuagint version as given in some copies, though the Vatican (considered as the oldest) text retains the comparative form of the original (ἢ θυσίαν), *rather* (or *more*) *than sacrifice*. The strong negative in Matthew may be either an adoption of the version current among Greek readers, or an authoritative change enhancing the original expression, as if he had said, 'I not only desire sacrifice less than mercy, but not at all when they are incompatible.' *Will have* in the original is simply *will*, not as an auxiliary but an independent verb meaning to desire, like the Hebrew one which it translates. *Sacrifice* (originally *slaying*) is here put for all ceremonial services and in antithesis to *mercy* or the exercise of kindness and benevolence towards those who suffer, and on God's part towards his sinful and unworthy creatures. The application evidently is, that the Pharisees ignored or violated this great principle in censuring our Lord for his association with the very persons whom he came to save. The figurative description of his work, in v. 12, is now followed by a literal one. The oldest manuscripts and latest critics read, *I came not to call the righteous, but sinners*. This, taken by itself, would seem to mean simply that his errand was to sinners, that his message was addressed to them. But the parallel passage in Luke (5, 32), as well as the received text of Mark and Matthew, adds the words, *to repentance*, thus giving to the verb *call*, at least in reference to the last clause, the specific sense of summoning, inviting, or exhorting. Some interpreters, suppose that this limitation of the meaning does not extend to the righteous, who are said to be called (or not called) in the vague sense above given— 'I came not to address the righteous, but to summon sinners to repentance.' There is something very harsh, however, in supposing the same verb to have two senses in one sentence without being even repeated. A far more natural construction is to give it the same sense in relation to both classes, or in other words, to let the additional phrase (*to repentance*) qualify the whole clause. 'I came not to call the righteous to repentance, but sinners.' To this it is objected that repentance is not predicable of the righteous. This depends upon the meaning of the latter term. If it denote, as some allege, comparatively righteous, i. e. less atrociously or notoriously wicked; or, as others think, self-righteous, righteous in their own eyes; then the righteous need repentance and the call to repentance just as much as others. If it mean absolutely righteous, i. e. free from sin, which is the proper meaning, and the one here required by the antithesis with sinners, it is true that such cannot repent, and need not be exhorted to repentance; but this is the very thing affirmed according to the natural construction. 'You reproach me for my intercourse with sinners, but my very mission is to call men to repentance, and repentance presupposes sin; I did not come to call the righteous to repentance, for they do not need it and cannot exercise it, but to call sinners as such to repentance.' By confining *to repentance* to the second member of the clause, the very thing most pointedly affirmed is either left out or obscurely hinted. Another error as to this verse is the error of supposing that our Saviour recognizes the existence of a class of sinless or absolutely righteous men among those whom he found upon the earth at his first advent. But the distinction which he draws is not between two classes of men, but between two characters or conditions of the whole race. By *the righteous* and *sinners* he does not mean those men who are actually righteous, and those other men who are actually sinners, but mankind as righteous and mankind as sinners. 'I came not to call men as unfallen sinless beings to repentance, which would be a contradiction, but as sinners, which they all are; and I therefore not only may but must associate with sinners, as the very objects of my mission; just as the physician cannot do his work without coming into contact with the sick, who are alone in need of healing.' He does not mean of course that his errand was to Publicans (as sinners), not to Pharisees (as righteous), but simply that the worse the former were, the more completely did they fall within the scope of his benignant mission.

14. Then came to him the disciples of John, saying, Why do we and the Pharisees fast oft, but thy disciples fast not ?

Near akin to the charge of undue condescension and familiar intercourse with sinners is that of a free and self-indulgent life, to the neglect of all ascetic mortifications. *The disciples of John* are by some regarded as worthy representatives of John himself, holding his doctrines and his relative position with respect to the Messiah. But this position was no longer tenable; the ministry of John was essentially prospective and preparatory; its very object was to bring men to Christ as the Lamb of God who taketh away the sin of the world (John 1, 29). Had all John's followers imbibed his spirit and obeyed his precepts, they would all have become followers of Christ, as some did. But even while John was at liberty, and in despite of his remonstrances, some of his disciples cherished a contracted zeal for him as the competitor of Christ (John 3, 26), and afterwards became a new religious party, equally unfaithful to the principal and the forerunner. These are the *disciples of John* mentioned in the gospel, after his imprisonment and the consequent cessation of his public ministry. Of their numbers and organic state we have no information. From the passage now before us, where they are connected with the Pharisees, not only by the history but by themselves, it is probable that John's severe means of awakening the conscience and producing deep repentance were continued as a ceremonial form after the spirit had departed. A remnant of this school or party reappears in Acts 19, 1–7, and with a further but most natural corruption in one or more heretical phenomena of later history. The neglect complained of would be equally offensive to the followers of John and to the Pharisees, however they might differ as to more important matters. *For what*, i. e. for what cause or reason? *Fast*, i. e. habitually, statedly, as a matter of observance, not as an occasional auxiliary to devotion, or a special means of spiritual discipline. The only stated fast prescribed in the Mosaic law is that of the great day of atonement, in which were summed up all the expiatory ceremonies of the year (Lev. 16, 29–34). But before the close of the Old Testament canon, we find traces of additional fasts added by the Jews themselves (Zech. 8, 19), and in the time of Christ an intimation by himself that the Pharisees observed two weekly fasts (Luke 18, 12). The Jewish traditions, though of later date, confirm the general fact here stated. The fasts observed by John's disciples were either the traditional ones common to all other

Jews, or formal repetitions of those used by John as temporary remedies, perhaps a servile imitation of his personal austerity and abstinence. We have no reason to believe, and it is highly improbable, indeed, that John himself established stated fasts, which would seem to be at variance with his intermediate position, as the last prophet of the old dispensation and the herald of the new, but commissioned neither to improve upon the one nor to anticipate the other. *But thy disciples fast not*, though a simple statement of a fact, derives from its connection a censorious character, as if they meant to say, how is this omission to be justified or reconciled with thy pretensions as a teacher sent from God? (John 3, 2.) In this case they complain to him of his disciples, as in that before it they complain to them of him (v. 11), and in the first which Mark records merely condemn him in their hearts without giving oral expression to their censures (v. 3, 4). This charge, though indirect and interrogative in form, may be regarded as confirming what we know from other quarters, and especially from Christ's own words below, that his life and that of his disciples were alike free from the opposite extremes of frivolous self-indulgence and austere moroseness.

15. And Jesus said unto them, Can the children of the bride-chamber mourn, as long as the bridegroom is with them? but the days will come, when the bridegroom shall be taken from them, and then shall they fast.

The reply to this charge is as unexpected and original in form as either of the others, and made still more striking by its being borrowed from familiar customs of the age and country, namely, from its marriage ceremonies, and particularly from the practice of the bridegroom bringing home his bride accompanied by chosen friends of either sex, rejoicing over them and for them. These, in the oriental idiom, were styled children of the bridal chamber, i. e specially belonging to it and connected with it, something more than mere guests or attendants at the wedding. The specific term *sons*, here used in all the gospels, designates the male attendants upon such occasions. *The bridegroom* is in Greek an adjective derived from *bride* and answering to *bridal, nuptial*. Used absolutely, it denotes *the bridal (man)*, or *bridesman*, called in English *bridegroom*, and differing from *husband* just as *bride* does from *wife*. They may be here a double allusion, first, to the favourite Old Testament figure of a conjugal relation between God and Israel (as in Ps. xlv. Isai. liv. Jer. ii. Hos. iii.), and then to John the Baptist's beautiful description of the mutual relation between him and Christ as that of the bridegroom and the bridegroom's friend (John 3, 29). The form of the question is highly idiomatic, being that used when a negative answer is expected. The nearest approach to it in English is a negative followed by a question—'they cannot—can they?' The incapacity implied is not a physical but moral one. They cannot be expected, or required to fast; there is no reason why they should fast. The general principle involved or presupposed is that fasting is not a periodical or stated, but a special and occasional observance, growing out of a particular emergency. This doctrine underlies the whole defence of his disciples, which proceeds upon the supposition that a fast, to be acceptable and useful, must have a reason and occasion of its own, beyond a general propriety or usage. It is also taught that fasting is not a mere *opus operatum*, but the cause and the effect of a particular condition, that of spiritual grief or sorrow. The duty of fasting being thus dependent upon circumstances, may and will become incumbent when those circumstances change, as they are certainly to change hereafter. The bridegroom is not always to be visibly present, and when he departs, the time of fasting will be come. To express this still more strongly, he is said to be removed or taken away, as if by violence. *Then*, at the time of this removal, as an immediate temporary cause of sorrow, not forever afterwards, which would be inconsistent with the principle already laid down, that the value of religious fasting is dependent on its being an occasional and not a stated duty. There is no foundation therefore for the doctrine of some Romish writers, who evade this argument against their stated fasts, by alleging that according to our Lord's own declaration, the church after his departure was to be a fasting church. But this would be equivalent to saying that the Saviour's exaltation would consign his people to perpetual sorrow. For he evidently speaks of grief and fasting as inseparable, and the two terms are here used as convertible.

16. No man putteth a piece of new cloth unto an old garment: for that which is put in to fill it up, taketh from the garment, and the rent is made worse.

Although Matthew has not yet recorded any of Christ's formal parables, he gives us in this passage several examples of his parabolical method of instruction, i. e. by illustration drawn from the analogies of real life. Having already employed some of the prevailing marriage customs to account for the neglect of all austerities by his disciples, he proceeds to enforce the general principle which he is laying down, by other analogies derived from the festivities of such occasions, and particularly from dresses and the drinks which were considered indispensable at marriage feasts. The first parable, as it is expressly called by Luke (5, 36), is suggested by the homely but familiar art of patching, and consists in a description of the general practice of what everybody does, or rather of what no one does, in such a matter. This appeal to constant universal usage shows, that however we may understand the process here alluded to, it must have been entirely familiar and intelligible to the hearers. The essential undisputed points are that he represents it as an unheard-of and absurd thing to combine an old and new dress, by sewing parts of one upon the other. The incongruity, thus stated by Matthew and Luke (5, 36), is rendered much more clear by Mark's explanation of a new dress, as meaning one composed of *unfulled cloth*, and therefore utterly unfit for the kind of combination here alluded to. Both the text and the construction of the next clause has been much disputed; but the true sense seems to be the one expressed in the common version, namely, that the new piece or filling up, by shrinking or by greater strength of fibre, loosens or weakens the old garment still more, and the rent becomes worse. The essential idea here expressed is evidently that of incongruity, with special reference to old and new. It admits of various applications to the old and new economy, the old and new nature of the individual, and many other contrasts of condition and of character. The primary use of it, suggested by the context and historical occasion, was to teach the authors of this charge that they must not expect in the Messiah's kingdom a mere patching up of what had had its day and done its office, by empirical repairs and emendations of a later date, but an entire renovation of the church and of religion; not as to its essence or its vital principle, but as to all its outward forms and vehicles. As the usages immediately in question were of human not divine institution, whatever there may be in this similitude of sarcasm or contempt, belongs not even to the temporary forms of the Mosaic dispensation, but to its traditional excrescences.

17. Neither do men put new wine into old bottles: else the bottles break, and the wine runneth out, and the bottles perish: but they put new wine into new bottles, and both are preserved.

The same essential truth is now propounded in another parabolic form, likewise borrowed from the experience of common life. Instead of old and new cloth, the antithesis is now between old and new skins as receptacles for new wine, the fermenting strength of which distends the fresh skins without injury, but bursts the rigid leather of the old ones. *Men*, as in 5, 15, and often elsewhere, represents the indefinite subject of the verb. The present tense denotes what is usually done in such a case. The word *bottles* is of course to be explained with reference to the oriental use of goat skins to preserve and carry water, milk, wine, and other liquids. The attempt to determine who are meant by the bottles, and what by the wine, proceeds upon a false assumption with respect to the structure and design of parables, which are not to be expounded by adjusting the minute points of resemblance first, and then deducing from the aggregate a general conclusion, but by first ascertaining the main analogy, and then adjusting the details to suit it. (See below, on 13, 3.) This is the method universally adopted in expounding fables, which are only a particular species of the parable, distinguished by the introduction of the lower animals, as representatives of moral agents. In explaining Æsop's fable of the Fox and the Grapes, no one ever thinks of putting a distinctive meaning on the grapes, as a particular kind of fruit, or on the limbs of the fox as having each its own significance. Yet this is the expository method almost universally applied to the parables. By varying the form of his illustration here, without a change in its essential import, he teaches us to ascertain the latter first, and then let the mere details adjust themselves accordingly. The last clause furnishes the key to both similitudes. New wine must be put into new bottles. In religion, no less than in secular affairs, new emergencies require new means to meet them; but these new means are not to be devised by human wisdom, but appointed by divine authority.

18. While he spake these things unto them, behold, there came a certain ruler, and worshipped him, saying, My daughter is even now dead: but come and lay thy hand upon her, and she shall live.

We now come to the narrative of two great miracles, woven together in the history as they were in fact, the one having been performed by Christ while on his way to work the other. *These things he saying to them* fixes the succession of the incidents, which is the same, though not so expressly stated, in the other gospels. *Ruler*, in Greek *Archon*, originally meaning one who takes the lead, applied in history to the chief magistrates of Athens. *A certain*, literally, *one*, the same unusual expression that occurs above in 8, 19, and here as there must be definitely understood as meaning one among so many, one out of a greater number, as if he had said, 'among those who applied to him for aid was one belonging to the class of rulers,' or as Mark explains it (2, 22), one of the *archi-synagogues* (or *rulers of the synagogue*), i. e. one of the national hereditary elders of the Jews, among whose functions was the local conduct of religious discipline and worship (see above, on 4, 23.) The idea of a separate organization and a distinct class of officers appears to have arisen after the destruction of Jerusalem, and could not therefore be the model of the Christian Church which had its pattern not in later Jewish institutions, but in the permanent essential part of the old theocracy, including its primeval patriarchal eldership, one primarily founded upon natural relations or the family government and thence transferred not only to the Jewish but to the Christian church-organization. Of such rulers there was always a plurality in every neighborhood, but not a bench or council of elective officers, uniform in number, as in the later synagogues, when the dispersion of the people had destroyed the ancient constitution and the present synagogue arrangement had been substituted for it. But as this arrangement is without divine authority, nothing is gained but something lost by tracing the New Testament church polity to this source, instead of tracing it back further to the presbyterial forms of the theocracy itself. The elders who were *ex officio* rulers of the synagogue, i. e. directors of its discipline and worship, had, both by birth and office, the highest rank and social position.

This application for assistance therefore came from the most respectable and influential quarter. The preservation of this ruler's name (Jairus) by Mark (5, 22) and Luke (8, 41), but not by Matthew, shows how far the others are from merely abridging or transcribing him. *Worshipped him*, or did him reverence, by falling at his feet (Mark 5, 22. Luke 8, 41). As to the import of this action, see above, on 8, 2. *Is even now dead*, literally, *just now died*, a strong expression of his fear that she must be dead by this time, and therefore not at variance with the more deliberate expressions in the other gospels (Mark 5, 23. Luke 8, 42.) The request in the last clause implies a belief that personal presence and corporeal contact were essential to the cure. This was the popular belief, to which the faith of the centurion rose superior (see above, on 8, 10), and which our Lord appears to have rebuked in a person of still higher rank. (See John 4, 46–54.) That the parent's faith in this case was not wholly wanting, appears from the request itself, and from the strong expression, *She shall* (i. e. certainly will) *live*, which may either mean, still live if yet alive, or live again, revive, if dead already.

19. And Jesus arose, and followed him, and (so did) his disciples.

Rising up, literally, raised or roused, i. e. from table in the house of Matthew (see above, on v. 10), who would therefore naturally have a vivid recollection of the whole scene. *His disciples*, in the wide sense of adherents, or at least of personal attendants, those who followed him from place to place, which was done, however, in the present instance by a great crowd (Mark 5, 24), probably of "publicans and others" who were eating with him (Luke 5, 29). We have seen, however, that a crowd was seldom far off, even in our Lord's most solitary and sacred hours. (See above, on 8, 1.)

20. And behold, a woman which was diseased with an issue of blood twelve years, came behind (him), and touched the hem of his garment.

While on his way to the house of Jairus he performs a miracle, the history of which is here inserted into that of the other by the three evangelists, precisely as it happened, a strong proof of authenticity and vivid recollection on the part of the eye-witnesses. *A woman* whose name, as usual, is not recorded (see above, 8, 2. 5. 28. 9, 2), that of Jairus being mentioned (in the parallels) on account of his official character and public station. *Having a flow of blood*, or *hemorrhage*, in Greek a single word of participial form. The precise nature of the malady, beyond this general description, is of no importance, even to physicians, much less to the mass of readers and interpreters. Instead of dwelling upon this point, the evangelist directs attention to its long continuance (*twelve years*). *Coming up* (or *to* him) *behind*, or more exactly *from behind,* i. e. approaching him in that direction, not by chance or from necessity, but for the purpose of escaping observation. *His garment,* not his clothes in general, which is the meaning of the plural elsewhere, but the robe or gown, which forms the outer garment in an oriental dress, and which the Greek word in the singular denotes. What she touched was not only this external garment, but its very edge or border, showing that her object was mere contact, so that the slightest and most superficial touch would be sufficient. The word translated *edge* is applied in the Septuagint to the fringe worn by the Jews at the corners of their garments (Num. 15, 38); but there seems to be no reason here for departing from its general and classical usage. It is important, though it may be difficult, to realize the situation of this woman, once possessed of health and wealth, and no doubt moving in respectable society, now beggared and diseased, without a hope of human help, and secretly believing in the power of the Christ, and him alone, to heal her, yet deterred by some natural misgiving and by shame, perhaps connected with the nature of her malady, from coming with the rest to be publicly recognized and then relieved. However commonplace the case may seem to many, there are some in whose experience, when clearly seen and seriously attended to, it touches a mysterious cord of painful sympathy.

21. For she said within herself, If I may but touch his garment, I shall be whole.

That she was not actuated merely by a sort of desperate curiosity, as might have been suspected from her previous history and present conduct, but by real confidence in Christ's ability to heal her, we are expressly taught by being made acquainted with her inmost thoughts before her purpose was accomplished. *For she said* (or *was saying,* as she made her way with difficulty through the crowd), not to others and aloud, but to or in herself. *If I only touch,* not *may touch,* which suggests too strongly the idea of permission or of lawfulness, whereas, the Greek expresses that of mere contingency. It is a slight but touching stroke in this inimitable picture, that she did not even choose the hem of his outer garment as the part which she would touch, but came in contact with it as it were by chance, desiring only to touch any of his clothes, no matter which or what. *I shall be whole,* literally *saved,* i. e. from this disease and this condition. The Greek verb is the one translated healed in Mark 5, 23 a needless variation, and indeed injurious to the beauty of the passage, as it mars the correspondence of these two expressions of reliance upon Christ, uttered almost simultaneously by persons probably entire strangers to each other.

22. But Jesus turned him about, and when he saw her, he said, Daughter, be of good comfort: thy faith hath made thee whole. And the woman was made whole from that hour.

Turning, or *being turned*, in Greek a passive form, but with an active or deponent sense. *When he saw her*, literally, *seeing her*, or looking at her. *Be of good comfort*, the precise word used in v. 2, and there translated, *be of good cheer*. In both cases, the affectionate address (*son, daughter*) is needlessly transposed in English. *Made whole*, literally, *saved*, as in the preceding verse. The essential part of this occurrence for Matthew's purpose was the healing wrought by simple contact with the Saviour's dress, which had precisely the same virtue as the touch of his hand in v. 25 below, and was afterwards renewed in the miracles of Paul (Acts 19, 11. 12). He therefore passes over the interesting circumstance, added by the other two evangelists (Mark 5, 30–33. Luke 8, 45–47).

23. And when Jesus came into the ruler's house, and saw the minstrels and the people making a noise.

Here again Matthew passes over the message received by the father on the way (Mark 5, 35. 36. Luke 8, 49. 50), as he does a similar trait in the case of the centurion (see above, on 8. 5), and hurries on to the principal occurrence, or the miracle itself. He does not even mention the three disciples whom he suffered to attend him, who are named in both the other gospels (Mark, 5, 37. Luke 8, 51.) It is a mere cavil to regard these omissions as implying that the facts were unknown to the writer or not found in the tradition which he followed. They only show that he selected his materials, instead of taking them at random, and so used them as form a compact and coherent narrative. The text of Matthew presents no deficiencies or chasms, and yet all the additions in the parallel accounts can be at once wrought into it. What stronger proof can be desired than that these writers used the same materials, but each with due regard to his own purpose? *Coming into the ruler's house, and seeing the pipers*, players on the flute, a common practice at the ancient funerals, *and the crowd* or promiscuous assemblage, *making a noise* (so Cranmer and Geneva) either that necessarily attending all crowds, or the uproar, clamour, such as commonly attend an oriental funeral.* Early burial was usual among the ancient Jews, because it was not properly interment, but a deposit of the body, frequently uncoffined. in tombs erected above ground, or lateral excavations in the rock, where the risk of death by premature burial was much less than it is among ourselves. Compare Acts 5, 6. 10, where an additional security against such a mistake existed in the certain knowledge which the apostles had, that Ananias and Sapphira were completely dead.

24. He said unto them, Give place: for the maid is not dead, but sleepeth. And they laughed him to scorn.

* Tyndale's version (*raging*) is too strong; the Rhemish (*keeping a stir*) approaches nearest to the true sense of the word ($\vartheta o\rho \nu \beta o\nu\mu\epsilon\nu o\nu$).

He says to them, the mourners thus employed in noisy lamentation. *Give place*, withdraw, retreat, a verb which has repeatedly occurred before, but in a different application (see above, on 2, 12. 13. 14. 22. 4, 12.) *Damsel*, a Greek diminutive of neuter form, but meaning a little girl. The word is confined in the older classics to the dialect of common life, as a familiar term of fondness and endearment; but the later writers use it in the more serious and elevated style. The Rhemish version has the old and now too coarse form wench. *Is not dead*, or *did not die* (when ye supposed), the same form that is used in Mark 5, 35. *But sleeps*, is sleeping, or asleep, the present tense denoting actual condition, as the aorist before it, strictly understood, denotes a previous occurrence. *She did not die but sleeps.* These words admit of two interpretations, each of which has had its advocates. The first assigns to them their strictest and most obvious sense, to wit that this was merely an apparent death, but really a case of stupor, trance, or syncope, which might, almost without a figure, be described as a deep protracted slumber. The other gives a figurative sense to both expressions, understanding by the first that she really was dead but only for a time and therefore *not dead* in the ordinary acceptation of the term; and by the second that her death, though real, being transient, might be naturally called a sleep, which differs from death chiefly in this very fact and the effects which flow from it. This last is now very commonly agreed upon by all classes of interpreters, German and English, neological and Christian, as the only meaning which the words will fairly bear. In favour of this sense is the fact that Jesus used the same expression with respect to Lazarus and expressly declared that in that case sleep meant death (John 11, 11-14), to which may be added that Mark is here recording signal miracles as proofs of Christ's extraordinary power, and that a mere restoration from apparent death would not have been appropriate to his present purpose. One of the best German philological authorities has paraphrased our Saviour's words as meaning, 'Do not regard the child as dead, but think of her as merely sleeping, since she is so soon to come to life again.' *And they* (i. e. the company, or those whom he had thus addressed) *laughed at him* (or *against him*), i. e. at his expense, or in derision of him. This idea is expressed in the English version by the added words, *to scorn*, which though not expressed in the original are not italicised because supposed to be included in the meaning of the compound Greek verb which, according to another usage of the particle with which it is compounded, might be understood to mean, *they laughed him down*, or silenced him by their derision.

25. But when the people were put forth, he went in, and took her by the hand, and the maid arose.

The people, literally, *the crowd*, a word in Greek suggesting the idea of confusion and disorder, in accordance with the previous description. *Put forth*, literally cast out, or as we say, turned out, to describe a peremptory dismission, whether accompanied by force or not. It is the term commonly applied to the expulsion of intrusive spirits (see above, on 7, 22. 8, 16. 31. and below, on vs. 33. 34). *Going in*, or having gone in, to the chamber where the child was lying, probably the large upper room (ὑπερῷον), which seems to have been used on such occasions. (Compare Acts 9, 37. 39.) *Took her by the hand* is not so strong as the original; which properly means *seized*, laid hold of. (Wiclif has, *held her hand*.) In condescension to the weakness of the father's faith (see above, on v. 18), our Lord here establishes a visible communication between himself and the person upon whom the miracle was to be wrought. For the same reason he made use of audible expressions serving to identify himself as the performer. These expressions, in the present case, have been preserved by Mark (5, 41), not only in a Greek translation, but in their Hebrew or Aramaic form, as originally uttered. Matthew, omitting all detail, records, in the most laconic manner, the result, to wit, that *the maid arose*, or retaining the exact form of the Greek, *was raised*, not only from her bed, but from a state of death. (See above, on vs. 5. 6. 7. 19.)

26. And the fame thereof went abroad into all that land.

The first words are more exactly rendered in the margin of the English Bible, *this fame*, or report, the Greek word being that from which the English *fame* is derived through the Latin, but originally meaning simply word or saying, from the verb to say. It is used in a general sense for good or bad report, and not restricted to the former as our *fame* is excepting in the combinations *common fame* and *ill fame*. *Went abroad*, went out, not only from the house, but from the city. *That land*, or country, an indefinite expression, which we neither need nor can define by geographical specifications.

27. And when Jesus departed thence, two blind men followed him, crying, and saying, (Thou) Son of David, have mercy on us.

Matthew here subjoins two miracles as following immediately the restoration of the ruler's daughter, without any contradiction from the other gospels, which omit them altogether. This freedom of insertion and omission shows that the evangelists, though working up the same material, do it not as abridgers or transcribers of each other, but as independent and inspired historians. The original construction is like that in 8, 23. 28, beginning with a dative as the object of the verb, but followed by a pleonastic repetition of the pronoun, *Jesus passing thence two blind men followed him*. The first verb is the same as that in v. 9, from its etymology implying that he did not go alone but as the leader of others. (Compare another compound of the same verb in 4, 23 above and v. 35 below.) The mention of two blind men has been added to the other cases of like nature (e. g. 8, 28 above) in proof of Matthew's disposition to see double, or his imaginative fondness for the number two. But as the fact itself is altogether natural, to wit, that sufferers, and more particularly blind men, should resort to Christ in pairs, the circumstance in question only shows that something in his habits or his turn of mind led Matthew to observe and remember the precise number, even when without historical importance and perhaps unnoticed by others. *Crying and saying,* may either mean *saying with a loud voice,* by the figure which the Greek grammarians called hendiadys; or the first word may denote an inarticulate cry of lamentation or complaint distinct from any verbal utterance. (See above, on 8, 29.) *Have mercy,* pity, show compassion, a verb corresponding to the noun in v. 13 above, and the adjective in 5, 7, where the verb itself appears in a passive form. *Son of David,* his descendant and successor on the throne of Israel, a remarkable acknowledgment of his Messiahship, according to our Lord's own exposition of the 110th Psalm. (See below, on 22, 41–45.) The title had been previously applied by the angel of the Lord to Joseph (see above, on 1, 20), through whom, as the husband of Christ's mother, he derived a legal right to the succession, as he did a natural or real one from his mother herself. (See above, on 1, 1. 16.)

28. And when he was come into the house, the blind men came to him : and Jesus saith unto them, Believe ye that I am able to do this ? They said unto him, Yea, Lord.

They not only followed him along the way but into the house to which he was going; whether that of Peter, or some other, in Capernaum or elsewhere, cannot be determined and is wholly unimportant. We have here another instance of the same pleonastic syntax, which is one of Matthew's chief peculiarities of language. *To (him) going into the house came to him the blind men.* How is it that this form of speech is found in Matthew only, if inspiration did not leave the peculiar habits of the sacred writers undisturbed, but used them all as mere machines and vehicles of one unvaried revelation ? This miracle is probably recorded to exemplify the way in which our Lord sometimes drew forth the profession of that faith which he prescribed as a prerequisite of healing. We thus learn what was really the object of that faith, to wit, his power or ability to work the wonder. (See above, on v. 22.) *Yea,* yes, the usual affirmative in Greek, though similar in form to one of our negative particles (*nay*). Cranmer avoids the use of it by a repetition of the verb (*Lord, we believe*).

29. Then touched he their eyes, saying, According to your faith, be it unto you.

Then has here the sense of afterwards, or in the next place, i. e.

after he had drawn forth this profession of the blind. *Touched their eyes*, as the parts immediately affected, so as to connect the cure still more distinctly with the person of the healed. *According to*, not on account of, as a meritorious ground, but in proportion and analogy to their belief, which he perceived to be sincere. For a different expression of the same idea in the case of the centurion, see above, on 8, 13. *Be it*, let it happen, come to pass, precisely the same form that is employed in the third petition of the Lord's Prayer. (See above, on 6, 10.)

30. And their eyes were opened ; and Jesus straitly charged them, saying, See (that) no man know (it).

The restoration of sight is described in a natural but figurative form, *their eyes were opened*, the inaction of the organ being conceived of as a shutting of the eye, not in the ordinary sense of covering the pupil with the eyelid, but in that of being closed to the perception of external objects. *Straitly* (i. e. strictly) *charged*, in the original a Hellenistic verb denoting strong emotion, and particularly grief or indignation, as in Mark 14, 5. John 11, 33. 38. Here (and in Mark 1, 43) it can only mean a threatening in case of disobedience, charging them on pain of his severe displeasure and disapprobation. The Vulgate and its copyists simply translated it *threatened (comminatus est)*. The form of the injunction is the same with that in 8, 4, but with the second verb in the third person. *See* (i. e. see to it, take care, be sure) *that no man* (more correctly, no one) *know* (*it*, or *of it*, as the older English versions have it).

31. But they, when they were departed, spread abroad his fame in all that country.

The result was the same as in the case of the leper, as described by Mark (1, 45), though not by Matthew (8, 4). Such prohibitions were uttered by the Saviour, not in conformity to any fixed rule, but for the general purpose of preventing the precipitate occurrence of events which according to his plan were to be gradually brought about. Hence we find him varying his practice as the circumstances of the cases varied, with the same independent and original authority which marked his public teaching. (See above, on 7, 29.) The evangelists describe him as exercising a divine discretion, which in every case determined whether the publication of his miracles required to be stimulated or retarded, though the grounds of the distinction may be now, and may have been at first, inscrutable to human wisdom. By this discretion the excessive zeal of those who witnessed his extraordinary works was checked and chastened, although not entirely suppressed. It may have been particularly needed in those cases where a miracle was wrought among a people less familiar with such wonders, and the more prone therefore to extravagant activity in spreading them abroad. *All that country* differs only in case from the phrase translated *all that land* in v. 26, and has the same indefinite meaning.*

32. As they went out, behold, they brought to him a dumb man possessed with a devil.

Matthew adds another miracle immediately ensuing. *as they (the blind men) went out*, literally, *they going out* or being in the act of doing so. *Behold* invites attention to this second case as not to be confounded with the first, nor indeed with another upon record, that in Mark 7, 32–35 being obviously different both in time and circumstances. That was a case of deafness and difficult articulation without any intimation of a preternatural cause. This was a case of demoniacal possession rendering the victim dumb. The other cases which most nearly resemble it are separately given by Matthew on account of other circumstances which distinguished them. (See below, on 12, 22. 17, 14.) The word translated *dumb* is elsewhere correctly rendered *deaf* (see below on 11, 5), and the classical usage is the same, which may be readily explained by the mutual relation of these two affections when congenital. In this case the sense of dumbness is required by the description of the cure (in v. 33). *They brought*, indefinitely, as in v. 2. *A man dumb (and) demonized*, implying that the one state was occasioned by the other. For the nature of the latter, see above, on 4, 24. 8, 16. 28, 33.

33. And when the devil was cast out, the dumb spake: and the multitudes marvelled, saying, It was never so seen in Israel.

The demon having been cast out, the dumb (man) talked, is not a sequence in time merely (when it was cast out), but in causation. As the demon was the cause of the man's dumbness, his expulsion was the cause of his recovering his speech. *The crowds wondered*, as at a new phase or exhibition of our Lord's extraordinary power. Some explain the next clause to mean, *never did he so appear*, i. e. so great, so glorious; but this would seem to be forbidden by the added words, *in Israel*, which are then almost unmeaning and superfluous. The true construction is no doubt the common one, which makes the verb indefinite, if not impersonal. *It never was so seen*, or so appeared, i. e. there never was such a sight or spectacle before, *in Israel*, among the chosen people, or in their history, their memory as a nation. This does not refer to the intrinsic greatness of the miracle, as compared with others, either in reference to the power displayed or the effect produced, but to its peculiarity in kind, arising from the complication of two such affections, which was probably the reason of its being here recorded.

* Wiclif's singular translation of the last verb (*and defamed him*) is only too exact a copy of the Vulgate (*diffamaverunt*), which is itself too close an adherence to the form of the original (διεδήμισαν), though justified by Latin usage.

34. But the Pharisees said, He casteth out devils, through the prince of the devils.

Another reason for recording this occurrence may have been, that it afforded an occasion for the first utterance of a blasphemous suggestion with respect to our Lord's miracles, which was afterwards repeated still more boldly, and led to a remarkable discourse recorded at full length below (12, 22–37). Being here only mentioned, as it were, in passing, the minute explanation of its terms may be reserved until we reach the passage just referred to. It will here be sufficient to observe that *the Pharisees* are not the same, as some have represented, in all cases, but such representatives of that great party as might happen to be present on different occasions. This is the less improbable as the name included the great body of the unbelieving Jews. (See above, on vs. 11. 14. and on 3, 7. 5, 20.) *Through the prince of the devils*, literally, *in the archon* (chief or leader) *of the demons* (see above, on v. 18), i. e. in intimate conjunction with him and reliance on him. (Tyndale: *by the power of the chief devil*.)

35. And Jesus went about all the cities and villages, teaching in their synagogues, and preaching the gospel of the kingdom, and healing every sickness, and every disease among the people.

This verse is almost perfectly identical in form, and altogether so in sense, with 4, 23. The name *Jesus* there stands later in the sentence, and is wholly omitted by the Codex Vaticanus and the latest critics, as they also do the last words of the sentence, *in* (among) *the people*. For *all the cities and villages* we there have *the whole* (*of*) *Galilee*, a difference which merely serves to show what cities and villages (or towns of every size) are here intended. With these exceptions, the two verses are identical, and it becomes an interesting question, how are they related to each other in the structure of the history? One view of this relation, and perhaps the one prevailing among readers and interpreters, is that which makes the passages descriptive of two successive circuits made by Christ through Galilee, being the first and third in order, while the second is exclusively preserved by Luke (8, 1–3). That Matthew, if he had described two, would most probably have introduced the third, although it cannot of itself refute this doctrine, certainly creates a strong presumption to its disadvantage, as the leaving out of one whole journey through the country is exceedingly improbable. And this presumption is strengthened by the use of the imperfect tense (περιῆγεν) and not the aorist, suggesting the idea of continued action, not on any one occasion but in general. This has led us to conclude already (see above, p. 98.) that 4, 23 is not an account of one particular mission, but a general description of our Lord's itinerant ministry, with its two great functions, working miracles and teaching. But if this be so, it seems to follow that the verse before us, with its marked similarity of form and substance, is a similar description of his ministry in general, and not that of a second or third circuit in particular. The question why this general description should be thus repeated almost *totidem verbis* may be readily answered, and the answer furnishes a key to the whole structure of this first great division of the history. The answer is, that Matthew, having executed his design of showing by examples how the Saviour taught and wrought in his great mission, now returns to the point from which he started in beginning this exemplification, and resumes the thread there dropped or broken by repeating his summary description of the ministry which he has since been painting in detail. This view of the connection is not only recommended by grammatical considerations, such as the imperfect tense and participles following in either case, but also by the clear light which it throws upon the structure of the book and the progress of the history. Even a mere hypothesis, which thus converts an incoherent series of details into a systematic well-compacted whole, can scarcely be denied as fanciful. According to this theory, the meaning of the verse before us is, 'and thus, or so it was, as I before said, that Jesus went about,' &c.

36. But when he saw the multitudes, he was moved with compassion on them, because they fainted, and were scattered abroad, as sheep having no shepherd.

A plausible objection to the view just taken of the preceding verse may seem to be presented by its close connection with the one before us, which can scarcely mean that he was always thus affected, and was always saying what is quoted in the next verse. This construction is indeed forbidden by the aorist (ἐσπλαγχνίσθη) in one case and the present (λέγει) in the other. But this change of tense, always significant in Greek, affords the key to the whole difficulty, showing as it does that after speaking of the whole course of Christ's ministry, and using for that purpose the imperfect tense with its dependent participles, Matthew now proceeds, by means of the aorist and present, to describe what took place upon one particular occasion. 'Thus did Jesus go about all Galilee, teaching and healing, and at one time he was moved with compassion,' &c. This does not imply that he was usually free from this affection, but singles out a special instance for the purpose of recording what he said to his disciples. *When he saw*, precisely the same words employed in 5, 1. and there more simply and exactly rendered *seeing*. *The multitudes*, the crowds, the promiscuous collections of the people from all quarters to attend his ministry, to hear his teachings, and to see his miracles. The particular point of time may be the same as that in 5, 1. when the concourse had attained its height, and thus occasioned the original delivery of the Sermon on the Mount. The heart, though properly the name of a bodily organ, is used in various languages to signify the seat of the affections, and sometimes the affections themselves. But the Greeks extended this figurative usage to all the higher or thoracic viscera, the liver, lungs,

&c., as distinguished from the lower or abdominal viscera, the former being also reckoned edible, the latter not. For want of a distinctive term, the English version uses the word *bowels*, even where the Greek noun (σπλάγχνα) has its figurative sense of feeling, and especially compassion. From this sense of the noun, later and Hellenistic usage formed a verb (σπλαγχνίζομαι) unknown to the Greek classics, and denoting, first the yearning of the bowels, or rather the commotion of the upper viscera, and then the emotion of pity or compassion. It is the passive participle of this verb that is here correctly paraphrased, *moved with compassion*. What excited his divine and human sympathy was not of course their numbers or their physical condition but their spiritual destitution. The figures of a shepherd and a flock to denote the mutual relation of religious guides and those who follow them are frequent in the Scriptures and too natural to need elucidation. On the other hand, the converse of this figure, or a flock without a shepherd, is the most affecting that can be employed to represent the want of nurture, guidance and protection, the extreme of weakness, helplessness, and imminent exposure both to force and fraud, dispersion and destruction. *Fainted*, in the margin, *were tired and lay down*. Both words in Greek are passive participles, the first, according to the common text (ἐκλελυμένοι), meaning *loosened out*, and then relaxed, exhausted (as in 15, 32, compare the figurative use in Heb. 12, 3. 5. Gal. 6, 9), but according to the reading now preferred (ἐσκυλμένοι), *vexed*, troubled, harassed (as in Mark 5, 35. Luke 7, 6. 8, 49). The other literally means *thrown*, cast, with the accessory ideas of being cast down, cast out, or cast about (scattered). The two together are intended to express the wretched state of sheep without a shepherd. At a later period, under similar impressions made by a great representative multitude, our Lord began immediately to teach them (Mark 6, 34), showing what he reckoned their most urgent want, and also that although it was his miracles of healing that had prompted them to follow him (John 6, 2), they were not without some just view of the intimate relations of his wonders to his doctrines, or at least not unwilling to receive instruction from the same lips which commanded with authority the most malignant demons and diseases.

37. Then saith he unto his disciples, The harvest truly (is) plenteous, but the labourers (are) few.

Then, at that time, upon that particular occasion, when he thus felt particularly moved with compassion, as described in the preceding verse. *Saith he*, he says, the graphic present, calling up the scene as actually passing, but referring to the same time as the aorist in v. 36, and not to the whole period embraced in the imperfect tense of v. 35. *His disciples*, those acknowledging him as a teacher, or perhaps more definitely, those who now attended him from place to place. (See above, on 5, 1. 8, 21. 23, 25. 9, 10. 11. 14. 19). Our Lord's authority and independence as a teacher, are evinced by his mastery of figurative language and his freedom from rhetorical preciseness as to change and mixture in his illustrations. What had just been represented as a flock of sheep without a shepherd, is now set before us as a harvest perishing for want of reapers. The previous context leaves no doubt that these expressions are to be applied, like those before them, to the crowds or multitudes of people who were dying without faithful spiritual guides and comforters. The specific thoughts suggested by the image of a harvest, as distinct from that of sheep without a shepherd, are those of [value], great abundance, waste, and loss, unless prevented by a timely ingathering to a place of safety. (See below, on 13, 30, and compare 1 Cor. 3, 9.) The sentence has the balanced form so common in Greek prose, the antithesis being marked by the corresponding particles, *indeed* (μὲν) and *but* (δέ). The first expresses a concession or admission, 'it is true, the harvest is abundant, but of what avail is that, if there are not enough to reap it?' The *few labourers* must not be understood too strictly as referring to our Lord and his immediate followers, though they are certainly included and particularly meant, but under a description of much wider application, and denoting all who could be figuratively represented as engaged in watching and securing the Lord's spiritual harvest.

38. Pray ye therefore the Lord of the harvest, that he will send forth labourers into his harvest.

This verse prescribes the remedy or cure of the great evil which had moved our Lord's compassion. There must be more labour brought to bear upon the harvest, i. e. more extensive human agencies employed in saving those who were now perishing, not among the heathen, but the Jews themselves, the chosen people, the theocracy, the church of God. This additional labour must be looked for not from strangers or intruders, but from *the Lord of the harvest*, its proprietor, its owner, him to whom it rightfully belongs and who is able to control it at its pleasure. This description, although really and specially appropriate to Christ himself, was not in the first instance so understood, or meant to be so understood by his disciples. It was a part of his humiliation, that many things, which he might have said directly of himself, he said as of another, or as here of God without respect to his own Godhead. The assistance of this great Proprietor could only be obtained by prayer, the warrant and encouragement for which had been so powerfully set forth in the Sermon on the Mount (7, 7–11). The verb here used originally means to *need* or *want*; and then, like the latter verb in English, to feel the necessity, to *desire*, and lastly, by a no less natural transition, to express that feeling by request, to *pray*, which is its only use in the New Testament, where it is confined, with this exception, to the dialect of Paul and Luke. The last clause gives the subject or the burden of the prayer enjoined. *Send forth*, is in Greek much stronger, meaning literally *cast* (or *drive*) *out*, as in v. 25, and frequently applied to the expulsion of intrusive demons, whereas here it signifies an earnest, prompt, authoritative mission of new labourers, by the great proprietor or owner, *into his own harvest*, which as such may claim to be protected and provided for. Wiclif's translation of these two verses is an interesting specimen of English. "Soothly (truly) there is much ripe corn but few workmen : therefore pray ye the Lord of the ripe corn, that he send workmen into his ripe corn."

CHAPTER X.

HAVING described our Lord's ministry in general terms (iv, 23–25), and then exemplified its two great functions by select examples of his teaching (v–vii) and his miracles (viii–ix), the evangelist now prosecutes his task by recording the organization of the twelve apostles, and the instructions under which they acted (x). We have first their general commission (1) and their names (2–4); then particular directions as to their immediate mission (5–15); and then a premonition of the treatment which awaited them thereafter, with appropriate instructions and encouragements (16–42). The last and largest portion of the chapter is peculiar to this gospel; the others are found both in Mark (vi) and Luke (ix). The position of this narrative is rather historical than chronological, that is to say, the writer's purpose is not simply to record certain incidents or acts in the order of their actual occurrence, but to present another striking feature in the ministry of Christ, to wit, the steps which he took towards the re-organization of the church, though not to be immediately accomplished by himself on earth for reasons which have been already given. (See above, p. 93.) These preparatory steps were first, the promulgation of the principles, on which his kingdom was to be established and administered; and secondly, the preparation of the men by whom it should be formally erected; which last is the subject of this chapter.

1. And when he had called unto (him) his twelve disciples, he gave them power (against) unclean spirits, to cast them out, and to heal all manner of sickness and all manner of disease.

Besides continuing his own itinerant ministry, our Lord now takes another step of great importance, by actually sending out the twelve whom he had previously chosen for the twofold purpose of being with him as disciples and going forth from him as apostles (4, 18. Mark 3, 14). It should be observed, however, that the mission here recorded was not the permanent and proper apostolic work, for which they were not qualified until the day of Pentecost (Luke 24, 49. Acts 1, 41), but a temporary and preliminary mission, to diffuse still more extensively the news of the Messiah's advent and the doctrine of his kingdom, attested by the same credentials which he bore himself. *Power*, i. e. derivative or delegated power, *authority*, conferred by a superior, not to be employed promiscuously or at random, but so as to promote the end for which it was bestowed. *Power of unclean spirits*, i. e. relating to them, and by necessary implication, *over* them, which is not expressed, however, but suggested by the context. *Unclean* is added as a qualifying term, because the noun includes all spirits, good and evil, whereas they were to have power only over fallen angels. Here, as elsewhere, the evangelists give special prominence to such dispossessions as the most extraordinary miracles of healing, and as such representing all the rest which were equally included in this apostolical commission, as expressed in the other clause. To *cast*, or more exactly, *so as to cast*, defining the indefinite expression, *power over unclean spirits*. It formed, as we have seen, no part of our Lord's personal errand upon earth to reorganize the Church, as this change was to rest upon his own atoning death as its foundation. For the same reason, he did not develop the whole system of Christian doctrine, but left both these tasks to be accomplished after his departure, yet preparing the way for both, by teaching the true nature of his kingdom, and by training those who should complete the Church, both as to its organization and its creed. This preparatory process was a very gradual one, as we learn from the occasional and incidental statements of the history, which nowhere gives us a connected and complete account of it. The first step which we can trace is his reception of two of John's disciples, first as guests or visitors, and then no doubt as friends and pupils, but as yet without requiring their continual attendance on his person (see John 1, 35–40). One of these two we know to have been Andrew (ib. 41), and the other is commonly believed to have been John the son of Zebedee, who never names himself in his own gospel. In pursuance of the Saviour's plan, each of these two introduced a brother (Simon and James). A fifth, directly called by Christ himself, was Philip (John 1, 44), who in his turn brought Nathanael, recognized by Jesus as an Israelite indeed, in whom there was no guile (John 1, 48), that is to say, a genuine, sincere adherent of the old theocracy, according to its true design and import as a preparation for Messiah's reign, and therefore ready to acknowledge him as soon as he should give some proof of his Messiahship (John 1, 49. 50). A seventh, called immediately by Christ himself, was Levi or Matthew (see above, on 9, 9). As the history of all these calls is only incidental, we may argue by analogy from one to the other, and as those first mentioned seem to have continued in their former occupations some time after their first introduction to their Master, it is not unlikely that the same happened in the other cases, though the writer's plan did not require it to be expressly mentioned. We have then two successive and distinct steps in the process of preparing men to organize the Church; first the personal vocation of at least seven persons into Christ's society, as friends and pupils; then a second call to constant personal attendance. The third step is that recorded here, to wit, the more formal designation of twelve persons to the Apostolic office. As we know that at least half of these had been previously called, and at least one fourth of them at two distinct times, it is highly probable that a like intimation had been given to the remaining six or seven. It would then be true of all, as it certainly is of those referred to, that the choice or calling here described did not take them by surprise, but merely carried out a purpose previously made known to them. Mark connects this designation of the twelve with the immense concourse just described, but only by juxtaposition, without any express specification of time. Luke (6, 12) does indicate the time, but very vaguely (*in these days*), and Matthew omits all mention of the twelve until he comes to their actual entrance on their work, which is a fourth stage in this gradual preparatory process. What is here described is neither the original vocation of the individual Apostles, nor their final going forth in that capacity, but the intermediate step of publicly embodying or organizing those who had been previously chosen one by one, or two by two, that they might now, as a collective body, be prepared for active service. This view of the matter is entirely consistent with Luke's statement that he chose them now (Luke 6, 13), for this was not an act that could not be repeated, and with Mark's (3, 13), that *he called to him whom he would*, which only excludes self-choice and popular election, but not a previous designation on his own part.

2. Now the names of the twelve apostles are these; The first, Simon, who is called Peter, and Andrew his brother; James (the son) of Zebedee, and John his brother;

We have four independent lists of the Apostles in the New Testament, differing chiefly in the order of the names, but also as to several of the names themselves. One of these catalogues is given here by Matthew, one by Mark (3, 16-19), and the remaining two by Luke (6, 14-16. Acts 1, 13). Bengel was probably the first to observe that although the arrangement of the names is so unlike in these four documents, the variation is confined to certain limits, as the twelve may be divided into three quaternions, which are never interchanged, and the leading names of which are the same in all. Thus Peter is invariably the first, Philip the fifth, James the ninth, and Iscariot the last, except in Acts, where his name is omitted on account of his apostasy and death. *Simon called* or *surnamed Peter.* We learn from John (1, 43), that the change of name was made at Simon's first introduction to the Saviour. But there is no improbability in the supposition that the words were repeated upon this, as they were upon a subsequent occasion (see below, on 16, 18). The name does not denote constancy or firmness, which were not peculiar traits of Peter's character, but strength and boldness, or the founding of the church upon a rock, as taught in the last cited words of Matthew. The new name did not wholly supersede the old one, as in the case of Saul and Paul (Acts

13, 9); for we find the latter still employed by Christ himself (see Mark 14, 37, and compare below 16, 16. 17. 17, 25. Luke 22, 31. John 21, 16. 17), as well as by the other Apostles (Luke 24, 34. Acts 15, 14). Throughout the Gospel of John (6, 8. 68, &c.) and in the opening words of Peter's second epistle, both names are combined. The place assigned to Peter, in all the lists of the Apostles and expressly here, is not fortuitous, nor founded simply on his being one of those first called; for Andrew then would take precedence of him. That it does not, on the other hand, imply a permanent superiority of rank or office may be argued from the fact that no such primacy is anywhere ascribed to him; that he was frequently betrayed into the gravest errors, both of judgment and of practice, and repeatedly rebuked with great severity by Christ himself; and lastly, that he alone of the eleven went so far as to deny his Master, and continued under the reproach of that apostasy until the risen Saviour condescended to restore him (John 21, 15–17). His true historical position is that of spokesman to the college of Apostles, like the foreman of a jury or the chairman of a large committee. This place was not assigned him for his own distinction, but for the convenience of his Master and his brethren, in whose name and behalf he often speaks, and is addressed in turn. He was qualified for the position, not by any moral superiority, but by his forwardness of speech and action, often accompanied by rashness and inconstancy of temper. Even after the effusion of the Holy Spirit, which corrected and subdued these constitutional infirmities, we find some trace of them in Peter's course at Antioch, reproved by Paul, and recorded in Gal. 2, 11–14. *James* and *John*, whose call has been already mentioned in 4, 21. 22. We here learn the name of their father, whom they then left with the hired men in the boat. James is described as the son of Zebedee, and John as the brother of James, apart from whom he is never mentioned. This is the more remarkable as James was the first and John the last of the Apostles who died. James was also the first martyr of the apostolic body (see Acts 12, 2). These illustrious brothers Mark puts next to Peter, whose own brother Andrew is thereby transferred to the fourth place; whereas Matthew names the two pairs of brothers in the order of their previous vocation as recorded in 4, 18. 21. Luke adopts the same arrangement in his gospel (6, 14), but in Acts (1, 13) agrees with Mark's.

3. Philip, and Bartholomew; Thomas, and Matthew the publican; James (the son) of Alpheus, and Lebbeus, whose surname was Thaddeus;

One observable distinction between Mark's and Matthew's lists of the Apostles is, that the latter arranges them in pairs throughout, while the former enumerates them singly, *and* being inserted between every two names. Such points of difference, however unimportant in themselves, are not without their value as proofs of distinct and independent origin, excluding the hypothesis of mere transcription or abridgment. *Andrew* and *Philip* are old Greek names, the former being found in Herodotus, and the latter everywhere in ancient history. These Apostles probably had Hebrew names besides, which had been gradually superseded by the Greek ones. It was very common for the Jews of that age to have double names, one native and one foreign. (Compare Acts 1, 22. 9, 36. 12, 12. 13, 1. 9.) Andrew and Philip were among the earliest of Christ's disciples. Andrew having previously followed John the Baptist, by whom he was led to Jesus as the Lamb of God, and not only followed him, but brought his brother Simon (Peter) to him (John 1, 41–43). Philip was called by Christ himself the next day, as he was about to remove from Judea into Galilee. Philip, though he seems to have been called in Judea, was a Galilean and a townsman of Andrew and Peter (John 1, 44. 45). He was himself the introducer of Nathanael, upon whom our Lord pronounced so high a commendation (John 1, 48), but who never afterwards appears by that name until after the resurrection, when we find him in company with four, and probably with six of the Apostles (John 21, 2). This has led to the not improbable conclusion that Nathanael was the person called *Bartholomew*, in all the lists of the Apostles, and in three of them placed next to Philip (compare Mark 3, 18. Luke 6, 14), while the fourth only introduces Thomas between them (Acts 1, 13). Nathanael was a resident of Cana in Galilee, the scene of Christ's first miracle (John 2, 1. 4, 46. 21, 2). *Matthew*, whose previous vocation is recorded in 9, 9. (Luke 5, 27), where he is called Levi; but he calls himself Matthew, in describing that event, and adds *the publican*, omitted by the others. *Thomas* was also called *Didymus*, the two names being Aramaic and Greek synonyms, both meaning a *twin*. Besides the lists of the Apostles, Thomas is named eight times in the Gospel of John (11, 16. 14, 5. 20, 24–29. 21, 2). *James* (*the son*) *of Alpheus*, as the ellipsis is no doubt to be supplied. The latter seems to be a Greek modification of an Aramaic name, of which *Clopas* (John 19, 25), is supposed to be another form. Now, as Clopas was the husband of the Virgin Mary's sister (John 19, 25), his son would be the cousin of our Lord, and might, according to a common Hebrew idiom, be called his brother. (See below on 13, 55, and compare Gal. 1, 19). *Thaddeus* occurs also in Mark 3, 18; it is given as the surname of *Lebbeus*, a name only mentioned here. But as both evangelists omit the name of *Judas* (*not Iscariot*, John 14, 22), which is given by Luke (6, 16. Acts 1, 13), it seems to follow that this Judas, Thaddeus, and Lebbeus were one and the same person. Some suppose the last two names to be synonymous, because derived from Hebrew or Aramaic words, meaning *heart* and *breast;* but this is doubtful. Luke describes him in both places as (*the son*) *of James*, if the ellipsis be supplied as in the case of *James* (*the son*) *of Alpheus*, or (*the brother*) *of James*, as most interpreters explain it and refer it to the James just mentioned. Judas may then be identified with Jude, the brother of the Lord, and the author of the short epistle near the end of the New Testament canon (see below, on 13, 55, and compare Jude, v. 1).

4. Simon the Canaanite, and Judas Iscariot, who also betrayed him.

Simon the Canaanite, not an inhabitant of Canaan (Cranmer), or of Cana (Tyndale), both which would be written otherwise in Greek, but a Zealot, as it is explained by Luke (6, 15. Acts 1, 13), and as the name itself, according to its Hebrew etymology, would signify. It may be descriptive of his personal character and temper, but much more probably of his connection with the sect or party of the Zealots, as fanatical adherents to the Jewish institutions and opponents of all compromise with heathenism, who assumed the right of executing summary justice after the example of Phineas (Numb. 25, 7. Ps. 106, 30), and by their sanguinary excesses caused or hastened the destruction of Jerusalem. To this party, of which traces may be elsewhere found in the New Testament (see below, on 27, 16, and compare Acts 23, 12), Simon may have been attached before he was named as an apostle. The juxtaposition of his name with those of James and Jude (see Luke, 6, 15. Acts 1, 13), exhibits a coincidence with 13, 55, which can hardly be fortuitous, and naturally leads to the conclusion that this Simon was also one of our Lord's brethren. *Iscariot* has been variously explained as an appellative, but is now commonly agreed to be a local name, denoting *man of Kerioth*, as the similar form *Istobos*, used by Josephus. means a *man of Tob*. As Kerioth was a town of Judah (Josh. 15, 25), Judas is the only one of the Apostles whom we have any reason to regard as not a Galilean. *Also*, i. e. besides being an Apostle, or although he was one, which was a fearful aggravation of his guilt. (See below on 26, 47, and compare Acts 1, 17. 25). *Betrayed*, though necessarily implied, is not the exact import of the verb, which simply means to give up or deliver into the power of another, by judicial process (see above, on 5, 25. 18, 34), or by recommendation to his favour. (Acts 14, 26. 15, 40.) But its constant application to the act of Judas in betraying Christ, has given it a secondary sense equivalent to the stronger terms employed by Luke (*betrayer, traitor*). The choice of this man to be one of the immediate followers of Christ, with perfect knowledge of his character and foresight of his treason (John 6, 64. 70. 71), is undoubtedly surprising, and at variance with the course which human wisdom would have marked out. But the foolishness of God is wiser than men (1 Cor. 1, 25), and it may have been a part of the divine plan to illustrate by the history of Judas the sovereignty of God in choosing even his most honoured instruments, without regard to any merit of their own, as well as to forewarn the church that absolute purity, although to be desired and aimed at, cannot be expected even in her highest places during her militant condition, or at least to guard her against terror and despair, when such defections do occur, by constantly reminding her that of the twelve whom Christ selected to be with him and to go out from him (Mark 3, 14), one was declared by himself to be a "devil," and a "son of perdition.' (John 6, 70. 17, 12.)

5. These twelve Jesus sent forth, and commanded them, saying, Go not into the way of the Gentiles, and into (any) city of the Samaritans enter ye not:

6. But go rather to the lost sheep of the house of Israel.

Their original commission was not ecumenical or catholic, but strictly national and theocratical, because the Christian church was to be founded on the Jewish. *Charging*, a Greek word primarily used of a military watchword or countersign, and therefore specially appropriate in this place, where the twelve are for the first time going forth as representatives and aids to their great leader. *The way of the Gentiles* is paraphrased by Tyndale, *the ways that lead to the Gentiles*. The Samaritans are added as half-heathen, or as the connecting link between the Jews and Gentiles. They were a mixed or as some suppose a purely heathen race, introduced by the Assyrians to supply the place of the ten tribes (2 Kings 17, 24), and afterwards partially assimilated to the Jews (ib. 25–41) by the reception of the law of Moses, and the professed worship of Jehovah on Mount Gerizim, involving a rejection of the sanctuary at Jerusalem, from the rebuilding of which, after the Babylonish exile, they were excluded by the restored Jews (Ezra 4, 1–3). At the time of the advent they were expecting the Messiah, but only, it should seem, in his prophetic character (John 4, 25), for which reason, and because of their entire segregation from the Jews (John 4, 9), our Saviour did not scruple to avow his Messiahship among them (John 4, 26. 29. 42), and to gather the first fruits of an extra-judaic church (ib. 39), with the promise of a more abundant harvest to be reaped by his apostles (ib. vs. 35–38). Of this promise the fulfilment is recorded in the eighth chapter of Acts; but as yet the apostles were restricted to the Jews. *Lost sheep*, wandering without a shepherd, in allusion to the figurative terms of 9, 36. *House of Israel*, family of Jacob, his descendants in the aggregate, considered as the chosen people, and represented by the whole tribes of Judah and Levi, with such members of the rest as had been incorporated with them. *A city of the Samaritans*, in striking contrast with the fact recorded in Acts 8, 5, where a kindred phrase is used (*a city of Samaria*) as if to show that the restriction here imposed had been removed by Christ's ascension and the giving of the Holy Ghost.

7. And as ye go, preach, saying, The kingdom of heaven is at hand.

The first word in Greek is the participle of the verb in the preceding verse—*go* . . . . *and going*, for the very purpose, and not as a mere incidental thing, which may be the idea suggested to some readers by the common version (*as ye go*). *Preach*, proclaim, announce, as in

3, 1. 4, 17. 23. The subject-matter of the proclamation is the same too as in Christ's first preaching, namely, the approach of the Messiah's kingdom. This confirms what has been already said, that the original or primary mission of the twelve was a preparatory one, not only restricted to the Jews, but even with respect to them intended mainly to arouse attention and prepare the way for more explicit teaching.

8. Heal the sick, cleanse the lepers, raise the dead, cast out devils : freely ye have received, freely give.

This verse describes the miraculous credentials by which their commission was to be attested. It gives the very words of the commission which had been described in v. 1. The acts commanded are the same which have already been repeatedly ascribed to Christ himself. (See above, 4, 23. 8, 16. 9, 35.) It is therefore a formal delegation of his own extraordinary powers to the twelve for a limited time and a specific purpose. It is also tacitly restricted by a reference to the circumstances under which they were to exercise these powers, namely, so far as they had occasion or were divinely guided. *Raise the dead* may, therefore, be a license which they never used, at least on this first mission, though the silence of the record as to such resuscitations, if they did take place, is easily explained by the consideration that the Gospel is the Life of Christ and not of his apostles, who are only introduced at all in order to complete his history. The words in question are omitted in most uncial manuscripts, while others place them before *cleanse the lepers*. *Freely* is properly an adjective meaning *gratuitous*, but like μακράν in 8, 30, used as an adverb, corresponding to the Latin *gratis*, which is actually introduced here by the Rhemish version. This last clause is a necessary caution against all mercenary selfish use of their extraordinary powers, which were not their own but merely lent for the good of others.

9. Provide neither gold, nor silver, nor brass in your purses ;

To their main commission is now added a special charge in reference to two points, their equipment for the journey, and their conduct towards the people with whom they came in contact. *Provide*, acquire, get (as in the margin of the English Bible). The idea of money is expressed by naming the three metals, of which it was then, as now, composed ; viz., gold, silver, and copper, which is the true sense of the word translated *brass*, an English term denoting the alloy of zinc and copper, which is said to have been unknown to the ancients, whereas that of tin and copper, commonly called *bronze*, was extensively employed, especially in works of art, and sometimes designated by the very word here used. *In your purses*, literally, *into your girdles*, the construction implying previous insertion, and the whole phrase a custom, still prevailing in the east, of using the belt which keeps the flowing dress together as a purse or pocket. Horace and Livy speak of money in the girdle, and Plutarch combines the very two Greek words employed by Matthew.

10. **Nor scrip for (your) journey, neither two coats, neither shoes, nor yet staves: for the workman is worthy of his meat.**

Not a scrip, an old word answering to bag, sack, wallet, used for carrying provisions. They were to take no such convenience with them *into the road*, or on their journey. *Nor two coats*, tunics, shirts, the inner garment of the oriental dress, worn next the skin and reaching to the knees. (See above, on 5, 40.) The thing prohibited is not the coat itself, but the additional supply or change of raiment. The idea of duplicity or plurality is probably to be extended to *shoes* or *sandals* (see above on 3, 11) and *staves*, as meaning extra or additional articles of that kind. The ground of these prohibitions is by no means an ascetic rigour, but the hurried nature of their errand, and the certainty that all their wants would be supplied by those who received their message and acknowledged their commission. *Worthy of*, entitled to, *his meat*, in the wide old English sense of *food* or, as the Greek word strictly denotes, *nourishment*. (See above, on 3, 4. 6, 25.) The meaning of the clause is that there could be no need of additional provision for their journey, since they were going forth as labourers (with obvious allusion to 9, 37), and as such would of course be fed by those among whom and for whom they laboured.

11. **And into whatsoever city or town ye shall enter, inquire who in it is worthy; and there abide till ye go thence.**

What is here said is explanatory of the charge immediately preceding. They had no need of luggage or provisions because they would be hospitably entertained at every stopping place. *Into whatever city or village*, i. e. large or small town, in the proper English (not New England) sense of that term. *Ye may go in*, a contingent form implying that he left the precise route or itinerary to their own discretion. *Inquire*, a stronger word in Greek, denoting a laborious searching out or discovery of the truth. *In it*, i. e. in the town, whether city or village. *Worthy*, entitled by his character and hospitable habits to be the entertainer of Christ's messengers. *There*, in the house thus pointed out or ascertained as the proper place of their abode. *Abide*, not in the modern sense of permanently dwelling, but in the vaguer one of staying or remaining, without reference to time. *Thence*, not from the house, but from the town or neighbourhood. The meaning of this charge is that, although they would be cheerfully received and entertained wherever there were true disciples, they must give no unnecessary trouble and attract no unnecessary notice by removals from one dwelling to another in the same place. (Compare Luke 10, 7.) They were not to be received as visitors but messengers or heralds, and must be content with what was absolutely requisite for their subsistence.

12. And when ye come into a house, salute it.

We have here more particularly stated than in either of the other gospels the precise mode in which the twelve were to take possession of their temporary homes. *When ye come* might be more exactly rendered *coming* (or *going*), i. e. in the very act of entering. *An house* should be *the house*, as the reference is specific and direct to the particular house ascertained and chosen in accordance with the previous directions (in v. 11). *Salute it,* greet it, a Greek word properly expressive of the welcome given to a person on his arrival, but here, by a natural inversion, used to denote the expression of a kindly feeling by the new-comer to his place of entertainment, and virtually therefore to his entertainers, though we need not formally assume a figurative substitution of the house for its inhabitants. The spirit of the precept is, express your good-will at the time of your arrival, and do not take possession of your quarters with a cold indifference, much less with an arrogant assumption of a right which does not really belong to you.

13. And if the house be worthy, let your peace come upon it: but if it be not worthy, let your peace return to you.

This sentence seems designed to obviate a silent or expressed objection on the part of the disciples, who might naturally feel unwilling to commit themselves by such a salutation till they knew by experiment how they would be received. 'But what if the house should prove unworthy, an unfit place even for our temporary residence?' The answer is that even in the case supposed, nothing would be lost by first saluting it. If the greeting did not profit those for whom it was intended, it would profit those who gave it. *Peace* means the peace which they had wished it, in allusion to the customary oriental form of salutation both in earlier and later times, namely, Peace be to you (or upon you). The *salaam alaikom* of the modern Arab is identical in letter and in spirit with the *shalom lakem* of the old Hebrew.* The future form adopted by the Vulgate, Luther, Tyndale, and some other versions (*shall come, shall return*), though really implied in the original, falls short of its full import. The imperative or hortatory form, correctly rendered in our Bible (*let your peace come, let your peace return*), conveys the additional idea, not suggested by the future, that they ought to let it be so, or consent to the result whatever it

---

* See Gen. 43, 23. Judges 6, 23. 19, 20. 1 Chron. 12, 18, and compare particularly 1 Sam. 25, 6 and Ps. 122, 7. 8.

might prove. 'Instead of anxiously withholding the expression of your good-will till you know how it will be received, impart it freely; and if they respond to it, let them enjoy the blessing you have called down on them; if they slight it or reject it, be content with having brought a blessing on yourselves by showing such a spirit and obeying my express command.' This explanation seems to agree better with the strong and positive expression, *let it turn back to you* (or *upon yourselves*), than the negative interpretation, 'let it be recalled, or consider it as unsaid.' There may be an allusion to the similar expression in Ps. 35, 13, as interpreted traditionally and no doubt correctly by the Jewish doctors.

14. And whosoever shall not receive you, nor hear your words, when ye depart out of that house or city, shake off the dust of your feet.

The foregoing directions presupposed that they would everywhere be well received; but they are now prepared to meet with marked exceptions, not in families or houses merely, but in towns and whole communities (Luke 9, 5). This we know was the experience of our Lord himself (see above on 8, 34, and compare Luke 9, 53), and he instructs the twelve how to act in all such cases. *Whosoever shall not receive you*, not as guests merely, but as teachers, *neither hear you*, speaking in my name, by my authority, and of my kingdom. *When ye depart*, or more exactly, *going out*, i. e. immediately when thus rejected. *Shake off* is the expression used by Luke (9, 5), whereas that of Mark (6, 11) and Matthew strictly means to *shake out*, though descriptive of the same act. *Dust* is also the expression used by Luke, while the one employed by Mark means strictly *earth* thrown up from any excavation, but appears to have acquired in the later Greek the sense of loose earth or flying dust. *Of your feet*, a supplementary specification, meaning that which adheres to the feet in walking. The act enjoined is a symbolical one, meaning that they would not even let the dust of the places where these people lived adhere to them, much less consent to come in contact with themselves, in other words, that they renounced all intercourse with them forever. The same essential meaning was expressed by the kindred act of shaking the garments. That both were practised by the apostles, even after Christ's ascension, we may learn from Paul's example at Antioch and Corinth (Acts 13, 51. 18, 6). The ancient Jews are said to have adopted the same method on returning to the Holy Land from foreign countries, to denote that they desired to abjure and leave behind all that cleaved to them of heathenism. In the case before us, it was reciprocal rejection of those by whom they were themselves rejected.

15. Verily I say unto you, It shall be more tolerable for the land of Sodom and Gomorrah in the day of judgment, than for that city.

The meaning of this verse is that the guilt of those who thus deliberately rejected Christ when offered to them was incomparably greater than the most atrocious sins of those who had enjoyed no such advantage. The case of Sodom and Gomorrah (Gen. 18, 20. 19, 24. 25) is a standing type in Scripture, both of aggravated sin and fearful retribution (Deut. 29, 23. Isai. 13, 19. Jer. 49, 18. 50, 40. Amos 4, 11). The threatening here implied, if not expressed, has reference to the last appeal which Christ was now about to make, the farewell offer of himself and his salvation, by the aid of the apostles to the whole population of the country, or at least of Galilee, before the days of his assumption should be filled and his face set for the last time towards Jerusalem (Luke 9, 51).

16. Behold, I send you forth as sheep in the midst of wolves: be ye therefore wise as serpents, and harmless as doves.

A question of some difficulty here arises, as to the connection of this verse with the foregoing context. The obvious and natural presumption is that it simply continues Christ's discourse at the first sending forth of the apostles, and that the remainder of the chapter, like the former part, refers directly to their original and temporary mission. But on looking at the passage in detail, we find some things which scarcely admit of such a reference, especially the warning against persecution which runs through the whole, and which was never realized till after the close of our Lord's personal ministry. This seems to point to the conclusion, that the charge relating to the first mission ends with the preceding verse, and that the one before us is the opening of a more general and prospective charge relating to their subsequent apostolical labours. This view of the connection is recommended, first, by its removing the apparent anachronism or incongruity already mentioned; then, by the slight but obvious appearance of a fresh start or a new beginning in the first words of this verse; and lastly, by the otherwise inexplicable fact, that neither Mark nor Luke records this latter charge, a circumstance which seems to favour the opinion that it was delivered on a different occasion, and only added here by Matthew, in accordance with his topical arrangement, to complete the history of the apostolical organization. But this, however probable, is not a necessary supposition, as the verse before us may be merely the transition from the immediate to the ulterior instruction of the twelve. *Behold* is then the mark of this transition, calling attention, as usual, to something new and unexpected. *I*, being expressed in Greek without grammatical necessity, must be emphatic and suggestive of the high authority by which they were commissioned. *Send you forth* is more significant in Greek, because the verb is that from which *apostle* is derived, and may, therefore, be regarded as equivalent to saying, 'I ordain (or constitute) you my apostles.' According to the view of the connection just presented, this expression may be still further amplified and paraphrased as follows: 'But your work is not to end with this immediate proclamation of the kingdom and the miracles attesting it. Behold, I have commissioned you as permanent apostles, to re-organize the church and to complete the revelation of its doctrine; and I now proceed to warn you of the treatment which you may expect, and of the conduct which you are to hold not merely now, but when I shall be taken from you.' The first fact stated, in the execution of this plan, is that the world would be their enemy, and that this relation would require peculiar qualities on their part. These ideas are expressed by figures borrowed from the animal creation, four species being mentioned, one to represent their enemies and three themselves. It is worthy of remark, too, even if fortuitous, that the symbols are borrowed from the three great classes of beasts, birds, and reptiles, and that both the familiar subdivisions of the first class (wild and tame) are represented. The contrast in the first clause is identical with that in 7, 15, *sheep* and *wolves* being specified as natural enemies, but here with special stress upon the circumstance that one is helpless and the other cruel. At the same time, the use of the term *sheep*, as usual, suggests the idea of comparative worth or value, and of intimate relation to the shepherd or proprietor. With due regard to these distinct aspects of the images here presented, the essential meaning of the clause, divested of its figurative dress, is, that he commissioned them, as his own cherished followers and servants, to go forth unarmed, and in themselves entirely helpless, in the midst of powerful and cruel foes. The last clause states the duty thence arising, and the means of security amidst such perils. *Therefore*, because you are so precious, yet so helpless, and because your enemies are so superior in strength and malice. *Be ye* is in Greek much more expressive, meaning properly, *become ye*, or begin to be,* implying the necessity of change to make them what they were not by nature or by habit. The contrast here is not, as in the first clause, between them and those who should oppose them, but between two different and at first sight inconsistent qualities, which they must have and exercise, in order to their safety. These were prudence or discretion, and simplicity or guilelessness of character and purpose. The idea is again conveyed by figures, and of the same kind as before; but the comparison is more explicit. In the first clause, the analogy was the familiar one between sheep and wolves, requiring no specification, as in this case, where the terms of the similitude are more unusual, and therefore, in addition to the names of the animals employed as emblems, the respective qualities denoted are expressly specified. He does not simply say, *as serpents*, but *wise as serpents*. The allusion is not merely to a popular belief, but to a well-known fact, that this part of the animal creation is peculiarly cautious in avoiding danger. It is this self-defensive and preservative faculty, and not the malignant cunning of the serpent (Gen. 3, 1), which is here presented as an emblem and a model to the twelve apostles. *Doves*, as a genus, without reference to nice zoolog-

---

* For the usage of the Greek verb (γίνομαι), see above, on 4, 3. 5, 45. 6, 16. 8, 24. 26. 9, 16.

ical distinctions, have in all ages been proverbial emblems of gentleness and innocence, especially in contrast with the sanguinary fierceness of those birds of prey by which they are persecuted and destroyed. But here a more specific sense attaches to the emblem, as suggested by the very derivation of the epithet employed, which primarily means *unmixed*, and in a moral application, free from all duplicity and disingenuous complexity of motive, corresponding thus exactly in essential meaning with the "single eye," of 6, 22. *Harmless* is therefore an inadequate and inexact translation, and the true sense given in the margin (*simple*), of the character required is not mere abstinence from injury to others, but that perfect simplicity and purity of motive, without which all the wisdom of the serpent would be unavailing.

17. But beware of men : for they will deliver you up to the councils, and they will scourge you in their synagogues.

What had just been briefly said in figurative form, is now repeated fully and in literal expressions. The wolves of the preceding verse were human wolves, and they must therefore be upon their guard against their fellow-men. *Beware of* is exactly the phrase used above in 7, 15, and there explained. *The men* is here generically used for mankind or the human race, as distinguished from the animals employed to represent them. As if he had said, 'remember that the wolves among whom I am sending you are men, and as such you must beware of them.' *Deliver you up* into the power of the magistrate by accusation and arrest, the same judicial use of the Greek verb that occurs above in 5, 25. (See also on 4, 12, and on v. 4 of this chapter.) *Into councils* (not *the councils*), the Greek word of which, *sanhedrim*, is a Hebrew or Aramaic corruption, and elsewhere applied to the supreme court or national council of the Jews, but in the plural to their local or provincial courts, the organization of which is differently stated by the ancient writers, and is wholly unimportant here, where the meaning is simply, into courts of justice, the preposition signifying not mere transfer or delivery, but introduction to their presence or arraignment at their bar. *Synagogues* might here seem to have its primary and wider sense of meetings or assemblies (see above, on 4, 23) ; but there are traces on the Jewish books of such a custom as the actual infliction of such punishments at public worship. The fulfilment of these warnings may be found recorded in the Acts of the Apostles (4, 1. 5, 17. 40. 16, 23. 22, 24).

18. And ye shall be brought before governors and kings for my sake, for a testimony against them and the Gentiles.

Governors and kings are here put for the whole class of individual rulers as distinguished from collective bodies, such as courts and councils. *For a testimony to them* (see above, on 8, 4), i. e. of the truth, and in behalf of Christ and his religion. *Against* is too specific and restricts the testimony to their unbelief and guilt; whereas it related chiefly to the truth which they rejected. *Gentiles* should here be *nations*, not only as the primary and strict sense of the Greek word (see above, on 4, 15. 6, 32), but as required by the obvious contrast between rulers and the nations over whom they ruled. The testimony thus borne was to reach not only to the head but to the body of the people.

19. But when they deliver you up, take no thought how or what ye shall speak: for it shall be given you in that same hour what ye shall speak.

20. For it is not ye that speak, but the Spirit of your Father which speaketh in you.

Such alarming premonitions required proportional encouragement; and this is here afforded in the promise of a special inspiration, to enable them to answer for themselves and for the truth when thus arraigned before judicial bodies or the masses of the people. (Compare Paul's experience of both, in Acts xxii. and xxiii.) *Take no thought* (as in 6, 25. 27. 28. 31. 34) means, be not solicitous, unduly anxious. *How* relates to the form, and *what* to the substance, of their public defences or apologies. The assistance promised should be so complete that they would be mere instruments or organs of the Spirit, who is called the Spirit of their Father, not merely as proceeding from him, but as given on account of their filial relation to God (see above, on 5, 16. 45. 48. and ch. vi. passim). This is so far from being a promise of divine assistance to unprepared and off-hand preachers, that it is not given even to the twelve indefinitely or forever, but expressly limited to one particular emergency, not only by the first words of v. 19 (*when they deliver you*), but also by the words, *in that hour*, or at that precise time (see above, on 8, 13. 9, 22). This promise gives the highest authority to all the apostolical defences upon record, and precludes the supposition of unhallowed anger in such cases as that of Paul's reply to Ananias (Acts 23, 3).

21. And the brother shall deliver up the brother to death, and the father the child : and the children shall rise up against (their) parents, and cause them to be put to death.

But, though they should be thus sustained, the trial would undoubtedly occur, and in the most distressing form, involving the dissolution of the tenderest relations. *Deliver up* is the same word and has here the same sense as in v. 17, of which this is a mere specification. The idea is not that of treachery but violence or open enmity, displayed by legal and judicial acts. The article inserted in the version weakens it. The literal translation (*brother* . . . . *brother, father* . . . . *child*) is at the same time more emphatic and impressive. *To death* suggests the thought of immediate execution; but the Greek phrase (εἰς θάνατον) that of the eventual result, or final object, as in 3, 11, *unto repentance*, i. e. with a view to it, and in v. 18 above, *for a testimony*, in all which cases the preposition is the same. There is a climax in the last clause, where the hatred just ascribed to brothers is affirmed of *children* (not *the children*) with respect to *parents* (not *their parents*.) *Shall rise up against* is a correct but feeble version of a doubly compound Greek verb (ἐπαναστήσονται), found only here and in Mark 13, 12, where the first verb is gratuitously rendered *betray*, although the original expressions are identical. *Put to death*, not directly, by killing them, but by occasioning their condemnation, to express which may have been the object of the periphrasis in the translation.

22. And ye shall be hated of all (men) for my name's sake : but he that endureth to the end shall be saved.

What had just been said in reference to the tenderest relations of domestic life is now repeated in a general and universal form, not exclusive of particular exceptions, but establishing the main fact, that the new religion was to meet with opposition, not in one place, or from one race merely, but throughout the world, because at variance with the natural corruptions of the human heart. *Of all men*, literally, *by all, men* being needlessly supplied by the translators. *For my name's sake*, on account of my name. does not mean merely for my sake or on account of me, nor even as bearing my name, or as Christians, but because of all that is denoted by that name, including his Messianic claims and his divinity, with all the sovereignty and absolute authority involved therein. The last clause shows that even this hostility would not be irresistible or necessarily destructive. *He that endureth*, not only in the sense of passively submitting to all these inflictions, but in the active one of persevering or persisting in the faith and conduct which provoke them. There is peculiar force in the aorist participle here used, *the* (one) *having endured*, i. e. the one that shall prove to have endured or persevered. *To the end*, not a fixed point but a relative expression, meaning the extreme or uttermost of the trials through which any one is called to pass. *Saved*, rescued, finally delivered from them. As this is a proverbial or aphoristic sentence, it is not surprising that our Lord should have employed it upon various occasions and in different connections, but without a change in its essential meaning (see below, on 24, 13).

23. But when they persecute you in this city, flee ye into another : for verily I say unto you, Ye shall not have

gone over the cities of Israel, till the Son of man be
come.

He now gives a particular direction how they were to exercise the
wisdom of the serpent under such distresses, namely, not by fanatically courting danger, or gratuitously staying where they could accomplish nothing, but by so far yielding to the pressure as to save their lives for future service. This is evidently not a rigid rule of uniform or universal application, but the allowance of a sound discretion. They were not to fly as soon as persecution showed itself (see Acts 8, 1. 13, 51. 18, 9. 19, 23), nor always to wait for its appearance, but to act upon the general principle of husbanding their lives and strength for the service of their master. *This city*, not the one in which he was then speaking, but any one in opposition to *another*. The meaning of the last clause seems to be that there were towns enough in Israel (or Palestine) for them to visit in succession on the principle just laid down, without ceasing wholly from their work, until the danger should be over and the kingdom of Messiah finally established. *Gone over* is a needless and enfeebling paraphrase, the true sense being given in the margin (*end* or *finish*). There is another explanation of this clause which refers it to Christ's following the twelve in their first mission, as he did the seventy (Luke 10, 1). The meaning then, is, that before they had fulfilled the task assigned them, he would be himself upon the spot to protect them or direct them further. The objection to this otherwise good sense is simply that it disregards the reasons which have been already given for considering this portion of the chapter as a subsequent or supplementary discourse relating not to the immediate mission then before them, but to later and more trying times. *Until the Son of man come*, an indefinite expression, meaning sometimes more and sometimes less, but here equivalent to saying, 'till the object of your mission is accomplished.'

24. The disciple is not above (his) master, nor the
servant above his lord.

25. It is enough for the disciple that he be as his
master, and the servant as his lord. If they have called
the master of the house Beelzebub, how much more
(shall they call) them of his household?

The object of this statement is to reconcile them to the trials just predicted, by reminding them that they were only to be sharers in the sufferings of Christ himself. Entire exemption from distress and persecution would give them an unseemly and unjust advantage over him. The sorest trials they had reason to expect would only put them on a level with him. They had every reason, therefore, to be satisfied with such companionship in sorrow. This general appeal to their affection for their master takes a more specific form in the last clause of v. 25, which gives a reason why they should especially submit to any kind or measure of misrepresentation and abuse, to wit, because this species of ill-treatment had been carried in the case of Christ himself as far as possible. The Son of God had been called Beelzebul, one of the most offensive terms that could be applied even to an idol or an imaginary being. This may either be a reference to something not recorded in the history, or to the charge of collusion with Beelzebul in working miracles recorded in ch. 12, 24 below. If the latter, which appears more probable, it furnishes another reason for believing that this last part of the chapter is of later date (see above, on v. 16). *Them of his household* corresponds to one Greek word, the nearest equivalent to which in English is *domestics,* now confined to servants, but originally signifying all the inmates of a house or members of a family.

26. Fear them not therefore: for there is nothing covered, that shall not be revealed; and hid, that shall not be known.

27. What I tell you in darkness, (that) speak ye in light: and what ye hear in the ear, (that) preach ye upon the housetops.

Here begins a positive and cheering exhortation not to be discouraged by the prospect of these trials, with a series of reasons drawn from various considerations. The first, suggested in these verses, is that this conflict with the world, however painful, was essential to the very end for which they were sent forth, and therefore could not be escaped without relinquishing the whole design. This was the promulgation of the truth or of the new religion. What they had learned of him in private was no esoteric doctrine to be cherished by a favoured few, but light to be diffused abroad for the dispelling of the universal darkness. (See above, on 5, 14–16.) This is clearly the meaning of the charge or precept in v. 27, and must therefore determine that of v. 26, which taken by itself might seem to mean that the crimes now secretly committed by the enemies of Christ and his disciples should hereafter be made public. But though the words might naturally bear this meaning, it would here be quite irrelevant, not only because this assurance was unsuited to console those who experienced or expected such ill treatment, but because the reference, throughout the passage, is not to secret but to public, and especially judicial persecution. The connection with the previous verses is not altogether clear; but on the whole, it is most probably the one already pointed out, to wit, that as the light must be diffused, and men love darkness rather than light because their deeds are evil (John 3, 19), opposition cannot be avoided without utterly abandoning the very end for which Christ came himself and sent forth his apostles.

28. And fear not them which kill the body, but are not able to kill the soul: but rather fear him which is able to destroy both soul and body in hell.

A second reason for not fearing even the most cruel and malignant human enemies, is that their power extends only to the body, leaving the nobler spiritual part, in which the personality resides, uninjured and untouched. *Soul* is the word correctly rendered *life* in 2, 20. 6, 25, but here determined to mean *soul* by the antithesis with *body*. But lest this should be understood as meaning that the soul is in no sense destructible, the last clause guards against this error, by expressly teaching that the soul may be destroyed, and that he who has the power of destroying it is properly an object of our fear. Another error here precluded is that of supposing that the body will escape in the destruction of the soul, whereas soul and body must eventually perish together. Besides this careful guarding against natural and common errors, there is great precision in the choice of terms, the term *kill* being only used in reference to the body as distinguished from the soul, while that employed in reference to the soul, even when reunited to the body, is *destroy*. *Hell*, the place of future torment. (See above, on 5, 22.) This last clause does not mean indefinitely, fear one who can do what these enemies cannot do, without implying that there is such a being. This is forbidden by the definite expression, *the* (*one*) *able*. It is a very old opinion that the person here referred to is the devil; but an exhortation to fear him would be irrelevant and out of place in this connection; and the power here ascribed to him he only possesses as an instrument or agent of the wrath of God, who must be reckoned therefore as the ultimate destroyer. The exhortation to fear him is really an exhortation to avoid displeasing him by disobedience, and is here peculiarly appropriate. As if he had said, 'instead of shrinking from your duty through fear of what these enemies can do to your bodies, be afraid of incurring God's displeasure by neglecting it.'

29. Are not two sparrows sold for a farthing? and one of them shall not fall on the ground without your Father.

A third reason for not shrinking from the execution of their great commission on account of the dangers which attended it. Not only was the power of their enemies restricted to the body, but their very bodies would be under God's protection. This is stated in a very striking form, not unlike that in 6, 26–30. Reduced to ordinary shape and order, the argument is this, that as God's protective care extends to the most insignificant and worthless of the feathered tribe, it must and does extend to man, and will especially extend to those who have been honoured with a most important mission. The actual order of these thoughts is, first, the little value of the sparrows, as indicated by the market price, two being sold for an *assarion*, a coin intermediate in value between our cent and an English penny; then the care of which they are the object. *Not one* (in opposition to the *two* of the preceding clause) *shall fall*, shall ever fall, and so by implication, can fall. There is no need of giving this the too specific meaning of falling into a snare, or of falling down dead. The idea is more general, that of any change occurring to them. *Without your father*, without his knowledge and permission. *Your father* again brings to mind their filial relation. He who thus protects the sparrows is your father.

30. But the very hairs of your head are all numbered.

31. Fear ye not therefore, ye are of more value than many sparrows.

This is a strong proverbial expression for minute knowledge and exact care. The hairs are numbered for the purpose of protection and careful preservation, so that if one be wanting, it is missed and looked for. It would be impossible to frame in human language a more forcible description of unerring oversight and sleepless care. V. 31 repeats the exhortation of v. 26, and formally propounds the reason really implied in the preceding verses, namely, the argument from less to greater, that as God takes care of sparrows, he will certainly take care of Christ's apostles.

32. Whosoever therefore shall confess me before men, him will I confess also before my Father which is in heaven.

33. But whosoever shall deny me before men, him will I also deny before my Father which is in heaven.

Another reason for discharging their commission without fear of man is, that on their fidelity in so doing must depend their treatment by the sovereign who commissioned them. *Whosoever therefore* is in Greek still stronger, *every* (one) *therefore, whosoever* (he may be), as if to cut off all exceptions to the rule here laid down. *Confess me*, literally, *in me*, which appears to be a Hebrew idiom, like the one in 5, 34. 7, 2. 6; or the preposition may indicate the subject of confession, *with respect* (or *in regard*) *to me*. The act itself is that of owning Christ as Lord and Master, with particular reference to the twelve, who were to go forth as his aids and representatives. The reciprocal act ascribed to him is that of owning as his follower, disciple, or apostle. (See above, on 7, 23, where the disowning act is itself called a confession.) *Before my father*, i. e. in heaven, not on earth; or at the final judgment; or perhaps more generally, in the most public, solemn manner. V. 33 repeats the same thing in the same words with respect to the denial or disowning of our Lord's authority by word or deed.

34. Think not that I am come to send peace on earth: I came not to send peace, but a sword.

35. For I am come to set a man at variance against his father, and the daughter against her mother, and the daughter in law against her mother in law.

36. And a man's foes (shall be) they of his own household.

Another reason for not shrinking from the fear of human opposition and divisions, is that these are not mere accidents but necessary consequences of the promulgation of the truth, and therefore to be looked for and manfully encountered by its advocates. *Think not that I came*, the same form of expression as in 5, 17, and in either case implying the existence of a disposition so to think, and act accordingly. *Send* is twice used to translate a much stronger Greek word meaning *throw* or *cast*, and here perhaps intended to suggest the idea of coercion or compulsion. 'I did not come to force men into peace and harmony.' But this can hardly be the meaning in the last clause where the same word governs *sword*. Another sense, admissible in both cases, is the figurative one of casting, violently throwing. The antithetical ideas of peace and war (or strife) are very differently expressed, the one literally, the other by a figure, but so natural and common as scarcely to be metaphorical. The reference is not to the legitimate effects of Christ's mission on the character and hearts of men, but to the abnormal consequences of their alienation and resistance. V. 35 is an amplification of the figurative term *sword*, as denoting separation and division of the tenderest relations, some of which are specified with antique and scriptural simplicity and force. The word translated *daughter-in-law* properly means *bride*, or young wife, but is here determined to a more specific sense by being placed in opposition to one meaning mother-in-law, the same that is translated *wife's mother* in 8, 14. V. 36 is a summing up of the previous details in a general declaration, that the most violent hostilities will sometimes exist within the limits of a single household, and engendered by the very cause which ought to have prevented them, and would have done so but for man's perverseness. This fearful picture has been often verified in actual experience. *A man's* should be *the man's*, i. e. those of the man who faithfully confesses Christ. *They of his own household* (the same Greek word that occurs in v. 25), namely, those just mentioned, not another class to be added to them.

37. He that loveth father or mother more than me is not worthy of me: and he that loveth son or daughter more than me is not worthy of me.

From this unavoidable division among near friends on the most important of all subjects would arise the painful necessity of choosing between them and Christ, and this would furnish an unerring test of their attachment to him, which in order to be genuine must be supreme. The principle propounded is the same with that in 9, 22, but in a form more general and absolute, as well as more explicit and unequivocal. *The (one) loving father or mother*, here correctly given as in Greek without the article (see above, on v. 21). *More than me*, literally, *above* (beyond) *me*. *Worthy of me*, i. e. fit to be my follower or disciple, much less my apostle and official representative. The same thing is then repeated as to son and daughter, the parental and filial relations, as the nearest ties of nature, being put for every other, such as those of marriage and remoter kindred.

38. And he that taketh not his cross, and followeth after me, is not worthy of me.

To the natural affections this was a hard saying, and might seem to ask too much of the disciple, since in many cases such a separation would amount to the severest punishment, and be in fact a sort of lingering death like that of crucifixion. But so far from recognizing this as an admissible objection or a valid ground of disobedience, Christ repeats it as a positive command, requiring just such crucifixion as a duty and a test of true discipleship whenever circumstances might demand it. Though the twelve may at the time have understood this merely as a beautiful allusion to the cross as an instrument of torture, or a mode of execution made familiar by its use among their Roman masters, we can now see, and they afterwards no doubt saw in it, a prophetic reference to his own death as the crown and consummation of his sufferings. He beholds himself as a convict on his way to crucifixion and his faithful followers bearing the cross after him. Whoever is not ready thus to share his sufferings, even at the cost of every natural affection, is not fit to be considered his disciple.

39. He that findeth his life shall lose it: and he that loseth his life for my sake shall find it.

A faithful acting out of the preceding requisitions might result in the loss of life itself and thus defeat the very object of discipleship. But even this extreme case obtains no relaxation of the rule already laid down. Life itself is not to be valued in comparison with faithfulness to Christ, but abandoned for the sake of it. This requisition is so utterly repugnant to the natural love of life that it might seem like exhorting men to self-destruction. In reality however it is only calling them to sacrifice a lesser for a greater good. *Lose* is a much stronger word in Greek and means *destroy*, the true antithesis to *save* in this connection. The form of the sentence is proverbial, and, as in many other cases of the same kind, uses the same word in two senses, or rather in a higher and a lower application of the same sense. *Life* is the correct translation in both clauses, but the life referred to very different. *The (one) finding his life* (i. e. his natural life, or the life of his body, for its own sake, as the highest good to be secured or sought) *will* (by that very act not only lose but) *destroy it*. He cannot perpetuate his life on earth, and by refusing to look higher, forfeits life in heaven. The converse is then stated as no less true and important. *The (one) who loses or destroys* (i. e. allows to be destroyed if needful) *his life* (in the lower sense before explained) *for my sake* (in my service and at my command), not only now while I am present upon earth, but even after my departure, for the sake of the gospel, the diffusion of the truth, and the erection of my kingdom, *he shall find his life* in losing it, or only lose it in a lower sense to save it in the highest sense conceivable. The difficulty of distinguishing precisely between life and life in this extraordinary dictum only shows that the difference is rather of degree than kind, and instead of weakening strengthens the impression.

40. He that receiveth you receiveth me ; and he that receiveth me receiveth him that sent me.

Having been led by a natural association into the previous discourse as to the test of true discipleship, our Lord reverts in conclusion to the principle laid down in vs. 24, 25, that what they did and suffered was as his representatives, and as identified with him. This is here applied to the authority with which they were to speak and act as his apostles, and the duty of receiving them as such. It is carried further than before, however, by applying the same principle to Christ's own ministry as one of delegated powers, so that they who acknowledged his apostles not only owned their commission as being sent from him, but his commission as being sent from God.

41. He that receiveth a prophet in the name of a prophet shall receive a prophet's reward ; and he that receiveth a righteous man in the name of a righteous man shall receive a righteous man's reward.

There are two interpretations of this verse and its connection with the one before it. Some regard it as a mere continuation of the promise, and the words prophet and righteous man as epithets applied to the apostles. Others make it an allusion to some well-known maxim or proverbial saying. As he that receives a prophet is to have a prophet's reward, so he that gives to drink, &c. There is also some obscurity and doubt as to the meaning of a prophet's reward and a righteous man's reward. It may mean, shall be rewarded by the prophet or the righteous man whom he receives, i. e. shall reap the benefit of so receiving him. Or it may mean, shall be regarded as possessing the same character with him whom he receives. The word *receive* is here used to translate two different Greek verbs, the one denoting active recognition, the other passive reception.

42. And whosoever shall give to drink unto one of these little ones a cup of cold (water) only in the name of a disciple, verily I say unto you, he shall in no wise lose he reward.

The most trifling acts of kindness to themselves on his account, he himself would note, and as it were acknowledge. *For whosoever shall* (whoever may) *give to drink*, a single word in Greek, analogous to our verb *to water*, but derived from the noun *drink*, and applied both to plants (by Xenophon) and to men (by Plato). From the same root comes the following noun, *cup*, or any drinking vessel, the same word that is used in Mark 7, 4. 8, and there explained. *A cup* (or *bowl*) *of water* is here mentioned as the cheapest of all bodily refreshments, and therefore suitable to represent the smallest acts of kindness done by man to man. *Verily* (Amen) *I say unto you*, implying that what follows is a certain and a solemn truth. *He shall not*, a particularly strong form of negation, being that employed in 5, 18, and there explained. *His reward*, i. e. the benefit of such regard to Christ, proved by kindness to his followers. The doctrine of legal merit is no more involved in this expression than in the many passages which teach that men are to be dealt with in proportion to their works, although salvation is entirely gratuitous.

CHAPTER XI.

It was very important, in any history of our Lord's official life, to define his position with respect to John the Baptist. This had been done, at an early period of the narrative, so far as the beginning of his ministry was concerned (4, 12), and also with respect to certain doctrines or practices of John's disciples (9, 14). But as John's life lasted longer than his ministry, and as he had some further intercourse with Christ, it was important that their mutual relation should be clearly pointed out before John's final disappearance from the scene. To do this may be fairly represented as the object of the passage comprehended in this chapter. After a sentence which is properly the close of the preceding chapter (1), we have first John's message from the prison and Christ's answer (2-6); then a discourse to the people, in which John's position is defined and his character described (7-15); then a parabolical description of the way in which their several ministries had been received (16-19). The unity of subject, and most probably of time, in this whole narrative is undisputed. Its connection with what follows, although not so obvious, is no less real. The ministry of John, though without miraculous credentials (John 10, 41), left the people inexcusable who did not receive him; how much more the ministry of Christ, with all its glorious attestations, to reject which was to court a doom beyond that of the most corrupted heathen (20–24). That any should continue blind, while others saw the great light, was a mystery of human depravity and of divine sovereignty (25–27), in view of which the Saviour earnestly and tenderly invites those groaning under legal bondage, whether ceremonial or moral, to exchange it for his salutary and delightful service (28–30).

1. And it came to pass, when Jesus had made an end of commanding his twelve disciples, he departed thence to teach and to preach in their cities.

The conventional division of the text is as injudicious here as in the case of ch. ix., and with the same effect, that of confusing the chronology by making this verse give the date or fix the time of what immediately follows; whereas it is the natural conclusion of what goes before, and the next verse opens an entirely new subject, without any mark of time whatever, and therefore without any contradiction of Luke's more chronological arrangement, which puts the message of John the Baptist early in the narrative. The verse before us is a winding up of the preceding chapter by the statement that our Lord, after organizing and commissioning the twelve, did not allow that act to interrupt his own itinerant labours, but as soon as he *finished charging or instructing* them (a military term in Greek, originally denoting the array and disposition of armed forces), *he passed on thence*, i. e. from the place where these instructions were delivered, and which cannot now be ascertained, though commonly supposed to be Capernaum or its neighbourhood. (See below, on v. 20.) The design of this departure was not rest but labour, *to teach and preach*, or, as the Greek construction necessarily suggests, (for the purpose) *of teaching and preaching*, or proclaiming and announcing the Messiah's kingdom (see above, on 3, 1. 4, 17. 23. 9, 35), *in their towns* (or *cities*), i. e. those of Galilee, the antecedent of the pronoun, although not expressed, being readily supplied from the whole preceding narrative, and more particularly from the previous descriptions of his ministry in 4, 23 and 9, 35, where the same form of expression is employed, a circumstance which shows that the writer here reverts to those descriptions of our Lord's itinerant labours, as the great theme of his narrative, which all the intervening statements were intended to illustrate and exemplify. This verse is therefore an important one, when replaced in its true position with respect to the preceding chapter, both as giving oneness and coherence to the whole composition, and as showing that, although the twelve were chosen and sent forth as aids and representatives of Christ in his announcement of the new dispensation, they were not intended to diminish, and did not in point of fact diminish in the least his own incessant and exhausting labours.

2. Now when John had heard in the prison the works of Christ, he sent two of his disciples,

The bad effect of the unfortunate division of the chapters is diminished, although not entirely removed, in the English version by the use of the word *now*, suggesting a transition, or the introduction of a new subject, though the Greek word is only the usual connective (δέ) elsewhere rendered *and* or *but*, and so translated here in all the older English versions, except Tyndale and Cranmer, who omit it altogether, making the transition still more marked and even sudden. It is very important that the reader should observe this relation of the verses, and should understand the second not as saying, that John then, i. e. after the mission and instruction of the twelve, sent two of his disciples, but that he did so once, or on a certain occasion, not exactly specified, but really anterior in date to the contents of the preceding chapter. There is nothing incorrect in this departure from the strict chronological order, or at variance with the practice of the best historians, when their purpose is not simply to detail events precisely as they happened, but to bring together illustrations and examples of some interesting topic, just as Matthew here defines our Lord's position with respect to John the Baptist, by recording facts which might have been introduced earlier or later, but are no doubt in their proper place with reference to his plan and purpose, or at least to that divine discretion in the exercise of which he placed them where they are and where we find them.* *Having heard*, through the report of his disciples (Luke 7, 18), *in the prison*, i. e. as we learn from Josephus, the fortress of Machærus on the border of Perea and the desert. The fact of John's imprisonment had been already mentioned in connection with the opening of Christ's Galilean ministry (4, 12), but without the particulars, which are given afterwards in speaking of his death (14, 3). *The works*, i. e. the miracles (Luke 7, 18), *of Christ*, not of Jesus as a private person, but *of the Messiah*, which he claimed to be, appealing to these very works in proof of his pretensions (John 10, 38. 14, 11. 15, 24). The meaning then is, that John heard in prison of miraculous performances appearing and purporting to be wrought by the Messiah. *His disciples*, those who still adhered to him after his mission had been merged in that of Christ himself, whom they refused to acknowledge as superior to John in opposition to his own most solemn declarations. (See above, on 3, 11. 14. 9, 14, and compare John 1, 20. 3, 25–30.) This fact betrays an obstinate persistency in error, inconsistent with right religious feeling, and deprives these disciples of all title to the honour which some would put upon them, as sincerely pious and as almost Christians. It also favours the opinion, which has been the common one since Hilary and Chrysostom, that this message was intended to remove their doubts, and not to satisfy

---

* Instead of *two* (δύο) the oldest manuscripts and latest critics read *through* (διά) *his disciples*, the number being known from Luke 7, 18, to which, it is supposed, the verse before us was assimilated by some ancient copyists.

the mind of John himself. There would, it is true, be no absurdity in holding that his faith was shaken for a moment in captivity, not as to the person of the true Messiah, which had been divinely indicated to his very senses (see above, on 3, 16. 17, and compare John 1, 32. 33), but as to his method of proceeding, so remote from the usages and associations of the old economy, of which John was a minister. The possibility of such misgivings is enhanced if we suppose that John's inspiration ceased with his official work for which it was intended to prepare him (Luke 1, 80. 3, 2). There is still, however, something in the tone of this inquiry, if expressive of John's own doubts, that can scarcely be reconciled with his strong and almost passionate asseverations of his own inferiority already cited. The necessity of all such undesirable assumptions is precluded by the ancient and prevailing supposition, just referred to, that the message was intended to remove the doubts of his disciples, or to bring them into contact with our Lord himself, and thus afford an opportunity of showing them the signs of the Messiah, as he actually did on this occasion. The objections to this view of the transaction, although not without weight, are entirely inconclusive. The apparent insincerity of asking such a question in his own name when he knew the truth already, may be either ascribed to the conciseness of the record, which has not preserved all the explanatory circumstances, or defended as a lawful means of bringing his disciples into contact with the object of their sceptical and envious misgivings. (See John 3, 26.) Though unwilling to resort to Christ as inquirers in their own behalf, they might consent to carry what appeared to be a challenge and expostulation from their master. There is still less force in the objection, that John would not have sent them to ask Jesus what he could have told them still more easily himself. He had already told them, but without effect, and he now wished to convince them, not by the words of Jesus merely, but by the "works of Christ."

3. And said unto him, Art thou he that should come, or do we look for another?

Said, through his messengers, a form of speech common in all languages, and throwing light upon the difference between Luke and Matthew in the case of the centurion's servant. (See above, on 8, 5.) *Art thou the (one) coming*, he whose coming has for ages been expected? This appears to have become almost a proper name of the Messiah. (See above, on 3, 11, and compare John 11, 27.) *Do we look?* is Cranmer's just correction of Tyndale's loose translation, *shall we look?* The contracted form in Greek ($\pi\rho o\sigma\delta o\kappa\tilde{\omega}\mu\epsilon\nu$) may be either subjunctive or indicative, and if the former, might be rendered *may* (or *must*) *we look?* But by far the simplest and most natural construction, and at the same time the most striking, is the usual one, *are we looking?* i. e. is it for another (not for thee) that we are looking? The phrase to *look for* is equivocal in English, being used to express the very different ideas of search and expectation. The latter predominates in early usage, and is here required by the unambiguous original. The sentence becomes still more pointed if we take another in the strong sense of the Greek word (ἕτερον), as strictly meaning of a different kind, another sort, although in general and later usage, it denotes mere numerical difference (like ἄλλος). The spirit of the question is, 'art thou indeed the Messiah, whose appearance Israel has so long expected?'

4. Jesus answered and said unto them, Go and show John again those things which ye do hear and see:

Instead of a direct and categorical reply in words, our Lord refers them to the testimony of their own senses, with a tacit reference to the prophecies which represent the Messiah as a wonder-worker (such as Isai. 35, 5. 6. 61, 1, &c.). The answer is addressed to John, from whom the question came, and therefore can determine nothing as to its true motive.

5. The blind receive their sight, and the lame walk, the lepers are cleansed, and the deaf hear, the dead are raised up, and the poor have the gospel preached to them.

This is a mere specification of *the (things) which ye hear and see*, not exhaustive but illustrative by means of a few signal instances. The raising of the dead may have been among the miracles they actually witnessed, or the reference may be to the resuscitation of the widow's son at Nain, which in Luke (7, 11–17) immediately precedes the narrative before us, and appears to be included among "all these things" which John's disciple reported to him (ib. v. 18). It is hardly natural, however, to apply the verb *hear* in v. 4 to the report of this and other miracles not actually seen by the disciples, since it rather has respect to what is mentioned in the last clause of the verse before us. *The poor are evangelized*, a most expressive phrase, which has been variously rendered: the glad tidings is preached to the poor (Tyndale)—the poor receive the gospel (Geneva)—the poor receive the glad tidings of the gospel (Cranmer)—to the poor the gospel is preached (Rheims). Wiclif's version (*poor men be taken to preaching of the gospel*) seems to be founded on Theophylact's construction of the Greek verb as a neuter or deponent not a passive; *the poor preach the gospel*, which, however, would not be insisted on as something new or strange, and is besides at variance with the obvious meaning of the prophecy referred to (see Isaiah 61, 1), where the Septuagint has the phrase (εὐαγγελίσασθαι πτωχοῖς). *Poor* is here to be taken in its pregnant and peculiar Hebrew or Old Testament meaning, as expressive, not of mere external destitution, but of that humility and sense of spiritual want which such a state often does and always should engender. (See above, on *poor in spirit*, 5, 3.)

6 And blessed is (he), whosoever shall not be offended in me.

This is a part of the reply, and not a mere reflection added to it. It states a general truth, leaving the application to the hearer or receiver. It proves nothing as to John's intention or his state of mind, which must be determined, if at all, on other grounds already mentioned. (See above, on v. 1.) The words apply to John himself, if his own faith wavered, but only upon that supposition. They are equally appropriate to his disciples, if the message was intended for their benefit. *Blessed*, truly fortunate or happy, with particular reference to the divine favour. (See above, on 5, 3.) *Whosoever*, a contingent expression, not necessarily implying that any one had actually been, but simply that some one might hereafter be *offended*, not in the popular or modern sense, *displeased*, but in the old sense, *stumbled*, made to fall, i. e. betrayed into sin and error. (See above, on 5, 29. 30.) *In me* (Geneva), not *by me* (Tyndale, Cranmer), but in reference to me as an occasion or example. (For a like use of the same preposition, compare Acts 4, 2.) This, though in form a beatitude or blessing, similar to those at the beginning of the Sermon on the Mount (5, 3–11), is, in substance and reality, a solemn warning against unbelief in the Messiahship of Jesus. At the same time, there is something truly admirable in the skill and delicacy, if we may apply such terms to the divine and gracious wisdom, with which Christ here treats the scruples and misgivings, whether of John himself or of his sceptical disciples. Without upbraiding, such as he employed soon after against open unbelievers (see below, on vs. 20–24), without even reasoning in direct opposition to the error which he has in view, he practically takes away its very basis, and benevolently warns against its ruinous results.

7. And as they departed, Jesus began to say unto the multitudes concerning John, What went ye out into the wilderness to see? A reed shaken with the wind?

Having sent this answer to John's question, he proceeds to guard against all false conclusions from it, as if John's testimony had been now retracted. This he does by showing that John was neither a capricious humourist nor a flattering parasite, but an eminent prophet, and himself a subject of prophecy, belonging indeed to the old dispensation, but the harbinger and herald of the new. *As they departed* (Tyndale), literally, *they departing*, i. e. just as they were gone or going, so as neither to appear to flatter John through his disciples, nor to leave him for a moment in a false position before the people. *Began* is not a pleonasm, but a natural expression of immediate action consequent upon another. No sooner had he finished his reply to John than he began his vindication of him. *To the multitudes* or *crowds*, not merely the great numbers, but the mixed promiscuous assemblage, in whose presence he had answered John's inquiry, and among whom there were many who might either take advantage of this message to invalidate John's well-known testimony to the Messiahship of Jesus, or be led by others into such a misconstruction of it. Here again the wisdom of the Master is conspicuous. Instead of positive assertion, he appeals to their own vivid recollections of the time, when the whole population had gone out into the wilderness adjacent to the Dead Sea and the Jordan, to see and hear the very man who now lay captive in Machærus. *What went ye out to see?* refers not so much to their previous expectation as to their actual experience, and is tantamount to saying, 'What did you see when you went out into the wilderness?' The word translated *see* is not the one commonly so rendered, but that employed in 6, 1, and denoting (as the etymon of *theatre, theatrical*, &c.) a more curious and eager gaze or contemplation. As if he had said, 'What spectacle or show did you go out to witness?' The question in the last clause is a virtual negation. 'Surely not a reed,' &c. There are two interpretations of the words themselves, one of which supposes *a reed shaken with the wind* (or more exactly, *by a wind*) to be referred to merely as an ordinary product of the desert of Judea, in one of its usual conditions. The meaning then is, that they surely had not gone out in such numbers to the wilderness merely to see its rustling reeds, which were always there and never worth seeing. It is therefore equivalent to saying, that they surely had not gone for nothing or without a motive. The objection to this explanation is, not that the sense which it affords is tame or flat, on which point tastes may naturally differ, but that it is not in keeping with the positive description in the next verse, which is evidently meant to be applied to John; and that it makes this verse irrelevant and useless as a part of our Lord's argument to prove that John's testimony to him had not been retracted or invalidated by his recent message. This required something more to sustain it than the bare fact that they went out to see something, or that John was not a mere nonentity or commonplace familiar object. It required an assertion of the fact that he was not a fickle, wavering, unstable character, who said and unsaid, or who now said one thing, now another. This is finely expressed, and in a way peculiarly adapted to impress an Oriental audience, by a figure borrowed from the very locality in question. 'When you went into the wilderness you surely did not find there one who wavered like its own reeds agitated by the wind.' With divine art he leaves them to apply the metaphor to John, who was notoriously any thing but such a reed, who on the contrary was well known to be firm, unbending, and unsparing in the work of his great office. The inference suggested, although not expressed, is that John was not the man to retract an attestation so deliberately, solemnly, repeatedly afforded. His message therefore could not be intended to invalidate his former testimony. All this is perfectly consistent with the supposition that John's question was expressive of his own misgivings, if these related only to Christ's method of proceeding, and not to his personal identity as the Messiah, of which John had been so clear and so definite a witness. At the same time, it must be admitted that the language of the verse before us, although not irreconcilable with this hypothesis, is far more favourable to the other, namely, that the message was designed to solve the doubts of those who bore it, not of John himself.

Scarcely one in a thousand of unbiassed readers would be led spontaneously to make the nice distinction between our Lord's Messiahship and Messianic working, or to understand him as admitting that John had experienced a lapse of faith as to the latter, and only denying such a lapse as to the former.

8. But what went ye out for to see ? A man clothed in soft raiment ? behold they that wear soft (clothing) are in kings' houses.

Supposing the question in v. 7 to be answered in the negative, he now puts an alternative interrogation. *But*, if not a reed shaken by the wind, *what went ye out to see*, or what did you see when you went out on that occasion ? *A man dressed in soft* (i. e. luxurious) *clothes*, the very opposite to John's dress, as described in 3, 4. That the reference, however, is not merely to ascetic and indulgent habits, is apparent from the next clause. *Behold*, an expression of surprise at the thought of finding such men in the wilderness. The place to seek them is the royal court, mentioned either in the general as the most luxurious form of human society, or with specific reference to the court of Herod. This suggests the idea of a courtier, proverbially akin to those of parasite and flatterer, a second character denied to John. As he was not a fickle changeling, blown about by every wind (Eph. 4, 14), neither was he a polite and courtly flatterer, whose testimony, given from an interested motive, was withdrawn or contradicted when that motive ceased to operate. On neither of these pretexts was there any ground for questioning the truth or the continued force of John's attestation of the claims of Jesus.

9. But what went ye out for to see ? A prophet? yea, I say unto you, and more than a prophet.

Both the foregoing questions being negatived, a third hypothesis is now presented. *But*, if not a courtier, what then ? What did you see when you went out into the wilderness? Discarding all ironical suggestions, he now anticipates the real universal answer to the question, 'We went out to see a prophet.' This he repeats in the form of an interrogation, as if about to question or deny it—' A prophet (do you say)?' but only for the purpose of a more emphatic affirmation. *Yea*, yes, most true; and what you thus say to me, *I say to you* in turn, and add to it what you cannot say with authority as I do, (*something*) *more*, literally, more abundant, more excessive than a prophet.

10. For this is (he), of whom it is written, Behold, I send my messenger before thy face, which shall prepare thy way before thee.

He was not only a prophet but a subject of prophecy, whose advent was predicted at the close of the Old Testament canon. *This is he*, or *this it is, of* (about, concerning) *whom it is written*, literally, *has been written*, in the perfect passive, a peculiarly expressive form, implying not only the existence of the passage and its ancient date, but its having been for ages upon record. (See above, on 2, 5.) We have here a most authoritative declaration as to the meaning and fulfilment of a prophecy still extant in the Hebrew text of Malachi (3, 1), and here quoted in a form varying, not only from the Septuagint version, but from the original, without change, however, of essential meaning. The words are here addressed to the Messiah himself as a pledge or promise, which though not expressed, is really implied in the original. *I send*, am sending or about to send, the verb from which *apostle* is derived, and suggesting (as in 10, 16) the idea of a public and official, not a personal or private mission. *My messenger*, the Greek word commonly translated *angel* (which is a mere abbreviation or corruption of it), but here used in its primary and wider sense. The original passage predicts the advent of two messengers or angels, the Angel of the Covenant, also represented as the Lord of the Temple, and another who was to prepare his way before him. These two are here identified, the one expressly and the other by necessary implication, with our Lord and his forerunner. *Before thy face* is not in the original; *before thee* there is literally *to my face*, in the first person. *Prepare*, an expressive Greek verb meaning to make fully ready, to equip, to furnish. *Thy way*, thy advent or appearance. The *for* at the beginning introduces this quotation as a proof that John was more than a prophet, i. e. more than any other that preceded him because standing nearest to the time of the fulfilment, and as being the immediate precursor of Messiah.

11. Verily I say unto you, Among them that are born of women there hath not risen a greater than John the Baptist : notwithstanding, he that is least in the kingdom of heaven is greater than he.

Verily, I say unto you, prepares the hearer and the reader for a still stronger statement, one that in itself might seem to savour of exaggeration, and could therefore only become credible by being uttered with divine authority. (See above, on 5, 18. 26. 6, 2. 5. 13. 16. 8, 10.) The paradoxical assertion thus enforced is, that John was not only more than a prophet, but equal to the greatest among men, not in personal qualities, however, but simply by position, from the rank assigned him in the history of the church and of the world. *There has not arisen*, or *been raised up*, called into existence (see below, on 24, 11, and compare John 7, 52). This is the first clause of the sentence in Greek and in most versions, the needless transposition in our Bible being introduced by Tyndale. *Among*, literally *in* (i. e. the number or the midst of) *the* (or *those*) *born of women*, an idiomatic phrase for mankind or the human race, the plural of one several times occurring in the book of Job.* *A greater* (*man* or *person*), or (*one*) *greater*, i. e. one more highly honoured by his relative position with respect to Christ himself. *But*, notwithstanding this exalted rank and unsurpassed pre-eminence. The superlative term *least* is one of the few groundless innovations introduced by the translators of King James's Bible, all the earlier versions, from Wiclif's to the Rhemish, having the literal translation, *less*. All that is really asserted is, that one inferior to John in some respect is greater in another. The most eminent Fathers, Greek and Latin, such as Chrysostom and Augustin, understand this of our Lord himself, who was John's inferior in the judgment of many, and really in age, to which the Greek word is frequently applied, though not in the New Testament, unless Mark 15, 40 be an instance. Thus understood, the sentence is a simple repetition of what John himself so often said, that one coming after him in time was his superior in rank and power. (See above, on 3, 11, and compare John 1, 15. 27. 30. 3, 28–31). The other and more common explanation among Protestants applies the words indefinitely to any one belonging to the kingdom of heaven, the new dispensation, or the Christian Church. The common version (*least*) supposes a comparison with other members of that body, and declares the humblest and least favoured among these to be superior in light and privilege to John the Baptist. This construction is of course preferred by those who understand the question in v. 2 to express John's own misgivings, and the verse before us to be Christ's apology or method of accounting for them, on the ground that John, with all his eminence among the prophets, was still like them of the old economy, and therefore less acquainted with the new than the weakest and most ignorant of those who had been brought into it. But not to insist upon the fact that the change of dispensations was not accomplished, and that consequently there were none of whom this could be said, this whole interpretation is at variance with the letter of the passage, which says nothing of *the least*, but only of *the less*, i. e. the less than John, unless we arbitrarily explain *the less* as meaning less than every other in the kingdom of heaven. These last words may be grammatically construed either with what follows or what goes before, 'he that is less (in the old dispensation or among the prophets) is greater in the kingdom of heaven'—or—'he that is less (i. e. younger, later) in the kingdom of heaven is greater than he.' On the whole, as *greater* refers not to age or chronological succession, but to dignity or rank, the collateral term *less* must have a corresponding import, and the most natural interpretation of the sentence is, that such would be the difference of light and privilege between the old and new economy, that one belonging to the latter, though inferior to John in every other particular, might in this, the most important, be considered greater.

12. And from the days of John the Baptist until now

* See Job 14, 1. 15, 14. 25, 4, in all which places the Septuagint version has γεννητὸς γυναικός.

the kingdom of heaven suffereth violence, and the violent take it by force.

The most probable connection here is that the eulogy on John the Baptist, interrupted by the last clause of the verse preceding, is resumed and continued by describing the effects of his ministry upon society at large. *From the days of John the Baptist*, i. e. from the time of his original appearance as a preacher of repentance and as Christ's forerunner. During this brief interval what changes had been wrought by the proclamation of Messiah's kingdom (Luke 16, 16)! The whole Jewish world had been thrown into commotion, and in spite of the resistance of its party leaders and its ruling classes, the new theocracy was welcomed by the masses, not with enthusiasm merely, but with a *furore* which could only be compared to the conquest of a kingdom by the violent irruption of a hostile army. This appears to be referred to, not as something new but well known to the hearers, as a proof that John the Baptist had retracted nothing, that although his active ministry was ended, the great work which he had begun was still in progress, and it was absurd to think of his abandoning it now, when it was at its height.

13. For all the prophets and the law prophesied until John.

As the *for* at the beginning of this verse assigns a reason for what goes before, it seems most natural to understand it as a general statement, that the whole preparatory system which preceded the Messiah's advent terminated in the person and the work of John, who therefore occupied a most peculiar and unique position in the history of redemption, as the last link in the long chain of Old Testament agencies, and in immediate contact with the first link of the new chain that succeeded and replaced it. This may be mentioned both as a further justification of the seeming paradox in v. 11, and as a further reason for believing that the man who held this high place in the scheme of the divine administration would not lightly undo all that he had done by retracting his official testimony to the person of his great superior. The form in which these ideas are expressed is peculiarly Judaic or Old Testament in character, but perfectly intelligible by the light of such associations. *The law and the prophets*, the Old Testament economy, the whole revelation of God's will in that form (see above, on 5, 17. 7, 12). *Until John*, as far as, down or up to John, as the last in the succession of such agencies. We have here another transposition introduced by Tyndale and retained by his successors. The sonorous close in the original is *prophesied*, i. e. executed their prophetic or preparatory office.

14. And if ye will receive (it), this is Elias, which was for to come.

This whole discourse respecting John the Baptist is concluded by repeating the authoritative statement of v. 10, in reference to another part of Malachi's prediction (4,5. 6. in the Hebrew text 3, 23. 24), at the very close of the Old Testament canon, where Elijah the Prophet is announced as the precursor of the "great and dreadful day of the Lord." This, we are here expressly told by Christ himself, was fulfilled in John the Baptist; and the same thing had been declared beforehand by the angel who announced his birth (Luke 1, 17). Whether this fulfilment was exhaustive or is yet to be succeeded by another, is a question which may be more conveniently considered in another place. (See below, on 17, 10–13.) The first clause of v. 14 implies that the prophecy was very differently understood, at least by many of our Saviour's hearers.

15. He that hath ears to hear, let him hear.

This idiomatic and proverbial formula, like many others of perpetual occurrence in our Lord's discourses, is never simply pleonastic or unmeaning, as the very repetition often tempts us to imagine. On the contrary, such phrases are invariably solemn and emphatic warnings that the things in question are of the most momentous import and entitled to most serious attention. They appear to have been framed or adopted by the Saviour, to be used on various occasions and in the pauses of his different discourses. There is something eminently simple and expressive in the one before us, which involves rebuke as well as exhortation. 'Why should you have the sense of hearing, if you do not use it now? To what advantage can you ever listen, if you turn a deaf ear to these admonitions? Now, now, if ever, he who can hear must hear, or incur the penalty of inattention!'

16. But whereunto shall I liken this generation? It is like unto children sitting in the markets, and calling unto their fellows,

Having defined John's position, and by necessary conseqrence his own, our Lord, by a natural transition, now refers to the characteristic difference between them, and to the reception which, in spite of this difference, they had both experienced, from the Jews, or rather from their leading men, the Pharisees and Scribes or Doctors of the law (Luke 7, 30). The conduct of the latter is presented in a parabolic form by means of an analogy derived from common life in one of its humblest and most familiar phases, that of child's play or infantile sports, a striking instance of our Saviour's condescension to the habits and associations of his hearers, even in expounding the most solemn truths. To this their attention is directed by himself in the opening question. *Whereunto*, to what, *shall I liken*, make like by comparison, *this generation*, not the Jewish race in general, for the Greek word (γενεά) has no such meaning, but the contemporary race, correctly rendered *generation*. As if he had said, 'it is impossible to represent correctly the behaviour of these spiritual leaders without drawing a comparison from the caprice and petulance of children.' *Markets* are mentioned not as places of traffic but of public concourse, an idea suggested by the derivation of the Greek word (ἀγορά from ἀγείρω, to assemble). *Sitting* denotes not merely the position, but the idle habit, dwelling, spending time there.*

17. And saying, We have piped unto you, and ye have not danced ; we have mourned unto you, and ye have not lamented.

Nothing could be more true to nature and experience than this trait of childish character and manners, which is daily verified in every nursery and playground. The complaint of those who here speak is that the others, or their comrades, had refused to do their part in some boyish ceremony, probably a mock funeral and wedding. *We piped*, or played the flute, the customary music both on joyful and sorrowful occasions (see above, on 9, 23), here restricted to the former by what follows, *ye did not dance*, to the music thus provided. (On the contrary) *we wailed*, a Greek word specially applied to lamentation for the dead, as performed by persons hired for the purpose, *and ye* (as the mourners) *did not beat* (your breasts), a common sign of grief on such occasions. It has been needlessly disputed which of the two sets of children here described represents the Scribes and Pharisees, and which our Lord and his forerunner. If the question required or admitted of an answer, it would be the one usually given or assumed, to wit, that the children introduced as speaking stand for John and Jesus, and those whom they address for the Scribes and Pharisees. The opposite hypothesis, ingeniously supported by some modern writers, turns the illustration upside down by making Christ himself the one who could be satisfied with nothing, and his enemies the party who complained of it. The reasons for preferring this ingenious paradox are wholly inconclusive, namely, that it is *this generation* that is said to be like the children speaking; that the *saying* of this verse must refer to the same subject as the *say* of the next; and that if Christ and John had been the speakers, the mourning would have come before the dancing. All this proceeds upon a false conception of the parable and an entire disregard of our Lord's practice with respect to it, which is to take the illustration as a whole and apply it as a whole to the thing signified. The same objections might be urged with far more plausibility and force against his own interpretation of the parable of the Sower (see below, on 13, 18–23.) The whole conduct of the leading Jews is here compared to that of the children in the market, the precise points of resemblance being left to be determined by the

---

* For *their fellows* (comrades, playmates), the latest critics have adopted the reading of the Vatican and many other uncial manuscripts, *the others*, corresponding to the *one another* found in Luke (7, 32). The variation has of course no effect upon the meaning.

hearer or the reader. As children are often hard to please even in their chosen sports, however varied, so the Scribes and Pharisees had treated John the Baptist and our Lord himself.

18. For John came neither eating nor drinking, and they say, He hath a devil.

This is our Lord's own application of the illustration given in the two preceding verses. I liken them to such children, *for*, because, *John came*, i. e. appeared in his official character, as sent by God. (Compare the use of the same verb in 3, 11. 5, 17. 7, 15. 9. 13. 10, 34, and vs. 3. 14 above.) *Neither eating nor drinking*, in the ordinary manner, and the customary meats and drinks of other men (Luke 7, 33), but locusts and wild honey (see above, on 3, 4). Another explanation of the words, as a hyperbolical description of John's abstinence, or of the small quantity of food which he consumed, is forbidden by its want of correspondence with what follows in relation to our Lord himself, which can not have respect to mere quantity. *And they say*, indefinitely, men say, people say, with special reference, however, to the Scribes and lawyers. *A devil*, or more properly, *a demon*, an evil spirit or fallen angel of inferior rank, permitted to invade the souls and bodies of men (see above, on 4, 24. 8, 16. 28. 9. 32). We thus learn that the same charge was alleged against our Lord and his forerunner. (See John 7, 20. 8, 48. 10, 20.) This shows that in John's case it was not a charge of demoniacal assistance in sustaining such a mode of life, but of demoniacal perverseness in adopting it. They may have thought it not unlike that of the Gadarene demoniacs as described above (8, 28) and in the parallels (Mark 5, 3–5. Luke 8, 27).

19. The Son of man came eating and drinking, and they say, Behold a man gluttonous, and a winebibber, a friend of publicans and sinners. But wisdom is justified of her children.

The Son of Man, the Messiah (see above, on 8, 20), of whom John was the forerunner, led a very different life as to external habits, and gave no occasion for the same reproach, but yet was equally condemned, though on another pretext. *Came*, appeared in his public and official character, as in v. 18. *Eating and drinking*, not simply more than John did, but like other men, subsisting on the same food, without any such ascetic singularity as answered an important purpose in the case of his forerunner. (See above, on 3, 4.) The essential point of the comparison is rather negative than positive. It is not so much our Lord's participation in the ordinary food of his contemporaries that is here presented for its own sake, as his freedom from those personal peculiarities which brought on John the charge of demoniacal possession. But the spite of his

14

opponents found another, resting on this very freedom from ascetic rigour. Because he ate and drank like other men, they called him a *glutton* (literally an *eating man*) and a *wine-bibber*, a felicitous translation of an Anacreontic word (οἰνοπότης). That it was not the mere quantity or even quality of our Saviour's meat and drink that angered them, but rather his unrestrained association with the masses, may be gathered from the next words, *a friend* (not merely a well-wisher, but a comrade, an associate, and perhaps more specifically still, a booncompanion) of *publicans and sinners*, a proverbial combination which has been explained already. (See above, on 9, 10–13.) The captious and unreasonable spirit of contemporary censors could not have been more vividly set forth than by thus pointing out their querulous dissatisfaction with two modes of life so utterly dissimilar as those of Christ and John the Baptist. When the one piped, there was no responsive joy, nor when the other wailed, responsive sorrow. Of the many senses put upon the last clause, there are only two which seem entitled to consideration; and these differ less as to the meaning of the words than in their application. The first, which is the common and most ancient one, regards this as a passing reflection of our Lord upon these spiteful and frivolous contemporary judgments, as compared with the true estimate of his course and of John's, as two successive and consistent parts of one great scheme, the proof and product of celestial wisdom, but an estimate confined to the children of that wisdom, its disciples or adherents. The wisdom of God displayed in these apparent contradictions, though condemned by the wisdom of the Jewish leaders, was acquitted and approved by all the truly wise. The only objection to the otherwise good sense thus put upon the clause is by no means a conclusive one, namely, that it seems to be a cold and unnecessary winding up of so lively an invective. This objection, which is wholly one of taste, and may therefore affect different minds differently, can be entirely removed, however, by the other explanation which has been referred to, but which rests entirely on its own intrinsic probability, there being no weight of authority in its favour. It agrees with the other in explaining *wisdom* to be that of God, as exercised and shown in the apparent contradiction of the life of John and that of Jesus, and in the two great systems which they symbolized or represented. (See above, on 3, 1.) They agree likewise in explaining *her children* to mean her adherents or disciples. But the explanation now in question differs from the other in applying this description, by a solemn irony, to the Scribes and Pharisees themselves, and in giving *justify* its earlier and wider sense of treating justly, doing justice. The clause will then be an indignant exclamation at the treatment which God's wise and gracious providence met with at the hands of those who claimed to be its reverent admirers and its authorized expounders. *And* (*so*) *was Wisdom justified on the part of* (ἀπό) *her* (favourite and honoured) *children.* Such justice does she meet with at the hands of those who claim to understand her best and ought to be her chief defenders.

20. Then began he to upbraid the cities wherein most of his mighty works were done, because they repented not:

Then, though sometimes indefinite, has commonly its strict sense, *at that time*, or *just afterwards;* nor is there any reason for departing from it here, as the connection with what goes before is obvious and natural, and an unbroken continuity appears to be required by the verb *began*, which is never wholly pleonastic (see above, on v. 7, and on 4, 17), and which would be misplaced at the beginning of an entirely new context. The connection seems to be, that he had no sooner ended his rebuke of the contemporary Jews for their unreasonable captious judgments with respect to John the Baptist and himself, than he began a more severe denunciation of those places, which had been particularly honoured by his presence and his miracles since the beginning of his Galilean ministry. That some of the expressions here used were repeated to the Seventy disciples (Luke 10, 13–15. 21. 22) is entirely in keeping with our Saviour's practice (see the introduction to the Sermon on the Mount, p. 105), but admits of another explanation, namely, that a part of what was actually spoken to the Seventy is given here by Matthew on account of its affinity with what precedes, and because the mission of the Seventy, as being something altogether temporary and without distinctive character, is nowhere else recorded in this Gospel. *To upbraid*, or cast reproach upon, including moral disapprobation and indignant feeling. The word is elsewhere used in a bad sense to denote the expression of human enmity and malice (see above, on 5, 11, and below, on 27, 44), but is here applied without essential change of meaning, to the mingled grief and anger of the Son of God (see Mark 3, 5) provoked by the impenitence and unbelief of those who had enjoyed the rarest opportunities of hearing his instructions and witnessing his miracles. *Mighty works*, literally *powers*, the cause being put for the effect. (See above, on 7, 22.) *The most*, in number, on account of his more frequent presence in the chief towns of the province. *Were done*, literally, were, became, or happened, came to pass. (See above, on 1, 22. 4, 3. 5, 18. 6, 10. 16. 8, 13. 9, 16. 10, 16. 25.) *Repented*, changed their minds, i. e. their judgments and their feelings, as to sin and their own sin, with a corresponding change of life. (See above, on 3, 2. 4, 17.)

21. Woe unto thee, Chorazin! woe unto thee, Bethsaida! for if the mighty works, which were done in you, had been done in Tyre and Sidon, they would have repented long ago in sackcloth and ashes.

The upbraidings described by the evangelist in v. 20, are now exemplified by quoting Christ's own words, addressed to three towns of Galilee, then flourishing, but now, and for ages past, no longer in existence. *Chorazin*, a name variously written in the oldest copies, and by

Origen as two words (Χώρα Ζίν), *the land of Zin,* a place known only from this passage and its parallel in Luke (10, 13), its very site being now uncertain. That assigned by Jerome (two Roman miles from Capernaum) is probably conjectural, the place having disappeared before his time. It is enough to know, however, as we do from this verse, that it was near enough to be grouped with Bethsaida and Capernaum, as salient points in the field of our Lord's Galilean ministry. *Bethsaida* (or *Bethsaidan,* as it is here written in the Greek text) is explained by the best geographical authorities to be the name of two towns, one on each side of the Sea of Galilee. This is the less surprising as the name denotes a fishery, and therefore would be apt to be repeated in a region so devoted to that business. The Bethsaida named in Luke, 9, 10. Mark 6, 45. 8, 22, was at the north-east end of the lake. The one here mentioned and in Luke 10, 13. John 1, 44. 12, 21, was on the west side, near Capernaum, the birthplace, or at least the former residence of three apostles, Philip, Andrew, and Peter (John, 1, 45). The last clause is a strong hyperbolical expression of the thought, that they were more obdurate even than the heathen. The question why our Saviour did not preach in Tyre and Sidon, if he knew that such would be the effect, was answered long ago by Augustin, because their inhabitants were not of the elect, and much more recently by a learned Romish writer, because his mission was at first to the Jews only (see below, on 15, 24). Both replies seem to assume, that the reference is here to the contemporary residents of Tyre and Sidon; but the mention of Sodom in the context seems to show that Tyre and Sidon are also used as historical types of the divine judgments, and as places which had already been destroyed in fulfilment of old prophecies. The reference then is not (as in Acts 12, 20) to the Tyre and Sidon which had risen from the ruins of the old, but to the old themselves, and *long ago* must be taken in a strong sense, as relating not to months or years but ages. Tyre and Sidon were the two famous cities of Phenicia, the narrow strip of sea-coast north of Palestine, distinguished in the ancient world for its maritime commerce. Sidon (or Zidon) was the more ancient, being mentioned both in Genesis (10, 19. 49, 13) and Homer, but was afterwards eclipsed by Tyre (Josh. 19, 29. Isai. 23, 8. Ezek. 27, 32). As the whole importance of Phenicia was derived from these two sea-ports, it is often designated by their joint names (Joel 3, 4. Jer. 47, 4. Zech. 9, 2. Acts 12, 20). *Sackcloth,* the coarsest kind of hair-cloth used for bags, and also for mourning, which in ancient times did not consist in finery of a certain colour, but rather in squalidity and seeming indifference to dress. *Ashes,* in which the mourner sat or with which he was sprinkled, as a sign of grief and desolation (see 2 Sam. 13, 9. Job 2, 8. and compare Josh. 7, 6. 2 Sam. 1, 2). These familiar badges of affliction were extended to religious sorrow and humiliation, and here used as symbols of repentance (Joel 1, 13. Jonah 3, 8).

22. But I say unto you, It shall be more tolerable for Tyre and Sidon at the day of judgment, than for you.

This is a simple repetition of the formula employed in 10, 15. to express the idea, that the guilt of unbelief in those who saw and heard Christ was immeasurably greater than it could be in the case of such as had enjoyed no such advantage. *But,* at the beginning of the verse, is not the usual connective (δέ), which occupies the same place in v. 16, nor the stronger adversative (ἀλλά) which holds the same position in vs. 8, 9, but a still stronger particle originally meaning *more,* nay more, and here equivalent to saying, 'but I say still more than this; not only is your sin more heinous than the sin of Tyre and Sidon, but your punishment shall be proportionally more severe.'

23. And thou, Capernaum, which art exalted unto heaven, shalt be brought down to hell : for if the mighty works which have been done in thee, had been done in Sodom, it would have remained until this day.

24. But I say unto you, That it shall be more tolerable for the land of Sodom in the day of judgment, than for thee.

Even Chorazin and Bethsaida, guilty as they were, were not the guiltiest of Galilean cities. There was one which Christ had chosen, in preference to Nazareth, his early home and second birthplace, as the seat and centre of his missionary labours, whence he went forth and whither he returned from his circuits of benignant toil (see above, on 4, 13), and where we know that he performed, not only several of the miracles recorded in detail, but multitudes of others which are only mentioned in the gross (see above, on 8, 5. 14. 16. 9, 2. 18. 25. and below, on 17, 24). The place thus highly honoured contained some true followers of Christ; but the mass of the people seem to have remained unmoved. *And thou* (or *thou too*), not as sharing merely in the guilt and condemnation of the other cities, but as far surpassing them, and therefore singled out for a distinct upbraiding.* The exaltation here referred to cannot be mere secular prosperity, but must be that resulting from the residence of Christ; and this determines the true meaning of what follows, *thou shalt be brought down,* or, according to the critics, *shalt descend* (or *go down*). *Hell* is not the word so rendered in 5, 22. 29. 30. 10, 28, and meaning the place of future torment, but another (ᾅδης) which, according to its etymology and usage in the classics, means the unseen world, the state of the dead, the world of spirits, without regard to difference of character or condition. This is also said to be

---

* The remainder of the first clause varies strangely in the oldest manuscripts, several of which read, *shalt thou be exalted to heaven?* but the latest critics only change the form and not the sense by reading ἢ ὑψώθης instead of ἡ ὑψωθεῖσα.

the meaning of the old English *hell*, though now used only in the sense of *gehenna*, which has led some to retain the Greek word *hades* in translation as a necessary means of avoiding error and confusion. It is here used simply in antithesis to *heaven*, and must be explained accordingly, as meaning the extremest degradation and debasement of a moral kind, but not perhaps without allusion to the loss of all external greatness, and oblivion of the very spot on which the city stood. The last clause and the next verse thus apply to Capernaum and Sodom what was said in vs. 21. 22. of Chorazin and Bethsaida, as compared with Tyre and Sidon.

25. At that time Jesus answered and said, I thank thee, O Father, Lord of heaven and earth, because thou hast hid these things from the wise and prudent, and hast revealed them unto babes.

If there were any chronological difficulty here in assuming an immediate succession, there would be no objection to our giving the words *in that time* a wider meaning. But as no such difficulty does exist; as the word translated *time* is one which strictly means a point or juncture, not a period; and as the nexus between this verse and the one before it is an obvious one; the only safe course is to give the terms their proper meaning as denoting that our Lord made this confession at the same time when he uttered the upbraiding just recorded. As the latter comprehended in its scope many learned and authoritative scribes, of whom there were some in every town of Galilee (see Luke 5, 17), it would naturally lead to precisely such reflections as are here recorded in the solemn form of an address to God. *Answering*, a word often used in Scripture without any words preceding (see below, on 22, 1. 28, 5, and compare Luke 14, 3. John 2, 18. 5, 17), and by some explained as perfectly synonymous with *saying;* but as this is almost always added, there would then be a deliberate tautology without example. Some suppose the answer to have reference to the thoughts, looks, or actions of the other party. Some prefer a wider reference to the occasion, whatever it may be, which bears the same relation to the words recorded, that an answer bears to the preceding question. In the case before us, on the supposition of unbroken continuity, the words of Christ are a reply to the impenitence and unbelief which called them forth. *Thank* is the verb correctly rendered by *confess* in 3, 6. and often elsewhere.* A more exact equivalent, however, is *acknowledged*, which may be applied both to sins and favours, in the sense of praise or thanks. It is here a most significant expression readily suggesting at the same time the ideas of praise, thanksgiving, and assent or acquiescence (as in Luke 22, 6, where it is translated *promised*, as the uncompounded verb is in 14, 7 below). It is not mere gratitude that Christ expresses as a man, but approbation

---

* See Mark 1, 5. Luke 10, 21. Acts 19, 18. Rom. 14, 1. 15, 9. Phil. 2, 11. Jas. 5, 16. Rev. 3, 5.

and concurrence as a divine person. 'I acknowledge to thee that thou hast done all things well.' He addresses God, first, as his Father, then as Lord of heaven and earth, thus claiming the most intimate personal relation to the sovereign ruler of the universe. This character or aspect of the divine nature is made prominent because he is about to cite a signal instance of God's sovereign independence of all human wisdom and authority. *That thou didst hide away*, conceal, *these (things)*, an indefinite expression, but with obvious reference to something previously said or done, and thus confirming the conclusion that this is not a new context, but a direct continuation of what goes before. *These things* most probably means all that made the difference between the classes here contrasted, i. e. spiritual knowledge of the truth, susceptibility of right impressions, and a just foresight of the consequences flowing both from faith and unbelief. The hiding here ascribed to God is only positive as being the fulfilment of his righteous judgment against sin, but negative as being only the withholding of that grace without which *these things* are invisible. *The wise and prudent* (or *intelligent*), not only in their own conceit but really in other matters, not excepting the letter of the law, of whose true spirit they knew nothing. *To babes*, infants, properly denoting children who have not yet learned to talk, and therefore an appropriate but strong description of the ignorant and weak, and more especially of such as feel themselves to be so in all spiritual matters, until God reveals them.

26. Even so, Father; for so it seemed good in thy sight.

Even so is Tyndale's version of the word translated *yea* in v. 9, and in 5, 37. 9, 28, and corresponding to the modern English *yes*, as a simple particle of affirmation. It may either be considered as expressive of assent, in which case our version is correct, or of emphatic repetition, with a verb to be supplied from the preceding verse. 'Yes (I do thank thee) that it has so pleased thee.' The latter explanation is preferred by the exact philologists; the other is the current one, in consequence of which this verse has now become a standing formula of acquiescence in the absolute and sovereign will of God. *So it seemed good in thy sight* is perhaps as near as we can come in English to the idiomatic form of the original, which strictly means, *so it became* (or *was*) *good pleasure* (or *complacency*) *before thee*. The Greek noun (εὐδοκία) expresses independent volition, sovereign choice, but always with an implication of benevolence, which sometimes becomes the predominant idea, as in Luke 2, 14.*

27. All things are delivered unto me of my Father:

---

* See also Eph. 1, 5. 9. Phil. 1, 15. 2, 13. 2 Th. 1, 11, and compare the cognate verb in 3, 17. above.

and no man knoweth the Son, but the Father; neither knoweth any man the Father, save the Son, and (he) to whomsoever the Son will reveal (him).

The emphatic recognition of the Father's sovereignty in the preceding verse required some definition of the speaker's Sonship to prevent all misconception of his own authority. This relation involves not merely delegation of authority in time, but community of nature from eternity. *All* (things) *were delivered* (or transferred, imparted) *to me by my Father,* i. e. all that he possesses in himself, except what constitutes the personal distinction between us. There is no inferiority implied in the reception, which is an eternal one. It follows, as a necessary consequence, that no one can be cognizant of this relation, that is, know it thoroughly (ἐπιγινώσκει) except those who are parties to it. The idiomatic use of *man* for *one*, which is no longer required by English usage, almost stultifies the sentence to the modern reader by appearing to call God a man. The last clause draws attention to the great and glorious truth, that as the Father, in that character, gives all things to the Son, it is a personal function of the Son, as the Divine Word, to reveal the Father.

28. Come unto me, all (ye) that labour and are heavy laden, and I will give you rest.

As the last words of the preceding verse implied the possibility of man in some sense knowing God the Father, but only through the intervention of the Son, and at his sovereign pleasure (*he to whomsoever the Son will reveal him*), our Lord offers, as it were, to exercise this gracious function, by inviting men to come to him, not in the way of speculation but of penitent submission, not as philosophers to be enlightened, but as sinners to be saved. There is exquisite beauty in this sudden but not harsh transition from the mysteries of the Godhead to the miseries of man. The Son is the revealer of the Father, not to stimulate or gratify a mere scientific curiosity as to the mode of the divine existence, but to bring the Godhead into saving contact with the sin-sick ruined soul. Having laid the foundation for what follows in his own eternal sonship and community of nature with the Father, he now turns the doctrine to a practical account, and calls men to avail themselves of its provisions. *Come*, the same invitatory adverb that was used above in 4, 19, and there explained as strictly meaning, *Here* (or *hither*) *after* (or *behind*) *me!* So in this place, with another preposition (πρός), it may be rendered, *Here* (or *hither*) *to me!* The invitation, although formally addressed to a certain class distinctly specified, is truly universal, since the qualities described belong to all men just so far as their consciences are sensible and active. *Ye that labour*, not in the mild sense of working, but in that of toiling, working hard, and suffering in consequence, all which is the essential meaning of the Greek word (κοπιῶντες). There may be no intentional allusion to self-righteousness, or efforts to work out our salvation in our own strength; but to nothing are the terms of the description more appropriate, not only as to this word, but the next, *heavy laden*, in Greek a single word applied in classical usage to the loading of a ship or beast of burden, and in this connection necessarily suggesting the idea of one weighed down by a burden far beyond his strength. Though exactly descriptive of man's general condition, as bound and yet unable to fulfil the law, and therefore groaning under its intolerable penalty and condemnation as a crushing load, this figure is peculiarly expressive of that form of legal bondage which oppressed the ancient Jewish church, and to which the same figure is applied by our Lord elsewhere (see below, on 23, 4), and by Peter in the council at Jerusalem (Acts 15, 10). *Give you rest*, another single word in Greek, and so translated in the older English versions (*ease you*). The exact sense is still more expressive, *I will make you cease*, i. e. cease to suffer from this thankless toil and this intolerable burden.

29. Take my yoke upon you, and learn of me; for I am meek and lowly in heart: and ye shall find rest unto your souls.

As in the Sermon on the Mount (5, 17), our Lord here guards against the natural tendency of all men to expect relief from legal bondage in the abrogation of the law itself. But what he there does by explicitly denying that he came for such a purpose, he does here no less effectually, although less directly, by inviting sinners, not to throw off the yoke entirely, but to take his yoke upon them, not a new law substituted for the old, but the old as interpreted and magnified by him, no longer as a method of salvation, but forever as a rule of life. The verb translated *take* has here its primary and proper sense of taking up and carrying, as in 4, 6. 9, 6. *Learn of me*, seems to mean, receive instruction from me, which is the idea probably conveyed to most English readers. But why should it be given as a reason for this precept that the teacher is *meek and lowly in heart?* However precious such a character may be, the main qualification of a doctrinal instructor must be wisdom, knowledge, and capacity to teach. The Greek suggests a somewhat different idea. 'Take a lesson from me,' as in 24, 32 below, where the same verb and particle occur together—'learn a parable of the fig-tree,' i. e. borrow an illustrative analogy from it. So here, take a lesson from my example. I am meek and lowly in heart, why should you refuse to be the same? I have condescended to be made under the law in its severest form and requisitions. Why should you scruple to submit to it with me as its interpreter and your assistant? Do this, and *you shall find* what you are vainly seeking elsewhere, *rest*, repose, relief, a Greek noun corresponding to the verb in v. 28. *To* (or *for*) *your souls*, not merely for your bodies, but relief from spiritual burdens and distresses which are otherwise incurable.

30. For my yoke (is) easy, and my burden is light.

Lest they should still imagine that they are invited only to exchange one hard yoke and one heavy burden for another, he assures them that his yoke is *easy*, a word elsewhere rendered *good* (1 Cor. 15, 33), *kind* (Ephes. 4, 32), *gracious* (1 Pet. 2, 3), but originally meaning *good for*, i. e. useful, beneficial, and never perhaps used without some reference to this its etymological import. This might seem to be its only meaning here, 'my yoke is good (for you), will do you good, however hard it may be.' But that the word was also meant to suggest the idea of gentleness and mildness, as opposed to harshness and severity, is evident, not only from its usage in the other places cited, but from the parallel expression in the other clause, *my burden is light*, the last word being wholly unambiguous and certainly the opposite of *heavy*, as appears, for example, from the antithesis in 2 Cor. 4, 17. The inconsistency which some have found between this declaration and the one in 7, 14 above, arises wholly from confounding the natural repugnance of the human heart to God's commandments with the weakness of the new man in obeying them. The former must be conquered or we cannot be saved. The latter needs only to be strengthened by divine grace, and the yoke of duty becomes easy to the humbled neck, the load of obligation light to the invigorated shoulders. This delightful invitation, still addressed to all who answer the description in the text, is remarkable, not only in itself as an expression of divine benignity and condescension, but historically also, as exactly suited to the time and circumstances in which it was uttered, after our Lord's appearance as a teacher, and yet long before his great atoning sacrifice. Without anticipating therefore what was not to be disclosed till after that great critical event, it nevertheless says enough to win the heavy-laden sinner, and to us, who read or hear it now contains the germ of all that has been since revealed.

CHAPTER XII.

It entered into the design of all the Gospels to exhibit the reception which our Saviour met with both from friends and enemies. The dark side of the picture has already been presented in the history before us, but only in occasional glimpses, as when it records the objection to his claiming the power of forgiveness, to his intercourse with publicans and sinners, to his free mode of living, and supposed neglect of all ascetic duties. In the present chapter the evangelist brings together other symptoms of increasing enmity, without much regard to chronological arrangement, but with great effect in showing from what quarters and by what means the opposition to our Lord's preliminary work proceeded. He first relates a charge of Sabbath-breaking brought ostensibly against his disciples, with his answer (1–8); then a second charge, connected with a miracle, and also followed by an answer (9–

13); then the organized opposition to which this led, and our Saviour's consequent retirement from the public view, without relinquishing his work, in which the evangelist points out the fulfilment of a signal prophecy (14–21). Another miracle, which led to a general inquiry whether he were not the Messiah, also led to a blasphemous charge of collusion with the Evil One, and this to an argumentative defence on his part, and a solemn warning against the unpardonable sin (22–37). Another form of opposition was the demand of a sign or miraculous proof of his Messiahship, which he refused, referring them to cases drawn from the Old Testament, as aggravations of their own misconduct, and concluding with a fearful and mysterious prediction of the ruin that awaited them (38–45). To these instances of opposition from his enemies, the historian adds one of interruption from his friends, which gave occasion to a memorable speech defining his social and domestic relations (46–50).

1. At that time Jesus went on the sabbath day through the corn; and his disciples were ahungered, and began to pluck the ears of corn, and to eat.

Matthew here resumes the history of the opposition to our Saviour which he had noticed incidentally before (see above, on 9, 3. 11. 14), in reference to his power of forgiveness, his intercourse with publicans, and his neglect of fasting. Another charge or ground of opposition to the Saviour, on the part of the more scrupulous and rigid Jews, was his alleged violation of the Sabbath, either in person or by suffering his followers to do what was esteemed unlawful. This divine institution, as already mentioned (see above, on 4, 23), being chiefly negative in its observance, was less affected by a change of outward situation than the legal ceremonies, most of which were limited to one place, and could not be performed without irregularity elsewhere. Hence the Jews in foreign lands, being cut off from the offering of sacrifices and the formal celebration of their yearly festivals, were chiefly distinguished from the Gentiles among whom they dwelt by two observances, those of circumcision and the Sabbath, and especially the latter, as the more notorious and palpable peculiarity of their religion. Hence the prophets who predict the exile, lay peculiar stress on the observance of the Sabbath, as the badge of a true Israelite. (Isa. 56, 2. 58, 13. Lam. 2, 6. Ezek. 44, 24. Hos. 2, 11.) After the restoration, when the same necessity no longer existed, the people were disposed to exaggerate this duty by gratuitous restrictions, and by pushing the idea of religious rest (which was the essence of the Sabbath) to an absurd extreme, at the same time losing sight of its spiritual purpose, and confining their attention to the outward act, or rather abstinence from action, as intrinsically holy and acceptable to God. One of the Jewish books enumerates thirty-nine acts, with many subdivisions, which were to be considered as unlawful labour, and the Talmud gives the most minute specifications of the distance which might be lawfully passed over, even in the greatest emergencies, as that of fire. With these distorted and corrupted notions of the Sabbath, they would soon find something to condemn in the less punctilious but more rational and even legal conduct of our Lord and his disciples. Two such attacks, with their historical occasions, are recorded here by Matthew. It is also given by Mark (2, 23–28) and Luke (6, 1–5), less minutely, and with some variation as to form and substance, but without the least real inconsistency. One of the points of difference is in the chronological arrangement. Matthew connecting what is here recorded with his previous context by the general formula, *in that time*, while Luke specifies the very Sabbath upon which it happened. As Mark has no indication of time whatever, it is clear that he is putting things together, not as immediately successive in the time of their occurrence, but as belonging to the same class or series, that of the objections made by the censorious Jews, on legal grounds, to Christ's proceedings. Hence this topic occupies an earlier place in Mark than in either of the other gospels, and when taken in connection with their marked agreement, even in minute forms of expression, proves that while they used the same material and aimed at the same ultimate design, each was directed to pursue his own plan independently of both the others. *Corn*, literally *sown* (*fields*), i. e. sown with corn, in the proper English sense of grain or breadstuffs, with particular reference to wheat and barley. That the corn was grown and ripe, though not expressly mentioned, is implied in all that follows. *On the Sabbath day*, literally, *the Sabbaths*, which may seem to indicate that this particular occurrence took place more than once, or that this clause is descriptive of a customary action. But the plural form of the Greek word is purely accidental, and arises either from assimilation to Greek names of festivals (compare John 10, 22), or from the fact that the Hebrew word *Sabbath* (שַׁבָּת) in its Aramaic form (שַׁבְּתָא) resembles a Greek plural (σάββατα), and is often so inflected, although singular in meaning. *His disciples*, his immediate personal attendants, probably those whose call has previously been recorded, Peter and Andrew, James, and John, and Matthew, perhaps with the addition of some others who received his doctrine, and were therefore *his disciples* in a wider sense. Our Lord appears to have been seldom free from the society of others, either friends or foes, so that he was sometimes under the necessity of escaping from them for a time, especially for devotional purposes. (See below, on 14, 22.) *Began* is not a pleonastic or superfluous expression, but suggests that they were interrupted, or that while they were so doing, the ensuing dialogue took place.

2. But when the Pharisees saw (it), they said unto him, Behold, thy disciples do that which is not lawful to do upon the sabbath day.

The Pharisees, i. e. certain of that class who seem to have been near at hand whenever Christ appeared in public. This will be less surprising if we consider that the Pharisees were not a small and select body, but the great national party, who insisted on the smallest points of difference between Jews and Gentiles, and most probably included the mass of the nation. (See above, on 3, 7.) The expression here used, therefore, is nearly equivalent to saying, certain strict punctilious Jews who happened to be present. Mark and Matthew represent them as complaining to the Master of his disciples; while according to Luke, the objection was addressed to the latter. Both accounts are perfectly consistent, whether we suppose Luke to describe the indirect attack upon them as a direct one, or, which seems more natural, assume that both our Lord and his followers were thus addressed by different persons, either at once or in succession. *See*, behold, implying something strange and hard to be believed. The simple act of plucking and eating was expressly allowed by the law of Moses (Deut. 23, 25). The unlawfulness must therefore have consisted either in wanton waste or in doing on the Sabbath what on any other day would have been lawful. But of waste or damage to the grain, the text contains no trace or intimation. It was therefore not the act itself, but the time of its performance, that gave occasion to the charge before us, as we learn from Maimonides that the tradition of the fathers reckoned the act here described as a kind of harvesting or reaping, and as such forbidden labour on the Sabbath.

3. But he said unto them, Have ye not read what David did, when he was ahungered, and they that were with him;

4. How he entered into the house of God, and did eat the shewbread, which was not lawful for him to eat, neither for them which were with him, but only for the priests?

By a combination of the three accounts we learn that Christ defended his disciples from this frivolous and malignant charge by five distinct arguments, two of which have been preserved by all three gospels, one by Mark alone, and two by Matthew alone. The first place is assigned by all to the same answer. This is drawn from the Old Testament history, and presupposes their acquaintance with it, and their habit of reading it. It also presupposes their acknowledgment of David as an eminent servant of God, all whose official acts, unless divinely disapproved, afford examples to those placed in similar situations. The narrative referred to is still extant in 1 Samuel 21, 1–6, which is thus proved to be a part of the canon recognized by Christ. *The house of God*, in which he dwelt among his people, an expression no less applicable to the tabernacle than the temple. As the ancient sanctuary, under both its forms, was meant to symbolize the doctrine of divine inhabitation and peculiar presence with the chosen people, it was moveable as long as they were wandering and unsettled; but as soon as they had taken full possession of the promised land, which was not till the reign of David, the portable tent was exchanged for a permanent substantial dwelling. At the time here mentioned the tabernacle was at Nob (1 Sam. 21, 1). The shew-bread, literally, *bread of presentation*, called in Hebrew, *bread of* (the divine) *face* (or *presence*), consisted of twelve loaves or cakes placed in rows upon a table in the Holy Place or outward apartment of the tabernacle, and renewed every Sabbath, when the old were eaten by the priests on duty (Lev. 24, 5–9). Whatever may have been the meaning of this singular observance, it was certainly a necessary and divinely instituted part of the tabernacle-service, resting on the same authority, though not of equal moment with the Sabbath. The relevancy of the case here cited is enhanced by the probability that David's desecration of the shew-bread was itself committed on the Sabbath, as the loaves appear to have been just renewed (1 Sam. 21, 6). *It was not lawful*, i. e. not according to the law of Moses, which our Lord and his disciples were accused of breaking. In either case, the positive observance, though legitimate and binding, must give way to the necessity of self-preservation.

5. Or have ye not read in the law, how that on the sabbath days the priests in the temple profane the sabbath, and are blameless?

Another argument against their formal and mechanical observance of the Sabbath, is that it was violated by the ritual itself, which they acknowledged to be no less binding. If all work on the Sabbath was forbidden absolutely, then sacrifices offered upon that day were unlawful, though required by express divine authority. This *reductio ad absurdum*, although perfectly consistent with the other arguments employed, has been preserved by Matthew only. *Profane*, make common or accessible to all. *Blameless*, because they are obeying an explicit divine precept.

6. But I say unto you, That in this place is (one) greater than the temple.

If the service of the temple justified a seeming violation of the Sabbath, how much more the presence and authority of one who was superior in dignity and value to the temple, because he realized in his own person what was only prefigured by the sanctuary, namely, the presence of God among his people. (Compare John 2, 21.)*

7. But if ye had known what (this) meaneth, I will

---

* Instead of the masculine form ($\mu\epsilon i\zeta\omega\nu$) *greater*, i. e. one greater, or a person greater, the latest critics have the neuter ($\mu\epsilon i\zeta o\nu$), i. e. something greater, which is more pointed, but without effect on the essential meaning.

have mercy, and not sacrifice, ye would not have condemned the guiltless.

Here the Saviour quotes a second time the words of God as recorded by Hosea (6, 6), and declaring the superior importance of benevolent affections to mere ritual observances however binding (see above, on 9, 13, where the words occurred before and were explained). That they were really uttered in both cases, is apparent from the different mode of introducing them. Before he told his enemies to go and learn the meaning of the prophet's language. Here he says that if they had known its meaning they would not have condemned the *guiltless*, the same word that is rendered *blameless* in v. 5, a needless variation which impairs the force, though it does not change the meaning of the sentence. The plural form refers to the disciples, who were the ostensible object of attack, although the censure was intended for their master, as sanctioning their conduct by his presence, if not his participation. (See above, on 9, 11, where the charge is made against himself, although addressed to his disciples).

8. For the Son of man is Lord even of the sabbath day.

For the Son of man is lord (not only of all other things affecting human happiness, but also or even) *of the Sabbath*, which you might suppose to be exempt from his control. Grotius and others have endeavoured to explain *Son of man*, in this place, as denoting any man or man in general. The sense will then be that as the Sabbath was appointed for man's benefit, it is his prerogative to regulate and use it for his own advantage. But to this construction, although specious, there are two invincible objections, one of form and one of substance. The sentiment expressed is not in keeping with the tenor of the Scriptures, which everywhere deny to man the right of abrogating or suspending a divine institution for his own good and at his own discretion. Such a prerogative can belong only to a divine person, i. e. to God as God, or to God incarnate in the person of Messiah. Besides, it is only to this person, the Messiah, that the usage of the Scriptures will allow the title Son of Man to be applied. (See above, on 8, 20.) The meaning of the sentence therefore must be, that the Sabbath having been ordained for man, not for any individual, but for the whole race, it must needs be subject to the Son of Man, who is its head and representative, its sovereign and redeemer. This implies that though the Sabbath, in its essence, is perpetual, the right of modifying and controlling it belongs to Christ, and can be exercised only under his authority. This sentence differs from the parallel in Mark (2, 28), only in the collocation of the words, the last words here being *Son of Man*.

9. And when he was departed thence, he went into their synagogue :

Matthew records another charge of Sabbath-breaking, probably to show how various were the outward occasions of such opposition; to illustrate the variety of Christ's defences; and to mark the first concerted plan for his destruction. *The synagogue*, most probably the one in Capernaum. The absence of any more specific note of time shows that exact chronological order was of small importance to the author's object. There is more precision as to this point in the parallel account of Luke (6, 11). There is no ground in the text of either gospel for the conjecture of some writers, that the presence of this sufferer had been contrived in order to entrap Christ. The constant application for his healing aid precludes the necessity of such a supposition, and indeed suggests that this was only one of many miracles performed at this time, and is recorded in detail on account of its important bearing on the progress of Christ's ministry.

10. And, behold, there was a man which had (his) hand withered. And they asked him, saying, Is it lawful to heal on the sabbath days? that they might accuse him.

Withered, literally, *dried*, or *dried up*, elsewhere applied to liquids, (Mark 5, 29. Rev. 16, 12), and to plants (Mark 4, 6. 11, 20. James 1, 11), but also to the pining away of the human body. The passive participle in Mark (3, 1), adds to the meaning of the adjective (*dry*) employed by Matthew and Luke, the idea that it was not a congenital infirmity, but the effect of disease or accident, the more calamitous because it was the right hand that was thus disabled (Luke 6, 6.) A similar affection, preternaturally caused, was that of Jeroboam (1 Kings 13, 4–6). We have here a striking indication that the opposition to our Saviour was becoming more inveterate and settled, so that his enemies not only censured what he did, but watched for some occasion to find fault with him. *Questioned*, or catechized, the vocal expression corresponding to the watching mentioned by Mark (3, 2). *Whether he would*, literally, *if he will*, a form of speech which represents the scene as actually passing. *On the Sabbath days*, literally, *the Sabbaths*, a form used above in v. 1, and there explained. The motive of their asking was not simply curiosity, but a deliberate desire to entrap him. *That they might accuse him*, not in conversation merely, but before the local judges, who were probably identical with the elders or rulers of the synagogue, or at all events present at the stated time and place of public worship. The subject of the verb is not expressed by Mark and Matthew, although easily supplied from the foregoing context (v. 2), and from the parallel account in Luke (6, 7), where the Scribes and Pharisees are expressly mentioned.

11. And he said unto them, What man shall there be among you that shall have one sheep, and if it fall into

a pit on the sabbath day, will he not lay hold on it, and lift (it) out?

12. How much then is a man better than a sheep? Wherefore it is lawful to do well on the sabbath days.

He exposes their formality and inconsistency, by showing that the right which they denied to him in public, and in reference to human subjects, they habitually exercised in private, and in reference to the lower animals. Whether this were done from disinterested kindness, or from regard to the value of the object, the conclusion was clear and irresistible in favour of extending the same practice to a suffering man. This conclusion is suggested in the first clause of v. 12, while in the other it is formally applied in answer to their captious question. *To do well*, does not mean to *do right*, which is always lawful, but to *do good*, to confer a benefit or favour upon others.

13. Then saith he to the man, Stretch forth thy hand. And he stretched (it) forth; and it was restored whole, like as the other.

There is here no mention of external contact, nor of any other order or command than that to stretch out the hand, which could only be obeyed when the miracle was wrought, and is therefore not required as a previous condition. This is often and justly used to illustrate the act of faith, which is performed in obedience to divine command and by the aid of the same power which requires it. *Whole*, in the old English sense of sound or healthy.

14. Then the Pharisees went out, and held a council against him, how they might destroy him.

One of the most important circumstances of this case, for the sake of which it was perhaps recorded, is the effect which it produced upon the Pharisees or High-Church Jewish party, whose religious tenets brought them into constant opposition to the Sadducees or latitudinarians (see above, on 3, 7). *Took counsel* is a phrase peculiar to Matthew (12, 14. 22, 15. 27, 1. 7. 28, 12), Mark's equivalent to which is *made counsel*, i. e. consultation. *How they might destroy him*, not for any past offences, but how they might take advantage of his words or acts to rid them of so dangerous an enemy. The motives of this concerted opposition were no doubt various, religious, political, and personal, in different degrees and cases. That it should have been deliberately organized at this time, out of such discordant elements (Mark 3, 7) and in the face of such conclusive evidence, can only be ascribed to the infatuation under which they acted (Luke 6, 11).

15. But when Jesus knew (it), he withdrew himself from thence : and great multitudes followed him, and he healed them all ;

In consequence of this combination and the dangers which arose from it, our Lord withdrew from Capernaum and other towns of Galilee, to the shores of the lake, where he would be less exposed to craft or violence, and better able to escape without a miracle. This retreat before his enemies was prompted, not by fear, but by that wise discretion which was constantly employed in the selection and the use of the necessary means for the promotion of the great end which he came to accomplish. As it entered into the divine plan that his great atoning work should be preceded by a prophetic ministry of several years' duration, the design of which was to indoctrinate the people in the nature of his kingdom, to prepare the way for its erection, and to train the men by whom it should be organized, it formed no small part of his work to check and regulate the progress of events, so as not to precipitate the consummation, but secure and complete the requisite preparatory process. That the movement here recorded was intended to elude his enemies, whose influence was greatest in the towns, and not to escape the concourse of the people, may be seen from the actual result as Mark describes it (3, 7). *And he healed them all,* i. e. all who needed and sought healing at his hands.

16. And charged them that they should not make him known :

This general statement is not inconsistent with the more specific one in Mark (3, 12) in reference to evil spirits. Mark has simply selected, in accordance with his previous details, which Matthew does not give, a single class out of many who were thus forbidden. While the sick in general were required not to make him known by giving undue or premature publicity to what they had experienced, a particular restriction was imposed upon the more specific testimony borne to his Messiahship by evil spirits. The word here rendered *charged* means originally to estimate or value ; then to impose a fine by way of punishment ; then to punish by reproof, which in its usual meaning (see above, on 8, 26, and below, on 16, 22. 17, 18. 19, 13. 20, 31). Here it can only mean to threaten with severe rebuke in case of disobedience.

17. That it might be fulfilled which was spoken by Esaias the prophet, saying,

18. Behold my servant, whom I have chosen ; my beloved, in whom my soul is well pleased : I will put my

Spirit upon him, and he shall shew judment to the Gentiles.

It is characteristic of this gospel, that while it passes over the minute details of Mark (3, 7–9) as to the concourse upon this occasion, it again pauses in the narrative to point out the fulfilment of an ancient prophecy, still extant in the writings of Isaiah (42, 1–4). The original passage exhibits to our view the servant of Jehovah, as the messenger or representative of God among the nations, and describes his mode of operation as not violent but peaceful, and the effects of his influence as not natural but spiritual. The quotation varies so entirely from the Septuagint version, even in expression where the meaning is the same, that it must be regarded as an independent and direct translation from the Hebrew. The literal meaning of the first verse is as follows:— " Behold my servant, I will hold him fast, my chosen one (in whom) my soul delights; I have given (or put) my spirit upon him; judgment to the nations shall he cause to go forth." The word *servant*, here as in the Septuagint, is the one employed above in 8, 6–13, and suggesting the idea both of son and servant, thus furnishing a link between the prophecy and its fulfilment. The only variation from the Hebrew in this sentence is the substitution of the verb to *choose* for one that means to *hold fast* for the purpose of sustaining. But this has no effect upon the general sense, and may be readily resolved into an authoritative modification of the text by a second inspired writer, as a sort of gloss or comment, expressing what is really implied in the original, and bringing out more prominently what was latent. Thus we learn in this case, that the servant of Jehovah was sustained because he was a chosen instrument or agent set apart for a specific service. There is an obvious allusion to this verse, or rather a direct application of it made by God himself, in the descent of the Holy Spirit on our Saviour at his baptism, and in the words pronounced from heaven then and at his transfiguration (see above, on 2, 17, and below, on 17, 5). The word *judgment* has been variously explained, but the most satisfactory interpretation is the common one, which understands the word as a description of the true religion, and the whole clause as predicting its diffusion. That Christ was sent to the Jews and not the Gentiles, is only true of his personal ministry on earth (see below, on 15, 24), and not of his whole work as continued by his followers (see below, on 28, 19). All that is here important is, that the evangelist applies to Jesus the prophetic description of the Messiah as a messenger from God to man.

19. He shall not strive, nor cry; neither shall any man hear his voice in the streets.

This is the main quotation, to which the preceding verse is merely introductory. The variations from the Hebrew are either wholly unimportant or explicable on the principle before laid down. Instead of two verbs meaning nearly the same thing, *to cry* and *to raise (the voice)*, only one is given and the other is replaced by the verb to *strive*, an intimation that the thing denied is not mere noise, but quarrelsome commotions. The quotation has sometimes been referred to our Saviour's mild and modest demeanor, but it rather has respect to the nature of his kingdom, and the means by which it was to be established. His forbidding the announcement of the miracle is not recorded simply as a trait of personal character, but rather as implying that a public recognition of his claims was not included in his present purpose.

20. A bruised reed shall he not break, and smoking flax shall he not quench, till he send forth judgment unto victory.

This verse continues the description of the mode in which the Messiah was to bring forth judgment to the nations, or in other words to spread the true religion. It was not to be by clamor or by violence. The first of these ideas is expressed in the preceding verse, the last in this. That such is the true import of the words, is clear from the addition of the last clause, which would be unmeaning if the words related merely to a compassionate and sympathetic temper. That this verse is included in Matthew's quotation, shows that he did not quote the one before it as descriptive of a modest and retiring disposition. For although such a temper might be proved by Christ's prohibiting the publication of his miracles, this prohibition could not have been cited as an evidence of tenderness and mildness. The only way in which the whole quotation can be made appropriate to the case in hand, is by supposing that it was meant to be descriptive, not merely of our Saviour's human virtues, but of the nature of his kingdom and of the means by which it was to be established. That he was both lowly and compassionate is true, but it is not the truth which he established by his conduct upon this occasion, nor the truth which the evangelist intended to illustrate by the citation of these words. As well in their original connection as in Matthew's application of them, they describe that kingdom which was not of this world; which came not with observation (Luke 17, 20); which was neither meat nor drink, but righteousness, and peace, and joy in the Holy Ghost (Rom. 14, 17); which was founded and promoted not by might nor by power, but by the Spirit of the Lord (Zech. 4, 6); and of which its founder said (John 18, 36), *If my kingdom were of this world, then would my servants fight, that I should not be delivered to the Jews, but now is my kingdom not from hence.* And again (John 18, 37), when Pilate said unto him, Art thou a king then? Jesus answered, *Thou sayest* (rightly) *that I am a king; to this end was I born, and for this cause I came into the world, that I should bear witness to the truth; every one that is of the truth heareth my voice.* How perfectly does this august description tally with the great prophetic picture of the Servant of Jehovah, who was to bring forth judgment to the nations, and in doing so was not to cry or raise his voice, or let men hear it in the streets, nor by brutal force to break the crushed reed or quench the dim wick, but to conquer by healing and imparting strength. Here again the variation from the Hebrew is explanatory, the obscure phrase (לֶאֱמֶת) *by* or *for the truth* being exchanged for the explicit one, *to victory,* triumphantly, the other idea having been sufficiently expressed in v. 18. This condensation and elucidation of the prophecy shows clearly that the changes in its form are not fortuitous nor inadvertent, but intentional and full of meaning. It is somewhat remarkable that the word in the original which means *dim* or feeble is translated *smoking* both in the Septuagint and Gospel, but by Greek words altogether different (καπνιζόμενον and τυφόμενον).

21. And in his name shall the Gentiles trust.

With the same disposition or determination to avoid the repetition of synonymous expressions, Matthew passes over the first clause in the next verse of Isaiah (42, 4), and closes his quotation with a paraphrase of the second. *In his name shall the Gentiles hope* is really equivalent in meaning *for his law shall the Gentiles wait.* The essential idea in both cases is the absolute dependence of the world at large upon the mission of Messiah for salvation. As the first part of the prophecy was cited as an introduction, so this last part is added to give roundness and completeness to the whole quotation. At the same time, these supplementary expressions, although not what the author meant especially to quote, serve the incidental but important purpose of suggesting, in the language of a prophet, the extent of the Messiah's mission and the ultimate conversion of the Gentiles.

22. Then was brought unto him one possessed with a devil, blind, and dumb: and he healed him, insomuch that the blind and dumb both spake and saw.

Then is here to be indefinitely understood as meaning either *at that time,* referring to the whole period of Christ's public ministry, or *afterwards,* and on a different occasion. This is not only agreeable to Matthew's usage and the method of his history, but removes all seeming discrepancy with the other gospels as to the date of the occurrence, which is here recorded as another instance of malignant opposition on the part of the Jewish leaders. The occasion was a miracle sufficiently remarkable even in itself considered, but which probably would not have been recorded in detail but for the reason just suggested, and the memorable warning which it drew from the lips of Christ. This is the more probable because of the resemblance which it bears to the miracle in 9, 32. 33, where demoniacal possession was combined with dumbness, to which blindness was added in the case before us.

23. **And all the people were amazed, and said, Is not this the Son of David ?**

Another reason for particularly mentioning this miracle was the effect it produced upon the people, not merely filling them with wonder, so that they were out of their normal state and as it were beside themselves (ἐξίσταντο), but leading them to ask whether this were not the Son of David, his descendant and successor, which, as we have seen (above, on 9, 27), had become a standing designation of the Messiah. This alarming question, showing whither the popular impressions were now tending, affords an explanation, not contained in Mark's account (3, 22), of the sudden and malignant accusation mentioned in the next verse.

24. **But when the Pharisees heard (it), they said, This (fellow) doth not cast out devils, but by Beelzebub the prince of the devils.**

The speakers are described by Luke (11, 15) as some of the multitude by whom the miracle was witnessed ; by Matthew more definitely as the Pharisees, or members of the rigorous Jewish party ; but by Mark (3, 22) still more precisely, as *the Scribes who had come down from Jerusalem*, perhaps on hearing of our Lord's return from his itinerant labours to Capernaum. The expression is too definite to be explained of a mere accidental presence, or a coming down on other business. Nor is it in the least unlikely, that the general agitation and excitement of the public mind by Christ's extraordinary words and works had now alarmed the rulers of the Jewish church, and led them to regard it as a public question of the highest national importance. This is rendered still more probable by John's account of the proceedings in the case of John the Baptist, when a deputation went into the wilderness to ask him whether he was the Messiah (John 1, 19. 24). The very answer which they then received (ib. 27, 28) must have made them more solicitous and watchful against new pretenders to the Messianic office. It is highly important to remember that our Lord did not appear abruptly on the scene as a new personage, entirely unconnected with the previous history of Israel, but claimed, first tacitly and then more openly, to be the great deliverer promised in the ancient Scriptures, and for ages looked for by the chosen people. Hence the growing agitation which his ministry occasioned was not regarded as a transient popular disturbance, but as the beginning of a national and spiritual revolution. But although the motive was the same in either case, the course now taken by the leading Jews was not entirely the same with that before adopted. Then, the messengers were sent directly to John, and demanded categorically who he was, or what he claimed to be (John 1, 19). Now, they are merely sent to watch our Lord's proceedings, and if possible to stem the mighty current of opinion which was setting in his favour, by insidious suggestion or malignant slander. Then, the persons sent were priests and

Levites; now they are only Scribes, but in both cases Pharisees, and sent directly from Jerusalem (compare John 1, 19. 24). It is possible, indeed, that even in the other point, though not expressly mentioned here, the deputations were alike; for as the Scribes, as the traditional expounders of the law, were mostly if not always Pharisees, so they were no doubt often, if not usually, priests or Levites, as the sacerdotal tribe was specially entrusted with the conservation and interpretation of the law (Lev. 10, 11. Deut. 24, 8. 2 Chr. 15, 3. 35, 3. Neh. 8, 7. Jer. 18, 18. Ez. 7, 26. Mal. 2, 7). It is a serious error to suppose that these descriptive titles are exclusive of each other, and denote so many independent classes, whereas they only denote different characters or relations, which might all meet in one and the same person, as being at the same time a priest and Levite by descent and sacred office, a Scribe by profession, and a Pharisee in sentiment and party-connection. These Scribes who had come down from Jerusalem, unable to deny the fact of the miraculous healing, used the only other means at their disposal to discredit him who wrought it, by malignantly accusing him of impious collusion with the very demons whom he dispossessed. This, while it shows their growing enmity and malice, also proves the weakness of their cause, and the reality of Christ's miraculous achievements, which they surely would have questioned if the evidence had not been overwhelming. Their very charge against him, therefore, may be reckoned as involuntary testimony to the truth of his pretensions to a superhuman power; and their failure or refusal to acknowledge this as an abundant confirmation of his Messianic claims can only be ascribed to their infatuation and judicial blindness (compare Luke 6, 11.) *Beelzebub*, or as it is written in all Greek manuscripts, *Beelzebul*. The latter is either a euphonic or fortuitous corruption of the former, or an intentional derisive change, like that of *Sychem* into *Sychar* (John 4, 5). On the latter supposition it is commonly explained as meaning *Dung-god*, an expression of contempt for Beelzebub, the *Fly-god* of the Philistines (2 Kings 1, 2. 3. 6), either so called as protecting his worshippers from noxious insects, or as being himself worshipped under an insect form. This contemptuous description of a heathen deity is perfectly agreeable to Jewish usage, and its application in the case before us a conclusive proof of the extreme to which these Scribes had carried their contempt and hatred of the Saviour, when they chose the grossest nickname of a false god to describe the unseen power by whose aid he wrought his miracles. The preposition (*in*, not *by*) denotes not mere alliance or assistance, but the most intimate personal union, such as existed in all cases of possession (9, 34.) 'It is by virtue of his union and identification with the ruler of the demons that he casts them out.' The word translated *prince* is properly a participle, meaning one who goes first, takes the lead, presides, or governs. As a noun, it denotes magistrates in general, and in Grecian history the *Archons*, or chief magistrates of Athens. It is applied in the New Testament to Moses, as the national leader (Acts 7, 35), to members of the Sanhedrim or national council (John 3, 1. 7, 50), and to the local elders or rulers of the synagogue (Luke 8, 41), but also to the Evil One, or leader of the fallen angels, as the "prince of this world" (John 12, 31. 14, 30. 16, 11), as the "prince of the power of the air" (Eph. 2, 2), and as the "prince of the devils" (9, 34). This last word is an inexact translation, as the Scriptures recognize only one *Devil*, but a multitude of *demons* (see Mark 5, 9. 15). The former is one of the names given to the Evil One by way of eminence, as the slanderer or false accuser of mankind, whereas *Satan* represents him as their enemy or adversary. (See above on 4, 1, and below on v. 26.) The other term, commonly translated *devils*, is properly an adjective, and originally means *divine*, or rather *superhuman*, comprehending all degrees and kinds of gods belonging to the Greek mythology, but specially applied to those of an inferior rank, and bearing some particular relation to individual men as their good or evil *genius*, in which sense Xenophon employs it to describe the tutelary monitor of Socrates. It is perhaps on account of this specific usage of the word that it is used in the New Testament to designate the fallen angels, or evil spirits, as connected with the history of our race, and especially as active in those singular affections which derive from them the name of "demoniacal possessions." Of these *demonia* or *demons*, Satan the Devil, is here called the prince or chief, but under the derisive and disgusting name *Beelzebul*, or *Dung-god*. It is a possible, though not a necessary supposition, that this application of the name was customary and familiar. It is more probable, however, as we do not find it in the oldest Jewish books now extant, that it was devised for the occasion, as a bitter sarcasm against Jesus, whom it virtually represents as united in the closest manner to the most unclean of spirits, and by his authority and power dispossessing his inferior agents. This view of the matter is important, as implying a terrific aggravation of the sin committed by these Scribes and Pharisees in representing the immediate acts of God as operations not of Satan merely, but of Beelzebub, which, though applied to the same being, is peculiarly insulting, as it identifies him with the Fly-god of the old Philistines, and the Dung-god into which this idol had been changed by the bitterness of Jewish controversial satire.

25. And Jesus knew their thoughts, and said unto them, Every kingdom divided against itself is brought to desolation ; and every city or house divided against itself shall not stand.

The first illustrative comparison is taken from *a kingdom*, a state, a body politic, implying not a mere aggregation of men, but organic life and unity of principle and interest. The fact alleged is not that all intestine strife or division is destructive to a state, which is not universally or always true, but that a state which wars against itself, so far as in it lies, contributes to its own destruction. If such a policy in human kingdoms would be justly reckoned suicidal, and at variance with the end for which the state exists, how can that which would be folly in a human sovereign be imputed to the most astute and crafty, as well as the most spiteful and malignant being in the universe? The argument involved in this comparison is not merely that the course supposed would be injurious, or ruinous, and therefore Satan cannot be supposed to take it, but that it would be self-contradictory and foolish, and at variance with the very end for which he has been plotting and deceiving since the world began. He is not too good to pursue such a course, but he is far too cunning. *Every kingdom, thus divided and at war against itself, is brought to desolation,* or as Mark has it (3, 24), *cannot stand,* an expression also used by Matthew in the latter clause of this verse, and more significant in Greek, because the form is passive, and although in usage substituted for the active, still retaining something of its proper force, and therefore suggesting the idea, that it cannot be established, made to stand, by such a process. The use of this expression shows still further, that the reference is not so much to strife between the subjects of a kingdom, which may sometimes be essential to its welfare, but to its waging war against itself, the state (as such) opposing its own interests and aiming at its own destruction. Such a case may be impossible, or never really occur; but if it should, the state would be its own destroyer. So would Satan, if he should do likewise. But that he who is called Apollyon, as the destroyer of others, should attempt self-destruction, is entirely inconceivable. Among men, suicide implies an utter ignorance or disbelief of all futurity; but no such incredulity or error is conceivable in one who knows already in his own experience what it is to perish and yet continue to exist; for as to this, as well as to the being and the unity of God, "the devils also believe and tremble" (James 2, 19). The same thing is true within a sphere still narrower, for instance in a family or household, when not only *divided,* i. e. composed of hostile and discordant members, but *divided against itself,* i. e. arrayed as a whole, or as a body, against its own interest or existence. That this is the true point of our Lord's comparison, is shown by the circumstance that both his illustrations are derived not from the case of individuals at strife, but from communities or aggregate bodies, large or small. The only analogous case that could have been adduced from the experience of a single person, is the strange one of a man divided against himself and striving for his own destruction. But leaving this to be completed by his hearers, he proceeds in the next verse to apply what he has said already.

26. And if Satan cast out Satan, he is divided against himself; how shall then his kingdom stand?

What is thus true of a kingdom and a household among men is no less true of Satan; for if he has risen up against himself, and been divided, he cannot possibly be made to stand, but has an end, or ceases to be what he is. Had the idea of division, in these various illustrations, been the simple one of some opposing others, our Lord would no doubt have applied his argument or principle to Satan's kingdom rather than himself; but as he here presents the paradoxical idea of Satan as an individual divided into two, and one arrayed against the other, we may safely infer, that this very paradox was meant to be the point of his whole argument. If they had said, Neither man nor devil can be thus divided so as to make war upon himself, he might have answered, How absurd then upon your part to allege such a division, by accusing me of being in alliance with my opposite! If Satan could be thus divided, he would not be Satan, but would have an end. (Mark 3, 26.)

27. And if I by Beelzebub cast out devils, by whom do your children cast (them) out? therefore they shall be your judges.

This is a second refutation of their charge, to wit, that by parity of reasoning it extended to their own exorcists, which they would not have been willing to admit. The Fathers understood by *your children* the Apostles; but it is not easy to see why they should be so called, or what force the argument could have in that case, since the twelve avowedly derived their miraculous power from their Master. On the other hand, the fact is certain, both from Scripture and Josephus, that exorcism was a common practice with the Jews. See Acts 19, 13, where *itinerant* (not *vagabond*) *exorcists* are found at Ephesus, the seven sons of a high priest, which may throw some light upon the term *sons* (or *children*) in the verse before us. It is of little moment whether they really exercised this power or not. If they professed and were believed to do so, this is all that is required to give force to the argument *ad hominem*. 'On what ground can you venture to accuse me of collusion with the devil, when your own sons claim to exercise the self-same power? *Therefore they shall be your judges*, to convict you of injustice and malignity in ascribing what I do to demoniacal collusion, when you make no such charge against them and their real or pretended dispossessions.'

28. But if I cast out devils by the Spirit of God, then the kingdom of God is come unto you.

But, on the other hand, a terrible alternative to these calumnious blasphemers, *if I cast out demons*, not by any such collusion as you impiously charge upon me, but *in* (possession of and union with) *the Spirit of God* (not merely as an attribute or influence, but as a divine person), then *has come upon you suddenly*, or unawares, surprised you by its unexpected coming, *the kingdom of God*, the reign of the Messiah, which the nation had been eagerly expecting for ages, but had now lost sight of its true nature, and were therefore liable and likely to be taken by surprise. *Come unto you* is entirely too weak a version both of the verb and preposition, one of which means always to prevent or anticipate, and the other implies superiority of some kind. There was solemn irony in this suggestion to the leading Jews, that in spite of their unwillingness to see or own it, the Messiah and his kingdom might be come after all.

29. Or else how can one enter into a strong man's house, and spoil his goods, except he first bind the strong man? and then he will spoil his house.

He adds an illustration from the experience of common life, to show the conclusion which they must have drawn in an analogous case, and which they therefore should have drawn in this. When a rich man, able to protect his goods, is robbed, no one imagines he has robbed himself, but every one regards it as the work, not only of an enemy, but also of an enemy superior in power. So, too, when they saw Satan's instruments and agents dispossessed and driven out by Jesus, instead of arguing that he and Satan were in league together, they ought rather to have argued that the prince of this world was cast out and judged (John 12, 31. 16, 11), that he had met his match, or rather come in contact with his conquerer. What clearer proof could be demanded, both of Christ's superiority and enmity to Satan, than the havoc which he made of Satan's instruments and tools, to which there may be some allusion in the word translated *goods*, which properly means vessels, utensils, or implements of any kind (see Mark 11, 16. Luke 17, 31. Acts 27, 17,) and may be well applied to those inferior demons of whom Satan was the prince and leader. *Or else* is in Greek simply *or*, and introduces a new supposition, as in v. 5, and in 7, 4. 9. 'Or if this analogy does not convince you, take another.'

30. He that is not with me is against me; and he that gathereth not with me scattereth abroad.

This is a proverbial expression, here appealed to as embodying the common sense of men upon a certain point, to wit, the fact that mere neutrality may sometimes be the worst hostility. In other circumstances the converse may be also true, and is accordingly embodied in another proverb (Mark 9, 40). So far are these two aphorisms from being contradictory, that both may be exemplified in the experience of the very same persons. For example, Nicodemus, by refusing to take part with the Sanhedrim against our Lord, although he did not venture to espouse his cause, proved himself to be upon his side; but if he had continued the same course when the crisis had arrived, he would equally have proved himself to be against him. The pretence of inconsistency between the words of this verse and the saying recorded in Luke (9, 50), is therefore as absurd as such a charge would be against Solomon's twin maxims (Prov. 26, 4. 5).

31. Wherefore I say unto you, All manner of sin and blasphemy shall be forgiven unto men: but the blasphemy (against) the (Holy) Ghost shall not be forgiven unto men.

Thus far the Lord has been refuting the absurdity of their malignant charge, without regard to its peculiarly offensive form; and as he uses the word Satan, not Beelzebub, it might appear that he intended to pass over the gross insult without further notice. But he now rebukes it, indirectly it is true, but with so awful a severity, that few can read the words and even partly understand them without shuddering. This passage, with its parallels in Luke and Mark, has been always and unanimously reckoned one of the most shocking and alarming in the word of God; but it acquires a new solemnity and terror when considered in its true connection with what goes before, and not as a mere insulated and detached expression of a mysterious and fearful truth. The Scribes had represented him as in collusion with the devil, under an unusual and most offensive name, importing that the spirit which possessed Christ was himself an unclean, nay, a filthy spirit. Instead of formally reproving them for this unparalleled affront to himself and to the Spirit who was in him, he describes to them the nature of the sin which they had almost, if not quite, committed, and the doom awaiting it hereafter. *Wherefore*, literally, *for* (or *on account of*) *this*, not what immediately precedes, but the whole foregoing context. As if he had said, 'in view of all this, and because your charge against me is so groundless and malignant.' *I say unto you* is an expressive formula too often overlooked as pleonastic, but containing two emphatic pronouns, 'I the Son of God, and yet the Son of Man, declare to you, my spiteful enemies and false accusers.' *All manner*, i. e. every kind, an explanation rather than a simple version of the Greek words, *every sin and blasphemy shall be remitted*, pardoned, left unpunished, *unto men*, not all the sins of every individual, but every kind of sin to some one. There is no sin (with the subsequent exception) so enormous that it shall not be forgiven to some sinner who commits it. This is said, not only of sin in general, but of a single class of sins, among the most appalling that can be committed or conceived of. (For the origin and usage of the words *blaspheme* and *blasphemy*, see above, on 9, 3.) This is specified, not merely to enforce the previous declaration by applying it to sins directly against God, and in the last degree insulting to him, but also to connect it with the case in hand, or the occasion upon which it was pronounced. The last clause gives the fearful and mysterious exceptions. *The blasphemy of the Spirit*, i. e. against the Holy Ghost, as more explicitly stated in the next verse. The solemn repetition or inversion of the formula in this clause gives it the impressive tone of a judicial sentence.

32. And whosoever speaketh a word against the Son of man, it shall be forgiven him : but whosoever speaketh against the Holy Ghost, it shall not be forgiven him, neither in this world, neither in the (world) to come.

This is a more explicit repetition of the statement in v. 31. The distinction here made seems entirely unaccountable if made between the second and third persons of the Godhead, simply as such, without any thing to qualify or specify the statement. This difficulty disappears, however, on observing that the person mentioned in the first clause is not the eternal Word or Son of God, but the Son of Man, and this, as we have seen (above, on 8, 20. 9, 6), describes the Saviour in his humiliation, in the form of a servant, as he was while resident on earth. To say a word against him while his Godhead was thus veiled and as it were in abeyance, was a very different offence from speaking with contempt and malice of the Holy Spirit in his clearest manifestations, especially those furnished by the words and works of Christ himself. The antithesis is then between contemptuous disparagement of Christ as he appeared in his humiliation, and the same treatment of him when his character and mission were attested by the Holy Ghost. *This world* and *the world to come* are common phrases with the Jews to denote the whole of existence or duration, as divided into two great parts or periods, the present and the future. They are here combined to produce an absolute negation and convey the idea that the sin described shall NEVER be forgiven. The word translated *world* properly denotes *duration*, sometimes definite, as an age, a lifetime, or a dispensation, but when limited by nothing in the context, indefinite and even infinite duration. This strongest sense would be implied here even if these words were not expressed. If some sins will be forgiven and some not, the latter must be co-extensive with the former; and as those forgiven are forgiven to eternity, those unforgiven must eternally remain so.

33. Either make the tree good, and his fruit good ; or else make the tree corrupt, and his fruit corrupt : for the tree is known by (his) fruit.

There is here an obvious recurrence to the principle laid down by Christ himself in the Sermon on the Mount (see above, on 7, 16–20), and there applied to the same class of persons whom he is addressing here. The obvious presumption therefore is that the same application is intended, and that the verse before us is an exhortation to bring their lives and their professions into harmony. But such a warning against false professions and appearances would seem to be misplaced in this connection, where the subject of discourse is open blasphemy, and after so terrible a warning against the unpardonable sin. Some writers therefore understand the words as a direct continuation of what goes before, and as having reference to their false estimate of Christ himself. Either admit the effect to be bad or the cause to be good. If the works which I perform are good works, how can they spring from collusion with the Evil One ? The sense thus put upon the verb to *make* is supposed to be justified by John's use of it in several places. (See John 8, 53. 10, 33. 19, 7. 1 John 1, 10. 5, 10.)

34. O generation of vipers, how can ye, being evil, speak good things ? for out of the abundance of the heart the mouth speaketh.

35. A good man out of the good treasure of the heart bringeth forth good things: and an evil man out of the evil treasure bringeth forth evil things.

Having thus rebuked their slanderous and blasphemous suggestions, he now, by a sudden apostrophe, declares them to be necessary products of their evil nature. *Generation* (brood) *of vipers* is the phrase applied by John the Baptist to the Pharisees and Sadducees who came forth to his preaching, and is here used to designate some of the same persons as belonging to the *seed of the serpent* (Gen. 3, 15), with whom Christ was necessarily in conflict, and over whom he must eventually triumph. *How can ye,* of yourselves, remaining as you are. The implied impossibility is then referred (in v. 35) to the general fact or principle, that language is the outflow, or as it is beautifully represented here, the overflow of inward dispositions, whether good or evil. This is then amplified and formally affirmed of either class (in v. 36). *Bringeth forth,* literally, *casts out,* expels, as if by an involuntary movement. *Treasure* is here used in its earlier and wider sense of store, deposit, without reference to value, so that it is applicable both to good and evil. These descriptions are of course not to be understood exclusively, but only in the general of the spontaneous expression of the inward dispositions in the language, when unrestrained by fear and undisguised by hypocritical professions, as appears to have been the case with these blasphemers.

36. But I say unto you, That every idle word that men shall speak, they shall give account thereof in the day of judgment.

This seems to be an answer to the tacit or audible objection, that too much stress was thus laid upon men's words as distinguished from their actions. The spirit of the answer is that language, for the reason just assigned, is an important criterion of character, and therefore a necessary element of judgment. *Idle,* unemployed, without work, is the proper meaning of the Greek word (ἀργόν) as applied to persons. (See below, on 20, 3. 6.) As here applied to words, some understand it as a strong meiosis or litotes like *unfruitful* in Eph. 5, 11. We have then a simple statement, that for every wicked word like that which they had just uttered against Christ, men must give account as well as for their overt acts. Most readers probably understand by *idle,* trifling, frivolous or foolish. A third interpretation makes it still mean trivial, but in the sense of unimportant. Even for such words men are held responsible.

37. For by thy words thou shalt be justified, and by thy words thou shalt be condemned.

Here, as in vs. 35. 36, what had been previously stated is reduced to the form of a general proposition. *By* does not convey the exact meaning of the Greek preposition, which is *from* or out of, as the source from which the judgment is to be derived. The meaning is not that the words of men are to be taken as the sole criteria of their character, to the exclusion of their other actions, which would be absurd and put it in the power of any man to settle his own destiny by sheer talking or profession. The meaning is the same as in v. 36, more formally propounded; namely, that the words, so far as they are real exponents of something inward, will be taken into the account in making up an estimate of each man's character, and not excluded or ignored, as many seem to imagine.

38. Then certain of the scribes and of the Pharisees answered, saying, Master, we would see a sign from thee.

Though the word *then* by itself would prove nothing as to chronological succession, its being before combined with *answered* makes it altogether probable that what is here related followed immediately the incidents recorded in the previous context. The speakers here are of the same class that blasphemed him, but not the same individuals (Luke 11, 16). The connection seems to be that they were not yet satisfied respecting the expulsion of the demons, and now ask *a sign from heaven*, as opposed to a sign from hell or one on earth, in proof of his Messiahship, before they would acknowledge his pretensions. Their addressing him as *Master*, i. e. Teacher, may be either hypocritical, intended to cajole and flatter, or ironical, intended to insinuate their doubts of his commission and authority. *We would see*, to a modern English reader, conveys very imperfectly the force of the original, the Greek word (θέλομεν), according to the lexicons, expressing not mere willingness or even inclination, but a decided choice and act of will, as if they had said, 'we choose (or we demand) to see a sign from heaven, in addition to these miracles on earth and possibly from hell.'

39. But he answered and said unto them, An evil and adulterous generation seeketh after a sign; and there shall no sign be given to it, but the sign of the prophet Jonas:

The answer, though addressed to them, is in the third person, as intended for a greater number, and because this form of speech has something disrespectful and contemptuous. He calls them *a generation*, as representing the great mass of the contemporary Jews. To the general term *evil* (i. e. wicked), he adds the specific one *adulterous*, literally, *adultress*, and in apposition with the feminine noun *generation*. This is not to be literally understood in reference to the prevalence of this particular iniquity, to which there is no allusion in the context, or any statement elsewhere in the Gospels. It is the well-known figure running through the Old Testament of a conjugal relation between God and the chosen people. Idolatry is often represented as a breach of this relation or as spiritual adultery. When idolatry ceased among the Jews, the same description would be naturally applied to other forms of unfaithfulness by which it was succeeded. There is no need of assuming (with Theophylact) that demons take the place of idols in this later usage. *Seeketh after,* an emphatic compound (ἐπιζητεῖ), used above (6, 32) to express the inordinate craving of the heathen after temporal advantages and comforts. *A sign shall not be given them,* i. e. such as they demand, to wit, a miracle of the kind prescribed or ordered by themselves, as the only proof of his Messiahship by which they would consent to be convinced. This refusal was justified, not only by the sovereign will of him who uttered it, but by the insolence of the demand itself, by the blasphemous aspersion which it presupposed, and by the general principle, continually recognized in the divine administration, that no one has a right to superfluous evidence of what has been sufficiently evinced already. (See below, on 21, 23-27, and compare Luke 16, 31.) The last clause is a sort of solemn irony equivalent to saying, 'unless they will accept the case of Jonah as such a sign.' It is not meant that it was such a sign as they demanded, but merely adds point to the previous refusal.

40. For as Jonas was three days and three nights in the whale's belly: so shall the Son of man be three days and three nights in the heart of the earth.

Instead of giving them a sign from heaven such as they demanded, he refers them to the sign of his own burial and resurrection, which he connects in an enigmatical manner with a well-known incident of Old Testament history, partly, no doubt, for the sake of the comparison that follows in the next verse. There are then two reasons for selecting this particular occurrence, first, the actual coincidence of outward circumstances, and secondly, the opposite effects in the two cases. The external resemblance was the burial for three days both of *Jonas* (the Greek form of *Jonah*) and of Jesus. *Whale* is gratuitously used in all the English versions for a Greek word meaning any great fish or sea-monster; so that the physiological objection, founded on the structure of the whale, is swept away. *Three days and three nights* are to be computed in the Jewish manner, which applies that formula to one whole day with any part however small of two others. This is not an invention of Christian apologists, but laid down as a rule in the Talmud: one hour more is reckoned as a day, one day more as a year. The existence of the usage may be seen by comparing the terms "after three days" and "until the third day" in 27, 63. 64 below. (See also Esther 4, 16. 5, 1). *The heart of the earth* is not *hades* (see above, on 11, 23), but the grave, so called in allusion to the words of Jonah (2, 2. 3. where *midst* is literally rendered in the margin, *heart*).

41. The men of Nineveh shall rise in the judgment with this generation, and shall condemn it: because they repented at the preaching of Jonas; and, behold, a greater than Jonas (is) here.

Besides the outward similarity just mentioned, there was a moral antithesis or contrast in the cases, which our Lord makes use of, to enhance the condemnation of the unbelieving Jews. The heathen to whom Jonah preached repented and were spared: the Jews to whom Christ preached were impenitent and perished. This of course has reference to the Scribes and Pharisees whom he addressed. The form of expression is similar to that in 10, 15. 11, 22. 24. *Rise in judgment* does not mean rise from the dead at the day of judgment, but stand at the bar to be tried. *With*, not against, but at the same time, or in company. *Condemn them*, not in words but by example. The last clause is similar in form and argumentative force to that of v. 6.

42. The queen of the south shall rise up in the judgment with this generation, and shall condemn it: for she came from the uttermost parts of the earth to hear the wisdom of Solomon; and, behold, a greater than Solomon (is) here.

As the mention of Jonah suggested the repentance of the Ninevites, in contrast with the unbelief of Christ's contemporaries, so the mention of the Ninevites suggests another case, not of repentance but of admiration for the wisdom of a mere man, as contrasted with the scorn of Scribes and Pharisees for that of a divine teacher. *The Queen of the South*, called in the Old Testament the *Queen of Sheba* (1 Kings 10, 1), supposed to be the southern part of the Arabian peninsula. *From the ends of the earth*, a hyperbole, found also in the best Greek writers, for a great distance. It may here be intended to suggest a difference of race and of religion.

43. When the unclean spirit is gone out of a man, he walketh through dry places, seeking rest, and findeth none.

As the preceding threatenings and denunciations had respect to the contemporary Jews, our Lord here gives a fearful view of their condition as compared with former generations. The similitude which he uses for this purpose is derived from demoniacal possessions, and is not to be regarded as a fiction but a fact, of real though perhaps of rare occurrence. The case described is that of a relapse into the demonized condition with its fearful aggravations and its hopeless issue. *Is gone out*, or more simply, *goes out*, either by a voluntary act or by coercive dispossession, a question of no moment in relation to what follows.

Walketh, a more specific term than the original which means no more than *goes*, or *passes through*. *Dry*, unwatered, without water, desert. It appears from the Apocrypha (Tobit 8, 3. Baruch 4, 35) that such places were regarded by the later Jews as the abode or the resort of demons, and the same thing is said of ruined Babylon in Rev. 18, 2. We have neither right nor reason to regard this as a mere superstition or poetical embellishment. Our Saviour's language, in the verse before us, warrants the belief that there is some mysterious fact at the foundation of all such allusions. *Rest*, not, as some suppose, another victim, or the pleasure of a new possession, but more generally, satisfaction and repose. The state described is that of restless discontent with present circumstances, urging to a prompt return to what preceded, as expressed dramatically in the next verse.

44. Then he saith, I will return into my house from whence I came out ; and when he is come, he findeth (it) empty, swept, and garnished.

My house, home, previous abode, to wit, the body and the soul of the demoniac. The description in the last clause has been variously understood. Some suppose the victim to be represented as entirely free from the Satanic influence, and in a state of spiritual health and purity; while others hold the opposite opinion, that he is described as ready for the re-possession; *empty, and swept* clean, not of demoniacal conditions, but of all that would prevent them; *garnished*, set in order or arranged, not for some higher end, but for the use of the returning demon. The former supposition makes the contrast more striking and the issue more terrific, by describing the reconquest as occurring just when every thing appeared to promise permanent deliverance. But the other agrees better with the application to the Jews, whose spiritual state before the great catastrophe could not be represented even comparatively as a pure one, unless we assume a specific reference to their freedom from idolatry, of which we may have more to say below.

45. Then goeth he, and taketh with himself seven other spirits more wicked than himself, and they enter in and dwell there : and the last (state) of that man is worse than the first. Even so shall it be also unto this wicked generation.

Then, when he sees the victim thus prepared for his reception. *He goeth* away in search of his companions. *Seven*, either as a definite number in some real case to which our Lord alludes, or as a proverbial form for an indefinite plurality, as in 18, 21. 22 below. *Worse*, more wicked, more of evil spirits, not collectively but severally. *Enter in*, a term used elsewhere to describe demoniacal possession. (See above on 8, 31. 32, and compare Mark 5, 12. 9, 25). *Dwell*, a Greek verb meaning properly to settle, take up one's abode, whether for a time or permanently, which last is here suggested by the context. *Last state*, literally, *last (things)*, circumstances, or conditions. This fearful picture, drawn perhaps from some notorious or well-remembered case of repossession, is expressly applied, in the last clause, to the contemporary race of Jews. It seems to be agreed on all hands that their *last state* was that following the national rejection of Messiah, and immediately preceding the destruction of Jerusalem, the dissolution of the Hebrew state, and the dispersion which has not yet ceased. We learn from their own historian that the people, and especially their leaders, were at that time filled with a fanatical insanity, not unlike that produced by demoniacal possession. The only difficulty is in ascertaining what is represented by the interval of dispossession, or in other words, when the unclean spirit can be said to have gone out of them. There are two ways of answering this question, one of which assumes a reference to some specific period in the history of Israel, and most probably to that which succeeded the Babylonish exile, one of the most singular effects of which was to extinguish idolatry among the people, who before were continually lapsing into it. The obvious objection to this explanation is that there was no return to idolatrous corruption, even in the *last state* of the Jewish nation, which in that respect was *better* and not *worse than the first*. To this it may be answered, not without some plausibility, that idolatry was not itself the demon that went out and afterwards returned, but only the specific temporary form of the possession, which might cease forever though the unclean spirit of malignant disobedience and unfaithfulness to God returned and showed itself in new and more atrocious forms of horrible corruption, such as worldliness, hypocrisy, cupidity, blindness to the truth, and rejection of their own Messiah. It might still be objected that the Jews would then be represented as entirely free from all corruption after the captivity; but this, though not absolutely true, was so far so as to justify the parabolical description, the design of which was simply to exhibit two successive changes, one for the better and the other for the worse. This is the ground assumed in the other explanation, which supposes what is here described to be no specific period in the history of Israel, but simply a process of deterioration, with occasional vicissitudes and fluctuations, but resulting in a state far worse than any that had gone before it. This is certainly the general impression made by the particular case stated, and it certainly applies with terrible exactness to the downward progress of the Jews, with partial interruptions, till the time of the great national catastrophe, the last generation being of course most severely punished, not only for their fathers's sins but for their own. (See below, on 23, 35).

46. While he yet talked to the people, behold, (his) mother and his brethren stood without, desiring to speak with him.

Having been led by a natural association under divine guidance to give some account of the effect produced by Christ's increasing popularity upon his most malignant enemies, the writer now returns to the effect upon his friends, especially those nearest to him. This view of the connection throws some light upon the conduct of his mother and his brethren, in disturbing him while publicly engaged in teaching. That they would venture to do so without a reason, or on ordinary business, or from personal affection, or from pride in their connection with him, although not impossible, is far less probable than that they were actuated by an anxious care for his own safety, and called for him in order to arrest what they regarded as a wild and dangerous excitement, both on his part and on that of the assembled masses. (Compare Mark 3, 21.) It may be difficult for us, with our habitual associations, to appreciate the motives of these anxious friends; but at the juncture here described, nothing could be more natural and pardonable than precisely such solicitude, which is perfectly compatible with true faith and affection, but imperfect views both of his person and his mission. The principal actor in this scene is his mother, the brothers merely following or attending her, but joining in her message and request. It has been a subject of dispute for ages, whether these brothers of our Lord were sons of Joseph and Mary, or of Joseph by a former wife, or nephews of either, all of which hypotheses have been maintained by high authorities. Some of the questions in relation to this topic will recur below (on 13, 55), and some have been considered in the exposition of 1, 25. All that is necessary here is to observe that they were certainly his near relations, and either by birth or by adoption members of his mother's family, so that they constantly attended her and acted with her upon this occasion. *Without*, either outside of the house, or more probably beyond the circle of his hearers in the open air.

47. Then one said unto him, Behold, thy mother and thy brethren stand without, desiring to speak with thee.

As there was a crowd about him (Mark 3, 32), they probably said it one to another till the nearest finally reported it to Jesus. There is no ground, therefore, for the singular opinion, that this person wished to interrupt our Lord's discourse as too alarming, by directing his attention to his friends who were present and inquiring for him.

48. But he answered and said unto him that told him, Who is my mother? and who are my brethren?

Our Lord takes occasion from this incident to teach them that his relative position in society was wholly different from that of others, his domestic ties, though real, being as nothing in comparison with those which bound him to his spiritual household. This is the meaning of the question here recorded. 'Do you think that my condition is the same as yours, and that the wishes of my mother and my brothers are as binding upon me as those of your own households are and ought to be on you?' There is no doubt an implied negation of the proposition thus suggested, as if he had said, 'You are mistaken in supposing that my family relations are the same as yours, or that my mother and brothers are what you express by those endearing names.' The contemptuous meaning put by some upon the words, as if he had intended to say, What are they to me? or what care I for them? is wholly foreign from the text and context.

49. And he stretched forth his hand towards his disciples, and said, Behold my mother and my brethren!

Mark and Matthew have preserved to us each a look or gesture of our Lord on this occasion. *He looked round about on them which sat about him* (Mark 3, 33), no doubt with affectionate and tender recognition, and *he stretched forth his hand toward his disciples*, as if to point them out to others. *See*, behold, (these are) *my mother and my brothers*, i. e. my family and nearest kindred. I am not bound, as you are, to a single household, but embrace as equally allied and dear to me, this vast assembly.

50. For whosoever shall do the will of my Father which is in heaven, the same is my brother, and sister, and mother.

Lest the comprehensive statement which immediately precedes should lead any to imagine that mere outward attendance on his teaching would entitle them to this distinction, he emphatically adds, that it belonged to none but those who acted out as well as listened to this doctrine. It was only he who did the will of God, as Christ announced it, that could claim the honour of this near relationship. But where this condition was complied with, even the poorest and most ignorant, and in themselves the most unworthy of his hearers, were as truly members of his household, and as affectionately cherished by him, as his highly favoured mother, who was blessed among women (Luke 1, 28), or his brothers and his sisters according to the flesh. This delightful assurance, far from abjuring his natural relations, only makes them a standard of comparison for others. Far from saying that he does not love his mother and his brethren, he declares that he has equal love for all who do the will of God. Such a profession from a mere man might be justly understood as implying a deficiency of natural affection, since so wide a diffusion of the tenderest attachments must detract from their intensity within a narrow sphere. Of Christ alone can it be literally true, that while he loved those nearest to him with a love beyond all human experience or capacity, and with precisely the affection due to each beloved object, he embraced with equal tenderness and warmth the thousands who composed his spiritual household, and will continue so to do forever. The implied reproof of his friends' interference with his sacred functions, was intended only for themselves. What he said to the multitude, instead of disparaging his natural relations, magnified and honoured them by making them the measure of his spiritual friendships; and even if he meant to say that those who did the will of God were the only relatives whom he acknowledged, he must still have given a high place among them to his mother, notwithstanding her anxieties on his behalf, and to his brothers also, if believers. If *brothers* be here taken in the wide sense of near relatives, or even in the narrower one of cousins, it is easy to imagine that while some belonging to this class were unbelievers (see John 7, 5), there were others at this time enrolled among his disciples, and some already known as his apostles. (See above, on 1, 25, and below, on 13, 55.)

CHAPTER XIII.

This division of the narrative is chiefly occupied with samples of our Lord's parabolic mode of teaching, of which seven are here brought together, in an order at once topical and chronological. In addition to the parables themselves, we have his own interpretation of two of them, not only enabling us to understand them in particular but also throwing light upon the true method of interpreting parables in general. The first and longest, that of the sower, shows the various receptions which the word or doctrine of the kingdom would meet with in the hearts of men (1–9). This is followed by a statement of his reason for employing this mode of instruction (10–17), and a formal explanation of the parable just uttered (18–23). The second parable is that of the tares, showing the mixed condition of the visible church, and the proper mode of dealing with it (24–30). This is followed by a double parable (the mustard-seed and leaven), showing, as usually understood, the expansive nature of the true religion (31–35). Then comes his private explanation of the tares to his disciples, at their own request (36–43). To these Matthew adds the parables of the hidden treasure and the pearl of great price, showing how the gospel should be valued and secured (44–46), and concludes the series with that of the net, of kindred import with the tares, but not without peculiar features of its own (47–50), and a brief conversation as to parables in general (51–53). The remainder of the chapter might have been connected with the next, as it has no relation to the Saviour's parables, but records his rejection by his old neighbours and acquaintances at Nazareth (54–58).

1. The same day went Jesus out of the house, and sat by the sea side.

2. And great multitudes were gathered together unto him, so that he went into a ship, and sat ; and the whole multitude stood on the shore.

Like Luke (8, 4) and (Mark 4, 1), Matthew records, as a sort of epoch or important juncture in his history, the beginning of our Saviour's parabolical instructions, as a part of the preparatory process by which he contributed to the reorganization of the Church, although he did not actually make the change during his personal presence upon earth, because, as we have seen, it was to rest upon his death and resurrection as its corner-stone. The other part of his preparatory work consisted in the choice and education of the men by whom the change was to be afterwards effected. (See above, on 4, 18. 9, 9. 10.) He had already taught the people publicly with great effect, but now began to teach them in a peculiar manner, with a special purpose to elucidate the nature of his kingdom, for the benefit of those who were to be his subjects, but without a too explicit and precipitate disclosure of his claim to the Messiahship. *By the sea-side*, or *along the sea*, i. e. the lake of Tiberias or Galilee (see above, on 4, 15), not only near it, but upon the very shore. *Multitudes*, or *crowds*, the Greek work indicating not mere numbers, but promiscuous assemblages (see above, on 4, 25). The situation is like that described in Mark 3, 9, where we read that he directed a small vessel to be ready, if the crowd should be so great as to prevent his standing on the shore with safety or convenience. Here we find him actually *entering into* (or *embarking in*) *the boat*, no doubt the one already mentioned as in readiness, and sitting there, i. e. upon the surface of the lake, while his vast audience was on the shore or beach. The scene thus presented must have been highly impressive to the eye, and still affords a striking subject for the pencil.

3. And he spake many things unto them in parables, saying, Behold, a sower went forth to sow :

Many things, of which only samples are preserved, even by Matthew, showing that the writer's aim was not to furnish an exhaustive history, but to illustrate by examples the ministry of Christ. *In parables*, i. e. in the form and in the use of them. *Parable* is a slight modification of a Greek noun, the verbal root of which has two principal meanings, to *propound* (throw out or put forth), and *compare* (throw together or lay side by side). The sense of the noun derived from the former usage, that of any thing propounded, is too vague to be distinctive, comprehending as it does all kinds of instruction, which, from its very nature, must be put forth or imparted from one mind to another. The more specific sense of comparison, resemblance, is not only sanctioned by the usage of the best Greek writers (such as Plato, Aristotle, and Isocrates), but recommended, not to say required by the employment of a corresponding Hebrew word (מָשָׁל from מָשַׁל to resemble) in precisely the same way. In its widest sense, a *parable* is any illustration from analogy, including the simile and metaphor as rhetorical figures, the allegory, apologue, fable, and some forms of proverbial expression. In a more restricted sense, the word denotes an illustration of moral or religious truth derived from the analogy of human experience. In this respect it differs from the fable, which accomplishes the same end by employing the supposed acts of inferior animals, or even those ascribed to inanimate objects, to illustrate human character and conduct. The only fables found in Scripture, those of Jotham (Judg. 9, 8–15) and Joash (2 Kings 14, 9), are given on human, not divine authority. The parable, in its more restricted sense, as just explained, is not necessarily narrative in form, much less fictitious, although this is commonly assumed in modern definitions of the term. There is good reason to believe that all the parables of Christ are founded in fact, if not entirely composed of real incidents. They are all drawn from familiar forms of human experience, and with one exception from the present life. This creates a strong presumption that the facts are true, unless there be some positive reason for supposing them fictitious. Now the necessity of fiction to illustrate moral truth arises, not from the deficiency of real facts adapted to the purpose, but from the writer's limited acquaintance with them, and his consequent incapacity to frame the necessary combinations, without calling in the aid of his imagination. But no such necessity can exist in the case of an inspired, much less of an omniscient teacher. To resort to fiction, therefore, even admitting its lawfulness on moral grounds, when real life affords in such abundance the required analogies, would be a gratuitous preference, if not of the false to the true, at least of the imaginary to the real, which seems unworthy of our Lord, or which, to say the least, we have no right to assume without necessity. In expounding the parables, interpreters have gone to very opposite extremes, but most to that of making every thing significant, or giving a specific sense to every minute point of the analogy presented. This error is happily exposed by Augustine, when he says, that the whole plough is needed in the act of ploughing, though the ploughshare alone makes the furrow, and the whole frame of an instrument is useful, though the strings alone produce the music. The other extreme, that of overlooking or denying the significance of some things really significant, is much less common than the first, and for the most part found in writers of severer taste and judgment. The true mean is difficult but not impossible to find, upon the principle now commonly assumed as true, at least in theory, that the main analogy intended, like the centre of a circle, must determine the position of all points in the circumference. It may also be observed, that as the same illustration may legitimately mean more to one man than to another, in proportion to the strength of their imaginative faculties, it is highly important that, in attempting to determine the essential meaning of our

Saviour's parables, we should not confound what they may possibly be made to mean, with what they must mean to attain their purpose. In addition to these principles, arising from the nature of the parable itself, we have the unspeakable advantage of our Saviour's own example as a self-interpreter. *Behold!* lo! see! both in Hebrew and Hellenistic usage, introduces something unexpected and surprising. Some take it even in its primary and strict sense, look! see there! implying that the object indicated was in sight or actually visible; in other words, that Christ was led to use this illustration by the casual appearance of a sower in a neighbouring field; and this is often represented as the usual occasion of his parabolic teachings. It seems, however, to regard them as too purely accidental, and too little the result of a deliberate predetermination, such as we cannot but assume in the practice of a divine teacher. A safer form of the same proposition is the one already stated that our Saviour's parables, though not invariably suggested by immediate sights or passing scenes, are all derived from the analogy of human experience, and in most instances of common life. Thus three here given by Matthew are designed not only to exhibit different aspects of the same great subject, the Messiah's kingdom, but to exhibit them by means of images derived from one mode of life or occupation, that of husbandry, with which his auditors were all familiar, and in which, most probably, the greater part of them were constantly engaged. But besides these objections to the general supposition that our Saviour's parables were all suggested casually, such an assumption is forbidden in the case before us by the form of expression used by all the evangelists with striking uniformity. It is not as it naturally would be on the supposition now in question. *See, a sower goes* (or *going*) *out*, but with the article, and in the aorist or past tense, *lo, the sower went out.* The Sower, like *the Fox* and *the Lion* in a fable, is generic, meaning the whole class, or an ideal individual who represents it. *Went out*, as we say in colloquial narrative, once upon a time, the precise date being an ideal one because the act is one of constant occurrence. As if he had said, 'a sower went out to sow, as you have often done and seen your neighbour do.' *To sow*, distinguishes his going out for this specific purpose from his going out on other errands. The sower went out as such, as a sower, to perform the function which the name denotes.

4. And when he sowed, some (seeds) fell by the way side, and the fowls came and devoured them up:

As he sowed, literally, *in the* (act of) *sowing*, and, therefore, in the field, not merely on the way to it. *By the way* must, therefore, mean *along the path* trodden by the sower himself and hardened by his footsteps, not along the highway leading to his place of labour. This idea is distinctly expressed by Luke (8, 5), *and it was trodden down*, i. e. it fell upon the path where he was walking. *Some* is understood by every reader to mean some of the seed which he was sowing, the noun, although not previously mentioned as it is in Luke (8, 4), being necessarily suggested by the kindred verb, *to sow, in sowing.* The principal circumstance in this part of the parable is not the treading of the seed, which Luke only adds to specify the place, but its lying exposed upon the trodden path, and there devoured by the birds. *Fowl*, now confined to certain species of domesticated birds, is co-extensive in old English with *bird* itself. *The birds* which his hearers well knew were accustomed to commit such depredations. The familiarity of this occurrence, and of those which follow, must have brought the illustration home to the business and bosoms of the humblest hearers, and, at the same time, necessarily precludes the idea of a fiction, when real facts were so abundant and accessible. It is idle to object that this particular sower never did go forth, when the opposite assertion can as easily be made, and when the terms employed, as we have seen, may designate the whole class of sowers, including multitudes of individuals, or any of these whom any one of the hearers might select as particularly meant, perhaps himself, perhaps some neighbouring husbandman. Such a use of language, when applied to incidents of every-day occurrence, is as far as possible remote from fiction.

5. Some fell upon stony places, where they had not much earth : and forthwith they sprung up, because they had no deepness of earth :

Others, i. e. other seeds fell upon *stony* (or rocky places), plurals equivalent to Mark's collective singulars (4, 5). The reference is not to loose or scattered stones, but to a thin soil overspreading a stratum or layer of concealed rock. *Immediately,* by Mark also, is emphatic, the rapid germination being a material circumstance, and seemingly ascribed to the shallowness of the soil, allowing the seed no room to strike deep root, but only to spring upwards. The same idea is suggested by the verb itself, a double compound meaning to *spring up and forth.* The cause assigned by Luke (8, 6), is not that of the speedy germination, but of the premature decay that followed it, as Matthew describes more fully in the next verse.

6. And when the sun was up, they were scorched ; and because they had no root, they withered away.

There is a peculiar beauty in the Greek here, which cannot be retained in a translation, arising from the use of the same verb (but in a less emphatic form) to signify the rising of the plant and of the sun, as both are said in English to be *up*, when one is above the surface of the earth and the other above the horizon. *Scorched* (or *burnt*) and *withered* (or *dried*, see above on 12, 10) are different effects ascribed to different causes. The first is the evaporation of the vital sap or vegetable juices by the solar heat ; the other their spontaneous failure from the want of a tenacious root. Together they describe, in a manner at once accurate and simple, the natural and necessary fate of a plant without sufficient depth of soil, however quick and even premature its vegetation.

7. And some fell among thorns ; and the thorns sprung up, and choked them :

Others, as in v. 5. *Into the thorns*, or in the midst of them, as it is more fully expressed by Luke (8, 7). *The thorns*, which happened to be growing there, or which are usually found in such situations. *Came up*, appeared above the surface, an expression constantly employed in English to denote the same thing. *Choked*, stifled or deprived of life by pressure. This word, though strictly applicable only to the suffocation of animal or human subjects (see Luke 8, 42), is here, by a natural and lively figure, transferred to the fatal influence on vegetable life of too close contact with a different and especially a ranker growth. Matthew uses an emphatic compound of the Greek verb, corresponding to our own familiar phrase *choked off*.

8. But others fell into good ground, and brought forth fruit, some a hundredfold, some sixtyfold, some thirtyfold.

9. Who hath ears to hear, let him hear.

Others, as in vs. 5, 7. It is a minute but striking proof that the evangelists wrote independently of each other, and that their coincidence of language arose not from mutual imitation, but from sameness of original material, that in these three verses Matthew always says *upon* (ἐπί), Mark *into* or *among* (εἰς). *Good ground*, in Greek, *the earth, the good*, earth or soil properly so called in distinction from the beaten, rocky, thorny places before mentioned. *Some*, the proportion stated being that of the seed sown to the ripe grain harvested. The productiveness ascribed to the nutritious grains in this place is by no means unexampled, either in ancient or modern times. It is indeed a moderate and modest estimate compared with some recorded by Herodotus, in which the rate of increase was double or quadruple even the highest of the three here mentioned, and the recent harvest in our western states affords examples of increase still greater. The particular attention of the hearers is invited to the parable in v. 9, by a formula occurring in 11, 15 above, and there explained.

10. And the disciples came, and said unto him, Why speakest thou unto them in parables ?

Disciples, not in the strict sense of apostles, but in that of friendly hearers and adherents. This is clear from Mark's description (4, 10) *those about him with the twelve*, i. e. those who in addition to the twelve were in habitual attendance on his person, following him from place to place ; or those who, upon this particular occasion, still remained about him after the dispersion of the multitude. Explained in either way, the words are probably descriptive of the same class, and imply that what now follows was addressed neither to the vast mixed multitude, nor to the twelve apostles only, but to an intermediate body, smaller than the first and larger than the second, but composed entirely of disciples (Luke 8, 9) or believers in his doctrine. They appear to have proposed to him two distinct inquiries; first, the general one, why he taught in parables at all; and then, the more specific one, what this first parable was meant to teach (Luke 8, 9). It is observable that Mark, although he gives the question in a single form, and that a vague one, gives the answers to the two inquiries really involved in it; a circumstance which all but hypercritical sceptics will regard, not as discrepancy, but agreement. The question thus interpreted shows that the parabolic method of instruction, as applied now for the first time to the doctrine of the kingdom, was obscure or unintelligible even to the more enlightened of our Saviour's hearers; a deficiency which furnished the occasion of his own authoritative exposition, making known not only the precise sense of the parable to which it was immediately applied, but also the more general principles and laws which are to govern the interpretation of all others.

11. He answered and said unto them, Because it is given unto you to know the mysteries of the kingdom of heaven, but to them it is not given.

We have here the answer to the first inquiry, namely, why he spake in parables at all. In answer to this question, he informs them that a sifting, separating process had begun already and must be continued, with the unavoidable effect of throwing all his hearers into two great classes, *those within* and *those without* the magic circle of his enlightening and saving influence. The difference between these classes was not one of personal intrinsic merit, but of divine favour. *To you it has been given*, the perfect passive form, implying an authoritative predetermination, being common to all three accounts, as in our Lord's assurance to the paralytic, *Thy sins have been forgiven thee* (see above, on 9, 2). *Given*, not conceded as a right, but granted as a favour. *To know*, i. e. directly, by explicit statement, either without the veil of parable, or with the aid of an infallible interpretation. *Mysteries*, in the usual sense of that word as employed in scripture to denote, not the intrinsic nature of the things so called, but merely their concealment from the human mind until disclosed by revelation. The mystery in this sense here particularly meant is that of the kingdom of God, to be erected by Messiah in the heart of man and of society, and to receive its final consummation in a future state of glory. The use of this expression (*of the kingdom*), common to all three accounts (see Mark 4, 11. Luke 8, 10), is not without importance, as evincing that the parables of Christ had reference, not merely to personal duty and improvement, but to the nature of his kingdom and the mode of its establishment, a reference too often overlooked or sacrificed to mere individual edification. To those without the sphere or scope of this illuminating influence, *it is not given*, i. e. in the same way, but by parables. (Mark 4, 11.)

12. **For whosoever hath, to him shall be given, and he shall have more abundance : but whosoever hath not, from him shall be taken away even that he hath.**

This aphorism Luke (8, 18) agrees with Mark (4, 25) in placing at the close of this important admonition. The question of arrangement is of less importance, as our Lord appears to have pursued the subject both before and after he explained the parable of the sower, and the only difference is in this relative position of the sentence. We may either suppose therefore that he uttered the words twice, or regard it as a matter of indifference whether they preceded or followed his infallible interpretation of the Sower. Applying the same rule of exposition as before, to wit, that the specific application of such maxims is to be determined by the context in every given case of their occurrence, we shall find that the one here uttered has respect not to grace or spiritual influence in general, but to illuminating grace or spiritual knowledge in particular. Our Lord exhorts them to attend to what he says, and lays it down as the foundation of ulterior attainments; for in this sense, too, it may be said, *Whoever has, to him shall be given,* i. e. whoever takes, keeps, and uses, what I tell him now, shall know still more hereafter. And the converse is, of course, true, *he who has not* (in possession and in use what I have previously taught him), *even what he has* (of previous knowledge and attainment, or even of this, as a mere speculative intellectual possession) *shall be taken from him*. This involves a threatening of divine retribution, but is strictly and directly the announcement of a general law, both intellectual and moral, namely, that the only choice is between loss and gain, advancement and recession; that there can be no stagnation or repose; that the only method of securing what we have is by improving it, the failure to do which is tantamount to losing it or throwing it away. It is only another aspect of the same important lesson, no doubt uttered by our Lord in some discourse upon this subject, and most probably in that before us, that we find in Luke's report of it (8, 18), namely, that the value of previous attainments in religious knowledge, unless thus improved and advanced upon, is only specious and apparent, and that even this, in case of failure to increase and grow, will be withdrawn, or seen in its true colours, for *whoever has not* (in possession and in use what I have taught him, but imagines that he can retain it as it is without its growing either more or less), *even what he* (thus) *seems to have* (or thinks he has of spiritual knowledge) *shall be taken from him*, not as an arbitrary punishment inflicted by authority, but as the necessary intellectual and moral product of his own neglect.

13. **Therefore speak I to them in parables : because they seeing see not ; and hearing they hear not, neither do they understand.**

Therefore, literally, *for this,* i. e. for this cause or reason, may refer grammatically either to what follows or what goes before. If the latter, it would seem to mean, 'according to the principle just laid down, or because to him who hath shall be given, &c.' If the latter, the expression simply means, 'I will tell you why I speak to them in parables.' In favour of the first construction is the intimate connection then existing between this verse and the one before it; while according to the other the transition is somewhat abrupt. Thus far it might have seemed that the obtuseness of the hearers to divine instruction was a mere misfortune, having no connection with their moral character and state. But now the Saviour represents it as the consequence of sin, left by God in his righteousness to operate unchecked in one class, but gratuitously counteracted in another. The terms of the description here are borrowed from that fearful picture of judicial blindness in Isaiah 6, 10. The quotation is recorded by the three evangelists, but much more formally and fully by Matthew. In this verse he anticipates it by a description of the actual condition of the people, showing that the prophecy applied to them. To see and not to see, hear and not hear, was a paradoxical Greek proverb, used by Demosthenes and Æschylus to signify a mere external sensuous perception without intellectual or moral conviction, as expressed in the last clause of the verse before us.

14. And in them is fulfilled the prophecy of Esaias, which saith, By hearing ye shall hear, and shall not understand; and seeing ye shall see, and shall not perceive :

Having first described their spiritual state in terms derived from Isaiah, he now quotes the prophecy itself, and declares it to be verified in them, but with a marked variation in the form of the expression. What the Prophet puts into the form of an ironical command or exhortation to do the very thing which would destroy them, our Lord, as Matthew here reports him, turns into a warning or prediction that they would so do. This is certainly involved in the original, and only drawn out here into a paraphrase. The Hebrew idiom is retained, which uses two forms of the same verb for intensity or more exact specification. *Seeing* indeed, or seeing still, or seeing clearly, so far as concerns the outward object. *Hearing* indeed, or still, or clearly, yet *they hear not,* with effect or to any useful purpose. *Neither do they understand* (or apprehend) the things heard in their spiritual import.

15. For this people's heart is waxed gross, and (their) ears are dull of hearing, and their eyes they have closed; lest at any time they should see with (their) eyes, and hear with (their) ears, and should understand with

(their) heart, and should be converted, and I should heal them.

The description of v. 13 is repeated, but with more exact adherence to Isaiah's words, which are given with little variation in the language of the Septuagint version. *Waxed gross*, grown fat, here a figure for inveterate insensibility. *Their ears are dull of hearing* is a paraphrase, the Greek words literally meaning *they have heard heavily with their ears. Closed*, literally, shut down, shut fast, or refused to open. The last clause gives the judicial end or purpose of their being thus abandoned, lest at any time (or some time), they should see and hear and understand and turn (or be converted), and be healed of their spiritual malady, or sin, by forgiveness, as the figure is explained by Mark (10, 12).

16. But blessed (are) your eyes, for they see: and your ears, for they hear.

17. For verily I say unto you, That many prophets and righteous (men) have desired to see (those things) which ye see, and have not seen (them); and to hear (those things) which ye hear, and have not heard (them).

In contrast with the spiritual blindness and stupidity of unbelievers he congratulates his own disciples, not the twelve, but all who acknowledged his authority, that their eyes see and their ears hear the glorious things revealed by him. In this they were more fortunate or highly favoured, not only than the blinded scribes and Pharisees around them, but also in comparison with better men of former times, who would have seen and heard these very things with thankfulness and joy, but died before the time. *Prophets and just men* seem to be combined as a description of the truly pious, or of good men, as in 10, 41 above.

18. Hear ye therefore the parable of the sower.

You, therefore, my disciples, as distinguished from the unbelieving world, and also from your less favoured predecessors, *hear the parable of the sower*, i. e. hear my explanation of it which you have requested. This explanation is not only in itself a model of conciseness, clearness, and superiority to all conceits and forced analogies, but from its source and author an invaluable rule and guide in all cases of the same kind, where we have not the advantage of an infallible interpretation. It becomes us, therefore, in the two authoritative expositions here recorded for our learning, to observe not only what our Saviour does but what he leaves undone, the neglect of which has led to the excesses and absurdities of ultra-allegorical interpretation. These are left without excuse by our Lord's condescending here to teach the fundamental principles of parabolical interpretation. It is impossible to overrate the value of this clew to guide us through the labyrinth of various and discordant expositions, or its actual effect, when faithfully employed, in guarding the interpreter against the opposite extremes of meagre generality and fanciful minuteness. It was not only placed here in the history, but uttered when it was, that it might serve as an example and a model in interpreting those parables which Christ has not explained himself. Some of the errors thus forbidden and condemned, if not prevented, will be noticed in expounding the ensuing verses.

19. When any one heareth the word of the kingdom, and understandeth (it) not, then cometh the wicked (one), and catcheth away that which was sown in his heart. This is he which received seed by the way side.

The characters about to be described are those whose case is represented by the falling of the seed upon the path. *This is he* (literally) *sown by the way*. The incongruity, alleged by some, of making the seed represent the man, and not the word is a mere rhetorical punctilio, and presents no difficulty to the mind of any unbiassed reader. The parable has answered its design for ages, notwithstanding this alleged flaw in its imagery, which probably occurs to none but hypercritics. When they (the persons represented in this portion of the parable) *hear* (or *have heard*) the word (just represented as seed sown), immediately comes the Evil One, elsewhere called the Devil (Luke 8, 12), and Satan, or the Adversary (Mark 4, 15). *Catcheth away*, in reference to the picking of grain by birds (see above on v. 4). *Sown in his heart*, a mixture of the sign and the thing signified, producing no confusion, and objectionable only on the ground of rhetorical preciseness. The influence here ascribed to Satan must be strictly understood as really exerted by him in the case of those who hear the word, but only as a persuasive, not a coercive power, and, therefore, exercised by turning the attention from the word as soon as uttered, and diverting it to other objects.

20. But he that received the seed into stony places, the same is he that heareth the word, and anon with joy receiveth it;

He now identifies the second class of fruitless and unprofitable hearers, those represented in the parable by the falling of the seed on stony places. Here again he seems to make the seed the emblem of the man himself, and not of the word preached to him, but with as little disadvantage to the force and clearness of the illustration as before, and in the exercise of that discretionary license which distinguishes original and independent thinkers, even among mere men, from the grammarians and rhetoricians. Every ordinary reader understands, without instruction, that *the (one) sown upon the rocky (places)* means those whose character and state are represented by the falling of the seed upon the rock, and not that the seed itself specifically represents the persons. The paraphrastic version in our Bible is entirely gratuitous. This portion of the parable, like that preceding it, exhibits a distinct class of hearers, and the influence exerted on them by the doctrine of the kingdom. The difference between the cases is that these go further, and not only hear the word, or passively receive it, but accept it as the word of God, and that not merely with a cold assent or forced submission, but with joy, as something addressed to the affections, no less than the reason and the conscience, and received accordingly, at once. *immediately*, which, though a favourite expression of Mark (1, 10. 18. 31. 42. 2, 2. 3, 6), is attested as genuine, not by his report alone (4, 16), which would have been sufficient for the purpose, but by that of Matthew. The obvious gradation in the parable not only renders it more perfect in a literary point of view, but increases its discriminating power as applied to individual and general experience, so that every class of hearers, even now, and still more in the time of Christ, might see itself as in a mirror. Indeed, nothing shows the wisdom of our Lord's instructions more impressively than the fact, confirmed by all experience for 1800 years, and receiving further confirmation every day, that all varieties of human and religious character may be reduced to some one or more of his simple but divine descriptions.

21. Yet hath he not root in himself, but dureth for a while: for when tribulation or persecution ariseth because of the word, by and by he is offended.

While the first seed was not even buried, but removed while on the surface, the second was not only sown, but came up prematurely and without a root, which same expression our Lord now applies to the class here represented, namely, those *who have no root in themselves*, i. e. what in our religious phraseology (here founded upon Job 19, 28) is called "the root of the matter," i. e. a principle of true religion, including or implying faith, repentance, and the love of God, producing an analogous external life. This shows in what sense Luke describes them (8, 13) as believing for a while, i. e. professing or appearing to believe while really without the root of true conviction and conversion. Matthew expresses the same thing more concisely in a single word, *temporary*, made up of the noun and preposition here employed by Luke, and elsewhere rendered *temporal* (2 Cor. 4. 18, as opposed to *eternal*), or paraphrased, *for a season* (Heb. 11, 25). *Distress* or *persecution*, kindred but distinct terms, one originally signifying *pressure*, and the other *pursuit*, the former comprehending providential chastisements. the latter denoting more specifically evils inflicted by the hands of human enemies. *For* (because or on account of) *the word*, the doctrine of Christ's kingdom, which they had so joyfully embraced, and for a time so openly maintained. *Ariseth* is in Greek an absolute construction, *being*, beginning to be, coming to pass, happening. *Immediately*, both in Matthew and Mark (4, 17), but with a difference of form (εἰθὺς and εὐθέως), the repetition showing that the real change for the worse is as sudden and as easy as the apparent change for the better. *Offended*, not in the ordinary modern sense of being displeased or alienated in affection, but in the Latin and old English sense of stumbling or being made to stumble. The nearest root or theme to which it can be traced in classic Greek, denotes a trap or snare, but in the Hellenistic dialect a stumbling block or hindrance in the path, over which one may fall. In like manner the derivative verb means to make one fall or stumble, a natural figure both for sin and error, and often representing both as commonly connected in experience. Another explanation of the usage, leading to the same result, gives *offend* its modern sense, but in reference to God, to offend whom is to sin, and then takes the verb here in a causative sense, *they are made to sin*, or betrayed into sinning against God. As the sin here meant is not such as even true believers may commit, but one arising from the absence of a root in the experience, Luke (8, 13) describes it by the stronger term, *apostatize* (or *fall away*), not from a previous state of grace or true conversion, which would imply the very thing explicitly denied in the preceding clause, to wit, the possession of a root, but from their ostensible and false profession.

22. He also that received seed among the thorns is he that heareth the word ; and the care of this world, and the deceitfulness of riches, choke the word, and he becometh unfruitful.

Another class of fruitless hearers represented in this parable *are those sown among the thorns*, i. e. those whose case is symbolized or emblematically set forth by the falling of a portion of the seed among thorns. The form of expression is the same as in vs. 19. 20. and is uniform in all the gospels, a sufficient proof that it is not an inadvertence or mistake of the historian, but at least in substance a deliberate expression of our Lord himself. Common to this with the other classes here described is the hearing of the word, because the very purpose of the parable is to exhibit different ways in which it may be heard with the effect upon the hearer. Some suppose the climax or gradation to be here continued, and this third class of hearers to be represented as going further than the second. But it seems more natural to make the two co-ordinate as different divisions of the same class, i. e. of temporary converts or believers, the difference between them being not that one continues longer than the other, but that one is scandalized by violence, the other by allurement or seduction. While the former yield to *distress and persecution*, these are rendered fruitless by the cares and pleasures of the world. *Care*, undue solicitudes, anxieties, and fears, as to the interests of this life. The corresponding verb (translated in our Bible by the old English phrase to *take thought*, i. e. to be over anxious) is applied by our Lord elsewhere in the same way (see above, on 6, 25–34, and compare Luke 10, 41). *Of this world* (or, according to the critics, *the world*), the same Greek word that was explained above (on 12, 32), as meaning properly *duration* or continued existence, either definite or indefinite, finite or infinite, according to the context. Some suppose it here to mean the old economy or dispensation, to which secular anxieties were more appropriate, and even necessarily incident, than to the new. But it is more natural to understand it of the present life, with its temporary interests and pleasures, as opposed to the future and eternal state. Besides the cares or anxious fears belonging to this mixed and in a certain sense probationary state, and relating chiefly to the means of subsistence, our Lord specifies another danger, *the deceit of wealth*, including both delusive hope and fanciful enjoyment, and applying, therefore, both to those who make haste to be rich, as being the true source of happiness, and those who reckon themselves actually happy because rich already. *Choke the word*, as in the parable itself (v. 7) the thorns *choked the seed*, another mixture of the sign and the thing signed, but still less confusing than in vs. 19. 20. because even in the parable *to choke* is a strong figure as applied to plants, requiring little modification to adapt it to spiritual subjects. The same thing substantially is true of the remaining clause, *and it becomes unfruitful*, i. e. the word or truth considered as a seed, because intended to produce beneficial effects upon the life and character of those who hear it.

23. But he that received seed into the good ground is he that heareth the word, and understandeth (it); which also beareth fruit, and bringeth forth, some a hundredfold, some sixty, some thirty.

Having thus applied the three ideal cases of unfruitful sowing to three well-known forms of human experience, our Lord concludes his exposition of the parable, by doing the same thing with respect to the one favourable case which it presented, but which really includes a vast variety, at least in the measure or degree of fruitfulness, denoted by the ratio or proportion of the fruit or ripe grain to the seed or sown grain. *The* (one) *sown*, as in v. 22, i. e. whose case is represented by the sowing upon good ground. These, like all the others, *hear the word*, receive instruction in the doctrine of the kingdom, and like two of the preceding classes, actively *accept* it, with assent and approbation, but unlike them all, escaping or resisting the occasions of unfruitfulness before described, retain it (Luke 8, 15) and *bear fruit*, not merely for a time, but in continuance, with perseverance, and yet with great diversity of actual attainment, corresponding to the different proportions which the crop bears to the literal seed sown, which Luke omits, but Mark and Matthew here repeat, though not in the same order (Mark 4, 20. *thirty, sixty, a hundred*). Even the most unreflecting reader cannot need to be reminded, that the numbers thus selected are intended to convey the general idea of proportional diversity, and not to limit that diversity to three specific rates. Hence our Lord, in expounding this part of the parable, simply repeats what he had said in the parable itself, without attaching a specific import to the several amounts, a lesson and example to inferior expounders, not only here but in all analogous cases. The same thing might be said in substance of the three cases of unfruitfulness, except that there is reason to believe that they are not given merely as selected samples, but as comprehensive heads to which all particular occasions of unfruitfulness in spiritual husbandry may be reduced.

24. Another parable put he forth unto them, saying, The kingdom of heaven is likened unto a man which sowed good seed in his field :

There is here no mark of time or of immediate succession, as in v. 1. and although the general presumption is in favour of the latter, yet the practice of Matthew and the structure of his gospel leave us at liberty to suppose that this parable was uttered on a different occasion, and only introduced here to complete the exemplification of our Saviour's parabolic mode of teaching. At the same time there is nothing to require this supposition but strong reasons for the contrary assumption, as we shall see below. *Put forth*, laid before (or by) them, a verb often used in reference to food (Mark 6, 41. 8, 6. 7. Luke 10, 8. 11, 6. Acts 16, 34. 1 Cor. 10, 27), and, therefore, specially appropriate in its figurative application to the furnishing of intellectual and spiritual aliment. This parable, like that before it, and another which occurs below (vs. 31. 32), is derived from the processes of husbandry, in which a large proportion of the hearers were no doubt employed, and with which all would be more or less familiar. *The kingdom of heaven*, as usual in this history, denotes the reign of the Messiah, or the new economy, with special reference, in this case, to its inception and its earlier stages. *Is likened*, literally, *was* (or *has been*) *likened*, which can hardly mean *compared*, or likened in discourse, as in 11, 16. where the active voice and future tense are used, but rather actual assimilation by the progress of events. The kingdom of heaven, even in that early stage of its development, had already begun to exhibit the unwholesome mixture which this parable describes. A third form of expression, which occurs below in 25, 1. refers the parable to changes not yet fully realized. *To a man*, that is, to the case, conduct, or condition of a man. The attempt to press the phraseology, as meaning that the man himself specifically represents the kingdom, is as false in taste as it is inconsistent with the masterly freedom of our Lord in the use of parabolic imagery. (See above, on v. 19, and on 9, 37.) *Which sowed,* literally, *sowing,* here expressive not of a habit or a custom, but of an act performed on a particular occasion, as appears from the whole narrative that follows. *Good seed,* not merely good of its kind, but of a good kind, of the right kind, some nutritious grain, as opposed to the poisonous or worthless weeds which are mentioned in the next verse.

25. But while men slept, his enemy came and sowed tares among the wheat, and went his way.

Literally, *in men's sleeping,* not on that occasion merely but in general, as a specification of the time, *when men sleep,* namely, in the night. It is not, therefore, an implied censure of the farmer or his servants, who in that case would have been more clearly pointed out, both in the parable itself and in the explanation of it. (See below, on vs. 38. 39.) The meaning obviously is, at the time when men as usual were sleeping, and in consequence unable to discover or prevent it. *His enemy,* no doubt an unfriendly neighbour, such as too often may be found in rural districts, as well as in the populous city. *Tares,* according to the Rabbins, a grain very similar to wheat, and not only worthless but injurious in its effects. Modern writers understand the Greek word as denoting a species of the darnel. The botanical question is of no importance to the meaning of the parable. *Among* is in Greek a strong expression (ἀνὰ μέσον) meaning *through* (or up and down), *the midst* (or middle) *of the wheat. And went away,* as secretly as he had come, without detection or discovery. This would also suggest the idea, that the work was done, the mischief was accomplished, and required no further care or labour, as the wheat did.

26. But when the blade was sprung up, and brought forth fruit, then appeared the tares also.

But (δέ), in contrast with this silent secret operation. Or the particle may be translated *and,* as in v. 7, and often elsewhere, and be taken as a mere connective. *Blade,* the word translated *grass* in 6, 30. but denoting in both places, that stage in the progress of the plant when it resembles grass externally. In 14, 19. *grass* is used correctly in its usual or proper sense. *Was sprung up,* came up, germinated, sprouted, *and brought forth,* literally, *made,* produced, fruit. *Appeared,* in Greek a passive form, was brought to view, was rendered visible, was made to appear, but constantly employed as a deponent, corresponding to the English word here used.

27. So the servants of the householder came and said unto him, Sir, didst not thou sow good seed in thy field? from whence then hath it tares?

So, the same connective (δέ) that is rendered *but* at the beginning of v. 25. The English word is also here used, not in its comparative and proper sense, but as a resumptive or continuative particle of constant use in our familiar narrative style. *Servants*, slaves, with special reference to those employed in field-work. The interrogation presupposes an affirmative answer, and is, therefore, equivalent to a positive assertion, which is made the ground of the ensuing real question, i. e. one intended to elicit information. *Whence*, from what source or quarter, by what means or agency? *Then*, therefore, since it had been sown with good seed. *Has it* (does the field contain and now exhibit) *tares* (as well as wheat)? There is something lifelike in the very simplicity of this brief dialogue, entirely in keeping with the supposition that this parable like all the rest relates a real incident. (See above, on v. 3.)

28. He said unto them, An enemy hath done this. The servants said unto him, Wilt thou then that we go and gather them up?

The particle translated *so* at the beginning of v. 27, is here omitted altogether. This was probably a mere inadvertence on the part of Tyndale, carelessly retained by Cranmer and the common version. It has no effect upon the sense, but renders the construction more abrupt than is usual either in Greek or Hebrew narrative. *An enemy*, in Greek, *an enemy* (or *hostile*) *man*, the first word being properly an adjective, though absolutely used, i. e. without a substantive, from Hesiod downwards. *Man* is here not simply pleonastic, but equivalent to saying, one who is an enemy or hostile, thus making somewhat prominent the attitude or character of enmity, whereas *an enemy* would put the emphasis upon the person. *Did this*, and by implication, did it at a certain time, to wit, before the wheat had come up. *Wilt thou*, is it thy desire or wish, not merely, art thou willing? (See above, on 12, 38.) The construction here is foreign from our idiom, though the sense is clear. *Wilt thou going we may gather them* (i. e. the tares)?

29. But he said, Nay ; lest while ye gather up the tares, ye root up also the wheat with them.

But, the particle omitted in v. 28, and rendered *so* in v. 27, but in Greek having precisely the same force in all these cases, namely, that of a connective or continuative particle. *Nay*, in modern English, *no*, in Greek and Latin, and some modern languages identical with *not*, and in all the correlative or opposite of *yea*, *yes* (*vai*, 5, 37. 9, 28. 11, 9. 26). *Lest*, that not, a compound particle originally meaning. *lest at any time* (or *some time*), and correctly so translated in 4, 6. 5, 25. and v. 15 above, but sometimes used with little or no reference to time, as in 7. 6. 15. 39. 25. 9 and the verse before us. *While ye gather*, literally, *gathering*, a favourite Greek construction and entirely consistent with our idiom, though almost constantly avoided in the old English versions. *Root up*, literally, *root out*, tear out by the roots, eradicate. *Also* is not expressed in Greek unless included in the adverb (ἅμα) meaning *at the same time*, simultaneously, which here and often elsewhere has the force of a preposition governing the dative (αὐτοῖς), *together* (at the same time) *with them*. The wisdom of this agricultural reason for refusing to allow the extirpation of the tares, is not without importance in its bearing on the spiritual application. (See below, on v. 40.)

30. Let both grow together until the harvest: and in the time of harvest I will say to the reapers, Gather ye together first the tares, and bind them in bundles to burn them: but gather the wheat into my barn.

Let, permit, suffer, but in Greek suggesting the original idea of the verb, which is to leave or let alone. (Compare 3, 15. 5, 40. 7, 4. 8, 22. with 4, 11. 20. 22. 5, 24. 8, 15.) *Grow together* is in Greek peculiarly emphatic, as being one compounded word (συναυξάνεσθαι). *Harvest*, a Hellenistic noun formed from the verb to reap or mow, here denoting not the season merely but the act or operation, as appears from the expression in the next clause, *time of harvest*. (Wiclif translates the first word, *reaping time*, the second, *time of ripe corn*.) *Reapers*, though entirely unlike in English, is a collateral derivative from the same Greek verb (θερίζω, θερισμός, θεριστής). Another pair of cognate words (δήσατε, δέσμας) is exactly and felicitously rendered by a corresponding pair in English (*bind* and *bundles*). As to the burning of the weeds, see above, on 6, 30. *First*, before the wheat is reaped, which was probably the customary order. *But*, when the worthless vegetation has been thus disposed of. *Gather*, not the same verb with the one in the first clause, but synonymous in usage, one originally meaning to lay or place, and the other to lead or bring, together. *Barn*, granary, or storehouse (see above, on 2, 12. 6, 36. in the former of which places it is rendered *garner*).

31. Another parable put he forth unto them, saying, The kingdom of heaven is like to a grain of mustard seed, which a man took, and sowed in his field:

This is a third parable derived from agricultural experience, to which Mark (4, 26–29) adds another, but omits that of the tares. This shows the independent choice of the evangelists in working up the same materials, and also the abundance of our Saviour's illustrations drawn from common life, of which these are probably mere specimens or samples. The kingdom of heaven is here itself said to be like a grain of mustard-seed, a form of expression which, as we have seen (on v. 24), is not to be unduly pressed, but which may here be strictly understood, as the truth taught is the expansive nature of religion, or of Christ's kingdom both in society at large and in the hearts of individuals. *A grain of mustard seed*, or single seed of mustard. Botanists are not agreed as to the plant here meant; but it is certain that an herb, of more than ordinary size, and bearing fruit resembling mustard, has been found by modern travellers in the Holy Land. *Taking sowed*, a pleonastic form, or rather fulness of description, not uncommon in colloquial narrative. *Field* is not exclusive but inclusive of what we call a garden, the Greek word denoting not the size but the fact of cultivation.

32. Which indeed is the least of all seeds : but when it is grown, it is the greatest among herbs, and becometh a tree, so that the birds of the air come and lodge in the branches thereof.

This is not a botanical dictum but a popular hyperbole, or rather a relative expression, meaning the smallest of domestic garden seeds in proportion to the size of the plant which it produces. *Greatest*, as in 11, 11. is an English superlative used to represent a Greek comparative. The literal translation is, *greater than the herbs*, i. e. the pot-herbs, garden vegetables, raised for domestic use. Even this phrase is substantially, though not in form, superlative, the meaning obviously being, *greater than the* (other, and by implication, all the other) *herbs*. But the form of expression in English is much stronger, and, therefore, not exact as a translation. *Becomes*, the true sense of the verb so often rendered by our verb *to be* (see on 4, 3. 5, 45. 6, 16. 9, 16. 10, 16. 12, 45. and v. 22 above). *A tree*, as distinguished from a mere plant or garden-herb in size. *Birds of the air*, literally, *of heaven*, as in 6, 26. 8, 20, where this form of expression is explained. *Come*, resort to it by choice as a convenient resting-place. *Lodge*, find shelter, the verb corresponding to the noun in 8. 20. The sense given in the older English versions (Tyndale, *build ;* Cranmer, *make their nests*) is too specific, and at variance with the fact as stated by the Spanish commentator Maldonatus, who observes that he had sometimes seen large groves of *sinapi* (or oriental mustard) and the birds sitting on the branches, but had never seen their nests there. Though we have not the advantage of our Lord's authoritative exposition of this parable, as in those of the sower and the tares, we have another, that of general and even universal agreement among all interpreters, that this one was intended to set forth, by lively and familiar images, the rapid progress of the true religion from what seemed to be feeble and contemptible beginnings, calling forth a repetition of the prophet's question, "Who hath despised the day of small things?" (Zech. 4, 10.) As this process, though in progress, was as yet very far from its completion, our Lord uses neither the past tense (as in v. 24) nor the future (as in 25, 1), but the comprehensive present, *it is like*, (already,) and will be still more like hereafter.

33. Another parable spake he unto them; The kingdom of heaven is like unto leaven, which a woman took, and hid in three measures of meal, till the whole was leavened.

To the three agricultural analogies just given, Matthew adds one borrowed from domestic life and female industry, as if to leave no part of every-day experience unemployed in the elucidation and enforcement of religious truth. The introductory formula is like that in vs. 24, 31, without chronological specification. Nor can any inference be drawn from the resemblance of this parable to that before it, since this very similarity may possibly have led to their juxtaposition without any chronological connection. The resemblance lies in the essential meaning, which is evidently that of an expansive spread or diffusion, corresponding to the growth of the mustard-plant. The figure here is that of *leaven*, yeast, or sour dough, with its familiar effect upon the meal into which it is kneaded. The measure mentioned is described by the rabbins as the third part of an ephah, and by Jerome, in his comment on this passage, as equivalent to one modius or Roman bushel (see above, on 5, 15) and a half. The precise capacity is unimportant to the meaning of the passage, though it may be worthy of remark, that three seahs or an ephah would seem to have been a customary quantity in household baking. (See Gen. 18, 6. Judges 6, 19.) The word translated *meal* is used in the classics to denote wheat flour, as distinguished from ground barley or other inferior grains. *Until* determines nothing as to the rapidity or slowness of the process, which is therefore not included in the import of the parable, or left to be supplied by the experience of the hearers. *The whole was* (or *it was all*) *leavened*, or retaining the Greek collocation, *it was leavened all (of it)*, or leavened wholly. This complete diffusion of the leaven, rather than the time required for the process, seems to be the main point in the parable. There is still an interesting question with respect to it, and one which admits of being plausibly argued upon both sides. Does this parable, like the one before it, set forth the diffusive quality or tendency of truth, and of the true religion, or the corresponding character of falsehood and corruption? In favour of the former supposition is the obvious presumption springing from the similarity of form, the want of any intimation to the contrary, the sameness of the prefatory formula, and chiefly the express use of the leaven to symbolize or represent "the kingdom of heaven." The two first of these reasons being negative, may be neutralized of course by positive considerations on the other side. The others, although strong, are not entirely conclusive, since the "kingdom of heaven" may be used, as in the Tares, to represent the whole state of the church in its present mixed and militant condition. In favour of the other explanation is the very strong fact, that leaven always in the Scriptures elsewhere (except Lev. 23, 17), is a figure for corruption, either in doctrine or affection. This usage, probably arising from the physical fact that fermentation is incipient putrefaction, may be traced in the exclusion of all leaven from the passover and other sacrificial rites of the Mosaic law, as well as in its figurative application both by Christ and Paul. (See below, 16, 6. and compare Ex. 12, 15. Lev. 2, 11. 1 Cor. 5, 6–8. Gal. 5, 9.) The usage is indeed so uniform and easily accounted for from rational considerations, that nothing can outweigh it but the equally uniform judgment of interpreters and readers in all ages that this is an exception to the general rule, and that leaven, in this one place and its parallel (Luke 13, 21), denotes the spreading or diffusive quality of truth and of the true religion. This alleged exception to so uniform an usage may seem less improbable if stated thus, that leaven, even in the other cases, is an emblem, not directly of corruption, but of fermentation and diffusion, and that this, which happens to be elsewhere applied only to false doctrine, or hypocrisy, or sin in general, is here no less properly applied to truth and goodness. The essential meaning of the symbol is unvaried, and the only difficulty in its applications is the very slight one which arises from the circumstance, that we have one example of the favourable sense and nearly half a dozen of the other. If this be so, the usual interpretation is entitled to the preference, as the safest on account of its antiquity and general adoption, while intrinsically it is scarcely if at all less eligible than the other.

34. All these things spake Jesus unto the multitude in parables; and without a parable spake he not unto them:

As these words do not necessarily relate to what was spoken upon any one occasion, they determine nothing as to the precise chronology of what precedes them, but might be considered as descriptive of our Saviour's customary method of instruction. The last clause must then be understood as meaning that he did not at the same time employ both the methods; or in other words, that when he taught in parables, he did not at the same time give the meaning in plain terms to the promiscuous multitudes, but only to his own disciples, in the wide sense of the term, in private and at their request, of which we have two instances in this one chapter (see above, on v. 10, and below on v. 36). The more obvious meaning of the clause, to wit, that he at no time taught the people without parables, is plainly contradicted by the whole course of the history before and afterwards. There is, however, a third explanation, which avoids this discrepancy no less than the first, and is perhaps more natural and easy, while it certainly agrees still better with the statement in v. 36, considered as relating to the time when the preceding parables were uttered. This explanation takes the last clause of the verse before us as referring only to that one occasion, and is recommended by its readily enabling us to hold fast the chronological as well as topical succession in this chapter, and at the same time to account for the crowding of so many parables in one discourse. It was the formal opening or inauguration of this method of instruction. See above, on v. 3, which he, therefore, exemplified by chosen samples, so that on this particular occasion, here remarked by the historian as a deviation from his ordinary practice. "he spake to the multitude in parables, and without a parable spake he not unto them."

35. **That it might be fulfilled which was spoken by the prophet, saying, I will open my mouth in parables; I will utter things which have been kept secret from the foundation of the world.**

Here again, as in 12, 17. the evangelist pauses in his narrative to point out the fulfilment of an ancient prophecy. The one here cited is the second verse of the seventy-eighth Psalm. The form of the quotation implies a knowledge of the Septuagint version without a necessary dependance on it, the first clause being taken from it word for word, the other varying in every word except the preposition (ἀπό) *from*. As the sense remains the same, this variation is important only as it shows the independence of the writer. The plural form, *parables*, occurring in both versions, is correct as representing a collective singular. The parallel term, *riddles*, translated in the Septuagint *problems*, is paraphrased by Matthew, *hidden (things)*. Instead of *utter*, he employs a much stronger word, originally meaning to vomit or belch forth, but in later usage fairly representing the Hebrew verb, which means to pour forth, or to cause to flow. The concluding words, *of old*, are strengthened by the Seventy, *from the beginning*, and still more by Matthew, *from the foundation of the world*, but without a material change of meaning. These are here described as the words of a prophet, of *the* (well known) *prophet*, i. e. Asaph, who is named as the author in the title or inscription (Ps. 78, 1), and spoken of in history (2 Chron. 29, 30) as a *seer*, an ancient synonyme of *prophet* (1 Sam. 9, 9). They seem at first sight inappropriate as an introduction to a psalm so purely historical; but this impression is removed when we consider, that the facts there stated had a typical significance and bearing on the advent and the reign of the Messiah, which is also the ground of what is here said by Matthew as to their fulfilment.

36. **Then Jesus sent the multitude away, and went into the house: and his disciples came unto him, saying, Declare unto us the parable of the tares of the field.**

Here, for the first time since the beginning of this chapter, there is a distinct indication of immediate chronological succession. (See above, on vs. 24. 31. 33. 34.) *Then*, by itself. might be indefinitely used; but the succeeding words can only be referred to the multitudes mentioned in the first verse, and the house from which he there came forth. This establishes the oneness of the narrative from that point, and makes it in a high degree improbable, if not impossible, that any of the intervening parables were not delivered on the same occasion. (See above, on v. 34.) *Sending away*, or letting go, permitting to depart. *The house*, most probably the one where he resided at Capernaum, perhaps that of Simon and Andrew. (See above, on 8, 14. and compare Mark 1, 29.) *His disciples*, not the twelve alone, but "they that were about him with the twelve" (Mark 4, 10), i. e. such as acknowledged his authority and owned him as a teacher come from God (John 3, 2). As this was not an organized body, it might here be represented by a few, who in addition to the twelve continued with him, and presented this request for further explanation. *Declare*, literally, *phrase* (φράσον), i. e. express in other words, that we may understand it.

37. He answered and said unto them, He that soweth the good seed is the Son of man ;

We have here a second model of parabolical interpretation from the lips of Christ himself, and like the former (see above on vs. 18–28), remarkable for clearness. brevity, and freedom from those fanciful inventions and infinitesimal minutiæ, which disfigure many uninspired expositions of these matchless lessons. Point by point, with one exception to be noticed presently, he goes through the parable, explaining its essential features in the fewest words possible. *The (one) sowing the good seed*, as related in v. 24. *The Son of Man*, our Lord himself as the Messiah, in his state of humiliation. (See above, on 8, 20. 10, 23. 11, 19. 12, 8. 32. 40.) This agrees with the past tense in v. 24, implying that the mixture represented in the parable had already taken place.

38. The field is the world ; the good seed are the children of the kingdom ; but the tares are the children of the wicked (one) ;

The field, in which the wheat and tares were both sown (vs. 24. 25), *is the world*, the present state of things, in the midst of which the church was to be planted. An apostle, writing at a later period, might have said *the Church;* but this was not yet organized upon its Christian basis, and is only mentioned rarely by prolepsis or anticipation. (See below, on 16, 18. 18, 17; the only two examples of the word ἐκκλησία in the Gospels.) *The children of the kingdom*, its possessors, not by mere hereditary claim (as in 8, 12), but by divine right and the grace of God. These are identified with the good seed, not as in the parable of the sower (see above. on v. 19), by a disregard of nice precision in the treatment of the figures, but in the strict sense of the terms, the good seed being really the emblem of the righteous. The *wicked (one)*, the name applied in v. 19 to the Devil. His children, those partaking of his nature, and belonging to him, as the seed of the serpent (see above, on 3, 7. 12, 34) and destined to be sharers in his punishment (see below, on 25, 41).

39. The enemy that sowed them is the devil; the harvest is the end of the world; and the reapers are the angels.

The enemy that sowed them, as related in the parable (v. 25). *The Devil,* slanderer, and false accuser (see above, on 4, 1), just described by his moral quality as the Evil or Wicked One, i. e. pre-eminently wicked in himself, and in some sense the author of all sin in others. The act here ascribed to him is that of introducing his own children and dependents among the children of the kingdom, which must be within the kingdom, i. e. the pale of the visible church. This extraordinary juxtaposition is among the most remarkable conditions of the church in this world, and naturally prompts the inquiry why it is permitted. And yet it is precisely here that our Saviour's exposition passes over a prominent feature · of the parable, and leaves it unexplained. The proposition of the servants to destroy the tares, and the refusal of the master, with the reason for it, are omitted in the commentary before us. We are, therefore, under the necessity of reasoning from analogy, and trying to explain this passage for ourselves, upon the principles propounded and exemplified by Christ himself. If the field is the world, or the present mixed condition of the church, and if the good and bad seed are the children of the kingdom and the wicked one respectively, the meaning of the dialogue in vs. 28–30 would appear to be, that such a mixture of the righteous and the wicked in society is not to be entirely avoided, and that any violent attempt at separation would be worse in its effects than their continued coexistence. The bearing of this doctrine upon church discipline has been a subject of dispute for ages. In the Church of Rome it has been made a question whether the tares and the children of the wicked one specifically mean heretics, and if so, whether their excision is forbidden in this passage. The most moderate have come to the conclusion that heresy is only one of many evils here denoted, and that excommunication is permitted where the wheat and tares are easily distinguished, the very thing which the parable itself represents as impossible. Among Protestants the question has been agitated, how far rigid discipline is reconcilable with what is here taught. Some reject it altogether, but the more judicious and considerate have always held in substance, that although the church is bound to aim at perfect purity, she is not to expect it as the product of mere discipline, nor ever to employ brute force, ecclesiastical or secular, in order to secure it. The entire separation of the two discordant elements, like that of the wheat and tares in the parable before us, however much to be desired and sought, is not to be expected till *the harvest.* This our Lord explains to be the end or consummation of the world, not the word so rendered in the verse preceding, though substantially synonymous, the one relating more to time, the other to place, but both denoting the present or existing state of things, including the material universe with its inhabitants ($κόσμος$), and time with its great divisions, whether natural or moral ($αἰών$). Of these two worlds, or of the world in these senses, the completion, consummation, winding up, denouement, or catastrophe, will be coincident if not identical. Then comes the time of clear discrimination and of final separation between those who are now mingled in society and even joined in one religious profession. The *reapers* in this *harvest*, or the agents in this sifting and dividing process, are to be, and are already by divine appointment *angels* (not *the angels*), i. e. spirits of a higher order, and exempt from all the complications and corruptions of our mortal state.

40. As therefore the tares are gathered and burned in the fire ; so shall it be in the end of this world.

The resemblance is to hold good, not only with respect to the discrimination, but to the destruction following. The correspondence here between the sign and the thing signified is pointed out more fully and distinctly in the form of a regular comparison. *Therefore*, since the points already mentioned correspond with such exactness, so must the remainder. *As the tares are gathered and burnt with fire*, a fact not expressed in the parable, but clearly implied in the command to bind them into bundles for that purpose. (See above, on v. 30.) *So*, in like manner, with a similar coincidence between the sign and the thing signified. *It shall be in the end of this world*, i. e. of the present creation and of time, not only as to what has been already mentioned, but in all that is to follow.

41. The Son of man shall send forth his angels, and they shall gather out of his kingdom all things that offend, and them which do iniquity ;

The sovereign agent in this final process is the Son of Man, the same despised Messiah who was now addressing them. The angels are now spoken of as his angels, subject to his orders and employed in executing his commands. *Send forth*, officially, the verb from which *apostle* is derived. (See above, on 10, 5. 16. 40.) The angels are on that great day to act as his apostles, his official aids and representatives. *Scandals*, the noun corresponding to the verb in 5, 29. 30. 11, 6. and strictly meaning snares or stumbling-blocks, whatever one falls into or falls over in his walk through life. It here means guilty causes or occasions of transgression on the part of others. That the reference is to persons, though the noun is neuter, may be gathered from the nature of the case, no other objects being liable to punishment, and also from the words that follow, *them that do* (those doing) *iniquity* or *lawlessness*, whatever is at variance with the law as the expression of the will of God. (See above, on 7, 33.) The only question as to this last phrase is whether it describes the same class as the word before it or another quite distinct. If the former, we must render the words, *making iniquity*, i. e. causing and promoting it in others, and the *and* must indicate a simple apposition, nearly equivalent to *even*, as it sometimes does. If we adopt the other and more obvious construction, *and* retains its usual connective force, and *doing iniquity* means *practising*, committing it, as something different from causing it in others.

42. And shall cast them into a furnace of fire: there shall be wailing and gnashing of teeth.

This is a simple but fearful amplification of the figure in v. 40. The wicked, like the tares, are to be cast into *a furnace of fire*, i. e. heated, burning, and destructive. As the form of the threatening is here suggested by the burning of the tares at the harvest, it may be considered as a figure for the most intense, intolerable sufferings, whether caused by material fire or not. It is worthy of remark, however, that the fire is here mentioned, not in the parable but in the exposition, and that if the Son of Man, the world, the children of the kingdom and the wicked one, the end of the world, and the angels, must be strictly understood, it would be arbitrary and confusing to suppose this one figure to denote itself, or in other words, that the figurative fire of the parable (v. 40) means a figurative fire in the explanations of the verse before us. But even granting a distinction, as in all the other cases, we have still no certain intimation of what is meant by a furnace of fire at the end of the world, beyond the vague but terrible idea of unutterable torment, which is further expressed, as in 8, 12, by the natural tokens of extreme distress, *weeping and gnashing of teeth*.

43. Then shall the righteous shine forth as the sun in the kingdom of their Father. Who hath ears to hear let him hear.

Then, when the wicked have been thus disposed of, shall the last stroke of the parable be verified, the gathering of the wheat into the barn (v. 30). This is here expressed by another figure, as the only explanation possible. The good seed, wheat, or children of the kingdom, are here called the *righteous*, as conformed to the divine will and enjoying his favour. Their future blessedness and glory is described as a resplendent shining like that of the sun, which may include not only the extreme of splendour but the accessory notion of imparting light to others. This glory is to take place in the kingdom of their Father, implying their hereditary and filial claim to it, and possibly the great mysterious truth revealed in 1 Cor. 15, 24, that when all Christ's enemies have been subdued, " he shall deliver up the kingdom to God, even the Father."

44. Again, the kingdom of heaven is like unto treasure hid in a field; the which when a man hath found, he

hideth, and for joy thereof goeth and selleth all that he hath, and buyeth that field.

The preceding verse forms so solemn a conclusion to the previous discourse, that one is tempted to regard what follows as a sort of appendix, adding certain parables not uttered on the same occasion, but appropriate to the writer's purpose of exemplifying this peculiar method of instruction as practised by the Saviour. But besides the general presumption in favour of continuous succession, and the reasons which have been already given for his uttering so many parables at once (see above, on vs. 34. 36), we have below (in v. 53) another statement, that can only be referred to a particular occasion, and would seem to imply the continuity and chronological arrangement of the intervening matter. It is safer, therefore, in the absence of all countervailing evidence, to hold fast to the natural presumption that the parables were uttered as they are recorded. If so, it will follow from v. 36, that those remaining were addressed to the disciples in the house, after the explanation of the Tares. But this is not at all unnatural, and is even rendered highly probable by an expression used below (in v. 51). *Again* does not mean that he said so on a different occasion, but that in the same discourse, he thus distinguished the successive parables, in order to avoid confusing the disciples by so rapid an enumeration (see the previous use of the same adverb in 4, 7. 8. 5, 33. and compare John 16, 16. 17. 19. 22–28. Rom. 15, 10. 11. 12. Heb. 1, 5. 6. 2, 13. 4, 5. 7). *The kingdom of heaven* has of course the same sense as in all the previous parables. (See above, on vs. 19. 24. 31. 33.) *Is like,* the same expression that is used in the parables of Mustard Seed and Leaven, more indefinite than that in the Tares, and not confined to any period in the progress of the kingdom. What is really here likened to a hidden treasure is the personal possession and enjoyment of the kingdom with its honours and immunities. The form of expression is not to be so strictly understood as in v. 38, but more so than in v. 19, where the character described is said to be himself the seed sown. Here, again, the image is derived from the experience of common life, such occasional discoveries of treasure being common in all ages, and in some productive of insane avidity, indulged in life-long searches after gold. It is not improbable that in the case before us there is reference to some recent case of treasure-trove, familiar to Christ's hearers. This hypothesis is favoured by the form of the original, in which the first verb is an aorist, *finding hid* (*again*), referring to what actually happened at a certain time, and thus determining the verbs that follow to be graphic presents, calling up the scene as actually passing, and not vague descriptions of what men usually do on such occasions. The case described is that of hidden treasure found. and then concealed again in order to secure it until legally acquired by purchase. The immorality, which some have seen in this transaction, even if real, would not vitiate the parable, which makes the man a model or an example only as to one point, the avidity with which he gave up all in order to secure this treasure.

This makes the application easy, even in the absence of a formal exposition by our Lord himself, to the eagerness with which men ought to seek, and often do seek, for admission to the kingdom of heaven. (See above, on 6, 33.) This, it will be observed, is an idea not directly suggested by any of the preceding parables, and therefore not a needless repetition, but an instructive variation of the one great theme; a circumstance which favours the opinion, that these parables were all delivered on the same occasion.

45. Again, the kingdom of heaven is like unto a merchantman, seeking goodly pearls:

46. Who, when he had found one pearl of great price, went and sold all that he had, and bought it.

Again, once more, to give you still another sample of this method of instruction. This parable resembles that before it very nearly, and was probably suggested by it; but they differ in one interesting point, the first representing the fortuitous discovery of treasure without seeking it, the second the success of a professional pearl-merchant in discovering a sample of extraordinary value, after which he does precisely like the other, i. e. gives up all in order to secure this single acquisition. While they both agree in this essential point, they differ as to the occasion, which admits again of easy application to men's conduct with respect to religion or salvation, when convinced of its paramount necessity and value, one apparently by accident or sudden revelation, another as the fruit of long-continued search, yet both alike renouncing all in order to secure it. The word translated *merchant* properly denotes a shipper or importer, but in later Greek a trader or trafficker in general, either of which senses would be here appropriate.*

47. Again, the kingdom of heaven is like unto a net, that was cast into the sea, and gathered of every kind:

48. Which, when it was full, they drew to shore, and sat down, and gathered the good into vessels, but cast the bad away.

Our Lord concludes the series of his parables with one resembling that of the Tares in meaning and design, yet differing from it in its images or figures, which are borrowed not from husbandry but fishing.

* The combination, *merchant-man*, resembling that in v. 28, has sometimes been described as a Hebrew idiom, but is found in the purest classics, and especially in Homer, e. g. ἄνθρωπος ὁδίτης, a traveller, which occurs in both the Iliad and Odyssey.

MATTHEW 13, 48. 49. 50.

This circumstance may help us to account for the addition of a parable so similar in import to one previously uttered on the same occasion. The mere difference of figurative dress would not sufficiently explain this, since the others might as easily have been thus varied. But he may have been induced, at least in part, by a desire to bring home this method of instruction to those of his disciples who had formerly been fishermen; and this we know to have been true of the four first who were called to actual attendance on him (see above, on 4, 18–22). As they were to be fishers of men (4, 19), such a parable as this would be peculiarly appropriate to their position. There may even be allusion to the very draught of fishes which accompanied the call of these disciples, as described by Luke (5, 1–11), which would account for the aorists in v. 48, more numerous than in v. 44, and here retained in the translation. The *net* here meant is a large seine or drag-net thrown into the sea and then drawn to the shore. *Every kind*, a popular hyperbole for various kinds, not only bad and good in quality, but actually different species. The scene so vividly presented in v. 48, is no doubt one often witnessed on the shore of Genessaret at the present day. *Bad*, literally rotten or decayed, but here used in a secondary wide sense, as in 7, 17. 18. 12. 33 above, where it is applied to living and productive but worthless trees. *Vessels*, a generic term, including baskets and all other receptacles employed for such a purpose.

49. So shall it be at the end of the world : the angels shall come forth, and sever the wicked from among the just,

50. And shall cast them into the furnace of fire : there shall be wailing and gnashing of teeth.

To this last parable our Lord seems to add an explanation; but it is only by repeating that appended to the Tares with little variation. The first clause of v. 49 is the last clause of v. 40, with the omission of the word *this* before *world;* and even this slight change is wanting in the Vatican and Beza copies. The remainder of v. 49 is only an abridgment of v. 41, from which the Son of Man, as the prime agent, and the particular description of the wicked, are to be supplied. The sending of the angels there corresponds to their going forth here to execute their dread commission. The only new trait is the final separation of the wicked from among the righteous, which is really the very burden of the other parable, and necessarily implied in the interpretation of it. V. 50 is identical with v. 42, thus giving to the passage a rhythmical or strophical unity by means of a refrain or burden. This not only finishes the proof that what we have before us is a regular discourse delivered at one time, but restores the solemn and sonorous close which seemed to have been lost by the addition of the last three parables. It was for the sake of this conclusion that he added a brief explanation of the net, and not because it needed formal exposition more than those preceding it.

51. Jesus saith unto them, Have ye understood all these things? They say unto him, Yea, Lord.

This verse discloses why the last three parables were added after the interpretation of the Tares, namely, as a sort of exercise or lesson in the heavenly art which he was teaching his disciples. Having given only an apparent explanation of the last, and none at all of the two others, he now asks them whether they had understood all these things, i. e. all these parables, not only those which he had formally expounded, but the others, also, and they answer no doubt truly, that they had, thus showing that his gracious condescension was not unavailing.

52. Then said he unto them, Therefore every scribe, (which is) instructed unto the kingdom of heaven, is like unto a man (that is) a householder, which bringeth forth out of his treasure (things) new and old.

Having taught them, both by precept and example, the divine art of parabolical instruction, and ascertained, by the inquiry in v. 51, that the experiment had been successful, he now intimates the use which he expected them to make of all such acquisitions. As he fed them, so they were to feed others, with the bread of truth and saving knowledge, and for this end were to lay it up in store and to dispense it, not indiscriminately or at random, but with a sound discretion and a bountiful economy, consulting the necessities of every person, and the exigencies of the times and seasons, so as to provide not only with abundance but variety for all whom they were called to serve. All this is beautifully set forth by the figure of a *householder* (i. e. a housekeeper or the head of a family) drawing from his treasury (or storehouse) things both new and old. Such a housekeeper must be *every scribe*, i. e. every official or professional expounder of the Scriptures, who is (not merely *instructed* but) *discipled*, introduced as a disciple, *into the kingdom of heaven*, or the church of the new dispensation, and employed there as a teacher. An allusion to the actual conversion of educated Scribes, as already past or future, such as that of Paul, although not essential to our Saviour's meaning, may appear to be suggested by his speaking of one who is a scribe already, being introduced into the church as a disciple. But the mere order of the words does not forbid the supposition that the discipleship precedes the scribeship. There is no one sentence in the Bible more instructive as to the duties of the ministry considered as a teaching office. It is connected by a *therefore*, or *for this (cause)*, with the previous context, as the practical improvement of the whole preceding lesson in the art of parabolical instruction.

53. And it came to pass, (that) when Jesus had finished these parables, he departed thence.

This verse affords a final proof that the preceding parables were actually uttered upon one occasion, by referring to them all collectively (*these parables*) without distinction or discrimination; by saying that he *finished* them, in Greek an aorist referring to some one time; and by adding that he then *departed thence,* implying unity of place also. Here the chapter should have ended, as already too long for convenience but containing one complete and undivided context, all relating to our Saviour's parables, and forming a fine counterpart or supplement to the previous example of his teaching in the Sermon on the Mount. By some inexplicable error of judgment, the divider of the text gratuitously added to the length of this division, and destroyed its unity of subject, by subjoining an occurrence which has no direct connection with what goes before.

54. And when he was come into his own country, he taught them in their synagogue, insomuch that they were astonished, and said, Whence hath this (man) this wisdom, and (these) mighty works?

This verse is not to be read as a direct continuation of the one before it, although actually printed so in some editions. The *and* at the beginning is the particle used even in the opening of books in the Old Testament (see above, on 9, 2), and, therefore, can prove nothing as to the connection here. *And coming,* as in many other cases, means no more than coming once, or at a certain time not specified. There is, therefore, no discrepancy between this narrative and Mark's (6, 1–6), which gives the following occurrence in immediate succession to the raising of the daughter of Jairus, which Matthew has recorded long before (see above, on 9, 18–26). The truth is, that neither of the two evangelists asserts an immediate consecution of events, but only, at the most, that one happened after the other, without saying that no other event intervened. It is only by neglecting this distinction that most charges of discrepancy between the Gospels can be rendered even plausible. Not the least striking and affecting part of Christ's humiliation was the treatment which he met with from his nearest friends, or those who might have been supposed to be such, either from natural relationship or from long association and acquaintance. We have already met with several indications of imperfect faith and narrow views upon the part of such; but the history of his mission would have been defective without a more detailed account of one extraordinary scene, in which the same thing took place on a larger scale and still more publicly. This was his reception on returning to the place where he had spent his childhood, and from which he came to be baptized in Jordan (see above, on 2, 23). The precise chronology of this transaction is of little moment, except as involved in the question of its identity with that recorded in a different connection by Luke (4, 16–31). As the scene of both is Nazareth, and the principal incident in both our Lord's rejection by his old acquaintances and neighbours there, the first presumption is, of course, in favour of their sameness. But this presumption of identity, is happily removed by Matthew, who affords a parallel to both the others in very different connections, thus establishing the fact of their diversity. Luke's account of the affair at Nazareth closes (4, 31) with a statement that he went thence to Capernaum, another town of Galilee, which formal and particular description shows that he is speaking of our Lord's removal to that place as the appointed centre of his future operations. Now this same removal is recorded with more brevity by Matthew, in immediate connection with our Lord's withdrawing from Judea into Galilee on John's imprisonment (see above, on 4, 12. 13). But here, much later in his narrative, he records a visit and rejection of our Lord at Nazareth, in terms almost identical with those of Mark (6, 1–6). It was, therefore, a second occurrence of the same kind, which is so far from being in itself improbable, that it would have been strange and out of keeping with the whole tenor of the Saviour's conduct, if in the course of his perpetual circuits through all Galilee, he never had revisited his old home and renewed the invitations which the people there had once rejected. Luke's silence in relation to this second visit is explained by his particular account of the first, whereas Matthew, having merely noted the removal, without any indication of the reasons, could describe the second visit without irksome repetition. The different connection in which Mark and Matthew introduce this narrative is unimportant, as the mere chronology was nothing to their purpose of exemplifying the reception and effect of our Lord's ministry in various cases. *His country* (fatherland, πατρίς from πατήρ), not in the wide sense now attached to this term, but in that of native place, ancestral residence. This description applied elsewhere (John 4, 46) to all Galilee, as distinguished from Judea, is here used, with equal propriety, to distinguish one town of Galilee from another. In the same sense that Galilee was his native province, Nazareth was his native town; for though not actually born in either, his parents (Luke 2, 27. 41) had resided there before his birth (Luke 1, 26. 27. 2, 4), and he had been brought up there from his infancy (2, 23. Luke 2, 51. 52), so that he was universally regarded as a Galilean and a Nazarene. *In their synagogue*, or stated meeting for religious worship, the Greek word, like its English equivalent and several others, such as *church, court, school*, being sometimes, but not necessarily or always, transferred to the place and even to the building. For a clear view of this natural transition, compare Luke 7, 5. where it could not be the meeting that was built, with Acts 13, 43. where it could not be the building that was broken up. We find here exemplified two of our Lord's habits, that of personal attendance on the synagogue worship, and that of official or authoritative teaching upon such occasions. This was allowed partly in accordance with a customary license of instruction, not entirely unknown among the modern Jews, but chiefly on account of Christ's miraculous credentials as a teacher come from God and recognized as such by other teachers even of the highest rank when free from party-spirit and malignant prepossession. *So that they were struck* (with wonder or amazement), the same phrase and descriptive of the same effect as that recorded in 7, 28, but very different as to the conclusion drawn from it. For in the former case it led the hearers to contrast him as a teacher with the Scribes very much to his advantage, while in this his old acquaintances compare his miracles and teachings with his humble origin and early residence among themselves, as a pretext for disparaging if not rejecting his pretensions. This unfriendly prepossession is expressed indirectly by their sneering questions. *Whence to this (one) this wisdom, and these powers*, thereby acknowledging his inspiration, but not without a sneer at his wisdom as belonging to another rather than himself. Nor do they venture to deny his miracles, but by wondering at them really bear witness to them. This is only one of many proofs that the reality of Christ's miraculous performances was never called in question either by his unbelieving friends or by his most malignant enemies (see above, on 12, 24). That this admission left them inexcusable both intellectually and morally for not receiving Jesus as the true Messiah, far from proving that they could not thus have spoken, only shows that their affections, envy, jealousy, and malice, were too strong for their rational convictions, so that in the very act of wondering at the proofs of his divine legation, they rejected and denied it. This inconsistency, instead of being "unpsychological" or contradicted by the laws of human nature, is continually verified in every day's experience, contributing with many other proofs to show the irrationality of unbelief and sin in general.

55. Is not this the carpenter's son ? is not his mother called Mary ? and his brethren, James, and Joses, and Simon, and Judas ?

56. And his sisters, are they not all with us ? Whence then hath this (man) all these things ?

The general expression of contemptuous incredulity is followed by a still more invidious allusion to his connections and associations, equivalent to saying, 'we know all about this boasted wonder-worker and instructor, who and what he is, and whence he drew his origin, that is, among ourselves, to whom he now assumes such vast superiority.' This is the language not of reason but of passion, since the circumstances mentioned only served to enhance the proof of that superiority which they repined at, though they could not question or deny it. *Is not this the carpenter's son?* The Greek word sometimes means an artisan or artificer in general, which some lexicographers consider its original import as indicated by its etymology (connecting it with τέχνη, *art*), and by its combination with the names of certain metals, to denote those who are constantly employed about them. Others explain this as a mere occasional extension of the usual and strict sense, which is that of any workman in wood, and still more specifically, a carpenter or joiner, which an uniform tradition represents as Joseph's occupation. It is not here spoken of as even a comparatively mean employment, that of building having always been regarded as among the most respectable and even intellectual of manual occupations. There was no intention, on the part of those here speaking, to put Jesus lower than themselves, but simply on a level with them. What they tacitly repudiate is not his claim to be their equal, but their better or superior in an infinite degree. This pretension, though attested by acknowledged miracle and inspiration, they endeavour, in a natural but foolish manner, to invalidate by urging his original equality in rank and occupation with themselves. Or rather it is not an argumentative objection, but a mere expression of surprise, like that which would be felt, though in a less degree, in any obscure neighbourhood, at the appearance of an old acquaintance in the new condition of a rich man or a nobleman. The immemorial dispute as to the brothers of the Lord has been already mentioned (see above, on 12, 46). Those who interpret that expression as denoting brothers in the strict sense, i. e. sons of the same mother (*fratres uterinos*), lay great stress upon the passage now before us and its parallel in Mark 16, 3. But even taken in the strictest sense it only proves that these were sons of Joseph, not necessarily by Mary, but perhaps by a former marriage, a traditional interpretation running back into remote antiquity. Others insist upon the wide use of *brother*, in the oriental idiom and in Scripture, to denote almost any near relation, whether natural or moral, such as that of fellow-men, otherwise called neighbours (5, 22), that of friends and associates (5, 47), that of fellow-Jews (Acts 2, 29), that of fellow-christians (Acts 1, 16), that of fellow-ministers (1 Cor. 1, 1). A word admitting of such various applications cannot of itself determine which is meant in any given case. Nor is there any principle or general law of language which forbids our giving to the term as here used the same meaning that it obviously has in Gen. 13, 8. 14, 14. 16. that of a near relative or kinsman. The presumption, however, here and elsewhere, is in favour of the strict construction; nor would any have doubted that the brothers of Christ were the sons of Mary, but for certain adventitious and collateral objections to that obvious interpretation. These are chiefly two, the one of great antiquity, the other of more recent date. The first is a repugnance to admit that Mary was the mother of any but of Christ himself. This repugnance, although found in connection with many superstitious notions in the Church of Rome, is not confined to it. Not only do the symbols or standards of the Lutheran and of some Reformed churches teach the perpetual virginity of Mary as an article of faith, but multitudes of Protestant divines and others, independently of all creeds and confessions, have believed, or rather felt, that the selection of a woman to be the mother of the Lord, carries with it as a necessary implication that no others could sustain the same relation to her; and that the selection of a virgin still more necessarily implied that she was to continue so; for if there be nothing in the birth of younger children inconsistent with her maternal relation to the Saviour, why should there be any such repugnance in the birth of older children likewise? If for any reason, whether known to us or not, it was necessary that the mother of our Lord should be a virgin when she bore him, what is there absurd or superstitious in assuming as a part of the divine plan that she should remain a virgin till her death? If, on the other hand, there be no real incongruity in holding that the mother of our Lord was afterwards an ordinary wife and parent, what incongruity would there have been in putting this extraordinary honour on the married state, by choosing one who was already in the ordinary sense a wife and mother? The question is not why it did not please God thus to order it, with which we have no right to intermeddle, but why the same minds which regard the perpetual virginity of Mary as a superstition, shrink with equal superstition from the bare suggestion that Christ might have been born of any but a virgin. The same feeling which revolts from one hypothesis in some revolts from both hypotheses in others, and the difference between them, as to this repugnance, is reduced to that of one and two, before and after, or at most to that of a consistent uniformity and arbitrary variation. After all, it is not so much a matter of reason or of faith as of taste and sensibility; but these exert a potent influence on all interpretation, and the same repugnance, whether rational or merely sentimental, which led fathers and reformers to deny that Christ had brothers in the ordinary sense, is likely to produce the same effect on multitudes forever until the question has received some new and unequivocal solution. The other and more recent ground of opposition to the strict sense of *brothers* in the case before us is the theory, by some connected with it, of extraordinary honours paid to one of these uterine brethren as such, though not one of the twelve apostles, i. e. James the brother of the Lord, whom Paul groups with John and Peter as a pillar of the church, and even names him first in the enumeration, which is natural enough if he was one of the apostles, and the one who specially presided in the church at Jerusalem; but if (as many now maintain) he was one of the Saviour's unbelieving brethren (John 7, 5), converted by our Lord's appearance to him after his resurrection (1 Cor. 15, 7), and then placed upon a level with the twelve on account of his relationship to Christ, the apostolical prerogative is sensibly impaired, and the door thrown open for an endless license of conjecture as to the men who were apostles, although not so dignified by Christ himself. An unwillingness to come to this conclusion has undoubtedly confirmed some in the old belief, that the brother of the Lord, of whom Paul speaks, was James the Less or James the son of Alpheus, at once an apostle and a relative of Christ, whether he were such as a nephew of the Virgin Mary, or of Joseph, or a son of Joseph by a former marriage. The additional hypothesis, that James and his brothers lived with Joseph after the decease of their own father, is not a necessary consequence of what has been already said, but merely an ingenious explanation of the fact that these brothers of Christ appear in attendance on his mother as members of her household. (See above, on 12,

46. and compare John 2, 12. Acts 1, 14.) In favour of identifying James the brother of the Lord (Gal. 1, 19) with James the son of Alpheus (see above, on 10, 3.) is the singular coincidence of names between the lists of the apostles and the passage now before us. In all we find a James and a Simon near together, and in Luke's two catalogues a Jude or Judas (not Iscariot), making three names common to the list of the apostles and of Christ's brothers. This may no doubt be fortuitous, the rather as the names were common, and the fourth here mentioned, which was less so, does not appear in any list of the apostles. Still on most minds the coincidence will have some influence, in spite of the objection that in John 7, 5. we are expressly told that his brethren did not believe on him. But if brethren means his near relations, surely some of them might be apostles, while the rest were unbelievers, even granting, what may well be questioned, that by unbelief in John 7, 5. we are to understand an absolute rejection of his claims and doctrines, rather than a weak contracted faith, with which he seems to charge his mother upon one occasion (John 2, 4), and the twelve on many. (See above, on 6, 30. 8, 26. and below, on 14, 31. 16, 8.) *His sisters*, is of course to be interpreted according to *his brothers*, the wide and narrow senses being applicable equally to either sex. *Here with us* (literally at us, close to us), i. e. still resident at Nazareth, which probably remained the permanent home even of his mother.

57. And they were offended in him. But Jesus said unto them, A prophet is not without honour, save in his own country, and in his own house.

Offended in him, i. e. made to stumble, or without a figure led into sin and error with respect to him. For the origin and meaning of the Greek term see above, on v. 21. Instead of resenting this reception as a personal offence and insult, which it certainly was, our Lord treats it merely as a single instance of a general and familiar fact, that God's most highly honoured instruments and agents are not only liable to be dishonoured by their fellow-men, but to be least respected on the part of those who know them best, and who would seem to be particularly bound to do them honour. The implied reason is that strangers judge of such a person only by his public acts or his official conduct, while his friends and neighbours, even the most friendly, have their minds so occupied with minor matters, that the greater are obscured if not distorted to their view. It is like looking at some noble structure from a distance where itself alone is visible, and near at hand, where the adjoining houses both distract the eye and lower the main object; so that he who sees the most in one sense sees the least in another. This familiar lesson of experience, and as such reduced to a proverbial form, is here applied especially to prophets, either because it had been actually verified in their experience more than that of others, or because it was our Lord's prophetic ministry and office which had been so contemptuously treated by his countrymen.

17

58. And he did not many mighty works there because of their unbelief.

The sad effect of this reception was the paucity of miracles at Nazareth, compared with those at other towns of Galilee, particularly at Capernaum (see above, on 8, 16. 9, 35). The people, having no faith in his healing power, or disdaining to receive the favours of one whom they knew so well, and were so unwilling to acknowledge as superior, did not present themselves as in other places. This is certainly more probable and pleasing than the supposition that our Lord, in this case, refused what he seems to have granted in all others.

CHAPTER XIV.

THE next incident recorded is the death of John the Baptist, introduced to explain the effect of our Lord's miracles on Herod (1–12), and followed by a new and most stupendous miracle, the feeding of five thousand (13–21), which was followed in its turn by that of walking on the water (22–27), to which Matthew adds the attempt of Peter to do the same, omitted in the other gospels (28–32), and concludes with a brief statement of our Lord's ensuing visit to the region of Gennesaret, and of the miracles performed there (33–36). It will be perceived, from the detailed interpretation of this chapter, that the chronological arrangement is adhered to with unusual exactness, and that it winds up what may be regarded as the first great division of the history, the second opening with a new series of assaults, and a fresh concourse of the multitudes to see and hear him.

1. At that time Herod the tetrarch heard of the fame of Jesus.

This was Herod Antipas, the second son of Herod the Great (2, 1. Luke 1, 5), and bearing the abbreviated name of his grandfather, Antipater, the Edomite or Idumean who had been the minister or confidential counsellor of Hyrcanus II., the last of the Maccabees or Hasmonean Kings, under whom, or rather through whom, Pompey the Great obtained possession of the Holy Land, and virtually, although not ostensibly, reduced it to a Roman province. Antipater, however, still continued to enjoy the favour of the conquerors, and his son Herod, after fleeing from the country to escape a sentence of the Sanhedrim, returned in triumph, having being acknowledged by the Senate, and crowned in the Capitol as king of the Jews. After reigning many years as a vassal of the empire, he bequeathed his kingdom to his three sons Archelaus, Antipas, and Philip, the first of whom was soon displaced by Roman governors, while both the others reigned much longer, as tributary sovereigns, but without the royal title, for which Augustus substituted that of *tetrarch*, which originally signified the ruler of a fourth part, or one of four associated rulers, as in ancient Galatia, but was afterwards applied in a generic sense to any ruler, and especially to tributary kings, immediately dependent on the Roman emperor. Hence Antipas, though usually called the *tetrarch* (14, 1. Luke 3, 1. 19. 9, 7. Acts 13, 1), is by Mark repeatedly described as *king*, which, though it seems at first sight an inaccuracy, really evinces his exact acquaintance with the titular rank of Herod, both in common parlance and in the actual arrangements of the empire. This prince, whose dominions comprised Galilee, Samaria, and Peræa, resided usually at Tiberias, a place from which the sea of Galilee derived one of its names (see above, on 4, 18), but which is not itself named in the New Testament, perhaps because our Saviour did not visit it, in order to avoid precipitating the catastrophe or crisis of his history, by being brought into collision with the court or person of this wicked ruler. But although they had not met, Herod, as might have been expected, *heard the fame*, literally, (*hearing*) *of him*, first by means of his own words and deeds incessantly reported far and wide by those who witnessed them, although this process was in some degree retarded by occasional injunctions not to make him known, and then by the preaching and the miracles of the twelve apostles who were sent forth for the very purpose.

2. And said unto his servants, This is John the Baptist; he is risen from the dead; and therefore mighty works do show forth themselves in him.

The effect produced by this increasing fame of Jesus on the mind of Herod, although strange, is not incredible, but true to nature and experience. His conclusion was that this was John the Baptist, who was indeed dead, but as the conscience-stricken king imagined, had been *raised from the dead*, from among them, their condition and society, not from death as an abstraction or a mere condition without reference to persons. The doctrine of a resurrection, although veiled, or only partially disclosed in the Old Testament, was now an article of faith with all the Jews except the Sadducees, who seem to have rejected it on philosophical rather than scriptural grounds. Even Herod, who seems elsewhere to be called a Sadducee (see Mark 8, 15), was either less incredulous on this point, or was scared out of his unbelief by guilty fear. This idea was the more strange because John performed no miracle (John 10, 41), and therefore miracles could be no proof of his resuscitation. But even as to this point the evangelist suggests without developing an explanation. *Therefore*, literally, *for* (or *an account of*) *this*, i. e. because he has appeared again, with some new message or authority, perhaps to punish those who would not hear him, or who slew him when he came before. Such an imagination was not wholly destitute of colour, since the prophecy of Malachi respecting John suggests the idea of successive advents, which might well be misconceived by Herod as relating to distinct appearances of one and the same person. (See above, on 11, 10. 14.) The expressions of the last clause are particularly strong in the original. *For this* (cause) *energize the powers in him*, i. e. miraculous or superhuman powers, not only *show forth themselves* (which conveys too little, and is neither the exact idea nor the form of the original), but *are busy, active, energetic,* which last is a word of kindred origin with that here used. The English version gives to *powers* the secondary meaning which it sometimes has of miracles, or mighty works, as the effects and proofs of superhuman power (see above, on 13, 54. 58); but the primary meaning is entitled to the preference as such and on account of its conjunction with a verb requiring it, as may be seen from the change which the translators have been forced to make in it, in order to retain their customary version of the noun, since a miracle cannot be said to act or to be active, which can be asserted only of the power that produces it. All that need be added as to this point is that, out of twenty places where the same Greek verb occurs in the New Testament, this and the parallel passage in Mark (6, 14) are the only ones in which it is not strictly rendered as expressive of efficient action. Thus explained the phrase before us is still more significant of Herod's guilty fears, occasioned by the very rumour of our Saviour's miracles, and uttered *to his servants*, literally, *boys*, or young men, for which usage see above, on 8, 6. 12, 18.

3. For Herod had laid hold on John, and bound him, and put (him) in prison for Herodias' sake, his brother Philip's wife.

One of the characteristics of a well-ordered history, as distinguished from mere chronicles or annals, is the way in which the writer interweaves his materials instead of simply throwing them together, going back to take up what has been allowed to drop, and introducing topics even out of their precise chronological arrangement, when required to complete or to illustrate the main narrative. The best historians in every language are remarkable for this constructive skill, which is rather natural than artificial, and is, therefore, often greatest where it shows the least. Some of the best samples of this quality are furnished by the sacred writers, whose simplicity is not, as some imagine, the effect of ignorance and inexperience, but of perfect skill; their artlessness is not opposed to art but to artifice, and often where the condescending critic pities the deficiency of purpose and coherent plan, it is the perfectness of both which has deceived him. Many instances of this kind are afforded by the gospels, one of which is now before us, in the different but equally artistic mode in which the writers introduce the narrative of John's imprisonment. Matthew and Mark defer it till they come to speak of Herod's terror when he heard of Jesus, where they are naturally led to give the causes of that strange impression by relating the whole story in connection. Luke relates the perplexity of Herod in the same way, but had no occasion to recount his previous treatment of the Baptist, having recorded it already in his narrative of John's appearance and official ministry. Now as both these methods are entirely natural and in accordance with the theory and practice of the best historians, and while the difference may serve to show the independence of the writers who exhibit it, the charge of incoherence against either is as groundless as against the best digested portions of Polybius or Gibbon. The *for* at the beginning of this verse refers to the phrase *risen from the dead* in the one preceding. To one acquainted with the previous facts this expression would need explanation, and Matthew now proceeds to give it. *Laid hold*, literally, *seizing* (or *arresting*), the verb explained above (on 9, 25. 12, 11) as denoting either violent or friendly seizure. *Bound*, either in the strict sense of *fastened*, chained, or in the wide one of *confined*, imprisoned, which the Greek sometimes seems to have. *In prison*, literally guard or ward, which may either mean the place or the condition of confinement. *For* (on account of) *Herodias*, the daughter of Aristobulus, son of Herod the Great, was married by her grandfather to his son Philip, not the tetrarch mentioned in Luke 3, 1. but another, who appears to have occupied no public station. Leaving him she married, in direct violation of the law, her uncle and brother-in-law Herod Antipas, who had divorced his own wife the daughter of Aretas, an Arabian king, supposed to be the same of whom Paul speaks in one of his epistles (2 Cor. 11, 32). This divorce involved him in a war from which he could be extricated only by the Roman arms. Enough has now been said to show the character not only of Herodias and of Antipas, but also of the whole Herodian race, whose history is stained with many odious imputations of adultery and even incest under the pretence of marriage.

4. For John said unto him, It is not lawful for thee to have her.

It is not without reason that Matthew speaks of John as being thrown into prison because Herod married Herodias; *for John said to Herod, it is not lawful* (or *permitted*) either by the law of nature or the law of Moses, *to have* (or hold in thy possession) the wife of thy own brother (Mark 6, 18). There is something very pleasing in this incidental glimpse of John's consistency and faithfulness in reproving sin without respect of persons, to which Christ himself seems to refer when he describes John as neither a reed shaken by the wind, nor a courtier in soft raiment 11, 7. 8. Luke 7, 24. 25). This description is emphatically verified by John's appearance in the scene before us, where the austere preacher of the wilderness, who so severely scourged both Pharisees and Sadducees, though enemies and rivals, as alike belonging to the seed of the serpent (Gen. 3, 15), or generation of vipers (3, 7. 12, 34), appears reproving Herod on his throne for his incestuous connection with his brother's wife, and all his other sins, of which this was the most flagrant and notorious, until he crowned all by his treatment of John himself (Luke 3, 19. 20).

5. And when he would have put him to death, he feared the multitude, because they counted him as a prophet.

We learn from Mark (6, 20) the interesting fact, that John the Baptist made a powerful impression upon Herod when brought into contact with him, and that Herod acknowledging his personal excellence and also his divine legation, kept or saved him for a time from the malice of Herodias, and did many things of those which John required or recommended. These promising appearances, however, were but temporary. Herod, whose character was weak as well as wicked, soon yielded to the constant influence of Herodias, and at length desired himself to kill John, but was deterred by his immense popularity and credit as a prophet. These accounts are perfectly consistent with each other and with the statement of Josephus, that Herod was afraid of some political excitement as the fruit of John the Baptist's preaching. Such men, in such emergencies, are usually actuated, not by simple but by complex motives, and the choice made by the different historians is just which might have been expected from their several views and purposes in writing. Here again the German notion of a contradiction between Mark and Matthew, is entirely at variance with our principles and practice as to evidence in courts of justice.

6. But when Herod's birthday was kept, the daughter of Herodias danced before them, and pleased Herod.

Birth-day is in Greek a word used by the older writers to denote a day kept in memory of the dead, but in the later classics and the Greek of the New Testament, confounded with a kindred form (γενέθλια) which means a birth-day, or rather its festivities, and, therefore, written in the plural. *The daughter of Herodias*, whose name, according to Josephus, was *Salome, danced*, not with others but alone, the dancing here intended not so much resembling the favourite amusement of the social circle as the professional exhibition of the theatre, and, therefore, never practised in the east or among the Greeks and Romans by women of respectable condition, so that this display was really a sacrifice of dignity and decency, intended to prevail upon the king by the seductions of an art, which he probably admired, and in which Salome may have had extraordinary grace and skill. All this is in the form of a preamble or preliminary statement of the circumstances in which the event about to be recorded took place.

7. Whereupon he promised with an oath to give her whatsoever she would ask.

The extravagance of Herod's admiration was evinced by his inconsiderate and lavish promise or agreement. (For the usage of the Greek verb, see above, on 7, 23. 10, 32.) *Ask* (*for herself*) as the middle voice in Greek denotes. Not content with this rash promise, he confirmed it by an oath.

8. And she, being before instructed of her mother, said, Give me here John the Baptist's head in a charger.

Before instructed, or rather, *instigated*, put forward, which agrees with Mark's account that there had been no previous understanding or agreement between them, but that the mother had employed the daughter's dancing to excite the liberality of Herod, whose infirmities she well knew, with the purpose of afterwards giving it the direction which she most desired and he least expected. The prompt laconic answer shows not only a predetermined plan, but a vindictive temper and an iron will. Her sanguinary purpose was expressed still more distinctly by requesting not the death of John the Baptist as a favour, but his head as a material gift. *Here*, on the spot, and by implication, now, without delay, as expressed in Mark (6, 25). *In a charger*, an old English word for a large dish, so called according to the etymologists from the load that it sustained. The Greek word originally means a board; then among other special applications of the term, a wooden trencher; and then any dish, without regard to the material. As Mark does not record this as a part of the suggestion of Herodias, it was probably added by the daughter of her own accord, as a hideous jest implying an intention to devour it.

9. And the king was sorry: nevertheless for the oath's sake, and them which sat with him at meat, he commanded (it) to be given (her).

This abrupt return of Herod to his senses is almost as clear a sign of intellectual and moral weakness as his foolish promise and his wicked oath. It also shows the motive of the eager promptitude with which his offer was embraced and acted on. This single scene affords a glimpse into the private life and character of this abandoned couple, fearfully in keeping with the history of their family as given by Josephus, though a flattering and interested writer. But Herod's sorrow, although probably sincere, was not sufficient to undo the mischief which his levity had done. For this, two reasons seem to be assigned, his conscience and his honour, a mistaken sense of duty and a feeling of false shame in reference to those around him. *For* (because of, on account of) *the oaths*, which may be taken either as a generic plural, equivalent in meaning to the singular, or as an inexact description of the promise and the oath (distinctly mentioned in v. 7) by a name strictly applicable only to the latter; or as referring to an eager repetition of his oath, not unlikely to have happened although not recorded. *And those reclining with him* (at his table, as his guests), before whom he had made the promise, and who may have affected to applaud his generosity and gallantry, and, therefore, might be probably expected to despise his fickleness and meanness if he broke it. The simplest construction is to take these as two distinct motives, a sincere belief that he was bound to keep his oath, and a morbid cowardly regard to the opinion of his company. It may be, however, that the two are to be more completely blended, and the one allowed to qualify the other, when the sense will be, that he considered his oath binding because publicly uttered, and that if it had been sworn in private he would not have scrupled to retract or break it. In either case the oath was an unlawful one on two accounts, because it was gratuitous, and, therefore, taking the Lord's name in vain (5, 34 Ex. 20, 7), and because it was dangerous, granting in advance what he might have no right to give, as the event proved to his sorrow and his cost. Although he could not, therefore, have broken his promise without guilt, he could not keep it without greater guilt, a choice of evils in which no man has a right to implicate himself by rash engagements.

10. And he sent, and beheaded John in the prison.

And sending he beheaded him, through an executioner (Mark 6, 27), but virtually with his own hands (see above, on 8, 5. 11, 3), *in the prison,* which, according to Josephus, was the fortress of Machærus on the southern frontier of Peræa near the Dead Sea. We must, therefore, either assume an interval of several days between the order and the execution, or suppose this feast to have been held at the fortress, during a visit of the tetrarch to that part of his dominions. The objection to the latter supposition, which is otherwise the most satisfactory, is that the company described by Mark (6, 21) are the lords, high captains, and chief estates, not of Herod's kingdom, but *of Galilee,* its north-western province, who would hardly be assembled on the southern frontier of Peræa, even if Herod would be likely to select a military station near the desert for the celebration of his birth-day.

11. And his head was brought in a charger, and given to the damsel : and she brought (it) to her mother.

This verse records the punctual performance of Herod's promise, and the exact execution of his orders, not excepting the dish, which with its ghastly contents was presented to the dancing-girl, whose fee it was, and by her to her mother, who, although behind the scenes, was the principal actor, or at least the manager of this whole tragedy. It may here be added, that she afterwards involved her husband in a ruinous attempt at further elevation, which was thwarted by her brother Herod Agrippa (the one whose death is recorded in the twelfth chapter of Acts), and resulted in the exile both of Herod and Herodias, first to Gaul, and then to Spain, where the former and most probably the latter died. Salome, true to her Herodian instincts, was married twice to near relations; first to her father's brother (and namesake) Philip the Tetrarch (see above, on v. 3, and compare Luke 3, 1), and after his death to Aristobulus, son of Herod king of Chalcis, to whom she bore three children. These facts are stated by Josephus, the contemporary Jewish historian ; the story of her death, preserved by the Byzantine writer Nicephorus, is commonly regarded as a later fiction.

12. And his disciples came, and took up the body, and buried it, and went and told Jesus.

His disciples, which might possibly mean those of Jesus, can have no such meaning in Mark (6, 29) where Jesus is not mentioned till the next verse, and in obvious connection with another subject. It must, therefore, signify John's own disciples, either those who had once been so before his imprisonment, or those who still professed to be so under some mistaken notion as to the relation which he bore to the Messiah, or some sceptical misgiving as to Jesus (see above, on 9, 14. 11, 2). It is possible however that it has a wider sense than either of those just proposed, and means some of the many who, without having ever been his personal attendants or disciples in the strict sense, had received his doctrines and his baptism. Of such disciples the whole land was full, and even on the outskirts of Peræa there could not be wanting some to pay this last respect to his decapitated body, and to announce his death to Jesus, who may now have been recognized by many for the first time as the Baptist's legitimate successor.

13. When Jesus heard (of it), he departed thence by ship into a desert place apart: and when the people had heard (thereof), they followed him on foot out of the cities.

We learn from Mark (6, 30) and Luke (9, 10), that the retreat here mentioned was immediately subsequent, not only to the death of John the Baptist, but to the return of the twelve from their first mission, and was partly intended to afford them some repose after their labours. *He withdrew*, retreated (see above, on 2, 12. 4, 12. 9, 24. 12, 15) *into a desert place by ship*, or rather (*in*) *a ship*, i. e. the one provided by our Lord's direction for his own exclusive use (Mark 3, 9). *Apart*, in private, privately, relating not so much to the mode of their departure as to its design and purpose. We know from other sources that the place to which they went was an unfrequented spot belonging to a town called Bethsaida (Luke 9, 10), on the other (or eastern) side of the sea of Galilee or Tiberias (John 6, 1). We are now approaching an occurrence so remarkable that all the four evangelists have given a detailed account of it. This not only furnishes a richer source of illustration than in any former case, but creates a strong presumption that the matter thus contained in all the gospels is, for some reason, worthy of particular attention. We have here a striking proof that our Saviour's popularity had not begun to wane when this occurrence took place; for not only did the multitudes still throng him when at home (Mark 6, 31), but no sooner had he pushed off in his boat to seek a momentary respite elsewhere, than the masses put themselves in motion to pursue or rather to outstrip him, so that when he reached his place of destination they were ready to receive him, and soon surrounded him as if he had not left them. As they went *on foot*, it is of course implied that they went *by land*, and some regard this as the meaning of the Greek word (πέζη) which is sometimes used in opposition to a voyage by water in Herodotus and Homer. But even in these cases the idea of a land-march or journey is rather necessarily implied than formally expressed. *From the towns* or cities in that region, not excluding the adjacent rural districts, which are generally represented as dependent on the nearest cities, as for instance in the case of Bethsaida and its desert (Luke 9, 10). We learn from John (6, 4) that all this happened just before the Passover, i. e. the third during our Lord's public ministry. (See John 2, 13. 23.)

14. And Jesus went forth, and saw a great multitude, and was moved with compassion toward them, and he healed their sick.

As these were not strangers or new-comers, but the same crowds who had pressed to see and hear him on the west side of the lake, their eager importunity excited our Lord's pity. *Going out* (from his boat, or from the place of his retirement, which however he had scarcely reached, as they outwent him) he saw *much people* (literally, crowd or concourse), *and was moved with compassion toward* (or *over*) *them,* the same peculiar idiom that was used above in 9, 36. and there explained. What excited his divine and human sympathy was not of course their numbers or their physical condition, but their spiritual destitution. At the view of this representative multitude, drawn from so many quarters, and perhaps swelled by the yearly stream of pilgrims to the Passover (John 6, 4), our Lord began without delay to teach them (Mark 6, 34), thereby showing what he reckoned their most urgent want, and also that although it was his miracles of healing that had prompted them to follow him (John 6, 2), they were not without some just view of the intimate relation of his wonders to his doctrines, or at least not unwilling to receive instruction from the same lips which commanded with authority the most malignant demons and diseases.

15. And when it was evening, his disciples came to him, saying, This is a desert place, and the time is now past; send the multitude away, that they may go into the villages, and buy themselves victuals.

When his discourse was ended, or perhaps while it was yet in progress, his disciples, i. e. the apostles (Luke 9, 12) began to be uneasy at the presence of so vast a multitude in a place which had been chosen for the very reason that it was secluded and remote from thoroughfares, though not cut off from all communication with the surrounding cultivated country. *Evening being come,* a verb employed before (8, 16) in reference to the lapse of time, and there explained. *H s disciples came to him,* probably while he was still engaged in teaching, with a view to interrupt him. *Saying desert is the place* (where we are now assembled) *and now* (already, or by this time), *the time is* now past. The word translated time is identical with the Latin *hora* and the English *hour*, but used in Greek with greater latitude of meaning, ranging from hours or even moments to the seasons of the year and time in general. (See above, on 8, 13. 9, 22. 10. 19.) Here it may either have the Latin sense or that of daytime. This anxious statement as to the lateness of the hour is followed by a proposition. *Send the multitude away*, dismiss, dissolve them as an audience or congregation (as the same verb means in Acts. 19, 41. 28, 25). This confirms the previous supposition that our Lord was still discoursing when the twelve made this suggestion, which was, therefore, tantamount to saying that he was detaining them too long, that it was time to pause and give them daylight to disperse in. The hint was no doubt well-meant and regarded by the men who made it as pre-eminently wise and prudent, little suspecting that their master, far from being at a loss as they were, had pursued this very course in order to convince them and others how little he depended on the ordinary means of subsistence. The disciples add a still more specific proposition, that the people be dispersed among the nearest farms and villages to buy provisions for themselves. *Buy*, in Greek a word peculiarly appropriate, because it originally means to *market*, and has primary reference to the purchase of provisions.

16. But Jesus said unto them, They need not depart; give ye them to eat.

17. And they say unto him, We have here but five loaves, and two fishes.

18. He said, Bring them hither to me.

We learn from John (6, 6), that Philip was the spokesman upon this occasion, and that our Saviour in this conversation tried the faith of his disciples, i. e. their confidence in his power to provide for all emergencies. John's additions to the narrative are not excluded, much less contradicted, by the others. *They* (the multitude) *have no need to depart* (or go away in search of food). *Give to them yourselves* (ὑμεῖς emphatic in itself and by position). In answer to their natural objection, that they have scarcely a sufficient provision for themselves (17), he simply orders it to be produced and placed at his disposal (18).

19. And he commanded the multitude to sit down on the grass, and took the five loaves, and the two fishes, and looking up to heaven, he blessed, and brake, and gave the loaves to (his) disciples, and the disciples to the multitude.

Having ordered the multitudes (*or crowds*) *to sit down*, literally, lie down, or recline, the customary posture even at table (see above, on 8, 11. 9, 10), but especially convenient in the open air, and when the food was spread upon the ground. *On the grass*, literally, *grasses*, a circumstance which not only adds to the beauty of the picture, and betrays a vivid recollection of the scene described, perhaps that of Peter (compare John 6, 10), but explains the word *desert* previously used (v. 13) as denoting not a barren waste, but only an unfrequented solitude, most probably an untilled pasture-ground. to which the corresponding Hebrew word is frequently applied in the Old Testament (e. g. Ps. 65, 13. Joel 2, 22.) He took the five loaves in succession, blessing each or all together. *Bread* and *loaf* are expressed by the same word in Greek as they are in French (*pain, pains*). *Looking up* is a natural and scriptural gesture in addressing God, whom all men as it were instinctively regard as dwelling in some special sense above them. *Heaven* denotes that distant place of God's abode, but also the visible expanse which seems to separate us from it (see above, on 3, 2. 16. 5. 26.) *Blessed*, a verb originally meaning to speak well of, but in usage applied to God's conferring favours upon men (25, 34), to men's invoking such favours upon others (Luke 2, 34), and to men's praising God particularly for such favours (Luke 2, 28). In the case before us these three senses may be said to meet; for as a man our Saviour gave thanks and implored a blessing, while as God he granted it. The intervention of the twelve in this distribution, while it answered the important but inferior purpose of securing order and decorum, also enabled them to testify more positively both to the scantiness of the provision and to the sufficiency of the supply. The particularity of this description corresponds to the deliberate and formal nature of the acts themselves, intended to arouse attention and preclude all surmise of deception or collusion. Nothing, indeed, could less resemble the confusion and obscurity of all pretended miracles, than the regular and almost ceremonious style in which this vast crowd was first seated and then fed, without the least disorder or concealment as to any part of the proceedings.

20. And they did all eat, and were filled: and they took up of the fragments that remained twelve baskets full.

The unequal division of the verses here is arbitrary and capricious and should serve to remind us that this whole arrangement is the work of a learned printer in the sixteenth century, and not entitled to the least weight in deciding the construction of a sentence or connection of a passage. *Did all eat* is in modern English an emphatic form, the auxiliary strengthening the verb, as if the fact had been denied or doubted; but it here represents the simple past tense, *all ate*, or retaining the Greek collocation, *ate all*. implying that the miraculous supply of food was limited only by the number of consumers. Nor was it a mere nominal supply in each case, but a full satisfaction of the appetite, even in the case of the most hungry. *Filled*, satisfied or sated, a Greek verb anciently confined to the feeding of the lower animals, but in the later writers (such as Arrian and Plutarch) extended to the human subject. We have here a remarkable example of our Saviour's provident discretion, even in the exercise of his almighty power. Had this miracle left no trace of itself except in the memory of men, it might have seemed like a dream or an illusion. But against this Jesus guarded in the most effectual manner, by commanding his disciples who had aided in the distribution, to collect the fragments which were left over after all were filled (John 6, 12). *And they took up*, and away with them, both which ideas are suggested by the usage of the Greek verb, and are equally appropriate, not only here but in 9, 6. 13, 12. and v. 12 of this chapter. *The abounding*, surplus, or excess of the *fragments* (from *frango*, to break, like κλάσματα from κλάω), broken pieces, scraps, or what are called in common parlance "broken victuals." The design of this command was threefold, first to discourage waste and teach a wise economy even in the lesser things of this life; secondly to show that in this case as in miracles of healing, the miraculous effect was to be instantly succeeded by the usual condition and the operation of all ordinary laws (see above, on 8, 15), so that although they had just seen a vast concourse supernaturally fed, they were themselves to use the fragments for their subsequent support; and thirdly, to preserve for some time in their sight and their possession the substantial memorials of this wonderful event, which was attested and recalled to mind by every crust and every crumb of which the company partook until the fragments were exhausted. And accordingly we find that our Lord, when afterwards reminding them of this great wonder and another like it, speaks expressly of the quantity left over after all were filled, as one of the most memorable circumstances in the case (see below, on 16, 9). It only remains to be considered whether these fragments were the refuse left by each partaker in the place where he had eaten, or the portions broken by our Lord for distribution and remaining untouched because more than was required to supply all present. The latter is not only a more pleasing supposition, but equally consistent with the terms of the narrative and the other circumstances of the case. That Jesus should have furnished an excessive or superfluous supply is not at variance with his wisdom or omniscience, as he may have done it for the very purposes before suggested. The word translated *basket* is used in a Latin form (*cophinus*) by Juvenal, as the usual baggage of the Jews when travelling. The number twelve has reference to the twelve apostles, so that each filled one, perhaps with some allusion to the symbolical import of the miracle.

21. And they that had eaten were about five thousand men, beside women and children.

This may either mean that there were none such present, or merely that they are not comprehended in the total of 5000. The latter is no doubt the true solution and to be explained by a fact already mentioned (see above, on 8, 11), that the men in ancient times as in the east at present ate together, and reclined at their repasts, while the women and children ate apart from them and in the ordinary sitting posture. Hence the companies or messes upon this occasion would be composed of men exclusively, and they alone could be numbered with facility from their distribution into fifties and hundreds (Mark 6, 40). It is not to be supposed, however, that the women and children would be overlooked in this benevolent provision, whether many or few, as some suppose upon the ground that the multitude was chiefly composed of pilgrims on their way to the passover (John 6. 4), which only males were required to attend (Ex. 23, 17. Deut. 16, 16.) But how is this to be reconciled with their having no provisions (see above, on v. 15, and compare Mark 6, 36), which seems rather to imply a concourse of people drawn too far from home by the excitement of pursuit (see above, on v. 13), and probably composed of men, women, and children. But whether these were few or many, it seems clear that they were not included in the number stated for the reason above given, whence it follows, either that those least able to dispense with food were thus provided, or that the number fed far transcended that recorded, which is *without* (i. e. exclusive of) *women and children*. Five thousand therefore is the minimum of those supplied by this stupendous miracle, being merely the number that could be determined at a glance from the methodical arrangement of the messes. Even at this rate, the original supply was only that of one loaf (and probably a small one) to a thousand men (besides women and children). But the greatness of the miracle consists not merely in the vast increase of nutritive material, but in the nature of the process which effected it, and which must be regarded as creative, since it necessarily involves not merely change of form or quality, or new combinations of existing matter, but an absolute addition to the matter itself. The infidel pretence that Christ is here described as visibly multiplying loaves and fishes in his own hands, so that every particle distributed was separately given out by him, is as groundless and absurd as it is impious in spirit and malignant in design. No such process of increase was presented to the eyes of the spectators, who saw nothing but the fact that the loaves and fishes still continued to be served until the whole multitude had been supplied. (Compare the miracles in 1 Kings, 17, 14. 2 Kings 4, 1–7.) Equally groundless yet instructive are the efforts of some sceptical interpreters to get rid of this miracle as originally a parable afterwards transformed into a history, or a myth founded on the story of the manna, or of Elijah fed by angels and ravens (1 Kings 17, 6. 19, 5), or on the doctrine of the living bread as taught by Christ (John 6, 48) and his apostles (1 Cor. 10, 16.) However specious these hypotheses may be, they are at bottom as gratuitous and hollow as the one of older date, now laughed at even by neologists themselves, that this is not recorded as a miracle at all, but merely as a figurative statement of the fact that by inducing his disciples to distribute their own scanty store, Jesus prevailed on others present who were well provided to communicate with others who had nothing. The only rational alternative is either to refute the overwhelming proof of authenticity and inspiration, or to accept the passage as the literal record of a genuine creative miracle, the first and greatest in the history, and therefore perhaps fully detailed in all the gospels.

22. And straightway Jesus constrained his disciples to get into a ship, and to go before him unto the other side, while he sent the multitudes away.

The effect of this transcendent miracle which, more than any that preceded it, appears to have convinced men of our Lord's Messiahship (John 6, 14), was immediately followed by another, more especially intended to confirm this impression on the minds of his disciples. This restriction of the circle of spectators was occasioned by his knowledge of a movement in the multitude to assert his regal claims as the Messiah (John 6, 15). To escape this dangerous and mistaken view of his pretensions, he withdrew himself at once into the highlands, on the verge of which the multitude had just been fed (John 6, 3). But first *he constrained* (compelled or forced) *his disciples to enter* (or embark upon) *the ship*, which waited on him for the purpose (Mark 3, 9), and *go before him* (literally *lead forward*, lead the way) to *the other side*, i. e. to Bethsaida of Galilee (Mark 6, 45). *He compelled them*, i. e. ordered them against their will, as they would naturally be averse to leave him, both on his account and on their own, a repugnance probably increased by the prospect of a nocturnal voyage on the lake where they had once been rescued from destruction by his presence (8, 23-26). Some assume, as an additional reason for sending the disples away, that they were disposed to join in the popular movement for making him a king. However this may be, he stayed behind *until he should dismiss* (dissolve, break up) *the crowds*, the same verb that is used above in v. 15. This was probably a matter of some difficulty, and requiring the exercise not only of authority but also of a superhuman influence.

23. And when he had sent the multitudes away, he went up into a mountain apart to pray: and when the evening was come, he was there alone.

Having sent them away he departed, went away, *into the mountain* (*not a mountain*, but the highlands or hill-country), which has been already several times mentioned (5, 1. 8, 1), and in which he was already (John 6, 3), so that he is only represented as penetrating further into its recesses, not for safety or repose, but *to pray*, a striking incidental notice of our Lord's devotional habits also given here by Mark (6, 46), and so far from being inconsistent with the statement made by John (6, 15) of his motive for retiring, that the two things were probably connected in the closest manner, as the plan for making him a king may have been both the occasion and the burden of his prayers at this time. There is something striking in the last words of this sentence: *Evening being come, he was alone there.* This double mention of the evening being come, both before and after the great miracle (see v. 15), has been misrepresented as an inadvertence springing from forgetfulness; whereas, it is in perfect keeping with the Jewish practice of reckoning two evenings (Ex. 12, 6. 29, 39. 41. Lev. 23, 5. Num. 9, 3. 5. 28, 4), one beginning at the first decline and the other at the setting of the sun. With this may be compared among ourselves the occasional or local use of evening to denote the afternoon.

24. But the ship was now in the midst of the sea, tossed with waves: for the wind was contrary.

Now, already, while he was still upon the shore. *In the midst of the sea*, not in its mathematical centre, or exactly half-way over, but out at sea, away from land, i. e. twenty-five or thirty stadia or furlongs (John 5, 19). *Tossed*, a very inadequate translation of a Greek word meaning properly *tormented* (see above on 8, 6. 29), here applied to the convulsive agitation of a vessel in a troubled sea and with an adverse wind. The same verb is applied by Mark (6, 48) to the disciples and translated *toiling*. The last clause gives the reason of their trying situation, *for the wind was contrary*, i. e. from the west or northwest.

25. And in the fourth watch of the night Jesus went unto them, walking on the sea.

The fourth watch of the night, according to the Roman division of the night into four watches of three hours each, which from the time of Pompey's conquest had supplanted the old Jewish division into three (Judg. 7, 19. Ps. 90, 6). The time here meant would be the three hours immediately preceding sunrise or perhaps the break of day, say from 3 to 6 o'clock A. M. *He came away* from the land *to* (or *towards*) *them*, where they were detained by the adverse wind, and making painful efforts to advance. *Walking*, originally *walking about*, or *to and fro* (hence *peripatetic*), but in the Greek of the New Testament simply walking, as opposed to other attitudes or motions. *On the sea*, not on the shore, as some absurdly fancy; for although the phrase sometimes has that meaning in both languages (as when we speak of a house or a town upon the sea), the other is equally justified by usage, is entitled to the preference, where other things are equal, as the primary or strict sense; and is required by the whole connection, by the obvious intention to relate a miracle, and by the fright of the disciples, which could not be owing to the sight of a man walking on the shore, even if he seemed to be walking in the water.

26. And when the disciples saw him walking on the sea, they were troubled, saying, It is a spirit; and they cried out for fear.

Seeing him, not merely *when they saw*, but in the very act of seeing him. *Were troubled*, i. e. violently agitated and disturbed at this most unexpected and inexplicable sight. *Saying that* (excluded by our idiom) *it is a phantom*. This last word is a corruption of the Greek word here employed (*phantasma*), both equivalent in meaning to the Latin *apparition*, i. e. an unreal appearance of a real person whether dead or living, commonly the former, but in the present case the latter. *Spirit* is here used in the specific sense, now attached to the synonymous term *ghost*, except when applied to the third person of the Trinity. *Cried out* (or *cried aloud*) *for fear*, the verb used elsewhere to describe the unearthly cries of evil spirits or of those whom they possessed. (See above on 8, 29, and compare Luke 4, 33. 8, 28.) These particulars are given both as vivid recollections of the memorable scene and as indications that the twelve, even after their first mission, still remained *in statu pupillari*, with many crude and childish views and even superstitious feelings, which were not to be entirely subdued till afterwards.

27. But straightway Jesus spake unto them, saying, Be of good cheer; it is I; be not afraid.

Although Jesus suffered them for wise and holy reasons to be momentarily alarmed, he did not leave them in this painful situation, but *immediately* (a circumstance here noted both by Mark and Matthew *spake* or *talked to them*, no doubt in his usual colloquial tone, with which they were now so familiar, and by which their superstitious fears would be instantly allayed, especially when uttering such cheering, reassuring words as those which follow. *Be of good cheer*, and *be of good comfort*, are the paraphrastic versions given in our Bible, of a single fine Homeric word (θάρσει pl. θαρσεῖτε), which might also be translated *cheer up*, or *take courage*. (See above, on 9, 2. 22. and compare Luke 8, 48. John 16, 33. Acts 23, 11, and 28, 15, where the corresponding noun appears.) It always presupposes some alarm or apprehension previously expressed or necessarily implied. *It is I*, literally *I am*, and therefore once translated *I am he* (John 4, 26), which is really the meaning in the other places also, i. e. *I am* (he that I appear to be, or he with whom you are so well acquainted). The coincidence of this familiar phrase with the divine name I AM (Ex. 3, 14) is extremely striking, even if fortuitous. (Compare Mark 14, 62.) *Be not afraid*, or frightened, fear not, an exhortation which implies, as something well known to them by experience, that his presence was enough to banish every danger.

28. And Peter answered him and said, Lord, if it be thou, bid me come unto thee on the water.

The narrative which follows is found only in this gospel, which is certainly remarkable, as Mark is supposed to have been aided by the memory of Peter, and as John has at least in one case supplied the name of that apostle when omitted by the others. (Compare John 18, 10 with Matt. 26, 51. Mark 14, 47. Luke 22, 50.) But even if this circumstance were more suspicious here than in the many other cases where a fact is only given in one gospel, all misgiving must be done away by the characteristic truth of the whole narrative so perfectly agreeable to what we know of Peter otherwise, that if the name had been omitted, it could be supplied at once by almost any reader. It is characteristic of the man, though perhaps belonging also to his office as the spokesman of the twelve, that he should answer first, and by a sort of challenge to the Master to make good his own identity on certain terms prescribed by Peter. *If it be thou,* literally, *if thou be,* corresponding to *I am* in the preceding verse. *Bid me,* order or command *me,* the verb used above in vs. 9. 19. *Water,* literally, *waters,* the origin of which plural form was explained above (on 5, 3).

29. And he said, Come. And when Peter was come down out of the ship, he walked on the water, to go to Jesus.

30. But when he saw the wind boisterous, he was afraid ; and beginning to sink, he cried, saying, Lord, save me.

Coming down from the ship, Peter walked upon the water, to go (i. e. intending or desiring so to do). Or the word may mean that he was actually going when his faith failed. *Seeing the wind strong,* the more exact though less emphatic marginal translation. *Boisterous,* however, conveys no idea not implied in the original. *He was afraid* is strictly passive both in Greek and English, where the last word is originally not an adjective (*fearful*), but a participle (*affrayed,* frightened). This alarm is perfectly in keeping with the character of Peter, which was more distinguished by impulsive ardour than by steady courage, whether physical or moral. *To sink* is also properly a passive, to be sunk, to be submerged, to be drawn beneath the surface. That his faith did not utterly forsake him is apparent from his cry for help to him who was at hand to give it.

31. And immediately Jesus stretched forth (his) hand, and caught him, and said unto him, O thou of little faith, wherefore didst thou doubt ?

Stretching forth the hand caught him, an expressive word in the original suggesting the idea that he seized him for himself, or took possession of him. (See above, on 6, 13.) *O thou of little faith,* a correct but necessarily diffuse translation of a single Greek work (see above, on 6, 30. 8, 26). The faith in which Peter was deficient was not justifying faith, nor general confidence in Christ's protection, but that specific faith which was essential to the miracle, a firm belief that what Christ had just commanded could be done and done by him and at that moment. (See above, on 8, 10. 9, 2. 22. 29, and below, on 15, 28. 17, 20. 21, 21.) *Wherefore*, not the ordinary phrase translated *why* 11 (9, . 14. 13, 10), but one occurring only here and meaning strictly, *as to what*, in reference to what cause, or from what consideration? *Doubt*, a Greek word, properly suggesting the idea of distraction or duplicity of mind and the uncertainty arising from it. It occurs in the New Testament but once besides, and that in this same gospel (see below, on 28, 17). After this most interesting episode, Matthew falls in with the narrative of Mark as if there had been no interruption.

32. And when they were come into the ship, the wind ceased.

33. Then they that were in the ship came and worshipped him, saying, Of a truth thou art the Son of God.

They coming, in the very act, or while they were so doing. *Ceased*, a most expressive word in Greek, denoting weariness or rest from labour, and employed by Mark not only here (6, 51), but in his history of the previous stilling of the storm (4, 39). The same evangelist describes, in very strong terms, the astonishment of the disciples at this double miracle, while Matthew speaks of *those in the ship*, which must either mean the passengers or crew, if any such there were besides them, as doing reverence to Jesus and acknowledging not merely his Messiahship, but his divinity. *Truly*, really, implies that he had previously claimed to be the Son of God. Such an acknowledgment might seem too much for any but his most enlightened followers, if it had not been already made by evil spirits. (See above, on 8, 29, and compare 4, 3. 6.) It is not easy to determine in such cases, how much meaning was attached to this mysterious title. On the whole, however, it is probable that those whom Matthew calls *the (people) in the ship* were identical with those whom Mark calls *the disciples*. (See above, on 8, 27, where a kindred form of speech is used by Matthew.)

34. And when they were gone over, they came into the land of Gennesaret.

And having crossed (the lake, from east to west) *they came to* (or upon) *the land of Gennesaret*, a small district four miles long and two or three wide, on the west side of the sea of Galilee, or lake of Tiberias, to which it gave one of its names. (See above, on v. 1 and on 4, 18.) Josephus describes this district as the garden of the whole land and possessing a fertility and loveliness almost unparalleled. Capernaum appears to have been in or very near this delightful region, so that John (6, 17) describes this same voyage as a voyage to Capernaum.

35. And when the men of that place had knowledge of him, they sent out into all that country round about, and brought unto him all that were diseased ;

The men of that place knowing (or recognizing) *him*, whom they had often seen before, as they lived so near his home and the centre of his operations. (See above, on 4, 13. 11, 23.) It is an interesting thought, very often incidentally suggested in the gospels, that during the three years of our Saviour's public ministry, his person must have become perfectly familiar to the great mass of the population, at least in Galilee. This, with the certainty that he retains his human body, and is to appear in it hereafter upon earth as he already does in heaven, should preserve us from a tendency to look upon all sensible and bodily associations with the person of our Lord as superstitious and irreverent, an error into which some devout believers are betrayed by their aversion to the opposite extreme of gross familiarity and levity in speaking of his glorified humanity. *That whole surrounding country*, an expression used in 3, 5, and there explained.

36. And besought him that thy might only touch the hem of his garment : and as many as touched were made perfectly whole.

This desire was only superstitious so far as it ascribed a magical effect to the mere touch, or regarded contact as essential to the healing power of the Saviour's word. It may have been his purpose to reach greater numbers in a given time without destroying all perceptible connection between the subject and the worker of the miracle. (Compare Acts 5, 15. 19, 12.) This is not a mere repetition of the statement in 8, 16. but designed to show that throughout the course as well as at the opening of our Saviour's ministry, his miracles were many, those recorded in detail being only a few selected samples, and also that his constant practice was to heal all who needed and desired it. *Made perfectly whole*, literally, *saved through*, brought through safe, i. e. through the danger or the suffering to which they were subjected. We are here brought back to the main theme of the history, to wit, the itinerant ministry of Christ in Galilee, to which the evangelist repeatedly reverts, as soon as he has finished any of the special topics comprehended in the plan of his gospel. We have such a description after the preliminaries in the four first chapters (4, 24) ; after the sermon on the mount and the series of miracles which follows it (9, 35) ; after the organization and commission of the apostolic body (11, 1) ; and now again after the formation of a systematic opposition, the exemplification of our

Saviour's parabolic teaching, the death of John the Baptist, the great creative miracle of feeding the five thousand, and the threefold miracle of walking on the water, saving Peter. and delivering the ship from danger. We have thus reached a resting-place, at which, without capricious violence, the book may be conveniently divided.

CHAPTER XV.

AFTER the manner of the best historians, Matthew now resumes the history of Christ's relations and behaviour to his enemies, especially the great Pharisaic party, taking up the subject where he laid it down, at the close of the twelfth chapter, for the purpose of exemplifying his peculiar mode of teaching the doctrine of his kingdom. He now records a fresh attack of the Pharisees and Scribes upon his unceremonial practice with respect to their traditional exaggeration and perversion of the Levitical purifications, with a full report of our Lord's authoritative teachings on the subject, both in public and private, to his own disciples (1–20). Connected with this, not only by immediate chronological succession, but in historical design and import, is the narrative of his one recorded visit to the Gentile world, with a miracle of dispossession there performed upon a Gentile subject, and among the most interesting in the Gospels, both for this and other reasons (21–28). Departing from his ordinary practice of detailing only select miracles, and those the most dissimilar, the evangelist here records a second instance in which Christ miraculously fed a multitude of people, for the very reason that the repetition of a wonder so stupendous entitled it to be again related (29–39).

1. Then came to Jesus Scribes and Pharisees, which were of Jerusalem, saying,

The immediate succession of events is not explicitly affirmed but highly probably from the marked chronological character of the whole context both in Mark and Matthew, though the first words here (*then came to Jesus*), in themselves considered, might refer to an entirely different time and occasion. *Scribes and Pharisees*, not wholly distinct classes, but the great religious party previously mentioned, with its official or professional leaders. The Scribes, or guardians and expounders of the law, were generally Pharisees and often Priests or Levites. See above, on 2, 4. 5, 20. 12, 38, and compare John 1, 19. 24.) 'Then came to him the Scribes and (other) Pharisees.' They are both described as *from Jerusalem*, which may either mean belonging to the Holy City (see above on 2, 1. 4, 25), or recently come down from it, as expressly stated by Mark (7, 1). It has even been supposed to denote a formal deputation from the Sanhedrim like that to John the Baptist (John 1, 19), and to Christ himself long afterwards (see below, on 21, 23). But this, though possible, is not the necessary meaning of the words. *To Jesus* may suggest, though it does not formally express, the idea of hostility (*against him*).

2. Why do thy disciples transgress the tradition of the elders? for they wash not their hands when they eat bread.

While Mark (7, 3–5) states with great particularity the Pharisaic usage as to washings, Matthew assumes it as already well known to his Jewish readers. This is one of many proofs that they wrote immediately for different classes. *Why*, literally, *for* (i. e. on account of) *what* (cause or reason), as in 9, 11. 14. 13, 10. *Thy disciples*, pupils, learners, so called because taught by thee, for whose behaviour thou art consequently answerable. This is the obvious spirit of the question, though civility or cowardice restricted it in form to the disciples. The question, as in all such cases (see above, on 9, 11. 14), though professedly a mere request for explanation, is in fact a challenge or demand by what right they thus acted, and by implication a denial that they had any right to do so. Whether *disciples* has its wider or its stricter application, is a point of no exegetical importance, as the meaning of the question is the same in either case. *Transgress*, violate, a form of expression claiming the authority of law for these traditions of the elders. *Tradition* means originally any thing delivered, in the way of precept (see 1 Cor. 11, 2. 2 Thess. 2, 15. 3, 6), but is specially applied to what is orally transmitted through successive generations. *Elders* may here have its official sense and designate the natural hereditary chiefs of Israel, as in 16, 21 below and often elsewhere. It will then denote the contemporary rulers of the Jews, by whose authority these uncommanded customs were enforced. More probably, however, there is reference also to the fathers of the nation, from whom the oral law had been transmitted. (See above, on 5, 21, and compare Gal. 1. 14.) *For* (introducing a specification of this general charge) *they wash not their hands when they eat bread*, in the strict sense, or partake of food in general, as bread was its principal though not its sole material in the case of the disciples. (See above, on 4, 3. 4. 6, 11. 7, 9.) The reference in this whole context is to washing, not as a means of cleanliness, but as a ceremonial or religious act, an uncommanded and traditional perversion of the legal ablutions or levitical purifications, as prescribed in Lev. xii–xv, and restricted to certain states of body representing the defilement of sin, but by the so-called oral law extended without meaning to the most familiar acts of life and even to the furniture of houses. (See Mark 7, 3. 4.)

3. But he answered and said unto them, Why do ye

also transgress the commandment of God by your tradition ?

Without denying their charge, he retorts it, with a fearful aggravation. 'What if my disciples do break the tradition of the elders; you do infinitely worse by breaking God's commandment for the sake of that tradition.' *Ye also*, you too, as well as they, are chargeable with such a violation, and that not of a human usage, but of a divine law. *By your tradition*, an inaccurate translation, founded upon that of Tyndale (*thorowe your tradition*), whereas all the other English versions (except that of the Geneva Bible) give the true sense of the preposition (διά) with the accusative (Wiclif and Rheims, *for;* Cranmer, *because of*). The meaning of the common version is a good one, but not that of the original, which represents their tradition as the motive, not the means, of their transgressing the divine commandment. The same idea is otherwise expressed by Mark (7, 9), " ye reject the commandment of God. that ye may keep your own tradition." Both forms of speech may have been actually used; or both may simply give the substance of our Saviour's answer; or one may give its substance and the other its form.

4. For God commanded, saying, Honour thy father and mother : and, He that curseth father or mother, let him die the death.

Not only in this one case of ceremonial baptisms did they thus reject and nullify God's precept, but in others of far more importance, because relating not to rites but moral duties, not to the abuse of positive and temporary institutions, but to the neglect of the most tender natural relations. Of this he gives a single instance, but a most affecting one, which utters volumes as to the spirit and the tendency of Pharisaic superstition. The sum and substance of it is that the observance of their vain tradition was considered and enforced by them as more obligatory than the sacred duty which the child owes to the parent, by the law of nature and the law of God. *For God commanded*, i. e. through Moses (Mark 7, 10). In these two parallels we have the clearest recognition of the code or system quoted in the next clause as the work of Moses and the law of God. He then quotes the first or preceptive clause of the fifth commandment (Ex. 20, 12. Deut. 5, 16), leaving out the promise or inducement as irrelevant to his present purpose, which relates exclusively to the precept, but substituting for it the severe law inflicting capital punishment on those who carried filial disobedience to the length of cursing or reviling, literally, speaking evil of, the opposite, both in etymology and usage, of the verb employed above in 5, 44. 14, 19, and there explained. Though here in strong antithesis to *honour*, it does not directly mean to *dishonour*, but denotes specifically one of the easiest and worst ways of doing so, to wit, by abusive and insulting language. *Whoso curseth*, literally, *the* (*one* or *the man*) *cursing* (or *reviling*) *father or mother*, an indefinite form used by both evangelists, and differing alike from the original and the Septuagint version, both which have the pronoun (*thy*). This exact agreement in so slight a difference is not to be explained by the hypothesis of servile imitation or transcription on the part of either, but by the supposition that these were the very words (or their exact equivalents) which Jesus uttered, and which therefore must have some significance, however faint the shade of meaning which they may express. That they do express one must be felt by every reader even of a literal translation, though it is not easy to subject it to analysis or definition. Perhaps it may be simply stated thus, that the definite expression in the other clause (*thy father and thy mother*) and in the original of this clause (*his father and his mother*) is designed to individualize, before the mind of every hearer or reader of the law, the very pair to whom he owes allegiance, while the vaguer phrase here used (*father* or *mother*) rather calls up the idea of parents in general as a class or species, but so as rather to enhance than to extenuate their claims upon their children, by presenting those claims in the abstract and the aggregate. As if he had said, 'he who can dishonour by his curses such a sacred object as a father or a mother.' *Let him die the death*, Cranmer's imitation of the Hebrew idiom which combines a finite tense and an infinitive of the same verb to express intensity, repetition, certainty, or any other accessory notion not belonging to the essential import of the verb itself. In the original passage our translators have expressed the qualifying adjunct (that of certainty) without copying the form (*shall surely be put to death*), while here the form is rendered prominent by a pretty close approximation to the Hebrew in the combination of the cognate verb and noun, a modification of the idiom not unknown in other languages. The imitation is indeed much closer than in Greek, where the verb is not the ordinary verb *to die*, but one which originally means to *end* or *finish*, often joined with *life*, and then elliptically used without it to express the same idea (that of ending life or dying). The strict translation of the whole phrase therefore would be, *let him end with death;* the meaning both of it and of the Hebrew. *let him surely die*. Tyndale has simply, *shall suffer death;* the Rhemish version, *dying he shall die*.

5. But ye say, Whosoever shall say to (his) father or (his) mother, (It is) a gift, by whatsoever thou mightest be profited by me;

The antithesis is still kept up between what God said and what they said, both being put into the form of a command or law. Having given that of God, with its tremendous sanction in the verse preceding, he now contrasts with it that of the traditional or oral lawyers. *But* (on the other hand, on your part) *ye say*, not in so many words, perhaps not formally at all, but practically by what you encourage and allow, both in yourselves and others. It pleased our Lord to put the spirit of their conduct and of the system upon which it rested into this technical and formal shape, in order more completely to expose its wickedness and folly. *Shall say* is too categorical and positive a version of the aorist subjunctive which denotes a hypothetical contingency, or something which may happen or may not. *To his father or mother*, literally, *the father or the mother*, the pronoun being still omitted, as in v. 4, but the article inserted. *A gift*, a word denoting gifts in general but specifically used in Homeric and Hellenistic Greek to mean a votive offering or a gift to God. In this restricted sense it answers to the Hebrew *corban*, here retained (Mark 7, 11), which according to its etymology means any thing brought near or presented, but in usage what is thus brought near to God. In this sense, it is applied, like the corresponding verb, to all the offerings of the Mosaic ritual, animal and vegetable, bloody and bloodless. (See Lev. 2, 1. 4. 12. 13. 7, 13. 9, 7. 15.) In the later Hebrew and Chaldee, it was applied still more extensively to all religious offerings, even those not sacrificial, but not to these exclusively, as some allege. This one word seems to have been the prescribed form in such cases, so that by simply saying "Corban," a man might devote the whole or any part of his possessions to religious uses, i. e. to the maintenance of the temple service by the purchase of victims or the sustentation of the priests and Levites. *Whatever thou* (the parent thus addressed) *mightest be profited by me* (i. e. whatever assistance or advantage thou mightest have derived from me) is Corban or devoted to religious uses like a sacrificial victim. That such things were permitted and applauded may be proved by certain dicta of the Talmud, and especially by a famous dispute between Rabbi Eliezer and his brethren, in which the very act here described was vindicated by the latter.

6. And honour not his father or his mother, (he shall be free). Thus have ye made the commandment of God of none effect by your tradition.

The division of the verses varies here in the editions of the Greek and English text, the former making what is here the first clause of v. 6 the last clause of v. 5, without effect upon the sense, but with advantage to the syntax. The English version makes this clause a part of what they said, and still dependent on the conditional phrase, *whosoever says* (or *shall say*). 'Whoever says this to his parents and refuses or neglects to honour them.' There is then an instance of the figure called aposiopesis, in which the apodosis, or logical conclusion of the sentence, is suppressed or left to be supplied by the reader. Such constructions, whether beauties or defects, occur in the best classical writers. The thought here supplied by the translators (in italics) is, *he shall be free* (i. e. to do so, or from punishment), in other words, he does no wrong, he does his duty. Another construction, found in Tyndale's version, and preferred by some philological authorities of later date, makes this clause our Lord's own statement of the consequence (*and so shall he not honour*). This, however, still supposes an aposiopesis in a different place, i. e. before instead of after the clause now in question. Having given this revolting instance of the practical result to which their treatment of God's precepts tended, he returns to the generic charge which it was stated to illustrate. *Thus* (literally *and*) *made void*, invalidated, nullified, a verb not used in classic Greek, but formed directly from an adjective familiarly applied by Plato and Thucydides to laws, and representing them (according to its etymology) as destitute of force, invalid, null and void. This was the actual effect, whatever may have been the purpose, of their ceremonial and traditional morality, by which they practically nullified the divine commandment. *By your tradition* should again be *for* (the sake or on account of) *your tradition*. The address may be either to the whole race as represented by his hearers, or to themselves as delivering and enforcing these traditions by authority.

7. (Ye) hypocrites, well did Esaias prophesy of you, saying,

8. This people draweth nigh unto me with their mouth, and honoureth me with (their) lips; but their heart is far from me.

Hypocrites, a Greek noun originally meaning one who answers or responds, with particular allusion to oracular responses, explanations, and advices; then one who answers in a colloquy or conversation, with particular allusion to dramatic dialogue; then one who acts upon the stage, an actor; then metaphorically one who acts a borrowed part; and lastly, a dissembler, a deceiver, one whose words and actions do not indicate his real thoughts and feelings. This last sense of the noun, the only one which it retains in modern languages, is not found in the classics; but the primitive or corresponding verb meant to dissemble at least as early as Demosthenes and Polybius. It is doubtful, however, whether the noun, even in the Greek of the New Testament, has always the strong sense which later usage puts upon it, and which sometimes does not seem entirely appropriate, as in Luke 12. 56, and here, in both which places the connection agrees better with the older sense of one who acts a part, who wears a mask, who is contented with an outside show, including not deliberate deceivers merely, but the self-deceived, or those who really mistake the outward for the inward, the apparent for the real. *Well*, not truly or correctly, which would be superfluous as an encomium on an inspired prophecy, both here and in Acts 28, 25, where Paul applies the same term to the Holy Ghost himself; but finely, admirably, or appropriately, exactly, in allusion to the singular coincidence between Isaiah's inspired description of his own contemporaries and the character and conduct of their children's children in the time of Christ. It is not however a mere accommodation of the passage to a foreign subject, since Isaiah's words are not con-

fined to those whom they immediately described; but this very fact,
that a description could be so framed as to represent with equal fidelity originals who lived so many centuries apart, is itself a proof of inspiration and a ground for the applause and admiration here expressed.
Esaias is the Greek form of *Isaiah*, like *Elias* for *Elijah* in 11, 14. As
Isaiah itself is a modification of the Hebrew form (*Jeshaiah, Jeshaiahu*),
it would have been better to employ either it or the Greek *Esaias* in
the version of both Testaments, the variation of the name confusing
uninstructed readers. This is still more true of *Jesus*, the Greek form
of *Joshua*, when used to designate the Son of Man (as in Acts 7, 45.
Heb. 4, 8). *Did Isaiah prophesy*, of old, so long ago. *Of* (i. e.
about, concerning) *you*, should be connected with the adverb, *well*.
The meaning is not that the Jews of Christ's time were the formal and the direct theme of the prophecy, which would not have
been spoken of as so remarkable, but rather that in speaking of his
own contemporaries, he drew an admirable picture of their children in the time of Christ. But although this does not require us to
interpret the original passage as a specific and exclusive prophecy respecting Christ's contemporaries, it does require us to interpret it so as
to include them, which can only be secured by making it descriptive of
the unbelieving Jews, not at one time merely, but throughout the period
of the old dispensation, an assumption perfectly confirmed by history.
The quotation is a free one from the Septuagint version of Isa. 29, 13,
the variations being unimportant to the Saviour's purpose. *Is far from
me*, in Hebrew, *it removes far from me;* but this variation is found
also in the Septuagint.

9. But in vain they do worship me, teaching (for)
doctrines the commandments of men.

But (or *and*), the usual connective (δέ), *in vain they worship me*, a
thought implied though not expressed in the original, and therefore
not improperly supplied by the Seventy and sanctioned by our Lord
or his biographers. The literal translation of the Hebrew words is,
and their fearing me (i. e. their worship) *is* (or *has become*) *a precept
of men, a thing taught*. This taken by itself might seem to mean that
they served God merely in obedience to human authority, and would
then imply no censure on the persons thus commanding, but only on
the motives of those by whom they were obeyed. But in our Saviour's
application of the passage to the hypocrites of his day, he has reference
particularly to religious teachers, as corrupting the law by their unauthorized additions.

10. And he called the multitude, and said unto them,
Hear, and understand:

Thus far he had addressed the Scribes and Pharisees themselves,
but now invokes a larger audience. *And calling to the crowd*, i. e. ad-

dressing them, or *calling the crowd to* (him), as in 10, 1, which does not necessarily imply a change of place, but merely a request for their particular attention, as expressed in the last clause. Still less is it implied that the multitude at large had not heard what is said in the preceding context. All that is meant is that, after having answered the demand of his opponents in the presence of the people, he now calls the attention of the latter to the same great subject, as one of practical and universal interest, because relating to the very principle of all morality. *Hear me*, listen to me, not an unmeaning form, but a distinct intimation that he had something of importance to communicate (see above, on 11, 15. 13, 9. 18. 43). *And understand*, give intelligent attention, not merely to my words but to their meaning.

11. Not that which goeth into the mouth defileth a man; but that which cometh out of the mouth, this defileth a man.

Having exposed the folly of the prevalent ceremonial superstition as to uncommanded baptisms or religious washings, and its wickedness in setting aside moral obligations, the Saviour now pursues the same course in a still more public manner with respect to the most prevalent and favourite of all merely ritual distinctions, that of clean and unclean meats, which had then become, and still continues, the chief bar to social intercourse between Jews and Gentiles. The very object of the law upon this subject (as recorded in Lev. xi. and Deut. xiv.) was to separate the chosen race from every other by restrictions on their food which should render it impossible for them to live together, or to interchange the ordinary courtesies of life, without a constant violation, upon one side, of religious duty. This effect had been abundantly secured for ages in the practice of all conscientious Jews, but with the necessary incidental evil of a constant disposition, even on the part of such, to mistake a positive and temporary regulation for a perpetual invariable law, and to regard the forbidden meats as having an intrinsic efficacy to defile, not only ceremonially but morally. In opposition to this groundless and pernicious error, Christ propounds the simple truth, but in a form adapted to arrest the popular attention and impress itself upon the memory by something of antithesis and even paradox. *A man*, literally, *the man*, which may either be the Greek equivalent to our generic " man " without the article, or be taken strictly as denoting the particular man eating or receiving food in any supposed case. *Entering into the mouth*, i. e. as food or nourishment. *Defiles him*, literally, *makes him common* or *profane*. This expression is derived from the ceremonial law, by which the Jews were separated from the other nations, and their sacred rites and utensils from all things, even of the same kind, which had not been thus sanctified or set apart to sacred uses as distinguished from all secular and common uses. Hence arises the antithesis, at first sight so surprising, between *holy* and *common*. *But* (the other branch of the antithesis) *the* (*thing*) *coming out of*, proceeding from (the exact correlative or opposite, in form as well as sense, of the preceding verb), *the mouth* in language, or more generally in conduct, as the expression of thoughts and character. The paradoxical character of this important statement arises from its solemnly affirming in a moral sense, what was not true if taken in a ceremonial sense, and therefore might at first sight seem, and did no doubt to many seem, directly contradictory to an express divine commandment. But this only deepened the impression of the true sense when discovered or revealed, as in all the paradoxes which may be said to form a striking characteristic of our Saviour's teachings, but which no mere man, at least no uninspired man, can imitate without the risk of doing far more harm than good, and of adding one more instance to the many which illustrate and confirm the fact that "fools rush in where angels fear to tread." What our Saviour here denies is not that the partaking of forbidden meats was ceremonially defiling, i. e. subjected those who did so to certain ceremonial disabilities and rendered necessary certain rites of purification; for all this was explicitly revealed in scripture and embodied in the practice of the Jewish church from the very beginning of the ceremonial dispensation, which was not yet at an end. Nor does he here deny that by transgressing this part of the law a man incurred the moral guilt of disobedience, which would have opened a wide door to lawless and ungodly license. It is not the authority or obligation of the precept that he calls in question, but its ground and purpose, as usually apprehended by the people and expounded by their spiritual leaders. Certain meats had been prohibited by Moses under the divine direction, for a temporary end of great importance but ere long to be forever superseded, i. e. to secure the separation of the Jews from other races till the change of dispensations, and in the mean time to symbolize the difference between heathenish corruptions and the holiness which ought to have adorned the church or chosen people. But by gradual departure from this clearly revealed purpose of the legal prohibitions now in question, they had come to look upon the unclean meats as *per se* morally defiling, and by necessary consequence, upon the strict use of the clean meats as intrinsically purifying, or at least meritorious in the sight of God. This is the error here refuted or condemned, and not obedience to the dietetic laws of Moses while the system was still binding, upon which these words of Christ have neither a remote nor an immediate bearing, as some eminent interpreters imagine, and as many of his hearers no doubt thought at that time, notwithstanding the admonitory warning against inattention and misapprehension, which we learn from Mark (7, 16) though not from Matthew, that he uttered upon this as on so many other similar occasions.

12. Then came his disciples, and said unto him, Knowest thou that the Pharisees were offended, after they heard this saying?

Then, i. e. after he had thus addressed the crowd or multitude at large, but in the presence of his Pharisaic censors. *Coming up,* or *coming to* (*him*), *his disciples,* either in the wider sense of those who took his part, were on his side, received his doctrine; or in the more specific sense of those who now attended him from place to place as learners. These, with their Jewish habits and associations, would naturally be disturbed at hearing the unfriendly and disparaging remarks of the leading men who were present in the audience, and would no less naturally tell their master, both as a warning to him and a relief to their own feelings. *Knowest thou,* in modern English do you know, are you aware? The question may perhaps imply that if he knew it, he would surely not continue to exasperate the enmity of such important men. *After they heard,* literally, *having heard* or *hearing* not by subsequent report or information, but upon the spot and with their own ears. *Offended,* i. e. stumbled, shocked, the figure being that of an obstacle or hindrance lying in the path. (For another application of the same essential meaning, see above, on 5, 29. 30. 11, 6. 13, 21. 41. 57.) Wiclif: thou knowest that if this word be heard, the Pharisees ben sclaundrid (are slandered)! The stumbling-block to these censorious hearers was the seeming nullification of the laws of clean and unclean food, as enacted by Moses and enlarged by the tradition of the elders.

13. But he answered and said, Every plant, which my heavenly Father hath not planted, shall be rooted up.

Our Lord's reply is twofold. In the first place, he assures his anxious followers that he had not spoken rashly or at random, but advisedly, in execution of a settled purpose to destroy the credit of these oral lawyers and traditional expounders, whose whole system of additions to the law was founded upon no divine authority, and therefore must be utterly destroyed to make way for the purer doctrine of the kingdom. This necessity is stated in a figurative form drawn from the vegetable world, and not unlike that used in several of the parables before recorded (chapter xiii). *Plant* seems to designate the individual, whereas Wiclif's version, *planting,* more correctly applies it to the whole traditional or Pharisaic system, theoretical and practical.

14. Let them alone : they be blind leaders of the blind. And if the blind lead the blind, both shall fall into the ditch.

This is the second part of our Lord's answer to the warning in v. 12. Although it was his purpose to destroy the credit of the Scribes and Pharisees as religious teachers, there was no need of violence, nor even of dispute, to bring about the end which he desired. It was enough to let his enemies alone in order to secure their ruin, and, alas, that of many whom they influenced and guided. Both were destitute of spiritual vision, and must therefore share the consequences of that destitution. The physical effect was not more certain in the case supposed (of blind men guided by a blind man) than the moral effect in the real case represented by it. *Let them alone,* or more exactly, *let them* (go on), *let them* (do as they are doing), *leave them* (to themselves), without attempting either to arrest or to accelerate their progress. (For the usage of the Greek verb, see above, on 3, 15.) *Be* is an indicative form common in old English and exactly equivalent to *are*. *The ditch* (or rather pit, hole), i. e. the one crossing the path in the case supposed.

15. Then answered Peter and said unto him, Declare unto us this parable.

Peter here speaks in the name of the disciples, and in the house after they had left the multitude (Mark 7. 17). *Declare,* the same verb that is so translated in 13, 36 above, though more emphatically rendered in the Romish versions by the word *expound*. It strictly means to *phrase*, or express in words, the idea of explanation being really suggested by the context. *This parable* might seem to mean the metaphor or simile just used in the preceding verse, to which the word is strictly applicable, as denoting an illustration from analogy (see above, on 13, 3). But our Lord's answer (in the following verses) seems to show that the inquiry has respect to his public declaration in v. 11, which can be called a *parable* only in the vague sense of something enigmatical, not obvious in meaning. (See above, on 13, 35.) It is possible, however, although not so probable, that Peter did intend to ask why our Lord compared the Pharisees to blind guides, and that he answers indirectly but emphatically by exposing the error which they entertained respecting the effect of food, and in which the disciples were still sharers. The plural form (*unto us*) shows that Peter spoke for all the rest, which agrees with Mark's account, and also with our Lord's reply, which was addressed not to Peter, but to the whole company.

16. And Jesus said, Are ye also yet without understanding?

Although this is not a harsh reproof, it certainly involves a censure on the followers of Christ for their continued share in the prevailing error which he had just refuted and denounced. This implies that what they failed to understand was not a mystery requiring special revelation to disclose it, ignorance of which could not have been condemned as culpable, but something clear already, if not from the nature of the case, from the word of God. *Jesus said* to them (in answer to their question or request for explanation). *Even ye* (or *ye also*) my most favoured and enlightened followers. *Yet,* the accusative of the noun *acme,* meaning full time; an adverb, just now; in later Greek, as here, *yet,* still. *Without understanding,* in Greek a single word which might be rendered *unintelligent* (the opposite in form as well as sense of that employed in 11, 25. Acts 13, 7. 1 Cor. 1, 19). It is applied by Paul (Rom. 1, 21. 31) to the irrationality of sin, but also in the same epistle (10, 19) to the ignorance and unintelligence of heathen or barbarians.

17. Do not ye yet understand, that whatsoever entereth in at the mouth goeth into the belly, and is cast out into the draught?

Do ye not perceive, a verb applied by Homer and Xenophon to bodily vision, but in the Greek of the New Testament to intellectual perception only, sometimes with the accessory notion of attention (see below, on 24, 15, and compare 2 Tim. 2, 7), which may also be included here (and in 16, 9 below). 'Are you not sufficiently attentive to perceive &c.?' This again implies that what they misconceived was no mysterious secret but an obvious and patent truth, which they could not have attentively considered without justly apprehending it, as almost self-evident, although the people had lost sight of it, and even the disciples did not see it clearly. Food does not affect the mind or soul, but only the corporeal organs, which are not moral agents or susceptible of moral changes. *The belly,* not the entire body, nor the abdomen exclusively, but the whole interior cavity (the Greek word originally meaning *hollow*), in which are lodged the organs of digestion here especially referred to, namely, the stomach and intestines. Mark has preserved the negative statement that the food never goes beyond the body or reaches the mind or soul, by suggesting that the whole course of the aliment, received through the mouth into the stomach and intestines, can be traced as all exclusively corporeal, from its entrance to its exit. How absurd then to imagine that the moral and spiritual state of man can be affected by the food which he consumes. *Draught,* drain, sink, or privy, a word belonging to the later Greek.

18. But those things which proceed out of the mouth come forth from the heart; and they defile the man.

This completes the antithesis, by adding to the negative account of what does not defile a man the positive description of what does. *The (things) coming out of the heart,* i. e. proceeding from it in a moral sense. The double *out* (ἐκ) prefixed in Greek both to verb and noun adds strength to the antithesis or contrast. *And they* (ἐκεῖνα, an emphatic pronoun meaning not what I have just described) *profane the man* (make him common or unholy in the proper sense). 'Food, when it enters, enters not into the soul but the stomach and the bowels; but there is something, in another sense proceeding from man, which does really defile him.' What it is, he teaches in the next verse.

19. For out of the heart proceed evil thoughts, mur-

ders, adulteries, fornications, thefts, false witness, blasphemies :

Out of the heart, the soul, the seat both of the intellect and the affections. *Proceed*, come out or forth, the same verb that is used in the preceding verse. *Thoughts*, not mere ideas or incoherent notions, but reasonings, calculations, plans, or purposes, implying action both of mind and heart in the restricted sense. Of these he now enumerates particular examples, in the plural number, either to denote the multitude of sinful acts included under each description or the variety of forms and circumstances under which each sin may be committed. *Murders*, unlawful and malicious homicides. *Adulteries*, violations of the marriage vow; *fornications*, violations of chastity by unmarried persons; both being breaches of the seventh commandment (Ex. 20, 14) as interpreted by Christ himself (see above, on 5, 28). These crimes, interpreted with proper latitude, include the worst offences against human justice and the order of society. *Thefts*, including all surreptitious violations of the property of others, and according to later Greek usage even those of a more violent and open nature, highway-robbers being still called *klephts* (essentially the same word here employed) in modern Greece. The opposite change has taken place in English, *thieves* and *robbers* being never now confounded as they often are in our Bible (see above, on 6, 19, and compare Luke 10, 30). In the place of *covetousness* (Mark 7, 22) Matthew substitutes *false testimonies*, both (or their equivalents in Aramaic) having probably been uttered by our Saviour, as well as several others here omitted but preserved by Mark. *Blasphemies*, another outward manifestation used to represent an inward disposition, namely, proud and spiteful anger, that which finds expression in reviling and abusive words not only against man but God (see above, on 12, 31). The allegation that Mark adds to Matthew's catalogue a number of irrelevant particulars, is perfectly gratuitous, as no rule can be laid down for determining how many might be given, and our Saviour may have uttered a still greater number, out of which one evangelist selected more, the other less, as best adapted to his own immediate purpose.

20. These are (the things) which defile a man : but to eat with unwashen hands defileth not a man.

The enumeration of particulars is followed by a summing up or repetition of the general statement which they were intended to exemplify. *These are the things (defiling) the man* (desecrating, rendering unholy), not ceremonially, but morally. To this is added, not by Mark but by Matthew, a correlative negation as to the effect of ceremonial washings or their omission, winding up the whole discourse and at the same time bringing it back to the point from which it set out in the first verse. *But to eat*, or *the (act of) eating, with unwashed hands*, i. e. ceremonially unwashed, without a previous ritual ablution, *does not profane* (or desecrate) the *man* (who so eats), or render him unholy in the sight of God.

21. Then Jesus went thence, and departed into the coasts of Tyre and Sidon.

Thence, i. e. from the place where the foregoing words were uttered. But where was this? The last particular place mentioned was Gennesaret (14, 34), but Mark speaks of his visiting "that whole surrounding country," and entering into "villages, cities, and fields" (Mark 6, 55. 56). This may seem to cut off the connection and prevent our ascertaining the locality referred to here. But as *thence* implies a definite place previously mentioned, and as Mark's statement is incidentally and parenthetically introduced, and relates not so much to what occurred at any one time as to the general and constant practice, as appears from the use of the imperfect tense, it is still most probable that the reference is here to the land (or district) of Gennesaret, or to the neighbouring city of Capernaum (see above, on 4, 13, and compare John 6, 17). *Departed*, or more exactly, *withdrew*, retreated (see above, on 2, 12. 4, 12. 12, 15. 14, 13), from the malice of his enemies, as some suppose, or as others, from the crowd and bustle even of his friends and followers. It is probable, however, that a higher and more important motive led to this retreat, to wit, the purpose to evince by one act of his public life that, though his personal ministry was to the Jews (see below, on v. 24. 26, and compare Rom. 15, 8), his saving benefits were also for the Gentiles. It is important to remember that these movements were not made at random or fortuitously brought about, as infidel interpreters delight to represent, and some of their believing admirers do not venture to deny, but deliberately ordered in accordance with a definite design, the reality of which is not affected by our being able or unable everywhere to trace it in the history. *Into* (not merely *to* or *towards*, which would be otherwise expressed). *The parts*, i. e. bordering or frontier parts (Mark 7, 24). *Tyre and Sidon*, the two great seaports of Phenicia, put for the whole country, which apart from them had no importance (see above on 11, 21). The whole phrase does not mean the region between Tyre and Sidon, but the boundary or frontier between Galilee and Phenicia.

22. And, behold, a woman of Canaan came out of the same coasts, and cried unto him, saying, Have mercy on me, O Lord, (thou) Son of David; my daughter is grievously vexed with a devil.

The remarkable circumstance in this case, which in part accounts for its insertion in the history, is that the woman here described was a Gentile, not only by residence, but by extraction. *A Canaanitish woman*, so called because Phenicia was peopled by the sons of Canaan, who had not been driven out as they were from Palestine. This is perfectly consistent with Mark's description of the same woman as a Syrophenician, i. e. a native or inhabitant of that Phenicia which was contiguous to Syria and dependent on it as a Roman province, and also as *a Greek*, in the Hellenistic sense of Gentile, even where the language was not actually spoken, as it may have been in this case. *Out of those borders*, i. e. frontier regions, the *parts* mentioned in the first verse. This phrase is not necessarily dependent in construction on the verb which follows it in Greek but comes before it in English. It may mean *coming out of those parts*, but it may also mean belonging to them (compare the like use of the preposition *aus* (or *out of*) in German), or residing in them. *Coming out* will then have reference to her house or place of residence. 'A woman from that region going forth (to meet him).' *Cried*, clamoured, made a noise. *Son of David*, a familiar name of the Messiah (see above, on 1, 1. 9, 27. 12, 23), in which character this Gentile woman recognizes Jesus. The last six words in English correspond to two in Greek which strictly mean *is badly demonized*, a verb repeatedly employed before by Matthew. (See above, on 4, 24. 8, 16. 28. 33. 9, 32. 12, 22.) Wiclif's version of the phrase is, *evil travailed of a fiend*.

23. But he answered her not a word. And his disciples came and besought him, saying, Send her away; for she crieth after us.

Another singularity of this case, which suggests a further reason for its being so minutely stated, is our Lord's refusal to perform the miracle, of which this is the first and only instance upon record. Even here, however, it was not an absolute and permanent refusal, but a relative and temporary one, designed to answer an important purpose, both in its occurrence and in the historical account of it. Matthew here records a circumstance not found in Mark, to wit, that her request was at first received in silence. *He did not answer her a word*, i. e. a single word or one word. The same expression occurs again in 22, 46 below, and the converse of it in 8, 8. 16 above. It here means simply that he did not answer her at all, in consequence of which she followed him continuing her outcries. This is not inconsistent with Mark's statement (7, 24) that he went into a house, which relates only to his first arrival in those parts, and cannot mean that he continued there indefinitely. *His disciples*, probably the twelve, who were again in attendance on him after their return from their temporary mission. (See above, on 14, 13, and compare Mark 6, 30.) *Coming up*, or *coming to* (him), i. e. nearer to him (as in v. 12). *Besought him*, literally, *asked him*, i. e. asked him whether he would not dismiss her, an absolute use of the verb *to ask* very common in Hebrew and the Greek of the New Testament. *Send away*, discharge, dismiss, a verb applied above (14, 15. 22. 23) to the dissolving of a large assembly, but elsewhere (1, 19. 5, 31. 32) to a single person. In itself it might here mean dismiss her without granting her petition; but our Lord's answer in the next verse presupposes that they asked him to get rid of her by granting it. *She crieth after us* is not, as it is sometimes represented, an expression of mere selfish regard to their own ease, as it may also indicate a care for the honour and the comfort of their master. Indeed there is no necessary reference whatever to the mere inconvenience of her crying after them. These words may be intended simply to describe her importunity and grief as a reason for granting her request. Thus explained they are equivalent to saying, 'Give her what she asks so earnestly, and with such evidence of suffering as well as of believing expectation.'

24. But he answered and said, I am not sent but unto the lost sheep of the house of Israel.

This is another interesting circumstance which Mark omits. Our Lord before answering the woman answers the disciples by reminding them that what they asked was not a thing of course or of usual occurrence, being not like his other miracles of healing and of dispossession a part of his ordinary work and mission, which was intended for the Jews and not the Gentiles. *Sent*, commissioned by my Father, in my Messianic character and office. The same application of the verb occurs above in 10, 40, while in vs. 5. 16 of the same chapter. it is applied to the apostles, whose official title is derived from it.* There seems to be an obvious allusion to their own commission as recorded in 10, 5. 6, as well as to the description in 9, 36. As explained by these analogies, the words may thus be paraphrased. 'How can you expect me to turn from the sufferers of my own race to strangers, when I forbade you to go to the Samaritans or Gentiles?' This is not a reason for refusing their request, but an intimation that in granting it he would be transcending the formal bounds of their commission and his own.

25. Then came she and worshipped him, saying, Lord, help me.

Not content with crying after him or to him from a distance, she drew near to him and worshipped him or did him homage (see above, on 2, 2. 4, 9. 8, 2. 9, 18. 14, 33). This may imply that he had stopped or stood still to receive her prayer. *Lord* is here a title of the most profound respect, if not a recognition of his deity. *Help*, rescue, a Greek word suggestive of extreme distress or danger, originally meaning to run in answer to a cry for succor.

---

* See also 13, 41. 20, 2. 21, 34. 22, 3. 23, 34. 28, 37. 24, 31, and compare John 1, 6. 3, 17. 23. 34. 5, 36. 6, 29. 57. 8, 42. 10, 36. 11, 42. 17, 3. 8. 18. 21. 23. 25. 20, 21.

26. But he answered and said, It is not meet to take the children's bread, and cast (it) to dogs.

Meet, i. e. suitable, becoming, handsome, which approaches nearest to the strict sense of the Greek word, namely, *fair* or *beautiful,* though commonly applied in Scripture to excellence or beauty of a moral kind. *To take,* not pleonastic, as it often is in English, but *to take away* from them and bestow it upon others. *The children's bread,* the bread intended and provided for them, and when actually given belonging to them. *Dogs,* a diminutive supposed by some to be contemptuous, like *whelps* or *puppies,* but by others an expression of affectionate familiarity, like *little daughter* (a Greek word of the same form) in Mark 7, 25. This question is connected with another, as to the sense in which dogs are mentioned here at all, whether simply in allusion to the wild gregarious oriental dog, regarded as an impure and ferocious beast, or to the classical and modern European notion of the dog as a domesticated animal, the humble companion and faithful friend of man. The objection to the former explanation is not only its revolting harshness, and the ease with which the same idea might have been expressed in a less unusual manner, but the obvious relation here supposed between the children and the dogs, as at and under the same table, and belonging as it were to the same household. John, it is true, uses dogs in the offensive sense first mentioned; but his language is "without are dogs" (Rev. 22, 15), apparently referring to the homeless dogs which prowl through the streets of eastern cities (and compare Ps. 22, 20. 59, 6. See above, on 7, 6. Phil. 3, 2); but here the dogs are represented as within, and fed beneath their master's table. The beauty of our Saviour's figure would be therefore marred by understanding what he says of savage animals, without relation or attachment to mankind. *Cast,* throw away, a term implying waste of the material as well as some contempt of the recipient. Like most of our Lord's parables or illustrations from analogy, this exquisite similitude is drawn from the most familiar habits of domestic life, and still comes home to the experience of thousands.

27. And she said, Truth, Lord : yet the dogs eat of the crumbs which fall from their master's table.

There is no dispute as to the meaning of this admirable answer, which might almost be applauded for its wit, if Christ himself had not ascribed to it a higher merit, as an evidence of signal faith, combined with a humility no less remarkable. There is, however, some dispute as to its form, particularly that of the first clause, which some explain as a denial of what he had said, and others more correctly as a partial affirmation or assent, but followed by a partial contradiction, as in our translation. The best philological interpreters are now agreed that *yet* is not a correct version of the Greek phrase (καὶ γάρ), which can only mean agreeably to usage, *for* or *for even.* The meaning of the answer then will be, 'Yes, Lord (or Sir), it is true that it would not be becoming to deprive the children of their food, in order to supply the dogs; for these are not to eat the children's bread, but the crumbs (or fragments) falling from the table.' The whole is therefore an assent to what our Lord had said, including his description of the Gentiles as the dogs beneath the table, and a thankful consent to occupy that place and to partake of that inferior provision. *Of* (literally *from*) *the crumbs* is not here a partitive expression, as it sometimes is, but simply indicates the source from which the nourishment is drawn. The idea suggested by an ancient and adopted by a modern writer, that the word translated *crumbs* here means the pieces of bread which the ancients used as napkins, is not only a gratuitous refinement, but a needless variation from the usage of the word, which is a regular diminutive of one itself denoting a crumb, bit, or morsel, especially of bread. *Their masters*, owners, or proprietors, either *the children* mentioned in v. 26, or the parents of those children (compare Mark 7, 28).

28. Then Jesus answered and said unto her, O woman, great (is) thy faith : be it unto thee even as thou wilt. And her daughter was made whole from that very hour.

Here again, as in the case of the centurion (see above, on 8, 10), our Lord commends the faith, not of the sufferer but of her representative and intercessor. It is worthy of remark that both the persons thus distinguished by the Saviour's praise were Gentiles. It was not however merely as such, or for Gentiles, that their faith was great, but even in comparison with the more highly favoured Jews. *Be it* (let it come to pass or happen) *to thee as thou wilt*, as thou desirest (Tyndale). *Healed*, i. e. delivered from the morbid state arising from the presence of the demon. (See above, on 4, 24.) *From that hour*, in the vaguer sense of *time* or the more specific one of *moment*. (See above, on 8, 13. 9, 22. 10, 19. 14, 15.) Tyndale's version of the preposition (*at*) is not only inexact, but fails to convey the idea of continuous or permanent recovery suggested by the strict translation (*from*). *Very* (Tyndale, the same) is an admissible but needless addition.

29. And Jesus departed from thence, and came nigh unto the sea of Galilee ; and went up into a mountain, and sat down there.

Passing (or *removing*) *thence*, from that place, i. e. from the region of Tyre and Sidon, where the preceding miracle was wrought. The point of departure and the route are more particularly specified by Mark (7, 31). *Along* (Wiclif, *beside*) *the Sea of Galilee*, otherwise called the lake of Tiberias or Genessaret. (See above, on 4, 15. 18. 14, 34, and compare Luke 5, 1. John 6, 1. 21, 1.) A circumstance which Mark omits is here recorded, namely, that on coming into these parts, he went up into *the mountain* (or the high lands) not *a moun*-

tain (see above, on 5, 1. 8, 1. 14, 23), and *sat there*, which would seem from the ensuing context, to denote, not the momentary act of sitting down on one occasion, but a more protracted period of residence or rest, an idea readily suggested by the verb *to sit* in Greek and Hebrew. (See above, on 4, 16. 11, 16.) As usual, however, this retirement and repose was soon interrupted by the never distant multitude, and by a great variety of cases for the exercise of healing power, one of which is singled out and related in detail by Mark alone (7, 32–37), while Matthew gives a general account of all the miracles performed at this time in the mountains of Decapolis.

30. And great multitudes came unto him, having with them (those that were) lame, blind, dumb, maimed, and many others, and cast them down at Jesus' feet; and he healed them:

As in other cases, where he wishes to describe the variety and number of our Saviour's miracles of healing, Matthew here names certain classes of disease or suffering and adds a general expression. Thus in 4, 24, he specifies the palsy, lunacy, and demoniacal possession, in connection with "divers diseases and torments," and the still more general terms, "every disease and every infirmity." In 8, 16, he adds to a particular case of fever the two great classes of demoniacs and sick. In 11, 5, he introduces Christ himself as enumerating to the messengers of John the Baptist, the blind, lepers, deaf, and dead, as the subjects of his healing and resuscitating power. So here the evangelist distinctly mentions, as the subjects of miraculous healing, the *lame, blind, deaf, and maimed,* a Greek word strictly meaning *crooked*, then more generally crippled by disease, in which sense it is joined with χωλός by Hippocrates. That these are only specimens or samples, may be seen not only from the other cases just referred to, but from the express addition of the vague but comprehensive phrase, *and many others.* The vast number of the cases may be gathered from the mention of those bringing them as *great multitudes* (or *many crowds*), the same expression as in 4, 25. 8, 1. 18. 12, 15. 13, 2, and the plural form of that in 14, 14. *Having with them*, i. e. bringing from their homes in the surrounding country, which would seem from this description to be one not previously visited. Some infer that they were rude mountaineers from the statement that *they cast* (or *threw*) *them down at Jesus' feet.* Others, however, understand this merely as a sign of haste and eagerness to bring as many as they could within the reach of our Lord's healing power. That this power was exercised in every case presented, may be safely gathered from the last clause, *and he healed them.* The miracle recorded here by Mark is taken from the third class specified by Matthew, and is one of the very few peculiar to Mark's Gospel.

31. Insomuch that the multitude wondered, when

they saw the dumb to speak, the maimed to be whole, the lame to walk, and the blind to see : and they glorified the God of Israel.

This verse describes the effect of the miracles on *the multitudes*, by whom the cases were presented. It would scarcely have been mentioned so particularly if the field were not a new one. The four classes mentioned in v. 30 are repeated in a different order, with the change wrought on each by the miracle of healing. A description similar in form but differing in details is given by our Lord himself in 11, 3 above. The effect itself was wonder, leading them to glorify or praise the *God of Israel*, a remarkable expression as applied to Jews, and almost justifying the conclusion, that these mountaineers were Gentiles, perhaps inhabiting the same tract where the demons took possession of the swine, and where our Saviour was desired by the people to depart on that occasion. (See above, on 8, 34.) If so, the passage has peculiar interest, as recording his return to the same region, and his joyful recognition by the people, not as a destroyer but a healer, which may possibly have ended in their general conversion to the true religion.

32. Then Jesus called his disciples (unto him), and said, I have compassion on the multitude, because they continue with me now three days, and have nothing to eat : and I will not send them away fasting, lest they faint in the way.

I have compassion, I am moved (or yearn) with pity, the peculiar idiom explained above (on 9, 36. 14, 14). The proposition is here made by Christ himself, as in John's account of the former miracle (John 6, 5), with which that of Matthew (14, 15) is perfectly consistent. *Because already three days they continue with me*, or according to the latest critics, *three days now continue*, i. e. the third day is passing. The three days are probably to be computed in the Jewish manner, i. e. reckoning each portion as a whole day, so that three days do not necessarily include more than one whole day and portions of two others. *To send them away*, dismiss, dissolve them (see above, on 14, 15. 22. 23), not as individuals merely, but as an assembly or a congregation, which implies that according to his custom he had taught as well as healed on this occasion. *Fasting*, hungry, without eating, without having eaten, a word found only in this passage and the parallel (Mark 8, 3). *I will not*, i. e. am not willing, do not choose to do so. *Lest they faint*, or be relaxed, debilitated, literally *loosened out*, a kindred verb to that translated *send away*, but strictly meaning to *dissolve*. The reference is, therefore, not to fainting in the modern sense of swooning, but to weakness occasioned by the want of food. *In the way*, in (or on) the way home.

33. And his disciples say unto him, Whence should we have so much bread in the wilderness, as to fill so great a multitude?

34. And Jesus saith unto them, How many loaves have ye? And they said, Seven, and a few little fishes.

Whence, not merely *how*, but more specifically, from what source or quarter? (*Are there*, or *can there be*) *to us*, i. e. how should we have so much bread (*so many loaves*). *Fill*, i. e. in the physical corporeal sense of satiating, filling the stomach, appeasing the desire for food. (For the primary and secondary usage of the Greek verb, see above, on 5, 6. 14, 20.) *In a* (not *the*) *desert*, which would therefore seem to mean a barren waste, and not a mere uncultivated solitude (see above, on 3, 1. 4, 1. 11, 7). The strangeness of the fact, that the disciples should have spoken thus after the first feeding of the multitude, though not to be denied, is not to be exaggerated. It is not said that they forgot the other miracle; but what right had they to expect its repetition, or what reason to believe that he would choose what was in some respects his most stupendous miracle to be repeated? Besides, the inconsideration of Christ's followers is always represented as extraordinary, almost preternatural, until they had received the Holy Spirit, And yet Moses represents himself as guilty of the same oblivion or unbelief (see Num. 11, 21. 22, and compare Ps. 78, 19. 20); and Israel displayed it upon all occasions from the departure out of Egypt till the entrance into Canaan. Even those who now reject the statement as incredible would probably have done the same if similarly situated. Now that we know Christ's purpose to renew the miraculous provision, it is easy to exclaim at those who did not know it and had really no reason to expect it. The number of loaves is here greater than before (14, 17), and the fishes are mentioned as few and small. These variations are exceedingly adverse to the hypothesis of one occurrence divided by tradition into two.

35. And he commanded the multitude to sit down on the ground.

36. And he took the seven loaves and the fishes, and gave thanks, and brake (them), and gave to his disciples, and the disciples to the multitude.

On the earth is substituted here for *on the grass* (14, 19), which might be regarded as substantially synonymous but for the expressions in v. 34 implying that this was a desert in the strict sense, i. e. wholly destitute of vegetation. Another circumstance omitted here in both accounts is the symmetrical arrangement of the multitude in companies or messes, which may either have been really dispensed with on this occasion, or left to be supplied from Mark (6, 39. 40). Another is the act of looking up to heaven (14, 19), while for that of blessing is here substituted that of giving thanks, unless both be considered as describing the same service, like the corresponding English phrase, to say grace. The usual and simple verb to *break* here takes the place of the emphatic compound used before.

37. **And they did all eat, and were filled: and they took up of the broken (meat) that was left seven baskets full.**

Instead of *twelve baskets full of fragments*, we have here *the remnant* (excess, superfluity) *of fragments, seven baskets*. Besides the difference of construction and of number, the word for *baskets* is entirely different in both evangelists from that before used (11, 20); and this distinction is observed in our Saviour's subsequent allusions to these two great miracles (see below, on 16, 10). The notion of some modern sceptics, that this difference betrays a difference of source or traditional authority, proceeds upon the monstrous supposition, that a writer capable of framing such a history as we have found this to be, could either ignorantly or deliberately introduce into his narrative, without the slightest intimation to the reader, two discordant statements of the same occurrence, with their variations both of form and substance, in a perfectly crude and unadjusted state. Such a postulate would not have been so long endured by Christian readers but for the unfortunate impression even among them, that the gospels are mere bundles of materials, out of which we are to frame a history, instead of being well-digested histories themselves. The consistent and uniform distinction made between the baskets makes it highly probable that different kinds were used upon the two occasions, though the difference itself may now be lost, as it certainly is wholly unimportant. Chrysostom suggests, however, that the baskets in the second case were probably larger, which makes the disproportion less, and seems to be confirmed by Acts 9, 25.

38. **And they that did eat were four thousand men, beside women and children.**

It is worthy of remark that this second narrative, so far from being an exaggeration or embellishment of the first, not only makes the numbers fed absolutely smaller, but the ratio or proportion to the food provided, thus diminishing the miracle so far as mere quantity is concerned. On what supposition can this strange fact be accounted for, except the supposition of historic reality, the simple supposition that the two events occurred precisely as Matthew here relates them? Had the two miracles been given each by one evangelist, there might have been some colour for the charge of two irreconcilable traditions; but as if to sweep away the very ground of such an allegation, both are recorded both by Mark and Matthew, so that the points of difference, instead of serving to discredit either, only prove that the events themselves were altogether different. The points are indeed as many and as marked as they could well have been, supposing that the same essential miracle was twice performed. The time, place, numbers, and proportions are all different; and it is surely not to be regarded as surprising that the people in both instances were hungry, that the food provided was their ordinary diet, that they leaned or lay upon the ground, that Christ pronounced or asked a blessing on the food, and employed the twelve disciples in its distribution. For how could any of these circumstances vary if he did repeat the miracle? His reasons for repeating it are not revealed, and need not be conjectured; but among them may have been the very feeling which now prompts the question. We have seen it already to be not improbable, that some of the accompanying acts in other miracles were varied for the purpose of evincing his own liberty and absolute discretion, as distinguished from the uniform routine to which men would have tied him. May he not, for the same reason, have repeated in a less imposing form, what they would rather have expected to see standing by itself in its unique sublimity, as something that could happen only once, and was wholly *sui generis?* But this may be undue refinement, and it may be better simply to regard it as an instance of authoritative action, independent of our finite views of what is right or needful. That both these miracles have been recorded notwithstanding their resemblance, is explained by that which seems to call for explanation. It is no doubt the practice of the sacred writers to avoid the repetition of identical or nearly similar events; but in a case of such surprising repetition of the acts themselves, the very sameness was a reason for recording both.

39. And he sent away the multitude, and took ship, and came into the coasts of Magdala.

Entered (embarked, went on board) not *a ship* but *the ship* (or *the boat*), i. e. the one before mentioned as attending him (see above, on 8, 23. 24. 9, 1. 13, 2. 14, 13. 22). in which he made his voyages from one point to another, and from which he sometimes taught the people. *The coasts* (borders, neighbourhood) *of* Magdala, the site of which has been determined on the west shore of the lake, a few miles north of Tiberias. The Codex Vaticanus and the Vulgate have *Magadan.*

CHAPTER XVI.

RESUMING his account of the concerted opposition to our Lord, Matthew now represents the two great rival sects or parties as uniting in a fresh demand for a certain kind of miracle, which they chose to make the test of his Messiahship, but which he again refused to furnish (1–4). A remarkable mistake of the disciples serves to show their backwardness in learning under such a teacher, and affords an opportunity of further admonition and instruction (5–12). During a circuit in the northern portion of Perea, he inquires into the opinions of his followers respecting him, and draws forth from the twelve a formal acknowledgment of his Messiahship (13–20). He then imparts to them, more clearly than before, the painful doctrine of his passion, and rebukes Peter for resisting it (21–23). This gives occasion to a public statement of the duty and necessity of self-denial, and the danger of denying Christ (24–27), winding up with a solemn and mysterious intimation of his coming in his kingdom as at hand (28). All these topics are connected by the twofold tie of chronological succession and of a natural association, proving anew the methodical coherence and organic oneness of the composition. There is a parallel in Mark to this whole chapter, and in Luke also to the latter part, though Matthew has in several places words and incidents not found in either of the others. The order of the topics is the same in all the Gospels.

1. The Pharisees also with the Sadducees came, and tempting, desired him that he would show them a sign from heaven.

The Pharisees, his prominent opponents, as the zealous adherents of the oral law or traditional theology, now combine with their own enemies and rivals, the sceptical and scoffing Sadducees (see above, on 3, 7, and below, on 22. 15. 23), in renewing a demand which had been made already by the Pharisees and Scribes on a previous occasion (see above, on 12, 38). *Tempting*, not in the ordinary sense of urging or enticing him to sin, but in the primary and wide sense of trying, putting to the proof, a process necessarily implying either doubt or unbelief of his pretensions. In this sense man is said to tempt God, who is incapable of tempting or being tempted in the other (James 1, 13). *Desired him*, literally, *asked* or *questioned*, as in 12, 10. *A sign from* (literally, *out of*) *heaven*, as distinguished from a sign on earth, such as his miracles of healing were, or a sign from hell, as they declared his dispossessions of the demons to be (see above, on 12, 24). *To show them*, i. e. to exhibit it for their satisfaction or conviction. This demand may have been prompted by a real belief that the Messiah's advent was to be announced by strange celestial phenomena; or it may have been a mere subterfuge, a cavilling demand for more proof when they had enough already, an attempt to escape from the convincing power of his miracles on earth by demanding one from heaven.

2. He answered and said unto them, When it is evening, ye say, (It will be) fair weather: for the sky is red.

Before repeating his refusal uttered on the previous occasion (12, 39), and here subjoined immediately by Mark (8, 12), our Lord rebukes their inconsistency or disproportionate regard to lower interests, by pointedly contrasting their facility and skill in judging of the weather, with their real or pretended want of evidence in his case. We have here another striking instance of his condescending wisdom in enforcing moral truth by illustrations drawn from the every-day experience of common life. *Evening being come*, or at the close of day, in reference no doubt to the later evening of the Jews (see above, on 8, 16. 14, 15. 23), or the interval from sunset until dark. *Ye say*, i. e. often or habitually say, are wont to say. The words thus put into their mouths were no doubt often heard in conversation, as the weather has in every age, despite the ridicule of mock-philosophers, afforded one of the most interesting subjects of colloquial discourse. What all men everywhere and always talk about, cannot be wholly unimportant or unworthy of attention. *Fair weather* is a single word in Greek, and a sort of exclamation, just as we say "a fine day!" without a verb expressed or understood. Here, however, there is more ground for assuming an ellipsis, as the reference is not to the present but the future. *Is red*, a Hellenistic verb (πυρράζει) derived from a classical Greek adjective (πυρρός) which properly means *fiery* in colour, and is peculiarly appropriate to the bright or flaming red with which the sky is often coloured at or after sunset.

3. And in the morning, (It will be) foul weather to-day: for the sky is red and lowering. O (ye) hypocrites, ye can discern the face of the sky; but can ye not (discern) the signs of the times?

4. A wicked and adulterous generation seeketh after a sign; and there shall no sign be given unto it, but the sign of the prophet Jonas. And he left them, and departed.

In the morning, one Greek word (πρωΐ), corresponding to the Latin *mane* and the English *early*, but more specific than the latter, which may be relatively used in reference to any portion of the day or night, whereas the Greek and Latin terms are restricted to the morning. The same description is repeated, but with an additional expression, *lowering* or *frowning*, which retains the participial form of the original, but may be rendered adjectively, *sullen*, angry. The original construction is, *reddens frowning*, without the *and* supplied in English, which conveys the true sense but enfeebles the expression.* We may either understand our Lord as meaning that these two appearances were usual at these two times of day respectively, or simply that they both

---

* The older versions have a rich variety of English phrases to express this appearance of the heavens. Wiclif, *heaven shineth heavily;* Tyndale, *the sky is cloudy and red;* Geneva, *red and cloudy;* Cranmer, *glowing red;* Rheims, *the element doth glow and lower.*

occurred at both, and are only distinguished for the sake of the emphatic repetition. There is nothing answering in Greek to *O ye*, which is no more necessary here than in ch. xxiii. (13. 14. 15. 23. 25. 27. 29), where the very same word is seven times translated simply *hypocrites*. This word has been here supposed to have the milder sense of persons wholly occupied with what is outward, in allusion to its primary (or secondary sense) of a masked actor or performer. But the usual unfavourable sense of a dissembler or deceiver is entirely appropriate to these men, who could confidently foretell the changes of the weather by its dubious and variable signs, and yet were constantly demanding some addition to the proofs already given that the fulness of the time was come, and that Jesus was the Christ long promised in the Scriptures and expected by the people. *Discern* (distinguish) *the face*, or *outward appearance* as Cranmer renders it. (Tyndale and Geneva have the old word *fashion*.) *Signs of the times*, miraculous and other indications that the days of the Messiah have arrived. The remainder of the answer (in v. 4) is the same, word for word, with that in 12, 39, and there explained. The variation in the epithets (*evil* and *wicked*) is confined to the translation. This exact repetition of his own words is so far from being improbable, that we may readily believe him to have uttered them in many other cases not recorded. (See above, on pp. 105–6.) The comparison with Jonah is not here carried out, as in the former instance, possibly because some of the same persons joined in the demand on both occasions. Instead of giving this addition, Matthew here says, that *leaving them behind, he went away*, which may imply an abrupt and indignant movement, corresponding to Mark's statement, that as he answered them, *he sighed* (or *groaned*) *in his spirit*, i. e. was internally and deeply moved with grief and anger at their obstinate and hopeless unbelief. (See Mark 8, 12, and compare Mark 3, 5.)

5. And when his disciples were come to the other side, they had forgotten to take bread.

The exact translation, *coming to the other side forgot*, seems to mean that they neglected, after their arrival on the other side, to make provision for their journey onward, which may have been into a desert region. *Bread*, in Greek the usual plural form, distinguishing the separate cakes or loaves, and here denoting the accustomed provision for the company, especially when going on a journey.

6. Then Jesus said unto them, Take heed and beware of the leaven of the Pharisees and of the Sadducees.

By what would be a curious coincidence where mere men were exclusively concerned our Lord begins, probably after they had thought of their neglect to carry bread and had begun to be solicitous about it, a parabolical discourse, in which he draws his illustration from the customary mode of making bread, i. e. with yeast or leaven. As this substance draws its useful quality from fermentation, and as this may be considered as incipient corruption, it affords a natural and striking emblem of the same thing in the moral world. Hence no doubt it was excluded from the sacrificial rites of the Mosaic law (Ex. 34, 25. Lev. 2, 11), and is employed so uniformly as a figure for depravity or depravation, that the only exception commonly admitted, the parable which Luke and Matthew join with that of the mustard seed (see above, on 13, 33), is thought by some to be no exception at all, but the reverse or wrong side of the parable just mentioned, and designed to show the spreading tendency of evil no less than of good, not only in the world but even in the church of God. However this may be, it is certain that our Lord here makes use of the emblem in a bad sense, when he tells his disciples to *beware of the leaven of the Pharisees.* Take *heed*, literally, *see*, i. e. see to it, be on your guard. *Beware of*, the expression used above, in 7, 15. 10, 17. and there explained. The particular corruption to which Christ applies this figurative term is that *of the Pharisees and Sadducees*, or according to Mark (8, 15), that *of the Pharisees and of Herod. The leaven of the Pharisees*, against which the disciples are here warned, is nothing peculiar to or characteristic of them, but something common to them with the Sadducees and Herod, and all others who professed the true religion without really possessing it. Our Lord might therefore have connected all these names, and others too, without the slightest incongruity, because he is referring to the points in which they are alike, and not the points in which they differ. What the point of contact and agreement was between these most dissimilar and hostile parties will be seen below (on v. 12). In the mean time their conjunction by our Saviour may be likened to the language of a zealous preacher now, who should exhort his hearers to be careful that their piety is not that of a Papist, a Jew, or a Mahometan, but that of a true Christian. The sense of such an exhortation would be evident, but who would charge it with confounding inimical, nay opposite religions?

7. And they reasoned among themselves, saying, (It is) because we have taken no bread.

Reasoned, reckoned, or considered through and through. *In themselves*, that is, each within his own breast, but also, as we learn from Mark (8, 16), *to* (or *with*) *each other.* This does not imply dispute, but only earnest conversation and comparison of views, in which they seem to have agreed, since they are all represented as saying, i. e. in substance: (it is, or he says this) *because we have not taken bread.* This little circumstance, which none but a true history would have given, speaks volumes as to the simplicity and ignorance of Christ's disciples, even after they had been so long in contact with him, and had gone forth from him as apostles preaching and performing miracles. With respect to the error here recorded, however childish it may now seem, it becomes us to remember that many who deride such blunders as absurd, if not impossible, would probably have made the same if placed in the same situation, with their thoughts running upon bread, and a mysterious intimation from their master about leaven. Accustomed as they were to hear him speak in riddles on the plainest subjects, why might they not without absurdity suppose him to be doing so now?

8. (Which) when Jesus perceived, he said unto them, O ye of little faith, why reason ye among yourselves, because ye have brought no bread?

But although not utterly irrational, and therefore not deserving our contempt, this error was still culpable and merited their Lord's rebuke. *When Jesus knew (it)* seems to imply that he afterwards discovered it, an idea not suggested by the Greek or by a close translation. *Jesus knowing*, i. e. on the same spot and at the moment, what they said, and what they thought. *Why reason ye because ye have not taken bread?* i. e. why connect what I have just said with your want of bread, and try to give my words a meaning in relation to that trifling matter? It is not their want of perspicacity in seeing what he meant for which he blames them, but the undue anxiety about mere temporalities which occupied their minds, and made them thus incapable of knowing what he meant, or at least that he was talking upon higher subjects.

9. Do ye not understand, neither remember the five loaves of the five thousand, and how many baskets ye took up?

10. Neither the seven loaves of the four thousand, and how many baskets ye took up?

Do ye not yet perceive the drift of my discourses, and the end to which my teachings are all tending, or comprehend at least my general purpose? If you have not strength of intellect sufficient to divine or comprehend my meaning, have you not at least some memory of what has passed so lately in your presence, before your eyes, and through your very hands? This reproach, it will be seen at once, relates not so much to their misapprehension of his words about the leaven, as to their extreme anxiety about the bread, which not only distracted and preoccupied their thoughts, but indicated want of faith in his capacity to help them and provide for them. Although he never performed miracles where ordinary means would answer the same purpose, they had surely no occasion to be troubled at the want of bread, when he had twice created it to feed not single individuals but thousands. As already hinted (see above, on 15, 37), the two kinds of baskets are distinguished here by both evangelists, as in the narrative itself, so that the difference cannot be unmeaning or fortuitous; and if the two accounts of the two miracles are merely two traditions of the same thing, then these words of Christ referring to them as distinct events must also be explained away. *The five loaves* of *the five thousand*, i. e. the five and the five thousand, the seven and the four thousand, now so memorable in my history and yours, but which you seem so strangely to have since forgotten.

11. How is it that ye do not understand that I spake (it) not to you concerning bread, that ye should beware of the leaven of the Pharisees and of the Sadducees?

12. Then understood they how that he bade (them) not beware of the leaven of bread, but of the doctrine of the Pharisees and of the Sadducees.

How is it that ye do not consider (or *perceive*), not my parables or enigmatical teachings till they are explained, but the design of my instructions, as relating not to bread but to religion, and the import of my miracles, as proving my capacity to feed you even by creating food, should that be needful. Had they duly considered what his miracles implied, they would not have had their minds engrossed by bread, or by the want of bread, when he was speaking, and would then have understood, if not precisely what he meant by leaven, yet at least that he did not mean the leaven used in making bread. This seems to be the natural connection of the thoughts, even in the narrative of Mark (8, 21), who stops short at this laconic question, without any further reference to the meaning of the leaven. This shows that his design was not to elucidate that figure, but to illustrate the condition of the twelve at this important juncture. But we here learn that before the conversation ended, they understood that by leaven he intended doctrine, not opinions or distinctive tenets, as to which the parties named could not have been described together, but their mode of teaching and expounding spiritual truth, which in all these cases was more or less external, superficial, ceremonial, and in that sense might be called hypocrisy, but also in the stronger sense of insincerity. (See above, on v. 3.)

13. When Jesus came into the coasts of Cesarea Philippi, he asked his disciples, saying, Whom do men say that I, the Son of man, am?

Here may be said to begin a new division of our Lord's official history, in which he prepared the minds of his disciples for the great events before them by imparting clear views of his own mission as a sufferer. This necessary process of instruction he begins by ascertaining how far they already recognized and understood his claims as the Messiah. Of this interesting conversation we have three harmonious accounts, Luke (9, 18) here again becoming parallel with Mark (8, 27) and Matthew. Neither evangelist assigns the date of this transaction, even by connecting it expressly with the previous context as immediately successive. The natural presumption is, however, in the absence of all indications to the contrary, that these disclosures followed, and most probably without an interval of any length, the miracles and teachings which immediately precede them in the narrative. The place (not specified by Luke) is given both by Mark and Matthew as the region or territory (Mark *villages*, Matt. *parts*) *of Cesarea Philippi* (i. e. *Philip's Cesarea*). This was a city of Upper Galilee, near one source of the Jordan, as the ancient Dan or Laish (Josh. 19, 47. Judg. 18, 27–29) occupied the other. It was at the foot of Hermon, and was called by the Greeks *Paneas*, a word still preserved by the local tradition as the name of a village (*Banias*) on the same site. To distinguish it from Cesarea on the sea-coast (*Cesarea of Palestine*, originally called *Straton's Tower*), so often mentioned in the Acts of the Apostles, it received the additional name *Philippi* (*Philip's* or of *Philip*) from the tetrarch of Iturea and Trachonitis (Luke 3, 1), brother of Antipas and husband of Salome (see above, on 14, 6), by whom it had been rebuilt or beautified, and named *Cesarea* in honor of Tiberius. Into the villages or towns dependent upon this important city Jesus came with his disciples, when or whence is not recorded. Most interpreters, however, inferring chronological succession from historical juxtaposition, understand this to have happened on a journey from Bethsaida Julias (see Mark 8, 22) to Cesarea Philippi. As a sample of the mode in which the ablest Germans harmonize the gospels, it may here be mentioned that De Wette represents as a material variation between Mark and Matthew, that the latter speaks of Jesus *having come* to the vicinity of Cesarea when he put this question, while the former says he asked it *in the way* (or *on the road*) to that place. Even if this were true, the usage of the participle aorist is wide enough to cover any discrepancy thence arising, *having come* and *coming* being almost convertible expressions. But the critic has himself fallen into the mistake which he imputes to the evangelist, by not observing that *in the way* is mentioned after the arrival at Cesarea, and refers not to the journey from Bethsaida thither, but to his visitation of the villages or parts dependent on the former town as a provincial capital. He came among those villages no doubt to exercise his ministry, and being in the way or on the road, i. e. travelling among them, for this purpose, he asked or questioned his disciples in the words recorded in the last clause. This is one of the imaginary discrepancies which even some Christian writers represent as quite irreconcilable without the use of disingenuous harmonical contrivances. *Whom do men say* (or declare) *me to be? the Son of Man?* This is the order of the words in Greek and the natural construction of the sentence. The common version makes it a description of himself, and some of the latest critics omit *me* altogether.

14. And they said, some (say that thou art) John the Baptist; some, Elias; and others, Jeremias, or one of the prophets.

Their answer brings to light the same diversity of judgment or conjecture before mentioned in the account of the effect produced on Herod by the miracles of Jesus (14, 2), but beginning with the notion there ascribed to Antipas himself, perhaps because it was maintained in such high places, or because it had also become dominant among the people. *Elias*, Elijah (see Mark 6, 15). *One of the prophets*, i. e. of the ancient or Old Testament prophets (Luke 9, 19), either in the vague sense of *some one*, or as this sense of the numeral is denied by eminent interpreters, *a certain one*, not named. It seems from this reply that notwithstanding the impression made by our Lord's miracles and teachings, and the convictions now and then expressed of his Messiahship, the great mass, even of those friendly to him, were disposed to look upon him rather as the Messiah's herald or forerunner than as the Messiah himself.

15. He saith unto them, But whom say ye that I am ?

16. And Simon Peter answered and said, Thou art the Christ, the Son of the living God.

In contradistinction from these popular impressions he demands of them, his personal attendants and more confidential followers, in what light they regarded him. As if he had said, 'these are the vague ideas of the multitude; but it is time to draw the line between them and yourselves by making a profession of your faith.' *But ye—whom do ye say* (or *pronounce*) *me to be?* Peter answers for the rest, not only from his rash and forward disposition, but because he was in fact their spokesman, recognized as such both by his master and his brethren, and particularly fitted for the office by the very disposition just referred to. (See above, on 10, 2.) As Mark (8, 29) introduces this confession merely to complete the chain of incidents, he gives Peter's answer in the briefest form, containing only the essential proposition, *Thou art the Christ*, the Messiah, which are Greek and Hebrew synonymes (see above, on 1, 1), while Luke (9, 20) employs the more emphatic phrase, *the Christ of God*, and Matthew the still more descriptive one, *the Christ, the Son of the living God*. (See above, on 4. 3. 8, 29. 14, 33.) The importance of this first express acknowledgment of Jesus as the Christ or the Messiah, even by his own chosen followers, arises from the fact that all his public actions hitherto implied a claim to that exalted character, and that in consequence the truth of this claim was essential to the proof, not only of his public mission but of his personal veracity. The claim itself had reference to the clear prediction of a Great Deliverer in the ancient prophecies, expressly called Messiah, or Anointed, both by David (Ps. 2, 2) and by Daniel (9, 25), and by implication so described in all the scriptures which exhibit him as filling the great theocratical offices of Prophet, Priest. and King, in which the previous incumbents only held his place till he should come, and to which they were set apart by unction, the appointed symbol of those spiritual gifts which fitted men for these high functions, and which he was to possess without measure. All this Jesus claimed, and all this Peter acknowledged him to be, not only as a private individual when the truth was first suggested to him by his brother Andrew (John 1, 41), but now as it were *ex officio*, in the name of all the twelve, and in response to an authoritative question from the Lord himself.

17. And Jesus answered and said unto him, Blessed art thou, Simon Bar-jona: for flesh and blood hath not revealed (it) unto thee, but my Father which (is) in heaven.

In reply to Peter's confession, our Lord, as it were, confesses Peter. (See above, on 10, 32.) *Blessed*, happy, with specific reference to the divine favour. (See above, on 5, 3.) Some suppose a reference to all the names here mentioned as significant, not only to *Peter*, but to *Simon*, as derived from the verb to hear and sometimes to obey, and *Bar-Jona*, son of a dove, denoting harmlessness (see above, on 10, 16), or used as a symbol of the Holy Spirit (see above, on 3, 16). Another explanation is, that the Son of Man was as certainly the Son of God as Simon was the Son of Jonah. *Bar* is the Chaldee word for *Son*, used in the prophecy of Daniel (7, 13), to which our Lord's question probably alludes. *Flesh and blood*, i. e. human nature, or humanity or man, as opposed to God. (See Gal. 1, 16. Eph. 6, 12. 1 Cor. 15, 50.) He had derived this knowledge from no human source, either in himself or others, but from a divine illumination. As the question of our Lord in v. 13 was addressed to all the twelve ($ὑμεῖς$), and as Peter, in this as well as other cases, speaks in the name of all, the blessing must be understood as equally extensive, though in form directed only to the spokesman. There is no ground whatever for assuming that the others did not share in his conviction, or that they obtained it in a different manner. (See above, on 14, 33, and compare John 1, 50.) Nor do the Saviour's words imply a sudden unexpected revelation of something entirely unknown before.

18. And I say also unto thee, That thou art Peter, and upon this rock I will build my church; and the gates of hell shall not prevail against it.

This is the passage upon which the Church of Rome rests its doctrine of the Papal Supremacy, in which it is assumed that the address is exclusively to Peter, not in his representative capacity, but as an individual apostle, and in reply to his personal confession. It is also assumed that he is here declared to be the foundation of the church, and that as the foundation of a building must be as lasting as the edifice itself, the promise is to Peter and the bishops of Rome as his successors. In opposition to this forced interpretation, many Protestants adopt one scarcely less so, namely, that the rock referred to in the promise is not Peter's person but his confession, or the doctrine which he had confessed, to wit, the Messiahship and deity of Jesus. To this construction there are two objections; first, that it is unnatural, and secondly, that it is needless. It is unnatural because it supposes an abrupt transition from one subject to another, without any thing to intimate it or prepare for it, to wit, from Peter's name to his confession, which is then moreover arbitrarily expressed by an unusual figure, not peculiarly adapted to suggest it. Such assumptions can be justified by nothing short of an extreme exegetical necessity, which does not here exist. For in the next place, this construction is not only unnatural but needless, even for the purpose of refuting the pretensions of the Papal See, which rest upon a series of gratuitous and false assumptions. Even granting all the rest that is assumed in this interpretation. it is false that the Popes are in any sense whatever the successors of St. Peter. It is false that the Apostle, as such, has or can have a successor. It is inconsistent with the very image here used of a rock or stone as the foundation of a building, which would then be represented, not as continuing unmoved forever, but as being constantly renewed and changed, which is absurd both in the sign and the thing signified. Another false assumption is that even if these words were addressed to Peter as an individual apostle, without reference to the rest, they necessarily imply a primacy or permanent superiority of rank or office. That no such consequence need follow even from the most exclusive application of the words, is clear from the equally legitimate and much more natural construction that may be put upon them; not, as some propose, that Peter was to lay the first stone of the church, which would represent him, not as a foundation but a founder; but that he was to be himself among the first stones laid by the great master builder, and that on him, as a part of the foundation, the church was to be reared by the accession of both Jews and Gentiles, as for instance on the day of Pentecost, and at the conversion of Cornelius. But although this is a far more natural interpretation of the words if addressed exclusively to Peter, than the Romish one, the fact that they are so addressed is far from being certain or beyond dispute. It is somewhat curious that the same interpreters who most gratuitously introduce a reference to the Popes, which is at variance with the very figure here employed, deny the obvious allusion to the twelve collectively or as a body. That our Lord's main purpose was not, as the Romanists allege, to honour and exalt this one Apostle at the cost of all the rest, is clear from its omission by the other two evangelists, who stop short at the end of Peter's own confession (Mark 8, 29. Luke 9, 20). This is something very different from the usual omissions in the parallel accounts. Had Mark and Luke omitted the occurrence altogether, or merely given it more briefly, no conclusion could be drawn from such a difference. But if Peter's exaltation is the main design of this address, what precedes (in vs. 13–16) is simply introductory. Now how can we believe that two of the evangelists would only give the introduction, and then leave out what it introduces? Another reason for believing that these words do not relate exclusively to Peter, if at all, may be derived from the continual allusions to the twelve as a collective body, even in the types of the Old Testament, especially the twelve tribes of Israel, as the framework of the old theocracy, but still more clearly in the promise to the apostolic body founded on this ancient constitution (Matt. 19, 28), in the repetition of the same thing in a different form elsewhere (Eph. 2, 20), and in the symbolical description of the twelve foundations of the New Jerusalem (Rev. 21, 14), of which it has been well said, that if one of the twelve stones is to be displaced and put beneath the rest, the whole will fall to pieces. But besides these analogies from other parts of Scripture, and the frequent appearances of Peter as the spokesman of the apostolic body (see above, on 10, 2), which create a strong presumption that he acts so here, we have sufficient ground for so affirming in the context, where we find that Peter's confession was in answer to a question addressed to the whole company (*whom say ye that I am?* v. 15). And what is here said of Peter is in substance elsewhere said of all, as we shall see upon the next verse. It will here be sufficient to refer to Eph. 2, 20, where believers (of whom the church is certainly composed) are said to be "built upon the foundation of the apostles and prophets (or inspired teachers)." What is there affirmed of all cannot here be said exclusively of one, and therefore, if these words relate to Peter at all, it can only be in common with the rest, and as their representative. But however possible or even probable this reference may be, it is not absolutely certain, but is open to some very strong objections, none of which can be regarded as conclusive in itself, nor perhaps in conjunction with the rest, but the aggregate of which does certainly make out a strong case in opposition to this doctrine. In the first place, the figure of a rock, although susceptible like others of indefinitely various applications, is especially appropriated in the Scriptures to the divine character and attributes, so that, as it has been well said by a living writer,* the spirit of the whole, and not of one place merely, is, "Who is a rock save our God?" See Deut. 32, 4. 15. 18. 30. 31. 37. 1 Sam. 2, 2. 2 Sam. 22, 2. 3. 32. 47. 23, 3. Ps. 19, 14. 28, 1. 31, 2. 3. 42, 9. 62, 2. 6. 7. 71, 3. 73, 26, 78, 37. 89, 26. 94, 22. 95, 1. Isai. 17, 10. 26, 4. 30, 29. 44, 8. Hab. 1, 12. Rom. 9, 33. 1 Cor. 10, 4. 1 Pet. 2, 8. In all these places the term rock is applied directly either to Jehovah or to Christ. Nor is it ever applied, even by the strongest figure, to a merely human subject. This remarkable usage is at least sufficient to create a strong presumption, that the figure here is not applied to any mere man. In the second place, it is exceedingly unusual, if not wholly unexampled, to employ the demonstrative (*this*) in application to the object of address; whereas our Lord repeatedly applies it to himself. See John 2. 19. 6, 5. Matt. 3, 3. 21, 44, in which last place, by a remarkable coincidence, he calls himself *this stone*. In the third place, the diversity of form

---

* Christopher Wordsworth.

and gender in the Greek words (πέτρος and πέτρα) is too abrupt and marked to be unmeaning and fortuitous, or explicable simply on the ground, that the masculine form was used in speaking of a man. But if they are synonymous, as commonly assumed, why should the feminine be used at all, the rather as it weakens and obscures the reference to Peter, if intended, which would certainly have been more clear and striking if the same Greek word had been repeated, " thou art Peter (i. e. rock), and on this Peter (i. e. rock) will I build my church." The assertion usually made, that this distinction exists only in the Greek, and that in our Lord's vernacular the same form was repeated, as it is in the Peshito, or old Syriac version, is doubly insufficient to effect its purpose; first, because it is gratuitous, assuming without proof the fact on which it rests; and then, because this fact, even if it be admitted, leaves the language used by Matthew unexplained. Without insisting, as some recent writers are disposed to do, that our Saviour uttered this address in Greek, or even that he introduced these two Greek words, a practice perfectly familiar to the Chaldee paraphrasts and Syriac translators, it is altogether arbitrary to assume that the Aramaic dialect of Palestine at that time could not furnish two equivalents to these two Greek words. It has even been alleged on high authority (Lightfoot) that *Cephas* itself bears the same relation to the Syriac word *Cepha* (ܟܐܦܐ) that *Petros* does to *Petra*, and that both may have been used on this occasion. But even granting that the same word was repeated, it might be, as in so many other cases, with a difference of meaning, not entirely clear at first, but having that peculiar enigmatical significance, which formed so prominent a feature in the Saviour's διδαχή or method of instruction. This double sense of one word has been sometimes preserved even in Greek (compare the double sense of *dead*, νεκρούς, in Matt. 8, 22 and the parallels, as commonly explained; that of ψυχή in 10, 39; that of ναός in John 2, 19. 20), while in the case before us the usage of that language furnished two forms to express the kindred but distinct ideas. The classical use of πέτρος and πέτρα is entirely distinct, the latter answering to *rock* and the former to *stone*, the two being scarcely ever interchanged even by poetic licence. See Passow (edited by Rost and Palen), Liddell and Scott, and all the late New Testament Greek lexicons, *sub vocibus*. This remarkable fact makes it still more difficult to understand why Matthew should have used both forms if Christ employed but one or only in one sense, when the masculine form (πέτρος) would have answered every purpose. If, on the other hand, this variation of the form is studied and significant, it serves to corroborate the previous objections to applying the term *rock* to Peter. By retaining the invariable classical distinction between πέτρος (stone) and πέτρα (rock), we not only adhere faithfully to usage (*penes quem est norma loquendi*), and do justice to the writer's careful choice of his expressions, but obtain a meaning perfectly appropriate and striking, namely, that while Peter was a stone, i. e. a fragment of the rock, his Master was the rock itself. The same contrast between Christ and the Apostles, or believers in general, as the rock and stones, or the chief corner-stone and those laid on it, reappears in Eph. 2, 20 and 1 Pet. 2, 4–8. This explanation, far from being new, is one of the most ancient upon record, being eloquently amplified by several of the Fathers,* and acknowledged even by the most ambitious of the Popes.† But if to any it should seem less natural than that which applies the figure of a rock to Peter, although contrary, as we have seen to settled usage, it has been already shown that there are cogent reasons for applying it to him in his representative capacity. But even if restricted to himself among the twelve, we have also seen that it implies no permanent superiority, and still less a derivative authority in any claiming to be his successors. It thus appears that whether *this rock* mean our Lord himself or Peter, it is easy to refute the papal claims, erected upon this expression, without resorting to any forced or fanciful construction. *I will build* (as something yet to be accomplished) *my church*, a Greek word, which according to its etymology means something *called out* or evoked, and by implication *called together* or convoked, as a separate assembly or society, selected from a greater number. As in the classics it denotes the popular assemblies of the Greek republics, and especially of Athens (compare Acts 19, 32. 39. 41), so in the Septuagint version it had long been used to represent a Hebrew word (קהל) denoting the host or congregation of Israel. To the Greek-speaking Jews, therefore, it had already a religious import, and would here be understood as meaning that the Saviour was about to found such a society, and to found it on the rock just mentioned. To this society he promises perpetual security. *Hell* is not the word so rendered in 5, 22. 29. 30. 11, 28, but that employed in 11, 23, and there explained to mean the unseen world, or the abode of disembodied spirits, the condition of the dead, without regard to their character and state of suffering or misery. It cannot therefore well be understood in this place as denoting what we call the powers of darkness, or the devil and his angels, but is rather a strong figure for death or destruction, corresponding to the *gates of the grave* in Isai. 38, 10, and *the gates of death* in Ps. 107, 18. The very combination here used is also found in Æschylus and Homer, and explained by an old Greek scholiast as a periphrasis for death (περίφρασις θανάτου). *Gates* has been variously explained to mean the entrance, the defences, the military force, and the judicial power. *Prevail against* is by some comparatively understood as meaning to be stronger than, but com-

---

* "*Petra* principale nomen est ; ideo *Petrus* a *Petra*, non *Petra* a *Petro*, quomodo non a Christiano Christus, sed a Christo Christianus vocatur. Tu es ergo, inquit, Petrus, et super hanc Petram, quam confessus es, super hanc Petram, quam cognovisti dicens, Tu es Christus filius Dei vivi, ædificabo ecclesiam meam, id est, super meipsum, Filium Dei vivi, ædificabo ecclesiam meam. Super me ædificabo te, non super te."—*Augustine*. (In his earlier expositions he applied the words to Peter) "Ecclesia Catholica super Petram Christum stabili radice fundata est."—*Jerome*..

† Baronius relates that when Hildebrand (Gregory VII.) deposed Henry IV., he sent a crown to Rudolph inscribed with this hexameter. "Petra dedit Petro, Petrus diadema Rodolpho."

monly as signifying victory or conquest. Whatever be the sense of the particular expressions, the essential meaning evidently is, that nothing should destroy the safety of the church to be erected on the rock here mentioned.

19. And I will give unto thee the keys of the kingdom of heaven : and whatsoever thou shalt bind on earth shall be bound in heaven ; and whatsoever thou shalt loose on earth shall be loosed in heaven.

The abrupt transition from the figure of a foundation-stone to that of a door-keeper, although not impossible or wholly unexampled in our Lord's discourses (see above, on 9, 36. 37. 13, 20), is not to be assumed without necessity, and therefore may be urged as an objection to the supposition that the *rock* of v. 18 is Peter. It is certainly no natural association of ideas, that the keys of a building should be given to the rock on which it rests. This may be neutralized, however, by observing that it is equally incongruous for a rock to give the keys as to receive them. All admit that this verse is addressed to Peter, as representing either his associates or successors. To the arguments against this last assumption, and in favour of the other, as already stated (on v. 18), may now be added, that the very grant here made to Peter is repeated almost in the same words in the next chapter (18, 18) and addressed to the whole body of apostles. The only question here is in relation to the power bestowed. The figure of a key would at once suggest the idea of admission and exclusion to or from the church here called the kingdom of heaven. (See above, on 3, 2. 4, 17. 5, 3. 10. 19. 20. 7, 21. 8, 11. 10, 7. 11, 11. 12. 13, 11. 24. 31. 33. 45. 47. 52.) Even as an individual apostle, Peter may be said to have exercised this power in the reception of the first converts, whether Jews or Gentiles, and in the exclusion of such false professors as Ananias and Sapphira and Simon Magus. Acts 2, 38—41. 5, 5. 9. 8, 21. 10, 48. As representing the whole body of apostles, he may be said, in a still wider sense, to have organized the church, deciding who should be and who should not be recognized as members, and performing all the functions properly belonging to the character and office of a founder. If this clause stood alone, there would perhaps be no dispute, except with respect to the extent of the grant here made, or the persons who received it. But a difficulty springs from the addition of the next clause, where the figure is distinct, and yet so much alike as to make it doubtful whether it denotes the same thing or another. The former is maintained by some upon the ground that doors were anciently tied fast and opened by untying or loosing. But even if the usage be admitted, the allusion to it here would seem to be precluded by the express mention of the key, which could scarcely be employed for the loosing of a knot. Another explanation seeks to gain the same sense by supposing bind to mean attach or fasten, and loose to separate, equivalent expressions for admission and exclusion. A third gives the words the more specific sense of remitting or not remitting (compare John 20, 23); a fourth, that of allowing and forbidding; while a fifth attempts to show by citations from the classics and Josephus, that to bind and loose was an idiomatic or proverbial expression for control or government in general. Diodorus Siculus gives an inscription on an image of Isis, in which she claims to be the queen of the whole country, adding, "What I shall bind, no one can loose." Josephus describes the Pharisees under Queen Alexandra, as managers of all affairs, who banished and restored whom they would, and adds, λυειν τε καὶ δεῖν. Even granting this to be the true sense of the figures, it is no proof of supremacy or even primacy, as here bestowed on Peter, since, as we have seen already, he is here addressed as representing the apostles, who are recognized by Protestants no less than Papists, as not only founders but chief rulers of the church; in which capacity, however, we deny that they can have successors.

20. Then charged he his disciples that they should tell no man that he was Jesus the Christ.

This prohibition is to be explained upon the same general principle with those addressed to evil spirits and to persons whom he healed (see above, on 8, 4. 9, 30), not as an absolute suppression of the truth, but such a gradual disclosure as might best secure the great ends of his advent, and especially postpone its final issue or catastrophe till all intermediate ends had been accomplished. The very verb translated *charged* (here and in Mark 5, 43. 7, 36. 8, 15. 9, 9) by its etymology suggests the idea of distinction or discrimination, and may serve to remind us that this practice rested upon no fixed law or general rule, but on the wisdom and authority of Christ himself. *That they should tell no man* (of him, Mark 8, 30), what they knew of him, particularly this which they had just confessed, to wit, that he was the Messiah.

21. From that time forth began Jesus to shew unto his disciples, how that he must go unto Jerusalem, and suffer many things of the elders and chief priests and scribes, and be killed, and be raised again the third day.

Having now drawn from them a profession of their faith in his Messiahship, he enters on the delicate and painful task of teaching them that although he was the Messiah, and by necessary consequence a king, the manifestation of his royalty must be preceded not only by prophetic but by priestly functions, or in other words that he must suffer before he reigned (see Luke 24, 26). This doctrine, though distinctly taught by Daniel (9, 26) and Isaiah (53, 4–10), had been gradually lost among the Jews, and was now confined to that small class who still looked for redemption in Jerusalem (Luke 2, 38). The teaching even of the Scribes presented the Messiah as a conqueror and an earthly monarch, who was to restore the throne of David and Solomon and the long lost privileges of the chosen people. This delusion seems to have been shared by the apostles, so far as they had any views upon the subject, and of this he now, *from this time*, began (and afterwards continued) to disabuse them, by foretelling his various sufferings, his rejection not by individuals but by the nation, represented in the Sanhedrim by the three great classes here distinctly named, and lastly, his resuscitation on the third day after his decease.

22. Then Peter took him, and began to rebuke him, saying, Be it far from thee, Lord : this shall not be unto thee.

The effect upon Peter, though denounced by some as improbable and inconsistent with his previous confession, is one of the most natural and lifelike incidents recorded in the Scriptures. Affectionate and ardent, but capricious and precipitate, imperfectly instructed even in the great truth which he had avowed in behalf of his brethren and himself, and no doubt elated above measure by the praise or rather blessing which the Lord had just bestowed upon him, although only in his representative capacity, he could not have betrayed his own infirmity in one act more completely than in that recorded here by Matthew and Mark (8, 32). *Taking him to* (himself or aside) as if to speak with him in private, not by the hand, which would be otherwise expressed. With our habitual associations, it may not be easy to see any thing in this procedure but absurd and arrogant presumption, which has led some to reject it as incredible. But when we take into consideration all the circumstances just suggested, and transport ourselves into the midst of them, as Peter was surrounded by them, we may see that the extraordinary scene presented in this passage, although one which no fictitious writer would have dreamed of, and which could not be the fruit of any mythical process, is nevertheless exquisitely true to nature, both to that of man in general and to that of Peter in particular. *Began to rebuke* (or *chide him*), as a friend entitled to such freedom, for indulging such unnecessary fears and gloomy apprehensions. *He began* to do this in the words preserved by Matthew, but was cut short by one of the severest answers ever uttered, which effectually taught him his mistake and brought him to his senses. *Be it far from thee* (Vulg. *absit a te*), literally, *propitious to thee*, which may either mean, God have mercy on thee, or spare thyself (Tyndale and Cranmer, *favour thyself*).

23. But he turned, and said unto Peter, Get thee behind me, Satan : thou art an offence unto me : for thou savourest not the things that be of God, but those that be of men.

But he (the Son of Man, thus corrected and patronized by one of his own followers) *turning* (to him, or upon him), *said to Peter : Get thee* (literally go, begone) *behind me* (out of my sight, away from me) *Satan*. These words are not only the same in both accounts of this transaction, but identical with those pronounced by Christ to Satan in the wilderness, according to the common text of Luke (4, 8), and according to the latest text of Matthew (4, 10). This coincidence affords a key to the true meaning of this sharp apostrophe, as not a mere expression of abhorrence or contempt, but a specific charge of imitating Satan as the tempter, and endeavouring to draw his master back from the very thing for which he came into the world, and for which his three years' ministry was but a preparation. As if he had said, 'What, is Satan come again to tempt me, as he did of old? Avaunt thou adversary, get thee hence!' Then addressing the astonished and no doubt affrighted Peter, in his own person, he describes the cause of the mistake which he had just made. *Thou art an offence*, i. e. a stumbling block, a hindrance, to me. (See above, on 13, 41). *Savourest*, an obscure English word, and expressing an idea not contained in the original, which means *thou mindest*, carest for, including both the thoughts and the affections. (Compare Rom. 8, 5. 1 Cor. 4, 6. Gal. 5, 10. Phil. 3, 19. Col. 3, 2.) *The things that be of God*, &c., in the original is simply, *the (things) of God, the (things) of men*, i. e. their respective interests, affairs, or claims. The meaning of the sentence seems to be, 'you look only at the human side of these transactions, and regard my death as a mere instance of mortality like that of other men, to be averted as a great calamity, whereas it is the means which God has chosen and appointed for the satisfaction of his broken law and the salvation of his elect people.'

24. Then said Jesus unto his disciples, If any (man) will come after me, let him deny himself, and take up his cross, and follow me.

The connection with what goes before is, that although the disciples were surprised to hear that he must suffer, they must now prepare to suffer too, the members with the head. *If any one* (whosoever, without any exception or reserve) *will* (i. e. wishes or desires to) *come after* (i. e. follow) *me* (as my dependent and adherent), not in public station merely, but among the humblest classes of my people. *Let him deny* (i. e. renounce, abjure) *himself* (as the great object of regard), *and let him take up his cross*, not merely a prospective or prophetic allusion to the mode of his own death, but a reference to the common practice of compelling malefactors to convey their own cross to the place of execution. Crucifixion being commonly regarded as at once the most painful and disgraceful way of dying, is here put for the worst form of suffering, and carrying the cross for humble, patient submission to it. *And let him follow me*, not merely in the general sense of service or the special sense of imitation, but in that of suffering with and like another. As if he had said, 'let him follow me to Golgotha.'

25. For whosoever will save his life shall lose it : and whosoever will lose his life for my sake shall find it.

This is one of our Lord's aphorisms, uttered upon more than one occasion, and already introduced by Matthew in a different connection and more briefly. (See above, on 10, 39.)

26. For what is a man profited, if he shall gain the whole world, and lose his own soul ? or what shall a man give in exchange for his soul ?

The loss in the case supposed is therefore no loss, as the gain in the other case is no gain. The terms are chosen from the dialect of ordinary secular business. *What is a man profited*, what will he gain, on ordinary principles of value or exchange, *if he gain*, acquire, in the usual commercial sense, the whole world, that is, all that it can offer as an object of attraction or desire, the aggregate, sum total, of enjoyment, whether sensual, ambitious, intellectual, pecuniary, *and lose* (a most emphatic passive form, be made to lose, be injured, ruined, with respect to) *his own soul,* the word before translated life, but here denoting rather that which lives, enjoys and suffers. What are enjoyments if there is no one to enjoy them, if the man himself is lost, i. e. lost to happiness for ever ? He pursues the awful supposition further, to the verge of paradox and contradiction, but with terrible advantage to the force of this transcendent argument. Suppose a man to lose his soul, his life, himself, in the sense before explained, how shall he recover it, redeem it, buy it back again, by giving an equivalent in value ? There is something unspeakably impressive in this method of suggesting the importance of eternal interests, by supposing the very life or soul itself to be lost to the possessor and an effort made to buy it back, and then propounding the question, where is the equivalent, or how shall it be rendered ? It is true that when the soul, or its eternal life, is lost, there is no one to attempt its restoration, for the subject or possessor is lost with it. But this is only stating in another form the very truth which Christ is here propounding, that a man may lose his present life and yet live on and have a better life in lieu of it ; but when he loses his eternal life, he is himself lost, lost forever, and the thought of compensation or recovery involves a contradiction.

27. For the Son of man shall come in the glory of his Father with his angels ; and then he shall reward every man according to his works.

The threatening against such as should be ashamed of Christ, recorded here by Mark (8, 38) and Luke (9, 26), having been substantially given by Matthew in a different connection (see above, on 10, 33), is here omitted, while the last clause of the verse as they report it (*when he shall come,* &c.) is amplified into a solemn prophecy that *the*

Son of Man (who now appears in the form of a servant) *will come in glory* (with a majesty the opposite of what you now behold, and that not his own glory merely but) *the glory of his Father, with* (attended by) the *angels*, whose reflected brightness will enhance that from which it is derived (Luke 9, 26). He will then come, no longer as a sufferer but a judge, empowered and prepared to deal with every man *according to his works*, literally, *practice* (πρᾶξιν), meaning his whole course of conduct.

28. Verily, I say unto you, There be some standing here, which shall not taste of death, till they see the Son of man coming in his kingdom.

This verse is one of the most difficult and disputed in the whole book, though the question is rather one of application than essential meaning. *Amen*, verily, assuredly (see above, on 5, 18. 13, 17). *I say unto you*, with emphasis on both the pronouns, *I* (the Son of Man) *to you* (my confidential followers). *There be*, not a subjunctive but an old indicative form equivalent precisely to the modern *are*. *Some of those here standing*, i. e. of the twelve then present and immediately addressed, or of the crowd referred to in Mark 8, 34. *Which*, applied in old English both to things and persons, but confined to the former in modern usage, which would here require *who*. *Shall not*, a peculiarly strong negative in Greek, the aorist subjunctive with the particle (μή) suggesting the idea, that they neither could, would, nor should do what the verb expresses. *Taste of death*, i. e. experience or partake of it, considered as a portion or a draught administered by God to man (see below, on 20, 22. 26, 39). Though the form of expression here is highly metaphorical, it can be referred to nothing but the literal decease of persons actually present. This restricts the meaning of what follows to a single generation or a single life-time, though it may have been a long one. *Till they have seen* (or *see*, behold, or witness) *the Son of Man* (now disguised in the form of a servant) *coming in his kingdom*, i. e. as a king in all his royal state and majesty. The essential meaning, as to which there can be no dispute, is that before all then present should be dead, there would be some convincing proof that the Messiah's kingdom had been actually set up, as predicted by the prophets and by Christ himself. The only doubt or difference of opinion is in reference to the nature of this evidence, or the particular event by which it was to be afforded. The solutions of this question which have been proposed are objectionable, chiefly because too exclusive and restrictive of the promise to a single point of time, whereas it really has reference to a gradual or progressive change, the institution of Christ's kingdom in the hearts of men and in society at large, of which protracted process the two salient points are the effusion of the Spirit on the day of Pentecost, and the destruction of Jerusalem more than a quarter of a century later, between which points, as those of its inception and its consummation, lies the lingering death of the Mosaic dispensation, and the gradual erection of Messiah's kingdom.

CHAPTER XVII.

The solemn confession and prediction in the preceding chapter seemed to intimate the close of our Lord's ministry in Galilee, the formal winding up of which is now recorded. This juncture in the history was marked, moreover, by a momentary anticipation of his glory, which three of the apostles were allowed to witness, after which the record of the Galilean ministry hastens to its close. The main subject of this chapter is the Transfiguration, with the accompanying incidents (1-21). The remaining verses, which describe our Lord's last circuit in Galilee and visit to Capernaum (22-27) are closely connected with the following chapter.

The Transfiguration (1-8). The time, place, and earthly witnesses (1)—the actual transfiguration (2)—the heavenly witnesses (3)—Peter's proposition (4)—the divine recognition (5)—the effect on the disciples (6)—their restoration (7)—the end of the vision (8).

The Descent (9-13). The prohibition (9)—the doctrine of the Scribes as to Elijah (10)—our Lord's confirmation of it (11)—the fulfilment of the prophecy (12)—its application to John the Baptist (13).

The Epileptic Demoniac (14-21). The return (14)—the description of the case (15)—the failure of the nine (16)—our Lord's expostulation (17)—the dispossession (18)—the inquiry of the nine (19)—the faith of miracles (20)—its spiritual aids (21).

The close of the Galilean ministry (22-27). The last circuit (22)—renewed prediction of his passion (23)—the last return to Capernaum (24)—Peter's conversation with the tax-gatherers (24)—our Lord's exemption from such charges (25. 26)—he waives his prerogative, and provides the sum required by miracle (27).

CHAPTER XVIII.

This chapter is entirely occupied with our Lord's discourses, or rather a single conversation (see below) to his disciples during his last circuit in Galilee, or perhaps during his last visit to Capernaum recorded at the close of Chapter XVII. These discourses relate chiefly to two topics; the nature of true greatness, or the dignity of Christ's little ones (1-14); and the nature of Christian discipline, or the divine law of censures and forgiveness (15-35). The first of these subjects was introduced by a question of the disciples, as to their relative rank in the Messiah's kingdom (1), which question was itself not improbably occasioned by our Lord's prediction of his passion in 17, 22. 23, though separated from it in the narrative by the account of an intervening incident (17, 24–27). To the question Christ gives first a symbolical answer (2), which he then explains in words, both negatively (3) and positively (4). The evil effects of such humility would be prevented by their bearing Christ's commission (5), which would make offences even against a child tremendous crimes (6, 7), which must therefore be avoided at any cost (8, 9). Another reason for respecting even the most childlike and defenceless of believers is the fact that they enjoy angelic guardianship (10), and are objects of Christ's saving mercy (11), valued not according to intrinsic worth, but as men value that which has been lost and is found (12–14). As there will be mutual collisions, however, even among true believers, our Lord shows how they should be dealt with; first, in the most private manner (15); then, if need be, in the presence of a few (16); and lastly, in the presence of the church (17), to which in the person of the twelve, he grants the necessary power of reception and exclusion (18), and of effectual united prayer (19, 20). All this has reference to the case of contumacious, obstinate offenders; but in answer to a question from Peter (21), our Lord teaches that the penitent offender is to be forgiven without limit. This he first expresses in a hyperbolical but not exaggerated answer to the question (22), and then enforces the necessity of such a temper in the parable of the two debtors (23–34), winding up with a solemn application to his hearers (35). There is not the slightest ground for doubting that this interesting conversation stands precisely in its proper place, i. e. its true chronological position, at the close of our Lord's residence and ministry in Galilee.

CHAPTER XIX.

As the two preceding chapters (XVII., XVIII.) record the close of our Lord's Galilean ministry, so the next two (XIX., XX.) contain the record of his last journey to Jerusalem. In the one before us, we see him actually crossing the Jordan into Perea (1) followed by a multitude in quest of healing (2), as well as by adversaries, who propound a difficult question in relation to divorce (3), which he answers by referring them to the creation of man (4), and the original institution of marriage (5), implying an indissoluble relation (6). In reply to a further question, as to the Mosaic law of repudiation (7), he represents it as a later regulation, rendered necessary by their own injustice and severity (8), and not at all justifying the prevailing licence of repudiation (9). In reply to a misgiving of the disciples as to marriage (10), he teaches them that there is no rule applicable to all cases (11), and enumerates several instances of lawful celibacy, closing with a repetition of his warning against indiscriminate judgments in such cases (12). The repulse of little children by his followers (13) leads to a gracious invitation on his own part (14), with obvious reference to his previous teachings (18, 2-4). Proceeding on his journey towards Jerusalem (15), he applies a searching test to a self-righteous seeker of eternal life (16-22), and takes occasion from it to declare the difficulties thrown by wealth in the way of men's salvation, which is stated both in literal and proverbial terms (23. 24); but immediately relieves the anxiety of his disciples (25), by referring all to the omnipotence of God (26). In reply to Peter's question as to those who, like the twelve, had stood the test of forsaking all for Christ (27), he utters a twofold promise, one specific and addressed directly to the twelve (28), the other general to all believers (29), closing with a proverbial intimation that there would be strange inequalities in its fulfilment (30). The obvious nexus between these discourses is a chronological one, that is to say, they are put together here because they were actually uttered in this order on the journey to Jerusalem.

CHAPTER XX.

This chapter continues and completes the last journey to Jerusalem. Its connection with the one before it is as intimate as possible. The proverbial maxim with which that concludes is here amplified into a parable, that of the labourers in the vineyard, at the close of which the aphorism is repeated (1-16). We then find him still on his way to Jerusalem with the multitude (17), and privately repeating to the twelve the premonition of his approaching passion (18. 19). This appears to have occasioned the ambitious application of the wife and sons of Zebedee, and Christ's mysterious answer and prediction with respect to the latter (20-23). The jealous emulation of the other ten apostles gives occasion to a statement of the difference between Messiah's kingdom and all others, as well as of the only means by which distinction in the former can be possibly attained (24-28). He has now reached the last stage on the journey to Jerusalem, and there performs a signal miracle of healing, the subjects of which join his retinue and accompany him towards the Holy City (29-34).

CHAPTER XXI.

THE next five chapters (XXI.-XXV.) record the winding up of our Lord's whole prophetic ministry on earth, first in public (XXI.-XXIII.) and then within the circle of his own disciples (XXIV., XXV.). In the one before us we find him at the end of his long journey, in the neighbourhood of Jerusalem (1), sending two of his disciples for an ass, in order to make his entrance in accordance with the well known prophecy of Zechariah (2-7). This first public claim to Messianic honours is acknowledged with enthusiasm by the crowd of worshippers going up to the passover (8-9). His arrival causes general commotion and inquiry as to his pretensions (10-11). He again exercises Messianic authority by clearing the temple of profane intruders, and by working miracles within its precincts (12-14). In reply to the remonstrances of the priests and scribes against these supposed disorders, he refers particularly to the acclamations of the children as a fulfilment of the Scriptures (15. 16). At night he withdraws to Bethany, and on his return early in the morning, blasts a fig-tree as a symbol of the judgment impending over the fruitless and unprofitable race of Israel (17-20). This leads to another brief discourse, in reference to the faith of miracles (20-22). At the temple he is met by a formal deputation from the Sanhedrim, demanding the authority by which he had so suddenly assumed prophetic if not Messianic powers (23). He replies by referring to the public testimony of his forerunner, whose divine legation they did not dare to call in question (24-27). He then shadows forth the coming changes in the parable of the Two Sons (28-32), and the fearful doom of the unfaithful Jews in that of the Husbandmen (33-41). He also applies to them and to himself the parabolic language of the eighteenth psalm (42-44). These open and severe denunciations of the theocratic rulers would have led to his immediate seizure, but for the popular belief in his prophetic mission (45-46).

CHAPTER XXII.

OUR Lord's great discourse to the heads of the theocracy as such (21, 23) is here completed by the parable of the marriage-feast (1-10) and wedding-garment (11-13), closing with one of his significant and solemn aphorisms (14). Here the chapter might have ended; for here begins a new series of attacks, not from the government or its members, in their official capacity, but from several leading classes of the people. The first attack proceeded from a coalition of the Pharisees and Herodians, intended to reduce him to a dilemma, in relation to the delicate political question upon which they were divided, the lawfulness of Jews submitting to a foreign and a heathen power, which our Lord answered with a wisdom so consummate as to command the admiration of his very tempters (15–22). The next attack was from the sceptical and latitudinarian Sadducees, and was not so much insidious as frivolous, designed to throw contempt upon the doctrine of the resurrection (23–28). To their scoffing question Christ replies with godlike dignity, correcting their false notion of a future state, and authoritatively laying down the doctrine of the resurrection, which they denied and laughed at (29–32). As this reply not only silenced his assailants, but produced a great impression on the people (33, 34), the Pharisees renewed their attack, not now as a political but as a religious party, putting forward one of their scribes or lawyers, with a question probably discussed in their schools, as to the relative importance of the precepts in the decalogue (35, 36). Neither evading it nor answering it formally, our Lord escapes their snare, and at the same time teaches them the true extent and import of the law, by citing the two precepts which contain its sum and substance (37–40). The last interrogation is from Christ himself, and marks the change in his position from defensive to offensive, charging home upon them their departure from the ancient Messianic doctrine, and opening the way for the terrible invective and denunciation which immediately follow (41–46).

CHAPTER XXIII.

Our Lord now turns from his assailants to the body of the people and to his own disciples, both in the narrower and wider sense (1). For their guidance he defines the official position of the Scribes and Pharisees, and their claim to obedience, but warns against copying their example (2–4). This he enforces by disclosing their true character and motives, the desire of human praise, as shown in several particulars, against which he forewarns his followers (5–12). He then turns, for the last time, to the Scribes and Pharisees themselves, against whom he utters the most terrible invective and denunciation upon record, summing up, at the close of his prophetic ministry, all that he had said against them during its previous course (13). The first ground of denunciation is their frustrating the very end of the theocracy committed to their charge (13). The second is their double profanation of religious worship as a cloak for their cupidity (14). The third is their proselyting zeal, not for good but for evil, and tending not to the salvation but the ruin and the ruinous influence of their converts (15). The fourth is their misguiding of the people, as to religious duties, with particular reference to oaths, either as a mere example, or as a specially prevailing evil (16–22). The fifth is their sacrificing the essentials of the law to its minutest ceremonial observances, and even to traditional and uncommanded usages, here expressed both directly and in strong proverbial language (23–24). The next two verses relate to the same thing, their merely outside righteousness, set forth under two striking and familiar images. The first is that of a dish clean upon the outside but dirty still within (25–26). The other is that of tombs or burial-houses, whitened on the outside, but within full of decayed or putrifying corpses (27–28). This comparison suggests the eighth and last denunciation, which was the more startling because founded upon what they no doubt looked upon as highly meritorious, their zeal in building monuments or tombs to the martyred prophets, and disclaiming all participation in the murderous fanaticism of their fathers. In opposition to this specious profession, our Lord represents them as the genuine descendants of the prophet-killers, and declares that they would yet commit the same sin upon those whom he should send unto them, and thus prove worthy to bear the burden of the whole race, not only as the last but as the worst generation (29–36). He then closes with a tender lamentation over the doomed race as represented by the Holy City, predicts its speedy desolation, and adds an enigmatical intimation of ulterior changes (37–39).

CHAPTER XXIV.

Though our Lord had solemnly concluded his public work as a teacher, and taken an affecting leave of Israel as a people (23, 37–39), his prophetic ministry was yet to be wound up, within a smaller circle, and by a prophetical discourse, in the strictest sense of the expression (XXIV., XXV.). A natural feeling of admiration in the twelve or some of them for the majestic structure of the temple leads him to predict its absolute destruction, and this to an inquiry as to the time and the premonitory signs of the great catastrophe of which they had so often heard obscurely (1–3). Instead of gratifying idle curiosity by positive details, our Lord begins by showing what would not be necessarily the signs of his return, however men might be inclined so to regard them, and impostors so to represent them (4, 5); such as wars and other national commotions and calamities, which instead of announcing the end, might be merely the beginning of sorrows (6–8). Even when assailed themselves, betrayed, and hated, they should still be rescued if they remained faithful during these sore trials, and the Gospel must be preached to every nation before the coming of the final consummation (9–14). Without distinguishing the different stages of his coming or the accompanying judgments, he instructs his followers what to do when the Romans should invest Jerusalem, viz., to flee without the least delay, the idea of precipitancy being variously and strikingly expressed (15–20). The reason given is the unparalleled severity of the judgments coming on the Jews, and only to be checked for the sake of true believers (21–22). Even at this fatal juncture there would not be wanting false pretenders to the prophetic, and even to the Messianic office, whom he solemnly charges his disciples not to listen to, either at home or abroad (23–26), assuring them that when he did come, it would be as conspicuously as the lightning, or the flight of eagles to their prey (27–28), and be followed by the most terrific changes in the frame of nature, and the final gathering of God's elect (29–31). Having answered their question as to the *signs* of his return in judgment, he now answers that as to the *time;* first, by telling them that these great changes were not arbitrary judgments, but the growth of moral causes, and could no more take place until these had done their work, than the fig-tree would bear fruit before the season (32–33); 2.—that in a certain sense, this whole prophetic scheme should be verified, before the end of the contemporary generation (34); 3.—that although the event was far more certain than the continuance of the frame of nature, the precise time of its occurrence was concealed alike from men and angels (35–36), and it would therefore come as unexpectedly at last as the flood upon the antediluvian sinners (37–39), but with a discrimination between individuals unknown in that case (40–41). Having thus disclosed as much as he thought fit with respect to his departure and return, our Lord now teaches his disciples how they ought to act during his absence, whether long or short. The first great duty is that of vigilance, enforced by a case of burglary, perhaps of recent date and well known to his hearers (42–44), and then by a supposed but most familiar case of a servant left to take care of his absent master's house (45–51). In carrying out this illustration, he exhibits in a plain but vivid manner, the conduct of a faithful and unfaithful servant in such circumstances, showing, however, by the fearful severity of the punishment, that he has his eye not so much upon the sign as the thing signified.

CHAPTER XXV.

HAVING taught them the necessity of vigilance after his departure, he now shows them that the vigilance required is not mere watchfulness but watchful preparation. This is beautifully set forth in the parable of the ten virgins, winding up with a solemn application to his hearers (1–13). His next lesson is that their vigilance must not be idle or unfruitful, but laborious and productive, in proportion to their several capacities and opportunities. This is taught in the parable of the talents (14–30). The last lesson has respect to the way in which they might testify their love to him while personally absent. By acts of kindness to his suffering people (31–46). This is enforced by a graphic scene which, standing as it does at the close of a series of parables, rising one above another, might itself be regarded as a parable, the imagery of which is borrowed from the future, like that of the Rich Man and Lazarus. But with a skill which in an uninspired writer would be called consummate, this passage also winds up the prophetic discourse in ch. XXIV., and thereby closes our Lord's personal work on earth as a prophet, even in the confidential circle of his own disciples.

CHAPTER XXVI.

HAVING finished his teaching work, our Lord now looks forward to his passion and connects it with the passover only two days off, thus for the first time fixing the precise date of that great event which he had so often more indefinitely foretold to his disciples (1, 2). The different lines of hostile influence which had long been converging towards his destruction now begin to show themselves in visible approximation. We find the Sanhedrim formally deliberating how they could despatch him without popular commotion, and abandoning the project until after the passover, for want of some auxiliary influence *ab intra*. How this aid was unexpectedly provided the evangelist informs us by relating how the disaffection of Judas had been brought to maturity and open outbreak a few days before at Bethany (6-13). This brought about the convergence which appeared to be indefinitely put off, and secured the espionage of a traitor within the narrow circle of our Lord's most confidential followers (14-16). He accompanies his Master and his brethren to the place appointed for the paschal feast; hears our Lord declare that one of them was to betray him, and pronounce a fearful woe on the betrayer, hears the eleven severally ask, Is it I? repeats the same inquiry and receiving an affirmative answer, silently withdraws, thus severing himself forever from the only Saviour (17-25). That Saviour then engrafts upon the last Jewish Passover the first Christian Eucharist, thus furnishing the link of transition and connection between the old and new economy (26-29). Withdrawing to the Mount of O.ives, he predicts the defection of his followers, but promises to meet them in Galilee after his resurrection (30-32). To Peter's vehement denial of our Lord's words, so far as they concerned himself, Christ repeats the prediction still more pointedly in reference to Peter, and receives a still more passionate denial, in which all the others join (33-35). Then comes the awful scene of anguish in Gethsemane, made more so by the insensibility and drowsiness even of his three chosen attendants (36-46). He is pointed out by Judas to the armed band who arrest him (47-50). He rebukes a feeble effort at resistance on the part of his disciples, and teaches them that his submission is entirely voluntary and intended to fulfil the Scriptures (51-55). His disciples now forsake him and are scattered, but Peter soon after follows at a distance to the house of the High Priest where his Master was arraigned before the Sanhedrim, and after several vain attempts, false witnesses were procured against him (57–61). On his refusing to defend himself, the High Priest puts him on his oath according to the solemn form of the Mosaic Law, and receives in answer the first public formal assertion of his Messiahship and Divinity, confirmed by a prediction of his second coming (62–64). The High Priest, both by symbolical action and by word, declares him guilty of blasphemy in their very presence, and the Sanhedrim accordingly condemns him to death and gives him up to the most unmanly treatment and cruel mockery especially of his prophetical pretensions (65–68). Here the historian pauses, at the most convenient place, to let us know that in the intervals of these proceedings Peter had been repeatedly accosted as a follower of Christ, and had as often denied him, until brought to himself and to repentance by hearing the appointed signal (69–75).

CHAPTER XXVII.

ALTHOUGH our Lord had been condemned to death for blasphemy by the highest tribunal of the Jews, that body re-assembles at an early hour, for the purpose of transferring him to the tribunal of the Roman Governor, who alone had power to execute the sentence (1–2). Before proceeding to record what took place there, the historian pauses to describe the miserable end of the betrayer; his remorse, his confession, his restitution of his wages, and his suicide (3–5). Then follows the debate among the priests as to the use to be made of the money, and their purchase of the Potter's Field (6–8). In all this the evangelist, according to his plan, points out the fulfilment of an ancient prophecy (9–10). Then resuming the account of our Lord's trial, he records his avowal of his kingship before Pilate, and his steady refusal to answer the accusations of the Jews (11–14). Pilate attempts to exchange him for another prisoner, according to a yearly usage, in which he is encouraged by a message from his wife; but the people, instigated by their rulers, choose Barabbas in preference to Christ (15–23). Pilate then, by word and symbolical act repudiates all responsibility, which the people, by an awful imprecation, take upon themselves (24–25). He is then abandoned to their will, mocked by the soldiery, and led to execution (26–33). The crucifixion is then described, with various circumstances serving to identify the sufferer as the subject of the ancient prophecies (34–35). The Roman watch, the inscription on the Cross, his fellow-sufferers, the scoffs of the passers-by, and the fearful insults of the priests, are all described with terrible distinctness (36–44). Then follow the extraordinary darkness, the desponding cry upon the Cross, the mockery even of this agony by some of the bystanders (45–49). The moment of his death is marked by various supernatural phenomena, producing conviction in the Roman soldiers who had charge of his execution that he was what he professed to be (50-54). Among the actual spectators of his death, the historian particularly mentions many women who had followed him from Galilee, several of whom he designates by name (55-56). The burial of our Lord is entrusted to an eminent [though hitherto a secret] disciple, who deposits the body in his own tomb, leaving two of the Marys as it were to watch it (57-61). A very different guard was provided the next day by the guilty fears of the Jewish rulers, who obtained from Pilate a detachment of soldiers, to prevent the body being stolen (62-66).

CHAPTER XXVIII.

The history now closes with the Resurrection and its accompanying incidents, the earthquake, the descent of the angel, the effect upon the guard (1-4); the encouraging address to the women who had come at an early hour again to see the sepulchre, the message sent through them to the disciples, its repetition by our Lord himself who meets them on the way (5-10), the report of the soldiers to the rulers, and the falsehood put into their mouths (11-15). The whole narrative is wound up by the rendezvous in Galilee, our Lord's assumption of supreme authority, his great commission to his followers, and the accompanying promise of his perpetual presence with them (16-20).

THE END.

www.ingramcontent.com/pod-product-compliance
Lightning Source LLC
Chambersburg PA
CBHW022132300426
44115CB00006B/153